READINGS IN MICROECONOMICS

READINGS IN
MICROECONOMICS

DAVID R. KAMERSCHEN, Editor

University of Missouri, Columbia, Missouri

JOHN WILEY & SONS, INC.

NEW YORK · LONDON · SYDNEY · TORONTO

BURGESS

10 9 8 7 6 5 4 3 2 1
Library of Congress Catalogue Card Number: 78-88550

SBN 471 45571 7 (cloth)   SBN 471 45572 5 (paper)

Printed in the United States of America

To Christine, Steve, Laura and Robert

PREFACE

The purpose of this volume of readings is to serve as a supplement to the material that is currently covered in the intermediate and graduate college courses in price theory. It might even prove useful in an "advanced" introductory course such as is found in the honors program at many fine universities. However, the intermediate market has been my primary aim. My survey of the leading textbooks in this field found many of the articles reprinted here on their suggested reading lists.

Although the articles reprinted in this volume have been arranged under eight separate topics, each makes its own contribution and can be read in any sequence. In the "Introduction" I shall indicate my own personal reasons for the numerical sequence of the articles. I have made some attempt to balance the articles—empirical and theoretical, orthodox and nonorthodox, "classical" and "neoclassical," etc.—so that the book is suitable for use with any of the standard microeconomic textbooks. On balance, however, the selections are biased on the theoretical side, as I think is appropriate for a price theory course.

All the selections in this volume have been previously published in professional economic journals, treatises, texts, or collections of essays. They are reprinted here, as originally published, with only minor typographical corrections. In general, the articles have been selected on the assumption that the typical intermediate price theory student has had relatively little mathematical training. Even in those few selections where training in mathematics or statistics is necessary to comprehend all the details, the reader without such training will generally have no trouble capturing the essence of the selection. My own experience has been that both intermediate and graduate students find the papers included here both enlightening and stimulating. Of course no selection of articles will exactly satisfy the desires of every instructor. I only hope that this volume will make the reading of "outside" assignments less onerous for the student.

In general I have tried to avoid duplicating articles that are already receiving fairly wide distribution—especially articles contained in the American Economic Association's two volumes: (1) George J. Stigler and Kenneth E. Boulding (eds.), *Readings in Price Theory* (1952); and (2) William J. Fellner and Bernard F. Haley (eds.), *Readings in the Theory of Income Distribution* (1946). This may explain why certain well-known articles are missing. However, the celebrated Jacob Viner article, "Cost Curves and Supply Curves," is so unanimously suggested reading in both undergraduate and graduate price theory textbooks that I included it here despite its inclusion in the American Economic Association's volume on price theory. In a few cases important articles have not been included because reprint permissions could not be obtained.

In the preparation of this book, I received help from numerous people. Professor Marshall Hall of Washington University and my colleagues at the University of Missouri were consulted and graciously gave their advice. I am grateful to the numerous people who have written me since this volume was first published in 1967 by the World Publishing Company for their encouragement and their suggestions. I am also indebted to the staff of John Wiley & Sons, Inc. In addition, I am obligated to the various authors and publishers who so readily permitted their material to be reprinted in this collection. Individual acknowledgment and the source are included at the beginning of each selection. If the author's present institutional location is different from that at the precise time when his publication first appeared in print, his previous affiliation is also identified.

David R. Kamerschen

Columbia, Missouri
April, 1969

TABLE OF CONTENTS

INTRODUCTION

The thirty-five selections collected in this volume have been arranged under eight separate headings.

Section I, "Introduction and Methodology," contains four papers. Lange's paper provides a nice introduction to the whole of economics from a somewhat "classic" methodological position. The Klappholz and Agassi paper discusses two of the newer views of methodology by Professors Friedman and Papandreou, and some of the more "classical" views such as Robbins'. The "new" methodology—and Friedman's paper in particular—has caused considerable controversy in economics. Samuelson's paper discusses the role—including the importance and limitations—of mathematics in economics. The last selection in the group, by Schumpeter, suggests that knowledge of the price system is invaluable regardless of the type of economic organization one lives in. I have found that students will appreciate the methodology articles even more after the basic materials in the course have been covered. I strongly recommended the rereading of these articles near the conclusion of the course.

The seven papers on "Demand and the Theory of Consumer Behavior," Section II, are theoretical in nature. What few empirical results are available are generally quite sophisticated mathematically and statistically. The first two are introductory and orthodox; the other five question the established theory and/or break new ground. The selections by Spencer and by Levenson and Solon are unusual in that they are not written for professional economists. They have been selected for their outstanding exposition. The Spencer piece is the finest elementary discussion of indifference curves that I have seen. The Levenson and Solon pages contain the best short statement I know of the consumer equilibrium conditions that point out explicitly the role of the assumption of diminishing marginal utility in determining equilibrium and the distinction between diminishing marginal utility and diminishing marginal rate of substitution. Although the pages employ calculus, I have found that students with a sufficiently good command of the economics—especially the definitions of complements, substitutes, and unrelated commodities—can benefit from the discussion. Similarly, the Kuhlman and Thompson selection employs mathematics and is concerned with complementarity and substitutability. Following Hicks, they demonstrate why complementarity and substitutability must be associated with both the direct ("own") and cross-price elasticities and the corresponding components of income elasticity. Whether the reader agrees with Mishan's conclusion or not, his article presents an excellent brief review, in basically nonmathematical terms, of both Hicks's indifference-preference and Samuelson's revealed-preference approaches. Friedman's article questions the conventional interpretation of the Marshallian demand curve as implying "money-income constant" and suggests "real-income constant" as more logical, as well as more in keeping with what Marshall said. Bailey takes Friedman's argument one step further by suggesting a "production frontier constant" demand curve as even more logical. Leibenstein adds to our theoretical tool kit by indicating how individual demand curves may still be aggregated into a market demand curve when interdependence is assumed. Strotz's article is a nonmathematical discussion of the von Neuman and Morgenstern utility index—i.e., it is concerned with the consumer's behavior in situations characterized by uncertainty.

Section III, "Supply and the Theory of the Firm," includes eight papers of both theoretical and empirical significance. The Viner paper on cost and supply curves has become basic reading in undergraduate and graduate microeconomic theory classes alike. Brumberg's short paper discusses the usually neglected "determinants" or "givens" employed in drawing supply curves. Leibenstein discusses a still unsettled controversy in economics regarding whether scale economies are a result of both proportions and absolute size or only proportions. Tangri's short exposition clarifies the usual textbook treatment of the Law of Variable Proportions with regard to cost and product relationships in the so-called Stage III, and the factor, but not product, symmetry of Stages I and III. The Levenson and Solon note claims to show: (1) marginal, not average, returns to scale determine isoquant spacing; and (2) the usual textbook treatment of the relationship between average returns to scale and isoquant spacing is accurate only for homogeneous production functions. [For a contrary view, see F. W. McElroy, *American Economic Review*, Vol. LVII (March, 1967), pp. 223-224.] The Apel paper is largely empirical in nature. It is concerned with reviewing the statistical findings that have been made on cost conditions. The Stigler and Nordquist selections provide a balanced look at the *modus operandi* of the firm. Stigler presents the traditional maximization of profits point of view, while Nordquist reviews the numerous antiprofit maximization works that have appeared.

Six papers appear in Section IV, "Market Organization." Machlup's note provides an interesting classification of market structure that has only partially been incorporated into the textbook literature. The two Stigler pieces are balanced by the two pieces by Bishop and Markham. Stigler suggests that: (1) imperfect competition has not been a very significant theoretical advance; (2) imperfect competition when found is generally undesirable; and (3) imperfect competition is not very important in our economy in terms of sheer numbers or economic results (especially "welfare losses"). The Bishop and Markham papers suggest that monopoly is theoretically and empirically important and perhaps even desirable, following the Schumpeterian arguments. Modigliani's paper reviews two recent contributions to oligopoly theory which have come to be known as the "Bain-Sylos" hypothesis.

The six papers in Section V, "Theory of Distribution," are primarily interested in theoretical issues in the microeconomic theories of distribution. Unfortunately, the present state of distribution theory is extremely unsatisfactory. In particular, there is at present no satisfactory theoretical explanation of the distribution of the national product between wages, profits, interest, and so on. Kaldor provides a historical review of some of the main contributors to distribution theory. Hirshleifer's article is an excellent synthesis of factor market equilibrium analysis. Although the famous Lester-Machlup debates on marginalism in firm and distribution theory are not directly included, the Nordquist article in Section III reviews this interesting tussle. Liebhafsky's paper is in a sense a continuation of this debate by defending the marginal productivity theory against more recent criticism. Reder's paper provides a summary of the various theories of distribution together with some empirical evidence relating to each. The Weston and Worcester articles survey, evaluate, and extend the profit and rent theories of functional distribution.

The single papers each in Sections VI, "Welfare Economics," VII, "Linear Programming," and VIII, "Econometrics," represent contributions in rapidly expanding areas of microeconomics. While all of these contain some amount of mathematics and/or statistics, they may still be read profitably by those without such training. The Bator article is a nice nonmathematical review of some elementary as well as some advanced propositions in "normative" or welfare economics. Dorfman's paper is outstanding in presenting a difficult topic that readily lends itself to mathematics in basically nonmathematical terms. The Fisher, Griliches, and Kaysen article is a most interesting application of elementary statistics to a real problem in price theory—the cost of annual model changes in automobiles. For the reader who does not have any knowledge of elementary statistics, the authors have written an abstract of their article; this abstract appears at the end of the full paper.

SECTION I

INTRODUCTION AND METHODOLOGY

1

THE SCOPE AND METHOD
OF ECONOMICS *

OSCAR LANGE, deceased, was in Washington, D.C.,
when this article was first published.

1. THE SUBJECT MATTER OF ECONOMICS

Economics is the science of administration of scarce resources in human society. Human beings, living within the framework of a given historical civilisation, experience various wants, such as of food, shelter, clothing, education, social prestige, entertainment, expression of religious, national, or political attitudes, and others. Some of the wants result from biological needs which must be satisfied for the very preservation of life. Most of them, however, are products of life in civilized society, frequently of the very existence of the means to satisfy them, and even the wants which result from biological needs assume forms determined by the standards of the particular civilisation under which the human beings live. The wants can be satisfied by means of appropriate objects called *goods*, e.g. land, coal, cattle, buildings, ships, railroads, machinery, stocks of raw materials and the uses of such objects or of persons called *services*, like of transportation, of housing, of workingmen, of teachers, of managers, and of artists, etc. The goods and services are the *resources* which serve to satisfy human wants. Some of the resources, air, for instance, are so plentiful that all wants dependent upon them can be fully satisfied. Others, however, e.g. oil or the services of human beings, exist only in quantities which are not sufficient to satisfy all wants dependent upon these resources. In this case, we say that the resources are *scarce*. When resources are scarce, certain wants must go unsatisfied. Men make decisions which, given the organisation and institutions of society, determine the distribution of the scarce resources among the different persons as well as the uses to which the scarce resources are put. In other words: the resources are administered. The study of the ways in which scarce resources are administered is the task of the science of economics.

The administration of scarce resources is influenced by the standards

* From *The Review of Economic Studies*, Vol. XIII (1945–1946), pp. 19–32. Reprinted by permission.

3

of civilisation and by the organisation and institutions of the society in which men live. The influence is a two-fold one. The wants which the resources serve to satisfy are products of standards of civilisation historically developed in society. The ways in which scarce resources are procured, adapted to various purposes, distributed among different persons are all results of social organisation and social institutions. Forms of ownership, institutions like corporations and banks, technical knowledge acquired in institutes of research and transmitted by schools, regulation by government agencies, habits and moral standards all influence the ways of administering scarce resources. Economics is thus a *social science*, i.e. it deals with a subject which depends on the standards and forms of life in human society. It differs from sociology, the science of social actions and relations (patterns of repeated social actions) between men, by being interested in the actions of men toward the scarce resources which serve to satisfy their wants. These actions are dependent upon social actions but are distinct from them. We shall call them *economic actions*. While dependent on social actions, economic actions, in turn, influence and even create social actions and relations. The last mentioned influence provides subject-matter for a special field of study. We might name it *economic sociology*, the science of the effect of economic actions upon social actions and relations. Subjects such as the sociology of industrial relations, bureaucracy in corporations, trade-unionism, belong to this field. The present essay is limited to economics, i.e. the study of economic actions. This includes a study of the influence of social organisation and institutions upon the ways and methods of administration of scarce resources.

Like any other science, economics is not content with merely descriptive knowledge. It tries to discern general patterns of uniformity in the administration of scarce resources. The possibility of establishing such patterns of uniformity is based on two observed facts. Human actions with regard to scarce resources are subject to uniform patterns of repetition. For instance, most people react to an increase in their income by spending more money on goods and services. Within the framework of given social organisation and institutions, the uniformities in economic action of individuals or groups of individuals produce certain uniformities in the distribution and use of scarce resources. Thus, an increase in the quantity of bank loans to businessmen or corporations makes them increase their demand for resources with a consequent rise in employment and/or prices. The branch of economics which deals with such patterns of uniformity and combines them in a coherent system is called *theoretical economics* or *economic theory* (also economic analysis). Statements enunciating the patterns of uniformity are referred to as *economic laws*. Economic laws are, like all other scientific laws, conditional statements. They assert that such and such happens regularly whenever such and such conditions are satisfied (i.e. whenever such and such other observations take place). No scientific law applies when its prerequisite conditions do not occur. Since the administration of scarce resources is influenced by social organisation and institutions, such organisation and institutions are among the conditions implied in economic laws. Consequently, economic laws which hold under one type of social organisation may fail to do so under another type. Most economic laws are thus "limited historically" to certain given types of social organisation and institutions. This, however, does not imply any basic difference between the laws of economics (or of other social sciences) and the laws of the natural sciences. The latter, too, are contingent upon conditions which are subject to change. Different laws of the natural sciences have different degrees of historic permanence, usually a much higher one than the laws of economics, though even this is not always the case (some laws of meteorology are less permanent than some laws of economics). The difference is but one of degree. Like all scientific laws, economic laws are established in order to make successful prediction of the outcome of human actions. In economics the laws serve to predict the result of policies, i.e. of actions of public or private agencies with regard to the administration of scarce resources. Such predictions, however, are difficult. This is due to the fact that the number of conditions circumscribing the validity of economic laws is very great, and it is difficult to ascertain whether they are all satisfied in any particular situation. Notwithstanding, some successful predictions are being made with the aid of economic science.

Theoretical economics does not exhaust the field of economic inquiry. Economics also studies and describes the particular ways and methods of administering scarce resources as they occur in the history of human society, past and present. Observations are made and classified and interpreted with the aid of the uniformities established by economic theory. This pursuit provides the subject-matter of *applied economics*. Applied economics is subdivided into several parts. The most important are economic history—the study of administration of scarce resources in the human societies of the past—and institutional economics, the study of the influence of particular social institutions upon the administration of scarce resources. The effect of trade-associations upon prices, quality and output of goods, or the effect of collective farming in agriculture on the efficiency of production are examples of problems which fall in the last-mentioned field.

Theoretical economics puts the patterns of uniformity in a coherent system. This is done by presenting the laws of economics as a deductive set of propositions derived by the rules of logic (and of mathematics) from a few basic propositions. The basic propositions are called assumptions or postulates, the derived propositions are called theorems. Theoretical economics thus appears (like all other theoretical sciences) as a deductive science. This, however, does not make it a branch of pure mathematics or logic. Like the rest of economics, economic theory is an empirical science. Its assumptions or postulates are approximative generalisations of empirical observations; e.g. the assumption that business enterprises act so as to maximise their money profit. Some inaccuracy of approximation (e.g. some considerations, like safety, may keep enterprises from maximising money profit) is accepted for the sake of greater simplicity. The theorems, in turn, are subjected to test by empirical observation. A deductive set of theorems to be subjected to empirical test is also called a *theory, hypothesis,* or a *model.* We can thus say that theoretical economics provides hypotheses or models based on generalisation of observations and subject to empirical test.

Since the assumptions (postulates) underlying a model are only approximative, the theorems do not correspond directly to results of empirical observations. In order to establish such a correspondence, special procedures must be observed. First, the concepts used in theoretical models are not adequate representations of empirical observation. For instance, a theoretical model speaks of "the price" of a specified good, but experience fails to produce anything like the specified "good" and its "price." There are hundreds of quality-grades and thousands of sellers each charging a different price. Experience is much richer than the language of science can make allowance for. In order to bridge the gap between theoretical concepts and empirical observations, it is necessary to have a procedure of *identification,* which contains rules establishing a correspondence between the two. Such procedures have to be provided by the different branches of applied economics. Furthermore, the theorems of theoretical economics are never borne out exactly by empirical observation. At best they do so only "approximately." This raises the question as to what is to be considered as an acceptable degree of approximation inducing us to accept a hypothesis as "true" and what degree of approximation is to be judged as insufficient, making us reject the hypothesis as "incompatible with the facts." The question can be answered only in terms of a procedure of *verification* (testing) which establishes rules according to which hypotheses are accepted as "empirically verified" or rejected as "empirically unverified" or "empirically refuted." A recently developed special branch of economics deals with such procedures of verification. It is called *econometrics* and is based on the principles of mathematical statistics.

The administration of scarce resources empirically observed can be evaluated in terms of certain social objectives. Such objectives may consist in the best satisfaction of the wants of private persons according to their own preferences or in marshalling scarce resources for certain collective enterprises—e.g. industrialisation of a country according to time-table, as in the Soviet Union, or successful prosecution of war, or enactment of certain ideas of social justice—or, finally, of a combination of all. The social objectives being given, rules of use of scarce resources can be found which are most conducive to the attainment of these objectives. The use of resources which follows these rules is referred to as the "ideal" use. The rules of "ideal" use of resources provide a standard by which the actual use can be evaluated as to its social desirability. The use of resources empirically observed may be compared with the "ideal" use and measures may be recommended to bring the actual use into closer correspondence with the "ideal" one. This provides subject-matter for another branch of economic science, usually called *welfare economics* (also normative economics or social economics). The rules of "ideal" use of resources are general statements; they express uniform patterns of economic action which, if adopted, are most conducive to the social objectives aimed at. They are conditional statements because they are valid only under given social objectives and given empirical conditions; they require empirical verification. (A rule of "ideal" use of resources may prove in practice not to be conducive to the social aims desired.) The rules of "ideal" use of resources can thus be considered as a special kind of economic laws. This makes it convenient to include welfare economics in theoretical economics as a supplementary branch of the latter.

2. THE OBJECTIVITY OF ECONOMIC SCIENCE

The statements of economic science have objective validity. This means that two or more persons who agree to abide by the rules of scientific procedure are bound to reach the same conclusions. If they start with the same assumptions, they are bound, by the rules of logic, to derive the same theorems. If they apply the same rules of identification and verification, they are bound to reach agreement as to whether the theorems should be accepted as "true" or rejected as "unverified" or "false." The test of verification decides whether the assumptions are adequate or not. In the latter case, they have to be replaced by new ones which lead to theorems able to stand the test of verification. The final verdict with regard to any statement of economic science is thus based upon an appeal to facts, i.e. to empirical observations. "The proof of the pudding is in the eating." This verdict has interpersonal validity because facts are interpersonal, i.e. can be observed by everyone. The interpersonal validity of statements holds also for welfare economics. There is no necessary interpersonal agreement about the social objectives which provide the standard of evaluation for welfare economics. Different persons, social groups and classes may, and frequently do desire different social objectives. Once, however, the objectives are stated and certain assumptions are made about empirical conditions, the rules of "ideal" use of resources are derived by the rules of logic and verified by the rules of verification. This procedure is interpersonally objective, i.e. everyone who applies it is bound to reach the same conclusions. The situation may be compared with that of two physicians treating a patient. There is no necessity of interpersonal agreement about the objective of the treatment. One physician may want to heal the patient, the other may want to kill him (e.g. the patient may be a Jew in a Nazi concentration camp; one physician may be a fellow prisoner who wants to help him, the other physician may be a Nazi acting under orders to exterminate Jews). But once the objective is set for the purpose under discussion (either of the two physicians may, of course, refuse to act upon it), their statements as to whether a given treatment is conducive to the end under consideration have interpersonal validity. Any disagreement between them can be settled by appeal to fact and to the rules of scientific procedure.

Our conclusion about the objectivity of economic science may seem startling. Economists are rather notorious for being unable to reach agreement and for being divided into opposing "schools of thought," "orthodox" and "unorthodox," "bourgeois" and "socialist," and many others. The existence of profound disagreement among economists, however, does not refute our thesis about the objectivity of economics as a science. The disagreements can all be traced to one or more of the following sources:

(1) Disagreement about social objectives. This is the most frequent source of disagreement, but acts as such only as long as it is implicit and unrecognised. If the social objectives are stated explicitly, the disagreement disappears. For any given set of social objectives and with given assumptions as to empirical conditions, conclusions are drawn with interpersonal validity by the rules of logic and of verification.

(2) Disagreement about facts. Such disagreement can always be resolved by further observation and study of the empirical material. Frequently, however, the empirical data necessary to resolve the disagreement are unavailable. In such cases the issue remains unsettled. The conclusion that the issue cannot be settled with the data available has interpersonal validity. Agreement is reached to withhold judgment.

(3) Failure to abide by the rules of logic, of identification and of verification. The disagreement can be removed by correct application of these rules.

The disagreements are thus all due to failure to abide by the rules of scientific procedure and can be resolved by strict application of these rules. Economists, as well as other scientists, however, are not automatons acting on the basis of the rules of scientific procedure. As human beings they are subject to a great multiplicity of influences, some conscious, most of them subconscious, which determine their conclusions as 1- id down in the literature of economics. There are influences, sociological and psychological, which sometimes are unfavourable and sometimes favourable to the application of scientific procedure. The persistence of disagreements indicates that the harmful influences are very strong. It is desirable to have a picture of these influences, harmful as well as helpful.

Economists, like other human beings, live under the institutions of a historic society and under the standards of its civilisation. They share in its beliefs and values, prejudices and interests, horizons and limitations. They depend for their living, advancement, and recognition on the institutions of the society in which they live, e.g. on universities, research institutes, publishers, press, government, and business establishments. Most of these institutions have other, more important, objectives than the "untrammelled pursuit of truth," and even those which have this objective are dependent on the rest of society and must make their adjustments and compromises. Furthermore, economists are brought up as members of a particular nation, social class, religious or philosophical group, and political tradition, etc. All this exposes economists, and also other scientists, to a multiplicity of influences other than the rules of scientific procedure. Those influences which are conscious are easily recognised and overcome if they interfere with honest application of scientific procedure. Though even in this case, many may choose to limit their scientific inquiry to "safe" fields where there is little danger of conflict with powerful and dominant interests and prejudices. The really important influences, however, are those which are subconscious. The economist subject to them is unaware of their existence; the influences operate through processes of rationalisation of subconscious motivations. The result is the production of *ideologies,* i.e. systems of beliefs which are held not on grounds of their conformity to scientific procedure but as rationalisations of subconscious, non-logical, motives. Idealogies have no interpersonal validity. They convince only those who share the same subconscious motivations and undergo the same processes of rationalisation.

The study of ideologies, of the conditions of their origins and influences, has become the subject-matter of a special discipline, the *sociology of knowledge*. This discipline has established valuable insights into the sociological and psychological conditions of scientific inquiry. Its most important contribution is the recognition of the fact that all scientific production contains an ideological element. This holds for the natural sciences as well as for the social sciences. The history of the Copernican theory in astronomy and of the theory of evolution in biology provides an example. For a long time the attitude of astronomers and of biologists to these theories was influenced by their general attitude, friendly or hostile, to dominant ecclesiastic doctrines and by their personal dependence or lack of dependence on ecclesiastic institutions. The history of economics is full of instances of the ideological element in economic science. The most important stepping-stones in the development of economics were not merely scientific but also ideological with far-reaching social consequences.

The existence of an ideological element in each science has caused some representatives of the sociology of knowledge to deny the objective validity of scientific statements, particularly in the domain of the social sciences. Such a conclusion is unwarranted. The validity of scientific statements can be ascertained with impersonal objectivity through an appeal to facts. Predictions derived from scientific statements are or are not borne out under the test of verification. The outcome is entirely independent of human motivations, conscious or subconscious; it depends entirely on the correctness of the scientific procedure applied in establishing the statements. Eclipses predicted do or do not occur, bridges stand the stress of traffic or break down, patients get healed or die, whatever the personal motivations of the astronomer, the engineering scientist or the medical man. Certain economic situations lead to unemployment or to inflation, whatever the economist's personal liking or disliking of the capitalist system. The validity of scientific statements does not depend on human motivations; it depends entirely on the observations of the rule of scientific procedure and is, therefore, interpersonal.

The ideological element in scientific inquiry need not always be a handicap in reaching interpersonally valid results. If this was not the case, little scientific progress would have been made. Ideological motivation may also stimulate the development of science. Discoveries have been made in physics and chemistry as a consequence of the desire to make profits or to promote national defence (indeed, the very development of these sciences is closely related to modern industry and warfare). Biological science has been stimulated by motivations of human sympathy for the sick and the suffering. Most important contributions

of the social sciences are due to passion for social justice and betterment. The discoveries of classical economics were thus ideologically
motivated by passion for freedom and justice as well as by the interest of
the industrial middle class. The progress of institutional economics was
substantially motivated ideologically by the desire for justice and for
the improvement of the lot of the industrial working class. Some relation seems to exist between the nature of the motivations and their
favourable or unfavourable influence upon the development of economics and other social sciences. "Conservative" motivations, i.e. motivations resulting from the desire to maintain established social
institutions and standards of civilisation tend to disfavour, while "progressive" motivations which result from the desire to change and improve social institutions and standards of civilisation tend to favour
the attainment of scientifically valid results in the domain of the social
sciences. For it is the desire for change and betterment, whether conscious or subconscious which creates the inquisitiveness of mind resulting in scientific investigation of human society.

3. THE UNITS OF ECONOMIC DECISION AND THEIR CO-ORDINATION

Administration of scarce resources, or economic activity, is carried on
by various units such as individual persons, families, business corporations, or agencies of the government. Each of these units has disposal
over certain resources and makes decisions as to their use. We shall call
them *units of economic decision* (or of economic activity). Three kinds
of use of resources are ordinarily distinguished: (1) *consumption* or the
use of resources for direct satisfaction of wants; (2) *production* or the
preparation and adaption of resources for the satisfaction of wants
through actions such as changing physical, chemical, and biological
qualities, changing location in space, and storing for future use; (3) *exchange* or the use of resources for procurement of resources from other
units of economic decision. Accordingly, the units of economic decision
are frequently classified as consumers and producers, respectively. These
classes, however, are not mutually exclusive. For the same unit is frequently a consumer and producer at the same time (a farm, for instance); almost all units in modern society engage in exchange. There
are practically no units engaging in exchange alone; e.g. commerce
involves always some change in location or some storage of resources.

A more important classification is one according to the objectives
which guide the decisions of the units. On this basis three types of units
can be distinguished:

(1) *Households*. The objective of the decisions of these units is con-

sumption, i.e. satisfaction of wants. Households may engage in exchange and in production, but these activities are undertaken with the purpose of providing for the satisfaction of wants of members of the unit. Households appear in different forms, namely, as individual persons, families, corporations, and even public agencies (e.g. a municipal orphanage). In our society, the family is the dominant form of a household.

(2) *Firms or Business Enterprises.* These are units which engage in exchange with the purpose of making a money profit, i.e. a difference between the money value of the resources sold and the money value of the resources bought. Firms are practically always producers; they are distinguished from other producers by the objective of their activity, namely the acquisition of money profit. Firms assume diverse forms: individual enterprises, business corporations, and also government agencies. In our present society, the corporate form is dominant.

(3) *Public Services.* These are agencies operated with the purpose of contributing to the attainment of certain social objectives (usually called public welfare). Instances of public services are schools, hospitals, research institutes, publicly owned and operated utilities, the post-office, the army and navy, etc. In most cases, public services are operated by some branch of government, national, state or local. But this is not always the case, e.g. privately endowed universities or hospitals. Certain public services are also operated jointly by two or several governments or by governments and private institutions.

The three objectives which serve as a basis for this classification can always be conceptually distinguished. Accordingly, each unit of economic decision will be considered as being either a household, a firm, or a public service. Under certain circumstances, the pursuit of one of these objectives may imply exactly the same actions as the pursuit of another one. Thus, a public service may, according to the social objective chosen, act exactly like a business enterprise. In such cases, it is necessary to ascertain the real objective of the decisions (e.g. attainment of a social objective or pursuit of money profit). This can be done by varying the circumstances hypothetically in such a way that the different objectives imply different actions and by inquiring into the actions which will be followed. It should also be noticed that individual persons may be members of several units of economic decision. For instance, a person can be a member of a household, and at the same time a member of several business firms.

The decisions of a unit may be independent of the decisions of other units and exert no influence on them. The unit is then said to be an isolated unit. Isolated units of economic decision are by necessity, households. In modern society, however, decisions of the various units influence each other; they are interdependent. The totality of inter-dependent units of economic decision is called an *economy* or an *economic system*. If the decisions of the different units in an economy are to be carried out, they must be consistent with each other. Thus, the quantity of resources which units wish to consume must be equal to the quantity which the same or other units wish to produce; the quantity of resources which units wish to acquire by exchange must be equal to the quantity which other units wish to give up in the exchange; the total quantity of a resource desired by the units must be equal to the quantity available in the economy. When the decisions of the various units in the economy are consistent with each other, the economy is said to be in *equilibrium*. Unless the economy is in equilibrium, the decisions of the units cannot all be translated into actions. In order for action to become possible, the decisions must be co-ordinated, i.e. brought into consistency with each other.

There are two principal methods by which decisions of the various units are co-ordinated. One is *planning*, i.e. co-ordination by a central authority with power to influence the decisions of the units. The means used by the planning authority to influence the decisions of the units are many. The planning authority can prescribe quotas, i.e. quantities of resources to be produced or consumed, bought or sold by each unit. It can also use more indirect means as, for instance, subsidies and taxes to encourage or discourage certain decisions. Another means of plan-ning is regulation, the setting of rules which the units must observe in their decisions and actions. The planning authority may extend over the whole economy or over a part of it. It may be public, e.g. an agency of government, or private, as for instance, a trade association or a cartel. We may, accordingly, distinguish between private and public planning.

The other method of co-ordination is the *market*. A market is a pat-tern of regular, recurrent exchange relations between units of economic decision. Regular exchange between a large number of units presup-poses the use of a generally accepted medium of exchange, namely of money. The units thus transact their exchange in two stages, sale and purchase; they sell their resources for money and buy with the money the resources desired. The ratio at which money and resources are ex-changed in the market is called the price. Meeting in the market, the various units match their offers and bids, their supplies and demands, against each other. They adjust and readjust their quantities offered and demanded and their prices, until co-ordination of their decisions is reached. Thus, through an interplay of the units in the market, equi-librium of the economy is attained. This happens quite unintentionally, as a by-product of the pursuit by each unit of its own individual goals (consumption, money profit, or public service). The market thus automatically produces a result equivalent to that of planning. Its operation has, therefore, been compared (by Adam Smith and others) to that of an invisible hand which produces co-ordination out of the autonomous decisions of many separate units. Not all markets, however, are able to produce such co-ordination, nor is the co-ordination obtained always consistent with accepted social objectives. In such cases, planning is used either to reach the co-ordination otherwise unobtainable or to correct the co-ordination produced by the "invisible hand" of the market.

Planning and the market do not exclude each other. Planning may utilise the uniformity of behaviour patterns of units operating in the market as one of the means of influencing their decisions. This happens, for instance, when the planning authority imposes tariffs or pays subsidies in order to influence the quantities bought or sold. Sometimes regulation—a special method of planning—is necessary in order to enable the market to achieve co-ordination of the units' decisions. The two methods of co-ordination co-exist with each other. However, in different historic societies, one or the other of these methods plays the preponderant role and appears as the chief means of co-ordinating all the units in the economy. The development of economics as a science is closely connected with the growing preponderance of the market in modern times. The co-ordinating operation of the market and, at times, the failure of the market to achieve co-ordination of decisions have posed the intellectual problems which have led to the emergence and growth of economic science.

4. CAPITALISM AND OTHER FORMS OF ECONOMIC ORGANISATION

The history of human society confronts us with different ways in which administration of scarce resources is organised. Of all types of economic activity, production is the one to which men devote their major time and attention. We, therefore, classify the forms of economic organisation according to the units of economic decision which are dominant in the performance of production. In older times, almost all producers were households; administration of resources was carried on in isolated units. Such a form of economic organisation is usually called a domestic economy. The growing interdependence of households through exchange of goods and services had led to the emergence of the firm or business enterprise as the dominant producing unit in the economy. At

present, in most of the advanced countries, production is done by firms.
Firms or business enterprises have as their objective one single magnitude, namely, money profit. In this they differ from households and public services. A household, for instance, desires to satisfy several wants, not to pursue merely one magnitude as an objective. Similar considerations hold for public services. Having one single magnitude for an objective, the firm attains the objective the better the greater the value of the magnitude attained. In other words: pursuing money profit for its objective, a firm wants to *maximise* it. It uses the resources at its disposal—its capital—in such a way as to obtain the greatest possible money profit. An economy in which all or most of production is done by firms is called a *capitalist economy*; the economic organisation which leaves production to firms is called *capitalism*. In our present economy, most of the firms or business enterprises are privately owned (most frequently they are private corporations). It is, however, possible to envisage an economic organisation in which production is assigned to publicly owned profit-maximising enterprises. We shall use the term *state capitalism* to denote such an economic organisation. For the sake of distinction, we may describe our present economic organisation as *private capitalism*. Since a publicly owned profit-maximising enterprise operates exactly like a private firm, this distinction is of no importance for economic theory, however significant it may be from the point of view of sociology or political science.

Pursuit of money profit implies participation in exchange. Firms regularly buy and sell resources. The market is, therefore, an integral part of the capitalist economy. It is, indeed, the chief method by which various units of decision in the capitalist economy are co-ordinated. Planning, however, is not excluded as a method of co-ordination under capitalism. It played an important part in early capitalism (mercantilist policy, e.g.) and increases steadily in importance in the present capitalist economy. The existence of the market is not sufficient for the economy to be capitalist; a market, for instance, exists in an economic organisation in which production is done by households which regularly exchange part of their products. For the economy to be capitalist, according to our definition, money profit must be the sole objective of the units engaged in production. This excludes an economy in which the satisfaction of wants competes with the profit-making objective. A craftsman may refuse to use an opportunity of making an additional money profit because it is not worth the effort involved or because he prefers to devote his time to the satisfaction of specific wants, such as company, entertainment, etc. A farmer may fail to maximise money profit because he prefers to

consume some of his products instead of selling them. In order that
the producing unit pursue money profit as its sole objective, it must
be entirely separated from the owner's (or owners') household and,
in addition, all services of persons employed by the unit must be
purchased in the market.

The condition that all services of persons employed by the producing
unit be purchased in the market implies that these persons do not
own the enterprise. They must be either pure labourers paid wages or
salaries or slaves purchased by the enterprise. In antiquity business
enterprises operated with slave labour played a considerable role.
Some authors, therefore, speak of capitalism in ancient Greece and
Rome. In modern times, however, business enterprises employ the
services of free wage and salary earners. The existence of a class of
labourers working for wages and salaries endows capitalism with
specific sociological features. Capitalism as a form of economic organisation is, therefore, a subject of study of economic sociology as
well as of economics.

Firms, as defined by us, are but approximate representations of certain units of economic decision found in experience. Although in
the present economy, money profit is the chief objective of most units
engaged in production, some other objectives are always co-existent.
Among these other objectives are, for instance, prestige, social standing, desire for a "quiet life," social responsibilities, and, most important of all, desire for safety, i.e. dislike of decisions involving risk.
Strictly speaking, the empirical units called "firms" or "business enterprises" are households which desire to satisfy these specific wants
alongside with making money profit; they are ready to sacrifice some
money profit to attain the other objectives. The pursuit of money
profit, however, dominates the other objectives to such an extent that
the units mentioned conform approximately to our theoretical concept of a firm. The extent of approximation between the theoretical
concept and its empirical counterpart justifies the assumption that
the units engaged in production pursue the single objective of money
profit as a useful simplification of analysis. The consequences of the
other objectives being present can be introduced at a later stage,
whenever necessary. However, the desire for safety may be of such
prominence that it sometimes becomes necessary to introduce it from
the very beginning in the analysis of the firm. This can be done by
redefining the firm as pursuing profit "discounted for risk" as a single
objective. The presence of a desire for safety among firms will be
considered as compatible with the capitalist character of the economy.

Another form of economic organisation to consider is *socialism*. This is an economic organisation where production is done by public services operated for the satisfaction of the wants of the community. Socialism is the objective of important social and political movements in many countries, e.g. the Labour Party in Great Britain, and in some of the Dominions, the Co-operative Commonwealth Federation in Canada, the socialist and communist movements in the various countries of Europe. One country, the Union of Soviet Socialist Republics, has established a socialist economy. In a socialist economy production is a public, not private, responsibility. All the units of economic decision charged with production need not be owned and operated by the central government. They may be owned and operated by branches of provincial and local government, by citizens' associations like co-operatives, unions, or collective farms, by special public service corporations, or foundations. There may be substantial decentralisation of units of decision in a socialist economy. All these units, however, must be public services, i.e they must be operated for the satisfaction of the wants of the whole community and not merely of members of the unit. In principle, the co-ordination of the decisions of the various units may be effected by either planning or the market. In practice, both methods prove necessary, as is similar under capitalism. Most socialists, however, assign planning a much greater role under socialism than it has under capitalism. In the U.S.S.R. planning serves as the basic method of co-ordination between producing units, the market playing an important subsidiary role in co-ordinating the decisions of households with the decisions of the producing units. If socialism is adopted by more countries, the socialist economies in different countries will probably differ substantially as to types of producing units, their degree of centralisation, and as to the relative importance of planning and the market as methods of co-ordination, just as the capitalist economy differs from country to country and in different historical periods.

History seldom confronts us with an economic organisation corresponding exactly to our theoretical classifications. In most cases, production is carried on by all three types of units of economic decision, by households, by firms, and by public services. Thus, in the United States at present, households like small farms or craftsmen and public services like publicly owned power plants or transportation services engage in production alongside with business enterprises. Elements of a domestic economy and of a socialist economy co-exist with those of a capitalist economy. But one of the three types (for instance, business enterprises in the United States) may be so dominant (in terms of the amount of resources at the disposal of units of this type) that the economy may be described as approximately domestic, capitalist, or socialist. For purposes of theoretical analysis, we then disregard the other elements and introduce them, if necessary, at a later stage. Such a procedure is sometimes called construction of "ideal types" of economic organisation. Economic theories can then be developed which describe the operation of such "typical" economies, e.g. the economics of capitalism or the economics of socialism. In some cases, however, this proves impossible because several types of units of economic decision are equally important in production, or although one type is dominant, some other type is too important to be disregarded even in a first approximation. For instance, in many countries of Europe big industry and finance are operated as public services, while medium-sized and small industry are operated by business enterprises; in addition, farming is frequently operated by households exchanging but a small part of their products in the market. In such case we speak of a *mixed economy*.

An instance of mixed economy occurs when the government chooses to leave production to private firms (or sometimes to households) or to conduct it through public services, depending upon, in each case, which course promises to contribute more to the satisfaction of the wants of the community. This may be called a *service economy* because production is assigned to the unit which best serves the social purpose. But it can be considered as a special kind of socialist economy. The purpose of production here is always satisfaction of the wants of the community; the operation of production is merely delegated to private firms if they do it better than, or at least, just as well as, public agencies. In such an economy private firms can be considered as a special kind of public service in which the managers are remunerated by being allowed to make whatever money profit they can. Furthermore, in a service economy the government must have the power to decide in each case whether a private firm or a public agency is to be charged with production. This presupposes an alignment of political power similar to that in a socialist society. The service economy type of socialism, rather than the "ideal type" excluding all forms of private business enterprise, is the objective of contemporary socialist movements; the political programmes of the socialist and communist parties are explicit in stating that private enterprise shall continue to operate under socialism in small farming, small trade, and small industry. It is, therefore, an important subject of study for economic science.

5. THE POSTULATE OF RATIONALITY

We have seen that the pursuit by firms of a single magnitude for an objective implies the desire to maximise it. A unit in pursuit of money profit but not desirous of maximising it obviously must be striving for additional objectives. It is ready to sacrifice some money profit for the attainment of some other objective or objectives. Thus, there appears to be an essential difference between firms and households. Firms pursue a single objective, a magnitude which they want to maximise; households, instead, are concerned with the satisfaction of many different wants, theirs being a multiplicity of objectives. However, since resources are scarce, wants must be weighed against each other and decisions must be made as to which wants to satisfy and to what extent; resources must be allocated accordingly. This implies the existence of given preferences which guide the houshold in choosing one allocation rather than another. We may now ask whether these preferences can be ordered along a scale. When this is possible, the household can be interpreted as pursuing a single objective, namely, the most preferred allocation of the resources among its different wants. The household appears then as maximising a magnitude. We call this magnitude *utility*. The decisions of the household are interpreted, in this case, in a way similar to those of firms, i.e. as resulting from the pursuit of a single objective.

The possibility of interpreting decisions of households in a way similar to decisions of firms suggests the adoption of a general postulate covering both cases. We call it the *postulate of rationality*. A unit of economic decision is said to act rationally when its objective is the maximisation of a magnitude. Firms thus act rationally, by definition, while households do so only when their preferred allocations of resources among different wants can be ordered along a scale. The postulate of rationality is the assumption that all units of economic decision act rationally. This assumption provides us with a most powerful tool for simplification of theoretical analysis. For if a unit of decision acts rationally, its decisions in any given situation can be predicted by mere application of the rules of logic (and of mathematics). In absence of rational action such prediction could be made only after painstaking empirical study of the uniformities in the decision patterns of the unit. For a unit which acts rationally, these uniformities or laws can be deduced immediately by logic and the decisions predicted, accordingly. Thus, the postulate of rationality is a short-cut to the discovery of laws governing the decisions of units and to the prediction of their actions under given circumstances.

Though a short-cut designed to save elaborate empirical investigation, the postulate of rationality, is nevertheless, but an empirical assumption. It is a hypothesis which, in each case, must be verified by confronting the logical deductions obtained from the postulate with the observations of experience. The use of the postulate is justified only when the logical deductions agree with the results of empirical observation with an acceptable degree of approximation. Otherwise, the postulate would lead us to make predictions which fail to be borne out by observed facts. This needs to be stressed because some economists believe that the postulate of rationality can be used as an *a priori* principle, not subject to empirical verification. In such case, however, the conclusions derived from the postulate of rationality could not have any empirical relevance, either. Theoretical economics would become a branch of pure logic or mathematics without empirical implications, whatsoever. If the laws deduced from the postulate of rationality are to serve as a basis of making predictions about the decisions of units encountered in experience, this postulate must be treated as an empirical hypothesis.

The hypothesis that producing units act rationally, i.e. with the objective of maximising money profit, is verified with satisfactory approximation in the capitalist economy. It serves, therefore, as a useful tool of simplification in the study of that economy. The situation is more doubtful with regard to households. Here the verification of the hypothesis is much more precarious, and we must expect much larger discrepancies between results of empirical observation and conclusions derived from the postulate of rationality. There seems, however, to be some difference between households operating in the capitalist economy and households of the domestic economy of precapitalist societies. The dominance of business enterprises with a tangible and quantified magnitude (money profit) as their objective has created a mental habit of considering all kinds of decisions as a pursuit of a single objective, expressed as a magnitude. Some authors call this mental habit the "capitalist spirit." It spreads beyond the specific decisions of business enterprises and affects the mode of operation of other units, including households. Under the influence of the mental habit mentioned, households are encouraged to order their preferences along a scale, i.e. to maximise utility. In capitalist society, therefore, the decisions of households are more likely to conform to the deductions derived from the postulate of rationality than in societies which preceded the rise of modern capitalism.

Public services act rationally when the social objective they aim at can be expressed as a single magnitude to be maximised. The magnitude is then called *public welfare*. Public welfare exists as a magnitude when the community, or more exactly the agencies of the community responsible for the judgment, have preferences as to the distribution of resources among members of the community as well as to the allocation of resources among the various wants of each member, and when, furthermore, these preferences can be ordered along a scale. In this case, the decisions of public services in any given situation can be derived by the rules of logic from the postulate of rationality. But the community seldom has such definite and ordered preferences. Because of this, the study of the operation of public services has to be based on the observations of institutional economics and economic history rather than on logical deductions from the postulate of rationality. However, there is a different way in which the postulate of rationality is useful in the study of public services. Instead of accepting it as an empirical hypothesis, we can consider conformity of public services with the postulate of rationality as a social objective. In other words: we can set up a chosen set of ordered preferences, i.e. some concept of public welfare, as our own (i.e. the student's) social objective and require that all public services be guided by this objective as a norm. This leads to rules of "ideal" use of resources and provides a basis for critical evaluation of the actual administration of resources by public services as well as by firms and households. The postulate of rationality becomes then the basis of a theory of welfare economics.

There is a difference between the rationality of households and firms and the rationality, whether (approximately) actual or normative (as in welfare economics) of public services. The first involves the pursuit of a private objective—utility or profit, respectively; the latter involves pursuit of a social objective, namely, public welfare. We can speak of *private* and *social rationality*, accordingly. Private rationality need not necessarily exclude social rationality. If the community's preferences as to allocation of resources among the various wants of each member coincide with the individual preferences of the members, then each member, by maximising his private utility, contributes to the attainment of maximum public welfare. Under certain conditions the maximisation of money profit by firms implies maximisation of public welfare too. In such cases, their own private rationality makes the members of the community act as if they were public services; private rationality then implies social rationality. The existence of such situations underlies the idea of the service economy. If all firms were always subject to these conditions, the capitalist economy could be considered as a special case of a service economy in which it is found expedient to delegate all production to private firms. This, indeed, is the famous doctrine of *laissez faire* which maintains that the capitalist economy, provided it is not hampered by government planning, spontaneously operates in such a way that it secures the maximum of public welfare. Accordingly, non-interference in the spontaneous operation of the capitalist economy is considered to be the best way of assuring the "ideal" use of resources. Most contemporary students of welfare economics consider this claim to be false and point out many conflicts between the private rationality of business enterprises and social rationality as postulated by welfare economics. The private rationality of business enterprises is also in conflict with the social objectives accepted by most citizens of modern democratic society. This accounts for the increasing tendency toward planning under contemporary capitalism and also for the socialist movements present in most capitalist countries.

A final observation has to be made about the procedure of verification of the postulate of rationality. There is some difference in procedure between firms, on the one hand, and households and public services on the other. Money profit is a quantity which can be observed empirically (like, for instance, velocity in physics). The theoretical concept of money profit, therefore, can be easily identified with corresponding empirical observations (the procedure of identification involves an interpretation of book-keeping categories). Direct observation tells, then, whether firms do or do not maximise money profit. Utility and public welfare, instead, are purely theoretical constructs; there are no empirical observations which would serve as their counterparts (just like in the case of the concept of potential in physics). But this does not preclude verification by indirect devices. The uniformities of decision patterns are different when utility or public welfare, respectively, are maximised than when they are not. This difference in the uniformities mentioned makes it possible to verify empirically the hypothesis of rationality of acts of households and of public services.

2

METHODOLOGICAL PRESCRIPTIONS IN ECONOMICS *

K. Klappholz teaches at the London School of
Economics & Political Science. J. Agassi teaches
at Boston University and The University of
Tel Aviv; he was formerly at the London School
of Economics & Political Science.

The two books under review [1] offer somewhat extreme examples of an impatience which is often to be found in methodological criticisms of economics. This impatience has a variety of targets, such as the "unnecessarily" slow progress in economics or the futility of much of the work done, and sometimes expresses itself in the complaint that economists often advance hypotheses which appear to be untestable, etc. And the impatience appears to give rise to the belief that, if only economists adopted this or that methodological rule, the road ahead would at least be cleared (and possibly the traffic would move briskly along it).

Our view, on the contrary, is that there is only one generally applicable methodological rule, and that is the exhortation to be critical and always ready to subject one's hypotheses to critical scrutiny. Any attempt to reinforce this general maxim by a set of additional rules is likely to be futile and possibly harmful.

To illustrate our contention we shall examine some of the methodological rules proposed not only in the books under review but also in some other recent writings on the methodology of economics. Our criticism will be based on our methodological point of view, which is that outlined in K. R. Popper's *Logic of Scientific Discovery*.

* From *Economica* N.S., Vol. XXVI (February, 1959), pp. 60–74. Reprinted by permission of the authors and the Economica Publishing Office.

[1] Sidney Schoeffler, *The Failures of Economics: a Diagnostic Study*, Harvard University Press, 1955. xv + 254 pp. 38s.
Andreas G. Papandreou, *Economics as a Science*, J. B. Lippincott Company, 1958. x + 146 pp.
We wish to thank Mr. L. P. Foldes and Professor L. Robbins for their valuable criticisms and suggestions.

I

We begin with Lionel Robbins' *Essay on the Nature and Significance of Economic Science* (second edition, 1935), since it is the first significant English work in this field in this century, and some subsequent discussions to which we refer can be viewed as (somewhat excessive) reactions to Robbins' attitude.

Even though Robbins' aim was "not to discover how Economics should be pursued" (p. 72), it is clear that methodological prescription was prominent in his *Essay*. We note, in particular, his suggestion that there should be an *a priori*, water-tight, separation between economics and other sciences. This amounted to the *a priori* decision to view certain variables of economics (e.g. tastes and technology) as essentially "exogenous", i.e. as not determined within economic models, rather than as not yet explained by any existing economic model. Robbins did not, of course, object to attempts to explain "tastes" psychologically or sociologically, but according to his view no explanation of them should contain (endogenous) economic variables. Secondly, he denied *a priori* the possibility of discovering "quantitative" laws in economics.

We find these suggestions unacceptable because they are designed to limit the fields of argument *a priori*. As a hypothesis, the view that tastes are independent of other economic factors could be subject to critical discussion; it could be countered by an alternative hypothesis describing conceivable relations between income, prices, tastes, etc. Robbins apparently did not advance his view that tastes are exogenous as a hypothesis, but rather as a methodological rule designed to delineate the area of economic discussion. The rule, in its turn, was based on more general considerations—on his general view of economics as a science.

Robbins regarded scientific laws as universal statements known with certainty to be true; laws were statements of the necessary aspects of natural phenomena. Examples of such laws in economics were the law of demand, the law of diminishing returns, and the quantity theory of money. How was knowledge of these laws obtained? It was derivable neither from history nor from controlled experiment, but rather obtained by a process of "deduction from a series of postulates. And the chief of these postulates are all assumptions involving in some way simple and indisputable facts of experience. . . . They are so much the stuff of everyday experience that they have only to be stated to be recognised as obvious" (pp. 78, 79).

Everyday experience might perhaps tell us that tastes are exogenous, but it certainly cannot tell us that tastes, or any other factor, must be regarded as exogenous in all future theories. The view, however, that economic laws are certain and must be based on everyday experience, does somehow entail that some factor or other must be exogenous.

The assertion that a law exists which describes the relation between the quantity of money in circulation and the price-level amounts to the claim that only a finite number of specifiable factors are relevant to this relation; for if a statement of this relation is made in which some relevant factors are overlooked, the statement will be refuted by showing the relevance of these factors. For example, a crude version of the theory ignored economic growth, and was thus refutable by showing that economic growth might prevent a rise in the price-level in spite of an increase of the quantity of money.

Thus a law, to be true, must correctly refer to all the relevant factors, which must of course be finite in number (since otherwise we could not mention them all). Now, if one defends a law one also implicitly defends the truth of the assertion that only a finite number of identifiable factors are relevant to the phenomena explained by it. One may, however, invert the procedure by asserting the following: even before we have any particular law we know that we can discover some laws, namely those explaining phenomena, which are subject to a finite number of identifiable factors. This view, when extended to all phenomena, is the view which J. M. Keynes, in his *Treatise on Probability,* called the *principle of limited variety.*[2] This principle amounts to the *a priori* assertion that every effect has a finite number of possible causes which are identifiable *a priori;* it thus implies that *all* laws are discoverable.

Now Robbins, unlike Keynes, did not accept the principle of limited variety as applicable to all cases. For example, he was agnostic as to the existence of quantitative laws, and merely claimed that we could not discover them. It seems, however, that Robbins did claim the following: since everyday experience reveals that certain economic phenomena are governed by a finite number of identifiable factors (since otherwise economic behaviour could not be rational), everyday experience guarantees the existence of laws which explain *some* phenomena. If one insists that only laws guaranteed by everyday experience will be found, one can hardly escape the conclusion that certain variables will inevitably remain exogenous.

One could criticise this position from a logical point of view, by arguing that empirical statements, however well-grounded in everyday experience (or in controlled experiment), are never indisputable; that

2 Pp. 234 *et seq.*; cf. Ch. XXIII.

we can never identify the relevant factors *a priori;* that many statements which were once considered to be quite indisputable were subsequently shown to be false. Yet such an attack, though logically
impeccable, would not be damaging to Robbins' position, which he
could retain with slight modifications. He could still claim that, although in principle all of economic theory is disputable, no reasonable
person would dispute such statements as the law of demand, and that
this law, and other similarly trivial statements, can explain much more
than meets the eye. (This is essentially Milton Friedman's position,
as we argue in section III).

We therefore dissent from Robbins' point of view rather than criticise his particular conclusions. We agree that many scientific statements
are accepted without debate, but we hold that such statements are of
little scientific interest. Scientific interest is aroused by controversial
statements, and by the controversy round them. Undisputed statements
are usually the product of qualifications of statements which were once
disputed, and the qualifications are accepted as the result of successful
criticism. For example, the quantity theory of money was once hotly
disputed; by now the accepted version is so well qualified (by conditional clauses regarding liquidity preference, unemployment, economic growth, etc.) that it is hardly of great *theoretical* interest. To
regain this interest, the theory would have to explain what we already
know by means of a less qualified, or more universal, statement.

Perhaps we should explain the sense in which we use the term "of
scientific interest". Clearly, the law of demand, the quantity theory of
money, and similar propositions are of the utmost importance for
economic policy. They are comparable, however, not to the laws of
physics which are now the subject of controversy, like quantum theory,
but rather to Gray's law of conductivity (metals conduct electricity),
which is obviously significant technologically. (See below, section III).
This law is as undisputed today as the law of demand, and equally
manifest in everyday experience. Yet this is precisely why Gray's law
is not of intellectual interest in current research in physics. Similarly,
the present wide acceptability of the law of demand renders it an
inadequate example of the significance of economic science. The
significance of economics, as of any other science, lies in its search for
new truths.

II

As we have said, we do not so much criticise Robbins' position from
a formal point of view, but rather from our view of what is of scientific

interest. An attempt at a formal criticism of Robbins was undertaken by T. W. Hutchison in his influential book, *The Significance and Basic Postulates of Economic Theory* (1938). Hutchison claimed that "propositions of pure theory" and "economic laws", as stated by Robbins and most other economists, were "tautologies" or "analytic truths". This appraisal was important since it was coupled with the prescription that scientific economic discussion should be confined to testable statements; for Hutchison has the great merit of having introduced (Popper's) falsifiability criterion into the discussion.

Hutchison's appraisal was based on the fundamental " 'division by dichotomy' . . . or exhaustive twofold classification of all propositions which have 'scientific sense' " (p. 26) into statements which are "conceivably falsifiable by observation" or *"forbid . . .* [some] conceivable occurrence", and statements which are not. The former are empirical statements and the latter logically true statements, or tautologies. All (scientifically meaningful) statements, he contended, fall into either of these two categories.

Hutchison took it for granted that the class of statements which are "conceivably falsifiable by observation" was identical with the class of those which *"forbid . . .* [some] conceivable occurrence"; which is a mistake. One can imagine a factually false statement which is irrefutable. Such a statement would *"forbid . . .* [some] conceivable occurrence", and yet would not be "conceivably falsifiable by observation". In this case these two classes of statements would not be identical. Hutchison argued, for example (Ch. II, 5), that since statements with unspecified *ceteris paribus* clauses are irrefutable, they are tautological (or logically true). Yet it can easily be proved that these unfalsifiable statements are not usually tautologies. Consider the two statements: *"ceteris paribus,* the imposition of a tax on cigarettes will raise their price", and *"ceteris paribus,* the imposition of a tax on cigarettes will *not* raise their price". These statements are untestable as long as the *ceteris paribus* clauses in them remain unspecified. But they are clearly not both tautologies, for they are incompatible with each other. Yet, according to Hutchison, both are tautologies. Thus Hutchison's identification of "conceivably refutable" with "possibly false" led him to the inconsistency of viewing as tautological all statements of economics which are qualified by unspecified *ceteris paribus* clauses.

To be sure, we do not claim that Hutchison was always mistaken in viewing propositions of pure theory as tautologies. Yet even where he is right, his argument depends on a particular interpretation of statements of pure theory, an interpretation which is neither necessary nor conventional. Often he criticised economists for uttering tautologies, when their utterances were not tautologies except on his interpretation. From his survey of economic theory one gets the impression that most economic theorists of his day uttered almost nothing but tautologies, although his book appeared two years after Keynes' *General Theory*. Yet Keynes was undoubtedly concerned with empirical issues.

We may give an example of Hutchison's imposition of his own meaning on other people's writings. Robbins had claimed that the quantity theory of money was indisputable and had predictive power (p. 117). Had Hutchison criticised this on the grounds that no theory is both indisputable and informative, we would have no comment. Yet we see no reason for his contention that "we find empirical content being read [by Robbins] into propositions of pure theory just because of their necessity and inevitability" (p. 65). The reference to "necessity and inevitability", which for Robbins was the necessity of a verified empirical law, was by no means sufficient ground for the claim that Robbins had stated the quantity theory of money as a tautology. If we understand him rightly, Hutchison argued (p. 66) that $"MV = PT"$, *is* a tautology, though $"M = kP"$ is not. This invites a few comments. First, since Robbins had referred to Sir William Petty's quantity theory of money, which is nearer to $"M=kP"$ than to $"MV=PT"$, Hutchison should have noticed that in Robbins' sense the theory was not a tautology, rather than blame Robbins for "reading content" into a tautology. Secondly, Hutchison did not show that $"MV=PT"$ was a tautology in all conventional interpretations. Thirdly, reading empirical content into a tautology is a perfectly respectacle procedure (at least since Hilbert's system of geometry was devised). True, the reading of content into a tautology renders it into a non-tautology, and robs it of its certitude; but it also does give it predictive power in many cases. Quite generally, we have great latitude in the interpretation of postulates. We often have the choice of viewing them either as tautologies or as hypotheses, as Hutchison himself pointed out (pp. 43, 44). Why then did he insist on viewing most of the "propositions of pure theory" as tautologies? The reason seems to be quite clear: he was driven to do so by the adoption of his dichotomy. He regarded most propositions of "pure theory" as untestable and, given the dichotomy, a statement which appeared to be untestable could be nothing but a tautology.

Hutchison adopted the dichotomy in order to propose the rule, "Do not argue about tautologies, but only about testable statements!" We have sought to show that Hutchison's dichotomy is false. If we still wished to follow his dictum, we should have to rule out as uninteresting not merely tautologies but also all untestable (or seemingly untestable) statements. This would amount to an undesirable restriction on the range of argument, especially since it is often difficult to know whether an important new idea is testable. It would surely be a mistake to rule such an idea out of court merely on the grounds that it did not appear to be testable.

Hutchison advocated the adoption of his rule in order to ensure adherence to the critical attitude. As we have already said, we do not think that the adoption of such rules necessarily has this result (for a discussion may still be *un*critical even though the rules are adopted). Hutchison was primarily concerned with the status (the testability) of statements, believing, apparently, that the restriction of discussion to testable statements would ensure that these statements would be tested and, if refuted, rejected. He seems to have held this view partly because (on the basis of the dichotomy) he thought that the *only* way to escape refutation of an empirical statement was to turn it into a tautology (p. 43). We have argued that this is not so. Yet it partly explains why Hutchison did not explicitly distinguish between the testability of a statement, and its being on the agenda for testing. Yet this distinction may be crucial. Our interest in testability is due to the fact that we are interested in testing. And our interest in testing stems from the fact that we learn by it. Yet in order to learn it is necessary that the test be such as to expose a hypothesis to the risk of falsification. Tests can easily be performed without any risk of falsification (for example, if we repeatedly "test" an astronomical hypothesis by deducing from it the prediction that the sun will rise tomorrow and testing his prediction); but nothing can be learnt from such testing. Moreover, there may be many testable statements which no one would trouble to test. In fact, neither the testability of a hypothesis nor its testing ensures the practical application of the critical attitude. Professor Popper has strongly emphasised this point, namely, that the critical attitude demands *severe* and *sincere* attempts to *falsify* our views, and he also stated the arguments against the dichotomy.

III

It seems to us that Milton Friedman's position, as outlined in the essay "The Methodology of Positive Economics" in his *Essays in Positive Economics* (1953), is an example of the acceptance of the methodological rules which are part and parcel of the critical approach, yet without the wholehearted adoption of the approach itself.

The central thesis of Friedman's essay is that much criticism of economic theory has been methodologically wrong-headed and misses the target, a thesis he easily establishes. Yet in his rebuttal of these misconceived criticisms, Friedman adopts a position which impedes criticism in general. We shall state three of his points, and then criticise them. *(a)* "A hypothesis can be tested *only* by the conformity of its implications or predictions with observable phenomena" (p. 40, our italics). *(b)* "Great confidence is attached to . . . [a hypothesis] if it has survived many opportunities for contradiction" (p. 9). This is apparently the case regarding "existing relative price theory", which is therefore "deserving of much confidence" (p. 41). *(c)* A new or rival theory "must have implications susceptible to empirical contradiction" before it can be regarded as interesting and important (p. 38).

(a) It is clear that empirical testing is the highest and most desirable form of critical argument concerning a theory; and it is also clear that in the history of economics too little attention has been paid to this form of critical argument. Yet it is a cardinal mistake to lay down the rule that empirical testing against observable phenomena should be the only acceptable method of criticism.[3] It seems important to emphasise this because, perhaps as a reaction against the manifestly insufficient attempts to test economic theories empirically, a mood is developing according to which empirical testing is regarded as the *sine qua non* of critical argument.

The insistence on empirical testing as the only form of acceptable criticism amounts to the assertion that untestable theories cannot be criticised and overthrown, which is historically untrue. For example, it is not clear whether Say's Law is empirically testable; yet in some sense it is considered as overthrown and given up. Again, some Mercantilist theories were abandoned as a result of heuristic criticism, rather than because of their conflict with observed phenomena. Furthermore, if we insist that as yet untestable theories cannot be successfully criticised, we are unlikely to develop testable theories at all. Testable theories are developed by a long process of arduous argument; we do not usually start an argument by producing an empirically testable hypothesis. Friedman tends to dismiss the theories of monopolistic competition and full-cost pricing on the grounds, among others, that they are untestable (p. 38, p. 33, note 25). Perhaps they are; but this is

[3] Since any criticism, other than proof of inconsistency, must somehow pertain to some facts, Friedman's dictum may be easily saved by using "empirical test" in a much wider sense than intended. Yet clearly our examples below are not "empirical tests" in the intended sense. Furthermore, one might criticise an explanation of some economic phenomena by pointing out that it unintentionally contained undesirable psychological implications, while if it were modified no such implications would follow and the explanatory power would remain unimpaired. But such kinds of criticism are hardly tests in the ordinary sense of the word.

not a reason for dismissing them, but rather a reason for criticising them in an attempt to make them testable. One of the problems which the theory of monopolistic competition was designed to tackle was the problem of "product competition". It is obviously an important problem, and one which has no place in the competitive model. The theory of monopolistic competition may not solve the problem, and may not even have tackled it sensibly. But at the very least it has drawn attention to the problem and provided a framework within which it can be discussed, which is sufficient reason for not dismissing the theory off-hand (especially as long as no alternative framework for the discussion of the problem is available).

There is also an "economic" argument against the insistence on testing as the only acceptable form of criticism. It is often possible to refute a hypothesis merely by a *Gedankenexperiment,* or by pointing out that it conflicts with an accepted hypothesis, or with known facts. For example, Galileo's hypothesis (which Friedman regards as "accepted" (p. 16) was shown to be unsatisfactory by *Gedankenexperimente* concerning the gravitation of the earth and the moon. If this can be done, it may be a more "economical" method of refutation than empirical testing.

(b) There are two different senses in which, according to Friedman, a hypothesis is "acceptable" as a result of ". . . its repeated failure to be contradicted" by experience (p. 23), (although he does not make this distinction). In the first sense he claims that the hypothesis is "acceptable" for technological purposes. In the second, he argues that it ought to be accepted in the sense that we ought to believe in its truth.

The two senses of "acceptability" cannot coincide since we have to disbelieve a refuted theory and yet may accept it for technological purposes (in physics as well as in economic policy). Newton's theory is accepted and widely used in technology because in technology we are not concerned with its (false) view of forces as acting at a distance, or that it is inapplicable to strong gravitational fields. At most a technologist who applies Newton's theory has to know that it is inapplicable where very high velocities are involved. Usually a theory accepted for technological purposes must command wide acceptance within the field of its practical application, for application may be dangerous as long as there is serious doubt concerning it. Yet this wide acceptability relates to highly qualified statements, and the qualifications, which are usually the result of past refutations, serve to delineate sharply the field of practical application.

The second sense is that of credibility, or high degree of belief, or

32 READINGS IN MICROECONOMICS

confidence in a scientific hypothesis, which results from a failure of attempts to refute it. We deny that this acceptability is compulsory. The refutation of a hypothesis does indeed compel us to reject it; but the absence of successful refutation of a hypothesis certainly does not prescribe belief or "confidence" in it. Confidence in a hypothesis is purely a matter of subjective estimate, and there are no rules or theorems which relate absence of refutation to desirable confidence in a hypothesis.

This is not the place to discuss this controversial philosophic issue.[4] We mention it in order to substantiate our claim that Friedman, in spite of his avowed intentions, does not wholeheartedly accept the critical approach. He wishes to use the absence of refutation as a credential for a theory, whereas the critical attitude is not particularly concerned with credentials but rather with argument. Friedman regards it as "trivial" that economic theory is open to criticism; it obviously offers a target for criticism "in a trivial sense", he says, because "any theory is necessarily provisional and subject to change with the advance of knowledge" (p. 41). This indeed may be trivial. It seems to us less trivial to stress the fruitfulness of criticism, or the fact that criticism may lead to the advance of knowledge. Criticism is an attempt to show that existing views require modification; if the criticism is successful it may lead to attempts at modification. And every modification of an existing view is itself an advance of knowledge. For this reason we are less impressed than Friedman by the absence of refutations.[5]

(c) The doctrine that the absence of refutation imposes a desirable degree of confidence in a hypothesis can be an impediment to critical argument. One way to stimulate argument against a hypothesis is to attempt to produce a rival one. Yet it is difficult to produce a rival hypothesis if it is claimed that existing unrefuted hypotheses must command confidence. If, in addition, one insists that a new rival hypothesis must be testable before it is an interesting subject for argument, the production of new hypotheses is made yet more difficult. Thus the doctrine of desirable confidence allied with the insistence on "testability here and now" may be a hindrance to scientific argument

[4] This issue is discussed in Popper's *Logic of Scientific Discovery*, Ch. X.
[5] We have said before (p. 30) that one can "test" a theory without exposing it to the risk of refutation, and that this is hardly an interesting or useful method of "testing". To avoid "testing" of this sort, Friedman holds that a hypothesis is particularly interesting if it ". . . yields . . . predictions about phenomena not yet observed" (p. 7), with which we quite agree. Yet Friedman does not adduce a single example of an economic theory which has been tested in this way. (The examples he mentions on pages 22-23 are not of this type).

and progress and a weapon for the defence of the scientific *status quo.* It is preferable, we think, to help our critic to formulate his rival hypothesis rather than to discourage him.

It seems clear that Friedman did not intend the consequences which we believe to result from his position. Possibly he overlooked them because of his view that the process of constructing new hypotheses "is a creative act of inspiration . . ." which ". . . must be discussed in psychological, not logical, categories" (p. 43). No doubt he is right. Yet there is also a logical category vitally relevant to the process of constructing new hypotheses, and that is criticism. Criticism fosters the creative inspiration which gives rise to the production of new hypotheses in at least two ways. It inspires new attempts, and it helps to eliminate errors which impede new inspiration. Since Friedman stresses the desirability of developing a more general theory of the allocation of resources than the present one, the purpose of his criticism of the theory of monopolistic competition is presumably to stimulate further attempts. Yet his criticism of the theory of monopolistic competition rests mainly on impatient methodology and is conservative and discouraging rather than stimulating.

IV

Although the preceding comments are occasioned by the two books under review, we must say straightaway that these books fall well below the high standards set by the authors we have considered so far. The two books invite criticism because the methodological faults which we have pointed out are here carried to almost incredible extremes.

Professor Papandreou's *Economics as a Science* conveys the following message: models are untestable unless the parameters in their equations are numerically determined. From this he concludes that all economics so far, including Keynesian models, is untestable and hence unscientific. The view that economics is a science is said to be sheer "folklore" and "myth". In fact his claim amounts to the assertion that unless we start doing econometrics we shall not engage in scientific activity.

We find it difficult to understand how this central thesis of the book could ever have been advanced. It is all the more puzzling since Papandreou seems to accept (pp. 81, 127) P. A. Samuelson's view that qualitative economics is testable to a certain extent *(Foundations,* pp. 7, 257).[6] The only clue seems to be a remark at the very end of the first (introductory) chapter. "Empirical meaningfulness in the

---

[6] One of Samuelson's main purposes seems to be the use of this testability to the utmost *(Foundations of Economic Analysis,* p. 284).

Samuelson sense", we read (on p. 11), "constitutes a program of research rather than an accomplished fact". Unfortunately, this statement is not substantiated anywhere in the book.

Yet this very statement, or the phrase "empirical meaningfulness"
in it, may provide a clue to our first puzzle: why does Papandreou
claim that economic models are untestable unless the parameters in
them are numerically determined? Our tentative answer may also
explain the purpose of the purely terminological discussion which fills
more than half of his volume. Although the author seems quite diffident
about the purpose of this lengthy discussion, it seems that he tries to
construct a language in which only testable statements are meaningful.
In this language expressions with unspecified parameters are not meaningful statements but merely statement-schemata (pp. 117–18).

This attempt may be criticised on at least three grounds. First, some
theories, which are meaningful in his language, may be untestable (for
example, a theory of an economy with 90 per cent unemployment),
while others, meaningless in his language, are testable (for example,
the models which Samuelson discusses). Secondly, there is no point
in forcing people to state only testable statements. As we have argued,
people's willingness to test hypotheses or to accept refutations will not
be increased merely by forcing them to utter only testable statements.
Thirdly, Papandreou only provides notations and definitions, but
he has not constructed a language. He does not specify rules of statement formation; and he does not provide rules of inference. It must
have been a slip of his pen when he writes (p. 128) of "derivation (as
defined in chapter 2)", for neither there nor elsewhere in the book
does he define "derivation".

Since the class notation which Papandreou introduces seems now to
be coming into vogue, we should warn the reader lest he be too impressed by it. We are rather indifferent to notation; we merely deny
that it necessarily adds to clarity or precision. A case in point is
Papandreou's own work which looks very impressive indeed. Yet the
bits of logic and mathematics it contains leave much to be desired.[7]

---

[7] The author's main concept is that of "generic element" (i.e. "variable"). It is
defined (pp. 60-61) with the help of the concept of "power set", but as the author
admits (footnote 1, p. 61) the definition is quite inadequate for his own purposes.
The proper definition is much simpler. The author's demand that the "social
space", as he defines it, should be used to specify the circumstances in which
the theory is supposed to apply is *apriorist*. For a theory is a *description* of the
"social space" whether or not it agrees with the author's definitions. Apart from
definitions, the only part of the mathematical exposition (pp. 39–100) which is of
substance is on pp. 87–89. The reader who wishes to understand these three pages
should consult Samuelson's *Foundations*, Ch. II, especially p. 10.

Prior to the mathematical exposition there is a discussion (pp. 13–38) of deduc-

On the whole, his nomenclature seems to reduce rather than increase both clarity and precision.

V

The second book under review also advances the thesis that there has been no economic science, but goes further and seeks to demonstrate that economics can never be scientific. Thus Professor Schoeffler's *The Failures of Economics* is not only completely outside the Weber-Robbins tradition in economics, which is shared by all other writers we mention, but advocates, moreover, that economists abandon this tradition.

Our reason for examining Schoeffler's work in some detail is that he provides persuasive rationalisations for widely prevalent but utterly dangerous muddles. In general, one prefers to ignore the confusions which occasionally creep into the literature, hoping that they will quietly lapse into oblivion without doing much harm. But this book is better not ignored. There is another reason for taking Schoeffler to task, namely that he fails to take his immediate predecessors seriously. He accuses economists of not having progressed since Mill (p. 1); we accuse him of regressing to Mill and even to ideas which Hume refuted. The demand for scientific progress may be an excessive demand; but the demand to avoid regression is not unreasonable, since it can be met simply by adhering to the vital tradition of not ignoring one's predecessors.

"So far, the most spectacular accomplishment of economics has been its failures . . .", writes Professor Schoeffler, referring to the deplorable inability of economists to make dependable predictions, for example, as to "where the Federal Reserve index of industrial production will stand six months hence" (p. 4). The purpose of his book is ". . . to inquire into the whys and wherefores of these failures . . . before searching for the appropriate curative treatments" (p. 6).

---

tive systems. This discussion is mainly concerned with formal (uninterpreted) systems—quite useless for economics, of course—and their subsequent interpretations. There is no discussion of deduction or derivation, not even mention of derivation as a truth-preserving transformation. The author stresses that the formulæ of a formal (uninterpreted) system "mean nothing" (p. 15), that its rules of transformation are "arbitrary within certain [?] bounds" (p. 14) and similar to the rules of chess (p. 16). Yet in his example of a formal (uninterpreted) system he has as a rule of transformation "if P and $P \longrightarrow Q$ are true, then Q is true" (p. 23)! The author is also confused about matters which are of importance for his discussion, e.g. the distinction between derivation and proof (pp. 17, 23).

All these confusions are particularly unfortunate since the author explicitly recommends his book "as an adjunct in classes in economic theory, economic method, and mathematical economics" (p. ix).

His diagnosis of the causes of these failures is quite simple. Economists have been looking for economic laws although it is clear that such laws do not exist. In so doing, they have been driven to commit a whole host of methodological "artificialities" which render economics useless for dependable prediction. Economists have failed to realise that their field is fundamentally different from that of the natural sciences, and requires a different methodology.

The following are his suggested remedies. Economists should stop attempting the impossible and give up the harmful pretence of being scientists engaged in the discovery of empirical laws. Instead, they should try to be useful and help to solve practical economic problems. This would indeed require prediction. Since the crux of Schoeffler's thesis is that there can be no economic laws, predictions in economics must be based on facts and on ". . . laws *already established by other sciences*" (p. 157, author's italics), and derived with the aid of inductive logic. The sciences which are to provide economists with laws are the natural sciences as well as "psychology, social psychology, and perhaps, sociology . . ." (p. 158). Professor Schoeffler nowhere explains why the other social sciences should be able to establish laws while economics cannot do so. Nor does he tell us what some of these laws are, except that "there is little doubt" that "dynamic laws of habit and attitude formation and change . . . actually exist" (p. 78). The main fountain of economic predictions, however, should be the rules of inductive logic which apparently enable us to make dependable predictions even without laws, although laws (from *other* sciences) may render the predictions even more dependable.

How does Schoeffler come to make such suggestions? Why does he hold that "the history of economic thought . . . constitutes a gigantic blind alley . . ." (p. 162)? This question leads us to his general view of science.

Professor Schoeffler is an inductivist. He believes implicitly in the possibility of making probabilistic predictions of some future events *solely* on the basis of past information, and that we can predict some future events with certainty on the basis of inductively verified laws. His view of verification closely follows Mill's: a law, he holds, is a statement whose ". . . validity conditions are fully stated; that is, it holds true, as it stands, under all possible surrounding circumstances. There should be no unstated validity conditions a change in which could, without previous notice, make the statement untrue" (p. 46). That is to say, we must consider *all* the circumstances which are relevant to a given relationship, and find out *all* the circumstances under which the relationship in question does not hold. As a result we should be able to state the circumstances in which the specified relationship *will always* hold, and this statement obviously would be a verified law. If we ignore *any* relevant circumstance, we no longer have a valid law, but merely assumptions or hypotheses which necessarily contain "artificialities", and are quite undependable for purposes of prediction.[8] This, as we noted, is Keynes' principle of limited variety (which, Keynes asserted, was implicit in Mill's doctrine).

Now, Schoeffler's thesis is that there can be no economic laws. In order to establish this, he tries to show that the economic system is "essentially open", where an "essentially open system" is defined as one regarding which ". . . we have *conclusive evidence* supporting the belief that . . ." it can never be law-abiding (pp. 49–50, our italics). It is not surprising that Schoeffler holds that we can have "conclusive evidence" concerning the question of whether a system is law-abiding, because he appears to take for granted the principle of limited variety. Yet when, after a lengthy series of definitions, he attempts to show that the "system" is "essentially open" (i.e. that we have "conclusive evidence" that it is lawless), he admits that "this assertion is easier to make than to prove" (p. 51). This amounts by (definition) to the admission that the "economic system" is *not* "essentially open"; nevertheless, after failing to prove his point, he proceeds as though it had been proved.

Clearly we can never have "conclusive evidence" that a system is or is not law-abiding (just as we can never verify any law). Consequently, Schoeffler has not advanced a methodological criticism of existing economic theories, as he thinks he has done, but rather an alternative (metaphysical) economic theory, the consequences of which he himself appears to find implausible.

Professor Schoeffler's theory is that no economic laws exist. It would follow that all "economic variables" are independent of each other, and therefore, for example, that the price-level is totally independent of the quantity of money. He may claim that he can escape this consequence by asserting that in an "essentially open system" the "variables" need not be totally independent; a system is "essentially open" if the relationships among its constituent "variables" are known to be "too weak or too few" (p. 50). But this is clearly inconsistent. However weak or few the relationships are, on

---

8 Undergraduates who complain that the social sciences can never be "scientific" seem implicitly to share Schoeffler's notions of what constitutes a scientific law.

"Artificialities" are false universal statements, like the hypothesis of profit maximisation. Since there are no economic laws, all economic models necessarily contain "artificialities".

38

his own view we could state a law which describes just these weak relationships.

Professor Schoeffler's discussion of the failures of economics and his analysis of the reasons for these failures are completed within 54 pages. The next 100 pages constitute so-called case-studies, in which one economic model after another is proved to contain "artificialities".[9] Usually the argument runs as follows: since the theory contains assumptions of economic laws of one kind or another, and since no economic laws exist, the model is false. This is, of course, *petitio principii* of the most obvious type.

We conclude that Schoeffler's attempted critique of economics fails entirely. Indeed, it seems to us utterly pointless to talk of "relevant variables" and "validity conditions" *except in the context of hypotheses*. Hence we can conceive of no other reasonable procedure in economics than the attempt to formulate hypotheses and to subject them to critical assessment. Schoeffler's alternative, namely the possibility of basing predictions solely on past information, is a myth which has been propagated by philosophers over the past two centuries. We find Hume's criticism of it wholly convincing. We are quite aware that some distinguished contemporary philosophers do not share our opinion; conspicuous among them Rudolf Carnap, from whom Schoeffler borrows his predictive model (cf. p. 185). This is not the place to debate this issue; moreover, Schoeffler himself grants that the application of his model is in any case impractical for the time being, if only for purely technical reasons. Still he offers the unabashed suggestion that economists should forthwith abandon their traditional (critical) method in favour of his.

VI

We have indicated our view of the proper place of methodological criticism at the beginning of this paper. We do not think this is a particularly unusual view; indeed, it was stated by Robbins in his *Essay* when he remarked that "economics is not one of those social sciences which are always discussing method before proceeding to deliver the

---

[9] If may be pointed out that some of the methods surveyed would hardly command the approval of most economists, e.g. some aspects of the statistical work of the N.B.E.R., some "business forecasting techniques", and the Dow Theory of stock exchange price movements. There are quotations from E. R. Dewey and E. F. Dakin, *Cycles: the Science of Prediction* which would make most economists wince, and one wonders why Professor Schoeffler thought it necessary to include *this* example in his "case studies". Even more surprising are his own indulgent comments on this particular work (p. 102).

goods" (pp. 115–16). We have sought to show that the practice of methodological criticism in economics often goes counter to this view, and that the cumulative effects of this may be undesirable. In doing so we may have unwittingly given the impression that we regard all methodological criticism as futile and, by implication, that we have found little of value in the writings to which we refer. This most certainly is not our position, and in conclusion we may state our view of the proper place of methodological criticism.

First and foremost, methodological argument can be used to advocate the critical attitude, by trying to demonstrate its fruitfulness or by arguing against different approaches. Given that the critical attitude is adopted, methodology can further its practical application by the appraisal of the "status of particular propositions". It is helpful to be told, for example, that one has unwittingly formulated a statement as a tautology, or rendered it untestable. It is useful to discuss explanatory power, informative content, and degrees of testability. (How much better Professor Papandreou's book would have been had he merely pointed out that the specification of parameters may increase the explanatory power and testability of some models). This sort of useful appraisal is, of course, to be found in the works we have mentioned in the earlier sections of this paper. Our objections were decidedly not directed against this kind of methodological criticism, but merely against the attempt to use this appraisal for the purpose of imposing rules intended either to enforce the critical attitude or, worse still, to undermine it. Above all, we contend that it is important to guard against the illusion that there can exist in any science methodological rules the mere adoption of which will hasten its progress, although it is true that certain methodological dogmas, such as the dogma that only theories pertaining to measurement are significant, or the dogma of inductivism, may certainly retard the progress of science. All one can do is to argue critically about scientific problems.

3

ECONOMIC THEORY AND
MATHEMATICS—AN APPRAISAL *

PAUL A. SAMUELSON teaches at Massachusetts
Institute of Technology.

It has been correctly said that mathematical economics is flying high
these days. So I come, not to praise mathematics, but rather to slightly
debunk its use in economics. I do so out of tenderness for the subject,
since I firmly believe in the virtues of understatement and lack of
pretension.

I realize that this is a session on methodology. Hence, I must face
some basic questions as to the nature of mathematics and of its application. What I have to say on this subject is really very simple—perhaps too brief and simple. The time that I save by brief disposal of the
weighty philosophical and epistemological issues of methodology I can
put to good use in discussing the tactical and pedagogical issues—or
what you might even call the Freudian problems that the mathematical
and nonmathematical student of economics must face.

THE STRICT EQUIVALENCE OF MATHEMATICAL
SYMBOLS AND LITERARY WORDS

On the title page of my *Foundations of Economic Analysis,* I quoted
the only speech that the great Willard Gibbs was supposed ever to
have made before the Yale faculty. As professors do at such meetings,
they were hotly arguing the question of required subjects: Should
certain students be required to take languages or mathematics? Each
man had his opinion of the relative worth of these disparate subjects.
Finally Gibbs, who was not a loquacious man, got up and made a four-
word speech: "Mathematics is a language."

I have only one objection to that statement. I wish he had made it
25 per cent shorter—so as to read as follows: "Mathematics *is* language." Now I mean this entirely literally. In principle, mathematics
cannot be worse than prose in economic theory; in principle, it cer-

* From the *American Economic Review,* Vol. XLII, No. 2 (May, 1952),, pp. 56-66.
Reprinted by permission.

tainly cannot be better than prose. For in deepest logic—and leaving out all tactical and pedagogical questions—the two media are strictly identical.

Irving Fisher put this very well in his great doctoral thesis, written exactly sixty years ago. As slightly improved by my late teacher, Joseph Schumpeter, Fisher's statement was: "There is no place you can go by railroad that you cannot go afoot." And I might add, "Vice versa!"

I do not think we should make too much of the fact that in recent years a number of universities have permitted their graduate students to substitute a reading knowledge of mathematics for a reading knowledge of one foreign language. For after all we run our universities on the principle that Satan will find work for idle hands to do; and the fact that we may permit a student to choose between ROTC and elementary badminton does not mean that these two subjects are methodologically identical. And besides, we all know just what a euphemism the expression "a graduate student's reading knowledge" really is. ◄

INDUCTION AND DEDUCTION

Every science is based squarely on induction—on observation of empirical facts. This is true even of the very imperfect sciences, which have none of the good luck of astronomy and classical physics. This is true of meteorology, of medicine, of economics, of biology, and of a number of other fields that have achieved only modest success in their study of reality. It used to be thought that running parallel with induction there runs an equally important process called "Deduction" —spelled with a capital D. Indeed, certain misguided methodologists carried their enthusiasm for the latter to such extremes that they regarded Deduction as in some sense overshadowing mere pedestrian induction.

Now science is only one small part of man's activity—a part that is today given great honorific status, but which I should like to strip of all honorific status for purposes of this discussion. However, to the extent that we do agree to talk about what is ordinarily called science —and not about poetry or theology or something else—it is clear that deduction has the modest linguistic role of translating certain empirical hypotheses into their "logical equivalents." To a really good man, whose IQ is 300 standard deviations above the average, all syllogistic problems of deduction are so obvious and take place so quickly that he is scarcely aware of their existence. Now I believe that I am uttering a correct statement—in fact, it is the only irrefutable and empty truth that I shall waste your time in uttering—when I say that not everybody, nor even half of everybody, can have an IQ 300 standard deviations above the mean. So there is for all of us a psychological problem of making correct deductions. That is why pencils have erasers and electronic calculators have bells and gongs.

I suppose this is what Alfred Marshall must have had in mind when he followed John Stuart Mill in speaking of the dangers involved in *long* chains of logical reasoning. Marshall treated such chains as if their truth content was subject to radioactive decay and leakage—at the end of n propositions only half the truth was left, at the end of a chain of $2n$ propositions, only half of half the truth remained, and so forth in a geometric multiplier series converging to zero truth. Obviously, in making such a statement, Marshall was describing a property of that biological biped or computing machine called *homo sapiens;* for he certainly could not be describing a property of logical implication. Actually, if proposition A correctly implies proposition B, and B correctly implies proposition C, and so forth all the way to Z, then it is necessarily true that A implies Z in every sense that it implies B. There can be no leakage of truth at any stage of a valid deductive syllogism. All such syllogisms are mere translations of the type, "A rose is a rose is a rose."

All this is pretty well understood when it comes to logical processes of the form: Socrates is a man. All men are mortal. Therefore, Socrates is mortal. What is not always so clearly understood is that a literary statement of this type has its complete equivalent in the symbolism of mathematical logic. If we write it out in such symbolism, we may save paper and ink; we may even make it easier for a seventeen-year-old freshman to arrive at the answer to complex questions of the type: "Is Robinson, who smokes cigarettes and is a non-self shaver, a fascist or is it Jones?" But nonetheless, the mathematical symbolism can be replaced by words. I should hate to put six monkeys in the British Museum and wait until they have typed out in words the equivalent of the mathematical formulas involved in Whitehead and Russell's *Mathematical Principia.* But if we were to wait long enough, it could be done.

THE CASE OF NEOCLASSICAL DISTRIBUTION

Similarly, in economics. The cornerstone of the simplest and most fundamental theory of production and distribution—that of Walras and J. B. Clark—is Euler's theorem on homogeneous functions. Now it is doubtful that Clark—who rather boasted of his mathematical innocence—had ever heard of Euler. Certainly, he cannot have known what is meant by a homogeneous function. But nonetheless, in Clark's theory, there is the implicit assumption that scale does not count; that what does count is the proportions in which the factors combine; and that it does not matter which of the factors of production is the hiring factor and which the hired. If we correctly interpret the implication of all this, we see that Clark—just as he was talking prose and knowing it—was talking the mathematics of homogeneous functions and not knowing it.

I have often heard Clark criticized for not worrying more about the exhaustion-of-the-product problem. He seems never to have worried whether rent, computed as a triangular residual, would be numerically equal—down to the very last decimal place—to rent calculated as a rectangle of marginal product. Like King Canute, he seems simply to have instructed his draftsman to draw the areas so as to be equal.

As I say, Clark has often been criticized for not going into this problem of exhaustion of the product. I myself have joined in such criticism. But I now think differently—at least from the present standpoint of the nature of true logical deductive implication as distinct from the human psychological problem of perceiving truth and cramming it into the heads of one's students or readers. Even if Euler had never lived to perceive his theorem, even if Wicksell, Walras, and Wicksteed had not applied it to economic theory, Clark's doctrine is in the clear. His assumptions of constant-returns-to-scale and viable free-entry ensure for him that total revenue of each competitive firm will be exactly equal to total cost. And with this settled in the realm of cost and demand curves, there is no need for a textbook writer in some later chapter of his book dealing with production to suddenly become assailed by doubts about the "adding-up problem of exhaustion-of-the-product."

Now let me linger on this case for a moment. Economists have carefully compared Wicksteed's and Clark's treatment of this problem in order to show that mathematics is certainly not inferior to words in handling such an important element of distribution theory.

What is not so clear is the answer to the reverse question: Is not literary economics, by its very nature, inferior to mathematics in handling such a complex quantitative issue. As one eminent mathematical economist put it to me: "Euler's theorem is absolutely basic to the simplest neoclassical theory of imputation. Yet without mathematics, you simply cannot give a rigorous proof of Euler's theorem."

Now I must concede that the economics literature does abound with false proofs of Euler's theorem on homogeneous functions. But what I cannot admit—unless I am willing to recant on all that I have been saying about the logical identity of words and symbols—I simply cannot admit that a rigorous literary proof of Euler's theorem is in principle impossible.

In fact, I tried a literary proof on my mathematical friend. He quite properly pointed out that it was not rigorous in the way it treated infinitesimals. I fully agree. My argument was heuristic. But I do claim that if my friend and I could spend a week or so talking together, so that I could describe in words the fundamental limit processes involved in the Newton-Leibniz calculus and derivatives, then this problem of lack of rigor could be met. In fact, much more subtle properties of Pfaffian partial differential equations are in principle capable of being stated in basic English. As Professor Leontief has pointed out, the final proof of the identity of mathematics and words is the fact that we teach people mathematics by the use of words, defining each symbol as we go along. It is no accident that the printer of mathematical equations is forced to put commas, periods, and other punctuation in them, for equations are sentences, pure and simple.

GEOMETRY IN RELATION TO WORDS AND MATHEMATICAL ANALYSIS

Today when an economic theorist deplores the use of mathematics, he usually speaks up for the virtues of geometrical diagrams as the alternatives. It was not always thus. Seventy years ago, when a man like Cairnes criticized the use of mathematics in economics, probably he meant by the term "mathematics" primarily geometrical diagrams. From the point of view of this lecture, the ancients were more nearly right than the modern critics. Geometry is a branch of mathematics, in exactly the same sense that mathematics is a branch of language. It is easy to understand why a man might have no use at all for economic theory, invoking, instead, a plague on mathematical economics, on diagrammatic textbooks, and on all fine-spun literary theories. It is also easy to understand why some men should want to swallow economic theory in all of its manifestations. But what is not at all clear—except in terms of human fraility—is why a man like Cairnes should be so enamored of literary theory and should then stop short of diagrams and symbols. Or why any modern methodologist should find some virtue in two-dimensional graphs but should draw the line at third or higher dimensions.

I suggest that the reason for such inconsistent methodological views must be found in the psychological and tactical problems which constitute the remaining part of my remarks.

But before leaving the discussion of the logical identity of mathematical symbols and words, I must examine its bearing on a famous utterance of Cairnes. He lived at a time when, as we now know, mathematics was helping bring into birth a great new neoclassical synthesis. Yet Cairnes went so far as to say: "So far as I can see, economic truths are not discoverable through the instrumentality of mathematics. If this view be unsound, there is at hand an easy means of refutation—the production of an economic truth, not before known, which has been thus arrived at." Now this view is the direct opposite of that of Marshall. Marshall in his own way also rather pooh-poohed the use of mathematics. But he regarded it as a way of arriving at truths, but not as a good way of communicating such truths—which is just the opposite of Cairnes's further remarks on the subject.

Well, what are we to think of the crucial experiment proposed by Cairnes? In the first place, he himself was both unable and unwilling to use the mathematical technique; so it might have been possible for us to produce a new truth which Cairnes could never have been capable of recognizing. Indeed, many have cogently argued that Jevons had in fact done so. However, from the methodological viewpoint that I have been expounding, it will be clear that any truth arrived at by way of mathematical manipulation must be translatable into words; and hence, as a matter of logic, could quite possibly have been arrived at by words alone. Reading Cairnes literally, we are not required to produce a truth by mathematics that could not have been proved by words; we are only required to produce one that has not, as a matter of historical fact, been previously produced by words. I suggest that a careful review of the literature since the 1870's will show that a significant part of all truths since arrived at have in fact been the product of theorists who use symbolic techniques. In particular, Walrasian general equilibrium, which is the peak of neoclassical economics, was already enunciated in Walras' first edition of the *Elements* at the time Cairnes was writing.

Jevons, Walras, and Menger each independently arrived at the so-called "theory of subjective value." And I consider it a lucky bonus for my present thesis that Menger did arrive at his formulation without the use of mathematics. But, in all fairness, I should point out that a recent rereading of the excellent English translation of Menger's 1871 work convinces me that it is the least important of the three works cited; and that its relative neglect by modern writers was not simply the result of bad luck or scholarly negligence. I should also add that the important revolution of the 1870's had little really to do with either subjective value and utility or with marginalism; rather it consisted of the perfecting of the general relations of supply and demand. It culminated in Walrasian general equilibrium. And we are forced to agree with Schumpeter's appraisal of Walras as the greatest of theorists—not because he used mathematics, since the methods used are really quite elementary—but because of the key importance of the concept of general equilibrium itself. We may say of Walras what Lagrange ironically said in praise of Newton: "Newton was assuredly the man of genius *par excellence*, but we must agree that he was also the luckiest: one finds only once the system of the world to be established!" And how lucky he was that "in his time the system of the world still remained to be discovered." Substitute "system of equilibrium" for "system of the world" and Walras for Newton and the equation remains valid.

SUMMARY OF BASIC METHODOLOGY

In leaving my discussion of Methodology with a capital M, let me sum up with a few dogmatic statements. All sciences have the common task of describing and summarizing empirical reality. Economics is no exception. There are no separate methodological problems that face the social scientist different in kind from those that face any other scientist. It is true that the social scientist is part of the reality he describes. The same is true of the physical scientist. It is true that the social scientist in observing a phenomenon may change it. The theory of quantum mechanics, with its Heisenberg uncertainty principle, shows that the same is true of the physical scientist making small-scale observations. Similarly, if we enumerate one by one the alleged differences between the social sciences and other sciences, we find no differences in kind.

Finally, it is clear that no a priori empirical truths can exist in any field. If a thing has a priori irrefutable truth, it must be empty of empirical content. It must be regarded as a meaningless proposition in the technical sense of modern philosophy. At the epistemological frontier, there are certain refined difficulties concerning these matters. But at the rough and ready level that concerns the scientist in his everyday work, the above facts are widely recognized by scientists in every discipline. The only exceptions are to be found in certain backwaters of economics, and I shall not here do more than point the finger of scorn at those who carry into the twentieth century ideas that were not very good even in their earlier heyday.

DIFFERENCES IN CONVENIENCE OF LANGUAGES

I now turn to the really interesting part of the subject. What are the conditions under which one choice of language is more convenient than another? If you are a stenographer required to take rapid dictation, there is no doubt that you will prefer shorthand to old-English lettering. No disinterested third party will ever be in doubt as to whether Roman numerals are less convenient than arabic numerals for the solution of problems in commercial arithmetic; and the same goes for a comparison between a decimal system of coinage and that used by the English.

A comparison between a language like French and one like German or English or Chinese is a little more difficult. We might concede that any proposition in one language is translatable into another. But that is not relevant to the psychological question as to whether one language is intrinsically more convenient for a certain purpose than another. We often hear it said that French is a very clear language, and that German is a very opaque one. This is illustrated by the story that Hegel did not really understand his philosophy until he had read the French translation!

I do not know whether there is anything in this or not. It seems to me that Böhm-Bawerk or Wicksell written in German is quite as straightforward as in English; whereas I find Max Weber or Talcott Parsons difficult to understand in any tongue. I suspect that certain cultures develop certain ways of tackling problems. In nineteenth century German economics it was popular and customary to ask about a problem like interest or value: What is the essence of interest or value? After this qualitative question is answered, then the quantitative level of the rate of interest or price-ratio can be settled. Now I happen to think that this is sterile methodology. But I cannot blame it on the German language.

It is interesting, however, that Menger wrote a letter to Walras on this very subject. As reported by Professor Jaffe's interesting article *(Journal of Political Economy, 1936)*, Menger said that mathematics was all very well for certain descriptive purposes, but that it did not enable you to get at the essence of a phenomenon. I wish I thought it were true that the language of mathematics had some special faculty of drawing attention away from pseudo problems of qualitative essence. For, unlike Menger, I should consider that a great advantage.

BACONIAN AND NEWTONIAN METHODS

There are many empirical fields where translation into mathematical symbols would seem to have no advantage. Perhaps immunology is one, since I am told not a single cure for disease—vaccination against smallpox, inoculation for diphtheria, use of penicillin and sulpha, and so forth—has been discovered by anything but the crudest empiricism and with sheer accident playing a great role. Here the pedestrian methods of Francis Bacon show up to much greater advantage than do the exalted methods of a Newton. If true, we must simply accept this as a fact. I am sure that many areas of the social sciences and economics are at present in this stage. It is quite possible that many such areas will always continue to be in this stage.

Pareto regarded sociology as being of this type. But curiously enough, he goes on to argue that the chief virtue of mathematics is in its ability to represent complexly interacting and interdependent phenomena. I think we must accept this with a grain of salt. Analogies with complicated interdependent physical systems are valuable if they alert us to the dangers of theories of unilateral causation. But after mathematical notions have performed the function of reminding us that everything depends upon everything else, they may not add very much more—unless some special hypotheses can be made about the facts.

On the other hand, there are areas which over the years have fallen into the hands of the mathematically anointed. Earlier I mentioned the case of symbolic logic. There are still some girls' seminaries where literary logic rules the roost; but no sensible man expects that in the centuries ahead the field of logic will be deloused of mathematics.

Another field is that of physics. Its capture by mathematics is a fact —as solid and irreversible as the second law of thermodynamics itself.

It is dangerous to prophesy. But I suspect that in some small degree the same will hold of the field of economic theory. For a century mathematics knocked at the door. Even today it has no more than a foot in the doorway. But the problems of economic theory—such as the incidence of taxation, the effects of devaluation—are by their nature quantitative questions whose answer depends upon a superposition of many different pieces of quantitative and qualitative information. When we tackle them by words, we are solving the same equations as when we write out those equations.

Now I hold no brief for economic theory. I think the pendulum will always swing between interest in concrete description and attempts to construct abstract summaries of experience, with one decade and tradition giving more emphasis to the one process and another time and place giving emphasis to the other. But I do think that when the pendulum is swinging in favor of theory, there will be kind of a Gresham's law operating whereby the more convenient deductive method will displace the less convenient.

CONVENIENCE OF SYMBOLS FOR DEDUCTION

And make no mistake about it. To get to some destinations it matters a great deal whether you go afoot or ride by a train. No wise man studying the motion of a top would voluntarily confine himself to words, forswearing all symbols. Similarly, no sensible person who had at his command both the techniques of literary argumentation and mathematical manipulation would tackle by words alone a problem like the following: Given that you must confine all taxes to excises on goods or factors, what pattern of excises is optimal for a Robinson Crusoe or for a community subject to prescribed norms?

I could go on and enumerate other problems. But that is not necessary. All you have to do is pick up a copy of any economic journal and turn to the articles on literary economic theory, and you will prove the point a hundred times over.

The convenience of mathematical symbolism for handling certain deductive inferences is, I think, indisputable. It is going too far to say that mathematicians never make mistakes. Like everybody else, they can pull some awful boners. But it is surprising how rare pure mistakes in logic are. Where the really big mistakes are made is in the formulation of premises. Logic is no protection against false hypotheses, or against misinterpretation of reality; or against the formulation of irrelevant hypotheses. I think it is one of the advantages of the mathematical medium—or, strictly speaking, of the mathematicians' customary canons of exposition of proof, whether in words or symbols—that we are forced to lay our cards on the table so that all can see our premises. But I must confess that I have heard of card games—in fact I have participated in them myself—where knowingly or unknowingly, we have dealt cards from the bottom of the deck. So there are no absolute checks against human error.

THE HUMAN DILEMMA

In conclusion, ask yourself what advice you would have to give to a young man who steps into your office with the following surprisingly common story: "I am interested in economic theory. I know little mathematics. And when I look at the journals, I am greatly troubled.

Must I give up hopes of being a theorist? Must I learn mathematics? If so, how much? I am already past twenty-one; am I past redemption?"

Now you could answer him the way Marshall more or less advised Schumpeter: forget economic theory. Diminishing returns has set in there. The world is waiting for a thousand important applications.

This of course is no answer at all. Either the young man disregards your advice, as Schumpeter did. Or he accepts it, and psychologically you have dealt him the cruelest blow of all.

I think a better answer might go somewhat as follows: Some of the most distinguished economic theorists, past and present, have been innocent of mathematics. Some of the most distinguished theorists have known some degree of mathematics. Obviously, you can become a great theorist without knowing mathematics. Yet it is fair to say that you will have to be that much more clever and brilliant.

It happens to be empirically true that if you examine the training and background of all the past great economic theorists, a surprisingly high percentage had, or acquired, at least an intermediate mathematical training. Marshall, Wicksell, Wicksteed, Cassel, and even such literary economists as Nicholson or Malthus provide examples. This is omitting economists like Edgeworth, Cournot, Walras, Pareto, and others who were avowedly mathematical economists.

Moreover, without mathematics you run grave psychological risks. As you grow older, you are sure to resent the method increasingly. Either you will get an inferiority complex and retire from the field of theory or you will get an inferiority complex and become aggressive about your dislike of it. Of course, those are the betting odds and not perfect certainties. The danger is almost greater that you will overrate the method's power for good or evil. You may even become the prey of charlatans who say to you what Euler said to Diderot to get him to leave Catherine the Great's court: "Sir, $(a + b^n)/n = x$, hence God exists; reply!" And, like Diderot, you may slink away in shame. Or reacting against the episode, you may disbelieve the next mathematician who later comes along and gives you a true proof of the existence of the Deity.

In short—your advice will continue—mathematics is neither a necessary nor a sufficient condition for a fruitful career in economic theory. It can be a help. It can certainly be a hindrance, since it is only too easy to convert a good literary economist into a mediocre mathematical economist.

Despite the above advice, it is doubtful that when you check back five years later on that young man he will be very different. Indeed, as I look back over recent years, I am struck by the fact that the species of mathematical economist pure and simple seems to be dying out and becoming extinct. Instead, as one of my older friends complained to me: "These days you can hardly tell a mathematical economist from an ordinary economist." I know the sense in which he meant the remark, but let me reverse its emphasis by concluding with the question: Is that bad?

4

THE NATURE AND NECESSITY OF A PRICE SYSTEM *

Joseph A. Schumpeter, deceased, taught at
Harvard University.

I

The reason why it may be useful to insert into our considerations a
few remarks on the nature of price, highly theoretical though they
may seem on the one hand and trivial though they may seem on the
other, is simply that recent discussion on fundamental economic re-
form has shown that some people take the view, not new, of course,
in itself, that prices and especially prices plus profits are nothing but
an incident in the life of acquisitive society, that they are an obstacle
to the full use of existing productive possibilities, and that they might
with advantage be done away with. Prices have been compared to tolls
levied for private profit or to barriers which, again for private profit,
keep the potential stream of commodities from the masses who need
them. The writer believes it to be a mistake to consider such views
as beneath discussion and thereby to insure their survival. Among the
theoretic tools needed in order to deal with this view are some of the
oldest of our science, dating back to the seventeenth century and also
some of the most recent ones which have been contributed to our
theoretic arsenal only in the last few years. As the problems involved
are familiar ground to economists, it will be possible to confine the
following remarks to a few points, in fact little more than headings
which could be worked out more fully.

The writer wishes to point out one thing at the outset: in the
course of progress of economic analysis during the last twenty years
or so, it has happened repeatedly that views largely held by practical
men or amateurs which bygone generations of economists have been
in the habit of disposing of as simply foolish have, by newer methods,
been shown to contain some element of truth after all, and sometimes
quite a large one. In no case that the writer knows of has the reasoning itself which led to such views been rehabilitated. But whilst its

* From *Economic Reconstruction* (New York: Columbia University Press, 1934), pp.
170-176. Reprinted by permission.

errors remained what they were, newer methods of analysis have repeatedly shown by other reasoning that there was yet something to the proposition which the wrong reasoning ineffectually tried to prove. It would be easy to give instances. Our problem is among them, for though as much economic insight as can be got out of an elementary course on economics would seem to be sufficient to refute that view on prices, recent investigations on limited-competition and short-period phenomena have yielded results which will go a long way toward justifying in some measure the practical implications involved in that view.

II

In order to show that price is a phenomenon incident to all forms of organization of society and to economic action in general, it is sufficient to look upon it as a coefficient of economic choice. That is to say, by paying a price for any commodity, buyers show a preference for that commodity as compared with other commodities which they could also buy if they wanted to, for the same money. At the point at which they stop buying, the price will exactly measure that preference for every one of them, and this is what is meant by calling price a coefficient of choice.

Now if we take the organization of a centralized socialist state as an example of non-capitalist forms of society, it stands to reason that the central management would have nothing to go by in its decisions on the questions of the what and how of production unless it gave the comrades an opportunity to express their preferences with quantitative precision. This is equivalent to saying that the coefficient of choice of the members of such a society would have to be found out somehow, for instance, by assigning to them a certain number of claims to units of product in general and allowing them to express their preferences for the various commodities by means of those units. If then prices can be considered to be coefficients of choice, then the coefficients of choice of the comrades would be essentially prices. Moreover, in order to choose between the various possible methods of production, it would be necessary for the managers to attribute values to the means of production at their command which it would be possible to deduce from the coefficients of choice expressed by the comrades. These values would be essentially the same thing as the prices of the means of production in a capitalist organization.

The last sentence already shows that the phenomenon of price covers in fact the whole range of economic action. If a man produces

whisky rather than bread from his rye, then what he does can be interpreted as bartering bread for whisky, and at the point at which he
stops doing this we shall again be able to obtain a quantitative expression of his preferences and again set a coefficient of choice which
in all respects is the same thing as price in a market. It is obvious that
the choice between these two alternatives is not determined by technical considerations. It should be equally obvious that economic considerations of precisely the same kind enter into the choice of the
method of producing either bread or whisky, and that it would be incorrect to say that the decision about the what of production is an
economic matter and the rest, namely, the decision about the how
of production, a technological matter. for whenever there is more
than one way of producing a thing, and methods of production differ
as to the relative quantities of the means of production they require,
it will be necessary to take account of their relative scarcity, or to put
it in another way, to consider how valuable the other products are
which could also be produced by the individual units of the means
of production which the producer contemplates using for a given purpose. These values of alternative production show themselves in
capitalist society in the money price of the means of production and
would show themselves in equivalent expressions in any other form
of society. This explains why technically backward methods of production may still be the most rational ones provided the more perfect
methods would require less of a plentiful factor and more of one
which is less plentiful, and why the technically most perfect method
of production is so often a failure in economic life. Hence rational production can never rest on exclusively technological considerations, at
least not as long as all means of production are not at the command
of a society in unlimited quantities. An economic dimension is, therefore, always necessary for the guidance of production, and this economic dimension at all times and under all circumstances finds expression in coefficients of choice which are fundamentally the same thing
as prices in capitalist society. Of course, this does not mean that these
coefficients would be numerically the same under all circumstances and
in all forms of society, but they would always be of the same nature
and fulfill the same purpose from which it follows that any attempt
to do without them would be devoid of sense.

III

Well-known arguments of very different degrees of scientific rigor have
been put forward to show that a régime of perfect competition would
invariably result in a maximum of welfare and also in a maximum

of total product. The first proposition is wrong but the second is correct, or at least nearly so, provided we define competition as a state of things in which no buyer and no seller of any commodity or productive service is big enough to exert by his own action any influence on the price of the product he sells or the price of the means of production he buys. For this case it can also be shown, at least as a matter of broad practical probability, that the sources of waste inherent in such a society are smaller than those inherent in others, that the process of saving would not create disturbances and, incidentally, that if free competition prevailed absolutely unfettered *all over the world,* the gold standard, although not functioning ideally, would yet not be the cause of any great or violent disturbances. But the great scientific interest of all those and many other conclusions is for practical purposes very much reduced by the fact that competition in that sense not only does not exist but under modern conditions of large-scale production could not exist. It is here that the practical man and the amateur score. For it is not true that what can be proved for the case of perfect competition holds approximately for the case of imperfect competition, as the older theory uncritically assumed. On the contrary, it has been proved of late that in important respects imperfect or monopolistic competition will produce exactly the opposite of those results which might be expected from free competition in the theoretic sense. Without going into the matter I refer to the literature of the subject, especially to the new book by Edward Chamberlin entitled *The Theory of Monopolistic Competition.* As the man in the street never meant anything else by competition but the absence of agreements or interference from outside, and as he certainly visualized monopolistic competition when he talked about competition in general, he is perfectly right in attributing to it all sorts of waste as well as a systematic tendency to stop short not only of any technical but also of the economic optimum of quantity of product. We need only go on to insert into our picture various kinds of inertia and friction in order to realize that whatever gain in life-likeness we thereby attain is exactly proportional to the distance we travel from the assumptions of rationality and free competition. We may add that under the conditions of limited competition profits emerge of a kind unknown to the system of free competition and that, however wrong it may be to consider the fact of profits as such, as an obstacle to economic progress, and however true it may be that some kinds of profits have been the prime movers of progress actually achieved, yet the profits of limited competition are precisely of the kind of which the first of these two statements would be true. Of course, factual investigation and analysis of the results obtained would still be necessary before we could compare those wastes and lags of the system we have with those of every one of the alternatives, all of which have sources of waste and lags of their own.

The diagnostic value of the theory of free competition in the pure sense is, however, not impaired by these considerations. It is still worth while not only to work it out but to present it in a simplified form to the public because it shows where the sources of trouble do *not* lie and therefore by implication where we are to look for them. We may indeed sum up by pointing to the more important possibilities:

(1) It can be shown that the mere fact of turning coefficients of choice into prices by expressing them in units of money does not alter their nature or the way in which they function. But this has nothing to do with the question whether the monetary and credit mechanism which determines the unit of price-accounting harbors sources of disturbance or not.

(2) The proof that competitive equilibrium is stable does not admit of extension to the case of limited competition. And all deviations from an unrealizable ideal state of competition may be so many causes of instability and disturbance.

(3) Even a perfectly competitive state of things would be exceedingly sensitive to disturbance from outside. Such disturbances, which obviously are very plentiful at present, must primarily be looked to if we are to understand the instabilities and troubles of the day. Among them we must not forget to glance at the general humor of the social environment which, quite apart from specific measures resulting from it, may injure the efficiency of the capitalist machinery in a thousand subtle ways by its general hostility to the forms of life and methods of business with which capitalist society works.

SECTION II

DEMAND AND THE THEORY
OF CONSUMER BEHAVIOR

5

DEMAND ANALYSIS: INDIFFERENCE CURVES *

MILTON H. SPENCER teaches at Wayne State
University; he was formerly at Queens College
of the City of New York.

We have already been introduced to the concept of demand. For
example, we know that a *demand schedule* is simply a list showing
the amounts that buyers would be willing to purchase of a certain
commodity at various prices. We know also that if we were to plot a
demand schedule on a graph, we would get a *demand curve,* such as
appears in Fig. 22–1.

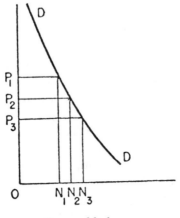

Figure 22–1

The first thing we should notice about this demand curve is that
it slopes *downward* from left to right. The question arises: Why does
it slope in this general direction? Why instead, doesn't it slope *upward*
from left to right, as does the usual supply curve?

* From *Basic Economics: A Book of Readings,* edited by Arthur D. Gayer, C. Lowell
Harriss, and Milton H. Spencer (Englewood Cliffs, N. J.: Prentice-Hall, Inc., 1951),
pp. 91–104. Reprinted by permission.

The answer, we have been told, lies in the fact that the lower the price, the more people will be willing to buy. There is, however, a more profound explanation of why a demand curve usually takes this shape. The explanation is found in a concept known as *"diminishing marginal utility."* Simply stated, this concept (or "law") means that the more we have of something, the less we want more of it.[1] Thus, the first unit of a commodity that we consume may give us much satisfaction, and the second unit may give us still more satisfaction than the first, but eventually (or rather very shortly), we reach a point where additional units of that commodity give us less and less satisfaction. That is, each additional unit gives us less satisfaction than did the previous unit.

Suppose now, that we already possess, say, three units of a certain commodity. If we are to consume a fourth unit, the satisfaction or marginal utility of that fourth unit will be less than the satisfaction or marginal utility of the third. In other words, we do not care as much for the fourth unit as we cared for the third. (Likewise, we would not care as much for a fifth unit as we cared for the fourth, if we already had four units and were contemplating the purchase of a fifth) and so on. It follows that if we are to be persuaded to purchase an additional unit of the commodity, the commodity will have to be offered to us at a *lower* price, so that the decrease in the price will offset the decrease in utility of the additional unit. Thus, if we look at the diagram, we see that as the price is lowered from OP_1 to OP_2 to OP_3, we are willing to increase our purchases from ON_1 to ON_2 to ON_3, etc. The demand curve, sloping downward from left to right, shows us, therefore, just how much will be purchased as the price is decreased.

There is, however, one major difficulty with this analysis. The difficulty lies in our *inability to measure utility*. We cannot measure just how much satisfaction an individual derives from the consumption of a commodity, as we can, for example, measure the distance between two points, or the weight of an object. We can measure distance in inches, feet, miles, etc., and we can measure weight in ounces, pounds, and tons, but we cannot measure satisfaction or utility in so precise a manner. It was largely because of this difficulty that economists devised a new technique for the purpose of explaining demand phenomena—a technique that makes use of a concept known as "indifference curves."

[1] Including the usual assumptions of constant tastes, incomes, etc.

INDIFFERENCE CURVES

THE PRICE LINE

Imagine a consumer possessing, say, two dollars, entering the market to spend his money on goods. He is confronted with two commodities, X and Y. The price of X is $2; the price of Y is $1. In other words, the price of X is twice the price of Y. Algebraically, if P denotes price, then $P_x = 2P_y$.

Now the consumer could spend his entire two dollars on X, in which case he could buy only one unit and have nothing left to spend on Y; or he could spend his whole two dollars on Y and have nothing left to spend on X. The following table shows some of the combinations of X and Y that he could purchase with his two dollars:

X	Y	Total amount spent
1	0	$2 + $0 = $2
$\frac{1}{2}$	1	$1 + $1 = $2
0	2	$0 + $2 = $2

Thus, for $2, with P_x equal to $2 and P_y equal to $1, our individual can buy any one of the above combinations, as well as any other combi-

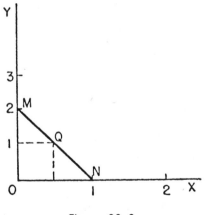

Figure 22-2

nations that will total two dollars. The diagram above illustrates this situation. From it, all of the possible combinations of X and Y that total two dollars can be derived.

OY represents the different quantities of commodity Y that the consumer could purchase at a price of \$1 a unit; OX shows the amounts of X that could be had at \$2 a unit.

If our consumer spends his entire two dollars on Y, he can purchase two units; or, what is the same thing, an amount equal to OM. If he spends the two dollars on X, he can purchase one unit; or an amount equal to ON. If we connect these two points with a line, the resulting MN is called a "price line."

Just what does this price line tell us? Essentially, it shows us all of the possible combinations of X and Y that could be purchased for a total of \$2, assuming that $P_x = \$2$ and $P_y = \$1$. Thus, point Q shows us that the consumer could purchase one unit of Y and one-half unit of X for a total of \$2. Likewise with any other point on MN. Notice, however, that as we move along the line from N to M, more of Y can be purchased and less of X. Moving from M to N, more of X can be purchased and less of Y. This is just as we should expect, for out of any given money income, the more we spend on one commodity, the less we have left to spend on other things.

Suppose now that our individual, instead of possessing only \$2, had say, \$4. Since he has twice as much money, he can buy twice as much of each commodity, provided that the prices do not change. Thus, for \$2, he was able to buy as much as $2Y$ or $1X$, or any combination in between. Now he can buy as much as $4Y$ or $2X$, or any combination in between. This fact is shown in Fig. 22–3, where $M'N'$ represents the new price line at an income of \$4, and MN the old price line at an

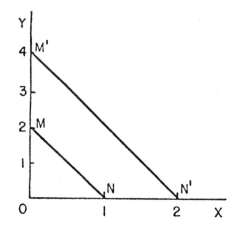

Figure 22–3

income of $2. Obviously, for every level of income, there would be a different price line corresponding to that income level. As income rises, so too does the price line. Therefore, just as there is an infinite number of income levels that are possible, so too there is an infinite number of price lines that are also possible.

INDIFFERENCE CURVES

When a consumer is confronted with two commodities, X and Y, he will probably not spend his entire income on only one of these commodities. Instead, he will probably purchase some combination of the two. Since there are many possible combinations of X and Y that can be purchased, the question is: Just which combination of the many possible combinations will he purchase?

Let us disregard the price relationships that were made in the previous section and pay attention solely to the satisfaction our consumer would derive from possessing commodities X and Y. That is, let us forget for the moment that $P_x = \$2$ and $P_y = \$1$, and that the consumer has a given income.

We start by constructing what is called an indifference schedule. This schedule is a list showing the various combinations of X and Y that would be equally satisfactory to the consumer. Column A of the following table is an example of a possible indifference schedule.

Combina-tions	A Indifference schedule	B Marginal rate of substitution of X for Y
1	60Y and 1X	10/1
2	50Y and 2X	9/1
3	41Y and 3X	8/1
4	33Y and 4X	7/1
5	26Y and 5X	6/1
6	20Y and 6X	5/1
7	15Y and 7X	4/1
8	11Y and 8X	3/1
9	8Y and 9X	2/1
10	6Y and 10X	1/1
11	5Y and 11X	

In this column, each combination of X and Y is equally satisfactory to the consumer. Thus, the consumer would just as soon have combination 1 of 60Y and 1X as he would combination 2 of 50Y and 2X, or combination of 3 of 41Y and 3X, and so on. This is true because each combination yields him the same total satisfaction or utility. Hence, he is completely *indifferent* as to which combination he prefers, for he prefers no one combination; they are all equally desirable because they all yield the same total utility.

Now there is this important thing to notice about an indifference schedule: Since each combination yields the same total utility, it follows that if the consumer were to increase his X intake by one unit at a time, he would have to decrease his Y holdings, in order that each successive combination continue to yield the same total utility. For example, when he possesses combination 1 of $60Y$ and $1X$, he derives a certain amount of total utility. If now he were to have $60Y$ and $2X$, his total utility would be greater than the total utility of $60Y$ and $1X$, for he would have the same amount of Y plus more of X. Therefore, in order to keep his total utility the same, he must give up a certain amount of Y for each unit increase in X. Column A shows this relationship.

Second, we should notice that as the consumer increases his X intake, the amount of Y that he is willing to give up *decreases*. Thus, when he possesses combination 1 of $60Y$ and $1X$, he is willing to give up ten units of Y for one unit of X, leaving him with $50Y$ and $2X$, or combination 2. At this point, he is willing to give up only nine units of Y for one more unit of X, which would leave him at combination 3. Column B indicates this relationship. It shows us the amount of Y he is willing to surrender for every unit increase in his X holdings, in order that the new combination yield him the same satisfaction as the previous one, *i.e.*, the same total utility.

The rate at which the consumer is willing to substitute X for Y is called the *marginal rate of substitution*. It may be defined as the change in Y (ΔY), which will just offset a unit change in X (ΔX), so that total utility remains the same.[2] In other words,

$$\text{marginal rate of substitution} = \frac{\text{change in } Y}{\text{change in } X}.$$

Since Y decreases as X increases, we may represent the change in Y as $-\Delta Y$, and the above equation, in abbreviated form, becomes

$$MRS = \frac{-\Delta Y}{\Delta X}.$$

---

[2] The Greek letter Δ, read "Delta," is a symbol used by mathematicians to denote a difference. Thus, if $X_2 = 8$ and $X_1 = 5$, then $X_2 - X_1 = \Delta X = 3$. If $X_2 = 4$ and $X_1 = 6$, then $X_2 - X_1 = \Delta X = -2$, or $-\Delta X = 2$. In this last case, it denotes a *decrement*. When positive, as in the first case, it denotes an *increment*.

We have just seen that as the consumer increases his X intake, the amount of Y that he is willing to surrender decreases. In other words, the MRS decreases as X is substituted for Y; i.e., as X increases and Y decreases. The precise amount by which the MRS decreases can be seen by referring to column 2 of the previous table.

Why does the MRS decrease? The reader will remember that the reason a demand curve sloped downward from left to right was that the marginal utility of the commodity decreased as more of the commodity was consumed. (The more we have of something, the less we want more of it.) We can also work the same idea backward by saying that the *less* we consume of something, the *greater* is our marginal utility of the commodity. (The less we have of something, the less we care to give up more of it.) In other words, we can start at the right end of the demand curve and work towards the left, instead of starting at the left and working towards the right. Thus, starting at the right and working left, the less we have of it, the more we are willing to pay for more of the commodity.

The concept of a decreasing MRS is similar to that of decreasing marginal utility. As X *increases* (one unit at a time), the marginal utility of X *decreases.* As Y *decreases,* the marginal utility of Y *increases.* Thus, the more we have of X, the less we want more of it, and the less we have of Y, the less we are willing to give up more of it. In other words, as we give up Y for X, the less of Y we are willing to give up for further units of X.

Thus, when the consumer possessed 60Y and 1X, he was willing to give up a relatively large amount of Y (10Y) for one unit of X. After that, he was willing to give up only nine units of Y, then 8Y, and so

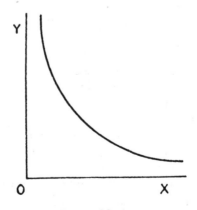

Figure 22–4

forth, for further units of X. This is because he cares less and less for additional units of X, and hence, is willing to give up less and less Y. (Or, conversely, he cares more and more for his smaller holdings of Y, and is willing to give them up at a slower and slower rate).

Suppose now that we were to extend our indifference schedule far enough and then plot the various combinations on a chart. We would get a curve similar to the one appearing in Fig. 22–4.

This curve is called an "indifference curve." Any point on the curve represents a combination of X and Y, and each combination is equally satisfactory, because each combination yields the same total utility.

Just as it is possible to have an infinite number of price lines, so too it is possible to have an infinite number of indifference curves.

Thus, in Fig. 22–5, point Q represents a combination of OM of X and ON of Y. This combination yields the same total utility as any other combination on the same curve. At point R, however, the con-

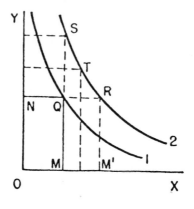

Figure 22–5

sumer possesses the same amount of Y, ON, plus more of X, OM'. Therefore, this combination must yield a higher total utility than any of the previous combinations to be found on curve 1. In other words, the higher the indifference curve (i.e., further to the right), the greater the total utility, for a higher curve will always have at least the same amount of one commodity plus more of the other.[3]

Since each curve will always represent a different total utility from any other curve, it follows that indifference curves can never intersect at any point. Also, since a higher indifference curve will have a higher

[3] Thus, at S there is the same amount of X plus more of Y. At any point between S and R, say T, there is more of both X and Y.

total utility, a consumer will always try to get himself onto the highest possible indifference curve, since we assume that he will always try to maximize his total satisfaction.

THE EQUILIBRIUM COMBINATION

Now let us combine the previous two sections dealing with price lines and indifference curves. Superimposing one diagram upon the other, we get a result such as in Fig. 22–6. The price line *MN* shows us the

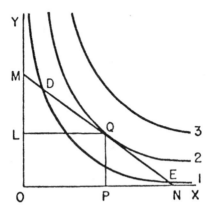

Figure 22–6

possible combinations of X and Y that could be purchased with given prices of X and Y, and a given income. The indifference curves, 1, 2, 3, show various combinations of X and Y that yield the same total utility. The higher the indifference curve, the higher the total utility; therefore, the consumer will always try to be on the highest possible indifference curve.

Now given these two sets of curves, price lines and indifference curves, precisely what combination of X and Y will be purchased?

The indifference curves represent the consumer's *subjective* valuations of X and Y, and have no relationship to the *objective* facts that X and Y have certain prices and that the consumer has a certain money income to spend. These objective facts are shown by the price line.

Subjectively, the consumer will try to be on the highest possible in difference curve; objectively, he is limited in doing so by the price line, for the price line is determined by the prices of X and Y, *and the consumer's income.*

Since the price line shows all of the possible combinations of X and

Y that can be purchased for a given money income, it follows that there will be only one point on the price line that will *also* be on the highest possible indifference curve. This is point *Q*, where the price line is tangent to curve 2. Point *Q*, therefore, shows the combination of X and *Y* that will be purchased—*OL* of *Y* and *OP* of X.

The consumer would not want to be on curve 1, where he would purchase a combination determined by *D* or *E*, because his purchasing power, as determined by the price line, permits him to be on a higher indifference curve. The *highest* curve that he can be on and yet *remain within his income as determined by the price line,* is curve 2, and the only place where the price line touches the highest indifference curve within the consumer's means is point *Q*. This point, therefore, indicates the combination of X and *Y* that will be purchased at the prevailing prices and income.

THE INCOME EFFECT

Suppose now that the consumer's income should increase while the price of X and the price of *Y* remain the same. The consumer could now purchase more of both X and *Y*. This condition is shown in Fig. 22–7, where the price line shifts to the right from *MN* to *M'N'* to

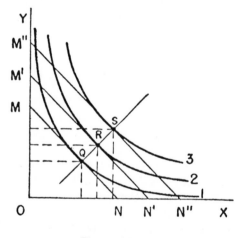

Figure 22–7

M"N", indicating that a greater combination of both commodities can be purchased. At each new level of income, there is a tangency with a new and higher indifference curve. Connecting these points of tangency, we get the line *QRS*, and dropping a perpendicular from each of these points to the X and Y axes shows us by how much the consumer increases his purchases of both X and Y as his income rises. This increase in purchases is called the "income effect," for it shows us the effect on consumption of an increase in income.

It is possible, however, that as income increases, the consumption of one commodity may increase while the consumption of the other commodity decreases. This is shown in Fig. 22–8a and Fig. 22–8b. In the

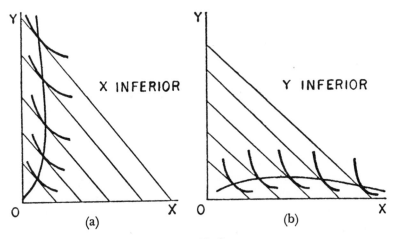

Figure 22–8

first case, as income rises, the consumption of Y also rises, and though X at first increases, it gradually falls off. The opposite is seen in 8b. As income rises, the consumption of both X and Y increase, but Y soon decreases.

The commodity whose consumption is *decreased* is called an "inferior" good, as compared to *superior* goods whose consumption increases as income rises. Inferior goods may be defined as goods whose consumption is decreased as income rises. Examples of such goods are margarine, potatoes, used clothing, and those goods consumed mostly by low income groups.

THE PRICE-CONSUMPTION LINE

Suppose that income remained constant and the price of Y remained constant, but the price of X decreased. The result is seen in Fig. 22–9. The price line shifts from MN to MN' to MN", indicating that as P_x falls, more of it can be purchased.

Working backwards, suppose that the price line to begin with was

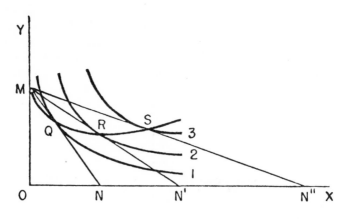

Figure 22-9

MN''. Then suppose that the price of X gradually rises while the price of Y and the consumer's income remain the same. As P_x rises, less of X can be bought, until finally the price of X is so high that it is not purchased at all, and the price line becomes OM, indicating that the consumer spends his entire income on Y.

Connecting the points of tangency, we get the line $MQRS$. This line is called a *price-consumption* line, for it shows us the rate at which X will be consumed as its price varies. Explained in this way, it is clear that the price-consumption line must also be the demand curve for X.

SUBSTITUTES AND COMPLEMENTS

We saw that as we increase our X intake, the rate at which we were willing to give up Y decreases; *i.e.,* there is a decreasing *MRS* of X for Y. In other words, the more X we had, the less Y we were willing to give up for further units of X.

Suppose now, that instead of Y being a commodity, we let it be money. In other words, suppose Y represented total purchasing power. It follows that the same relationship would prevail as before. That is, there would still be a decreasing *MRS* of X for Y (money), for the more X we had, the less Y (or money) we would be willing to give up (or spend) for further units of X. This is, in fact, the case; if there were no decreasing *MRS* of X for money, we would spend all of our money on the one commodity we desired most of all. It is only because additional units of a commodity yield us *less* satisfaction (and because the smaller amount of money we have left over after purchasing the commodity means that we have a *greater* marginal utility for the money left over) that we stop purchasing one commodity and start purchasing another. In other words, commodities compete with one another for our money.

We see, then, that there will be a decreasing MRS of X for money, for as we increase X, we are willing to give up less and less money for further units of X. Thus, we could derive an indifference curve for money and X, just as we derived an indifference curve for two commodities. The same relationships would hold true.

Now let us suppose that instead of Y representing money, we let Y represent a commodity, just as before. Instead of money being denoted by the letter Y, we will denote it by the letter M. In other words, X and Y are commodities, and M is money (or total purchasing power). We know, now, that there will be a decreasing MRS of X for M. (As X increases, the amount of M we are willing to give up decreases). Now if X and Y were both similar in use to one another, *i.e.*, substitutes, it follows that just as we are willing to give up less and less M for further units of X, so too we would be willing to give up less and less M for further units of Y. In other words, since the commodities are similar to one another, what is true of X will be true of Y, so far as our spending money for them is concerned. The more we have of X, the less we want more of it, and since X and Y are similar, the more we have of X, the less we want more of Y. Therefore, just as there is a decreasing MRS of X for M, so too there is a decreasing MRS of Y for M. The more we have of either one, the less we want more of the other. We may define substitute commodities as follows:

X and Y are substitutes if there is a decreasing MRS of Y for M as X is increased and M is decreased in order to maintain the same level of total utility.[4] In other words, as X is increased, there will be a decreasing MRS of X for M. If, during this process, there is also a decreasing MRS of Y for M, then X and Y are substitutes.

Examples of substitute commodities are leather gloves and woolen gloves, new text books and used ones, Coca-Cola and Pepsi-Cola, etc. Obviously, two commodities cannot be *perfect* substitutes, for if they were, they would be identical products and, therefore, they would be the *same* product.

Two goods are complementary when, the more we have of one, the *more* we want of the other. The MRS of Y for M would *increase* as X is increased and M is decreased in order to maintain the same total utility.

[4] Cf. J. R. Hicks, *Value and Capital*, 2nd ed., p. 44.

Examples of complementary goods are left shoes and right shoes, wrist watches and watch bands, good girdles and sleek dresses. The more we have of one, the more we want of the other. As we increase X, we are willing to give up *more* M for further units of Y. There will be an *increasing MRS* of Y for M.

CONCLUSION

In the indifference curve approach, we need assume only that the consumer knows his preferences: he must know whether he prefers one combination of goods to another, or whether he regards them as equivalent.[5] He does not have to know by *how much* he prefers one combination to another. Thus, the older approach to demand theory, which assumed a cardinal relationship (1, 2, 3, etc.), is replaced by a more realistic approach, which assumes an ordinal relationship (1st, 2nd, 3rd, etc.). The inability to measure utility is no longer a problem, for such a measure is no longer needed.

[5] Thus, the consumer is in a position not unlike that of Buridan's ass, at least in some respects. The ass, it will be remembered, stood equidistant between two equal bundles of hay, and finally died of hunger because it couldn't decide which bundle to choose. Likewise, all combinations on any one indifference curve are equally desirable, and it is the price line that is the determining factor.

6

CONSUMER EQUILIBRIUM *

ALBERT M. LEVENSON and BABETTE S. SOLON
teach at Queens College of the City University
of New York.

1. CARDINAL UTILITY APPROACH

Assume that there are but two commodities, A and B, with prices P_a and P_b and that the individual has an income, I, which he spends on the two commodities.

$$I = AP_a + BP_b \quad \text{Income constraint} \tag{A4A.1}$$

$$U = U(A, B) \quad \text{Utility function} \tag{A4A.2}$$

We may rewrite equation A4A.1 as

$$\frac{I - AP_a}{P_b} = B \tag{A4A.3}$$

and then rewrite equation A4A.2 as

$$U = U\left(A, \frac{I - AP_a}{P_b}\right) \tag{A4A.4}$$

Let

$$\mu_a = \frac{\partial U}{\partial A}$$

and

$$\mu_b = \frac{\partial U}{\partial B}$$

We now compute

$$\frac{dU}{dA} = \mu_a + \mu_b\left(-\frac{P_a}{P_b}\right) \tag{A4A.5}$$

Set this expression equal to zero:

$$\mu_a + \mu_b\left(-\frac{P_a}{P_b}\right) = 0 \tag{A4A.6}$$

$$\mu_a = \mu_b \left(\frac{P_a}{P_b} \right) \tag{A4A.7}$$

or

$$\frac{\mu_a}{\mu_b} = \frac{P_a}{P_b} \tag{A4A.8}$$

or

$$\frac{\mu_a}{P_a} = \frac{\mu_b}{P_b} \tag{A4A.9}$$

Expression A4A.9 which states that for utility to be maximized the marginal utility of the goods consumed must be proportional to their prices, is a necessary but not a sufficient condition for maximization of utility. This condition ensures only that an extreme—either a maximum or a minimum—has been found. To ensure a maximum a "second order" condition must be fulfilled (that is, a condition involving second partial derivatives).
Let

$$\mu_{aa} = \frac{\partial^2 U}{\partial A^2}$$

$$\mu_{bb} = \frac{\partial^2 U}{\partial B^2}$$

$$\mu_{ab} = \frac{\partial^2 U}{\partial A \, \partial B}$$

For a maximum to exist, the following must be true:

$$\frac{d^2 U}{dA^2} = \left[\mu_{aa} + 2\mu_{ab}\left(-\frac{P_a}{P_b} \right) + \mu_{bb}\left(-\frac{P_a}{P_b} \right)^2 \right] < 0$$

$$= \left[\mu_{aa} + 2\mu_{ab}\left(-\frac{P_a}{P_b} \right) + \mu_{bb}\left(\frac{P_a^2}{P_b^2} \right) \right] < 0 \tag{A4A.10}$$

Multiply by $(P_b)^2$ and the inequality remains.

$$[(\mu_{aa}P_b^2 - (2\mu_{ab}P_a P_b) + (\mu_{bb}P_a^2)] < 0 \tag{A4A.11}$$

If an additive utility function is assumed, so that the utility of each commodity is independent of the utility of the other commodities (this was generally assumed by the founders of utility theory), μ_{ab} would be 0. If then we assume diminishing marginal utility to hold for both commodities, that is, $\mu_{aa} < 0$, $\mu_{bb} < 0$, then the entire expression on the left is negative and the second condition for a maximum is fulfilled. The role of the assumption of diminishing marginal utility is therefore to ensure that the "second order" condition will be met.

It can be seen, however, that in our general utility function this condition could be fulfilled even if $\mu_{aa} > 0$ and $\mu_{bb} > 0$, provided that $\mu_{ab} > 0$ (complements) and the negative middle term were large enough to overpower the end terms. It could also be fulfilled if one commodity displayed diminishing marginal utility and the other did not if the sum of the negative terms were greater (in absolute terms) than the positive terms. On the other hand, if μ_{ab} is negative (substitutes) the entire expression may be positive even when $\mu_{aa} < 0$ and $\mu_{bb} < 0$. From these considerations it is clear that diminishing marginal utility is necessary and sufficient in order that the second order conditions for maximum total utility be fulfilled only in the case of an additive utility function (a function in which the utilities of the goods are assumed independent).

Indifference curve analysis permits a less restrictive assumption to be made. . . .

2. ORDINAL UTILITY APPROACH

The condition of diminishing absolute MRS_{xy} is not the same as that of diminishing marginal utility; it is less restrictive.

By definition the level of satisfaction along an indifference curve is constant; this means that the total differential is zero. Using some of the symbols used in Appendix 4A [Sec. 1 above], we have

$$\mu_a dA + \mu_b dB = 0 \qquad (A5.1)$$

or

$$-\frac{dB}{dA} = \frac{\mu_a}{\mu_b} \qquad (A5.2)$$

This simply says that the absolute slope of the indifference curve is equal to the ratio of the marginal utilities of the commodities.

We want to know what happens to MRS_{xy} as we move along the indifference curve and so we differentiate μ_a/μ_b again.

Decreasing MRS_{xy} means that

$$\frac{d}{dA}\left(-\frac{dB}{dA}\right) = \left\{\frac{1}{\mu_b^3}\left[\mu_{aa}\mu_b^2 - 2\mu_{ab}\mu_a\mu_b + \mu_{bb}\mu_a^2\right]\right\} < 0 \qquad (A5.3)$$

From Appendix 4A [Sec. 1 above] we have:

$$\mu_a = \mu_b\left(\frac{P_a}{P_b}\right) \qquad (A4A.7)$$

We substitute this in expression A5.3 above and obtain

$$\left\{\frac{1}{\mu_b^3}\left[\mu_{aa}\mu_b^2 - 2\mu_{ab}\left(\mu_b\frac{P_a}{P_b}\right)\mu_b + \mu_{bb}\left(\mu_b\frac{P_a}{P_b}\right)^2\right]\right\}$$

This simplifies to

$$\left\{ \frac{1}{\mu_b}\left[\mu_{aa} - 2\mu_{ab}\left(\frac{P_a}{P_b}\right) + \mu_{bb}\left(\frac{P_a}{P_b}\right)^2 \right] \right\} < 0$$

We now multiply and divide the expression by P_b^2, which leaves the inequality unchanged:

$$\left\{ \frac{1}{\mu_b P_b^2}\left[\mu_{aa}P_b^2 - 2\mu_{ab}P_aP_b + \mu_{bb}P_a^2 \right] \right\} < 0 \qquad (A5.4)$$

The first term on the left must be positive if the commodity is an economic, utility-yielding commodity selling at a positive price. The condition, therefore, that the expression on the left be negative amounts to saying that the second and bracketed expression must be negative. But we have shown above in Appendix 4A [Sec. 1] that this is exactly the second-order condition for maximum utility. Furthermore, we have shown that it does not necessarily imply diminishing marginal utility.

7

SUBSTITUTION AND VALUES
OF ELASTICITIES *

JOHN M. KUHLMAN teaches at the University of
Missouri at Columbia; RUSSELL G. THOMPSON
teaches at Texas A. and M.; he was formerly at
the University of Missouri.

It is commonplace in intermediate price-theory texts, as well as elementary texts, to explain variations in the coefficient of price elasticity
in terms of the number and closeness of substitute products. That is,
a relatively large number of close substitutes results in a large (in absolute value) coefficient of price elasticity, and a relatively small number
of substitutes results in a small coefficient of price elasticity.

To take a recent example (and other examples can be found in nearly
any intermediate theory text), consider Professor Watson's approach to
the concept. He says:

> If a commodity has many close substitutes, its demand is
> almost certain to be elastic; perhaps highly so. If price goes
> up, consumers buy less of the commodity and buy more of
> its substitutes. If its price goes down, consumers desert the
> substitutes and buy the commodity in (relatively) much
> larger quantities [2, p. 40].

Later, in describing the causes of variations in the coefficient of cross
elasticity, Professor Watson makes the following statement:

> The closer two commodities are as substitutes for each
> other, the greater is the size of the cross-elasticity coefficient.
> Close substitutes have high cross elasticities of demand. Two
> commodities are poor substitutes for each other, if the cross
> elasticities are low [2, p. 100].

After encountering practically the same explanation for the two
different concepts, a reader might question the usefulness of the coefficient of cross elasticity. If the degree of substitutability is expressed in

* From the *American Economic Review*, Vol. LV, No. 3 (June, 1965) pp. 506–510.
Reprinted by permission.

the coefficient of price elasticity, why introduce another elasticity coefficient to represent the same phenomenon?

Watson, as well as other authors of intermediate theory texts, face the problem of incorporating the basic concepts of substitutability and complementarity into the theory of demand. They have tried to accomplish this integration using the Marshallian approach based upon the constant marginal utility of money. Hicks demonstrated that this approach neglects the income effect; and hence substitutability and complementarity can only be treated in a satisfactory method if the income effect is included.

Using Hicks's results, we will show why substitutability must be associated with both the (direct and cross) price elasticities and corresponding components of the income elasticity. It is the only way in which one can accurately discuss substitutability of two goods in the consumer's market basket whenever the income effect is significant.

Our argument will be based upon the Fundamental Equation of Value [1, p. 309]. Using Hicks's notation, the substitution term, X_{ij}, can be expressed as follows:

(1) $$X_{ij} = \frac{\partial x_i}{\partial p_j} + x_j \frac{\partial x_i}{\partial M} \text{ where } i, j = 1, 2, \ldots, n.$$

It can be shown that the substitution term has the following properties:

(2) $$X_{ii} < 0 \quad \text{for } i = 1, 2, \ldots, n$$

(3) $$X_{ij} = X_{ji} \quad \text{for } i, j = 1, 2, \ldots, n \text{ and } i \neq j$$

(4) $$\sum_{j=1}^{n} p_j X_{ij} = 0, \qquad i = 1, 2, \ldots, n.$$

Stating the first set of equations in matrix terms, we have:

(1') $$(X_{ij}) = \begin{bmatrix} X_{11} & X_{12} & \ldots & X_{1n} \\ X_{21} & X_{22} & \ldots & X_{2n} \\ \cdot & \cdot & \cdot & \cdot \\ X_{n1} & X_{n2} & \ldots & X_{nn} \end{bmatrix} = X$$

The matrix X, commonly referred to as the Slutsky matrix, has all negative terms on the diagonal. Hence for each good, the direct substitution effect is always negative.

The matrix X is symmetric; that is, the substitution effect of the ith good for the jth good is equal to the substitution effect of the jth good for the ith good.

Substituting the respective Slutsky term in (4), we obtain:

$$p_1 \left[\frac{\partial x_1}{\partial p_1} + x_1 \frac{\partial x_1}{\partial M} \right] + p_2 \left[\frac{\partial x_1}{\partial p_2} + x_2 \frac{\partial x_1}{\partial M} \right] + \ldots + p_n \left[\frac{\partial x_1}{\partial p_n} + x_n \frac{\partial x_1}{\partial M} \right] = 0$$

$$(5) \quad p_1 \left[\frac{\partial x_2}{\partial p_1} + x_1 \frac{\partial x_2}{\partial M} \right] + p_2 \left[\frac{\partial x_2}{\partial p_2} + x_2 \frac{\partial x_2}{\partial M} \right] + \ldots + p_n \left[\frac{\partial x_2}{\partial p_n} + x_n \frac{\partial x_2}{\partial M} \right] = 0$$

$$\cdot \quad \cdot \quad \cdot \quad \cdot \quad \cdot \quad \cdot \quad \cdot \quad \cdot \quad \cdot \quad \cdot \quad \cdot \quad \cdot$$

$$p_1 \left[\frac{\partial x_n}{\partial p_1} + x_1 \frac{\partial x_n}{\partial M} \right] + p_2 \left[\frac{\partial x_n}{\partial p_2} + x_2 \frac{\partial x_n}{\partial M} \right] + \ldots + p_n \left[\frac{\partial x_n}{\partial p_n} + x_n \frac{\partial x_n}{\partial M} \right] = 0$$

If we assume that a positive quantity of each good is demanded (i.e., $x_i > 0$ for all i), we can divide the first equation in (5) by x_1, the second by x_2 and so on. Doing this division and completing the multiplication we obtain:

$$\left[\frac{p_1}{x_1} \frac{\partial x_1}{\partial p_1} + \frac{p_1 x_1}{x_1} \frac{\partial x_1}{\partial M} \right] + \left[\frac{p_2}{x_1} \frac{\partial x_1}{\partial p_2} + \frac{p_2 x_2}{x_1} \frac{\partial x_1}{\partial M} \right] + \ldots$$
$$+ \left[\frac{p_n}{x_1} \frac{\partial x_1}{\partial p_n} + \frac{p_n x_n}{x_1} \frac{\partial x_1}{\partial M} \right] = 0$$

$$\left[\frac{p_1}{x_2} \frac{\partial x_2}{\partial p_1} + \frac{p_1 x_1}{x_2} \frac{\partial x_2}{\partial M} \right] + \left[\frac{p_2}{x_2} \frac{\partial x_2}{\partial p_2} + \frac{p_2 x_2}{x_2} \frac{\partial x_2}{\partial M} \right] + \ldots$$

$$(6) \quad\quad\quad\quad + \left[\frac{p_n}{x_2} \frac{\partial x_2}{\partial p_n} + \frac{p_n x_n}{x_2} \frac{\partial x_2}{\partial M} \right] = 0$$

$$\cdot \quad \cdot \quad \cdot \quad \cdot \quad \cdot \quad \cdot \quad \cdot \quad \cdot \quad \cdot \quad \cdot \quad \cdot \quad \cdot$$

$$\left[\frac{p_1}{x_n} \frac{\partial x_n}{\partial p_1} + \frac{p_1 x_1}{x_n} \frac{\partial x_n}{\partial M} \right] + \left[\frac{p_2}{x_n} \frac{\partial x_n}{\partial p_2} + \frac{p_2 x_2}{x_n} \frac{\partial x_n}{\partial M} \right] + \ldots$$
$$+ \left[\frac{p_n}{x_n} \frac{\partial x_n}{\partial p_n} + \frac{p_n x_n}{x_n} \frac{\partial x_n}{\partial M} \right] = 0$$

The first term in each bracket in (6) is a direct or cross price elasticity of demand. The other terms become economically recognizable if we consider the components of the income elasticity of demand for the ith good:

$$(7) \quad \frac{p_1 x_1}{x_i} \frac{\partial x_i}{\partial M} + \frac{p_2 x_2}{x_i} \frac{\partial x_i}{\partial M} + \ldots + \frac{p_n x_n}{x_i} \frac{\partial x_i}{\partial M} = \frac{M}{x_i} \frac{\partial x_i}{\partial M},$$
$$i = 1, 2, \ldots, n.$$

The sum of all of the fractional components of the income elasticity for the ith good equals the income elasticity for the ith good. So letting

$$\epsilon_{ii} = \frac{p_i}{x_i}\frac{\partial x_i}{\partial p_i}, \quad \epsilon_{ij} = \frac{p_j}{x_i}\frac{\partial x_i}{\partial p_j}, \quad \epsilon_{iM} = \frac{M}{x_i}\frac{\partial x_i}{\partial M} \text{ and } \eta_{ij} = \frac{p_j x_j}{x_i}\frac{\partial x_i}{\partial M},$$

we can write (6) as follows: [1]

$$(\epsilon_{11} + \eta_{11}) + (\epsilon_{12} + \eta_{12}) + \ldots + (\epsilon_{1n} + \eta_{1n}) = 0$$

$$(\epsilon_{21} + \eta_{21}) + (\epsilon_{22} + \eta_{22}) + \ldots + (\epsilon_{2n} + \eta_{2n}) = 0$$

(8) $\cdot \quad \cdot \quad \cdot \quad \cdot \quad \cdot \quad \cdot \quad \cdot \quad \cdot \quad \cdot \quad \cdot \quad \cdot \quad \cdot \quad \cdot \quad \cdot \quad \cdot$

$$(\epsilon_{n1} + \eta_{n1}) + (\epsilon_{n2} + \eta_{n2}) + \ldots + (\epsilon_{nn} + \eta_{nn}) = 0$$

where

$$\sum_{j=1}^{n} \eta_{ij} = \epsilon_{iM} \text{ for all } i = 1, 2, \ldots, n.$$

The η_{ij} represents the contribution of the jth good to the income elasticity of the ith good, ϵ_{iM}. (It might be looked upon as the percentage change in demand for the ith good relative to the percentage change that income is of the expenditures upon the jth good.) Hence, the terms in each parenthesis in (8) are price (direct and cross) elasticities and the fractional components of income elasticity.

Hicks [1, p. 311] defines two goods x_1 and x_2 to be substitutes if the substitution term $X_{ij} > 0$ and to be complements if $X_{ij} < 0$. Using these definitions, the above relationships imply for all i, j:

(9) $(\epsilon_{ij} + \eta_{ij}) < 0$ if $i = j$.

(10) $(\epsilon_{ij} + \eta_{ij}) > 0$ if i and j are substitutes and $i \neq j$.

(11) $(\epsilon_{ij} + \eta_{ij}) < 0$ if i and j are complements and $i \neq j$.

Hence, commodity i can be a substitute for commodity j in each of the following cases $(i \neq j)$.

(12) $\epsilon_{ij} < 0, \eta_{ij} > 0$ and $|\epsilon_{ij}| < |\eta_{ij}|$

(13) $\epsilon_{ij} > 0, \eta_{ij} < 0$ and $|\epsilon_{ij}| > |\eta_{ij}|$

(14) $\epsilon_{ij} > 0$, and $\eta_{ij} > 0$

Moreover, they also imply that commodity i can be a complement of commodity j if $|\epsilon_{ij}| > |\eta_{ij}|$ in (12), $|\epsilon_{ij}| < |\eta_{ij}|$ in (13), and the inequalities are reversed in (14).

Using Hicks's definitions, the above argument demonstrates whenever two goods are compared that they can be substitutes even though

[1] The reader should recall that

$$\sum_{j=1}^{n} p_j X_{ij} = 0; \quad \text{so} \quad \sum_{j=1}^{n} \frac{p_j}{x_i} X_{ij} = \sum_{j=1}^{n} (\epsilon_{ij} + \eta_{ij}) = 0, \quad i = 1, 2, \cdots, n.$$

the cross elasticities are negative. Furthermore, it shows that two goods can be complements when the cross elasticities are positive.

Considering a definition such as the first one cited above (referring to price elasticity and many substitutes) and the relationships in (8), another inconsistency may be noted. We can illustrate this if we rewrite those relationships as follows:

$$(15) \qquad \sum_{\substack{j=1 \\ \& \ i \neq j}}^{n} (\epsilon_{ij} + \eta_{ij}) = - (\epsilon_{ii} + \eta_{ii}), \quad i = 1, 2, \ldots, n.$$

Suppose now that the commodity i has many substitutes as well as many complements and that the sum on the left in (15) is 0.1. Further suppose that the contribution of commodity i, η_{ii}, to its income elasticity, ϵ_{iM}, is 0.1. Then it follows that the coefficient of price elasticity, ϵ_{ii}, must equal $-.2$, an extremely inelastic (price) demand. Hence, it is possible for a commodity to have many substitutes and many complements and still have an inelastic price demand.

Use of elasticities to classify substitutes and complements can result in classifications contrary to common sense and everyday observation. For example, a price decline in hamburger could enable a poor person to eat more beefsteak. The utilization of the cross-elasticity definition would classify these obvious substitutes as complements, while Hicks's definition would not. The explanation, of course, is the income effect. Hicks formulated his definitions in terms of the substitution effect to overcome pitfalls such as this.

8

THEORIES OF CONSUMER'S BEHAVIOUR: A CYNICAL VIEW *

EDWARD J. MISHAN[1] teaches at The London
School of Economics & Political Science.

Since the popularization in the Eighteen Seventies of the concept
of marginal utility, theories of consumer's behaviour have come to
occupy one of the central positions in that corpus of economic analysis
which, before the war at any rate, was customarily referred to as the
theory of value. It is surely a tribute to the influence of a powerful
tradition raised on the authority of such names as Jevons, Marshall and
Edgeworth, and, more recently, Hicks and Samuelson, to mention only
those in the English-speaking assemblage, that although frequently
questioned and sometimes challenged, theories of consumer's behaviour continue to form a necessary part of the syllabus of all students
specializing in economics. And if with the older techniques, marginal
utility and indifference-preference fields, the interest in such theories
eventually appeared to languish, the invention of revealed preference
has revived our spirits wonderfully by providing us with a rather impressive technique in which to express familiar theorems and in which
to carry on the staple controversies of old.

I must, therefore, reconcile myself to being regarded as something of
a killjoy when I propose that we abandon all this; that we seek to
dislodge such theorems from their hold on our imagination and to
face the fact that though fascinating in themselves they form an unnecessary adornment on the apparatus of economic analysis. Recognizing the strong intellectual vested interest in the current doctrines I
cannot, of course, expect the reader to fall in with these proposals unless cogent reasons are adduced for them. To that extent this paper
constitutes an essay in persuasion. My aim is to convince the reader
that, after all the display of technical virtuosity associated with such
theorems, there is nothing the practising economist can take away with

---

* From *Economica* N.S., Vol. XXVIII (February 1961), pp. 1–11. Copyright © by
London School of Economics and Political Science. Reprinted by permission of the
author and the Editorial Board, *Economica*.

[1] I am deeply indebted to W. J. Corlett for pointing out several errors in a first
draft of this paper.

him to help him come to grips with the complexity of the real world. Indeed, he would be no worse off if he remained ignorant of all theories of consumer's behaviour, accepting the obviously indispensable "Law of Demand" on trust [2].

I

As a matter of chronological order and convenience we shall examine the propositions arising from Hicks' indifference-preference hypothesis [3] and from Samuelson's revealed preference hypothesis in that order.

The explicit assumptions in *Value and Capital* are (i) that utility is any monotonic increasing function of all goods—measurement is ordinal, not cardinal—and (ii) that the individual maximizes satisfaction subject to his budget constraint. Tacit assumptions are (iii) transitivity, and (iv) convexity of the indifference surfaces.[4] The chief propositions

[2] It is well known that Gustav Cassell rejected the current marginal utility theory of Marshall on the grounds, among other things, that it was quite superfluous in economic science. See his *Theory of Social Economy*, Vol. I (London, 1932), pp. 80 *et seq.*

[3] Several of the propositions to be found in *Value & Capital* have been re-stated in Hicks' *Revision of Demand Theory* using the new language of price-quantity data. With my present aim in mind there is nothing to be gained by making any appraisal of Hicks' second thoughts on this subject or in trying to gauge his present position. I shall take the version given in *Value & Capital* as fully representative of the indifference-preference hypothesis as originally proposed by Allen and Hicks in *Economica*, February 1934 (and anticipated, as it transpired, by Slutsky in 1915).

[4] In the appendix to his *Value & Capital*, Hicks derives what he calls the Fundamental Equation of Value Theory:

$$\frac{\partial x_s}{\partial p_r} = -X_r \frac{\partial x_s}{\partial Y} + \mu \frac{U_{rs}}{U}$$

In the special case of the response of the good x_r to the price p_r, the last term in the equation becomes U_{rr}/U which, it has been shown, is always negative. This negative term carries the interpretation that the response of the consumer's demand for x to a change in the price of x_r, all other prices remaining constant, is always negative in so far as substitution alone is concerned.

Since a negative U_{rr}/U is in this appendix, a corollary of the sufficient conditions for a (local) maximum, it was inferred that these conditions—referred to by Hicks as "the stability conditions" of the consumer's equilibrium—ensured the negative substitution effect and that, therefore, convexity of the indifference surfaces was not an independent postulate but in fact could be inferred from the "stability conditions". This, however, is not the case. The adoption of the calculus, which does not lend itself to corner solutions of a constrained extremum, is to be interpreted as a clear *assumption* that the solution is at a point of tangency; in economic terms, that the individual purchases, in general, some of all

which, in their more general formulation, may be derived mathematically from this set of assumptions are to be found in a few pages of the appendix to that work.[5] They are (a) that the substitution effect on the quantity of good x of a change in its price is always negative; (b) the rate of substitution of a good x in response to a change in the price of y is equal to the rate of substitution of a good y in response to a change in the price of x; (c) in response to a rise in the price of x alone, the sum of the substitution effects on all goods other than x, weighted by their corresponding prices, is equal and opposite to the substitution effect on x weighted by its price; (d) if we divide the number of goods into two groups, the sum of the rates of substitution of all goods in the first group, each with respect to a change in the price of every good belonging to the second group, is always positive, provided that each such effect is weighted by the product of the corresponding pair of prices, and (e) the sum of the changes in all prices times the corresponding change in their substitution effects is always negative—the general statement of the negative substitution effect.[6]

We do well to notice from the start that all these implications involve substitution terms only and hold only for small movements about the individual's "equilibrium". If there are income effects—and they can hardly be avoided in any real situation—the resultant direction of response in any of the above propositions is no longer certain. For this reason, if for no other, such implications are difficult to put to the test. This difficulty increases if, as is usual, our test draws upon aggregative data, for a good which is observed to have a zero income effect for the whole population may not have a zero effect for each individual. And, if we are to be strict in our test, it is the latter condition which must be met if we are to measure unadulterated substitution effects.

However, if such propositions as these are difficult to test it is not

---

the goods. Since the condition of a tangency solution to the constrained maximum in question is convexity of the indifference surfaces, the latter must be considered as an independent assumption of the hypothesis. The negative substitution effect is, then, *not* inferred; it is a postulate of the model.

[5] *Value and Capital* (2nd Edition), pp. 305–311.

[6] Using Hicks' notation in the appendix to *Value and Capital, loc. cit.,* where in general x_{rs} is the consumer's substitution of a good s in response to a change in the price of a good r, these propositions may be represented as:

$$\text{(a)} \quad x_{rr} < 0, \quad \text{(b)} \quad x_{rs} = x_{sr}, \quad \text{(c)} \quad \sum_{s=1}^{n} p_s x_{rs} = 0,$$

$$\text{(d)} \quad \sum_{s=1}^{m} \sum_{s=m+1}^{n} p_r p_s x_{rs} > 0, \quad \text{and} \quad \text{(e)} \quad \sum_{r=1}^{n} dx_r dp_r < 0.$$

likely that the practising economist suffers much frustration on this account. Other than (a), which forms the basis of the demand curve and which we examine later, such propositions do not provide the kind of knowledge that the economist interested in prognostication is likely to be seeking.[7] Inasmuch as he is interested in the consequences which stem from changes in one or two variables on one or two other variables, such propositions—even if he sees fit to ignore the impact of income effects—are of little use to him. In (c), (d), and (e), for instance, he cannot predict the substitution effect on a chosen good given its change of price unless he already has knowledge of the substitution effects on all other goods with respect to the prices that have changed: to predict anything he must have discovered almost everything to begin with. It is not surprising that there is no evidence of any attempts to make practical use of such propositions.

Another group of implications in terms of elasticities, though of comparable peculiarity, can also be derived from the same hypothesis, and in particular from the assumption that the individual's total expenditure is equal to his income and from the implication that, for the individual, demand functions are homogeneous of degree zero in prices and income. Some of these describe the relationships between individual elasticities and those of the market; e.g., that the income elasticity of the *market* demand for a good is the averages of the elasticities of the *individuals*, each such elasticity weighted by the income of the corresponding individual. This is obvious, perhaps, but of little use to the economist who wishes to obtain a measure of the market elasticity. Other such propositions trace a relationship for the individual between price elasticities, between income elasticities, or between both. Typical are propositions such as (a) the sum of the income elasticities of demand for each good in the individual's budget, weighted by the fraction of total expenditure on it, sums to unity, or (b) that the sum of the elasticities of demand for a good x with respect to the price of each good in question is equal, and opposite in sign, to the income elasticity of demand for x.[8]

The comments on the previous group of propositions apply with equal force to this group. It may be urged that such relationships serve as a rough check on the statistical estimation of elasticities. But the number of other elasticities required in order to check the one reduces

[7] (b) might be thought fairly simple to test. The idea is simple enough, but we must remember that we want pure substitution effects for two goods whose prices change when all others remain and that, moreover, the theorem holds for the consistent individual whose tastes remain unchanged, and not for the market.
[8] For a fairly exhaustive account of elasticity relationships, see H. Wold's *Synthesis of Pure Demand Analysis*, especially pp. 90-108.

the practical value of such a check to something approaching zero. Even if we play down the problem of the probable errors in the estimation of a host of elasticities, the cost in time and effort of calculating the relevant elasticities for each good, or for each group of goods, in the economy would be incomparably greater than the cost of direct applications of any statistical refinements.

II

Since the term revealed preference was introduced into economics by Samuelson in 1938, there has been a proliferation of papers making use of its basic technique. One may legitimately surmise that it was the fascination of the relational algebra which inspired most of the contributions rather than an inherent interest in economic theory. At all events, the economic content of such contributions has, in the main, been slight. Indeed, in so far as the subject matter of economics is taken to be a study of market behaviour, revealed preference has yielded no more useful empirical implications than the indifference-preference hypothesis that preceded it.

The term, revealed preference, is not altogether satisfactory since the basic notion is merely that of consistent choice. If an individual chooses a batch of goods Q_2 rather than the batch Q_1 in circumstances in which both batches are available, provided his tastes remain unaltered consistency demands that in such circumstances he never chooses Q_1. This somewhat tautological statement is translated into an index number theorem—a theorem couched in terms of prices and quantities, since these are the only data we observe directly. According to this theorem, if we observe that $\Sigma P_2 Q_2 \geqq \Sigma P_2 Q_1$, where Q_1 and Q_2 are the batches of goods chosen in the I and II situations in which respectively the price sets P_1 and P_2 prevail we can infer from our observation that if both batches of goods were available he would choose Q_2. In other words, since he would not choose Q_1, $\Sigma P_1 Q_1 \geqq \Sigma P_1 Q_2$. That is, we should also observe $\Sigma P_1 Q_1 < \Sigma P_1 Q_2$.

The idea of consistent choice [9] and the index number theorem derived therefrom are what we start with. How far do they take us?

[9] Unless we seek to 'rationalize' the individual's behaviour, the mere fact of choosing Q_2 rather than Q_1 does not oblige us to interpret this choice as revealing a preference for Q_2. Indeed, this recklessly non-operational interpretation has long been abandoned by those concerned to preserve their methodological chastity. In deference to established custom, however, the term revealed preference continues to be used rather than a more accurate form of designation such as revealed choice.

Developments have in fact branched off in three directions. Two appear to lead nowhere in particular though the traffic along these routes is still heavy. The third development leads directly to a demand theorem of sorts but, alas, not one of much use to the economist.

Of the two developments which I have suggested are blind alleys, the first constitutes an endeavour to derive from the basic idea of consistent choice in alternative budget situations, a set of indifference surfaces for the individual having the familiar properties of ordinal ranking, convexity, and non-intersection. This has been accomplished by Little, by Samuelson, and by Houthakker, in each case in a slightly different way from the others.[10] The question of integrability arose as, indeed, it did in the indifference-preference hypothesis, for unless the integrability conditions are satisfied there is, apparently, no assurance that the individual might not contradict himself. In the event, and after some bewilderment, Houthakker, adopting an axiom of "semi-transitivity"—an axiom which asserts that if batch 1 is revealed preferred to batch 2, batch 2 revealed preferred to batch 3, and so on down to batch n-1 revealed preferred to batch n, then batch n cannot be revealed preferred to batch 1—deduces transitivity, and therefore integrability, for the indifference surfaces which he generates.

That this integrability issue should have arisen at all, points to a prepossession with mathematical problems rather than with economic ones. After all, if the real concern in our model is that economic man does not contradict himself, why should we not demand this attribute of him from the outset? What argument can there be to prevent our requiring of all the economic men we shall have occasion to deal with that their choices be transitive (and, therefore, consistent)? If we can go along with Houthakker and slip in semi-transitivity to help us along, on what methodological grounds are we inhibited from introducing the axiom of full transitivity? Whether or not there is a convincing answer to this question [11] this issue—apart from some bickering on the side lines as to how well Houthakker managed the

10 I. M. D. Little, "A Reformulation of the Theory of Consumer's Behaviour," *Oxford Economic Papers,* January 1949.

P. A. Samuelson, "Consumption Theory in Terms of Revealed Preference," *Economica,* November 1948.

H. S. Houthakker, "Revealed Preference and the Utility Function," *Economica,* May 1950.

11 It is surely paring things too fine with Occam's razor to save on an axiom—or, rather, half an axiom, since Houthakker starts off with the axiom of "semi-transitivity"—at a cost of several pages of close reasoning when, in the end, the implications for consumer's behaviour, slight enough as we shall see, are no different.

proof [12]—appears to be at an end. Assuming for the time being that an indifference map is a desirable construct, was it ever necessary?

The advantages of constructing an indifference map from the axioms of revealed preference rather than from those of the indifference-preference hypothesis of consumer's behaviour, or from a direct description of the properties of such a map, has been argued most lengthily by Little.[13] He demonstrates a method of constructing what is, in effect, a system of indifference curves from hypothetical observations of price-quantity data using only four assumptions—fewer, he alleges, than are required in the Hicksian model.[14] He is emphatic, however, in calling the curve he generates a "behaviour line"—a boundary above which all batches are preferred to some given batch, say Q_1, and below which all batches are rejected for Q_1—since the concept of an indifference curve is rejected by him as non-operational. Indifferent behaviour, he states, is not observed in the market.[15]

Now it is true, at least for single choice situations to which we confine ourselves in the theory of demand, that we cannot observe indifferent behaviour. But then we are not required to observe it. In the implications for market behaviour—which behaviour we *do* observe—indifference certainly does not feature. After all, the implications we seek to observe from the indifference-preference hypothesis are always

[12] See, for instance, H. A. John Green, "Some Logical Relations in Revealed Preference Theory," *Economica*, November 1957, and Peter Newman, "A Further Note on Revealed Preference," *Economica*, May 1959.

[13] *Loc. Cit.*

[14] Little's assumptions are (i) the individual never chooses a smaller collection if a larger one is available; (ii) all collections which are available are chosen in some price-income situation; (iii) if the individual chooses collection A to B, he will always choose A to B; (iv) transitivity of choices. Presumably (iii) can be subsumed under (iv), and, as for (ii), his argument seems to call rather for an axiom which asserts that in any price-income situation one, and only one, collection of goods is chosen, which is more restrictive than (ii).

Hicks' explicit assumptions are (i) that utility is any monotonic increasing function of all goods, and (ii) that the individual maximizes subject to his budget constraint. Tacit assumptions are (iii) transitivity, and (iv) convexity.

The demonstrations of both Hicks and Little also require the assumption of differentiability of the utility function of the first and second order.

On the test of counting axioms, then, Little appears to win by a nose, having one axiom the fewer. It is difficult to be impressed by this.

[15] Little further alleges that the index number criterion of revealed preference is "fundamental," indifference curves being derivable therefrom. The deriviation of indifference curves from index number data does not, however, suffice to bear out this contention. In any event, Hicks, in his "Valuation of the Social Income" (*Economica*, May 1940) shows how the index number theorem may be derived from the logic of indifference curve analysis.

of a price-quantity nature, in principle observable enough, and in any case no different from the implications which are derivable from the model constructed by Little. However, since we can generate a consistent set of indifference surfaces using the axioms of revealed preference, it follows that all those implications which flow from the indifference-preference analysis, and which I have suggested are rather sterile, may be said to flow also from the revealed preference hypothesis.

III

The second branch of development of the revealed preference technique has forked off into welfare economics. Since I wish to limit the scope of my arguments to positive economics, little will be said here about this development. On the one hand, there have been attempts to state anew propositions which have been known for more than half a century, but in terms of consistent choice,[16] or else to attire in a panoply of symbolism contributions of little more than footnote stature.[17] On the other hand, since hypothetical price-quantity data is employed directly in this technique, it is not surprising that we have witnessed attempts to use index numbers as indicators of change in the welfare of the community.[18] From the trend of recent contribu-

[16] For a recent instance, see Kelvin Lancaster, "Welfare Propositions in Terms of Consistency and Expanded Choice," *Economic Journal*, September 1958.

[17] As an example, the proposition that a system of taxes which causes the ratio of the commodity prices to deviate yet further from the individual's no-tax optimum, further reduces his welfare. For an attempted rigorous proof of this proposition see McManus, "A Theorem on Undercompensated Price Changes", *Economica*, November 1959. That this theorem has no application to the community at large, even within the familiar static analysis, may be gathered from my paper, "A Reconsideration of the Principles of Resource Allocation", *Economica*, November 1957.

[18] Unless such index numbers propositions can be generalized successfully so as to encompass the community at large they are, however, of little use to economists. Yet the only serious attempt to face up to the difficulties of making the transition from the individual to society was made by Hicks in his "Valuation of Social Income" paper *(loc. cit.)*. It was a gallant and ingenious attempt but, for all that, it failed. Let us recall, briefly, why.

If the index numbers revealed that $\Sigma P_2 Q_2 \geqq \Sigma P_2 Q_1$ then, according to Hicks, the welfare situation in Q_2 was to be regarded as an improvement for the community compared with Q_1. For with the P_2 prices—the prices ruling in the Q_2 situation—each person in the community can be made worse off with the Q_1 collection of goods than he would be in the Q_2 situation. However, after the controversy which flared up eight years later in *Economica*, in which Kuznets, Hicks, and Little took part (and which controversy was to some extent summarized in Samuelson's "Evaluation of Real Income", *Oxford Economic Papers*, January 1950),

tions, however, it seems fairly clear that the revealed preference technique adds nothing new to welfare economics. It provides only alternative formulations of familiar welfare propositions.

IV

Finally, revealed preference opens up a direct route to the demand curve, the original *raison d'être* of theories of consumer's behaviour. The best known theorem is that of Samuelson [19] which builds on the axioms (i) that the individual behaves consistently, (ii) that he chooses only one collection in every budget situation, and (iii) that he prefers more goods to less. It states that if an individual buys more of a good when his income rises he will buy less of it when the price of that good rises. The diagrammatic exposition is straightforward enough and will suffice for the purpose in view. In Fig. 1, the individual is purchasing a batch of goods Q_2 along his budget line YP_2. The price of X rises to P_1, the new budget line facing him being YP_1. We are to show that Q_1, that batch of goods chosen in this new situation, is to the left of Q_2.

First, "overcompensate" the individual for the rise in price of X by giving him just enough additional income, Y_1Y, to enable him to continue purchasing Q_2 if he wishes. His opportunities can therefore be represented by Y_1P_1', parallel to YP_1, which passes through Q_2.

Since Q_2 was chosen to all other points in the area YOP_2, he cannot forgo Q_2 for a point along Q_2P_1'. He either stays at Q_2 or else takes up a position along Q_2Y_1. Suppose he does the latter and chooses the batch Q_2'. We now subtract the original compensation Y_1Y, so that he is faced with YP_1 again, the original position with the price of X raised. His income effect on X being assumed positive, he reduces his consumption of X and therefore chooses a position Q_1, along YP_1, that is to the left of Q_2'.

Since the amount of X in Q_1 is, by assumption, less than that in Q_2', and the amount of X in Q_2' is, by consistent behaviour, less than

---

it transpired that this criterion was no less vulnerable than the original Kaldor-Hicks compensation test of which, indeed, it was but a variant. Thus, owing to the intimate connection between welfare distribution and the relative valuation of goods, data which revealed the simultaneous existence of $\Sigma P_2Q_2 \geqq \Sigma P_2Q_1$ and of $\Sigma P_1Q_1 \geqq \Sigma P_1Q_2$ pointed to no inconsistency in the behaviour of individuals in the community. In consequence, however, no unambiguous index of an improvement in welfare emerged either.

This matter is further explained and illustrated in my "Survey of Welfare Economics, 1939-1959", *Economic Journal*, June 1960, p. 231, n. 2.

[19] "Consumption Theorems in Terms of Overcompensation rather than Indifference Comparisons", *Economica*, February 1953.

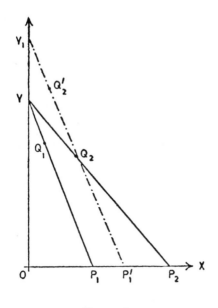

Figure 1

or equal to that in Q_2, the amount of X in Q_1 is less than that in Q_2. *Q.E.D.*

We may, in passing, compare this theorem with an analogous one derivable from the individual's indifference map. An exact income compensation now being possible, the form it takes is somewhat less restrictive: if the price of a good rises less of it will be bought by the individual if its income effect is *non-negative*.[20]

V

We cannot fail to notice that such demand theorems are conditional theorems, not universal ones. If the income effect is not positive— or, in the one derivable from the indifference map, the income effect is negative—we can say nothing of the response of the individual to a change in the price of a single good.

[20] In his review article, "Revising Demand Theory", *Economica*, November 1957, Lancaster has suggested that this kind of theorem can be derived from the consideration of consistency alone and offers a similar proof which omits Samuelson's axiom (iii), above, the so-called non-saturation axiom, in this way allowing for the possibility that the individual may choose a collection of goods *inside* the budget

More important yet, such theorems have reference only to the individual. Even if we managed to derive downward-sloping demand curves for X for each individual in the economy, it does not follow that the market demand curve for X slopes downward. True, the

---

frontier. His argument can be depicted graphically in much the same way as Samuelson's argument, which procedure it follows.

We start the individual with a budget line YP_1 in Fig. 2, but, since we have discarded the non-saturation axiom, we have him choose q_1 *inside* his budget frontier. The price of X now falls to p_2. We must show that the new collection of goods he buys, q_2, contains more of X; i.e., q_2 is to the right of q_1.

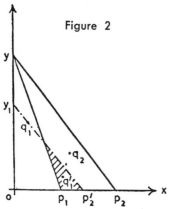

Figure 2

We subtract from his income an amount equal to yy_1 so that he can just continue to buy q_1 if he wishes. y_1p_2' is, therefore, drawn parallel to yp_2 and passes through q_1. Consistency of choice requires that the individual either remain at q_1 or choose a point q_1' within the shaded triangle. Suppose he chooses q_1'. We now restore yy_1 income. Since we assume observation of a positive income effect for X, he chooses some batch of goods, q_2, outside the shaded triangle and to the right of q_1'.

Since q_2 is to the right of q_1' which itself is equal to or to the right of q_1, q_2 must be to the right of q_1.

However, on reflection it can be appreciated that the choice of a collection of goods *inside* the budget frontier violates the axiom of consistency in such a theorem. For, supposing he chooses q_2 when his budget frontier is yp_2, a small enough increment in his income would—unless the income effect were zero on all goods—impel him to choose some point other than q_2 inside the frontier yp_2. But this behaviour is not consistent with the proposition that he chooses q_2 above all other collections within the triangle oyp_2. Nor can we allow a zero effect on all goods, for if we allow a zero income effect on X we will not be able to generate the inverse price-quantity relationship.

It might yet be argued that if we observe *discontinuities* in the income effect on *all* goods about such chosen points as q_1 and q_2, we might yet reconcile consistency with a choice of goods within the budget frontier. Whether so peculiarly contingent a theorem is worth any attention is a moot point. For, although consistency might be preserved if such comprehensive discontinuities were in fact observed, we now have to put up with the implication that *not all reductions* in the price of X lead to an increase in the quantity purchased.

If, however, as all empirical evidence suggests, we can ignore the suggestion of discontinuities in the income effects on all goods, we are left with an inconsistency in choice when we drop the non-saturation axiom. Apparently then, the requirement of consistency in this theorem relegates non-saturation from an axiom to an implication—unless, that is, the individual does choose a collection of goods along his budget frontier he is not behaving consistently.

frequently invoked clause of *ceteris paribus* lays it down that for the market demand curve all other prices remain unchanged. But while no exception need be taken to this procedure in so far as the demand curve of the individual is concerned, it cannot in general be maintained for a market demand curve without violating logical necessity. If the price of X falls on the market, we cannot hold all other prices constant unless the supply curves of all other goods are infinitely elastic. In general, then, product prices alter. So also do factor prices; which is to say that the distribution of real income in the community is altered. Though each individual have a downward-sloping demand curve for this good X, redistributions of real income can be envisaged which issue, for some range of prices, in an upward-sloping demand curve for the market.

We may be justified in believing that this contingency is highly unlikely; that market demand curves are always, or almost always, downward-sloping. However, we are constrained to acknowledge that this supposition in no way derives from our theorizing, but only from intuition and observation. In consequence, then, we are advised to join hands with Gustav Cassel and begin our analysis of the demand side, in the theory of value, with the "law of demand".

This sort of disappointment is not unusual in much of the traditional theory of value. We begin by aiming at a theory which will yield some transparently modest implication—one which sets limits to the direction of change in the price or quantity variables. Quite often, we already suspect the direction of change from intuitive considerations or from casual observation. Yet once we start to explore the theory we discover, to our chagrin, that the customary postulates concerning behaviour, technology and institutions, yield implications which in fact cover all the logical possibilities. We may, of course, obtain what we are looking for by imposing more restrictive assumptions—though recourse to this treatment is open to the charge of 'cooking up' the theory to account for the observed or suspected relationships. Alternatively, we can escape this impasse by explicit use of the taxonomic method which in effect makes our theorems conditional upon the prior fulfilment of one or more particular provisions, a procedure which, though frequently necessary, obviously limits the applicability of economic theory and increases the difficulty of testing it.

In the last resort we might think to justify theories of consumer's behaviour as useful exercises in economic thinking, in which case even manifestly false theories might qualify in our syllabus. A less exceptionable argument might be that when all is said and done the indifference-preference hypothesis does provide us with some very fruitful suggestions. The distinction between substitution and wealth effects, for instance, runs right through price economics. It helps to organize our thinking on complex questions.

I have sympathy with this view, but it cannot be decisive. For until we have tested the implications of those theorems which utilize this distinction we cannot legitimately vouch for the advantages of having our thoughts organized in this particular way.

9

BANDWAGON, SNOB, AND VEBLEN EFFECTS IN THE THEORY OF CONSUMERS' DEMAND *

HARVEY LEIBENSTEIN teaches at Harvard University; he was formerly at Princeton University.

I. THE NATURE OF THE PROBLEM [1]

The desire of some consumers to be "in style," the attempts by others to attain exclusiveness, and the phenomena of "conspicuous consumption," have as yet not been incorporated into the current theory of consumers' demand. My purpose, in this paper, is to take a step or two in that direction.

1. "NON-ADDITIVITY" IN CONSUMERS' DEMAND THEORY

This enquiry was suggested by some provocative observations made by Professor Oskar Morgenstern in his article, "Demand Theory Reconsidered." [2] After examining various aspects of the relationship between individual demand curves and collective market demand curves Professor Morgenstern points out that in some cases the market demand curve is not the lateral summation of the individual demand curves. The following brief quotation may indicate the nature of what he calls "non-additivity" and give some indication of the problem involved. "Non-additivity in this simple sense is given, for example, in the case of fashions, where one person buys because another is buying the same thing, or vice versa. The collective demand curve of snobs is most likely not additive. But the phenomenon of non-additivity is in fact much deeper; since virtually all collective supply curves are non-additive it follows that the demand of the firms for their labor, raw

* From *The Quarterly Journal of Economics*, Vol. LXIV (May, 1950), pp. 183–207, copyright © 1950 by the President and Fellows of Harvard College. Reprinted by permission of the author and the Harvard University Press.

1 The writer wishes to take this opportunity to thank Professor Ansley Coale and Messrs. Carey P. Modlin and Norman B. Ryder for their painstaking criticism of an earlier draft of this paper.

2 This *Journal*, February 1948, pp. 165–201.

materials, etc, is also non-additive. This expands the field of non-additivity enormously." [3]

Since the purpose of Professor Morgenstern's article is immanent criticism he does not present solutions to the problems he raises. He does clearly imply, however, that since coalitions are bound to be important in this area only the "Theory of Games" (developed by Von Neumann and Morgenstern) is likely to give an adequate solution to this problem.[4] The present writer is not competent to judge whether this is or is not the case, but he does believe that there are many markets where coalitions among consumers are not widespread or of significance, and hence abstracting from the possibility of such coalitions may not be unreasonable. Should this be the case we may be able to make some headway through the use of conventional analytical methods.

What we shall therefore be concerned with substantially is a re-formulation of some aspects of the static theory of consumers' demand while permitting the relaxation of one of the basic implicit assumptions of the current theory—namely, that the consumption behaviour of any individual is independent of the consumption of others. This will permit us to take account of consumers' motivations not heretofore incorporated into the theory. To be more specific, the proposed analysis is designed to take account of the desire of people to wear, buy, do, consume, and behave like their fellows; the desire to join the crowd, be "one of the boys," etc.—phenomena of mob motivations and mass psychology either in their grosser or more delicate aspects. This is the type of behaviour involved in what we shall call the "bandwagon effect." On the other hand, we shall also attempt to take account of the search for exclusiveness by individuals through the purchase of distinctive clothing, foods, automobiles, houses, or anything else that individuals may believe will in some way set them off from the mass of mankind—or add to their prestige, dignity, and social status. In other words, we shall be concerned with the impact on the theory created by the potential nonfunctional utilities inherent in many commodities.

2. THE PAST LITERATURE

The past literature on the interpersonal aspects of utility and demand can be divided into three categories: sociology, welfare economics, and pure theory. The sociological writings deal with the phenomena of fashions and conspicuous consumption and their relationship to social

[3] *Ibid.*, p. 175 n.
[4] *Ibid.*, p. 201.

status and human behaviour. This treatment of the subject was made famous by Veblen—although Veblen, contrary to the notions of many, was neither the discoverer nor the first to elaborate upon the theory of conspicuous consumption. John Rae, writing before 1834, has quite an extensive treatment of conspicuous consumption, fashions, and related matters pretty much along Veblenian lines.[5] Rae attributes many of these ideas to earlier writers, going so far as to find the notion of conspicuous consumption in the Roman poet Horace; and a clear statement of the "keeping up with the Joneses" idea in the verse of Alexander Pope.[6] An excellent account of how eighteenth and nineteenth century philosophers and economists handled the problem of fashion is given in Norine Foley's article "Fashion."[7] For the most part, these treatments are of a "sociological" nature.

The economist concerned with public policy will probably find the "economic welfare" treatment of the problem most interesting. Here, if we examine the more recent contributions first and then go backward, we find examples of current writers believing they have stumbled upon something new, although they had only rediscovered what had been said many years before. Thus, Professor Melvin Reder in his recent treatment of the theory of welfare economics claims that ". . . there is another type of external repercussion which is rarely, *if ever*, recognized in discussions of welfare economics. It occurs where the utility function of one individual contains, as variables, the quantities of goods consumed by other persons."[8] It can only be lack of awareness of the past literature that causes Reder to imply that this consideration has not been taken up before. Among those who considered the problem earlier are J. E. Meade,[9] A. C. Pigou,[10] Henry Cunynghame,[11] and John Rae.[12]

The similarity in the treatment of this matter by Reder and Rae is at times striking. For example, Reder suggests that legislation forbidding "invidious expenditure" may result in an increase in welfare by

---

[5] John Rae, *The Sociological Theory of Capital* (London: The Macmillan Co., 1905), especially Chap. XIII, "Of Economic Stratification," and Appendix I, "Of Luxury," pp. 218–276.

[6] *Ibid.*, pp. 249 and 253.

[7] *Economic Journal*, 1893, pp. 458–474.

[8] *Studies in the Theory of Welfare Economics* (New York: Columbia University Press. 1947), p. 64. Italics mine.

[9] "Mr. Lerner on the Economics of Control," *Economic Journal*, 1945, pp. 51–56.

[10] *The Economics of Welfare* (4th Edition, 1929), pp. 190–192, 225–226, 808.

[11] "Some Improvements in Simple Geometrical Methods of Treating Exchange Value, Monopoly, and Rent," *Economic Journal*, 1892, pp. 35–39.

[12] Rae, *op. cit.*, pp. 277–296.

freeing resources from "competitive consumption" to other uses.[13] In a similar vein Rae argued that restrictions on the trade of "pure luxuries" can only be a gain to some and a loss to none, in view of the labor saved in avoiding the production of "pure luxuries." It is quite clear from the context that what Rae calls "pure luxuries" is exactly the same as Reder's commodities that enter into "competitive consumption." [14]

One reason why the interpersonal effects on demand have been ignored in current texts may be the fact that Marshall did not consider the matter in his *Principles*. We know, however, from Marshall's correspondence,[15] that he was aware of the problem. Both Cunynghame and Pigou pointed out that Marshall's treatment of consumers' surplus did not take into account interpersonal effects on utility. Marshall seemed to feel that this would make the diagrammatical treatment too complex. Recently, Reder [16] and Samuelson [17] noticed that external economies and diseconomies of consumption may vitiate or, at best, greatly complicate their "new" welfare analysis, and hence, in true academic fashion, they assume the problem away. This, however, is not the place to examine the question in detail.

The only attack on the problem from the point of view of pure theory that the writer could find [18] is a short article by Professor Pigou.[19] In this article Pigou sets out to inquire under what circumstances the assumption of the additivity of the individual demand curves "adequately conforms to the facts, and, when it does not so conform, what alternative assumption ought to be substituted for it." [20] It is obvious that the particular choice of alternative assumptions will determine (a) whether

---

[13] Reder, *op. cit.*, pp. 65–66.

[14] Rae, *op. cit.*, pp. 282–288.

[15] Pigou, *Memorials of Alfred Marshall*, pp. 433 and 450. These are Marshall's letters to Pigou and Cunynghame which indicate that Marshall had read the articles (*E. J.* 1892, and *E. J.* 1903), where Pigou and Cunynghame consider the matter.

[16] Reder, *op. cit.*, p. 67. "We shall assume, throughout its remainder, that the satisfaction of one individual does not depend on the consumption of another."

[17] *Foundations of Economic Analysis*, p. 224.

[18] James S. Duesenberry, in his recent book, *Income, Saving, and the Theory of Consumer Behavior* (Harvard University Press, 1949), considers problems of a somewhat similar nature but handles them in quite a different manner. Chapter VI on interdependent preferences and the "new" welfare analysis is especially worthy of mention. Duesenberry's treatment of the problem helps considerably to fill an important gap in the current theory. Unfortunately, Mr. Duesenberry's work came to the attention of the writer too late to be given the detailed consideration it deserves.

[19] "The Interdependence of Different Sources of Demand and Supply in a Market," *Economic Journal*, 1913, pp. 18–24.

[20] *Ibid.*, p. 18.

a solution can, given the existing analytical tools, be obtained, and (b) whether such a solution is relevant to the real world. Pigou's treatment of the problem is, unfortunately, exceedingly brief. He attempts to deal with non-additivity in both supply and demand curves within the confines of six pages. In examining the additivity assumption he points out that it is warranted when (1) the demand for the commodity is wholly for the direct satisfaction yielded by it or, (2) where disturbances to equilibrium are so small that aggregate output is not greatly changed. After briefly suggesting some of the complexities of non-additivity he concludes that the ". . . problems, for the investigation of which it is necessary to go behind the demand schedule of the market as a whole, are still, theoretically, soluble; there are a sufficient number of equations to determine the unknowns." [21] This last point, which is not demonstrated in Pigou's article, is hardly satisfying since it has been shown that the equality of equations and unknowns is not a sufficient condition for a determinate solution, or indeed for any solution, to exist.[22]

3. THE APPROACH AND LIMITS OF THE ENSUING ANALYSIS

It should, perhaps, be pointed out at the outset that the ensuing exposition is limited to statics. In all probability, the most interesting parts of the problem, and also those most relevant to real problems, are its dynamic aspects. However, a static analysis is probably necessary, and may be of significance, in order to lay a foundation for a dynamic analysis. In view of the limitations to be set on the following analysis, it becomes necessary to demarcate clearly the conceptual borderline between statics and dynamics.

There are, unfortunately, numerous definitions of statics and there seems to be some confusion on the matter. In view of this it will not be possible to give *the* definition of statics. All that we can hope to do is to choose *a* definition that will be consistent with and useful for our purposes—and also one that at the same time does not stray too far from some of the generally accepted notions about statics. Because of the fact that we live in a dynamic world most definitions of statics will imply a state of affairs that contradicts our general experience. But this is of necessity the case. What we must insist on is internal consistency but we need not, at this stage, require "realism."

21 *Ibid.*, p. 24.
22 On this point cf. Morgenstern, "Professor Hicks on Value and Capital," *Journal of Political Economy*, June 1941, pp. 368–376. See also part of an article by Don Patinkin, "The Indeterminacy of Absolute Prices in Classical Economic Theory," *Econometrica*, January 1949, pp. 310–311, which sets out the conditions under which systems of homogeneous equations will possess no solution.

Our task, then, is to define a static situation—a situation in which static economics is applicable. Ordinarily, it is thought that statics is in some way "timeless." This need not be the case. For our purposes, a static situation is not a "timeless" situation, nor is static economics timeless economices. It is, however, "temporally orderless" economics. That is, we shall define a static situation as one in which the order of events is of no significance. We, therefore, abstract from the consequences of the temporal order of events.[23] The above definition is similar to, but perhaps on a slightly higher level of generality than, Hicks's notion that statics deals with "those parts of economic theory where we do not have to trouble about dating." [24]

In order to preserve internal consistency, it is necessary to assume that the period of reference is one in which the consumer's income and expenditure pattern is synchronized. And, we have to assume also that this holds true for all consumers. In other words, we assume that both the income patterns and the expenditure patterns repeat themselves *every* period. There is thus no overlapping of expenditures from one period into the next. This implies, of course, that the demand curve reconstitutes itself every period.[25] The above implies also that only one price can exist during any unit period and that price can change only from period to period. A disequilibrium can, therefore, be corrected only over two or more periods.

II. FUNCTIONAL AND NONFUNCTIONAL DEMAND

At the outset it is probably best to define clearly some of the basic terms we are going to use and to indicate those aspects of demand that we are going to treat. The demand for consumers' goods and services may be classified according to motivation. The following classification, which we shall find useful, is on a level of abstraction which, it is hoped, includes most of the motivations behind consumers' demand.

        A. Functional
        B. Nonfunctional
           1. External effects on utility

[23] An excellent discussion of the above problem, the relationship between the notions of time in economics and various definitions of statics and dynamics, can be found in W. C. Hood, "Some Aspects of the Treatment of Time in Economic Theory," *The Canadian Journal of Economics and Political Science,* 1948, pp. 453–468.

[24] *Value and Capital,* p. 115.

[25] The above assumptions are necessary in order to take care of some of the difficulties raised by Professor Morgenstern in "Demand Theory Reconsidered."

      (a) Bandwagon effect

      (b) Snob effect

      (c) Veblen effect

   2. Speculative

   3. Irrational

By functional demand is meant that part of the demand for a commodity which is due to the qualities inherent in the commodity itself. By nonfunctional demand is meant that portion of the demand for a consumers' good which is due to factors other than the qualities inherent in the commodity. Probably the most important kind of nonfunctional demand is due to external effects on utility. That is, the utility derived from the commodity is enhanced or decreased owing to the fact that the commodity bears a higher rather than a lower price tag. We differentiate this type of demand into what we shall call the "bandwagon" effect, the "snob" effect, and the "Veblen" effect.[26] By the bandwagon effect, we refer to the extent to which the demand for a commodity is *increased* due to the fact that others are also consuming the same commodity. It represents the desire of people to purchase a commodity in order to get into "the swim of things"; in order to conform with the people they wish to be associated with; in order to be fashionable or stylish; or, in order to appear to be "one of the boys." By the snob effect we refer to the extent to which the demand for a consumers' good is *decreased* owing to the fact that others are also consuming the same commodity (or that others are increasing their consumption of that commodity). This represents the desire of people to be exclusive; to be different; to dissociate themselves from the "common herd." By the Veblen effect we refer to the phenomenon of conspicuous consumption; to the extent to which the demand for a consumers' good is increased because it bears a higher rather than a lower price. We should perhaps emphasize the distinction made between the snob and the Veblen effect—the former is a function of the consumption of others, the latter is a function of price.[27] This paper will deal almost exclusively with these three types of nonfunctional demand.

For the sake of completeness there should perhaps be some explanation as to what is meant by speculative and irrational demand. Specula-

---

[26] It is assumed from here on that the reader will be aware that these terms will be used in the special sense here defined, and hence the quotation marks will hereafter be deleted.

[27] Some writers have not made the above distinction but have combined the two effects into what they termed "snob behaviour" (see Morgenstern, *op. cit.*, p. 190). The above does not imply that our distinction is necessarily the "correct" one, but only that it is found useful in our analysis.

tive demand refers to the fact that people will often "lay in" a supply
of a commodity because they expect its price to rise. Irrational demand
is, in a sense, a catchall category. It refers to purchases that are neither
planned nor calculated but are due to sudden urges, whims, etc., and
that serve no rational purpose but that of satisfying sudden whims and
desires.

In the above it was assumed throughout that income is a parameter.
If income is not given but allowed to vary, then the income effect on
demand may in most cases be the most important effect of all. Also, it
may be well to point out that the above is only one of a large number
of possible classifications of the types of consumers' demand—classifications that for some purposes may be superior to the one here employed.
We therefore suggest the above classification only for the purposes at
hand and make no claims about its desirableness, or effectiveness, in
any other use.

III. THE BANDWAGON EFFECT

1. A CONCEPTUAL EXPERIMENT

Our immediate task is to obtain aggregate demand curves of various
kinds in those cases where the individual demand curves are non-additive. First we shall examine the case where the bandwagon effect is important. In its pure form this is the case where an individual will
demand more (less) of a commodity at a given price because some or all
other individuals in the market also demand more (less) of the commodity.

One of the difficulties in analyzing this type of demand involves the
choice of assumptions about the knowledge that each individual possesses. This implies that everyone knows the quantity that will be
demanded by every individual separately, or the quantity demanded
by all individuals collectively at any given price—after all the reactions
and adjustments that individuals make to each other's demand have
taken place. On the other hand, if we assume ignorance on the part of
consumers about the demand of others, we have to make assumptions
as to the nature and extent of the ignorance—ignorance is a relative
concept. A third possibility, and the one that will be employed at first,
is to devise some mechanism whereby the consumers obtain accurate
information.

Another problem involves the choice of assumptions to be made
about the demand behaviour of individual consumers. Three possibilities suggest themselves: (1) The demand of consumer A (at given

prices) may be a function of the total demand of all others in the market collectively. Or, (2) the demand of consumer A may be a function of the demand of all other consumers both separately and collectively. In other words, A's demand may be more influenced by the demand of some than by the demand of others. (3) A third possibility is that A's demand is a function of the number of people that demand the commodity rather than the number of units demanded. More complex demand behaviour patterns that combine some of the elements of the above are conceivable. For present purposes it is best that we assume the simplest one as a first approximation.[28] Initially, therefore, we assume that A's demand is a function of the units demanded by all others collectively. This is the same as saying that A's demand is a function of total market demand at given prices, since A always knows his own demand, and he could always subtract his own demand from the total market demand to get the quantity demanded by all others.

In order to bring out the central principle involved in the ensuing analysis, consider the following *gedankenexperiment*. A known product is to be introduced into a well-defined market at a certain date. The nature of the product is such that its demand depends partially on the functional qualities of the commodity, and partially on whether many or few units are demanded. Our technical problem is to compound the non-additive individual demand curves into a total market demand curve, given sufficient information about the individual demand functions. Now, suppose that it is possible to obtain an accurate knowledge of the demand function of an individual through a series of questionnaires. Since an individual's demand is, in part, a function of the total market demand, it is necessary to take care of this difficulty in our questionnaires. We can have a potential consumer fill out the first questionnaire by having him assume that the total market demand, at all prices, is a given very small amount—say 400 units. On the basis of this assumption the consumer would tell us the quantities he demands over a reasonable range of prices. Subjecting every consumer to the same questionnaire, we add the results across and obtain a market demand curve that would reflect the demand situation if every consumer believed the total demand were only 400 units. This, however, is not the real market demand function under the assumption of the possession of

---

[28] As is customary in economic theory the ensuing analysis is carried out on the basis of a number of simplifying assumptions. The relaxation of some of the simplifying assumptions and the analysis of more complex situations must await some other occasion. The present writer has attempted these with respect to some of the simplifying assumptions but the results cannot be included within the confines of an article of the usual length.

accurate market information by consumers, since the total demand (at each price) upon which consumers based their replies was not the actual market demand (at each price) as revealed by the results of the survey. Let us call the results of the first survey "Schedule No. 1."

We can now carry out a second survey, that is, subject each consumer to a second questionnaire in which each one is told that schedule No. 1 reflects the total quantities demanded, at each price. Aggregating the replies we obtain schedule No. 2. Schedule No. 1 then becomes a parameter upon which schedule No. 2 is based. In a similar manner we can obtain schedules No. 3, No. 4, . . . , No. n in which each schedule is the result of adding the quantities demanded by each consumer (at each price), *if each consumer believes that the total quantities demanded (at each price) are shown by the previous schedule.* Now, the quantities demanded in schedule No. 2 will be greater than or equal to the quantities demanded in schedule No. 1. for the same prices. Some consumers may increase the quantity they demand when they note that the total quantity demanded, at given prices, is greater than they thought it would be. As long as some consumers or potential consumers continue to react positively to increases in the total quantity demanded the results of successive surveys will be different. That is, some or all of the quantities demanded in schedule No. 1 will be less than the quantities demanded at the same prices, in schedule No. 2, which in turn will be equal to or less than the quantities demanded, at the same prices, in schedule No. 3, and so on.

At this point it is appropriate to introduce a new principle with the intention of showing that this process cannot go on indefinitely. Sooner or later two successive schedules will be identical. If two successive surveys yield the same market demand schedules, then an equilibrium situation exists since the total quantities demanded, at each price, upon which individual consumers based their demand, turns out to be correct. Thus, if schedule No. n is identical with schedule No. n-1, then schedule No. n is the actual market demand function for the product on the assumption that consumers have accurate information of market conditions.

The question that arises is whether there is any reason to suppose that sooner or later two successive surveys will yield exactly the same result. This would indeed be the case if we could find good reason to posit a principle to the effect that for every individual there is some point at which he will cease to increase the quantities demanded for a commodity, at given prices, in response to incremental increases in total market demand. Such a principle would imply that beyond a point incremental increases in the demand for the commodity by others have a decreasing influence on a consumer's own demand; and, further, that a point is reached at which these increases in demand by others have no influence whatsoever on his own demand. It would, of course, also be necessary to establish that such a principle holds true for every consumer. It would not be inappropriate to call this the principle of diminishing marginal external consumption effect. Does such a principle really exist? There are some good reasons for believing that it does. First, the reader may note that the principle is analogous to the principle of diminishing marginal utility. As the total market demand grows larger, incremental increases in total demand become smaller and smaller proportions of the demand. It sounds reasonable, and probably appeals to us intuitively that an individual would be less influenced, and indeed take less notice of, a one per cent increase in total demand, than of a ten per cent increase in total demand, though these percentage increases be the same in absolute amount. Second, we can probably appeal effectively to general experience. There are no cases in which an individual's demand for a consumer's good increases endlessly with increases in total demand. If there were two or more such individuals in a market then the demand for the commodity would increase in an endless spiral. Last but not least, the income constraint is sufficient to establish that there must be a point at which increases in a consumer's demand must fail to respond to increases in demand by others. Since every consumer is subject to the income constraint, it must follow that the principle holds for all consumers.[29]

Now, to get back to our conceptual experiment, we would find that after administering a sufficient number of surveys, we would sooner or later get two surveys that yield identical demand schedules. The result of the last survey would then represent the true demand situation that would manifest itself on the market when the commodity was offered for sale. We may perhaps justly call such a demand function the equilibrium demand function—or demand curve. The equilibrium demand curve is the curve that exists when the marginal external consumption effect for every consumer, but one,[30] at all alternate prices is equal to zero. All other demand curves may be conceived as disequilibrium curves that can exist only because of temporarily imperfect knowledge

[29] If the reader should object to our dignifying the diminishing marginal external consumption effect by calling it a principle or a law, we could point out that if it is not a "law," then it must be an equilibrium condition.

[30] The fact that the marginal external consumption effect of one consumer is greater than zero can have no effect on the demand schedule since total market demand, at any given price, cannot increase unless there are at least two consumers who would react on each other's demand.

by consumers of other people's demand. Once the errors in market information were discovered such a curve would move to a new position.

2. THE BANDWAGON EFFECT—DIAGRAMMATICAL METHOD

The major purpose of going through the conceptual experiment with its successive surveys was to illustrate the diminishing marginal external consumption effect and to indicate its role in obtaining a determinate demand curve. There is, however, a relatively simple method for obtaining the market demand function in those cases where external consumption effects are significant. This method will allow us to compare some of the properties of the "bandwagon demand curve" with the usual "functional" demand curve and, it will also allow us to separate the extent to which a change in demand is due to a change in price, and the extent to which it is due to the bandwagon effect.

Given a certain total demand for a commodity as a parameter,[31] every individual will have a demand function based on this total market demand. Let the alternative total market demands that will serve as superscripts $a, b, \ldots n$ (where $a < b < \ldots < n$). Let the individual demand functions be $d_1\ d_2, \ldots d_n$; where every subscript indicates a different consumer. Thus d_3^a is the individual demand curve for consumer 3 if the consumer believes that the total market demand is a units. Similarly d_{500}^m is the individual demand curve for the 500th consumer if he believes that the total market demand will be m units. We could now add across $d_1^a, d_2^a, d_3^a, \ldots, d_n^a$ which will give us the market demand curve D^a, which indicates the quantities demanded at alternate prices if all consumers believed that the total demand was a units. In the same manner we can obtain $D^b, D^c, \ldots, D^n$. These hypothetical market demand curves $D^a, D^b, D^c, \ldots, D^n$ are shown in Figure 1. Now, if we assume that buyers have accurate knowledge of market conditions (*i.e.*, of the total quantities demanded at every price) then only one point on any of the curves $D^a, D^b, \ldots, D^n$ could be on the real or equilibrium demand curve. These are the points on each curve $D^a, D^b, \ldots, D^n$ that represent the amounts on which the consumers based their individual demand curves; that is, the amounts that consumers

---

[31] The reader should note that the analysis in the following pages is based on a somewhat different assumption than the *gedankenexperiment*. In the diagrams that follow each demand curve (other than the equilibrium demand curve) is based on the assumption that consumers believe that a fixed amount will be taken off the market at all prices. There is more than one way of deriving the equilibrium demand curve. The earlier method helped to bring out the nature of the central principle that is involved, while the method which follows will enable us to separate price effects from bandwagon effects and snob effects, etc.

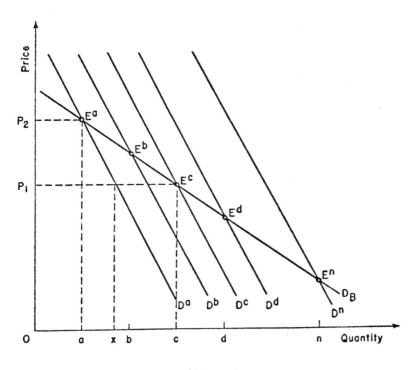

Figure 1

expected to be the total market demand. These points are labeled in Figure 1 as E^a, E^b, . . . , E^n. They are a series of virtual equilibrium points. Given that consumers possess accurate market information, E^a, E^b, . . . , E^n, are the only points that can become actual quantities demanded. The locus of all these points D_B is therefore the actual demand curve for the commodity.

It may be of interest, at this point, to break up changes in the quantity demanded due to changes in price into a price effect and a bandwagon effect; that is, the extent of the change that is due to the change in price, and the extent of the change in demand that is due to consumers adjusting to each other's changed consumption.[32] With an eye

[32] We are now really in the area of "comparative statics." It may be recalled that we defined statics and our unit period in such a way that only *one* price holds within any unit period. Thus, when we examine the effects of a change in price we are really examining the reasons for the differences in the quantities demanded at one price in one unit period and another price in the succeeding unit period.

on Figure 1 consider the effects of a reduction in price from P_2 to P_1.
The increase in demand after the change in price is ac. Only part of
that increase, however, is due to the reduction in price. To measure
the amount due to the reduction in price we go along the demand curve
D^a to P_1 which tells us the quantity that would be demanded at P_1 if
consumers did not adjust to each other's demand. This would result in
an increase in demand of ax. Due to the bandwagon effect, however,
an additional number of consumers are induced to enter the market or
to increase their demands. There is now an additional increase in demand of xc after consumers have adjusted to each other's increases in
consumption. Exactly the same type of analysis can, of course, be carried
out for increases as well as for decreases in price.

We may note another thing from Figure 1. The demand curve D_B is
more elastic than any of the other demand curves shown in the diagram. This would suggest that, other things being equal, the demand
curve will be more elastic if there is a bandwagon effect than if the
demand is based only on the functional attributes of the commodity.
This, of course, follows from the fact that reactions to price changes are
followed by additional reactions, *in the same direction,* to each other's
changed consumption.

3. SOCIAL TABOOS AND THE BANDWAGON EFFECT

Social taboos, to the extent that they affect consumption, are, in a sense,
bandwagon effects in reverse gear. That is to say, some people will not
buy and consume certain things because other people are not buying
and consuming these things. Thus, there may not be any demand for a
commodity even though it has a functional utility, although, apart
from the taboo, it would be purchased. Individual A will not buy the
commodity because individuals B, C, and D do not, while individuals
B, C, and D may refrain from consumption for the same reasons. It is
not within the competence of the economist to investigate the psychology of this kind of behaviour. For our purposes we need only note that
such behaviour exists and attempt to analyze how such behaviour affects
the demand function.

We can proceed as follows. Let d_1^x be the demand curve of the least
inhibited individual in the market, where the superscript x is the total
quantity demanded in the market upon which he bases his individual
demand. Suppose that at market demand x consumer 1 will demand at
some range of prices one unit of the commodity, but at no price will he
demand more. If he believes, however, that the total market demand is
less than x units he will refrain from making any purchases. Since, *ex*

hypothesi, consumer 1 is the least inhibited consumer, he will, at best, be the only one who will demand one unit of the commodity if consumers expect the total market demand to be x units. It must be clear, then, that x units cannot be a virtual equilibrium point, since only points where the total expected quantity demanded is equal to the actual quantity demanded can be points on the real demand curve, and the quantity x cannot at any price be a point where expected total demand is equal to actual total demand. Now, if the total expected demand were $x + 1$ the actual demand might increase, say, to 2 units. At expected total demands $x + 2$ and $x + 3$, more would enter the market and the actual demand would be still greater since the fear of being different is considerably reduced as the expected demand is increased. With given increases in the expected total demand there must, at some point, be more than equal increases in the actual demand, because, if a real demand curve exists at all, there must be some point where the expected demand is equal to the actual demand. That point may exist, say, at $x + 10$. That is, at an expected total demand of $x + 10$ units a sufficient number of people have overcome their inhibitions to being different so that, at some prices, they will actually demand $x + 10$ units of the commodity. Let us call this point "T"—it is really the "taboo breaking point." The maximum bid (the point T^1 in Figure 2) of the marginal unit demanded if the total demand were T units now gives us the first point on the real demand curve (the curve D_B).

How social taboos may affect the demand curve is shown in Figure 2. It will be noted that the price axis shows both positive and negative "prices." A negative price may be thought of as the price it would be necessary to *pay* individuals in order to induce them to consume in public a given amount of the commodity; that is, the price that it would be necessary to pay the consumers in order to induce them to disregard their aversion to be looked upon as odd or peculiar.

As we have already indicated, the point T in Figure 2 is the "taboo breaking point." T represents the number of units at which an *expected* total quantity demanded of T units would result in an *actual* quantity demanded of T units at some *real* price. Now, what has to be explained is why an expected demand of less than T units, say $T - 3$ units, would not yield an actual demand of $T - 3$ units at a positive price but only at a "negative price." Let the curve D^{T-3} be the demand curve that would exist if consumers thought the total demand was $T - 3$. Now, at any positive price, say P_3, the amount demanded would be less than $T - 3$, say $T - 7$. The price P_3 can therefore exist only if there is inaccurate information of the total quantity demanded. Once con-

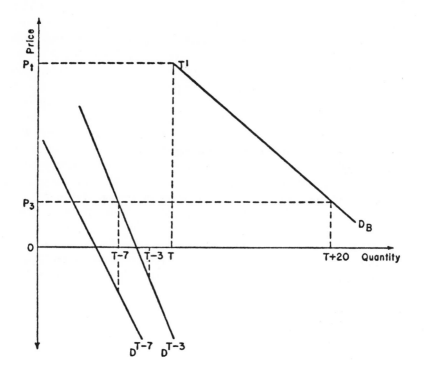

Figure 2

sumers discovered that at P_3 only $T - 7$ was purchased, and believed
that this was the demand that would be sustained, their demand would
shift to the D^{T-7} curve. At P_3 the amount purchased would now be less
than $T - 7$ and demand would now shift to a curve to the left of the
D^{T-7} curve. This procedure would go on until the demand was zero at
P_3. We thus introduce a gap into our demand function and focus attention on an interesting psychological phenomenon that may affect
demand. What we are suggesting, essentially, is that given "accurate
expectations" of the total quantity demanded on the part of consumers,
there is a quantity less than which there will not be any quantity demanded at any real price. In other words, this is a case in which a commodity will either "go over big" or not "go over" at all. It will be noted
that at P_3 zero units or $T + 20$ units (Figure 2) may be taken off the
market given "accurate expectations" of the total quantity demanded.
It would seem, therefore, that "accurate expectations" of the total

quantity demanded at P_3 can have two values depending upon whether people are generally pessimistic or optimistic about other consumers' demands for the commodity in question. If everybody expects that everybody else would not care much for the commodity, then zero units would be the accurate expectation of the total quantity demanded; if everybody, on the other hand, expects others to take up the commodity with some degree of enthusiasm,[33] then $T + 20$ units would be the accurate expectation of the total quantity demanded. The factors that would determine one set of expectations rather than the other are matters of empirical investigation in the field of social psychology. The factors involved may be the history of the community, the people's conservatism or lack of conservatism, the type and quantity of advertising about the commodity under consideration, etc.

The really significant point in Figure 2 is T^1, the first point on the real demand curve D_B. As already indicated, it is the point at which the maximum bid of the marginal unit demanded is P_t and the total market demand is T units. If the price were higher than P_t, the Tth unit would not be demanded and all buyers would leave the market because of the effect of the taboo at less than a consumption of T units.[34] By way of summary we might say that the whole point of this section is an attempt to show that in cases where social taboos affect demand, the real demand curve may not start at the price-axis but that the smallest possible quantity demanded may be some distance to the right of the price-axis.

IV. THE SNOB EFFECT

Thus far, in our conceptual experiment and diagrammatic analysis, we have considered only the bandwagon effect. We now consider the reverse effect—the demand behaviour for those commodities with regard to which the individual consumer acts like a snob. Here, too, we assume at first that the quantity demanded by a consumer is a function of price and of the total market demand, but that the individual consumer's demand is negatively correlated with the total market demand. In the snob case it is rather obvious that the external consumption effect must reach a limit although the limit may be where one snob constitutes the only buyer. For most commodities and most buyers, however, the motivation for exclusiveness is not that great; hence the

---

[33] If consumers have accurate expectations of the degree of enthusiasm with which others will take up the product, then they will expect demand to be $T + 20$ units.

[34] This is a "pure" case where *all* buyers are governed by taboo considerations.

marginal external consumption effect reaches zero before that point. If the commodity is to be purchased at all, the external consumption effect must reach a limit, at some price, where the quantity demanded has a positive value. From this it follows that after a point the principle of the diminishing marginal external consumption effect must manifest itself. We thus have in the snob effect an opposite but completely symmetrical relationship to the bandwagon effect.

The analysis of markets in which all consumers behave as snobs follows along the same lines as our analysis of the bandwagon effect. Because of the similarity we will be able to get through our analysis of the snob effect in short order. We begin, as before, by letting the alternate total market demands that serve as parameters for alternate individual demand curves be indicated by the superscripts $a, b, \ldots , n$ (where $a < b < n$). Let the individual demand functions be $d_1, d_2, \ldots d_n$, where there are n consumers in the market. Again, d_3^a signifies the individual demand curve for consumer 3 on the assumption that he expects the total market demand to be "a" units. By adding

$$d_1^a + d_2^a + \ldots + d_n^a = D^a$$
$$d_1^b + d_2^b + \ldots + d_n^b = D^b$$
$$\cdot \qquad \cdot$$
$$\cdot \qquad \cdot$$
$$\cdot \qquad \cdot$$
$$d_1^n + d_2^n + \ldots + d_n^n = D^n$$

we obtain the market demand functions on the alternate assumptions of consumers expecting the total market demands to be $a, b, \ldots , n$. Due to snob behaviour the curves $D^a, D^b, \ldots , D^n$ move to the left as the expected total market demand increases. This is shown in Figure 3. Using the same procedure as before we obtain the virtual equilibrium points $E^a, E^b, \ldots , E^n$. They represent the only points on the curves $D^a, D^b, \ldots , D^n$ that are consistent with consumers' expectations (and hence with the assumption of accurate information). The locus of these virtual equilibrium points is the demand curve D_S.

Now, given a price change from P_2 to P_1 we can separate the effect of the price change into a price effect and a snob effect. In Figure 3 we see that the net increase in the quantity demanded due to the reduction in price is ab. The price effect, however, is ax. That is, if every consumer expected no increase in the total quantity demanded then the total quantity demanded at P_1 would be Ox. The more extreme snobs will react to this increase in the total quantity demanded and will leave the market.[35] The total quantity demanded

---

[35] The other snobs will, of course, reduce their demand but not by an amount large enough to leave the market.

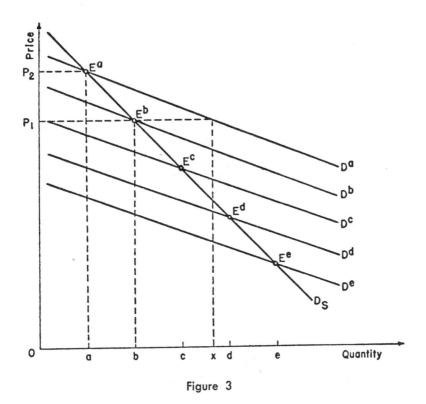

Figure 3

will hence be reduced by *bx*. The net result is therefore an increase in demand of only *ab*.

It may be of interest to examine some of the characteristics of the curves in Figure 3. First we may note that all the points on the curves other than D_S (except E^a, E^b, . . . , E^n) are theoretical points that have significance only under conditions of imperfect knowledge. Second, we may note from the diagram that the demand curve for snobs is less elastic than the demand curves where there are no snob effects. The reason for this, of course, is that the increase in demand due to a reduction in price is counterbalanced, in part, by some snobs leaving the market because of the increase in total consumption (*i.e.*, the decrease in the snob value of the commodity). It should be clear, however, that the snob effect, as defined, can never be in excess of the price effect since this would lead to a basic contradiction. If the snob effect were greater than the price effect, then the quantity demanded at a lower price would be less than the quantity demanded at a higher price. This implies that some of the snobs in the market at the higher price leave the market when there is a reduction in the total quantity demanded; which, of course, is patently inconsistent with our definition of snob behaviour. It therefore follows that the snob effect is never greater than the price effect. It follows, also, that D_S is monotonically decreasing if D^a, D^b, ..., D^n are monotonically decreasing.[36]

Finally, it may be interesting to note another difference between the usual functional demand curve and the D_S curve. In the usual demand curve the buyers at higher prices always remain in the market at lower prices. That is, from the price point of view, the bids to buy are cumulative downward. This is clearly not the case in the D_S curve. Such terms as intramarginal buyers may be meaningless in snob markets.

V. THE VEBLEN EFFECT

Although the theory of conspicuous consumption as developed by Veblen and others is quite a complex and subtle sociological construct we can, for our purposes, quite legitimately abstract from the psychological and sociological elements and address our attention exclusively to the effects that conspicuous consumption has on the demand function. The essential economic characteristic with which we are concerned is the fact that the utility derived from a unit of a commodity employed for purposes of conspicuous consumption depends not only on the inherent qualities of that unit, but also on the price paid for it. It may, therefore, be helpful to divide the price of a commodity into two categories; the real price and the conspicuous price. By the real price we refer to the price the consumer paid for the commodity in terms of money. The conspicuous price is the price other people think the consumer paid for the commodity [37] and which therefore determines its conspicuous consumption utility. These two prices would probably be identical in highly organized markets where price information is common knowledge. In other markets, where some can get "bargains" or special discounts the real price or conspicuous price need not be identical. In any case, the quantity demand by a consumer will be a function of both the real price and the conspicuous price.

The market demand curve for commodities subject to conspicuous consumption can be derived through a similar diagrammatical method

---

[36] We shall see below however that the snob effect plus the Veblen effect combined can be greater than the price effect.

[37] More accurately, the conspicuous price should be the price that the consumer thinks other people think he paid for the commodity.

(summarized in Figure 4). This time we let the superscripts 1, 2, ..., n stand for the expected conspicuous prices. The real prices are P_1, P_2, ..., P_n. The individual demand functions are d_1, d_2, ..., d_n. In this way d_6^3 stands for the demand curve of consumer number 6 if he expects a conspicuous price of P_3^e.[38] We can now add across $d_1^1, d_2^1, \ldots, d_n^1$ and get the market demand curve D^1 which indicates the quantities demanded at alternate prices if all consumers expected a conspicuous price of P_1^e. In a similar manner we obtain D^2, D^3, ..., D^n. The market demand curves will, of course, up to

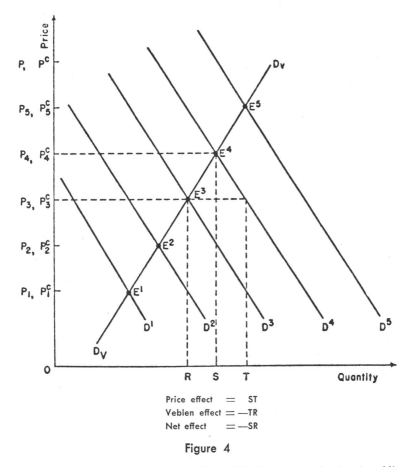

Price effect $=$ ST
Veblen effect $=$ —TR
Net effect $=$ —SR

Figure 4

[38] The expected conspicuous prices are distinguished from the real prices by adding the superscript c to the P's. Thus, to the range of real prices P_1, P_2, ..., P_n, we have a corresponding range of conspicuous prices denoted by P_1^c, P_2^c, ..., P_n^c.

a point, shift to the right as the expected conspicuous price increases. Now on every curve D^1, D^2, . . . , D^n in Figure 4 only one point can be a virtual equilibrium point if we assume that consumers possess accurate market information—the point where the real price is equal to the conspicuous price (that is, where $P_1 = P_1^c$, $P_2 = P_2^c$, . . . , $P_n = P_n^c$). The locus of these virtual equilibrium points E^1, E^2, . . . , E^n gives us the demand curve D_V.

As before, we can separate the effects of a change in price into two effects—the price effect, and, what we shall call for want of a better term, the Veblen effect. In Figure 4, it will be seen that a change in price from P_4 to P_3 will reduce the quantity demanded by RS. The price effect is to increase the quantity demanded by ST; that is, the amount that would be demanded if there were no change in the expected conspicuous price would be OT. However, at the lower price a number of buyers would leave the market because of the reduced utility derived from the commodity at that lower conspicuous price. The Veblen effect is therefore RT.

It should be noted that unlike the D_S curve, the D_V curve can be positively inclined, negatively inclined or a mixture of both. It all depends on whether at alternate price changes the Veblen effect is greater or less than the price effect. It is possible that in one portion of the curve one effect may predominate while in another portion another may predominate. It is to be expected, however, that in most cases, if the curve is not monotonically decreasing it will be shaped like a backward S, as illustrated in Figure 5A. The reasons for this are as follows:

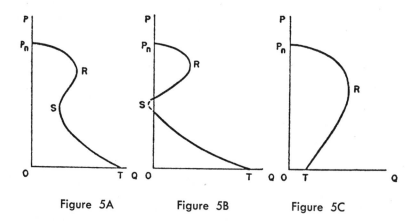

Figure 5A   Figure 5B   Figure 5C

First, there must be a price so high that no units of the commodity will be purchased at that price owing to the income constraint (among other reasons). This is the price P_n in Figure 5A, and it implies that there must be some point at which the curve shifts from being positively inclined to being negatively inclined as price increases. Second, there must be some point of satiety for the good. This is the point T in Figure 5A. It therefore follows that some portion of the curve must be monotonically decreasing to reach T if there exists some minimum price at which the Veblen effect is zero. It is of course reasonable to assume that there is some low price at which the commodity would cease to have any value for purposes of conspicuous consumption. If this last assumption does not hold, which is unlikely, then the curve could have the shape indicated in Figure 5C. Otherwise, it would have the general shape indicated in Figure 5A, or it might be in two segments as illustrated in Figure 5B.

VI. MIXED EFFECTS

Any real market for semidurable or durable goods will most likely contain consumers that are subject to one or a combination of the effects discussed heretofore. Combining these effects presents no new formal difficulties with respect to the determination of the market demand curve, although it complicates the diagrammatic analysis considerably. The major principle, however, still holds. For any price there is a quantity demanded such that the marginal external consumption effect (or the marginal Veblen effect) for all buyers but one, is zero. This implies that for every price change there is a point at which people cease reacting to each other's quantity changes, regardless of the direction of these reactions. If this is so, then for every price there is a determinate quantity demanded, and hence the demand curve is determinate.

Now, for every price change we have distinguished between the price effect and some other, such as the snob, the Veblen, or the bandwagon effect. In markets where all four effects are present we should be able to separate out and indicate the direction of each of them that will result from a price change. That is, every price change will result in two positive and two negative effects—two which, other things being equal, will increase the quantity demanded, and two which, other things being equal, will decrease it. Which effects will be positive and which will be negative will depend on the relative strength of the Veblen effect as against the price effect. The Veblen and the price effects will depend directly on the direction of the price change. An increase in price will therefore result in price and bandwagon effects that are negative, and in Veblen and snob effects that are positive, provided that the price effect is greater than the Veblen effect; that is, if the net result is a decrease in the quantity demanded at the higher prices. If, on the other hand, the Veblen effect is more powerful than the price effect, given a price increase, then the bandwagon effect would be positive and the snob effect negative. The reverse would of course be true for price declines.

The market demand curve for a commodity where different consumers are subject to different types of effects can be obtained diagrammatically through employing the methods developed above—although the diagrams would be quite complicated. There is no point in adding still more diagrams to illustrate this. Briefly, the method would be somewhat as follows: (1) Given the demand curves for every individual, in which the expected total quantity demanded is a parameter for each curve, we can add these curves laterally and obtain a map of aggregate demand curves, in which each aggregate curve is based on a given total quantity demanded. (2) The locus of the equilibrium points on each aggregate demand curve (as derived in Figure 1) gives us a market demand curve that accounts for both bandwagon and snob effects. This last curve assumes that only one conspicuous price exists. For every conspicuous price there exists a separate map of aggregate demand curves from which different market demand curves are obtained. (3) This procedure yields a map of market demand curves in which each curve is based on a different conspicuous price. Employing the method used in Figure 4 we obtain our final market demand curve which accounts for bandwagon, snob, and Veblen effects simultaneously.

VII. CONCLUSION

It is not unusual for a writer in pure theory to end his treatise by pointing out that the science is really very young; that there is a great deal more to be done; that the formulations presented are really of a very tentative nature; and that the best that can be hoped for is that his treatise may in some small way pave the road for future formulations that are more directly applicable to problems in the real world.[39] This is another way of saying that work in pure theory is an investment in the future state of the science where the returns in terms of applications to real problems are really very uncertain. This is probably especially true of value theory where the investment in time and effort is more akin to the purchase of highly speculative stocks rather than the purchase of government bonds. Since this was only a brief

[39] See, for example, Samuelson, *Foundations of Economic Analysis*, p. 350, and Joan Robinson, *Economics of Imperfect Competition*, p. 327.

essay on one aspect of value theory, the reader will hardly be surprised if the conclusions reached are somewhat less than revolutionary.

Essentially, we have attempted to do two things. First, we have tried to demonstrate that non-additivity is not necessarily an insurmountable obstacle in effecting a transition from individual to collective demand curves. Second, we attempted to take a step or two in the direction of incorporating various kinds of external consumption effects into the theory of consumers' demand. In order to solve our problem, we have introduced what we have called the principle of the diminishing marginal external consumption effect. We indicated some reasons for believing that for every individual, there is some point at which the marginal external consumption effect is zero. We have attempted to show that if this principle is admitted, then there are various ways of effecting a transition from individual to collective demand curves. The major conclusion reached is that under conditions of perfect knowledge (or accurate expectations) any point on the demand curve, for any given price, will be at that total quantity demanded where the marginal external consumption effect for all consumers but one, is equal to zero.

In comparing the demand curve in those situations where external consumption effects are present with the demand curve as it would be where these external consumption effects are absent, we made three basic points. (1) If the bandwagon effect is the most significant effect, the demand curve is more elastic than it would be if this external consumption effect were absent. (2) If the snob effect is the predominant effect, the demand curve is less elastic than otherwise. (3) If the Veblen effect is the predominant one, the demand curve is less elastic than otherwise, and some portions of it may even be positively inclined; whereas, if the Veblen effect is absent, the curve will be negatively inclined regardless of the importance of the snob effect in the market.

10

THE MARSHALLIAN DEMAND CURVE *

MILTON FRIEDMAN † teaches at the University of
Chicago.

Alfred Marshall's theory of demand strikingly exemplifies his "impatience with rigid definition and an excessive tendency to let the context explain his meaning." [1] The concept of the demand curve as a functional relation between the quantity and the price of a particular commodity is explained repeatedly and explicitly in the *Principles of Economics:* in words in the text, in plane curves in the footnotes, and in symbolic form in the Mathematical Appendix. A complete definition of the demand curve, including, in particular, a statement of the variables that are to be considered the same for all points on the curve and the variables that are to be allowed to vary, is nowhere given explicitly. The reader is left to infer the contents of *ceteris paribus* from general and vague statements, parenthetical remarks, examples that do not purport to be exhaustive, and concise mathematical notes in the Appendix.

In view of the importance of the demand curve in Marshallian analysis, it is natural that other economists should have constructed a rigorous definition to fill the gap that Marshall left. This occurred at an early date, apparently without controversy about the interpretation to be placed on Marshall's comments. The resulting definition of the demand curve is now so much an intrinsic part of current eco-

---

* From *Journal of Political Economy*, Vol. LVII (December, 1949), pp. 463–495, copyright © by The University of Chicago Press. Reprinted by permission.

† I am deeply indebted for helpful criticism and suggestions to A. F. Burns, Aaron Director, C. W. Guillebaud, H. Gregg Lewis, A. R. Prest, D. H. Robertson, G. J. Stigler, and, especially, Jacob Viner, to whose penetrating discussion of the demand curve in his course in economic theory I can trace some of the central ideas and even details of this article. The standard comment that none is to be held responsible for the views expressed herein has particular relevance, since most disagreed with my interpretation of Marshall as presented in an earlier and much briefer draft of this article.

[1] C. W. Guillebaud, "The Evolution of Marshall's *Principles of Economics*," *Economic Journal*, LII (December, 1942), 333.

nomic theory and is so widely accepted as Marshall's own that the assertion that Marshall himself gave no explicit rigorous definition may shock most readers.

Yet why this particular interpretation evolved and why it gained such unquestioned acceptance are a mystery that requires explanation. The currently accepted interpretation can be read into Marshall only by a liberal—and, I think, strained—reading of his remarks, and its acceptance implicitly convicts him of logical inconsistency and mathematical error at the very foundation of his theory of demand. More important, the alternative interpretation of the demand curve that is yielded by a literal reading of his remarks not only leaves his original work on the theory of demand free from both logical inconsistency and mathematical error but also is more useful for the analysis of most economic problems.

Section I presents the two interpretations of the demand curve and compares them in some detail; Section II argues that a demand curve constructed on my interpretation is the more useful for the analysis of practical problems, whatever may be the verdict about its validity as an interpretation of Marshall; Section III demonstrates that my interpretation is consistent with Marshall's monetary theory and with his work on consumer's surplus; and Section IV presents the textual evidence on the validity of my interpretation. Finally, Section V argues that the change that has occurred in the interpretation of the demand curve reflects a corresponding change in the role assigned to economic theory.

I. ALTERNATIVE INTERPRETATIONS OF MARSHALL'S DEMAND CURVE

The demand curve of a particular group (which may, as a special case, consist of a single individual) for a particular commodity shows the quantity (strictly speaking, the maximum quantity) of the commodity that will be purchased by the group per unit of time at each price. So far, no question arises; this part of the definition is explicit in Marshall and is common to both alternatives to be discussed. The problem of interpretation relates to the phrase, "other things the same," ordinarily attached to this definition.

In the first place, it should be noted that "same" in this phrase does not mean "same over time." The points on a demand curve are alternative possibilities, not temporally ordered combinations of quantity and price. "Same" means "same for all points on the demand curve"; the different points are to differ in quantity and price and are not to differ with respect to "other things." [2] In the second place, "all" other things cannot be supposed to be the same without completely emasculating the concept. For example, if (a) total money expenditure on all commodities, (b) the price of every commodity other than the one in question, and (c) the quantity purchased of every other commodity were supposed to be the same, the amount of money spent on the commodity in question would necessarily be the same at all prices, simply as a matter of arithmetic, and the demand curve would have unit elasticity everywhere. [3] Different specifications of the "other things" will yield different demand curves. For example, one demand curve will be obtained by excluding b from the list of "other things"; another, quite different one, by excluding c.

A. The Current Interpretation

The current interpretation of Marshall's demand curve explicitly includes in the list of "other things" (1) tastes and preferences of the group of purchasers considered, (2) their money income, and (3) the price of every other commodity. The quantities of other commodities are explicitly considered as different at different points on the demand curve, and still other variables are ignored. [4]

---

[2] Of course, when correlations among statistical time series are regarded as estimates of demand curves, the hypothesis is that "other things" have been approximately constant over time or that appropriate allowance has been made for changes in them. Similarly, when correlations among cross-section data are regarded as estimates of demand curves, the hypothesis is that "other things" are approximately the same for the units distinguished or that appropriate allowance has been made for differences among them. In both cases the problem of estimation should be clearly distinguished from the theoretical construct to be estimated.

[3] Yet Sidney Weintraub not only suggests that Marshall intended to keep a, b, and c simultaneously the same but goes on to say: "Clearly Marshall's assumption means a unit elasticity of demand in the market reviewed and no ramifications elsewhere; that was why he adopted it" ("The Foundations of the Demand Curve," American Economic Review, XXXII [September, 1942], 538–52, quotation from n. 12, p. 541). Weintraub even adds the condition of constant tastes and preferences to a, b, and c, speaking of a change in tastes as shifting the demand curve. Obviously, a, b, and c together leave no room for tastes and preferences or, indeed, for anything except simple arithmetic.

[4] Explicit definition of the demand curve in this way by followers of Marshall dates back at least to 1894 (see F. Y. Edgeworth, "Demand Curves" [art.], Palgrave's Dictionary of Political Economy, ed. Henry Higgs [rev. ed.; London: Macmillan & Co., 1926]). Edgeworth's article apparently dates from the first edition, which was published in 1894. While Edgeworth does not explicitly attribute this interpretation to Marshall, it is clear from the context that he is talking about a Marshallian demand curve and that he does not regard his statements as incon-

On this interpretation it is clear that, while money income is the same for different points on the demand curve, real income is not. At the lower of two prices for the commodity in question, more of some commodities can be purchased without reducing the amounts purchased of other commodities. The lower the price, therefore, the higher the real income.

B. AN ALTERNATIVE INTERPRETATION

It seems to me more faithful to both the letter and the spirit of Marshall's writings to include in the list of "other things" (1) tastes and preferences of the group of purchasers considered, (2) their real income, and (3) the price of every closely related commodity.

Two variants of this interpretation can be distinguished, according to the device adopted for keeping real income the same at different points on the demand curve. One variant, which Marshall employed in the text of the Principles, is obtained by replacing "(2) their real income" by (2a) their money income and (2b) the "purchasing power of money." Constancy of the "purchasing power of money" for different prices of the commodity in question implies compensating variations in the prices of some or all other commodities. These variations will, indeed, be negligible if the commodity in question accounts for a negligible fraction of total expenditures; but they should not be disregarded, both because empirical considerations must be sharply separated from logical considerations and because the demand curve need not be limited in applicability to such commodities. On this variant all commodities are, in effect, divided into three groups: (a) the commodity in question, (b) closely related commodities, and (c) all other commodities. The absolute price of each commodity in group b is supposed to be the same for different points on the demand curve; only the "average" price, or an index number of prices, is considered for group c; and it is to be supposed to rise or fall with a fall or rise in the price of group a, so as to keep the "purchasing power of money" the same.

The other variant, which Marshall employed in the Mathematical Appendix of the Principles, is obtained by retaining "(2) their real

sistent in any way with Marshall's *Principles*. Though no explicit listing of "other things" is given by J. R. Hicks, *Value and Capital* (Oxford, 1939), the list given above is implicit throughout chaps. i and ii, which are explicitly devoted to elaborating and extending Marshall's analysis of demand. For statements in modern textbooks on advanced economic theory see G. J. Stigler, *The Theory of Price* (New York: Macmillan Co., 1946), pp. 86–90, and Kenneth E. Boulding, *Economic Analysis* (rev. ed.; New York: Harper & Bros., 1948), pp. 134–35.

income" and adding (4) the average price of all other commodities. Constancy of real income for different prices of the commodity in question then implies compensating variations in money income. As the price of the commodity in question rises or falls, money income is to be supposed to rise or fall so as to keep real income the same.

These two variants are essentially equivalent mathematically,[5] but

[5] Let x and y be the quantity and price, respectively, of the commodity in question; x' and y', the quantity and price of a composite commodity representing all other commodities; and m, money income. Let

$$x = g(y, y', m, u) \tag{1}$$

be the demand curve for the commodity in question, given a utility function,

$$U = U(x, x', u), \tag{2}$$

where u is a parameter to allow for changes in taste, and subject to the condition

$$xy + x'y' = m. \tag{3}$$

From eq. (3) and the usual utility analysis, it follows that eq. (1), like eq. (3), is a homogeneous function of degree zero in y, y', and m; i.e., that

$$g(\lambda y, \lambda y', \lambda m, u) = g(y, y', m, u). \tag{4}$$

On the current interpretation, a two-dimensional demand curve is obtained from eq. (1) directly by giving y' (other prices), m (income), and u (tastes) fixed values. A given value of y then implies a given value of x from eq. (1), a given value of x' from eq. (3), and hence a given value of U (i.e., real income) from eq. (2). The value of U will vary with y, being higher, the lower y is.

On my alternative interpretation, u and U are given fixed values and x' is eliminated from eqs. (2) and 3). This gives a pair of equations,

$$x = g(y, y', m, u_0), \tag{5}$$

$$U_0 = U_0\left(x, \frac{m - xy}{y'}, u_0\right), \tag{6}$$

where the subscript 0 designates fixed values. The two-dimensional variant involving compensating variations in other prices is obtained by eliminating y' from eqs. (5) and (6) and giving m a fixed value; the variant involving compensating variations in income, by eliminating m from eqs. (5) and (6) and giving y' a fixed value.

The homogeneity of eqs. (5) and (6) in y, y' and m means that x is a function only of ratios among them. Thus eqs. (5) and (6) can be written:

$$x = g(y, y', m, u_0) = g\left(\frac{y}{m}, \frac{y'}{m}, 1, u_0\right) = g\left(\frac{y}{y'}, 1, \frac{m}{y'}, u_0\right), \tag{5'}$$

$$\left.\begin{array}{l} U_0 = U_0\left(x, \frac{m - xy}{y'}, u_0\right) = U_0\left(x, \frac{1 - x\dfrac{y}{m}}{\dfrac{y'}{m}}, u_0\right) \\[3em] \qquad\qquad\qquad = U_0\left(x, \frac{m}{y'} - x\frac{y}{y'}, u_0\right). \end{array}\right\} \tag{6'}$$

The choice of price-compensating variations is equivalent to selecting the forms of these two equations in the next to the last terms of eqs. (5') and (6'); of income-compensating variations, to selecting the forms in the last terms.

the assumption of compensating variations in other prices is easier to explain verbally and can be justified as empirically relevant by considerations of monetary theory, which is presumably why Marshall used this variant in his text. On the other hand, the assumption of compensating variations in income is somewhat more convenient mathematically, which is presumably why Marshall used this variant in his Mathematical Appendix.

On my interpretation, Marshall's demand curve is identical with one of the constructions introduced by Slutsky in his famous paper on the theory of choice, namely, the reaction of quantity demanded to a "compensated variation of price," that is, to a variation in price accompanied by a compensating change in money income.[6] Slutsky expressed the compensating change in money income in terms of observable phenomena, taking it as equal to the change in price *times* the quantity demanded at the initial price. Mosak has shown that, in the limit, the change in income so computed is identical with the change required to keep the individual on the same level of utility (on the same indifference curve).[7] It follows that a similar statement is valid for compensating changes in other prices. In the limit the change in other prices required to keep the individual on the same indifference curve when his money income is unchanged but the price of one commodity varies is identical with the change in other prices required to keep unchanged the total cost of the basket of commodities purchased at the initial prices, that is, to keep unchanged the usual type of cost-of-living index number.

C. COMPARISON OF THE INTERPRETATIONS

The relation between demand curves constructed under the two interpretations is depicted in Figure 1. Curve Cc represents a demand curve of an individual consumer for a commodity X drawn on the current interpretation. Money income and the prices of other commodities are supposed the same for all points on it; in consequence, real income is lower at C than at P, since, if the individual sought to

[6] Eugenio Slutsky, "Sulla teoria del bilancio del consumatore," *Giornale degli economisti*, LI (1915). 1-26, esp. sec. 8. [A translation of this article is now available in American Economic Association, *Readings in Price Theory* (Chicago: Richard D. Irwin, Inc., 1952), pp. 27-56.]

[7] Jacob L. Mosak, "On the Interpretation of the Fundamental Equation of Value Theory," in O. Lange, F. McIntyre, and T. O. Yntema (eds.), *Studies in Mathematical Economics and Econometrics* (Chicago: University of Chicago Press, 1942), pp. 69-74, esp. n. 5, pp. 73-74, which contains a rigorous proof of this statement by A. Wald.

buy *OM* of *X* at a price of *OC*, he would be forced to curtail his purchases of something else. As the curve is drawn, of course, he buys none of *X* at a price of *OC*, spending the sum of *OHPM* on other commodities that his action at a price of *OH* shows him to value less highly than he does *OM* units of *X*. The ordinate is described as the ratio of the price of *X* to the price of other commodities. For the demand curve *Cc* this is a question only of the unit of measure, since other prices are supposed to be the same for all points on it.

From the definition of the demand curve *Cc*, *OC* is obviously the maximum price per unit that an individual would be willing to pay for an infinitesimal initial increment of *X* when his money income and the prices of other commodities have the values assumed in drawing *Cc*. Let us suppose him to purchase this amount at a price of *OC*, determine the maximum price per unit he would be willing to pay for an additional increment, and continue in this fashion, exacting the maximum possible amount for each additional increment. Let these successive maximum prices per unit define the curve *Cv*. The consumer obviously has the same real income at each point on *Cv* as at *C*, since

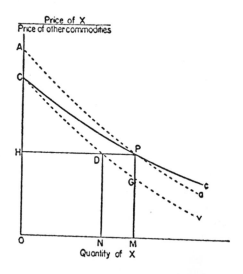

Figure 1. Comparison of demand curves constructed under
the two interpretations

the maximum price has been extracted from him for each successive unit, so that he has gained no utility in the process.

Cv is now a demand curve constructed according to my interpreta-

tion of Marshall. If other prices are supposed to be the same, the necessary compensating variations in money income as the price of X falls
are given by triangular areas exemplified by HCD for a price of OH:
OH is the maximum price per unit that the individual will give for an
additional infinitesimal increment of X when he has spent OCDN for
ON of X out of his initial income of, say, m; but his situation is exactly the same if, when the price of X is OH, his income is (m − HCD)
and he spends OHDN on X; he has the same amount left to spend on
all other commodities, their prices are the same, and he has the same
amount of X; accordingly, his demand price will be the same, and he
will buy ON of X at a price of OH and an income of (m − HCD).[8]

If compensating variations in other prices rather than in money
income are used to keep real income the same, the absolute price of
neither X nor other commodities can be read directly from Figure 1.
For each ratio of the price of X to the price of other commodities, the
quantity of X purchased will be that shown on Cv. But the prices of
other goods will vary along Cv, rising as the relative price of X falls,
so the absolute price of X can no longer be obtained by multiplying
the ordinate by a single scale factor.

Figure 1 is drawn on the assumption that X is a "normal" commodity, that is, a commodity the consumption of which is higher, the

[8] In the notation of n. 5, except that u is omitted for simplicity, the quantities of
X and X′ that will be purchased for any given values of y and $y′$ and any given
real income, U_0, are obtained by solving simultaneously:

$$\frac{U_x}{U_{x'}} = \frac{y}{y'},\qquad(1)$$

and

$$U(x, x') = U_0,\qquad(2)$$

where U_x and $U_{x'}$ stand for the partial derivatives of U with respect to x and x',
respectively, i.e., for the marginal utility of X and X′. The solution of these equations gives the demand curve on my interpretation of Marshall, using compensating variations in money income.

$U_0 (0, m/y')$ is the utility at C in the diagram. For any given amount of X
and given value of y', the amount of X′ purchased is obtained by solving

$$U(x, x') = U_0\left(0,\frac{m}{y'}\right),\qquad(3)$$

which is identical with eq. (2). The amount paid for X (the area under Cv) is

$$m - x' y'.\qquad(4)$$

The maximum price that will be paid per unit of X is the derivative of eq. (4), or

$$y = -\frac{dx'}{dx}y' = \frac{U_x}{U_{x'}}y',\qquad(5)$$

which is identical with eq. (1). It follows that Cv is a demand curve constructed
on my interpretation of Marshall.

higher the income. This is the reason Cv is drawn to the left of Cc—at every point on Cv other than C, real income is less than that at the corresponding point on Cc; hence less X would be consumed.

Curve Aa represents a demand curve on my interpretation of Marshall for a real income the same as at point P on Cc; it is like Cv but for a higher real income. Real income is higher on Aa than on Cc for prices above OH, lower for prices below OH, which is the reason Aa is to the right of Cc for prices above OH and to the left of Cc for prices below OH.

D. WHY TWO INTERPRETATIONS ARE POSSIBLE

The possibility of interpreting Marshall in these two quite different ways arises in part from the vagueness of Marshall's exposition, from his failure to give precise and rigorous definitions. A more fundamental reason, however, is the existence of inconsistency in the third and later editions of the *Principles*. In that edition Marshall introduced the celebrated passage bearing on the Giffen phenomenon. This passage and a related sentence added at the same time to the Mathematical Appendix fit the current interpretation better than they fit my interpretation. Although these are the only two items that I have been able to find in any edition of the *Principles* of which this is true, they provide some basis for the current interpretation. A hypothesis to explain the introduction of this inconsistency into the *Principles* is offered in Section IV, E, below.

II. THE RELATIVE USEFULNESS OF THE TWO INTERPRETATIONS

The relative usefulness of the two interpretations of the demand curve can be evaluated only in terms of some general conception of the role of economic theory. I shall use the conception that underlies Marshall's work, in which the primary emphasis is on positive economic analysis, on the forging of tools that can be used fairly directly in analyzing practical problems. Economic theory was to him an "engine for the discovery of concrete truth." [9] "Man's powers are limited; almost every one of nature's riddles is complex. He breaks it up, studies one bit at a time, and at last combines his partial solutions with a supreme effort of his whole small strength into some sort of an attempt at a solution

---

[9] Alfred Marshall, "The Present Position of Economics" (1885), reprinted in *Memorials of Alfred Marshall*, ed. A. C. Pigou (London: Macmillan & Co., 1925), p. 159.

of the whole riddle." [10] The underlying justification for the central role of the concepts of demand and supply in Marshall's entire structure of analysis is the empirical generalization that an enumeration of the forces affecting demand in any problem and of the forces affecting supply will yield two lists that contain few items in common. Demand and supply are to him concepts for organizing materials, labels in an "analytical filing box." The "commodity" for which a demand curve is drawn is another label, not a word for a physical or technical entity to be defined once and for all independently of the problem at hand. Marshall writes:

> The question where the lines of division between different commodities should be drawn must be settled by convenience of the particular discussion. For some purposes it may be best to regard Chinese and Indian teas, or even Souchong and Pekoe teas, as different commodities; and to have a separate demand schedule for each of them. While for other purposes it may be best to group together commodities as distinct as beef and mutton, or even as tea and coffee, and to have a single list to represent the demand for the two combined.[11]

A. THE DISTINCTION BETWEEN CLOSELY RELATED AND ALL OTHER COMMODITIES

A demand function containing as separate variables the prices of a rigidly defined and exhaustive list of commodities, all on the same footing, seems largely foreign to this approach. It may be a useful expository device to bring home the mutual interdependence of economic phenomena; it cannot form part of Marshall's "engine for the discovery of concrete truth." The analyst who attacks a concrete problem can take explicit account of only a limited number of factors; he will inevitably separate commodities that are closely related to the one immediately under study from commodities that are more distantly related. He can pay some attention to each closely related commodity. He cannot handle the more distantly related commodities in this way; he will tend either to ignore them or to consider them as a group. The

---

[10] Alfred Marshall, "Mechanical and Biological Analogies in Economics" (1898), *ibid.*, p. 314.

[11] Marshall, *Principles of Economics* (8th ed.; London: Macmillan & Co., 1920), p. 100 n. All subsequent page references to the *Principles*, unless otherwise stated, are to the eighth and final edition.

formally more general demand curve will, in actual use, become the kind of demand curve that is yielded by my interpretation of Marshall.

The part of the Marshallian filing box covered by *ceteris paribus* typically includes three quite different kinds of variables, distinguished by their relation to the variable whose adaptation to some change is directly under investigation (e.g., the price of a commodity): (*a*) variables that are expected both to be materially affected by the variable under study and, in turn, to affect it; (*b*) variables that are expected to be little, if at all affected by the variable under study but to materially affect it; (*c*) the remaining variables, expected neither to affect significantly the variable under study nor to be significantly affected by it.

In demand analysis the prices of closely related commodities are the variables in group *a*. They are put individually into the pound of *ceteris paribus* to pave the way for further analysis. Holding their prices constant is a provisional step. They must inevitably be affected by anything that affects the commodity in question; and this indirect effect can be analyzed most conveniently by first isolating the direct effect, systematically tracing the repercussions of the direct effect on each closely related commodity, and then tracing the subsequent reflex influences on the commodity in question. Indeed, in many ways, the role of the demand curve itself is as much to provide an orderly means of analyzing these indirect effects as to isolate the direct effect on the commodity in question.

The average price of "all other commodities," income and wealth, and tastes and preferences are the variables in group *b*. These variables are likely to be affected only negligibly by factors affecting primarily the commodity in question. On the other hand, any changes in them would have a significant effect on that commodity. They are put into the pound in order to separate problems, to segregate the particular reactions under study. They are put in individually and explicitly because they are so important that account will have to be taken of them in any application of the analysis.

Price changes within the group of "all other commodities" and an indefinitely long list of other variables are contained in group *c*. These variables are to be ignored. They are too numerous and each too unimportant to permit separate account to be taken of them.

In keeping with the spirit of Marshallian analysis this classification of variables is to be taken as illustrative, not definitive. What particular variables are appropriate for each group is to be determined by the problem in hand, the amount of information available, the detail required in results, and the patience and resources of the analyst.

B. CONSTANCY OF REAL INCOME

It has just been argued that any actual analysis of a concrete economic problem with the aid of demand curves will inevitably adopt one feature of my interpretation of Marshall—consideration of a residual list of commodities as a single group. For somewhat subtler reasons this is likely to be true also of the second feature of my interpretation of Marshall—holding real income constant along a demand curve. If an analysis, begun with a demand curve constructed on the current interpretation, is carried through and made internally consistent, it will be found that the demand curve has been subjected to shifts that, in effect, result from failure to keep real income constant along the demand curve.

An example will show how this occurs. Let us suppose that the government grants to producers of commodity X a subsidy of a fixed amount per unit of output, financed by a general income tax, so that money income available for expenditure (i.e., net of tax and gross of subsidy) is unchanged. For simplicity, suppose, first, that no commodities are closely related to X either as rivals or as complements, so that interrelations in consumption between X and particular other commodities can be neglected; second, that the tax is paid by individuals in about the same income class and with about the same consumption pattern as those who benefit from the subsidy, so that complications arising from changes in the distribution of income can be neglected; and, third, that there are no idle resources. Let DD in Figure 2 be a demand curve for commodity X, and SS be the initial supply curve for X, and let the initial position at their intersection, point P, be a position of full equilibrium. The effect of the subsidy is to lower the supply curve to $S'S'$. Since we have ruled out repercussions through consumption relations with other markets and through changes in the level or distribution of money income, it is reasonable to expect that the intersection of this new supply curve and the initial demand curve, point P', will itself be a position of full equilibrium, involving a lower price and larger quantity of X. Yet, if the demand curve is constructed on the current interpretation and if the supply curve is not perfectly inelastic,[12] point P' is not a position of full equilibrium. This can be seen most easily by supposing DD to have unit elasticity, so that

---

[12] If it is perfectly inelastic, neither the price nor the quantity of X is changed, so the new position of equilibrium coincides with the old; but the demand curve will pass through the initial position of equilibrium whether constructed on the current interpretation or on mine; hence the two coincide at the one point on them that is relevant.

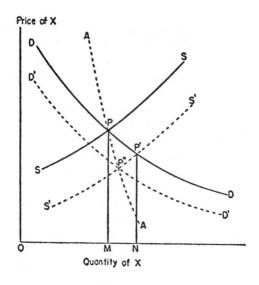

Figure 2. Illustrative analysis of effect of subsidy

the same amount is spent on X at P' as at P. The same amount is then available to spend on all other commodities, and, since their prices are supposed to be the same for all points on DD under the current interpretation, the same quantity of each of them will be demanded. But then where do the resources come from to produce the extra MN units of X? Obviously, our assumptions are not internally consistent. The additional units of X can be produced only by bidding resources away from the production of other commodities, in the process raising their prices and reducing the amount of them produced. The final equilibrium position will therefore involve higher prices and lower quantities of other commodities. But, on the current interpretation, this means a shift in the demand curve for X—say, to D'D'—and a final equilibrium position of, say P".[13]

The assumption that the elasticity of DD is unity is not, of course, essential for this argument. If the elasticity of DD is less than unity, a

[13] D'D' will not necessarily be to the left of DD even for a "normal" commodity. The reason is that the ordinate of Fig. 2 measures the absolute price of X, so that ordinates of the same height on DD and D'D' represent different ratios of the price of X to the price of other commodities. If the ordinate measured the ratio of the price of X to the price of other commodities, D'D' would always be to the left of DD for "normal" commodities, always to the right for "inferior" commodities.

larger amount than formerly is available to spend on other commodities; at unchanged prices this means a larger quantity demanded. In consequence, while the additional amount of resources required to produce the increased amount of X demanded is smaller when DD is inelastic than when it has unit elasticity, this is counterbalanced by increased pressure for resources to produce other commodities. Similarly, when DD is elastic, the additional amount of resources required to produce the increased quantity of X demanded is larger than when DD has unit elasticity, but some resources are released in the first instance from the production of other commodities.

No such internal inconsistency as that just outlined arises if the demand curve is constructed by keeping real income the same. Curve AA is such a demand curve. At prices of X less than PM, prices of other commodities are supposed to be sufficiently higher than at P to keep real income the same, which involves the release of just enough resources so that the position of final equilibrium, P'', lies on the demand curve so constructed—at least for small changes in the price of X.[14]

The fundamental principle illustrated by this example can be put

[14] Let X' be a single composite commodity representing all commodities other than X; x and x', the quantities of X and X'; and y and y', their prices. Let the subscript 1 refer to values at the initial position of equilibrium, P; the subscript 2, to values at the final position, P''. The condition of constant total expenditures means that

$$x_1 y_1 + x_1' y_1' = x_2 y_2 + x_2' y_2'. \tag{1}$$

As was pointed out above (Sec. I, B), in the limit, holding real income constant is equivalent to holding constant the cost of a fixed basket of commodities. Thus, if P'' is considered close to P,

$$x_1 y_1 + x_1' y_1' = x_1 y_2 + x_1' y_2'. \tag{2}$$

In the neighborhood of P, y_1 can be regarded as the cost per unit of producing X; y_1', as the cost per unit of producing X'. The condition that sufficient resources be released to permit the production of the requisite additional amount of X is therefore

$$(x_2 - x_1) y_1 = - (x_2' - x_1') y_1', \tag{3}$$

which is equivalent to

$$x_1 y_1 + x_1' y_1' = x_2 y_1 + x_2' y_1'. \tag{4}$$

But, in the limit, eqs. (1) and (2) imply eq. (4), as can be seen by subtracting eq. (2) from eq. (1) and replacing y_2 and y_2' in the result by $(y_2 - y_1 + y_1)$ and $(y_2' - y_1' + y_1')$, respectively.

More generally, constant real income [with constant total expenditures] involves keeping a price index unchanged; constant use of resources involves keeping a quantity index unchanged; and, in the limit, a constant price index and constant total expenditures imply a constant quantity index.

Note that AA need not be steeper than DD in a graph like Fig. 2. The point in question is that commented on in n. 13.

more generally. The reason why a demand curve constructed under the current interpretation fails to give the correct solution even when all disturbing influences can be neglected is that each point on it implicitly refers to a different productive capacity of the community. A reduction in the price of the commodity in question is to be regarded as enabling the community, if it so wishes, to consume more of some commodities—this commodity or others—without consuming less of any commodity. But the particular change in supply whose consequences we sought to analyze—that arising from a subsidy—does not make available any additional resources to the community; any increase in the consumption of the commodity in question must be at the expense of other commodities. The conditions for which the demand curve is drawn are therefore inconsistent with the conditions postulated on the side of supply. On the other hand, if the demand curve is constructed by keeping "real income" the same, no such inconsistency need arise. True, constant "real income" in the sense of "utility" and constant "real income" in the sense of outputs attainable from a fixed total of resources are different concepts, but they converge and can be treated as the same in the neighborhood of a position of equilibrium.

Of course, not all shifts in supply that it is desired to analyze arise in ways that leave the productive capacity of the community unaltered. Many involve a change in productive capacity—for example, changes in supply arising from improvements in technology or the discovery of previously unknown resources. Even in these cases, however, a demand curve constructed on the current interpretation will not serve. There is no reason to expect the differences in productive capacity implicit in constant money income and constant prices of other goods to bear any consistent relation to the change in productive capacity arising on the side of supply.[15] The better plan, in these cases, is to allow separately and directly for the increase in productive capacity by redrawing the demand curves to correspond to an appropriately higher real income and then to use a demand curve on which all points refer to that higher real income.

The main point under discussion can be put still more generally. The opportunities open to a consumer to satisfy his wants depend principally on two factors—the total resources at his disposal and the terms on which he can exchange one commodity for another, that is, on

[15] Note the difference from the previous case of constant productive capacity. As stated above, there is reason to expect constant real income along a demand curve to bear a consistent relation to constant productive capacity in the neighborhood of equilibrium. The reason, in effect, is provided by one of the conditions of equilibrium: the tangency of consumption and production indifference curves.

his real income and on relative prices. The form of analysis that is now fashionable distinguishes three effects of changes in his opportunities—the income effect arising from changes in his money income; the income effect arising from changes in the price of a commodity, with unchanged money income and prices of other commodities; and the substitution effect arising from a change in the relative price of a commodity, with unchanged real income.

The distinction between the so-called "substitution" and "income" effects of a change in price is a direct consequence of defining the demand curve according to the current interpretation of Marshall. Its basis is the arithmetic truism that at given prices for all commodities but one, a given money income corresponds to a higher real income, the lower the price of the remaining commodity—at a lower price for it, more of some commodities can be purchased without purchasing less of others. In consequence, a decline in the price of a commodity, all other prices constant, has, it is argued, two effects: first, with an unchanged real income, it would stimulate the substitution of that commodity for others—this is the substitution effect; second, if the money income of the consumers is supposed to be unchanged, the increase in their real income as a result of the decline in price causes a further change in the consumption of that commodity as well as of others—this is the income effect.[16]

The two different kinds of income effects distinguished in this analysis—one arising from a change in money income, the other from a change in the price of one commodity—are really the same thing, the effect of a change in real income with given relative prices, arising in different ways. It is hard to see any gain from combining the second income effect with the substitution effect; it seems preferable to combine the two income effects and thereby gain a sharp contrast with the substitution effect.

It has often been stated that Marshall "neglected the income effect."[17] On my interpretation of his demand curve, this statement is invalid. One must then say that Marshall recognized the desirability of separating two quite different effects and constructed his demand curve so that it encompassed solely the effect that he wished to isolate for study, namely, the substitution effect. Instead of neglecting the income effect, he "eliminated" it.

[16] See Slutsky, *op. cit.;* Henry Schultz, *The Theory and Measurement of Demand* (Chicago: University of Chicago Press, 1938), pp. 40–46; J. R. Hicks and R. G. D. Allen, "A Reconsideration of the Theory of Value," *Economica*, XIV (1934), 52–76 and 196–219; Hicks, *op. cit.*, Part I.

[17] Hicks, *op. cit.*, p. 32.

The conclusion to which the argument of this section leads is identical with that reached by Frank H. Knight in a recent article, in which he says:

> We have to choose in analysis between holding the prices of all other goods constant and maintaining constant the "real income" of the hypothetical consumer. . . . The treatment of the Slutsky school adopts the assumption that . . . the prices of all other goods (and the consumer's money income) are constant. Hence, real income must change. Of the two alternatives, this seems to be definitely the wrong choice. . . . The simple and obvious alternative is to draw the demand curves in terms of a change in *relative* prices, i.e., to assume that the value of money is held constant, through compensating changes in the prices of other goods, and not that these other prices are held constant.[18]

III. THE CONSISTENCY OF THE ALTERNATIVE INTERPRETATION WITH OTHER PARTS OF MARSHALL'S WORK

Marshall's demand curve is part of a coherent body of thought; it is designed to fit into the rest of his structure of analysis; and it is used extensively in developing and applying this structure. It would take us too far afield to demonstrate in detail that my interpretation of his demand curve is consistent with the rest of his work. However, two special topics call for some explicit consideration: (1) the relation between the demand curve and Marshall's theory of money, because, in my view, this explains the particular device that he adopted for holding real income constant; and (2) the concept of consumer's surplus, because this is one of the most important applications of the demand curve and certainly the most controversial and because the passages in the later editions of the *Principles* that are inconsistent with my interpretation were introduced into the discussion of consumer's surplus.

A. THE THEORY OF RELATIVE PRICES AND THE THEORY OF MONEY

Granted that real income is to be held constant along the demand curve, why do so by holding money income and the purchasing power

[18] "Realism and Relevance in the Theory of Demand," *Journal of Political Economy*, LII (December, 1944), 289–318, esp. Sec. III, "The Meaning of a Demand Curve," pp. 298–301. Quotation from p. 299.

of money consant rather than, for example, by holding prices of other goods constant and permitting compensating variations in money income? What reason is there to treat the prices of all other commodities as moving inversely to the price of the commodity in question?

The answer to these questions is given, I think, by one of Marshall's basic organizing principles, namely, the separation of the theory of relative prices from monetary theory, the theory of the level of prices. The *Principles* is devoted to the theory of relative prices under given monetary conditions; *Money, Credit, and Commerce* to the analysis of monetary conditions and their effect on the "purchasing power of money." With *given monetary conditions*, is it possible for the prices of all commodities other than the one in question to remain the same, on the average, while the price of this one rises or falls? Will not a rise or fall in the price of the commodity in question set in motion *monetary* forces affecting other prices? A complete answer requires explicit specification of the content of "given monetary conditions" and perhaps also of the source of the initial price change.

Marshall's selection of a constant purchasing power of money as a means of impounding monetary forces is presumably the end result of a chain of reasoning about the influence of monetary forces, not the direct content that he gave to "given monetary conditions." The beginning of the chain of reasoning may well be his own version of the quantity theory of money. According to this version, "the value of money is a function of its supply on the one hand, and the demand for it, on the other, as measured by 'the average stock of command over commodities which each person cares to keep in a ready form.' " [19] Given monetary conditions would then imply a given stock of money and a given desired "average stock of command over commodities." A decline in one price alone, all other prices remaining the same, is inconsistent with these "givens." It would increase the real value of a fixed (nominal) stock of money, leave the community with a larger "stock of command over commodities" than previously, and establish an incentive (reflecting "monetary" forces) to increase expenditures and thereby raise prices until the fixed stock of money again represented the same "stock of command over commodities," that is, until the "purchasing power of money" reached its former level.[20] This argument suggests that not only

---

[19] J. M. Keynes, "Alfred Marshall, 1842–1924," *Memorials*, p. 29.

[20] C. W. Guillebaud has pointed out to me that Marshall typically supposed the desired "stock of command over commodities" to be a given fraction of real income (see *ibid.*) and that the argument in the text might not apply if this fraction were taken as the fundamental given. The monetary effects of a change in one price, other prices given, would then depend on the source of the initial price change. If this involved no change in aggregate real income (e.g., arose from

was constant purchasing power of money a device for separating the theory of relative prices from monetary theory; it was also a bridge between the two. Marshall separated the two theories in his attempt to reduce problems to manageable proportions, but he constructed them in such a way as to make them mutually consistent and thus facilitate ultimate combination.[21]

Marshall was, of course, very much aware of the interaction between real and monetary factors. The 1879 *Economics of Industry* contains an extremely interesting discussion of the trade cycle, part of which Marshall thought sufficiently important to quote at length in 1886 in answering questions circulated by the celebrated Royal Commission on the Depression of Trade and Industry.[22]

Marshall's decision to keep the purchasing power of money the same for different points on a demand curve may not be the device best

---

a shift in demand), the argument in the text would remain unchanged. If it did involve a change in aggregate real income (e.g., arose from an invention reducing the cost of producing the commodity in question), no inconsistency need arise, since the desired "stock of command over commodities" would change in proportion to the change in real income. These considerations account for the phrase "perhaps also of the source of the initial price change" at the end of the preceding paragraph of the text.

[21] This interpretation would, of course, be contradicted if Marshall had devised his theory of money after he had substantially completed his theory of relative prices, as might be inferred from the fact that *Money, Credit, and Commerce* was not published until 1923, thirty-three years after the first edition of the *Principles*. But in Marshall's case, the order of publication is a poor guide to the order of construction. Keynes tells us that the essence of his quantity theory of money is contained in a manuscript "written about 1871"; that "by 1871 his progress along" the lines of the material contained in the *Pure Theory* "was considerably advanced"; that the *Pure Theory* itself was "substantially complete about 1873," though not printed even for private circulation until 1879; that "in 1877 he turned aside to write the *Economics of Industry* with Mrs. Marshall"; and that Mrs. Marshall said "Book III on Demand was largely thought out and written on the roof at Palermo, Nov. 1881—Feb. 1882" (*Memorials*, pp. 28, 21, 23, 39 n.). These dates are extremely suggestive, particularly since the constancy of the purchasing power of money is not explicitly mentioned in the *Pure Theory*, which Marshall was presumably working on at about the same time that he was developing his monetary theory, while it is explicitly mentioned in the 1879 *Economics of Industry*, begun some years later. See also nn. 36 and 37.

[22] See Alfred Marshall and Mary Paley Marshall, *Economics of Industry* (London: Macmillan & Co., 1st ed., 1879; 2d ed., 1881), Book III, chap. i, pp. 150–57. This and all later references are to the first edition. "Answers to Questions on the Subject of Currency and Prices Circulated by the Royal Commission on the Depression of Trade and Industry (1886)," *Official Papers by Alfred Marshall* (London: Macmillan & Co., 1926), pp. 7–9. See also "Remedies for Fluctuations of General Prices" (1887), *Memorials*, pp. 189–92.

suited to abstract from monetary factors. It serves, however, to emphasize the necessity of considering explicitly the monetary arrangements under which the forces affecting relative prices are supposed to operate. The best apparatus for tackling problems of relative prices cannot be determined independently of these arrangements and of their mode of operation. Though price theory and monetary theory can be separated, they are not basically independent. From this point of view it is entirely natural that the recent development of alternative monetary theories should have stimulated re-examination of price theory.

B. Consumer's Surplus

Marshall's discussion of consumer's surplus constitutes one of the most extensive applications that he made of his demand curve and has probably given rise to more controversy and discussion than any other part of his theory. Recently, consumer's surplus has come in for renewed attention, primarily as a result of J. R. Hicks's attempt to rehabilitate and reinterpret the concept.[23] The reason for commenting on it here is not to contribute to the discussion or to evaluate the merits or demerits of the concept but rather to show the relation between Marshall's treatment of consumer's surplus and my interpretation of his demand curve.

Marshall's treatment of consumer's surplus might, offhand, seem inconsistent with my interpretation of his demand curve for either of two different, and almost opposed, reasons. In the first place, consumer's surplus refers to a difference in real income under different situations. But, on my interpretation, all points on the demand curve are to be regarded as corresponding to the same real income. A movement along such a demand curve cannot, therefore, involve a change in consumer's surplus. Does this not eliminate the entire notion of consumer's surplus and make Marshall's entire discussion of it pointless? The answer is clearly "No," the reason being that the two situations compared need not correspond to two points on the *same* demand curve, even

[23] See Hicks, *op. cit.*, pp. 38–41; "The Rehabilitation of Consumers' Surplus," *Review of Economic Studies*, VIII (February, 1941), 108–16; "Consumers' Surplus and Index Numbers," *ibid.* (summer, 1942), 126–37; "The Four Consumer's Surpluses," *ibid.*, XI (winter, 1943), 31–41. See also A. Henderson, "Consumer's Surplus and the Compensating Variation," *Review of Economic Studies*, VIII (February, 1941), 117–21; Knight, *op. cit.*; Kenneth E. Boulding, "The Concept of Economic Surplus," *American Economic Review*, XXXV (December, 1945), 851–69, reprinted in American Economic Association, *Readings in the Theory of Income Distribution* (Philadelphia: Blakiston Co., 1946), pp. 638–59; E. J. Mishan, "Realism and Relevance in Consumer's Surplus," *Review of Economic Studies*, XV (1947–48), 27–33.

though a single demand curve is used to *estimate* the difference in real income between the two situations.

In the second place, Marshall regarded his analysis of consumer's surplus as valid only for commodities that account for a small part of total expenditure. He makes this restriction in order to justify neglecting changes in the marginal utility of money. But, if all points on the demand curve correspond to the same real income, does it not then follow that the marginal utility of money is the same everywhere on the demand curve? And does it not also follow that his estimate of consumer's surplus is exact, so that the assumption that a negligible proportion of expenditures is devoted to the commodity in question becomes unnecessary? Again the answer is "No," and for much the same reason. If the two situations compared differ in real income, the fact that real income is the same along the demand curve becomes something of a vice in using it to measure consumer's surplus. The assumption that a negligible proportion of expenditures is devoted to the commodity in question cannot be dispensed with on my interpretation; indeed, if anything, it is even more necessary than on the current interpretation.

To explain and justify these cryptic answers, it will be necessary to examine Marshall's definition of consumer's surplus, his suggested estimate of its magnitude, and the relation of this estimate to the correct value under the two alternative interpretations of the demand curve.

Marshall is more explicit and complete in defining consumer's surplus than was his wont, and his definition admits of little ambiguity: "The excess of the price which he would be willing to pay rather than go without the thing, over that which he actually does pay, is the economic measure of this surplus satisfaction. It may be called *consumer's surplus.*" [24]

Marshall then proceeds to argue that consumer's surplus can be *estimated* by the famous triangle under the demand curve. As Hicks remarks, this "association of Consumer's Surplus with the curvilinear triangle under the demand curve . . . is not a definition; it is a theorem, true under certain restrictive assumptions, but only true if these assumptions are granted." [25] The confusion of the suggested estimate with the definition is perhaps the chief source of misunderstanding on this exceedingly complex subject.

Figure 1, introduced in Section I, C, above to illustrate the relation between demand curves drawn on the current and on my interpretation, can also be used to show the relation between consumer's surplus

[24] *Principles*, p. 124.
[25] "The Rehabilitation of Consumers' Surplus," *op. cit.*, p. 109.

as defined and estimates of it obtained from demand curves constructed according to the two interpretations. Curve Cc, it will be recalled, is a demand curve for the commodity X constructed according to the current interpretation. Money income and all other prices are the same for all points on it. Aa and Cv are demand curves constructed according to my interpretation—Aa for a real income the same as at P on Cc; Cv for a real income the same as at C on Cc. At point P on Aa and at point C on Cv, money income and all other prices are the same as on Cc. At other points other prices are sufficiently different, or money income is, to compensate for the difference in the price of X and thereby keep real income the same.

Now consider the consumer's surplus obtained from this commodity when the consumer is at P.[26] This is *defined* as "the excess of the price which he would be willing to pay rather than go without the thing, over that which he actually does pay." "Price" is here to be interpreted as "total amount" rather than "price per unit." [27] Further, it is clear that the sum he would pay rather than go without is to be determined for circumstances otherwise the same as at P; in particular, his money income and the other prices are to be the same as at P.[28] Now the amount that he actually does pay for OM of X is given by the rectangle $OHPM$ in the figure. By the argument of Section I, C, the maximum amount that he would be willing to pay for OM of X rather than go without any of it is given by the area under Cv between O and M, or $OCDGM$. The triangular area CDH *minus* the triangular area DPG therefore gives the consumer's surplus. This area is necessarily positive; we know he is willing to pay at least $OHPM$ for OM of X; hence $OCDGM$ must be greater than $OHPM$.

Marshall's *estimate* of the maximum sum is the area under the demand curve: $OCPM$ if we use the current interpretation, $OAPM$ if we use the alternative interpretation. For a "normal" commodity, the case for which the figure is drawn, both are clearly too large. How large the

---

[26] For simplicity, the discussion is restricted to the consumer's surplus obtained from the entire amount of X consumed; and to facilitate this, the demand curves have been drawn to cut the price axis.

[27] See Mathematical Note II of the *Principles* (p. 838), in which Marshall defines p as "the price which he is just willing to pay for an amount x of the commodity" and then differentiates p with respect to x to get the price per unit.

[28] None of the reasons cited earlier for keeping real income the same along the demand curve applies here. The question being asked is purely hypothetical; no other reactions need be allowed for. Further, to keep his real income the same when he has none of X as when he has OM of X would make the entire discussion of consumer's surplus pointless. The whole point of the discussion is to measure the difference in real income between the two situations.

142 READINGS IN MICROECONOMICS

error is depends on the difference between *Aa* and *Cc*, on the one hand, and *Cv*, on the other. Now we have seen (in Sec. I, C) that these differences arise entirely from differences in the real income associated with the different curves; if real incomes differ little, so will the curves. Here is where Marshall's assumption about the fraction of expenditures devoted to the commodity enters the picture. If this fraction is small, the differences in real income will tend to be small, and both estimates will approach the correct value.[29] Since the error is larger for *Aa* than for *Cc*, it is clear that Marshall's assumption is, if anything, even more necessary on my interpretation of the demand curve than on the current one.[30]

[29] This statement is not rigorous. As the fraction of expenditures devoted to the commodity diminishes, so will aggregate consumer's surplus. It is not enough that the error becomes small in absolute terms; its ratio to the correct value must become small. This, in general, will occur, as is well known. The chief qualification has to do with the behavior of a demand curve constructed under the current interpretation (e.g., *Cc*) for small quantities of *X*. The crucial question is the difference in real income between *P* and *C*. Expenditure on the commodity might be a small fraction of total expenditure at *P;* yet, if the demand curve constructed under the current interpretation were extremely inelastic, not near *C*. In this case the difference in real income might be large.

This qualification is emphasized by Marshall. For example: "If however an amount *b* of the commodity is necessary for existence, $f(z)$ [*sic*] [ordinate of the demand curve] will be infinite, or at least indefinitely great, for values of *x* less than *b*. We must therefore take life for granted, and estimate separately the total utility of that part of the supply of the commodity which is in excess of absolute necessaries" (p. 841). See also pp. 133 and 842. $f(z)$ clearly should be $f(x)$, as it is in the first four editions of the *Principles*. See appendix to this paper.

This discussion of the role of the assumption that the commodity absorbs only a small fraction of income throws some light on an issue about which there has been considerable discussion, namely, whether Marshall assumed the marginal utility of money to be roughly constant with respect to a change in price or a change in income. The above analysis suggests that he assumed constancy with respect to a change in income. This is also Hicks's conclusion (*Value and Capital*, p. 40; "The Rehabilitation of Consumers' Surplus," *op. cit.*, p. 109). Samuelson denies this and asserts that he assumed constancy with respect to a change in price (see Paul A. Samuelson, "Constancy of the Marginal Utility of Income," in *Studies in Mathematical Economics and Econometrics*, p. 80).

[30] The argument can be easily extended to "inferior" goods. The order of the three curves in Fig. 1 is then reversed; the estimates then become too small, instead of too large; but the error under the alternative interpretation remains larger in absolute value than under the current interpretation.

In the terminology used by Hicks in "The Four Consumer's Surpluses," what I have called the consumer's surplus is what Hicks calls the "quantity-compensating variation." The estimate of consumer's surplus derived from the demand curve constructed under my interpretation (the area *APH*) Hicks calls the "quantity-equivalent variation." The area *CDH* in Fig. 1, Hicks calls the "price-compensat-

IV. TEXTUAL EVIDENCE ON WHAT MARSHALL REALLY MEANT

Marshall's writings on demand bear on three different problems: (1) the definition of the demand curve—the problem of form; (2) the shape of the demand curve—the problem of content; and (3) the use of the demand curve—the problem of application. In his usual manner Marshall gives precedence to the problem of content and does not explicitly separate his discussion of content from his discussion of form. His definitions are characteristically given parenthetically and implicitly. He went to extreme lengths to present his tools in the context of concrete problems, so that definitions grew out of the uses to be made of them.[31] His discussion of utility and diminishing utility in the chapter of the *Principles* which introduces the concept of a demand curve (Book III, chap. iii, "Gradations of Consumers' Demand") is part of the discussion of content, even though it precedes his definition. It is the means whereby he rationalizes his "one general *law of demand:*—The greater the amount to be sold, the smaller must be the price at which it is offered in order that it may find purchasers." [32] It is not part of his definition of the demand curve.

Similarly, one of the major applications that Marshall made of the demand curve was his analysis of consumer's surplus. This analysis, too, must be distinguished from his definition of the demand curve. Assumptions made in his discussion of consumer's surplus cannot, without ad-

---

ing variation." Hicks's fourth concept, "price-equivalent variation," is not shown directly in Fig. 1. It is obtained by drawing a horizontal line through C. Designate by E the point at which this line cuts Aa. The "price-equivalent variation" is then equal to the area APH minus AEC. These relations can be checked by noting that curve *mep* in Hicks's Fig. 3 is Aa in our Fig. 1; his curve PCM is Cv in our Fig. 1. Further, in comparing the two figures, the part of Hicks's diagram for quantities less than hN should be neglected. That is, his point P is equivalent to our point C, his p to our P. Our Fig. 1 is also equivalent to Fig. 3B in Boulding, "The Concept of Economic Surplus."

31 Cf. J. M. Keynes, *Memorials,* esp. pp. 33–38; see also Guillebaud, *op. cit.*

32 *Principles,* p. 99. Note that on my interpretation this is truly a *general* law, not subject to the exceptions that have been made in recent literature. It depends for its validity only on (a) the postulate that consumers can be treated as if they behaved consistently and attempted to maximize some function of the quantity of commodities consumed; (b) the observed fact that consumers choose a higher income in preference to a lower, other things the same; and (c) the observed fact that consumers do not spend all their income on one commodity. For proof that a demand curve constructed on my interpretation must slope negatively see Slutsky, *op. cit.,* sec. 8.

ditional evidence, be supposed to apply equally to other applications
of the "demand curve."

A. The Central Passages in the Text of the *Principles*

The central passages in the text of the eighth and final edition of the
Principles bearing on the other things to be kept the same seem to me
to be three: one governing the entire volume, and two essentially parenthetical comments in his discussion of the demand curve:

> We may throughout this volume neglect possible changes
> in the general purchasing power of money. Thus the price
> of anything will be taken as representative of its exchange
> value relatively to things in general [p. 62].

> The larger the amount of a thing that a person has the
> less, other things being equal (i.e. *the purchasing power of
> money, and the amount of money at his command being
> equal*), will be the price which he will pay for a little more
> of it: or in other words his marginal demand price for it
> diminishes [p. 95; italics added].

> The demand prices in our list are those at which various
> quantities of a thing can be sold in a market *during a given
> time and under given conditions.* If the conditions vary in
> any respect the prices will probably require to be changed;
> and this has constantly to be done when the desire for any-
> thing is materially altered by a *variation of custom, or by a
> cheapening of the supply of a rival commodity, or by the in-
> vention of a new one* [p. 100; second set of italics added].

For our purposes the critical part of the second quotation is the italicized parenthesis and, of the third, the second set of italicized phrases.

Though these quotations are taken from the eighth edition of the
Principles, their substantive content is contained in Marshall's earliest
published work on the theory of demand. All except the constancy of
the purchasing power of money is in *The Pure Theory of (Domestic)
Values,* printed for private circulation in 1879 [33] but, according to
Keynes, "substantially complete about 1873";[34] and the constancy of the
purchasing power of money is in his and Mrs. Marshall's *The Econom-*

---

[33] Reprinted, together with the companion paper, *The Pure Theory of Foreign
Trade,* by the London School of Economics and Political Science (1930).

[34] *Memorials,* p. 23.

ics of Industry, published in 1879.³⁵ The actual wording of the first and third quotations can be traced back to the first edition of the *Principles* (1890), of the second quotation, to the second edition (1891).³⁶

---

³⁵ This work should not be confused with the condensation of the *Principles,* published, under the same title but with Alfred Marshall as sole author, in 1892.

³⁶ In all editions of the *Principles* the statement corresponding to the first quotation is in a subsection dealing with the meaning of the word "value." In the first (1890), second, (1891), and third (1895) editions, the subsection on "value" is at the end of Book I, "Preliminary Survey," chap. i, "Introduction," and contains the statement: "Throughout the earlier stages of our work it will be best to speak of the exchange value of a thing at any place and time as measured by its price, that is, the amount of money for which it will exchange then and there, and to assume that there is no change in the general purchasing power of money" (p. 9, all three editions). In the first edition this assumption is repeated at the beginning of the chapter on "The Law of Demand" (Book III, chap. ii): "The purchasing power of this money may vary from time to time; but in these early stages of our work we assume it to be constant" (1st ed., p. 151). This repetition was eliminated in later editions, apparently in the process of introducing into the second edition the chapter on "Wants in Relation to Activities." In the fourth edition (1898), the subsection on "value" was split, part remaining at the end of Book I, chap. i, the remainder, including the material on the purchasing power of money, being transferred to the end of Book II, "Some Fundamental Notions," chap. ii, "Wealth." The wording was changed to essentially its final form; the only difference is that the first sentence is in the passive voice, reading: "Throughout this volume possible changes in the general purchasing power of money will be neglected" (4th ed., p. 130). In the fifth edition (1907), the rest of the subsection on "value" was transferred to the end of Book II, chap. ii, and the quotation revised to its present form; even the page number is the same in the fifth and eighth editions (p. 62).

In both editions of *The Economics of Industry,* subsection 4 in Book II, "Normal Value," chap. i, "Definitions. Law of Demand," contains essentially the same material as the subsection on "value" in the *Principles* referred to in the preceding paragraph, including the following statement: "But while examining the theory of Normal value we shall, for convenience, assume that the purchasing power of money remains unchanged. So that a rise or fall in the price of a thing will always mean a rise or fall in its general purchasing power or exchange value" (pp. 68–69). No corresponding statement appears in *The Pure Theory.*

The italicized parenthesis in the second quotation is identical in the second and all later editions of the *Principles.* The remainder of the quotation was worded as follows in the second edition: "An increase in the amount of a thing that a person has will, other things being equal . . . diminish his Marginal Demand-price for it" (p. 152). In the third edition, the words "marginal" and "demand" were not capitalized, and the hyphen was eliminated after "Demand" (p. 170). In the fourth edition the end of the statement was expanded to read, "diminish the price which he will pay for a little more of it: or in other words diminishes his marginal demand price for it" (pp. 169–70). In the fifth edition the quotation takes its present form, except for the addition of a comma, even the page num-

[Footnote 36 continued on p. 146]

B. The Bearing of These Passages on the Two Interpretations

The "other things" listed in the three passages cited above are as follows:

    1. "Purchasing power of money"
    2. "Amount of money at his command"
    3. "Custom"

[Footnote 36 continued from p. 145]

ber being the same as in the eighth edition (p. 95). In all editions from the second on, the indicated quotations are in Book III, chap. iii, the chapter first introducing the demand curve. This chapter is entitled "The Law of Demand" in the second and third editions, "Gradations of Demand" in the fourth, and "Gradations of Consumers' Demand" in the fifth and later editions.

The absence of the statement from the first edition reflects a difference in exposition, not in substance. As noted above, an explicit statement that the purchasing power of money is assumed constant appears in the chapter on "The Law of Demand" in the first edition. In all editions this chapter contains a statement covering the second part of the italicized parenthesis, which is worded as follows in the first edition: "Every increase in his resources increases the price which he is willing to pay for any given pleasure. And in the same way every diminution of his resources increases the marginal utility of money to him, and diminishes the price that he is willing to pay for any pleasure" (p. 156). The only change in this statement in later editions was the substitution of "benefit" for "pleasure" (8th ed., p. 96).

The Economics of Industry also contains a statement anticipating the second part of the italicized parenthesis: "The price which he is willing to pay for a thing depends not only on its utility to him but also on *his means;* that is, the amount of money or general purchasing power at his disposal" (p. 70).

In all editions of the *Principles* the statement corresponding to the third quotation is in the final subsection of the chapter first introducing the demand curve (1st ed., Book III, chap. ii; in later editions, Book III, chap. iii). In the first edition it reads: "It must be remembered that the demand schedule gives the prices at which various quantities of a thing can be sold in a market during a given time and under given conditions. If the conditions vary in any respect the figures of the schedule will probably require to be changed. One condition which it is especially important to watch is the price of rival commodities, that is, of commodities which can be used as substitutes for it" (p. 160). A footnote is attached to the word "rival," the first sentence of which reads: "Or to use Jevons' phrase (*Theory of Political Economy,* Ch. IV), commodities that are nearly 'equivalent' " (1st ed., p. 160, n. 2).

The part of the second sentence of the third quotation following the semicolon assumed its final form in the second edition (p. 157), the footnote reference to Jevons being dropped. The rest of the quotation is the same in the second and third editions as in the first and assumes its final form in the fourth (p. 174). The change made in the second sentence from the first to the second edition

[Footnote 36 continued on p. 147]

4. Price of "a rival commodity" (to avoid "cheapening of the supply of a rival commodity")
5. Range of rival commodities available (to avoid "invention of a new one") [37]

[Footnote 36 concluded]

argues that the list was not intended to be exhaustive, but illustrative. No change in substance is involved (see 1st ed., p. 155). In all editions the quoted statement is followed by the example of tea and coffee to illustrate the necessity of assuming the prices of rival commodities to be known; in the second edition the example of gas and electricity was added, and in the third edition the example of different varieties of tea. The passage itself, the changes in it, and the examples all indicate that Marshall considered the price of "rival" commodities particularly important. The examples, together with the footnote in the first edition, make it clear that he meant "close" rivals.

For a statement in the *Pure Theory* covering the substance of these quotations, except the constancy of the purchasing power of money, see n. 37 below.

[37] The adequacy of this list as a summary of Marshall's views may be checked by comparing it with two others in Marshall's writings. In *The Pure Theory of (Domestic) Values*, he writes: "The periods with which we are concerned . . . are sufficiently long to eliminate . . . casual disturbances. . . . But they are sufficiently short to exclude fundamental changes in the circumstances of demand and in those of supply. On the side of demand for the ware in question it is requisite that the periods should not include (i) any very great change in the prosperity and purchasing power of the community; (ii) any important changes in the fashions which affect the use of the ware; (iii) the invention or the great cheapening of any other ware which comes to be used largely as a substitute for it; (iv) the deficiency of the supply of any ware for which the ware in question may be used as a substitute, whether this deficiency be occasioned by bad harvests, by war, or by the imposition of customs or excise taxes; (v) a sudden large requirement for the commodity, as e.g. for ropes in the breaking out of a maritime war; (vi) the discovery of new means of utilizing the ware, or the opening up of important markets in which it can be sold" (p. 15).

Item i in this list presumably corresponds with 2 in my list; ii corresponds with 3, and iii and iv with 4 and 5, iii excluding a fall in the price of a rival commodity and iv a rise. Items v and the first part of vi would seem to be contained in 3 and largely redundant with ii. The rest of vi is presumably covered by the restriction of the discussion to a demand curve for a particular market.

The other list is in Marshall's discussion in the *Principles* of the difficulties of the statistical study of demand (Book III, chap. iv), where he writes: "Other things seldom are equal in fact over periods of time sufficiently long for the collection of full and trustworthy statistics. . . . To begin with, [a] the purchasing power of money is continually changing. . . . Next come the changes in [b] the general posperity and in the total purchasing power at the disposal of the community at large. . . . Next come the changes due to [c] the gradual growth of population and wealth. . . . Next, allowance must be made for changes in [d] fashion, and taste and habit, for [e] the opening out of new uses of a commodity, for [f] the discovery or improvement or cheapening of other things that

[Footnote 37 continued on p. 148]

1. *The current interpretation.*—The current interpretation of Marshall's demand curve treats item 2 as referring to the money income of the group of purchasers to whom the demand curve relates, item 3 to their tastes and preferences, and item 4 to the price of every other commodity rather than of *rival* commodities alone. It ignores entirely items 1 and 5.

Item 2 is not entirely unambiguous. It might be interpreted as referring to the cash balances of the purchasers or to their wealth instead of, or in addition to, their income. On the whole, the most reasonable course seems to be to interpret it as referring to both income and wealth,[38] particularly since wealth qualifies for the list of "other things" by virtue of its possible importance as a factor affecting consumption. This expansion of the current interpretation does not alter it materially; it merely transfers "wealth" from the category of "other things" implicity supposed to be the same to the list of things mentioned explicitly.

Item 3 requires no discussion, since the only reasonable interpretation of it is that it refers to tastes and preferences.[39]

The important defect of the current interpretation is its treatment of item 4, which is, in turn, responsible for the neglect of items 1 and 5.

[Footnote 37 concluded]

can be applied to the same uses with it" (*Principles*, pp. 109–10; letters in brackets added). This statement dates from the first edition (pp. 170–71); only trivial editorial changes were made in later editions.

Item *a* in this list corresponds with 1 in my list; *b* with 2; *d* and presumably *e* with 3; and *f* with 4 and 5. Item *c* is presumably in part covered by restriction of the discussion to a demand curve for a particular market; in part it contains an item that may deserve to be added to the list, namely, "wealth." The wording of *f* is ambiguous, since it could refer to substitutes for the good in question, to complements, or to both. The subsequent text and the examples cited make it clear that it refers to substitutes; one example, of petroleum and petroleum lamps, itself ambiguously worded, suggests that it may refer to complements as well.

[38] In the quotations from Book III, chap. iv, in the preceding footnote, "wealth" is mentioned explicitly, though separately from "general prosperity" and "total purchasing power." See also the quotations in the fourth and fifth paragraphs of n. 36. Marshall repeatedly refers to "rich" and "poor" rather than to high- and low-income people (e.g., pp. 19, 95, 98). However, in an illustrative case, a rich man and a poor man are identified by their annual incomes (p. 19). And in Book III, chap. vi, he remarks: "We have throughout this and preceding chapters spoken of the rich, the middle classes and the poor as having respectively large, medium and small incomes—not possessions" (p. 134).

[39] See n. 37 above. In discussing the law of diminishing marginal utility, Marshall says: "We do not suppose time to be allowed for any alteration in the character or tastes of the man himself" (p. 94).

"Rival commodity" is replaced by, or read to mean, "any other commodity," and hence item 4 is taken to mean that the price of every other commodity is to be supposed the same. For example, Henry Schultz says, as if it were obvious and without citing any statements of Marshall: "Marshall also assumes, in giving definite form to the law of demand for any one commodity, that the prices of all other commodities remain constant." [40] Numerous other statements to the same effect could be cited. It is an amusing commentary on our capacity for self-delusion that the only reference to Marshall for support that I have seen are to the page containing the third quotation in Section IV, A, above—the source of the words quoted in item 4.[41] The first set of italicized words in that quotation are the only words on the page even remotely supporting the substitution of "any other" for rival. The specific examples that follow the quotation—tea and coffee, gas and electric lighting, different varieties of tea, beef and mutton—make it clear that Marshall was using the word "rival" in a narrow sense and not in that broad sense in which it may be said that all commodities are "rivals" for the consumer's income.[42] Whatever the merits of the current interpretation, it cannot be found explicitly in Marshall.

The interpretation of item 4 as referring to all other commodities makes item 5 unnecessary and contradicts item 1. Item 5 is unnecessary because the introduction of a new commodity is equivalent to a decline in its price from infinity to a finite amount; hence is ruled out if the

[40] *Op. cit.*, p. 53. Immediately after making this statement he quotes from Edgeworth's article on "Demand Curves" cited in n. 4 above, not as evidence for the validity of his interpretation of Marshall but rather as an indication of the difficulties that it raises.

[41] Joan Robinson states without citation: "Marshall instructs us to draw up a demand schedule on the assumption that the prices of all other things are fixed" (*The Economics of Imperfect Competition* [London: Macmillan & Co., 1934], p. 20). Paul Samuelson says, also without citation: "All other prices and income are held constant by *ceteris paribus* assumptions" in the "Marshallian partial equilibrium demand functions" (*Foundations of Economic Analysis* [Cambridge: Harvard University Press, 1947], p. 97). In an unpublished exposition of income and substitution effects prepared for class use about 1939, I stated, also without citation: "There is no question but that it [the Marshallian demand curve] was not intended to be . . . interpreted" as "showing the effect of *compensated* variations in price." Similar statements, all citing p. 100 of the *Principles* as authority, are made by Robert Triffin, *Monopolistic Competition and General Equilibrium Theory* (Cambridge: Harvard University Press, 1940), p. 44; Ruby Turner Norris, *The Theory of Consumer's Demand* (New Haven: Yale University Press, 1941), p. 82; and Weintraub, *op. cit.*, p. 539.

[42] If any doubt remains, it is removed by the footnote in the first edition attached to the word "rival" referring to Jevons' phrase "commodities that are nearly 'equivalent' " (see n. 36).

price of every other commodity is to be unchanged. Item 1 is contradicted because, if all other prices are unchanged, the purchasing power of money will be lower, the higher the price of the commodity in question. The purchasing power of money cannot, therefore, be the same for all points on the demand curve.

The redundancy of item 5 on this interpretation of item 4 is unimportant; this item is in a list that is illustrative rather than exhaustive, and there is no reason why Marshall should have scrupulously avoided overlapping. The logical inconsistency between items 1 and 4 cannot, however, be dismissed so lightly. Retention of the current interpretation requires either that item 1 be eliminated, on the grounds that the quotations on which it is based are exceptional and peripheral, or that Marshall be convicted of logical inconsistency on a fundamental point in his theory of demand.[43] Item 1 cannot, I think, be eliminated. The constancy of the purchasing power of money is clearly fundamental in Marshall's thought, probably more fundamental than any other item on our list.[44]

One excuse for retaining the current interpretation of Marshall, despite the logical inconsistency that it introduces, is to suppose that Marshall intended to restrict the use of his demand curve to commodities that account for only a small fraction of total expenditures. A change in the price of such a commodity would have only a small effect on the purchasing power of money, and it could be argued that Marshall neglected it as a "second-order effect." On this rationalization, item 1 becomes redundant, but, in the limit, not logically inconsistent with an item 4 taken to refer to all other commodities.

I do not believe that Marshall intended to restrict the use of the demand curve to commodities accounting for only a small fraction of

[43] The extent to which the current interpretation dominates economic thought could not be more strikingly illustrated than by the fact that so acute an economic theorist as J. R. Hicks can write: "No doubt it [the constancy of the marginal utility of money] was . . . associated in his [Marshall's] mind with the assumption of a constant value of money (constant prices of other consumers' goods than the one, or sometimes ones, in question)" ("The Rehabilitation of Consumers' Surplus," *op. cit.*, p. 109). Hicks here treats constancy of all other prices as an alternative statement of item 1, when, in fact, it is logically inconsistent with item 1.

[44] See nn. 36 and 37. Note also that constancy of the purchasing power of money was a standard assumption of economic theory long before Marshall's day. It was made by Ricardo in his price theory, and Marshall refers to Cournot's discussion of the reasons for making this assumption (see Marshall, *Principles*, pp. ix, 62; Augustin Cournot, *Researches into the Mathematical Principles of the Theory of Wealth* [1838], trans. Nathaniel Bacon [New York: Macmillan Co., 1897], p. 26).

total expenditure. He speaks of a demand curve for wheat (p. 106), for houseroom (p. 107), and for other commodities that he cannot have regarded as unimportant. He first explicitly introduces the restriction to unimportant commodities in connection with his discussion of consumer's surplus, which comes well after the initial discussion of the demand curve—in the eighth edition, three chapters later; and the restriction is repeated at most points at which the argument depends on it. At one point the restriction is said to be "generally," not universally, justifiable. This evidence may not be conclusive, but it certainly establishes a strong presumption that Marshall did not intend the restriction to carry over to all uses of the demand curve.[45]

It should be noted that Marshall's explicit introduction of the restriction to unimportant commodities has no bearing on the relative validity of the two interpretations of his demand curve. The restriction is necessary on either of the two interpretations at each point at which Marshall explicitly makes it. So the restriction cannot be regardad as called for by the inconsistency of items 1 and 4 on the current interpretation of 4.

[45] In connection with the discussion of consumer's surplus and the assumption of a constant marginal utility of money implicit in that discussion, Marshall says: "The assumption . . . underlies our whole reasoning, that the expenditure on any one thing . . . is only a small part of his whole expenditure" (p. 842). The first sentence of the paragraph from which this quotation is taken explicitly limits it to "the discussion of consumers' surplus" (p. 842). The quotation is followed by a cross-reference to the part of Marshall's famous analysis of the process by which equilibrium is reached in a corn market in which he discusses "the latent assumption, that the dealers' willingness to spend money is nearly constant throughout" (p. 334). "This assumption," he says, "is justifiable with regard to most of the market dealings with which we are practically concerned. When a person buys anything for his own consumption, he generally spends on it a small part of his total resources" (p. 335).

Nowhere in Book III, chap. iii, does Marshall explicitly restrict his discussion to unimportant commodities. The one statement in that chapter that might be regarded as so restricting the discussion is the statement on p. 95 that "the marginal utility of money to him is a fixed quantity." But the context argues and Note II in the Mathematical Appendix demonstrates that this is merely a verbal statement of an identity (if income is unchanged, so is marginal utility of money), and thus is not really relevant to the issue. In the eighth edition, Note II is referred to only at the end of the subsection following the paragraph containing the passage quoted. However, in the first edition, the corresponding note (Note III) is referred to at the end of the paragraph containing the passage quoted, and hence clearly covers it (pp. 155-56, 737-38).

The above quotations are essentially unchanged from the first edition on. The restriction to unimportant commodities is, however, mentioned neither in Marshall and Marshall, *Economics of Industry*, nor in the *Pure Theory*.

2. *The alternative interpretation.*—My interpretation of the Marshallian demand curve resolves almost all the difficulties that plague the current interpretation, since it accepts at face value the five "other things" listed at the beginning of Section IV, B. Marshall's words can be taken to mean what they say without uncomfortable stretching, and there is no logical inconsistency in the constancy of both item 1, the purchasing power of money, and item 4, the prices of rival commodities. Item 5, the range of rival commodities available, is still redundant, since, if "rival" has the same meaning in 4 and 5, the invention of a new rival commodity means a change in its price from infinity to a finite value.

My interpretation explains also the precise wording of the second quotation in Section IV, A, which reads, in part: "The larger the amount of a thing that a person has the less . . . will be the price which he will pay for a little more of it." This is a curious form of phrasing on the current interpretation. Why emphasize the amount of a thing that a person has and the marginal expenditure that he can be induced to make rather than the amount he purchases and the average price he pays? On my interpretation, this phrasing follows directly from the argument of Section I, C, above (and Note II of Marshall's Mathematical Appendix), according to which a demand curve constructed on my interpretation can be viewed as showing the maximum price per unit that a person can be induced to pay for successive increments of the commodity.

One minor puzzle remains on my interpretation. Why does Marshall restrict his attention to "rival" commodities? Why not to "closely related" commodities, whether rivals or complements? His use of the word "rivals" in discussing the demand curve is apparently not a mere verbal accident. He uses the word repeatedly; almost all his examples deal with the effect of, or through, substitutes. I have no very good answer to this puzzle; the only one that seems at all persuasive is that he thought the concept of "joint demand" and the associated analytical apparatus better suited to problems involving complementary goods.[46]

My interpretation follows so directly from Marshall's words that further defense of it would be unnecessary were it not for the unquestioned dominance of the current interpretation in the economic think-

[46] In Note VII of the Mathematical Appendix, Marshall qualifies a suggested formula for combining consumer's surplus from different commodities by saying: "if we could find a plan for grouping together in one common demand curve all those things which satisfy the same wants, and are rivals; and also for every group of things of which the services are complementary (see Book V, chap. vi) . . ." (p. 842). Box V, chap. vi, contains the discussion of joint demand. The qualification quoted appears first in the third edition.

ing and writing of the past half-century. This circumstance explains the
presentation of additional textual evidence bearing on the validity of
the alternative interpretation.

C. Counterevidence from the Text of the *Principles*

I have been able to find only one passage in the text of the eighth edition of the *Principles* that is in any way inconsistent with my interpretation of Marshall. This is the celebrated passage, adverted to above,
which deals with the so-called "Giffen phenomenon" and which was
first introduced in the third edition:

> For instance, as Sir R. Giffen has pointed out, a rise in the
> price of bread makes so large a drain on the resources of the
> *poorer labouring families* and raises so much the marginal
> utility of money to them, that they are forced to curtail their
> consumption of meat and the more expensive farinaceous
> foods: and bread being still the cheapest food which they
> can get and will take, they consume more, and not less of it
> [p. 132; italics added].

This passage clearly offsets an income effect against a substitution
effect, whereas, on my interpretation of Marshall, real income is the
same at all points on the demand curve, so there is no "income effect"
(see Sec. II, B, above). The passage is thus in the spirit of the current
interpretation. Yet the words I have italicized indicate that it does not
necessarily contradict my interpretation of Marshall. The purchasing
power of money and the real income of the community at large may
remain constant; yet the real income of a particular group in the community that has a special consumption pattern may be adversely affected
by the rise in the price of a particular commodity.[47]

D. The Evidence of the Mathematical Appendix

The Mathematical Appendix to the *Principles* confirms and extends
the evidence already presented from the text of the *Principles* and from
Marshall's other writings. Note II (III in the first edition) explicitly
derives a relation between price and quantity demanded that is identical with a demand curve on my interpretation, in which real income is
kept constant by compensating variations in money income. Indeed, my
derivation of such a demand curve in Section I, C, above is a verbal

---

[47] See Marshall's explicit discussion of, and emphasis on, this possibility in "Remedies for Fluctuations of General Prices" (1887), *Memorials*, p. 207.

paraphrase of Marshall's mathematics. Marshall does not explicitly say that the relation he derives is a demand curve, but Note II is attached to his initial discussion of the demand curve (Book III, chap. iii, in the eighth edition) and is given as the authority for statements made about the demand curve; hence there can be no doubt that it presents the pure theory of his demand curve.

In all editions of the *Principles* Note VI, attached to Marshall's discussion of consumer's surplus, contains a sentence that is definitely wrong on the current interpretation of his demand curve but correct on my interpretation.

Finally, a sentence added to Note VI in the third edition, referred to in the text of the *Principles* in connection with the material added on the Giffen phenomenon, contains an implicit mathematical proposition that is correct on the current interpretation but incorrect on my interpretation. The mathematical point in question is considerably more subtle than those referred to in the two preceding paragraphs, so it cannot be given the same weight.

These two notes are examined in some detail in the appendix to this paper, to which the reader is referred for proof of the above statements.

E. A Synthesis of the Evidence

There are two differences between the current interpretation of Marshall's demand curve and my interpretation: (1) On the current interpretation, account is taken of the price of each other commodity individually; on my interpretation, only of the average price of all commodities other than the one in question and its close rivals. (2) On the current interpretation, real income varies along the demand curve with the price of the good in question; on my interpretation, real income is constant along the demand curve.

On the first, and less important, point, it is mathematically convenient to consider each other price separately, and this procedure might well have recommended itself to the writer of mathematical Notes XIV and XXI. On the other hand, it is impossible to consider each price separately in a practical analysis; so the use of an average price would clearly have recommended itself to the writer of the text of the *Principles* and is entirely in the spirit of Marshall's explicit methodological statements (see Sec. II, A, above). Marshall does not discuss this point explicitly; hence the textual evidence is all indirect.

On the second and basic point of difference the evidence leaves little room for doubt: Marshall's theory of demand, in the form in which it is presented in the first edition of the *Principles,* is explicitly based on constancy of real income along the demand curve. This interpretation not only is consistent with both the letter and the spirit of the entire text of the first edition of the *Principles* but is almost conclusively established by the evidence cited above from two notes in the Mathematical Appendix of the first edition. In his determined effort to be persuasive and to make his work accessible to educated laymen, Marshall might well have been vague in his verbal presentation, though even there it seems unlikely that he would have been logically inconsistent. It is hardly credible that he would have been not merely vague but downright wrong on simple mathematical points stated in mathematical language, especially since the mathematical points in question could hardly even have arisen if he had been explicitly using the current interpretation of the demand curve.

I am inclined to believe, however, that by the time Marshall made the revisions incorporated in the third edition of the *Principles*—presumably between 1891, when the second edition appeared, and 1895, when the third edition appeared—he had himself been influenced by the current interpretation, probably without realizing that it was different from his own. This conjecture is based primarily on the two passages cited above as inconsistent with my interpretation: the passage dealing with the Giffen phenomenon and the last sentence of Note VI of the Mathematical Appendix. Both were added in the third edition— and these are the only passages I have been able to find in any edition of the *Principles* that fit the current interpretation better than they fit my interpretation. Further, both show some evidence of confusion about the fine points of his theory of demand (see last paragraph of appendix to this paper).

The hypothesis that Marshall did not recognize the contradiction between the current interpretation and his earlier work would hardly be tenable if the lapse of time between the work incorporated in the first and the third editions of the *Principles* were as short as between their publication. But, as already noted, this is not the case. The essence of both his theory of demand and his analysis of consumer's surplus is contained in the *Pure Theory of (Domestic) Values*, which, though not printed until 1879, "must have been substantially complete about 1873." [48] The one important point in the theory of demand that is not in the *Pure Theory*—explicit mention of constancy of the purchasing power of money—is in the 1879 *Economics of Industry*. The only important addition in the *Principles* is the concept of "elasticity of demand"; and even this concept, which is not relevant to the present problem, was worked out in 1881–82.[49] No important substantive changes were made in the theory of demand in successive editions of

[48] Keynes, *Memorials*, p. 23.
[49] *Ibid.*, p. 39, n. 3.

the *Principles,* though the exposition was amplified and rearranged, the wording changed in detail, and some examples modified. The only important change of substance introduced into the discussion of consumer's surplus (in the third edition was in connection with a point that has no bearing on the present issue.[50]

Marshall himself writes: "My main position as to the theory of value and distribution was practically completed in the years 1867 to 1870. . . . By this time [from the context, 1874] I had practically completed the whole of the substance of my Mathematical Appendix." [51] Thus Marshall appears to have completed his fundamental work on the theory of demand in the early 1870's and to have made no important substantive changes thereafter. The third edition appeared some twenty or more years later—an ample lapse of time for the precise details of an essentially mathematical analysis to have become vague and their difference from a superficially similar set of details to pass unnoticed. This seems especially plausible in view of the acceptance of the current interpretation by others and the absence of controversy about it.

[50] This change does not reflect favorably on Marshall's willingness to admit error. The first edition states: "Subject to these corrections then we may regard the aggregate of the money measures of the total utility of wealth as a fair measure of that part of the happiness which is dependent on wealth" (pp. 179–80), the corrections referred to being for "differences in the wealth of different purchasers" (p. 178) and "elements of collective wealth which are apt to be overlooked" (p. 179). A footnote to the first quotation refers to mathematical Note VII, in which he says, subject to the same two qualifications: "if a_1, a_2, a_3 . . . be the amounts consumed of the several commodities of which b_1, b_2, b_3 . . . are necessary for existence, if $y = f_1(x)$, $y = f_2(x)$, $y = f_3(x)$ . . . be the equations to their demand curves . . . , then the total utility of his wealth, subsistence being taken for granted, is represented by

$$\sum \int_b^a f(x)\, dx"$$

(1st ed.; p. 741)

The eighth edition does not contain the first statement. Instead, the text contains an explicit warning against adding consumer's surpluses for different commodities, and a footnote says: "Some ambiguous phrases in earlier editions appear to have suggested to some readers the opposite opinion" (p. 131). Note VII in the Mathematical Appendix was modified by replacing "his wealth" by "income" and, of more importance, "is represented" by "might be represented" and by adding after the formula the significant qualification, "if we could find a plan for grouping together in one common demand curve all those things which satisfy the same wants, and are rivals; and also for every group of things of which the services are complementary. . . . But we cannot do this; and therefore the formula remains a mere general expression, having no practical application" (p. 842). As noted, these changes date from the third edition.

[51] Letter to J. B. Clark, *Memorials,* p. 416.

Further circumstantial evidence that Marshall did not recognize the contradiction between the current interpretation and his earlier work is provided by the apparent absence of any explicit discussion of the question in the writings of either Marshall or the more prominent of his students or even of any comments that could reasonably be interpreted as implying recognition of the existence of alternative interpretations of the demand curve. Yet, as noted earlier (n. 4), the current interpretation is explicitly given by Edgeworth as early as 1894 in an article on "Demand Curves" in *Palgrave's Dictionary of Political Economy* that Marshall must be presumed to have read. Though the assumption of constant prices of commodities other than the one in question is not explicitly attributed to Marshall, most of the article is based on Marshall; and there is no suggestion that this assumption does not apply to Marshall's demand curve. Further, Walras' definition of the demand curve, which presumably influenced Edgeworth, is identical with the current interpretation of Marshall's demand curve, and Marshall refers to Walras several times in the first edition of the *Principles,* though it seems clear that Marshall developed his theory of demand independently of Walras.[52] So Marshall must have been exposed to a definition of the demand curve corresponding to the current interpretation at a time when he was still making substantial revisions in the *Principles.* If he had recognized that this interpretation was incorrect, would he not have taken the opportunity to clarify his statements in later editions?

V. ALTERNATIVE CONCEPTIONS OF ECONOMIC THEORY

There remains the mystery how the current interpretation of Marshall's demand curve gained such unquestioned dominance at so early a date and retained it so long, not only as an interpretation of Marshall, but also as "the" definition of "the" demand curve.

One obvious explanation is that mathematical economists were more likely than others to state explicitly and precisely their assumptions about the behavior of other prices; that mathematical economists were likely to be familiar with Walras' independent definition and to take it as a point of departure; and that, in any event, the current interpretation is mathematically more convenient. Other economists, it could be argued, followed the lead of the mathematical economists, and thus the current interpretation was taken for granted and accepted without question.

52 *Principles* (1st ed.), pp. xi, xii, 425; Keynes, *Memorials,* pp. 19–24; Marshall's letter to J. B. Clark, *ibid.,* pp. 416–18.

This explanation seems to me a significant part of the answer; however, I do not believe that it is the entire answer. If, as I have argued above, my interpretation of Marshall is more useful for most practical problems, why has its use been so rarely proposed; why has there been no general feeling of dissatisfaction with the current interpretation? There must, it would seem, be something about the role that has been assigned to economic theory that has made the current interpretation acceptable.

I am inclined to believe that this is, in fact, the case; that, by slow and gradual steps, the role assigned to economic theory has altered in the course of time until today we assign a substantially different role to theory than Marshall did. We curtsy to Marshall, but we walk with Walras.

The distinction commonly drawn between Marshall and Walras is that Marshall dealt with "partial equilibrium," Walras with "general equilibrium." This distinction is, I believe, false and unimportant. Marshall and Walras alike dealt with general equilibrium; partial equilibrium analysis as usually conceived is but a special kind of general equilibrium analysis—unless, indeed, partial equilibrium analysis is taken to mean erroneous general equilibrium analysis. Marshall wrote to J. B. Clark in 1908: "My whole life has been and will be given to presenting in realistic form as much as I can of my Note XXI." [53] Note XXI, essentially unchanged from the first edition of the *Principles* to the last, presents a system of equations of general equilibrium. It ends with the sentence: "Thus, however complex the problem may become, we can see that it is theoretically determinate, because the number of unknowns is always exactly equal to the number of equations which we obtain." [54] The explanation given above why Marshall might have decided to hold the purchasing power of money constant was entirely in terms of constructing the demand curve so that it would be consistent with general equilibrium in those parts of the system not under direct study.

The important distinction between the conceptions of economic theory implicit in Marshall and Walras lies in the purpose for which the theory is constructed and used. To Marshall—to repeat an expression quoted earlier—economic theory is "an engine for the discovery of concrete truth." The "economic organon" introduces "systematic and organized methods of reasoning." Marshall wrote:

> Facts by themselves are silent. . . . The most reckless and
> treacherous of all theorists is he who professes to let facts

[53] *Memorials*, p. 417.
[54] *Principles*, p. 856. This note was numbered XX in the first edition.

and figures speak for themselves, who keeps in the background the part he has played, perhaps unconsciously, in selecting and grouping them, and in suggesting the argument *post hoc ergo propter hoc.* . . . The economist . . . must be suspicious of any direct light that the past is said to throw on problems of the present. He must stand fast by the more laborious plan of interrogating facts in order to learn the manner of action of causes singly and in combination, applying this knowledge to build up the organon of economic theory, and then making use of the aid of the organon in dealing with the economic side of social problems.[55]

Economic theory, in this view, has two intermingled roles: to provide "systematic and organized methods of reasoning" about economic problems; to provide a body of substantive hypotheses, based on factual evidence, about the 'manner of action of causes." In both roles the test of the theory is its value in explaining facts, in predicting the consequences of changes in the economic environment. Abstractness, generality, mathematical elegance—these are all secondary, themselves to be judged by the test of application. The counting of equations and unknowns is a check on the completeness of reasoning, the beginning of analysis, not an end in itself.

Doubtless, most modern economic theorists would accept these general statements of the objectives of economic theory. But our work belies our professions. Abstractness, generality, and mathematical elegance have in some measure become ends in themselves, criteria by which to judge economic theory. Facts are to be described, not explained. Theory is to be tested by the accuracy of its "assumptions" as photographic descriptions of reality, not by the correctness of the predictions that can be derived from it. From this viewpoint the current interpretation of the demand curve is clearly the better. It is more general and elegant to include the price of every commodity in the universe in the demand function rather than the average price of a residual group. Any price may affect any other, so a demand equation including every price is a more accurate photographic description. Of course, it cannot be used in discovering "concrete truth"; it contains no empirical generalization that is capable of being contradicted—but these are Marshallian objections. From the "Walrasian" viewpoint, to take one other example from recent developments in economic theory, it is a gain to eliminate the concept of an "industry," to take the individual firm as the unit of analysis, to treat each firm as a monopoly, to confine

55 The quotations are all taken from Marshall, "The Present Position of Economics" (1885), *Memorials*, pp. 159, 161, 164, 166, 168, 171.

all analysis to either the economics of the individual firm or to a general
equilibrium analysis of the economy as a whole.[56] From the Marshallian
viewpoint this logical terminus of monopolistic competition analysis is
a blind alley. Its categories are rigid, determined not by the problem at
hand but by mathematical considerations. It yields no predictions,
summarizes no empirical generalizations, provides no useful framework
of analysis.

Of course, it would be an overstatement to characterize all modern
economic theory as "Walrasian" in this sense. For example, Keynes's
theory of employment, whatever its merits or demerits on other
grounds, is Marshallian in method. It is a general equilibrium theory
containing important empirical content and constructed to facilitate
meaningful prediction. On the other hand, much recent work based on
Keynes's theory of employment is Walrasian.[57]

VI. CONCLUSION

Modern economic theory typically defines the demand curve as showing
the relation between the quantity of a commodity demanded and its
price for given tastes, money income, and prices of other commodities.
This definition has also been uniformly accepted as a correct interpretation of the demand curve defined and used by Alfred Marshall in his
Principles of Economics. Rarely has the view been expressed that a
different definition would be preferable.

Despite its unquestioned acceptance for over half a century, this
interpretation of Marshall is, in my view, wrong. Marshall's early writings, the text of the *Principles,* and, even more definitely, the Mathematical Appendix provide almost conclusive proof that Marshall's
demand curve differs in two respects from the one commonly used and
attributed to him: first, commodities other than the one in question
and its close rivals are treated as a group rather than individually, and
only their average price is explicitly taken into account; second, and
far more important, real income is considered the same at all points on
the demand curve, whereas constant money income and other prices
imply a higher real income, the lower the price of the commodity in
question. Two variants of Marshall's demand curve can be distinguished: one, employed in the text of the *Principles,* uses variations in
the prices of other commodities to compensate for variations in the
price of the commodity in question and thereby keeps the purchasing power of money constant; the other, employed in the Mathematical

[56] See Triffin, *op. cit.* pp. 188–89.
[57] O. Lange, *Price Flexibility and Employment* (Bloomington, Ind.: Principia Press, 1944), is perhaps as good an example as any.

Appendix, uses variations in money income to compensate for variations in the price of the commodity in question.

The only textual evidence that conflicts with this interpretation is a passage in the text and a related sentence in the Mathematical Appendix that were added to the third edition of the *Principles*. The inconsistency of these with the rest of the *Principles* can be explained by the hypothesis that Marshall himself was after a point influenced by the current interpretation of the demand curve without recognizing its inconsistency with his earlier work. Some circumstantial evidence also supports this hypothesis.

The alternative interpretation of the demand curve not only is faithful to both the letter and the spirit of Marshall's work but also is more useful for the analysis of concrete problems than is the demand curve commonly employed. The acceptance of a less useful definition seems to me to be a consequence of a changed conception of the role of theory in economic analysis. The current interpretation of the demand curve is Walrasian; and so is current economic theory in general.

APPENDIX ON TWO NOTES IN THE MATHEMATICAL APPENDIX TO THE *PRINCIPLES*

I. NOTE II OF THE EIGHTH EDITION

This note is numbered III in the first edition of the *Principles*, II in the rest. In the first edition the relevant parts are worded as follows (pp. 737–38):

"If m is the amount of money or general purchasing power at a person's disposal at any time, and μ represents its total utility to him, then $d\mu/dm$ represents the marginal utility of money to him.

"If p is the price which he is just willing to pay for an amount x of the commodity which gives him a total pleasure u, then

$$\frac{d\mu}{dm} \Delta p = \Delta u; \text{ and} \qquad \frac{d\mu}{dm} \frac{dp}{dx} = \frac{du}{dx}. \ldots$$

"Every increase in his means diminishes the marginal utility of money to him; . . .

"Therefore, du/dx, the marginal utility to him of an amount x of a commodity remaining unchanged, an increase in his means . . . increases dp/dx, that is, the rate at which he is willing to pay for further supplies of it. Treating u as a variable, that is to say, allowing for possible variations in the person's liking for the commodity in question, we may regard dp/dx as a function of m, u, and x. . . ."

The wording in the eighth edition is identical except that "marginal

utility of money" is replaced by "marginal degree of utility of money"
and that "du/dx" and the words "Treating u . . . in question" are
omitted from the last paragraph quoted (pp. 838–39). The changes were
first made in the third edition.

In the second sentence of this note the word "price" is to be interpreted as "total amount," not as "price per unit." This is clear from
the context and is demonstrated by the equation that follows and the
designation of dp/dx as "the rate at which he is willing to pay for
further supplies of it." The words "just willing" in the second sentence
and the equations that follow demonstrate that p is the maximum
amount he can pay for an amount x and have the same utility as if he
had none of the commodity. Thus Marshall is describing a process like
that outlined in Section I, C, of this paper, whereby the maximum
possible amount is extracted from the individual for each successive
increment of the commodity, the individual retaining the same "real
income," that is, remaining on the same indifference curve, throughout
the process.

The last sentence quoted shows that u is to be regarded as a parameter to allow for changes in tastes. The rest of that sentence simply
describes a function like that obtained by eliminating y' from equations
(5) and (6) of note 5 of this paper. The parameter m in Marshall's
function takes the place of U_o in our footnote, since dp/dx is still to be
regarded as the price per unit paid for an additional increment of the
commodity rather than as the price per unit at which any amount can
be purchased. In consequence, no explicit statement is needed as yet
about the compensating variations in income that are implicit in Marshall's analysis.

The word "demand" does not appear in this note. But the note is
attached to the chapter in the *Principles* in which Marshall first introduces the demand curve (Book III, chap. ii, in the first edition; Book
III, chap. iii, in later editions) and is cited as proof of statements about
the demand curve; hence there can be no doubt that the "function"
mentioned in the last sentence quoted is the counterpart of Marshall's
demand curve.

I have been able to construct no interpretation of this note that
would render it consistent with the current interpretation of Marshall's
demand curve.

II. Note VI

This note has the same number in all editions. In the first edition the
relevant parts are worded as follows (p. 740):

"If y be the price at which an amount x of a commodity can find purchasers in a given market, and $y = f(x)$ be the equation to the demand-curve, then the total utility of the commodity is measured by

$$\int_0^a f(x)\, dx\,,$$

where a is the amount consumed.

"If however an amount b of the commodity is necessary for existence, $f(x)$ will be infinite, or at least indefinitely great, for values of x less than b. We must therefore take life for granted, and estimate separately the total utility of that part of the supply of the commodity which is in excess of absolute necessaries: it is of course

$$\int_b^a f(x)\, dx \dots.$$

"It should be noted that, in the discussion of Consumers' Rent, we assume that the marginal utility of money to the individual purchaser is the same throughout. . . ."

Only trivial changes were made in these sentences in subsequent editions: a typographical error in the fifth edition, which remained uncorrected thereafter, substituted $f(z)$ for $f(x)$ in the second sentence; and "consumers' surplus" replaced "Consumers' Rent." In the third edition the following sentence was added at the end of the note:

"If, for any reason it be desirable to take acount of the influence which his expenditure on tea exerts on the value of money to him, it is only necessary to multiply $f(x)$, within the integral given above by that function of $xf(x)$ (i.e. of the amount which he has already spent on tea) which represents the marginal utility to him of money when his stock of it has been diminished by that amount" (3d ed., p. 795). The only subsequent changes were the addition of a comma after "reason" and the deletion of the comma before "within" (8th ed., p. 842).

In its final form Note VI seems internally inconsistent: the second sentence is wrong on the current interpretation of Marshall's demand curve, correct on my interpretation; the final sentence, added in the third edition, seems correct on the current interpretation, wrong on my interpretation.

A. *The second sentence.* The second sentence is wrong on the current interpretation, which holds money income and other prices constant along the demand curve, since the ordinate of the demand curve for any quantity x cannot then exceed money income divided by x, and this is not "indefinitely great" for a fixed value of x—say, x_0—*whether*

x_o is greater or less than b. True, $f(x)$ might approach infinity as x approaches zero, but this is not what Marshall says; he says it is "indefinitely great, for values of x less than b," i.e., for any particular value of x less than b—say, $x_o = 0.99b$.

On the variant of my interpretation involving compensating variations in money income—the variant that the note numbered II in the eighth edition leads me to believe Marshall used in the Mathematical Appendix—this sentence is entirely valid. As x declines from a value larger than b, the compensating variation in money income required to keep the individual's real income the same becomes larger and larger, approaching infinity as x approaches b, the minimum amount necessary for existence. This permits the ordinate of the demand curve likewise to approach infinity as x approaches b. On the variant involving compensating variations in other prices—the one Marshall used in the text —the definition of the demand curve breaks down for values of x less than b: for a finite price of the commodity in question, sufficiently high so that the given money income could purchase only a quantity x less than b, there will exist no set of nonnegative prices for the remaining commodities that will keep the purchasing power of money constant in the sense of enabling the same money income to provide the same level of utility; money income and real income cannot both be held constant and at the same time all prices be kept nonnegative. This sentence can therefore be defended as valid on either variant of my interpretation.

One possible ground for dismissing this sentence as evidence against the current interpretation is that the so-called "error" on that interpretation is of my own making, arising from a too subtle and too literal reading of the note. Marshall, it could be argued, was using "demand curve" to mean "utility curve" and $f(x)$ to mean "marginal utility," and therefore he did not consider whether the sentence would be valid if $f(x)$ were to be interpreted literally as the ordinate of the demand curve. A note that Marshall published in 1893 on "Consumer's Surplus" could be cited as evidence for the contention. In this note he quotes part of Note VI as follows: " 'If, however, an amount b of the commodity is necessary for existence, [the utility of the first element] a will be infinite.' "[58] The bracketed expression that Marshall substituted for $f(x)$ would support the notion that he was using "demand curve" and "utility curve" interchangeably.

[58] "Consumer's Surplus," *Annals of the American Academy of Political and Social Science*, III (March, 1893), 618–21 (brackets in original). This note is a reply to some comments by Simon Patten. The letter a after the brackets which appears in the *Annals* note does not appear in the *Principles*, and I can explain it only as a typographical error.

I do not myself accept this argument; it seems to me to do much less than justice to Marshall. In the first place, I am inclined to give little weight to an incidental, explanatory, phrase inserted by Marshall as late as 1892 or 1893, some twenty years after the fundamental analysis incorporated in Note VI had been completed. I have noted above and shall presently cite evidence that Marshall may have been somewhat confused about the fine points of his own theory of demand by the early 1890's. In the second place, and more important, Marshall clearly distinguishes in the earlier notes in the Mathematical Appendix between a utility curve and a demand curve, repeatedly using the word "utility," and in the first sentence of Note VI says that "the total utility of the commodity is *measured by*

$$\int_0^a f(x)\,dx'$$

(1st ed., p. 740; italics added). If he had been using $f(x)$ to stand for marginal utility, the words I have italicized could have been omitted. Finally, Note VI, like most of the rest of the Mathematical Appendix, summarizes a subtle, closely reasoned, and by no means obvious, mathematical argument, in which, so far as I know, few errors have ever been found. Is it credible that it would have been worded as loosely and carelessly as the argument being criticized requires; or that, if at one stage it had been, Marshall would have failed to see the simple mathematical error implicit in a literal reading of his words on the current interpretation of the demand curve? It seems to me far more credible that he meant what he said and that the correctness of what he said on my interpretation of his demand curve is strong evidence for that interpretation.

B. *The final sentence.* The explanation that follows of the final sentence added to Note VI in the third edition, though not completely satisfactory, is reasonably so, and I have been able to construct no other even remotely satisfactory explanation.

Let U be the utility function of the "individual purchaser" and U_x the marginal utility of x units of tea to him, i.e., the partial derivative of U with respect to x. Now the increase in utility attributable to having a rather than b units of tea—consumer's surplus in utility units—is given by

$$\int_b^a U_x\,dx\,, \tag{1}$$

where the integral is computed for constant quantities of other commodities equal to the amounts consumed when a units of tea are consumed and other conditions are those corresponding to the demand curve $y = f(x)$.

At every point along the demand curve,

$$U_x = ny = n(x) f(x), \tag{2}$$

where n is the marginal utility of money—itself, of course, a function of x along the demand curve. Integrating both sides of equation (2) gives

$$\int_b^a U_x dx = \int_b^a n(x) f(x)\, dx . \tag{3}$$

The left-hand side of equation (3) is symbolically identical with equation (1); yet there is an important difference between them. In equation (1), U_x is computed, holding the quantities of other commodities constant as x varies; in equation (3), U_x is computed, holding constant whatever is held constant along the demand curve (money income and other prices on the current interpretation; real income on my interpretation). In general, quantities of other commodities vary along the demand curve (on either interpretation), and U_x may depend on the quantities of other commodities, so the U_x in equation (3) may be numerically different from the U_x in equation (1) for a value of x other than a. This difficulty disappears if U_x is supposed to be independent of the quantities of other commodities—an assumption that Marshall pretty clearly makes as a general rule (e.g., see Notes I and II of the Mathematical Appendix). On this assumption, then, the right-hand side of equation (3) measures consumer's surplus in utility units.

It is at this point that difficulties of interpretation arise; for the right-hand side of equation (3) is obtained by multiplying "$f(x)$ within the integral given above by that function of" x "which represents the marginal utility . . . of money." Why does Marshall say "that function of $xf(x)$" rather than of x alone? And is it valid to make this substitution? One can argue that to each value of x there corresponds a value of $f(x)$ and hence of $xf(x)$, so that the two forms of statement are equivalent: Marshall has simply made the transformation $z = xf(x)$ and converted $n(x)$ into $n(z)$. This argument is not, however, rigorous. In general, x will not be a single-valued function of z; hence to any given value of z there may correspond more than one value of x and hence more than one value of n. The two forms of statement are equivalent if and only if n is a single-valued function of z, i.e., if $n(x)$ is the same for all values of x for which $xf(x)$ is the same.

Given independence between the marginal utility of tea and the quantity of other commodities, this condition is always satisfied on the current interpretation of the demand curve but not on the alternative interpretation. Let x' stand for the quantity of a composite commodity representing all commodities other than tea, y' for its price, and $U_{x'}$ for its marginal utility. At each point on the demand curve,

$$\frac{U_x}{y} = \frac{U_{x'}}{y'} = n.$$

On the current interpretation of the demand curve, money income and the prices of other commodities are the same for all points on the demand curve. It follows that, for all values of x that yield the same value of $xf(x)$, the same amount will be spent on other commodities; so x' is the same (since y' is by definition); so $U_{x'}$ is (since, on the assumption of independence, $U_{x'}$ depends only on x'); and so n is. Marshall's use of $xf(x)$ instead of x is thus valid on the current interpretation of the demand curve.

On my interpretation, either money income varies along the demand curve, so as to keep real income constant, or other prices do; hence the preceding argument is no longer valid. That the two forms of statement are no longer always equivalent can be shown by a counterexample. If other prices are held constant and compensating variations of income are used to keep real income constant,

$$U = \sqrt{x} + \sqrt{x'}$$

is a utility function that gives different values of n for different values of x yielding the same value of $xf(x)$. If money income is held constant and compensating variations of other prices are used to keep real income constant,

$$U = 3 + x - \tfrac{1}{10} x^2 + \sqrt{x'}$$

is such a utility function. Hence Marshall's use of $xf(x)$ instead of x is invalid on either variant of the alternative interpretation.

This explanation leaves a number of Marshall's verbal statements wrong or ambiguous, whichever interpretation of the demand curve is accepted. (1) The parenthetical explanation of the meaning of $xf(x)$ seems wrong—why the word "already"? If one is thinking of going through the process of extracting as much as possible from the consumer for each successive unit of tea and is supposing the maximum price that he will pay for successive units to be given by the demand curve, then

$$\int_b^v f(x)\,dx$$

and not $xf(x)$ is the amount he has "already spent on tea." If one is thinking of the amount spent on tea at a given price for tea, then $xf(x)$ is the amount spent when the price is $f(x)$, not the amount "already spent." The explanation offered above accepts the latter rendering of the parenthesis, i.e, supposes the word "already" omitted. (2) The last clause—"when his stock of money has been diminished by that amount" —is ambiguous. To make it consistent with the explanation offered above, one must add "and tea is unavailable, so that the balance is spent solely on other commodities at the prices assumed in drawing the demand curve for tea." The reference to "stock of money" suggests that Marshall was supposing money income constant and so, independently of the rest of the quotation, would tend to rule out compensating variations in money income. It should be noted that there are no such ambiguities in the original version of Note VI, either in the parts quoted above or in the parts not quoted.

11

THE MARSHALLIAN DEMAND CURVE *

MARTIN J. BAILEY [1] is affiliated with the Department of Defense; he was formerly at The Johns Hopkins University.

In an article with the above title, Professor Friedman [2] has urged that a constant-real-income demand curve is a more satisfactory tool for economic analysis than the customary constant-other-prices-and-money-incomes demand curve and that, at least in the first two editions of the *Principles*, this was the type of demand curve which Marshall really had in mind. On the latter, historical question nothing will be said here; but on the former, analytical question I shall contend that Friedman did not make the best choice of a curve as an improvement on the conventional one and that the constant-real-income curve, strictly interpreted, does not on balance possess the superiority he claims for it. Of the various interesting alternative types of demand curve which can be defined, one at least possesses most, if not all, of the advantages which Friedman can claim for any type of constant-real-income demand curve and none of its disadvantages.

In his argument in support of the constant-real-income demand curve Friedman demonstrated that the use of an ordinary demand curve in a demand-supply diagram to show the effects of a subsidy on a given commodity fails to take account of the necessary withdrawal of resources from other uses; on the other hand, the constant-real-income demand curve, which in the limit is an approximation of what the community can actually have, allows for this withdrawal of resources and therefore presents a better picture of the final outcome.[3]

* From *Journal of Political Economy*, Vol. LXII (June, 1954), pp. 255–261. Copyright © by The University of Chicago Press. Reprinted by permission.

[1] I wish to thank Mr. Amotz Morag and Professors Arnold C. Harberger and Carl F. Christ for their helpful advice and criticisms of early drafts of this note; and I wish to thank Professor Milton Friedman for his advice and criticism at a later stage. Specific acknowledgments to Professor Friedman appear at appropriate points in the text of this note. Responsibility for such errors as remain is, of course, my own.

[2] Milton Friedman, "The Marshallian Demand Curve," *Journal of Political Economy*, LXII (1949), 463–95.

[3] *Ibid.*, pp. 467–74.

While Friedman's analysis does not contain any errors, it is liable to serious misinterpretation if its assumptions and their relevance are overlooked; on the other hand, with a different type of demand curve which I shall propose the pitfalls can be avoided, and an analytically superior tool can be had in the bargain.

DEMAND CURVES AND PRODUCTION POSSIBILITIES

Suppose, for simplicity of arrangement, that a fully employed community has the production possibilities between its two competitively produced commodities X and Y as shown by the opportunity-cost curve ST in Figure 1A. Money, different from either commodity, is used as a unit of account only; money incomes are assumed to be spent in full, and the absolute price level to be determined arbitrarily.[4]

From the community indifference curves (for the moment assumed to be defined unambiguously) shown in Figure 1A, we may derive the two demand curves mentioned so far (the constant-real-income and the other-things-equal demand curves) in the customary manner. DD in Figure 1B is defined by the price-consumption line PC in Figure 1A, and RR is obtained from the equilibrium indifference curve I_1 by noting the quantity of X at which I_1 has any given slope (i.e., marginal rate of substitution, interpreted as a price ratio, P_x/P_y).

Suppose now that the government pays a subsidy on production of X; the apparent effect after production adjusts itself to the new conditions will be to lower the price of X by some fraction of the amount of the subsidy, changing the price line from $S'T'$ to $S'L$ in Figure 1A, and to leave the price of Y and money income unchanged. Given this apparent opportunity, the community would like to consume to the point C in Figure 1A, that is, to the point W in Figure 1B. However, as Friedman pointed out, this is clearly impossible. Physical supplies are not available, and corresponding to this lack there is an inflationary gap equal to the going amount of the subsidy; also the relative price of Y must fall owing to the shift of production toward more X.

Hence we must further suppose that the government imposes an income tax always equal to the subsidy. The final equilibrium point is found where a price line which is tangent to an indifference curve where it crosses the production frontier differs in slope from the slope of the production frontier at that point by an amount corresponding to the subsidy. $S'L$ will "shift" to MN, where it is tangent to the indifference curve I_0, lower than I_1, at A. This equilibrium point is only

---

[4] Friedman's assumption of a fixed supply of factor services is retained here, since its retention does not cause any loss of generality in the argument.

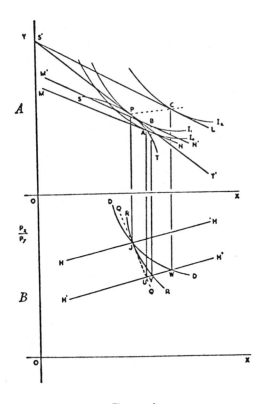

Figure 1

slightly distant from B, the point at which $M'N'$ is tangent to I_1. ($S'L$, $M'N'$, and MN have it in common that each one's slope differs by the rate of subsidy from the slope of the production frontier beneath the point where each one is tangent to an indifference curve.)

It can be seen from this result that neither DD nor RR, in Figure 1B, shows the final outcome correctly. The correct outcome could be obtained only from another type of demand curve, the "production-frontier" demand curve, which would show, for each amount of X, the marginal rate of substitution of the indifference curve which crosses the production frontier at the point where that amount of X is produced. This demand curve is shown as QQ in Figure 1B; if X is not an inferior good, QQ must lie to the left of both RR and DD below J and must lie between them above J (where J in Fig. 1B corresponds to P in Fig. 1A). Its intersection with $H'H'$ at U, corresponding to A in

Figure 1*A*, shows the true outcome as the result of the imposition of the combination subsidy and income tax.

The production-frontier demand curve is clearly the one hypothetically most desirable for use in the comparative statics of demand analysis, since it shows what in fact the community will take when the repercussions on the production of other commodities are taken into account. Its weakness is that it is defined only for given production conditions. Presumably tastes are relatively constant, whereas real or apparent production conditions are always changing because of fluctuations in weather and crops, changes in government policy, and other factors. Data on market behavior may, to the extent that this is true, be supposed to tell us something about consumer preferences but to tell us little about production conditions. At any moment of time, however, production conditions are in some sense fixed; and for economic analysis it would be desirable to take these conditions into account in analyzing demand. Lacking knowledge of these conditions of the moment, we must adopt some more or less arbitrary method of approximating the effects of a change in policy or the like.

Friedman argues in effect that RR (in Fig. 1*B*) is a better approximation to QQ than is DD, since I_1 is tangent to ST at P and so approximates it in the limit, whereas PC has no such limiting property. That is to say, RR is tangent to QQ, but DD is not. This is correct, as long as the community preference field (the function represented by the indifference map) is innocent of any discontinuities in the first and all higher derivatives. Though I suppose there is no reason to doubt its innocence for practical purposes, this qualification should be recognized as relevant. But other arguments developed below substantially weaken the case for the constant-real-income demand curve.

THE CONSTANT-REAL-INCOME CONCEPT

The argument so far has been greatly aided by the use of unexplained community indifference curves. It is now necessary to investigate the meaning of these curves of constant community real income and of the idea of a constant-real-income demand curve. The construction of community indifference curves will not be repeated here; suffice it to say that constant community real income means constant real income for *every individual* in the community.[5] The relevant construction necessarily implies the existence of different distributions of money incomes

[5] William J. Baumol, "The Community Indifference Map: A Construction," *Review of Economic Studies*, XVII (1949–50), 189–97; and E. J. Mishan, "The Principle of Compensation Reconsidered," *Journal of Political Economy*, LX (1952), 514–17.

at different points along a given community indifference curve; the reason for this will become clear in the following discussion.

Consider, in Figure 2, the indifference curves of two individuals whose money incomes are equal.[6] When the two indifference maps are

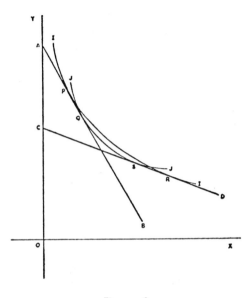

Figure 2

superimposed on one another, their opportunity lines will coincide, as, for example, in *AB*. The individual *I* will be in equilibrium at *P*, and the individual *J* will be in equilibrium at *Q*, given the opportunity line *AB*. Now for an arbitrary change in the price of, say, commodity *Y*, what price change of *X* will keep both individuals on the same levels of real income *J* and *I*? It is at once apparent that there need not be *any* price change of *X* which will do the trick. If the price of *Y* should rise until the given money income of each individual could purchase only *OC* of *Y*, then a price of *X* corresponding to the opportunity line *CD* would do it, since *CD* happens to be tangent to both *I* and *J* at *R* and *S*, respectively. But the set of points *C* through which a line can be drawn tangent to both indifference curves is in general a finite set (the principal exception being the case where the two indiffer-

6 For persons with different money incomes, the scales of *X* and *Y* quantities for the person with the larger income may be compressed (in the same proportion) until the two opportunity lines coincide when the indifference maps are superimposed. The argument in the text then applies without change to this case.

ence curves coincide) and may be empty, aside from the point A. A price compensating constant-real-income demand function for the two individuals must remain undefined except at points such as C—that is, we cannot, in general, have a constant-real-income demand "curve" at all, as long as money incomes are held constant.

On the other hand, if money income changes are used—in general, a different change for each individual—then it will always be possible to find an income change for each individual that will just offset any price change (or set of price changes) and permit him to achieve the same indifference curve as before. This, in effect, is what is done in defining community indifference curves.

But if the method of compensating price changes is used, there is no such thing as a constant-real-income demand curve for two individuals taken together. Such a curve can be defined for each one, but the curves cannot be aggregated because the price changes of Y offsetting a given price change of X would be different for the two individuals. This would be true a fortiori for a larger community; and it would continue to be true whatever the number of commodities.

It should be clear, then, that a constant-real-income demand curve for a community cannot be defined in terms solely of offsetting price movements for all possible price changes of a given commodity unless everybody's tastes are, in effect, identical. In fact, identity of tastes is not sufficient when money incomes are different. What is required is that the indifference curve on which each individual finds himself in equilibrium must be an exact projection of the corresponding indifference curve of every other individual. Unless all indifference systems were homogeneous, identity of tastes would guarantee this coincidence only for an equal distribution of income.

TWO APPROXIMATIONS: CONSTANT APPARENT REAL INCOME AND CONSTANT APPARENT PRODUCTION

The objections against a constant-real-income demand curve, as I have so far defined it, are for any practical purpose overwhelming; recourse may be had, however, to an approximating concept which avoids these objections.[7] This concept is that of the constant-*apparent*-real-income demand curve, which can be defined for constant-money incomes all around and with no particular knowledge of individual consumer preferences. In Figure 3A the point P represents, as before, the initial equilibrium point, and $S'T'$ is the equilibrium price line. If the price

[7] In his text Friedman uses the constant-apparent-real-income demand curve (*op. cit.*, pp. 466–67).

of X is lowered, the consumers' real income will "apparently" be the same if the price of Y is raised to the point where the consumers are just able to buy the same bill of goods they bought before; that is, the new price line $M''N''$ should pass through P. This, to a first order of approximation, cancels out the income effect to consumers in the aggregate [8] but allows them a small gain in "real income" by substituting X for Y; the new bill of goods they would choose if they had this opportunity would be B', on the community indifference curve I_3, higher than I_1.

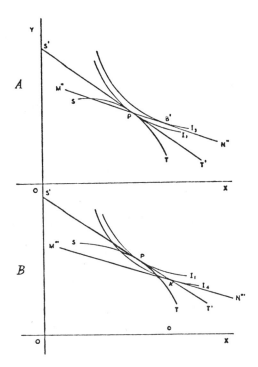

Figure 3

[8] If individual incomes are not adjusted, then "income effects" are not removed by this procedure even to a first order of approximation for individuals, since no individual need be consuming the two commodities in the same proportions as they are consumed by the whole community.

However, this consideration may be ignored for the constant-apparent-real-income demand curve, if we like, whereas in the nature of the case it cannot be ignored for the "true" constant-real-income demand curve. Furthermore, if we choose not to ignore it, we need only to know the original quantities bought by each consumer in order to define the constant-apparent-real-income demand curve, whereas for the constant-real-income demand curve one must know the shape and position of each consumer's relevant indifference curve. Similar re-

The demand curve derived in this way is not the same thing as the true constant-real-income demand curve as previously defined (which depended on the shape of I_1 only), but it can be proved to be a first-order approximation of it,[9] just as the true constant-real-income demand curve is a first-order approximation of the production-frontier demand curve. It follows that the constant-apparent-real-income demand curve is a first-order approximation of the production-frontier demand curve. Furthermore, it does not suffer from the difficulties of definition of the other curve, since it can unambiguously be defined in terms of constant-money incomes for every individual.

In practice, something in the nature of a constant-apparent-real-income demand curve could be derived statistically from ordinary total market data; whereas a true constant-real-income demand curve could not but would require data on every individual. With a statistically derived demand curve in our hands, we would not know what values of the price variables (if any) would give every consumer the same real income (for a constant-money income) as some other set of values of the price variables. However, it would be a simple matter to choose a set of price variables giving the same *apparent* real income (as here defined) to the community as some other set; all that has to be done is to choose a set of prices which keeps a base-weights price index unchanged in value.[10]

However, the possibilities for better practical approximation of the production-frontier demand curve are not yet exhausted. We may with comparable simplicity define a constant-apparent-*production* demand curve; and this will be the best approximation of the lot. In Figure 3B the line $S'T'$ represents the equilibrium price line as before, and, being tangent to the production frontier ST at P, it represents a local approximation of ST, just as does I_1. A useful demand concept is defined by moving along $S'T'$: for any given price ratio for X and Y, we obtain

---

marks apply to the constant-apparent-production demand curve discussed below in the text.

So far as I can see, the production-frontier demand curve has the disadvantage that there is no logical way to define it for each individual in the community—it is a purely aggregate function, and any relative income distribution is consistent with its definition. This disadvantage is the antithesis of the disadvantage of the constant-real-income demand curve, which in effect is defined only for the individual.

My earlier omission of the points in this footnote was brought to my attention by Friedman.

[9] See Jacob L. Mosak, "On the Interpretation of the Fundamental Equation of Value Theory," in O. Lange *et al.* (eds.), *Studies in Mathematical Economics and Econometrics* (Chicago: University of Chicago Press, 1942), p. 73 n.

[10] Friedman, *op. cit.*, p. 467.

from the community indifference map that bill of goods among those along $S'T'$ which the community would prefer; that is, we find the community indifference curve I_4, which at its point of crossing of $S'T'$ has the same slope as the given price line, $M'''N'''$.

We may now compare the different conceptions of demand set forth here; the curves are illustrated in Figure 4, which is derived from Figures 1A, 3A, and 3B in the same manner as Figure 1B is derived

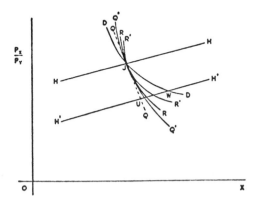

Figure 4

from Figure 1A. The curves DD, RR, and QQ in Figure 4 are the same as in Figure 1A; the new curves $R'R'$ and $Q'Q'$ are the approximations —constant *apparent* real income and production, respectively—discussed in this section.

The curves $R'R'$, RR, and $Q'Q'$ are all tangent to QQ at J, a condition which will hold provided the necessary continuity obtains in preference and production; and it can also be seen that $R'R'$, RR, and $Q'Q'$ are successively better approximations in that order to QQ, which represents the demand derived from what the community can actually have. (The relative positions of the various curves depend on the assumption that commodity X is not inferior.) No importance should be attached to the absolute curvatures of the different curves, which depend on the conditions of preference and production; but under the assumed conditions it is necessarily true that QQ, $Q'Q'$, RR, and $R'R'$ are successively more concave upward and that $Q'Q'$ is the best approximation to the shape of QQ.

The constant-apparent-production demand curve can, like the constant-apparent-real-income demand curve, be derived from market data on quantities sold and prices. Just as the constant-apparent-real-income

demand curve is obtained from the knowledge of the original equilibrium quantities and of the relevant part of the consumer preference
field as revealed in market data, so the constant-apparent-production
curve is obtained from a knowledge of the original equilibrium *prices*
and of the relevant part of the consumer preference field. The first
involves keeping a base-weights price index constant; the second involves keeping a base-weights quantity index constant. Such awkward-
ness of definition as exists in the constant-apparent-production
demand curve disappears if the Continental procedure of expressing
prices as a function of quantity is adopted.[11]

The constant-apparent-production curve has the advantage, however,
that it represents the true possibilities closer than does the constant-
real-income demand curve. *It utilizes information which the latter
curve does not use, namely, that the equilibrium price ratio is itself an
approximation of the alternative bills of goods which the community
can in fact have.*

There is one other point on which the suggested "improvement" of
the conventional demand curve might be rejected: the conventional
demand curve is unambiguous about how "other prices" behave,
whereas none of the other demand curves is. If there are several commodities, a given change in the price of commodity X may be offset
by price changes in other goods in any of a number of different ways
still meeting the specifications of the other four types of demand
curves. It may make a good deal of difference to the demand for X
whether the prices of closely competing or complementary goods are
changed a little or a lot to compensate for the change in the price of X.
If any demand curve other than the all-other-prices-and-incomes-equal
demand curve is used, some arbitrary specification must be made as to
how other prices are to change to offset changes in the price of X, such
as that all other prices change in the same proportion. It should be
recognized that such a solution *is* arbitrary, since whatever choice is
made does not necessarily have any connection with the way these
prices would really change if, say a subsidy were imposed on commodity X. The conventional demand curve solves this problem (also
arbitrarily, of course) by assuming that other prices do not change at
all.

FINAL COMMENT

The conclusion of the above remarks finds me substantially in agreement with Friedman's argument in favor of revising the conventional

[11] I am indebted to Friedman for this point.

notion of a demand curve when we desire to analyze the effects of an excise tax or subsidy, although I have come out in favor of even greater revision than he suggested. In the policy problem in question, the community's production opportunities are unaffected, but *apparent* supply conditions are changed. Therefore, it is simplest to use a demand curve along which true supply conditions are (exactly or approximately) unchanged. The conventional demand curve does not meet this specification; consequently, in the problem under consideration one must show a shift in such a demand curve, as well as in the apparent supply curve, as the effect of the policy action.[12] If market data are sufficiently informative, both demand and supply conditions are hypothetically ascertainable, and the production-frontier demand curve may be used. If not, the approximations discussed here may be used, the better of which is the constant-apparent-production demand curve.

The situation is not the same if the problem under consideration involves changes in actual supply conditions such as (a) changes in technique, (b) crop variations and the like, and (c) changes in government activity, altering the availabilities to the private sector of the economy. In any such case the relevant demand curve would change, that is, would "shift." This is true of the production-frontier demand curve and of all three of its approximations. It is possible that, by coincidence, the new equilibrium might be on the old price-consumption line (PC in Fig. 1A); and in this case the conventional demand curve would give the true result without shifting. No such coincidence is possible for the other four demand curves if the new production frontier lies entirely above or below the old one. Beyond this, however, nothing can be said as to whether the outcome of a change in conditions can or cannot be approximated with any single demand curve defined here.

It is therefore evident that the choice of a demand curve for purposes of analysis should depend on the problem in hand; and for some problems no demand curve will perform with the simplicity we might desire. It should therefore also be evident that the use of general equilibrium diagrams such as Figure 1A is an important supplement to clear and accurate analysis. With such diagrams it is still necessary to state the relevant qualifications regarding income distribution, but subject to this the interrelationships between different types of changes in conditions can be shown.

12 Friedman, *op. cit.*

12

CARDINAL UTILITY *

Robert H. Strotz is Dean of the College of Arts
and Sciences at Northwestern University; he was
formerly on the staff at Northwestern University.

This paper is concerned with the recent revival of the proposition
that utility is measurable.[1] This is an old issue and one on which our
opinion has been largely reversed during the past few years. Initially
we accepted the concept of utility as measurable, then we rejected it,
and now we are in the process of accepting it again.

Utility was originally conceived as a psychic quantity, which, while
it may not have been easily measured, was regarded as measurable, at
least in principle. The notion of diminishing marginal rate of utility
came quite naturally for it appears to have had considerable appeal to
one's intuition. Although the acceptance of a cardinal utility of this
sort had been questioned earlier, that doctrine was not effectively in-
terred until 1934, largely as a consequence of the work of Allen and
Hicks. ("A Reconsideration of the Theory of Value," *Economica,* February, May, 1934.) Utility then came to be regarded as an ordinal
sort of thing, subject to ranking but not to measurement. The principle of Occam's Razor lent sanctity to the new approach because it
was found that ordinal utility served very well for the treatment of the
problems to which utility theory was conventionally applied. The
assumption of the cardinal, quantitative character of utility, doubtful
and unneeded, was largely abandoned. The word utility persisted in
our literature, however, but only as an indicator enabling us to say
that if a consumer prefers A to B to C he derives greater utility from
A than from B or C and greater utility from B than from C. But we
denied that any meaningful statements could be made about whether
the difference in the utilities provided by A and B is greater or less
than the difference in the utilities provided by B and C. Utilities could
be compared but differences between utilities could not.

This paved the way for a behavioristic rather than a hedonistic interpretation of utility. Utility no longer had to be thought of as a psycho-

* From the *American Economic Review*, Vol. XLII (May, 1953), pp. 384–397, Reprinted by permission.
[1] This paper is included in *Cowles Commission Paper*, "New Series," No. 75.

logical entity measurable in its own right. It could now be regarded as simply a convenient label for the explicit value of a function which described consumer behavior. The definition of a utility that consumers maximized had become tautologous. The utility function was simply any function that was maximized and the empirical significance of the theory of consumer behavior resided in the qualitative restrictions that were imposed on the form of the utility function itself, notably by the requirement of the diminishing marginal rate of substitution. Professor Stigler could write in his *Theory of Competitive Price:* "It does not affect the formal theory of demand in the least whether the individual maximizes wealth, religious piety, the annihilation of crooners, or his waistline." (Page 64.) This statement clearly requires that no judgment be made as to whether utility be measured in dollars or in days indulgence, in octaves or in inches, and there certainly is no presumption that utility is to be measured in some psychological unit.

In 1945, however, with the publication of the *Theory of Games and Economic Behavior,* by von Neumann and Morgenstern (second edition, Chapter III and Appendix), measurable utility was resurrected, but only as a result, it should be understood, of a quite different and superior understanding of the meaning of measurement. Measurable utility in the von Neumann-Morgenstern sense bears little resemblance to the measurable utility that was discarded during the past two decades. During the interregnum from Allen and Hicks to von Neumann and Morgenestern such debate as existed between the vanishing cardinalists and the ascendant ordinalists was concerned essentially with the philosophical question of whether cardinality or quantifiability could reasonably be regarded as an intrinsic property of the entity called utility.[2] From the modern point of view, we now realize that this philosophical question of whether utility is intrinsically measurable is a spurious one and that measurement has meaning, not as a property of things, but as a predictive procedure. Crucial to an understanding of this entire subject is the realization that measurement is always invented and never discovered!

Consider for a moment the question of measuring length. Suppose that there are two carpenters each of whom has the task of placing

[2] This appears to be the case, for example, in O. Lange, "The Determinateness of the Utility Function," *Review of Economic Studies,* June, 1934; W. E. Armstrong, "The Determinateness of the Utility Function," *Economic Journal,* September, 1939; F. H. Knight, "Realism and Relevance in the Theory of Demand," *Journal of Political Economy,* December, 1944; and, more recently, D. H. Robertson, "Utility and All That," *Manchester School,* May, 1951.

two boards end to end and then sawing a third board that will exactly cover the combined length of the first two. The first carpenter proceeds as we would. He measures the length of a board by counting the number of times he can lay down on it, end to end, a rule of unit length, where the unit is arbitrarily defined. If the rule can be placed end to end three times on the first board, he declares that board to be three rule-lengths, or, let us say, 3 feet long. Now this statement is arbitrary. He might just as well have said that the length of the board is the-square-root-of-three feet long or the-square-of-three feet long or any-other-function-of-three feet long. But his convention is a useful one, especially for the problem at hand. Finding the first board to be 3 feet long and the second board to be 4 feet long, he knows that the board to be cut must be $3 + 4$ or 7 feet long. He need only know how to add to make a good prediction.

The second carpenter, having been apprenticed in a strange land, measures the first board in a different manner. His measure is the square of our measure. When he lays the rule down again and again he counts "1, 4, 9" and declares the board to be 9 feet long. The second board is measured by counting "1, 4, 9, 16." To determine then how long a board he should cut, he calculates $(\sqrt{9} + \sqrt{16})^2 = 49$, and so measures off a length of 49 counting "1, 4, 9, 16, 25, 36, 49." Forty-nine being the square of 7, his answer is really the same as that of the first carpenter. The method of the second carpenter requires somewhat better knowledge of arithmetic than the method of the first, as he must square a sum of square roots rather than simply add. But his method is not incorrect; it is simply awkward.

Suppose now that these two carpenters were given another assignment. This time they are to place the first two boards at right angles and saw a third board to form the hypothenuse of a right triangle. The first carpenter performs the calculation $\sqrt{3^2 + 4^2} = 5$; the second carpenter, $9 + 16 = 25$. Twenty-five being the square of 5, both methods are correct, but this time it is the method of the first carpenter which is awkward. In short, one method of measurement may be more convenient than another for some purposes and less convenient for other purposes. A vast variety of methods may, however, all be correct.

Why do we customarily use the measure of the first carpenter rather than that of the second? I suppose the answer is that we more commonly encounter problems of placing lengths end to end than problems of constructing right triangles. But the important point is this: our choice of a measure is largely a matter of convenience or manageability.

An equally important point, of course, is that a measure which makes computation convenient must also work. If, for example, we found that although a board 7 feet long exactly covers the combined length of one 3 feet long and one 4 feet long, a board 70 feet long exceeds the combined length of boards 30 and 40 feet long, then the particular formula we use, namely, simple addition, would be incorrect and unsatisfactory. In short, what we want is to invent some arbitrary method of measuring things which, coupled with a simple formula, will enable us to make correct predictions.

Now the very same thing is true of utility. We want to find an arbitrary measure of utility so that we can under frequently encountered conditions predict consumer behavior by use of a simple formula.

An early example of this approach is to be found in Samuelson's essay entitled, "Constancy of the Marginal Utility of Income" (in O. Lange *et al., Studies in Mathematical Economics and Econometrics*). Here the following problem was raised.

Marshall found that a good deal of the analysis of consumer behavior could be greatly simplified by assuming that the marginal utility of income is constant. Now, the marginal utility of income is clearly a measure. Could we then invent a measure of utility so that the marginal utility of income would in fact be constant?

If so, we should then want to determine whether this measure would imply anything about reality that we might put to test, and, if there are any empirically testable theorems implicit in our acceptance of this measure, we should then want to know whether these theorems correspond to reality. Before pursuing the question of whether we can invent an acceptable measure of utility for which the marginal utility of income is constant, we must note, as Samuelson has pointed out, that the phrase, "the constancy of the marginal utility of income," is subject to diverse interpretations. For our illustrative purpose here, we propose the following particular interpretation. By "the marginal utility of income" let us mean the common value of the ratios of the marginal utilities of commodities to their prices. By "constancy" let us mean constancy with respect to independent changes in the various prices of commodities and in income. Now, we may see clearly what our problem is. As is well known, there is an infinite number of utility functions that will serve equally well to describe the behavior of a given individual. This is so because for any one of these functions that will describe his behavior any other function that increases, decreases, or stays the same whenever the first one increases, decreases, or stays the same will describe the consumer's behavior just as well.

Two functions which are related in this way are called "monotonically increasing functions of each other." The reason why any member of this family of monotonically increasing functions may be selected as the utility function is because a consumer who may be said to maximize any one of them subject to his budget may be said to maximize any other for they all go up and down together. Can we find among this infinite number of acceptable utility functions one that has the property that the marginal utility of income will remain constant for a change in any price or for a change in income? If so, we can define a measure of utility (that is, we can select this particular utility function) so that it is permissible to assume that the marginal utility of income is constant. What Samuelson then proceeded to show is that no such function is available. (This is analogous to showing that for no measure of length will the third side of a triangle, which is not necessarily a right triangle, be equal to the sum of the other two sides.)

Let us next change the problem a bit by changing our definition of constant to mean constant with respect to a change in any commodity price, although not constant with respect to a change in income. In answer to this problem Samuelson showed that a total utility function might be specified so that the marginal utility of income is constant in this sense. But he found, moreover, that there is an empirically testable proposition implicit in the acceptance of such a total utility function; namely, that the income elasticity of the demand for each commodity is unitary. This, clearly, does not square with the facts. To summarize, the question was whether a measure of total utility could be devised so that the marginal utility of income would be constant with respect to price changes. What was shown was that any measure that would satisfy this condition would entail the empirical restriction that income elasticities be unitary. Since income elasticities are not all unitary, we conclude that no such measure can be defined.

Just as it suits the Marshallian demand analysis to assume a total utility function for which the marginal utility of income is constant, so von Neumann and Morgenstern also had a purpose in assuming the existence of a total utility function with a convenient property. Dealing to a considerable extent in their *Theory of Games* with choices in situations involving risk, they found that it would be quite helpful to have a utility function that would make possible the use of a simple formula to describe an individual's choices among various risks. How nice it would be to say that every gamble can be reduced to a certainty equivalent, where the certainty equivalent would be that certain income (increment of income) which provides a utility equal to a weighted average of the utilities resulting from different possible outcomes of the gamble, the weights being probabilities. For example, it would be convenient if we could say that an individual would evaluate a 1/5 to 4/5 chance of winning either $0 or $10 as follows: If he in fact wins nothing his utility will be, say, 0; if he in fact wins $10 his utility will be, say 1. The weighted average utility will therefore be $1/5 \cdot 0 + 4/5 \cdot 1 = 4/5$.

Now, we should like to continue, the individual will be indifferent between this particular gamble and any other gamble that provides a weighted average utility of 4/5 and he will be indifferent between this class of gambles and any certain awards that provide the same utility. The weighted average is known as his mathematical expectation of utility or, in Bernoulli's terms, his moral expectation. It is to be distinguished from the utility of the mathematical expectation of his winnings which would be the utility of the weighted average of the possible winnings; that is, the utility of $1/5 \cdot \$0 + 4/5 \cdot \$10$ or the utility of $8. We can make this distinction in more familiar terms. The mathematical expectation of utility or moral expectation we might call simply the "average utility of the winnings" or just "average utility." The utility of the mathematical expectation of the winnings we shall call the "utility of the average winnings."

Suppose the individual prefers the certainty of $8 to the 1/5-4/5 chance of nothing or $10. The utility of the average winnings is then greater than the average utility of the winnings. Suppose, however, that he is indifferent between the gamble and the certainty of $6. The utility of $6 is then equal to his average utility from the gamble, which is 4/5.

This defines three points on a utility curve (Figure 1): for zero income, zero utility; for $10 income, 1 unit of utility; and for $6 income,

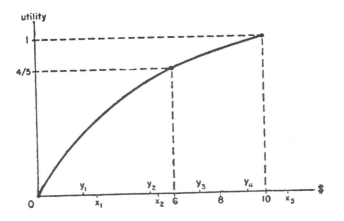

Figure 1

4/5 of a unit of utility. The first two points are arbitrarily defined; the last is obtained by finding the certain income which is equivalent to the gamble, the utility of which has been computed to be the weighted average utility of the possible outcomes.

By varying the probabilities in the gamble and setting the average utility which we can compute equal to the utility of the certain payment to which the individual is indifferent (the certainty equivalent) his entire utility curve can be constructed between $0 and $10, and by the same general method the curve can be extended still further. Such a curve is a Neumann-Morgenstern utility function. There are, of course, many such functions but they differ one from another only in the choice of a unit of measurement and the location of zero. They are all related to one another in the same way that the centigrade thermometer is related to the Fahrenheit thermometer.

Once we have constructed a Neumann-Morgenstern utility function it should, to be useful, enable us to answer all possible questions we can put to it about the choice that an individual would make among various gambles offered to him. If, for example, an individual had a choice between a gamble in which he might win any one of the amounts x_1, x_2, x_3 with various probabilities and a gamble in which he might win any one of the amounts y_1, y_2, y_3, y_4 with various probabilities, it should follow that he will choose the gamble for which the average utility of the possible outcomes is the greater. Now, it is certainly conceivable that we might find someone whose behavior in situations involving risk could not be predicted from this function by use of the simple formula of average utility or moral expectation. But the possibility that we may not be able to make correct predictions indicates simply that the von Neumann-Morgenstern postulate has empirical content and is not an empty formalism. For the postulate to be significant, one must run the risk that it might be proved wrong.

What does our intuition tell us about this matter? Is it self-evident that people who are not pathological will order their preferences among gambles so that the existence of a Neumann-Morgenstern function will be assured? I am afraid my intuition tells me very little. It is not self-evident to me that this function either does exist or does not exist.

What then can be done to answer this question? We may move in either of two directions: First, we may replace the hypothesis that there exists a Neumann-Morgenstern utility function with an axiomatic system that implies this statement as a theorem. That is, we may seek a set of statements (axioms) which are logically equivalent to the statement that a Neumann-Morgenstern utility function exists. The existence of this function is then a theorem which can be logically derived from these axioms. The purpose of finding such axioms which really say the same thing as the theorem is that it may be easier for our rather opaque intuition to accept or reject the axioms than to accept or reject the theorem itself. A Supreme Being would have no need for axioms, but they are often found quite useful for mere men. Von Neumann and Morgenstern have provided us with an axiomatic system for their utility measure as have several other writers.[3] Let me sketch one of these systems, that of Professor Marschak, in a rather carefree fashion to indicate the main idea.

Marschak's axioms or postulates are as follows:

1. An individual's preferences are completely ordered. Any two "prospects," be they gambles or certainties, can be compared in the sense that one will be either preferred or indifferent to the other. Furthermore, the ranking of prospects is transitive, which means that if A is preferred to B and B preferred to C, A is preferred to C.

2. If A is preferred to B and B to C, then there exists a probability p between 0 and 1 such that the gamble A with probability p and C with probability $1 - p$, which we shall represent as $[pA + (1 - p)C]$, will be indifferent to B. This means that some probability combination of something better and something worse can be found to make such a gamble indifferent to something in between.

3. For any object of choice or "prospect" A and for any probability p (between 0 and 1) one can specify another prospect B such that A will not be indifferent to the probability combination $[pA + (1 - p)B]$. That is to say, for example, that if A is \$10 and p is ½, one can find a sum of money such that a fifty-fifty chance of \$10 or that other sum is either better or worse than \$10. The real significance of this is that a gamble in which the probability of a given prospect of A is not 1, however close to 1 it may be, cannot always be regarded as equivalent to the certainty of A.

4. If A and B are indifferent and p is between 0 and 1, then for any prospect C, $[pA + (1 - p)C]$ is indifferent to $[pB + (1 - p)C]$. This has caused some confusion because of the possibility that B and C may be more complementary than are A and C so that one would prefer to have B and C to having A and C. This complementarity is irrelevant, however, because in a gamble of the sort considered one gets either one outcome or the other, but not both.

These axioms have strong intuitive appeal. It would seem that every

[3] Notably Jacob Marschak, "Rational Behavior, Uncertain Prospects, and Measurable Utility," *Econometrica*, April, 1950; I. N. Herstein and John Milnor, "An Axiomatic Approach to Measurable Utility," *Econometrica*, forthcoming.

normal person would clearly accept them as precepts of behavior. Now, Marschak shows that these axioms are just another way of saying that a Neumann-Morgenstern utility function exists. If you accept the axioms you are then logically required to accept the Neumann-Morgenstern theorem which can be derived from them.

Earlier I said that resort to the use of axioms is one of two methods of considering the validity of the Neumann-Morgenstern hypothesis. Another way is to find some concrete choice situations where the violation of the Neumann-Morgenstern hypothesis seems plausible or is actually revealed by observation. The following case will illustrate what I mean.

Suppose an individual is confronted with choices among these alternatives:

$$A = (\$0, p = 1)$$
$$B = (\$5, p = 1)$$
$$C = (\$10, p = 1)$$
$$D = (\tfrac{1}{2} \cdot \$0 + \tfrac{1}{2} \cdot \$10)$$
$$E = (\tfrac{1}{2} \cdot \$0 + \tfrac{1}{2} \cdot \$20)$$
$$F = (\tfrac{2}{3} \cdot \$0 + \tfrac{1}{3} \cdot \$25)$$

and that he orders these alternatives as follows, where a letter higher on the page is preferred to one that is lower.

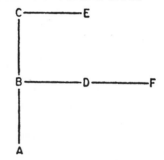

Is there anything preposterous or pathological about a person arranging his preferences in this way? Are we prepared to say that such a person would hardly be found walking the streets? I am not myself prepared to say this.

Suppose now we attempt to construct a Neumann-Morgenstern utility function for this person (Figure 2). Let the utility of A be 0 and the utility of B be 1. Then the utility of \$10 must be 2 because D is indifferent to B. The utility of \$20 must be 4 because E is indifferent to C. The utility of \$25 must then be 3 because F is indifferent to B. But

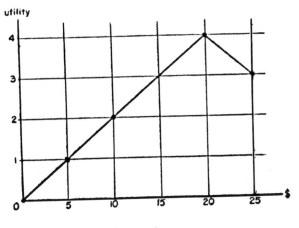

Figure 2

this says that the utility of $25 is less than the utility of $20, which is an absurdity.

Is there something unbelievable about this person's preferences or is there something unrealistic about the Neumann-Morgenstern hypothesis? This much we can note. Because E is indifferent to C and because C enters into the probability combination D, we may substitute E for C ($10) in D. This describes a new prospect $D' = [\frac{1}{2} \cdot 0 + \frac{1}{2} (\frac{1}{2} \cdot \$0 + \frac{1}{2} \cdot \$20)]$ which is a fifty-fifty chance of winning nothing or of winning a lottery ticket which provides in turn a fifty-fifty chance of winning nothing or of winning $20. Using Marschak's fourth axiom, D' is then indifferent to D. Now D' may be written more simply as $[\frac{3}{4} \cdot \$0 + \frac{1}{4} \cdot \$20]$. Transitivity requires that since D' is indifferent to D and D is indifferent to F, D' must be indifferent to F. But this means that the individual does not prefer F to D' or does not prefer having the amount to be won increased from $20 to $25 simultaneously with an increase of the probability of winning from $\frac{1}{4}$ to $\frac{1}{3}$. In other words, F differs from D' only by offering a higher probability of winning more. F would, therefore, clearly be preferred to D'. The conclusion from the axioms that F and D' are indifferent therefore involves us in a contradiction.

Is there something irrational about a man's holding these preferences and contradicting the axioms of choice which we reviewed a bit ago? The rationality of these axioms seemed self-evident, but we ought now explain just what the meaning of rational is. A test for the propriety of using the word rational here is the following. Consider any person not deemed insane who holds contradictory preferences such as those illustrated here. Imagine that we explain to this person the nature of the contradiction, pointing out clearly how his preferences violate our axioms. Will he in consequence of understanding the nature of the contradiction decide that his preferences are ill-founded and proceed to change them, or will he persist in his original preferences even though it is entirely clear to him exactly what precepts his preferences violate. If for nearly every person holding contradictory preferences an understanding of the character of the contradiction induces him to straighten out his preferences, then the Neumann-Morgenstern axioms may properly be regarded as precepts of rational choice. My own feeling is that it would be a strange man indeed who would persist in violating these precepts once he understood clearly in what way he was violating them.

But to conclude that the Neumann-Morgenstern hypothesis provides a principle of rational behavior is not to conclude that it is empirically valid. My own casual impression of human nature does not permit me to deny a priori the existence of contradictory choice structures. Even after accepting the Neumann-Morgenstern principle as a rational one, choice among risks may not be an easy thing for an untutored man to keep straight and self-contradictory preferences like faulty arithmetic may not be uncommon. This is, of course, an empirical question and one might hope that future empirical work will shed some light on this subject. I should not want to prejudge the final answer. To emphasize the possibility that the Neumann-Morgenstern theory may be an incorrect generalization about reality is, of course, also to emphasize that it is a meaningful proposition that has something to say about reality.

Here is an interesting way to illustrate the fact that the Neumann-Morgenstern hypothesis has empirical content. Consider all possible risks which entail only some probability of winning some single amount of money. Any such risk may be represented by a point on the graph (Figure 3) where the amount to be won is measured horizontally and the probability of winning that amount is measured vertically along a logarithmic axis. For example, A is a gamble offering a $1/10$ chance of winning $100. Consider now the indifference curves of an individual among these various gambles. (The probability of winning may be regarded as one commodity and the amount to be won as another). If the individual is rational according to the Neumann-Morgenstern axioms, these indifference curves will all be vertical displacements of one another, as drawn. This may be demonstrated as follows: Con-

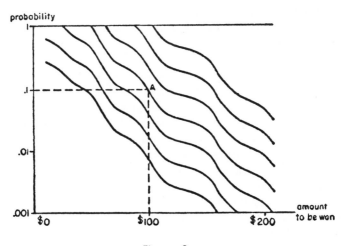

Figure 3

sider any two indifference curves such as those shown in Figure 4 and lottery tickets $A = (p_a \cdot x_a)$ and $B = (1 \cdot x_a)$, and any $C = (p_c \cdot x_c)$ which is indifferent to B. To establish that the indifference curves are vertical displacements of one another we need only show line $DC = AB$. Since A is the probability p_a of winning x_a and B the certainty of x_a we may substitute the "sure" ticket B for x_a in ticket A. A can therefore be regarded as a lottery ticket offering the probability p_a of win-

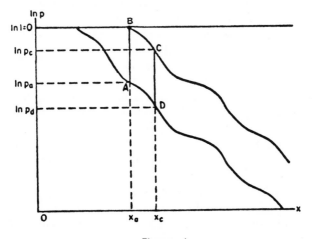

Figure 4

ning the "sure" ticket B; i.e., $A = [p_a \cdot (1 \cdot x_a)]$. Using the fourth of Marschak's axioms we may substitute C for B in A because C and B are indifferent. This defines a new lottery ticket

$$D = [p_a \cdot (p_c \cdot x_c)] = (p_a p_c \cdot x_c) = (p_d \cdot x_c)$$

which is indifferent to A. We must now show $\ln p_c - \ln p_d = \ln 1 - \ln p_a$. Since $\ln p_d = \ln p_a + \ln p_c$ and $\ln 1 = 0$, this is straightforward. Therefore, $DC = AB$, as required. Another way of stating this is that the marginal rate of substitution between the logarithm of probability and the amount to be won must be independent of the probability.

There are several further aspects of the topic being discussed here and only a few of them can yet be considered even briefly.

One question concerns the extent to which the "love of gambling" has been ignored by the theory. The "love of gambling" as a "love of danger" is clearly ruled out as behavior inconsistent with the theory (Marschak, *op. cit.*, pages 138, 139). Neumann-Morgenstern people do not play Russian Roulette. They may or may not commit suicide but they certainly do not prefer a $1/6$ probability of death to either the impossibility or the certainty of death. The cylinders of their revolvers are either completely empty or fully loaded. The attraction of gambling which derives from the pleasure of the game, the spinning of the wheel, the bouncing of the dice, the party—these things are either abstracted from or included as part of the pay off. But the desire to gamble, even when gambling is dull, is not excluded. It is, as a matter of fact, one of the main things that the theory is about. The person who takes the dull gamble with a negative expected return is said to gamble because of increasing marginal utility which means that he finds the average utility of the possible outcomes to exceed the utility of the average outcome. It is a major contribution of the theory that it provides a hypothesis to explain this.

A related point refers to the fascinating psychological experiments conducted by Ward Edwards, of Johns Hopkins, in a paper entitled, "Experiments in Economic Decision-Making in Gambling Situations" (presented at the September, 1952, meetings of the Econometric Society). Edwards observed the preferences of subjects among various lottery tickets and found that he could explain their choices very neatly (in my opinion, more neatly than the von Neumann-Morgenstern utility function could explain them) in terms of assumed preferences for certain probabilities and dislikes of other probabilities. His subjects seem to have been attracted by certain probabilities and repelled by others independently of the winnings associated with them. Only small amounts of money were involved, however, and the probability preferences he found may well have been inconsequential and overpowered by Neumann-Morgenstern considerations had larger amounts been at stake.

Granted the existence of a Neumann-Morgenstern utility function, we have only found a particular measure of utility that proves to be highly manageable for dealing with problems of risk. We have in no way denied that other utility functions which are not Neumann-Morgenstern functions may just as correctly be defined. If U_1 in Figure 5 is a Neumann-Morgenstern function in terms of which we can predict a person's choices, then U_2, which is not a Neumann-

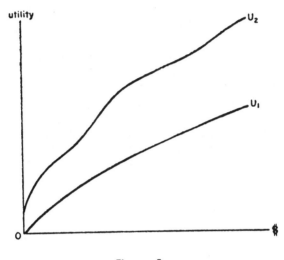

Figure 5

Morgenstern function but which increases monotonically with U_1, will be equally correct. It will simply be more cumbersome in making the same predictions. This everyone has come to recognize, especially since William Baumol's note which insisted on the point ("The Neumann-Morgenstern Utility Index—An Ordinalist View," *Journal of Political Economy,* February, 1951). This means we have not reverted to the concept of a unique measure of utility in the sense in which cardinal utility was originally conceived. The behavioristic definition of utility as the value of any function the individual may be said to maximize has not been scuttled for the earlier, hedonistic concept of utility as a psychological quantity. The measure of utility provided by von Neumann and Morgenstern cannot therefore rehabilitate the utilitarian brand of welfare economics which requires the maximization of some scalar function of the cardinal utilities of the individuals in a society. For welfare economics there is no more reason to accept U_1 than to accept U_2.

Furthermore, the acceptance of the von Neumann-Morgenstern measure does not preclude the definition of still other measures. It is true that the von Neumann-Morgenstern measure is convenient and manageable for the class of problems involving risk, but it need not prove convenient for all classes of utility problems that may conceivably arise. Nothing rules out the usefulness of another measure for another purpose. And certainly no hypotheses about measurable utility can rebut the merits of the ordinal, indifference curve analysis of consumer behavior under certainty which seems to require the definition of no particular measure and which therefore does not impose unnecessary further restrictions on the nature of reality.

I should not want these final cautions concerning the use of the Neumann-Morgenstern measure to detract from the significance of this subject. Von Neumann and Morgenstern have given us an empirically meaningful and provocative hypothesis about economic behavior that may contribute substantially to a broad area of economic analysis. They have also straightened out the thinking of economists about the meaning of measurement and cleared aside the major misunderstanding that hampered the earlier disputations of cardinalists and ordinalists.[4]

[4] The reader who is interested in reading further on this subject is referred to the references already cited and in addition to J. Marschak, "Why 'Should' Statisticians and Businessmen Maximize Moral Expectation?" in J. Neyman, ed., *Proceedings of the Second Berkeley Symposium on Mathematical Statistics and Probability*, 1951; Milton Friedman and L. J. Savage, "The Utility Analysis of Choices Involving Risk," *Journal of Political Economy*, August, 1948; Frederick Mosteller and Philip Nogee, "An Experimental Measurement of Utility," *Journal of Political Economy*, October, 1951; and Milton Friedman and L. J. Savage, "The Expected-Utility Hypothesis and the Measurability of Utility," *Journal of Political Economy*, December, 1952.

SUPPLY AND THE THEORY OF THE FIRM

13

COST CURVES AND SUPPLY CURVES *

JACOB VINER is Professor Emeritus at Princeton University; he was formerly at the University of Chicago.

It is the primary purpose of this article to develop a graphical exposition of the manner in which supply curves are dependent upon the different possible types of technological and pecuniary cost situations, under the usual assumptions of atomistic competition and of rational economic behavior on the part of the producers. No attempt is made here at realistic description of the actual types of relationship between costs and supply, and the purpose is the more modest one of presenting the formal types of relationship which can be conceived to exist under certain simplifying assumptions. Analysis of this kind derives obviously from the path-breaking contribution of Alfred Marshall in his Principles of Economics. Interest in this type of problem has been largely confined to the Anglo-Saxon countries, and in these countries there has been a tendency until recent years for economists to accept and reproduce the general lines of Marshall's analysis somewhat uncritically and without much further elaboration. I have no very serious fundamental criticism to make of Marshall's analysis of the supply side of the exchange value problem. But Marshall's treatment is highly elliptical. A striking illustration of his tendency to telescope his argument is his common practice in his graphs of labelling cost curves and supply curves alike with the symbols *ss*, conventionally used for supply curves, and thus diverting the attention of his readers, and perhaps also occasionally his own attention, from the necessity of selecting from among the many possible types of cost curve that one which in the given circumstances alone has claims to being considered as also a supply curve. Marshall, moreover, although he made valuable additions to the conceptual terminology necessary for analysis of this type, nevertheless worked with vocabulary lacking sufficient terms to distinguish clearly from each other all the significant types of cost phenomena, and here also the terminological poverty tended to lead to inadequate classifica-

* From *Zeitschrift für Nationalökonomie*, Vol. III (September, 1931), pp. 23–46. Reprinted, by the courtesy of Springer-Verlag and the author, without change from the original text, with the addition of a supplementary note.

tion not only on the part of his followers but on his own part. Marshall's analysis was excessively simple even on the basis of his own simplifying assumptions, and inadequately precise in formulation, and his followers have standardized an even simpler type of exposition of the relationship of cost to price.

In recent years a number of English economists, notably Pigou, Sraffa, Shove, Harrod and Robertson, have presented in the Economic Journal a series of criticisms, elaborations, and refinements of the Marshallian analysis which, in my opinion, go a long way both towards bringing out clearly the contribution contained in its implications as well as in its explicit formulations, and towards completing and correcting it where that is necessary. The indebtedness of the present paper to their writings is considerable and is freely acknowledged. But I have been presenting charts such as those contained in this article to my students at the University of Chicago for a long period antedating the writings referred to above, and if in the course of years these charts have undergone substantial revision and, as I am convinced, correction, chief credit is due to the penetrating criticisms of my students.

The analysis which follows is based on the usual assumptions and presuppositions of the Marshallian type of economics. As compared to the Lausanne School type of analysis, it contents itself with examination of the conditions of a partial equilibrium of a special sort, and does not inquire into the repercussions of the postulated changes in cost or demand conditions on the general equilibrium situation. Like all partial equilibrium analysis, including the allegedly "general" equilibrium theories of the Lausanne School, it rests on assumptions of the *caeteris paribus* order which posit independence where in fact there is some degree of dependence. For such logically invalid assumptions there is the pragmatic defense that they permit of more detailed analysis of certain phases of economic interdependence than would be possible in their absence, and that to the extent that they are fictions uncompensated by counterbalancing fictions, it is reasonable to believe that the errors in the results obtained will be almost invariably quantitative rather than qualitative in character, and will generally be even quantitatively of minor importance. As compared to the Austrian School, there is, I believe, no need either for reconciliation or for apology. On the somewhat superficial level on which analysis of the present type is conducted the basic issue as between the English and the Austrian Schools does not enter explicitly into the picture, and in so far as it has any bearing on the conclusions, this bearing is again quantitative rather than qualitative in character. The Austrian School starts with the assumption, usually tacit, never emphasized, that the supplies of all the elementary factors of production are given and independent of their rates of remuneration. The English School emphasizes, perhaps overemphasizes, the dependence of the amounts of certain of the elementary factors, notably labor and waiting, on their rates of remuneration. The techniques of analysis of each school are in essentials identical, and each school, if it were to apply its techniques to the situation postulated by the other, would reach identical conclusions. The difference in the assumptions of the two schools has bearing on the quantitative but not on the qualitative behavior of the prices of the elementary factors and therefore also of the money costs of their products, as the demands for these factors and products change. The conflict between the two schools has greater significance for the theory of the value of the elementary factors of production, i.e., for the theory of distribution, than for the theory of particular commodity price determination. For the present analysis, where it is assumed either that the prices of the elementary factors remain unaltered or that they undergo changes of a kind consistent with the basic assumptions of either school, the differences between the two schools would not affect qualitatively the character of the findings. All of the propositions laid down in this paper should, I believe, be acceptable to, or else should be rejected by, both schools.

The procedure which will be followed, will be to begin in each case with the mode of adjustment of a particular concern to the given market situation when the industry as a whole is supposed to be in stable equilibrium. This particular concern is not to be regarded as having any close relationship to Marshall's "representative firm." It will not be assumed to be necessarily typical of its industry with respect to its size, its efficiency, or the rate of slope of its various cost curves, but it will be assumed to be typical, or at least to represent the prevailing situation, with respect to the general qualitative behavior of its costs as it varies its own output or, in certain situations, as the industry of which it is part varies its output. All long-run differences in efficiency as between concerns will be assumed, however, to be compensated for by differential rates of compensation to the factors responsible for such differences and these differential rates will be treated as parts of the ordinary long-run money costs of production of the different concerns. In the long-run, therefore, every concern will be assumed to have the same total costs per unit, except where explicit statement to the contrary is made. It will be assumed, further, that for any industry, under long-run equilibrium conditions, the same relationships must exist for every concern between its average costs, its marginal costs, and market place, as for the particular concern under special examination. But the reasoning of this paper will still hold if the realistic concession were made that in every industry there may be a few concerns which are not typical of their industry with respect to the qualitative behavior of their costs as output is varied either by themselves or by the industry as a whole, and which therefore do not wholly conform to these assumptions. It may be conceded, for instance, that in an industry in which for most producers expansion of their output means lower unit costs there should be a few producers for whom the reverse is true.

SHORT-RUN EQUILIBRIUM FOR AN INDIVIDUAL CONCERN

Chart I, which represents the behavior of money costs in the short-run for a single concern with a plant of a given scale, is the fundamental graph, and is incorporated in or underlies all the succeeding ones.[1] It

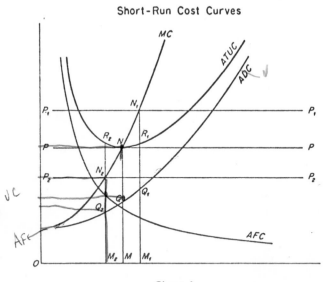

Short-Run Cost Curves

Chart I

[1] The charts were drawn for me by Y. K. Wong of the University of Chicago. Where in any chart one curve is derived from another or a combination of other curves presented in the same chart, it is drawn mathematically to scale. No attempt has been made, however, to maintain the same scales as between different charts. An attempt has been made to use mnemonic symbols for the various curves, MC for instance indicating marginal cost, P indicating price, and so forth. It is hoped that this will facilitate reading of the charts.

is assumed that this concern is not of sufficient importance to bring about any change in the prices of the factors as a result of a change in its output. Since unit money costs of production are the sum of the products of the amounts of the factors used in the production of one unit multiplied by the prices of the factors, any change in unit money costs as output varies must in this case be due, therefore, to changes in the amounts of the factors required for the production of one unit, or, to use Walras' term, to changes in the "technological coefficients of production." The "short-run" is taken to be a period which is long enough to permit of any desired change of output technologically possible without altering the scale of plant, but which is not long enough to permit of any adjustment of scale of plant. It will be arbitrarily assumed that all of the factors can for the short-run be sharply classified into two groups, those which are necessarily fixed in amount, and those which are freely variable. "Scale of plant" will be used as synonymous with the size of the group of factors which are fixed in amount in the short-run, and each scale will be quantitatively indicated by the amount of output which can be produced at the lowest average cost possible at that scale. The costs associated with the fixed factors will be referred to as the "fixed costs" and those associated with the variable factors will be called the "direct costs." It is to be noted that the "fixed costs" are fixed only in their aggregate amounts and vary with output in their amount per unit, while the "direct costs" are variable in their aggregate amount as output varies, as well as, ordinarily at least, in their amount per unit. Amounts of output are in this as in all the succeeding charts measured along the horizontal axis from O, and money costs and prices along the vertical axis from O.

The curve AFC represents the trend of the average fixed costs per unit as output is increased. Since these are the costs associated with the parts of the working combination which, by hypothesis, are absolutely fixed in their aggregate amount, this curve must be a rectangular hyperbola.[2] The curve ADC represents the trend of average direct costs per unit as output is increased. Since the increase in output is the result of the application, to a constant amount of "fixed" factors, of increased amounts of the variable factors, the law of diminishing returns, if it is operating, should make the output per unit of the variable factor employed diminish, i.e., should make the "direct" technical coefficients of production increase, as total output increases. As the prices of the factors by assumption remain constant, the average direct costs must also increase as output increases, if the law of diminishing returns is operative. It is assumed, not, I believe, without justification,

[2] I.e., the equation to the curve will be of the form $xy = c$.

that within the useful range of observation the law of diminishing returns is operative, and the average direct cost curve is therefore drawn positively inclined throughout.[3] The curve *ATUC* represents the trend of average total (i.e., fixed plus direct) unit costs as output is increased, and is, of course, the sum of the ordinates of the *ADC* and *AFC* curves. It is necessarily *U*-shaped for all industries having any substantial fixed costs, and is in this respect a universal short-run curve qualitatively descriptive of the short-run behavior of average costs of practically all concerns and all industries which cannot quickly and completely adjust the amounts of all the factors they use to variations in their rates of output. But the relative lengths and the relative rates of inclination of the negatively inclined and the positively inclined portions of the curve will differ from concern to concern and from industry to industry, depending upon the relative importance of the fixed to the total costs and upon the degree of sharpness with which the law of diminishing returns is operative for the variable factors. The curve *MC* represents the trend of marginal costs as output is increased. Any point on it represents the increase in aggregate costs as output at that point is increased by one unit.[4]

The marginal cost curve must cut the average cost curve at the lowest point of the latter. At the point of intersection, average cost and marginal cost are of course equal. But average cost is equal to marginal cost only when average cost is constant, i.e., when the average cost curve is a horizontal line.[5] The point of intersection of the marginal cost curve with the average cost curve when the latter is concave

---

[3] It is also drawn concave upward, to indicate the progressively sharper operation of the law of diminishing returns as the fixed factors are more intensively exploited.

[4] If y_a = average fixed cost per unit, y_b = average direct cost per unit, and x = output, then ATUC = $y_a + y_b$, and $MC = \dfrac{d[(y_a + y_b)x]}{dx}$. It is important to note that no consideration need be given to the fixed costs, if they really are absolutely fixed, in computing the marginal cost. Since $xy_a = c$, and $\dfrac{dc}{dx} = o, \ldots \dfrac{d[(y_a + y_b)x]}{dx} = \dfrac{d(xy_b)}{dx}$.

[5] If x = output, and y = average cost, marginal cost = $\dfrac{d(xy)}{dx}$. If $y = c$, then $\dfrac{d(xy)}{dx} = y$. If y is an increasing function of x then $\dfrac{d(xy)}{dx} > y$. If y is a decreasing function of x, then $\dfrac{d(xy)}{dx} < y$.

upwards must therefore be at the lowest point of the latter, where its tangent is a horizontal line.[6]

If this particular producer is an insignificant factor in his industry, i.e., if atomistic competition prevails, he may reasonably assume that no change in his output, and especially no change consistent with the maintenance of the scale of plant at its original level, will have any appreciable effect on the price of his product. Under these conditions, the partial demand curve for his product may be taken as a horizontal line whose ordinate from the base is equal to the prevailing price.[7] It will be to his interest to carry production to the point where marginal cost equals price, i.e., his short-run MC curve will also be his rational short-run supply curve. If price is MN, this will mean an output of OM and no extra profit or loss on his operations, i.e., the quasi-rent on his fixed investment per unit of output, NQ, would be equal to the fixed costs per unit. If price is P_1, output will be OM_1, and the quasi-rent per unit of output, N_1Q_1, will be in excess of the fixed costs per unit, R_1Q_1. If P_2 is the price, the output will be OM_2, and the quasi-rent per unit of output will be N_2Q_2, or less than the fixed costs per unit, R_2Q_2. All of these situations are consistent with short-run equilibrium, which, as far as individual producers are concerned, requires only that marginal cost equal price. The short-run supply curve for the industry as a whole is not shown in this chart, but is simply the sum of the abscissae of the individual short-run marginal cost ($=$ individual supply) curves.[8]

LONG-RUN EQUILIBRIUM

The long-run is taken to be a period long enough to permit each producer to make such technologically possible changes in the scale of his plant as he desires, and thus to vary his output either by a more or less intensive utilization of existing plant, or by varying the scale of his plant, or by some combination of these methods. There will therefore be no costs which are technologically fixed in the long-run,[9] and

---

[6] For a mathematical proof, see Henry Schultz, "Marginal Productivity and the Pricing Process," *The Journal of Political Economy,* Vol. XXXVIII (1929), p. 537, note 33.

[7] This is equivalent to saying that the partial demand for his product has infinite elasticity.

[8] It is shown in Chart II.

[9] This is, of course, not inconsistent with the proposition that at any moment within the long-run there will be costs which from the short-run point of view are fixed.

if in fact the scale of plant is not altered as long-run output alters, it will be the result of voluntary choice and not of absolute technological compulsion. For an industry as a whole long-run variations in output can result from more or less intensive use of existing plants, or from changes in the scale of plants, or from changes in the number of plants, or from some combination of these. Under long-run equilibrium conditions changes in output, whether by an individual producer or by the industry as a whole, will be brought about by the economically optimum method from the point of view of the individual producers, so that each producer will have the optimum scale of plant for his long-run output. To simplify the analysis, it will be assumed that in each industry the optimum type of adjustment to a long-run variation in output for that industry as a whole will not only be alike for all producers but will involve only one of the three possible methods of adjustment listed above; namely, change in intensity of use of existing plants, change in scale of plants, and change in number of plants. The theoretical static long-run, it should be noted, is a sort of "timeless" long-run throughout which nothing new happens except the full mutual adjustment to each other of the primary factors existing at the beginning of the long-run period. It is more correct, therefore, to speak of long-run equilibrium in terms of the conditions which will prevail after a long-run, rather than during a long-run. Long-run equilibrium, once established, will continue only for an instant of time if some change in the primary conditions should occur immediately after equilibrium in terms of the pre-existing conditions had been reached. The only significance of the equilibrium concept for realistic price theory is that it offers a basis for prediction of the direction of change when equilibrium is not established. Long before a static equilibrium has actually been established, some dynamic change in the fundamental factors will ordinarily occur which will make quantitative changes in the conditions of equilibrium. The ordinary economic situation is one of disequilibrium moving in the direction of equilibrium rather than of realized equilibrium.

For long-run equilibrium not only must marginal cost of output from existent plant equal price for each individual producer, but it must also equal average cost. If this were not the case, there would be either abnormal profits or losses, which would operate either to attract capital into the industry or to induce withdrawal of capital from the industry, and in either case would tend to bring about a change in output. For long-run equilibrium it is further necessary not only that each producer shall be producing his portion of the total output by what is for him, under existing conditions, the optimum method, but that no other producer, whether already in the industry or not, shall be in a position to provide an equivalent amount of output, in addition to what he may already be contributing, at a lower cost. The relations of costs to supply in the long-run will depend on the technological conditions under which output can be most economically varied, and the succeeding discussion will consist in large part of a classification and analysis of these conceivable types of technological conditions.

"RICARDIAN" INCREASING COSTS

Chart II illustrates a special case corresponding to the Ricardian rent theory in its strictest form. Let us suppose that a given industry is already utilizing all of the supply available at any price of a necessary factor of production, so that the output of the industry as a whole can

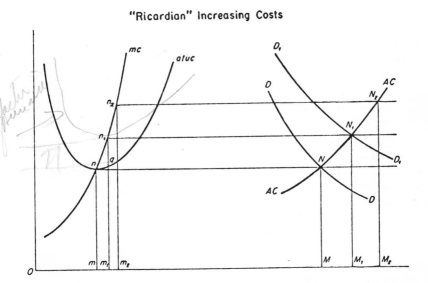

"Ricardian" Increasing Costs

Chart II

be increased only by the more intensive utilization of the absolutely limited factor. Suppose also that no appreciable economies are to be derived, whatever the output of the industry as a whole, by a combination into larger productive units, or a subdivision into smaller productive units, of the existing concerns. In order further to simplify the analysis, it is assumed that the identical portions of the working-

combination which in this case remain technologically fixed in amount
whatever may be the short-run variations in output also remain economically fixed in amount whatever long-run variations in output may
occur. If the particular concern whose costs are indicated in the left-
hand portion of Chart II and the particular concern with which Chart
I is concerned were identical, and if the two charts were drawn to the
same scale, the MC curve in Chart I and the mc curve in Chart II
would be identical, although the former represents the short-run trend
and the latter represents the long-run trend of marginal costs as output
is varied, i.e., for these assumptions, the short-run and the long-run
marginal cost curves would be identical. The $atuc$ curve in Chart II,
continuing these assumptions, would simply represent the short-run
variations in average cost for this particular concern as output was
varied, when long-run price was mn or MN,[10] and would be in all
respects identical with the $ATUC$ curve of Chart I. When long-run
price was MN, this concern would be in both short-run and long-run
equilibrium when its output was Om, and its average cost, its marginal
cost, and price were all equal.

Suppose now, that owing to a long-run increase of market demand
from DD to D_1D_1, long-run price rises to M_1N_1. It will pay our producer to increase his output to Om_1, at which point the new marginal
cost, m_1n_1, will be equal to the new price. If the prices of all the factors remain the same, the new price will be higher than the new average cost m_1q. But it is impossible, for a case such as this, to adhere to
the assumption that the prices of all the factors remain the same.
Given an absolutely limited amount of one of the factors, no change
in the prices of the other factors, and a rise in the long-run demand for
and in the long-run price of its product, and the long-run price of this
absolutely scarce factor must rise. Let us suppose that the fixed factor
is land. Its price or rent will rise until there ceases to be any excess of
marginal over average cost. The $atuc$ curve in Chart II therefore has
only short-run significance. A long-run increase in the price of the
product will cause an increase in the price of land-use, and therefore a
rise in the entire $atuc$ curve. The increase in land-rent, however, will
have no effect on marginal costs, and therefore on the long-run mc
curve, for it will be due to the increase in price of the product and not
to the increase in output of this particular concern. Even if this producer maintained his output at Om, after long-run price had risen to
M_1N_1, the $atuc$ curve would rise in the same manner and degree. It
would always shift upward in such a way, however, that the mc curve

---

[10] The qualifying phrase in italics is important. Its significance is explained in the
next paragraph of the text.

would intersect it at its lowest point,[11] i.e., rent for land would rise just sufficiently to make the new lowest average cost equal to the new equilibrium marginal cost. When the long-run price was M_1N_1, therefore, average cost, marginal cost, and price would be equal for each producer under long-run equilibrium.

The AC curve in the right-hand portion of Chart II represents the long-run supply curve for the industry as a whole, and is simply the sum of the abscissas of the individual mc curves. It is also a long-run average cost curve for the industry as a whole inclusive of rent, and a long-run marginal cost curve for the industry as a whole exclusive of rent. For the individual producer, the changes in rent payments required as demand changes are due primarily to the changes in demand, secondarily to the changes in output of the industry as a whole, and only to an insignificant degree to his own changes in output. The individual will therefore not take the effect on his rent payments of increased output on his own part into account, and the supply curve for the industry as a whole will therefore be the marginal cost curve for the industry as a whole exclusive of rent.[12]

This appears to be the case usually designated in the textbooks as the case of "increasing costs." I have labelled it as "Ricardian increasing costs" to indicate its close relationship to the Ricardian rent theory. It is to be noted that as output increases the long-run average costs rise even if the increase of rents is disregarded and that there are increasing unit technological costs, therefore, whether the technical coefficients are weighted by the original or by the new prices of the factors. There are increasing marginal costs in every possible sense of the term costs.

11 Each successive short-run $atuc$ curve of a particular producer, as the long-run price of his product rises, consists of the ordinates of his former $atuc$ curve plus a new rent charge fixed in total amount regardless of his output, and therefore of the form $xy = c$. As was pointed out in note 4, page 202, the vertical addition of a rectangular hyperbola to an average cost curve does not affect the marginal cost curve derivable from it. The same mc curve can, therefore, continue to be the short-run marginal cost curve, even when the short-run average cost curve is undergoing long-run changes consistently with the conditions assumed in this case.

12 For the industry as a whole, however, the increase of output as demand increases will affect rent, on the one hand by influencing price and gross receipts, and on the other hand by influencing gross expenses. Depending upon the shift in position and the elasticity of the demand curve and upon the rate of slope of the industry marginal cost curve exclusive of rent, an increase of output when demand increases may make rent either greater or less than if output were kept constant. But under atomistic competition the possible results of keeping output constant when demand rises will play no part in the determination of output, of price, or of rent.

If mc were the short-run marginal cost curve for a scale adapted to a long-run equilibrium output of Om, and if not all the factors which were technologically fixed in the short-run remained economically fixed in the long-run as output was increased, then, since there would be less scope for the operation of the law of diminishing returns, the long-run marginal cost curve for the particular concern would be different from and less steeply inclined than the mc curve, and the new short-run $atuc_1$ curve for a long-run equilibrium scale of output of, for example, Om_1 would have no simple relationship to the $atuc$ curve in Chart II. Similarly, the long-run supply curve for the industry as a whole, since it is the sum of the abscissas of the individual long-run marginal cost curves, would then also be less steeply inclined than the AC curve in Chart II, which would then be only a short-run supply curve for the industry as a whole, when the long-run equilibrium output of the industry was OM.

CONSTANT COSTS

In the short-run, for industries which have any fixed costs whatsoever, constant marginal costs as output is varied are wholly inconceivable if the law of diminishing returns is operative, and constant average costs are inconceivable if there are increasing marginal costs as required by the law of diminishing returns.[13]

In the long-run, however, constant costs are theoretically conceivable under two kinds of circumstances. The first case is when each producer can vary his scale of production without affecting his long-run average costs. The situation in this case for any individual concern will be as represented in Chart III. The curves $atuc_1$ and mc_1 represent, respectively, the short-run trends of average and marginal costs as output is varied from a plant of scale OA. The curves $atuc_2$ and mc_2, similarly represent, respectively, the short-run trends of average and marginal costs as output is varied from a plant of scale OB; and similarly, for scales OC and OD. In the long-run any output would be produced from the optimum scale for this output. The long-run average cost curve would therefore be the horizontal line AC, which passes through the lowest points of all the short-run $atuc$ curves. Where

---

[13] Let x = output, y_a = average fixed costs per unit, y_b = average direct costs per unit, and c and k be two different constants. Suppose that short-run average costs are constant, i.e., that $y_a + y_b = k$. But $xy_a = c$. Then $xy_b = kx - c$, and marginal cost, or $\dfrac{d(xy_b)}{dx} = \dfrac{d(kx - c)}{dx} = k$, which is inconsistent with the law of diminishing returns.

Constant Costs

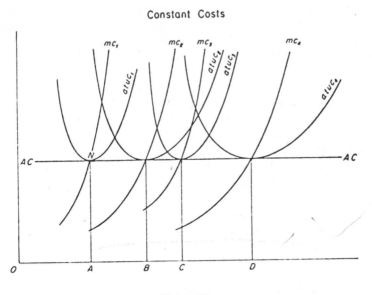

Chart III

average costs are constant as output varies, average cost and marginal cost are always identical.[14] This horizontal line would therefore also be the individual producer's long-run supply curve.

This case presents certain difficulties when perfect competition prevails which make it impossible to indicate graphically the relationship between the long-run supply curves of the individual concern and the industry as a whole. Read as an ordinary supply curve, the AC line indicates that in the long-run this concern would be unwilling to operate at any price under AN, would be willing to produce any amount at a price AN, and would be anxious to produce unlimited quantities at any price over AN. If the costs of different producers in the industry are not uniform, then the lowest cost concern would tend to monopolize the industry. If the costs of different producers are uniform, the supply curve for the industry would be indefinite, and in the long-run there would be a constant tendency toward overproduction, with consequent losses and a reaction toward underproduction. Actual long-run price and output would be unstable, but would oscillate above and below stable points of equilibrium price and equilibrium output.

14 See note 5, page 202.

The second conceivable case of long-run constant costs, not illustrated graphically here, would be presented by a situation in which all of the concerns within the industry and an indefinite number of potential members of the industry can operate at long-run minimum average costs uniform as between the different concerns, but with average costs increasing for each as its output increases. The long-run output of the industry would then consist of the sum of the outputs of all the member concerns, each operating at that scale at which its costs are at the minimum common to all, and variations of output for the industry as a whole would result wholly from variations in the number of producers, each of whom would maintain a constant output while he remained in the industry. For the industry as a whole, therefore, long-run production would take place under conditions of constant long-run average and marginal cost, uniform for all producers and equal to each other, although each concern would be operating subject to short-run increasing average and marginal costs. Here also actual long-run price and output for the industry as a whole would tend to be unstable, but would oscillate above and below stable points of equilibrium price output.

The situation would in these two cases be somewhat analogous to that of a thermostatic control which aims at maintaining a uniform temperature, which is stimulated into operation only when there is a significant degree of variation from the desired temperature, and which succeeds only in keeping the ever-present variations from the desired temperature from exceeding narrow limits in either direction. Completely stable equilibrium under constant cost conditions is only conceivable on the assumption of some departure from perfect competition, in consequence of which variations in output by individual producers, or entrance into the industry by new producers or withdrawal of old, are subject to some difficulty even in the long-run after the equilibrium price and output have once been momentarily established.

NET INTERNAL ECONOMIES OF LARGE-SCALE PRODUCTION

We owe to Marshall the important distinction between the "internal" and the "external" economies resulting from increased output. For present purposes we will use the term "net internal economies of large-scale production" to mean net reductions in costs to a particular concern resulting from a long-run expansion in its output when each output is produced from a plant of the optimum scale for that output. The word "net" is introduced to make it clear that increase in output may result at the same time in economies and in diseconomies and that it is only the excess of the former over the latter to which reference is made here. Internal economies of large-scale production are primarily a long-run phenomenon, dependent upon appropriate adjustment of scale of plant to each successive output. They should not be confused with the economies resulting from "spreading of overhead," which are a short-run phenomenon, represented by the negative inclination of the average fixed cost curve in Chart I. Internal economies of large-scale production need not be relatively greater for those particular costs which in the short-run are the fixed costs than for those particular costs which in the short-run are the direct costs. In the long-run, in any case, there are no technologically fixed or overhead costs, if the definitions here followed of "long-run" and of "fixed costs" are adhered to. Internal economies of large-scale production are independent of the size of output of the industry as a whole, and may be accruing to a particular concern whose output is increasing at the same time that the output of the industry as a whole is undergoing a decline. It is for this reason that Marshall gave them the name of internal, to distinguish them from the external economies which are dependent on something outside of the particular concerns themselves, namely, the size of output of the industry as a whole.

Internal economies may be either technological or pecuniary, that is, they may consist either in reductions of the technological coefficients of production or in reductions in the prices paid for the factors as the result of increases in the amounts thereof purchased. Illustrations of technological internal economies would be savings in the labor, materials, or equipment requirements per unit of output resulting from improved organization or methods of production made possible by a larger scale of operations. Pecuniary internal economies, on the other hand, would consist of advantages in buying, such as "quantity discounts" or the ability to hire labor at lower rates, resulting from an increase in the scale of purchases.[15]

Chart IV illustrates the behavior of the cost curves for a particular concern which enjoys net internal economies of large-scale production. As in Chart III the *ac* curves and the *mc* curves represent the short-run variations in average and marginal costs respectively, as output is varied from plants of each indicated scale. The *AC* curve represents the long-run trend of average costs, that is, the trend of average costs when

---

15 Pecuniary internal economies are, theoretically, as likely to result from expansion of output from a given plant as from expansion of output brought about by increase of scale of plant. But it is only the latter form of expansion of output which is likely to be great enough to result in significant pecuniary internal economies.

Net Internal Economies of Large-Scale Production

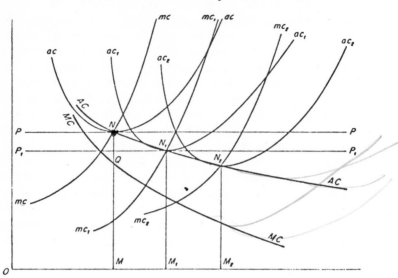

Chart IV

each output is produced from a plant of the optimum scale for that output, and is drawn so as to connect the points of lowest average cost for each scale of plant.[16] The MC curve is the long-run marginal curve for this particular concern when the AC curve is interpreted as a continuous curve. It represents the increment in aggregate costs resulting from a unit increase in output, when each output is produced from a plant of the optimum scale for that output. It is to be noted

[16] The AC curve would represent a continuous trend only if it is assumed that scale of plant can be modified by small increments. If the curve is interpreted as a discontinuous one, then only the points N, N_1, N_2, . . . on it are significant, and the significant long-run costs for the intervals between are the lowest short-run average costs available for the indicated outputs. It may be noticed that at certain points the short-run ac curves are drawn so as to sink below the long-run AC curve. If the AC curve is interpreted as having significance only at the N points, this is of no consequence. But if the AC curve is interpreted as a continuous curve, this is an error. My instructions to the draftsman were to draw the AC curve so as never to be above any portion of any ac curve. He is a mathematician, however, not an economist, and he saw some mathematical objection to this procedure which I could not succeed in understanding. I could not persuade him to disregard his scruples as a craftsman and to follow my instructions, absurd though they might be.

that while the short-run marginal cost curves are positively inclined, the long-run marginal cost curve is negatively inclined.[17]

The familiar proposition that net internal economies of large-scale production and long-run equilibrium are inconsistent under competitive conditions is clearly illustrated by this chart. When price is MN, this concern, if operating with the scale of plant represented by the short-run curves ac and mc, is in short-run equilibrium when its output is OM, for its short-run marginal cost is then equal to price. It will not be in long-run equilibrium, however, for its long-run marginal cost will then be only MQ, or less than price. Provided that no change in its output will affect market price, it will pay this concern to enlarge its plant whatever the price may be, and whatever its existing scale of plant may be. If thereby it grows so large that its operations exert a significant influence on price, we pass out of the realm of atomistic competition and approach that of partial monopoly. Even then, however, it would still be profitable for this concern to enlarge its plant and increase its output as long as long-run marginal cost was lower than long-run marginal revenue, or the increment in aggregate receipts resulting from a unit increment in output, after allowance for any reduction in price.[18]

[17] If y, y_1, y_2, are the short-run average costs for scales of plant, OM, OM_1, and OM_2, respectively, as indicated by the ac curves; Y = long-run average cost, as indicated by the AC curve; x = output; mc, mc_1, and mc_2 indicate the short-run marginal costs as represented by the mc curves; and MC indicates the long-run marginal cost, as represented by the MC curve, then:

$$mc = \frac{d(xy)}{dx}; \ mc_1 = \frac{d(xy_1)}{dx}; \ mc_2 = \frac{d(xy_2)}{dx}; \text{ and } MC = \frac{d(xY)}{dx};$$

$$\text{and } \frac{d^2(xy)}{dx^2} > 0; \text{ and } \frac{d^2(xY)}{dx^2} < 0.$$

[18] If Y_p = long-run price, X = long-run output, and Y_c = long-run average cost, long-run marginal cost would be $\frac{d(XY_c)}{dX}$, long-run marginal revenue would be $\frac{d(XY_p)}{dX}$, and it would pay to carry production to the point where long-run marginal cost equalled long-run marginal revenue, or $\frac{d(XY_c)}{dX} = \frac{d(XY_p)}{dX}$. Under atomistic competition, $\frac{d(XY_p)}{dX} = Y_p$, which is independent of this particular concern's output. Whatever the price, therfore, this concern would always have an incentive to increase its long-run output as long as long-run marginal cost remained less than that price. If partial monopoly resulted, however, marginal revenue, or $\frac{d(XY_p)}{dX}$, would become a function of market demand and of competi-

For any particular concern operating under these conditions, and *a fortiori* for an industry as a whole consisting of such concerns, there is no definite long-run supply curve. At any price *MN* higher than the asymptote of the *AC* curve, this producer will be willing to produce any quantity not less than *OM*.

To negatively-inclined long-run cost curves such as the *AC* and *MC* curves in Chart IV, Marshall has denied the characteristic of "reversibility," i.e., of equal validity whether output is increasing or decreasing, on the ground that some of the economies accruing when the output of a concern, or of an industry as a whole, is increased will be retained if the output of the concern or of the industry returns to its original dimensions.[19] This reasoning appears to involve a confusion between static and dynamic cost curves. The reductions in costs as output is increased indicated by curves such as the *AC* and *MC* curves in Chart IV are purely functions of size of output when scale is adjusted to output and not of lapse of actual time during which improved processes may happen to be discovered. The economies associated with output *OM* are economies which are not available for any output less than *OM*. The only basis on which the irreversibility of these curves, as static curves, could logically be posited would be the existence of possible economies of a type adapted to any scale of output but discoverable only when output is great, where invention, but not its exploitation, was a function of scale of output.

NET INTERNAL DISECONOMIES OF LARGE-SCALE PRODUCTION

Cases are clearly conceivable where increase of scale of plant would involve less efficient operation and consequently higher unit costs. The prevailing opinion in the United States that for most types of agriculture the one-family farm is still the optimum mode of agricultural organization would indicate that in this country at least agriculture was subject to net internal diseconomies of large-scale production after an early stage in the size of the farm-unit had been reached. But when increase of output by means of the increase of scale of existing plants involves a substantial increase in unit costs, it will always be possible

tor's supply and would be smaller than Y_p, and a point of stable long-run equilibrium might exist, depending on how the other producers reacted to variations in output by this one. If complete monopoly resulted, there would probably be a definite point of stable equilibrium. These questions, however, are beyond the range of this paper.

[19] *Principles of Economics*, 8th ed., 1922, p. 808.

for the industry as a whole to avoid the net internal diseconomies of large-scale production by increasing its output through increase in number of plants without increase in their scale.[20] This case has no practical importance, therefore, except as it represents an economic barrier against increase in scale of plants, and it is not worth while to illustrate it graphically.

NET EXTERNAL ECONOMIES OF LARGE PRODUCTION

External economies are those which accrue to particular concerns as the result of the expansion of output by their industry as a whole, and which are independent of their own individual outputs. If an industry which enjoys net external economies of large production increases its output—presumably through increase in number of plants—the average costs of the member concerns of that industry will fall even though each concern maintains a constant scale of plant and a constant output. Like internal economies, external economies may be either technological or pecuniary. Illustrations of technological external economies are difficult to find, but a better organization of the labor and raw materials market with respect to the availability of laborers and materials when needed by any particular plant, and improvement in productive technique resulting from "cross-fertilization," or the exchange of ideas among the different producers, appear to be possible sources of technological external economies resulting from the increase in size of the industry as a whole. Illustrations of pecuniary external economies would be reductions in the prices of services and materials resulting from the increase in the amounts of such services and materials purchased by the industry as a whole. Pecuniary external economies to industry A are likely to be internal or external economies to some other industry B. If industry A purchases materials in greater quantity, their price may fall because industry B can then produce them at lower unit cost. But cases are theoretically conceivable where pecuniary external economies to industry A may not be economies to any other industry, as, for instance, if laborers should have a preference, rational or irrational, for working in an important rather than in a minor in-

---

[20] Increase of scale should be distinguished from increase in output from the same scale of plant. In the former, all the factors are increased in about the same proportions; in the latter some factors remain fixed in amount. Whenever it is generally possible to increase all the factors in about the same proportion, i.e. to increase scale of plant, it is also possible, alternatively at least, to increase the number of plants.

Net External Economies of Large Production

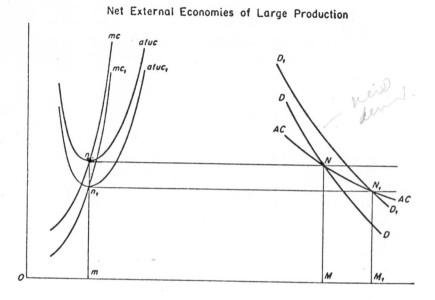

Chart V

dustry, and should therefore be willing to accept lower wages as the industry expands.

Chart V illustrates the case of net external economies of large production, irrespective of whether these economies are technological, or pecuniary, or both. As always, each concern will in the long-run tend to produce its output from the optimum scale for that output, and given that scale, to carry production to the point where its average and marginal costs are both equal to price. If Om represents the optimum scale of plant for the particular producer, i.e., the scale at which he can produce at the lowest average cost, if the long-run price is mn or MN, and if the long-run output for the industry as a whole is OM, this producer will be in long-run equilibrium when his output is om, and his average and his marginal cost are both mn. Suppose now that long-run demand rises from DD to D_1D_1, and that long-run output of the industry as a whole increases, as the result of increase in the number of producers, from OM to OM_1. Since, by assumption, this industry is subject to net external economies of large production, the short-run average and marginal cost curves of each particular concern will fall in the manner indicated in the left-hand portion of Chart V. This particular concern will be in long-run equilibrium with the new situation when its output is *om,* as before, but its long-run average and marginal costs will have fallen from *mn* to mn_1. The *AC* curve represents the trend of the individual average (and also marginal) costs as output of the industry as a whole changes by the amounts indicated on the horizontal axis. Any point on this curve represents the long-run average cost for every individual producer, and therefore for the industry as a whole, when the output of the industry as a whole is as indicated. It is theoretically the same as the supply curve for the industry as a whole. The long-run marginal cost curve for the industry as a whole is not shown on the chart. It would fall below the *AC* curve.[21] Its only relationship to the short-run marginal cost curves of the individual concerns would be that it was a function of the downward shifting of the lowest points on the individual short-run *atuc* and *mc* curves as the output of the entire industry increased. Under atomistic competition this marginal cost curve would have no influence on supply, since individual producers would not take it into account in deciding either upon their continuance in or their entrance into the industry or upon their scale of output when in the industry.[22]

NET EXTERNAL DISECONOMIES OF LARGE PRODUCTION

Although it has not ordinarily been given consideration, the case of net external diseconomies of large production is of indisputable practical importance. Pecuniary diseconomies of this kind will always tend to result from the expansion of output of an industry because the increased purchases of primary factors and materials which this entails must tend to raise their unit prices. In order that pecuniary diseconomies shall not result from the expansion of an industry's output, it is necessary, for both primary factors of production and materials, that the increase in demand by this industry shall be accompanied by a corresponding and

[21] If X = output of the industry as a whole, and Y_a = long-run average cost for the industry as a whole as represented by the *AC* curve, the *MC* curve for the industry as a whole would be $\dfrac{d(XY_a)}{dX}$, $< Y_a$. If average cost for a particular producer = y_a, then $y_a = f(X)$, and at long-run equilibrium, $y_a = Y_a$.

[22] Employing terminology resembling that used by Pigou in his *The Economics of Welfare,* the marginal private net cost would exceed the marginal industry net cost. If the output of an additional producer be represented by ΔX, and the average cost of his output and of the outputs of the other producers by $y_a = f(X)$, then the marginal private net cost would be y_a, and the marginal industry net cost would be $\dfrac{\Delta(XY_a)}{\Delta X}$, $< y_a$.

simultaneous decrease in demand by other industries or increase in supply of the factors and materials themselves, or, failing this, that the materials, because of net external or internal economies in the industries producing them, should have negatively inclined supply curves.[23] These pecuniary external diseconomies, however, may be more than counterbalanced by technological external economies, and need not necessarily result therefore in net external diseconomies. External technological diseconomies, or increasing technical coefficients of production as output of the industry as a whole is increased, can be theoretically conceived, but it is hard to find convincing illustrations. One possible instance might be higher unit highway transportation costs when an industry which provides its own transportation for materials and products expands its output and thereby brings about traffic congestion on the roads.

Chart VI illustrates the case of net external diseconomies of large production, whether technological or pecuniary. When the long-run equilibrium outputs of the industry as a whole are OM and OM_1, respectively, the $atuc$ and $atuc_1$ curves represent the respective trends of short-run average costs, the mc and mc_1 curves represent the trends of short-run marginal costs and mn and mn_1 represent the long-run equilibrium average and marginal costs, for one individual producer. The reverse of the conditions when net external economies of large production are present, in this case the long-run equilibrium average and marginal costs of the individual concern, rise as the output of the

---

[23] It is worth pointing out that negative supply curves for the primary factors of production will not prevent an increased demand for them from a particular industry from resulting in an increase in their unit prices and therefore are not a barrier to pecuniary external diseconomies for that industry in so far as their primary factor costs are concerned. The negatively inclined supply curves of primary factors have a different meaning from the negatively inclined supply curves for commodities. If labor has a negatively inclined supply curve that means not that willingness to hire labor in greater quantities will result in a fall in the wage-rate, but, what is very different, that fewer units of labor will be offered for hire when a high rate of wages is offered than when a lower rate is offered. In the case of commodities, any point on a negatively inclined supply curve must be interpreted to mean that at the indicated price, the indicated quantity or more of the commodity can be purchased. In the case of labor, any point on a negatively inclined supply curve must be interpreted to mean that when the indicated wage-rate is obtainable, the indicated quantity of labor, but no more, will be available for hire. If the negatively inclined supply curve for labor has an elasticity of less than unity, as seems probable, it must be assumed that labor will prefer a high wage rate and partial employment to a low wage rate and fuller employment, and therefore will resist any movement toward the lower points on its supply curve.

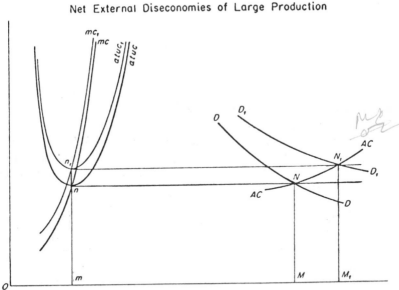

Net External Diseconomies of Large Production

Chart VI

industry as a whole increases. The *AC* curve represents the trend of
the individual average (and also marginal) long-run costs and therefore
also of the industry long-run average cost as the industry as a whole
varies its output. This is also the long-run supply curve for the industry
as a whole. The long-run marginal cost curve for the industry as a
whole is not shown on the chart. It would rise above the *AC* curve.[24]
Since the individual producers will not concern themselves with the
effect on the costs of other producers of their own withdrawal from or
entrance into the industry, and since in this case it is assumed that variation in output takes place only through variation in number of producers, the marginal cost curve for the industry as a whole will, under
competitive conditions, have no influence on output.[25]

[24] As for Chart V, if X = output of industry as a whole and Y_a = long-run average
cost for industry as a whole, as represented by the AC curve, the marginal cost
curve for the industry as a whole would be $\frac{d(XY_a)}{dX}$. If for the individual concern,
y_a = average cost, then $y_a = f(X)$, and at long-run equilibrium $y_a = Y_a$.

[25] In Pigou's terminology, the marginal industry net cost would exceed the marginal
private net cost. If the output of an additional concern be represented by ΔX,
and his average cost by $y_a = f(X)$, then the marginal private net cost would be
y_a, and the marginal industry net cost would be $\frac{\Delta(XY_a)}{\Delta X}$, $> y_a$.

PARTICULAR EXPENSES CURVES

In the foregoing analysis of the relation of cost to supply, it has been throughout maintained, explicitly or implicitly, that under long-run static competitive equilibrium marginal costs and average costs must be uniform for all producers. If there are particular units of the factors which retain permanently advantages in value productivity over other units of similar factors, these units, if hired, will have to be paid for in the long-run at differential rates proportional to their value productivity, and if employed by their owner should be charged for costing purposes with the rates which could be obtained for them in the open market and should be capitalized accordingly. In the short-run, the situation is different. There may be transitory fluctuations in the efficiency of particular entrepreneurs or of particular units of the factors, and it would neither be practicable nor sensible to recapitalize every unit of invested resources with every fluctuation in their rate of yield. Even in the short-run, there must be equality as between the marginal costs of different producers under equilibrium conditions,[26] but there may be substantial variations as between the average costs, and therefore as between the net rates of return on original investment, of different producers.

Statistical investigations of individual costs in the United States, based in the main on unrevised cost accounting records, have shown that the variations in average costs as between different producers in the same industry at the same time are very substantial, and that ordinarily a significant proportion of the total output of an industry appears to be produced at an average cost in excess of the prevailing price. To some extent these variations in cost can be explained away as due (1) to different and, from the point of view of economic theory unsatisfactory, methods of measuring costs, and especially the costs associated with the relatively fixed factors of production, (2) to regional differences in f.o.b. factory costs and in prices which, in an area as large as the United States, can be very substantial for bulky commodities without

[26] Since a time-interval is always present between the sale contract and at least some of the stages of hiring of factors and of actual production, there is opportunity under short-run equilibrium for some divergence between price and marginal cost, and therefore, between the marginal costs of different producers. It would be a more precise way of formulating the short-run theory to say that since all producers, if acting rationally, carry production to the point where anticipated marginal cost will equal anticipated price, and since price, in a perfect market, is uniform for all, marginal cost tends to be uniform for all producers, and variations as between different producers result only from errors in anticipation.

implying the absence of keen competition and (3) to the absence of atomistic competition. But even aside from such considerations, it should be obvious that such findings are in no way inconsistent with the propositions of equilibrium price theory as outlined above. Under short-run equilibrium the average costs, including the fixed costs, of any particular producer need bear no necessary relationship to price, except that the average direct costs must not exceed price. These statistical costs, moreover, are not the equilibrium costs of the theoretical short-run, but are the costs as they exist at an actual moment of time when short-run equilibrium with the fundamental conditions as they exist at the moment may not have been attained, and when these fundamental conditions are themselves liable to change at any moment.

It may be worth while, however, to show the relationship of the distribution of particular average costs within an industry at particular actual moments of time to the general supply conditions of the industry under assumptions of long-run equilibrium. To a curve representing the array of actual average costs of the different producers in an industry when the total output of the industry was a given amount, these individual costs being arranged in increasing order of size from left to right, Marshall gave the name of "particular expenses curve," [27] and American economists have called such curves "bulk-line cost curves," [28] "accountants' cost curves," and "statistical cost curves." In Chart VII, the curves AN, BN_1, and CN_2 are supposed to be the appropriate particular expenses curves for an industry subject to net external economies of large production, when the output of the industry as a whole is OM, OM_1, and OM_2, respectively. Because the industry is subject to net external economies, the entire particular expenses curves are made to shift downward as the output of the industry expands. (If the industry were subject to net external diseconomies of production, the particular expenses curves would shift upwards as the output of the industry expands. Corresponding modifications in the chart would have to be made as other assumptions with respect to the conditions under

---

[27] See *Principles*, 8th ed., Appendix *H*, p. 811. It will be noticed that his particular expenses curve, *SS* is drawn so as to project somewhat beyond the point of total output for the industry as a whole *A*. This is an error, and no significance can be given to the part of the curve projecting beyond the point of total output of the industry as a whole. If the output of the industry were to increase up to the terminal point of this curve, the entire curve would acquire a different locus.

[28] "Bulk-line cost curves" because if a perpendicular is dropped to the horizontal axis from the point of intersection of the price-line and the curve, the greater part or the "bulk" of the output would be to the left of this "bulk-line." See F. W. Taussig. "Price-Fixing as seen by a Price-Fixer," *The Quarterly Journal of Economics*, Vol. XXXIII.

Particular Expenses Curves

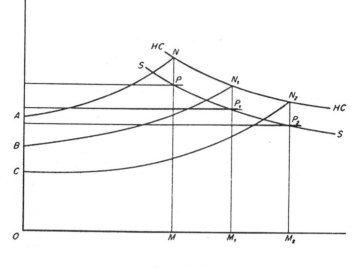

Chart VII

which the industry can expand its output were introduced.) It is to be
understood also that no dynamic changes in prices of the factors or in
average technological cost conditions for the industry as a whole are
occurring except such as are associated with variations in output of the
industry as a whole.

The HC curve is a curve connecting the points of highest-cost for
each successive output. These highest-costs, though often so designated,
are not marginal costs in the strict sense of the term, but are in each
case simply the average costs of that producer whose average costs are
the highest in the industry. If the statistical indications and also certain
a priori considerations are to be followed, these highest average costs
are likely to be, except in "boom years," distinctly higher than the true
marginal costs,[29] and are so drawn in this graph. The P, P_1, P_2 lines
represent price, and are drawn to intersect the particular expenses

---

[29] If the AN, BN_1, and CN_2 curves were the actual particular expenses curves
when the actual outputs of the industry as a whole were OM, OM_1 and OM_2
respectively, the actual marginal cost curve for the industry as a whole would be
a curve representing the differences per unit increase of output between the
aggregate costs represented by the successive areas, $AOMN$, BOM_1N_1, COM_2N_2,
. . . as output was increased from OM to OM_1, to OM_2, to . . . . It would be
negatively inclined, and would be much below the HC curve.

curves below their highest points, in conformity with the statistical findings. The curve SS, drawn through the P, P_1, P_2 points representing actual prices prevailing when the outputs are OM, OM_1 and OM_2, respectively, is a sort of actual semi-dynamic [30] supply curve.

What is the ordinary relationship between the HC curve and the SS curve under fully dynamic conditions cannot be postulated on *a priori* grounds, and only statistical investigation can throw much light on it. American investigators of particular expenses curves believe that they have already demonstrated stable and predictable relations between them and price, but a reasonable degree of scepticism still seems to be justified. One point, however, is clear on *a priori* even more than on inductive grounds. If the SS in Chart VII were not ordinarily below, and substantially below, the HC curve, the familiar and continuously present phenomenon of bankruptcy would be inexplicable.

It is possible, moreover, to devise a theory of even long-run static equilibrium which still leaves room for an excess of the HC over the SS curves, and therefore for bankruptcy as a phenomenon consistent with long-run equilibrium. For such a theory, however, long-run equilibrium would apply only to the industry as a whole, and would be a sort of statistical equilibrium between rate of output and rate of consumption. None of the individual producers under this theory need be in long-run equilibrium at any time. At any moment, some producers would be enjoying exceptional profits, and others incurring heavy losses. The particular expenses curve could remain positive in its inclination and fixed in its locus, but there would be necessarily a constant process of shifting of their position on that curve on the part of the individual producers, and an equality in rate of withdrawal of producers from the industry through bankruptcy or otherwise, on the one hand, and of entrance of new producers into the industry, on the other hand. A theory of this sort would leave room for pure profits even in a static state.

---

[30] "Semi-dynamic" because certain types of dynamic changes have been assumed not to occur.

SUPPLEMENTARY NOTE (1950) *

I do not take advantage of the opportunity to revise my 1931 article. Even the error in Chart IV (page 212) is left uncorrected, so that future teachers and students may share the pleasure of many of their predecessors of pointing out that if I had known what an "envelope" was I would not have given my excellent draftsman the technically impossible and economically inappropriate assignment of drawing an AC curve which would pass through the lowest cost points of all the ac curves and yet not rise above any ac curve at any point. It is left also to the reader to modify the general contour of the ATUC curve of Chart I in conformity with the evidence which inductive studies seem to provide that the trough of this curve has a negative inclination throughout almost all of its possible course.

I feel it incumbent upon me, however, so as to avoid propagating serious error, to carry the analysis of costs a stage further in one respect by departing here from the traditional Marshallian pattern of assumptions to which the article adheres. The partial-equilibrium nature of the Marshallian assumptions leaves a wider range of possibilities to the long-run tendencies of costs for an expanding industry than is consistent with general-equilibrium analysis. I first saw this in 1938, and thereafter pointed it out to my students at the University of Chicago. But the first, and, to my knowledge, still the only, analysis in print similar to what I have in mind is in Joan Robinson's excellent article, "Rising Supply Price," *Economica,* VIII, February, 1941, which has not attracted the attention which in my opinion it eminently deserves. What follows is, I think, in substantial harmony with her argument, but is so presented as to provide a link with the analysis in my 1931 article.

The most significant long-run behavior of costs for many applications of value theory to concrete economic issues is the trend of unit costs, average or marginal, for a particular commodity (or group of commodities) as the total output of such commodity expands while the

* Reprinted from *Readings in Economic Analysis,* ed. by R. V. Clemence, Addison-Wesley Press, Cambridge, 1950, Vol. II, pp. 31-36, by the courtesy of the publisher and the author.

economy as a whole remains stable (or relatively stable), so that the expansion of output of this commodity is of necessity simultaneous with a corresponding contraction of output of all other commodities considered in the aggregate. Let us assume that in an otherwise stable economy a shift of wants occurs from other commodities to cloth, with a consequent expansion in the output of cloth. Except by coincidence, and even that conceivable only at a "point" rather than over a substantial range, the cloth industry will be using the various "factors" (or "ingredients," or "resources," or "input items") in proportions somewhat different from those in which the economy as a whole, and the contracting section of it, uses them. As the cloth industry expands, therefore, and bids for more factors, the contracting industries will not, at prevailing prices for the factors, be releasing factors in the same proportions in which the cloth industry is trying to acquire them; at prevailing prices for the factors, those which the woolen industry uses relatively heavily will be in short supply while those which it uses relatively lightly will be in excess supply. There will consequently occur a realignment of the prices of the factors, with those used relatively heavily by the cloth industry rising in price and those used relatively lightly by it falling in price.

Thus all industries must tend to be subject to "external net pecuniary diseconomies of large production" when they expand relative to the economy of which they are a part. The entrepreneurs in an expanding industry, to lessen the impact of these pecuniary diseconomies, will endeavor to reduce the ratio of their use of the factors which have risen in price to their use of the factors which have fallen in price. But the extent to which such change in the proportions in which the factors are combined is technically feasible and economically profitable is limited by the operation of the law of diminishing returns, i.e., increase in the relative use of the cheaper factors results in decreased ratios of output to input of these factors. It is not possible therefore completely to escape the pecuniary diseconomies resulting from the relative changes in the prices of the factors by altering the proportions in which the factors are used, if it is assumed, as I do here, that the law of diminishing returns is operating in the long run.

There is presented on page 227 an arithmetical illustration of the conclusions derivable from this reasoning with respect to money costs per unit of product and allocation of resources as between different industries when in an economy of stable size a shift of wants of given extent in favor of cloth results in an expansion of the cloth industry. Case I represents what are for present purposes the essential characteristics of the assumed original equilibrium of the economy as a whole, and Case II represents a possible new equilibrium, consistent with all the assumptions made, after there has been full adjustment to the shift in wants. It is assumed in Case II that all the factors are fixed in amount, and also that the total national income remains at $320. There are in Case II as compared to Case I: an increase in the output of cloth; a rise in the price of factor B used relatively heavily by the cloth industry and decreases in the prices of other factors; a relative decrease in the use of factor B as compared to other factors for each industry (although not for all industry in the aggregate); a rise in the average cost and in the price of cloth (there would also be a rise in the marginal cost of cloth but this is not brought out explicitly in the illustration) and falls in the average costs and prices of all other commodities taken as a whole. The degrees of change from Case I indicated in the illustration are in every instance arbitrary, though consistent with equilibrium for the economy as a whole, but the directions of change are in every instance necessary ones.

The assumption that the factors are fixed in amount, i.e., that the amounts offered for hire are independent of their rates of remuneration, is an unnecessary one; though for fortuitous historical reasons it is a popular assumption in economic theory and even sometimes presented as dogma which it is not respectable to depart from, it is in fact wholly arbitrary and unrealistic. It is easy to modify the arithmetical illustration, however, to adapt it to other types of assumptions as to the character of the supply functions of the factors. I will not take the space required to do this here, but will confine myself to a summary account of the character of the necessary changes in the results which follow changes in the assumptions as to the supply functions of the factors, all other assumptions remaining as before.

Case III. Assume that each of the factors has a supply function such that the quantity offered for hire is an increasing function of the rate of remuneration. All price and cost changes as compared to Case I will be the same in direction as in Case II, but less in degree. The total quantity of factor B used by the economy as a whole will be greater and of factors B and C will be less than in Case I or Case II.

Case IV. Assume that factor B has a fixed supply, while the amounts offered of factors A and C are increasing functions of their rates of remuneration. The cost and price of cloth will rise more than in Cases II or III and the cost and prices of other commodities will fall less than in Cases II or III.

Case V. Assume that the quantity of factor B offered for hire is an increasing function of its rate of remuneration, while the supplies of factors A and C are fixed. The cost and price of cloth will rise, but less

Factor	Rate of remuneration per unit	Total quantity of factors used			Total payments to factors	Industry	Output: units	Input per unit of output ("technical coefficients")			Average cost = price
		By cloth industry	By other industries	By all industries				A	B	C	
						Case I					
A	$4.00	1	29	30	$120	Cloth	4	$\frac{1}{4}$	$\frac{5}{4}$	$\frac{2}{4}$	$8.00
B	4.00	5	15	20	80	Other	36	$\frac{29}{36}$	$\frac{15}{36}$	$\frac{28}{36}$	8.00
C	4.00	2	28	30	120	All	40				8.00
				80	$320						
						Case II					
A	$3.40	6	24	30	$102	Cloth	8	$\frac{6}{8}$	$\frac{8}{8}$	$\frac{5}{8}$	$10.30
B	5.50	8	12	20	110	Other	30	$\frac{24}{20}$	$\frac{12}{30}$	$\frac{25}{30}$	7.92
C	3.60	5	25	30	108	All	38				8.42 +
				80	$320						

than in Cases II, III, or IV, while the prices of other commodities will fall more than in Cases II, III, or IV.

Case VI. Assume that the supply functions of all of the factors of production can be represented graphically by "rising-backward" curves, i.e., that as higher rates of remuneration are offered for them smaller quantities are supplied.[31] The rise in the cost and the price of cloth would be greater and the fall in the costs and prices of other commodities would also be greater than in any of the preceding Cases II to V.

In all these cases an increase in the long-run output of cloth can occur only at higher cost, and these or allied cases cover all the assumptions as to the supply functions of the factors which seem to me to be conceivable as realities if the possibility of migration of factors to or from the economy in question is excluded. If the reasoning here presented is valid, there is therefore a universal long-run "law" of increasing money costs as output changes in response to shifts in wants in an economy of constant national money income. The "law" will operate unambiguously, however, only after the expanding industry has reached the stage beyond which there are no net technological or efficiency advantages of increasing the scale of plants in order to increase output of the particular commodities concerned as compared to increasing the number of plants, i.e., where there are no "net technological economies of large-scale production." When this stage is ordinarily reached is a question of fact, but I know of no convincing evidence that the optimum-efficiency size, as measured by the ratio of optimum-plant-capacity to total output of the industry, is not quite moderate for any industry of appreciable size outside the fields of transportation and communication, where "plant" is difficult to define.

[31] "Rising-backward" supply curves need to be interpreted differently from ordinary negatively-inclined Marshallian supply curves, even when they are geometrically identical. In the former case each point on the curve represents a maximum quantity; in the latter case each point on the curve represents a minimum quantity. Negatively-inclined supply curves of the second type for basic factors of production seem to me so improbable as to make analysis of their consequences pedantic.

14

CETERIS PARIBUS FOR SUPPLY CURVES *

RICHARD E. BRUMBERG,[1] deceased, taught at The
Johns Hopkins University when this article was
written.

§1. In any empirical study of economic phenomena, such as partial
equilibrium supply curves, some conditions are assumed to be unchang-
ing. It is the purpose of this note to make explicit the more important
constants that must be considered in the investigation of supply, to
indicate that the list generally considered is incomplete and to discuss
the relative merits of two alternative means of rectifying an inconsistency in the completed list. The note deals with empirical supply
curves of products—that is, of commodities that have undergone some
sort of transformation or production.

In order to study the effects of changes in demand by consumers, it
is desirable that, during the investigation, any alterations in quantity
and price be attributable only to these demand changes. By using a
supply schedule that shows the relation of the minimum prices at
which different amounts are offered by producers when faced with
different demands, it is possible to determine the consequences of the
changes in demand. It is desirable that the supply schedule itself
should be immutable during the analysis so that the effects of demand
changes may be isolated from other variations.

As quantities and prices are assumed to vary along the supply schedule in a determinate manner, a mathematical model may be envisioned
that will "explain" the relationship. In price theory this model is one
of maximising behaviour on the part of the individual firm. The firm
operates within such limitations as existing technology and the supply
conditions of productive services. Some features of these limitations are
not allowed to vary; they are the parameters of the model. These parameters have been assigned a variety of names in the literature of

* From *The Economic Journal,* Vol. LXIII (June, 1953), pp. 462–467. Reprinted by
permission of the Royal Economic Society.

[1] The author is very grateful to Professor Milton Friedman, of the University of
Chicago, and to Professors D. H. Flanders and E. T. Weiler, of the University
of Illinois, for their criticisms and many valuable suggestions.

economics, such as the "givens," "predetermined variables," "other things being equal" and "things impounded in *ceteris paribus.*"

Any list of parameters is necessarily arbitrary. However, this note will try to define those variables that seem to be impounded in *ceteris paribus* in current price theory.

§2. Professor Milton Friedman has suggested classifying impounded variables as follows: (*a*) variables that both affect and are affected by the variable under study; (*b*) variables that are little affected by the studied variable, but materially affect it; (*c*) variables that neither significantly affect the variable under study nor are significantly affected by it.[2] This classification will be useful for discriminating the long-run from the short-run parameters.

§3. Two theoretically distinct, although empirically arbitrary curves will be discussed—the short- and long-run curves. The short run is that interval in which there is time to vary production, but not enough time to alter the plant to adjust to a different level of output. All goods in this time period are newly produced for sale: there is no reservation demand. The long-run period is defined to be that time long enough to use any of the known productive combinations (and, hence, a more elaborate production function than in the short run), but not long enough for all productive services to become almost perfect substitutes. If factors did become perfect substitutes, the supply curve would have infinite elasticity. This extreme is uninteresting from the viewpoint of empirical work.

SHORT-RUN SUPPLY CURVE *CETERIS PARIBUS*

§4. To the author's knowledge, the most complete discussion available of the *ceteris paribus* for supply curves is in an unpublished paper by Milton Friedman.[3] In it, Friedman suggests that the parameters for the short run are: (1) the state of the arts, (2) the prices of products that are either close substitutes or highly complementary in production, and (3) the supply curves of factors of production for the product considered.

Friedman's third point needs no explanation; the first two require examination. The significant part of the "state of the arts" which must remain constant is simply the production function for the product. This function, in the short run, includes all possible productive combinations that do not require changing the plant. Other changes in tech-

---

[2] Milton Friedman, "The Marshallian Demand Curve," *Jour. Pol. Econ.*, Vol. LVII, No. 6 (December 1949), p. 470.

[3] Milton Friedman, "The Relationship Between Supply Curves and Cost Curves" (notes used in advanced-price theory course, The University of Chicago, 1950), pp. 2 f. (Hectographed.)

nology in the society, which affect neither the quality nor price of the factors nor the ways of combining them, may vary in any way whatsoever. These changes belong to the third class mentioned above (§2).

Products that are either close substitutes or highly complementary in production belong to the first class of variables. While it may be useful for some problems to hold their prices constant, it is not necessary to do so. It is also possible to impound the quantities of these products; while a third alternative is that the demand curves for the closely related products remain unchanged. The first two choices of impounding prices or quantities really reduce to perfectly elastic and perfectly inelastic demand curves for the products. While these extremes are improbable, they should not be forgotten as approximations in empirical work.

A fourth parameter is expectations. Although supply curves are treated within a static framework, perfect foresight is neither basic nor desirable for the theory.[4] Consequently, expectations must be introduced into the analysis. If the expectations change during the period of analysis, the supply curve is no longer determinate. Thus, in Hicksian phraseology, there must be a constant elasticity of expectations.[5] Although it is not necessary, this elasticity is usually considered to be unity.[6]

An example may clarify the meaning of these four impounded variables. Suppose a scholar produces two products, text-books and original work. If the supply schedule of text-books from this producer is to be described, it is reasonable that the production function remain constant during the period (*i.e.*, the scholar must not suddenly become more intelligent). Secondly, let the demand for related products be impounded (were the scholar to receive greater remuneration for his original work, he might stop producing text-books entirely). Furthermore, the supply schedules of productive services should not change (such as a fall in wages making possible the employment of a secretary). Finally, were the scholar subject to fluctuating expectations about college enrolment, the supply schedule would be indeterminate.

CETERIS PARIBUS FOR THE LONG RUN

§5. Short-run supply curves have been dealt with in an unequivocal manner. Long-run curves present greater difficulties. In particular,

[4] Nicholas Kaldor, "The Equilibrium of the Firm," *Economic Journal*, March 1934, p. 70.
[5] J. R. Hicks, *Value and Capital* (2nd. ed., London, Oxford University Press, 1946), p. 205.
[6] Fritz Machlup, "The Theory of Foreign Exchanges," *Readings in the Theory of International Trade* (Philadelphia, The Blakiston Company, 1949), p. 109.

long-run studies become involved in phases of general equilibrium analysis. Some variables which, in the short run, neither affected nor were affected by output changes and had been in Friedman's third category (§2) now fall into the second as they affect the supply schedule.

6§. For the short period, only those supply curves of productive services used in the fixed-plant production functions for the product are in the second category. All other factors are in the third class (*i.e.,* shifts of curves in the markets of these variables do not affect the product under study). However, this separation does not exist in the long run.

Many productive services may be transformed into other productive services in the long run; consequently, a change in the demand or supply of a productive service not used in making the product will affect at least some supplies of those productive services that are used. A striking example is a change in demand or preference for one type of labor and the resultant changes in the supply of other kinds of labor.

If these productive-service markets are to be impounded, then certain general equilibrium qualifications are inherent in long-run partial equilibrium analysis. This proposition is neither new nor revolutionary;[7] what is of interest is the actual selection of the general equilibrium conditions. Although the author believes the set of constants that follows is almost too extensive and confining for empirical work, it does seem to be the set implied by neo-classical thinking. A set that could be more closely approached in the real world would be preferable.

§7. Suppose a quasi-stationary state is postulated in which the only independent variable is tastes and preferences for final products. These demand changes may be broken into three types. The first is a change in demand for the product considered. It is this movement that traces out the supply curve. The second is a change in taste for other products that does not involve any net movements in the demands for individual productive services. The third is one which does not immediately affect the demand for the product, but does cause changes in the prices of productive services. Such an influence, acting through the ultimate substitute or complementary relationship of almost all productive services, would cause the product supply curve to shift. Therefore, although this kind of alteration is common in the real world, it must be excluded in the model.

If this sort of stationary state is accepted, then two other parameters may be listed. These parameters are in Friedman's second class.

§8. Most, if not all, technological change is to be impounded. Any advance in technology would change some demands for productive

[7] George J. Stigler, *The Theory of Price* (New York, Macmillan Co., 1948), pp. 28 f.

services and, by the reasoning above (§6), would affect those factor-supply schedules that must be held constant.

§9. It is also necessary to consider money income. According to Keynesian analysis, a change in money income would alter the rate of interest and, thus, the price of a productive service.[8] For the neo-classicist, there would be a direct price movement. If all prices rose by the same percentage, there would be a parallel vertical movement of the product supply curve; under any other circumstance the shift of the curve cannot be determined *a priori*. Either of these two lines of thinking leads to the conclusion that it is necessary to impound money income.

To summarise: if the supply schedules of productive services used in the product are not to change in the long run, then it is necessary to impound: (1) variations in taste not directed towards the product, but altering the demand schedules of productive services; (2) money income; and (3) technology.

§10. These parameters all seem to be necessary; yet, reflection quickly shows a theoretical inconsistency. This inconsistency, and two alternative assumptions which will rehabilitate the system, may now be demonstrated.

When demand changes for a product, quantity can only increase by a decreased use of resources in other production. Money is diverted from these other uses, and the system will reach a new equilibrium with unchanged technology (§8) and unchanged money income (§9). Under the definition of the long-run time period (§3), however, productive services are not perfect substitutes. From this definition (which is basic to neo-classical price theory), it is implied that the supply schedule will take on different shapes, depending upon the resources that are released. For if the resources which go into a given dollar's worth of product A are imperfect substitutes for an equal money's worth of product B, there is no reason whatsoever to assume a shift in demand from A to C will result in the same output of C as an equal shift from B to C. For example, a shift from cigars to cigarettes would yield a different output of cigarettes than if the shift had been from chewing gum.

§11. There are two solutions to this apparent impasse. The first suggestion is one that seems to be implicit in neo-classical theory. Marshall's customary treatment of small industries with no great peculiarities may be interpreted as implying the assumption that the resources released are equally substitutable, regardless of the product from which they are released.

The rationalisation for this assumption is a bit nebulous (and it may

---

[8] John Maynard Keynes, *The General Theory of Employment Interest and Money* (New York, Harcourt, Brace and Company), Bk. IV.

be for this reason that the statement has been avoided). In the first place, by definition, productive services cannot be perfect substitutes; nevertheless, they must be substitutes to some degree if the supply curve is not to be perfectly inelastic. An intermediate degree is required. This degree would be achieved if the released resources are technologically at a distance so great, that by the time the reactions and interactions have filtered through the economy, the effect on the factors used in the product is essentially the same, regardless of the particular resources freed in the first instance. This author has been unable to find or develop a more rigorous statement justifying the assumption.[9]

§12. The alternative to the Marshallian assumption is one that provides for the release of resources from all other products. Rather than the shift from a single distant product, resources from all other products may be freed in some standard fashion. The simplest assumption is a uniform release from other products. An example of this kind of release would be a government maintaining a balanced budget in a closed economy. If the government were to finance its expenditure upon a product by means of a sales tax on all products, then a unique supply curve may be traced for the product. A variation of this assumption would be a redirection of income: the demand for other products would shift because of the income effects of the decreased expenditure apportioned them. The analogue of the above example would be an income tax financing the government's purchases of the product.

There is no way of telling the exact relationship between the supply curves formed under the Marshallian assumption and from one of the "all products" assumptions. In conjunction with the parameters stated above (§6–9), the use of either kind of assumption will yield a consistent supply curve.

---

[9] The assumption may be made a little more palatable by impounding a specific list of products that are closely related in production, as was done for the short-run curve. This restriction would at least force some filtering on the system. Friedman has done a similar thing, for a different reason, with closely related commodities in demand for his exposition of the demand curve. Milton Friedman, "The Marshallian Demand Curve," *op. cit.*, p. 465.

15

THE PROPORTIONALITY CONTROVERSY AND THE THEORY OF PRODUCTION *

HARVEY LEIBENSTEIN teaches at Harvard University; he was formerly at Princeton University.

In the theory of the firm much is made of the observation that certain factors are lumpy. In fact, many writers have gone so far as to attribute both increasing and decreasing returns solely to this phenomenon. Professor Chamberlin challenged this view in a well known article, but defenders of what may be called the "proportionalist position" were quick to reply.[1] (By the "proportionalist position" we refer to the notion that, given divisibility, the multiplication or division of all factors by a constant will yield proportional returns; in other words the idea that, given divisibility, production functions are necessarily homogeneous.)[2] A recent article by Messrs. Whitin and Peston reinforces the Chamberlinian view by describing "several situations where the rational entrepreneur will vary certain factors less than proportionately with output."[3] But in these discussions an important methodological point has been missed. In this note we shall explore this point and show how it can help to clarify some aspects of the problem.

One of the reasons why controversies on theoretical issues are often difficult to settle is that the theory, in its development towards greater and greater generality, becomes so terse that it does not permit certain

---

* From *The Quarterly Journal of Economics*, LXIX (November, 1955), pp. 619–25. Copyright © 1955 by the President and Fellows of Harvard College. Reprinted by permission of the author and the Harvard University Press.

[1] E. H. Chamberlin, "Proportionality, Divisibility and Economies of Scale," this *Journal*, Feb. 1948, pp. 229–62; "Comments" by A. N. McLeod and F. H. Hahn, "Reply" by E. H. Chamberlin, *ibid.*, Feb. 1949, pp. 128–43. The first article is incorporated in *The Theory of Monopolistic Competition*, 6th ed., as Appendix B.

[2] What the outcome of the debate has been is not at all clear. If the writer can judge on the basis of conversations he has had with some economists on the problem, he must conclude that the "proportionalist position" is still held quite tenaciously in some quarters.

[3] T. M. Whitin and M. H. Peston, "Random Variations, Risk, and Returns to Scale," this *Journal*, Nov. 1954, pp. 603–12.

significant distinctions to be made. As a result implicit assumptions go
unrecognized and appear to lead inevitably to what are in fact wrong
conclusions. We suggest that this is the case with the conventional
theory of production of the firm. When the necessary distinctions are
made, some of the central issues in the controversy are clarified, and we
shall see that, once these distinctions are accepted, the "proportionalist
position" becomes untenable.

1. THE ISSUE

According to the proportionalist argument if the factors of production
are infinitely divisible then this inevitably leads to long-run constant
costs. Since there is some optimum combination of the factors that will
yield an output at lowest average unit cost, then, given infinite divisibility, it follows that we could obtain greater or lesser outputs at the
same average cost simply by dividing or multiplying the optimum combination by an appropriate constant. At first blush this appears to be
an eminently reasonable point of view. Yet it is quite incorrect.

2. THE MEANING OF FACTOR DIVISIBILITY

Before embarking on our analysis proper we have to indicate what is
meant by a fractional unit of a factor. Assuming that all units are
homogeneous, the question that arises is how to define half units where
it is not meaningful to divide a unit physically. In this case we may, for
the sake of argument, accept what appears to be the "proportionalist
position" and define half units in terms of efficiency. Namely, one hundred half-men are equivalent to fifty whole men, and this equivalence
is in terms of what they can do. Thus, the entrepreneur who hires one
hundred half-men, is just as well off as he who hires fifty whole men or
two hundred quarter-men, etc. In other words, our definition implies
that *under similar circumstances* fractional units, no matter how finely
divided, operate just as efficiently as whole units. Surely this meets the
proportionalist ideal of perfect divisibility, and yet we shall see that
proportional returns to scale do not follow.

Before presenting the elements of our model two aspects of the problem must be made explicit. First, it must be understood that the controversy is about the divisibility of *factors* and its consequences, and not
about *other* aspects of the productive process. In other words, when
writers on the subject speak of the divisibility of factors we assume that
we are to take them literally and that they *are* speaking about factors
of production. Second, we assume that the theory we are considering is

not merely a formal matter but that it has to do with the productive process as it exists in the real world, although the theory may abstract from many aspects of that process.

3. THE PRODUCTION MODEL

The theory of production is in terms of two polar categories, inputs and outputs. While it is true that writers on production theory are aware that there is more to the process than merely combining inputs and obtaining outputs, and they sometimes allude to intervening elements, it nevertheless remains the case that the formal theory is usually presented in terms of inputs and outputs. For many problems the input-output approach is sufficient. But with respect to the controversy under discussion a model in which the intervening categories are made explicit is the more adequate.

Recalling that the issue at stake is the contention that complete divisibility is a sufficient condition for constant long-run average costs, it follows that to disprove this proposition we need conceive of merely a single possible case in which this is not so. Thus, if we can visualize a model of the production process in which the proposition at issue need not hold, then we have proven our case.

And now to our model. The definitions of the basic categories of our model follow:

(1) A *commodity* is the entity that is the object of the productive process, and that has a specific set of attributes or specifications.

(2) An *activity* is our primitive concept. It refers to those necessary acts carried out by a factor, or functions of a factor, necessary in the productive process. We define a set of related activities as an *operation*.

(3) A *process* is any specific set of operations used to produce the commodity in question. There may be a number of possible alternative processes.

(4) A *factor* is an entity, units of which can be purchased on the market, that has the capacity to carry out one or more activities.

(5) By a *firm* we refer to the entity that purchases factors, creates commodities, and sells commodities.

Our vision of the productive process is this: The firm purchases all the necessary factors. The firm's purpose in doing so is to create some quantity of a commodity which can be defined in terms of a set of attributes. The attributes are created by a set of operations. We refer to any specific set of operations as a process. The operations are performed by or made up of activities. Our notion of an activity is a rather broad one so that it contains any contribution to the creation of the commodity. For example, we conceive of some specific raw material, say a piece of wood, as capable of performing the activity of becoming the necessary physical matter out of which the commodity, say a bench, is made.

Since we assume perfect divisibility, the firm can purchase its factors in any conceivable combination. For some given output the commodity is produced at minimum costs for that output and with a specific ratio of the factors. The question is whether the firm can also produce any other output at the same cost per unit if the factors are purchased in exactly the same proportion as the alternative outputs. The answer depends on whether the quantity of any activity that has to be carried on is a function of the output of the commodity. Now clearly in any conceivable productive process *not all activities or operations need be functions of output.* Indeed, it is unlikely that there is any modern productive process in which *all* the activities or operations depend entirely on the quantity produced. Once we accept this possibility then we can quite readily see that perfect divisibility of *factors* (provided we accept the distinctions between factors, activities, and operations) is not a sufficient condition for long-run constant costs.

The number of times any activity has to be performed may vary directly with the amount of any given factor that is hired, the variety of the factors, the number of operations, or the number of other activities. The relationship need not be a proportional one. For example, the activities of starting and stopping may be functions of the number and variety of operations that are performed. Nor need we assume that any particular activity need always be carried on for any particular output. Some activities may have to be carried on regardless of output while other activities and operations may be required when some other variable in the production process reaches a certain minimum size, while still others may grow or decline in a nonproportional fashion to other variables. The extent to which the condition just alluded to holds depends on the nature of the productive process.

The critical reader may assert that all we have done is simply to shift our grounds from lumpy factors to "lumpy activities" and operations. But this is not the point. For what we come out with is that there is something inherent in the productive process and not in the divisibility of factors that is the cause of nonhomogeneous production functions.

Furthermore, we have not really shifted ground by changing the definition of a factor, for the issue is one of *meaningfulness* and not of definition. There is meaning to a "lumpy factor" but there is *no* meaning to a "lumpy activity" or to a "divisible activity." Consider, for example, the production process of publishing a book. One of the activities is proofreading. Once it is done it need be done no more, regardless of the number printed, the thickness of the pages, or any other quality of the book. It is meaningless to say that proofreading is a lumpy or indivisible activity. It is simply an activity determined by the technical requirements of producing a book. The fact that it has to be done only once irrespective of the number of copies produced is entirely unrelated to the bulkiness or divisibility of the factors of production employed. It is just as meaningless to half proofread something as it is to half kick a ball. You either kick it or you do not. An activity is either performed or it is not. The fact of its performance has nothing to do with the size of the ball, the size of the kicker, or their divisibility or lack of it. Something is not proofread if only half the pages are read. In a similar vein to "half-switch" on a light is a meaningless idea. Without belaboring this notion further it should be clear that some combinations of words simply have no meaning and it is a methodological error to act as though they had. By making inadequate distinctions, or by leaving certain elements implicit, some writers seem not to have realized that they were indirectly advocating combinations of ideas that really make no sense.

An objection that may be raised is that our definition of a factor involves an unnecessary distinction; that the firm really purchases the activities performed, and therefore, the activities and the factor are one and the same thing.

In reply we argue that it is surely legitimate to distinguish what is in fact distinguishable. The factors of production that are hired in the market are in fact not the same thing as the uses to which they are put. The factors may be divisible and yet the activities that they perform are discreet. It may take multiple (or fractional) units of a factor to carry out an activity. Under such circumstances we do not violate the assumption of the divisibility of a factor.

But even if we think of factors solely in terms of the bundle of activities performed it does not change the basic argument. The crucial distinction to be recognized is that the nature of the factors supplied must be separated conceptually from the nature of the activities *needed* in the production process. The nature of the factors supplied is determined by conditions outside the production method under consideration. For example, the attributes and specifications of the commodity need not, and do not, determine the characteristics of the factors. But, the attributes and specifications of the commodity do determine, in part at least, the activities and operations necessary for the production of that commodity. That is, the activities and operations required in the production process are determined, to some

extent, by technical considerations. Furthermore, the technical considerations may be such that they require operations and activities to be
performed that are nonproportional to output.

In order to sharpen the argument it may be useful to classify activities into three categories. (1) Direct proportional activities: those
activities which are involved in operations on the commodity in question, and where the quantity of the particular activity is proportional
to output. (2) Direct nonproportional activities: these are activities
that are directly connected with producing the commodity but where
the amount of the activity is not proportional to output. (3) Indirect
activities: here we have in mind activities such as personnel administration, record keeping, and others that do not involve contact with
the commodity but are necessary to the operation of the firm.

Now the implicit assumption of the "proportionalist position" must
be that if factors were completely divisible then *all* activities would be
direct proportional activities. This implies that all direct nonproportional activities and all indirect activities carried on by firms at the
present time are entirely due to the indivisibilities of factors. But this
last implication of the "proportionalist position" is most difficult to
believe if we consider some of the specific nonproportional activities
that have to be carried on by firms. For example, such activities as
production planning, the issuance of orders to personnel, keeping records, the channelling and collecting of information internal to the firm,
the channelling and collecting of information external to the firm,
the administration of personnel, the administration of credit and finance,
as well as a host of similar control activities need not be, and
probably are not, directly proportional to output. Many of these
activities have to be carried on regardless of output and one cannot see how the fact that factors were divisible would either eliminate
their need or transform them to proportional activities. Consider
factors that have some degree of durability. Surely the appropriate
depreciation formula would not always be of the form $D = NQ$, where
D is the amount of depreciation and Q the quantity produced. The
"proportionalist" view would imply not only that all depreciation costs
are user costs, but also that user costs are always proportional to output
if factors are divisible. But the fact of the matter is that the physical
nature of durable goods is not of this kind. Some depreciation takes
place for reasons other than use. The case is especially clear with respect to obsolescence. The risks of obsolescence, and the fact of obsolescence, surely do not depend on the divisibility of factors. Another interesting possibility is a chemical process where a catalytic agent is
involved. Again, the amount of the catalytic agent need not be propor-

tional to output. This is a matter of the laws of chemistry and not of economics or of the divisibility of factors. Other interesting examples in this vein, especially for cases where risk and random variations are involved, are mentioned in the article by Whitin and Peston.[4]

In sum our argument boils down to the fact that many production processes necessitate indirect activities and operations, as well as direct nonproportional activities. The issue at stake is not a matter of definition. Essentially, it is both an empirical matter and a question about the meaningfulness of ideas. The empirical aspect depends on what the firm has to do in order to produce a commodity and maintain the firm as a continuing entity, and this does not depend entirely on the divisibility of factors. It does depend on the objective nature of commodities and production activities, and on the technical requirements of production processes, which in turn depend in part on the laws of physics and chemistry and on the arts of engineering and administration.

The lack of meaningfulness of some of the assertions about the consequences of factor divisibility have not been recognized heretofore because they were based on a theory in which there are inadequate distinctions. As a result it was not recognized that certain implicit elements in the argument implied combinations of ideas that were in essence nonsensical. By breaking down the theory into more elements we are enabled to make these necessary distinctions and thus bring to the fore the meaningless nature of some of the arguments. Specifically, we have seen that while it may often be sensible to speak of the divisibility of the factors it is quite meaningless to think even implicitly in terms of divisible activities. And since activities need not be proportonal to output if factors are divisible, then factor divisibility need not lead to constant returns to scale.

4 Whitin and Peston, *op. cit.*

16

OMISSIONS IN THE TREATMENT OF THE LAW OF VARIABLE PROPORTIONS *

OM P. TANGRI [†] teaches at the University of
Manitoba, Winnipeg, Canada.

The purpose of this paper is to clarify two points with respect to the treatment of the Law of Variable Proportions (hereafter referred to as the Law) in most economics textbooks. The first concerns cost and product relationships in Stage III, commonly called the "irrational" region [1] of production, and the second deals with the symmetry of Regions I and III.

Although Stage III is an irrational area of production, it is not uncommon for firms lacking perfect knowledge actually to produce in that region, particularly in agriculture. As Bishop and Toussaint note [1, p. 41]: [2]

> . . . evidence of production in Region III is often noted. For example, during the late summer and fall months, we frequently have evidence of too many cattle on a given quantity of pasture, resulting in overgrazing of pastures and less production than could have been obtained with fewer cattle. Also, we find evidence of overcrowding of broilers and layers in poultry houses.

Regardless of the empirical incidence, however, the chief reason for examining cost curves in Stage III lies in presenting a complete and

* From the *American Economic Review*, Vol. LVI, No. 3 (June, 1966), pp. 484–493. Reprinted by permission.

[†] Martin Ulrich, a graduate student in my seminar, started me on this paper by expressing skepticism on the standard treatment of cost-product relationships. My thanks to him and to Surendra Kulshrestha, both of whom assisted me by running the necessary input-output computations (not included in this paper). Thanks also to the referee, my colleagues at the University of Manitoba, and my brother at Wayne State University.

[1] The terms "stage," "region," and "phase" are used interchangeably in this paper.
[2] For additional examples, see Heady [3, pp. 94 and 170].

consistent treatment of the product-cost relationships in all three phases of the Law.

Most of the textbooks on economics discuss the various product functions and their interrelationships for all three phases of the production function in considerable detail. However, the corresponding cost functions are derived only for the first two phases of the Law and the relationship between product and cost functions in Stage III has been neglected, stated ambiguously, or misinterpreted.

The common practice is to draw a standard sigmoid-type total cost function and its corresponding average and marginal cost functions. This tends to leave the reader either wondering as to the product-cost relationships in the third phase or under the erroneous impression that the total, average, and marginal cost functions as drawn are for all phases of the Law and that they continue to have a positive slope, even though the total product function assumes a negative slope in the third region.[3] The writer has found both undergraduate and graduate students curious and confused about this.

The cost-product diagram (Figure 1) reproduced from a recent textbook on agricultural economics by Snodgrass and Wallace [6, p. 235] will show that the confusion is not confined to students alone. In providing a vivid illustration of the cost-product relationships, the authors completely overlook the point that the AVC function cannot continue to rise with a positive slope, as shown in Figure 1, for the output beyond point C on the TPP function or on the MPP function, because from C onwards the TPP is falling and the MPP is negative. It is true that the authors recognize "that the horizontal and vertical axes in each of the three figures [panels a, b, and c, in Figure 1] . . . are not comparable on a quantitative basis [but] the importance is to show the relationship between various points on the physical product curves and the cost curves . . ." [6, p. 235]. However, it is in this effort to show the relationship between various points on the product and cost functions that they either make the said error or at least fail to warn the reader anywhere in the book that such an error is due to the lack of exact quantitative correspondence between the horizontal and vertical axes of the three panels of the figure.

---

[3] Heady's book [3, p. 94] is one of the few texts which advises the reader explicitly that the stages of increasing average and diminishing total returns are not drawn in subsequent chapters of the book. To the best of my knowledge, Vickrey [8, pp. 159–60] is the only author who makes a brief reference to and draws very tiny portions of the backward-rising AVC and TVC functions. However, he does not show the complete interrelationships between various product and cost functions.

I. INTERRELATIONSHIPS BETWEEN PRODUCT AND COST FUNCTIONS

Figures 2 and 3 illustrate product-cost relationships for all phases of the Law. The product functions in Figure 2 are based on the production function: [4]

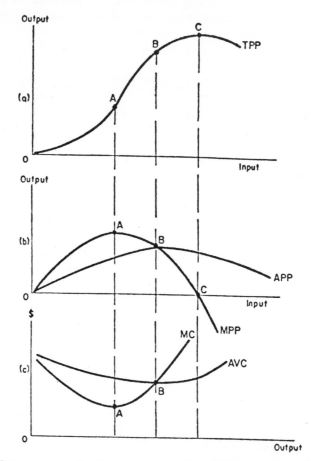

Source: Reproduced from Fig. 13-2 (p. 235) *Agriculture, Economics, and Growth* by Milton M. Snodgrass and Luther T. Wallace. Copyright © 1964 by Meredith Publishing Company. Reproduced by permission of Appleton-Century-Crofts, Division of Meredith Publishing Company.

Figure 1. Product and cost curves

[4] This production function is taken from Heady's book [3, p. 39, n.1], except that the constant term, 40, has been dropped in order to keep our TPP function similar to the familiar textbook TPP which usually starts from the origin.

(1) $$Y = 4.0X + .5X^2 - .15X^3$$

where Y represents total physical product (TPP), and X stands for the variable input which is being applied to a fixed amount of another in-

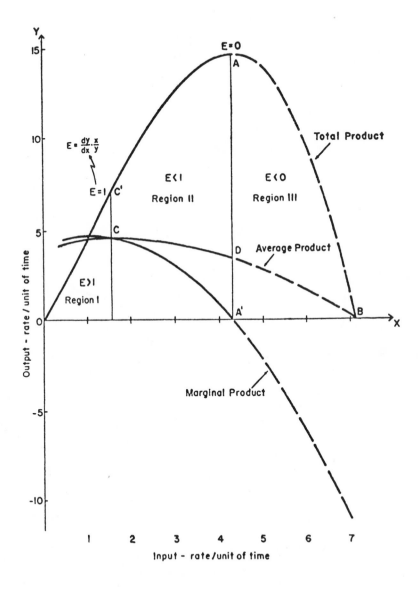

Figure 2. Factor-product relationships

put. This fixed input (not explicitly included in the production function) is assumed to be perfectly divisible and adaptable. The marginal physical product (MPP) function, therefore, is given by

(2) $dY/dX = 4 + 1.0X - .45X^2.$

In deriving cost functions (Figure 3) from product functions (Figure 2) it is assumed that the input market is perfectly competitive, so that the variable factor of production can be purchased at a constant price per

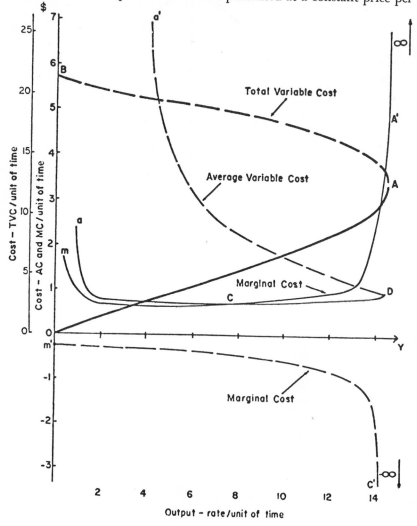

Figure 3. Cost-product relationships

unit of the input, irrespective of its quantity bought. The assumed input price, $P_x = \$3.00$ per unit.

From Figures 2 and 3 it will be noted that when Region III, the area of diminishing *total* returns, is included in the cost analysis, the various standard cost functions take on some peculiar attributes. In Figure 3, the total variable cost function (TVC) no longer remains single-valued; instead it becomes bi-valued. The TVC for all phases of the Law is denoted by OAB; the broken segment AB represents TVC for Stage III. Notice that in this region, TVC continues to rise until point B, a point representing a high positive cost but zero output, and has a negative slope because output is continuously falling, a phenomenon quite consistent with Stage III.

The average variable cost (AVC) function in Figure 3, represented by aDa', develops a cusp at D, a point representing the end of Stage II and beginning of Stage III. After this point, the broken line Da' denotes AVC for Stage III. In this region, since output begins to fall after point D, Da' assumes a negative slope. It is of the same general shape as the AVC function, aD, in Stages I and II, but is at a higher cost level.

Again, diminishing *total* returns in production cause a discontinuity in the marginal cost (MC) function. The complete MC function for all regions of the Law is shown by $mCA'C'm'$ (Figure 3), where mCA' represents the MC function for Stages I and II, and $C'm'$ denotes MC for Stage III. It will be noted from Figure 3 that at point A' (maximum output), the MC function attains a value of $\pm \infty$. Therefore after A', the MC function for Stage III, $C'm'$, is (1) a discontinuous function at the maximum output level, and (2) is negative over the entire region (III) because the associated MPP function for this region in Figure 2 is negative.

In our traditional treatment of costs, we usually do not think in terms of negative costs. Negative MC is not to be construed to mean that for a certain rate of output the cost rate is negative (i.e., the entrepreneur is saving) but implies, instead, that after a certain point (A') if an effort is made to increase output, cost changes are positive even though output changes are negative, a phenomenon quite consistent with the input-output behavior, and the total cost-total product relationship in Stage III.

II. SYMMETRY OF REGIONS I AND II

This paper will conclude with clarification and elaboration of two final properties of the Law, viz., (I) interfactoral symmetry [5] (or reversibility)

[5] The term "symmetry" is used here to imply reversibility of factor proportions (or factor position) rather than strict mathematical symmetry.

in Regions I and III, and (2) the relationship, if any, between factor symmetry and product symmetry in Regions I and III. As early as 1936, Cassels in his celebrated article [2, p. 108] remarked: "The most important thing to observe about this law is that it is symmetrical and consequently the third phase is simply the converse of the first." Yet, most textbooks make scanty or no reference to this point.[6] Furthermore, of the writers who do discuss the symmetrical nature of the Law, few, including Cassels, bring out the practical significance of the Law. Except for suggesting one operational aspect, namely, that total output can be increased in either Region I or Region III by reducing the relative intensity of the excessive factor, most writers leave the reader with the impression that symmetry of the Law is a mere theoretical nicety.

In our analysis of factor-product relations, Figure 2, it would be recalled that factor X (explicitly included in the production function) was treated as a variable factor of production. It was applied in equal incremental units to a given amount of some other factor (not explicitly included in the production function) which was treated as a fixed factor of production. Thus, in Region I, where the ratio of the variable factor to the fixed factor is relatively low, the marginal physical product for the variable factor is positive and greater than the average physical product (until $MPP_X = APP_X$ at the outer boundary of Region I).[7] In Region III, however, where the ratio of the variable factor to the fixed factor is relatively high, MPP of the variable factor is negative and below the APP of this factor.

By reversing the positions of these factors, one can easily see that a low variable-fixed factor ratio in Region I means a high fixed-variable factor ratio in the same region. Accordingly, when the MPP for our variable factor is positive in this region, it is negative for the other input in the same region. Likewise, in Region III a high variable-fixed factor ratio means a low fixed-variable factor ratio in the same region. Thus, when the MPP for our variable factor is negative, it is positive for the other factor. In short, Region I for one input is Region III for some other input, and vice versa.[8]

---

[6] Of some 15 texts consulted, only a few, viz., Heady [3, pp. 76–78], Leftwich [4, pp. 116-21], and Stigler [7, p. 125] discuss this point adequately. Even as good a text as Samuelson's [5, pp. 518–19] devotes only $5\frac{1}{2}$ lines to this point.

[7] It is recognized that the location of the boundary between Regions I and II at the point where MPP = APP holds true only when the production function is homogeneous of the first degree. If either diminishing or increasing returns to scale are present, the boundary between Regions I and II will not be marked by the equality of MPP and APP.

[8] For an excellent graphic and tabular illustration of this point, see Leftwich [4, pp. 116–21].

The importance of factor reversibility lies not only in deciding *when* a particular factor of production should be decreased to increase production, but also in deciding *what* factor of production should be treated as variable or fixed in a given economic environment. These are not easy decisions. They confront not only entrepreneurs at the individual level but also policy makers at the national level whenever they are concerned with optimum resource allocation. An example from Heady [3, p. 77] will illustrate the point.

> Within a cropping year, a farmer may consider hog numbers as fixed and corn as variable; he can either sell the year's corn crop or feed it in varying amounts to a given number of spring-farrowed pigs. Or, he can consider the corn crop as fixed and vary the number of hogs in proportion to it; the corn can be stored into the next year and opportunities will be open for farrowing more pigs. At the national level, food emergencies may arise which call for either feeding more or less grain to a given number of hogs within a year or storing the corn and increasing the number of hogs to which it might be fed. Which system will give greatest profits to the farmer or food to the nation?

Answers to such complicated problems can be determined only by an analysis of both the physical and economic relationships. The important point is that reversibility of the technical inputs not only allows the interchange of factor positions but also provides the necessary, though not sufficient, basis on which this choice is exercised. The usual textbook discussion of symmetry and optimum factor proportions then becomes meaningful.

The second point concerns the relationship, if any, between factor symmetry and product symmetry in Regions I and III. Having read the class assignment on the symmetry of the Law in standard sources, many students ask: If Regions I and III are symmetrical, why doesn't the TPP curve in Region III have an inflection point corresponding to the inflection point in Region I? In terms of the MPP function, why doesn't it achieve a maximum negative value in Region III corresponding to the maximum positive value in Region I, and reverse its direction toward zero (B, Figure 2) as it does toward the zero value (A' Figure 2)?

These questions reveal a confusion between factor symmetry and product symmetry in Regions I and III. Even though factor symmetry makes Regions I and III the converse of each other, it does not necessarily mean that the *rate* of increase in total product in Region I must be symmetrical to the *rate* of product loss in Region III. Hence the difference in the exact behavior and shapes of the TPP and MPP curves in Regions I and III.

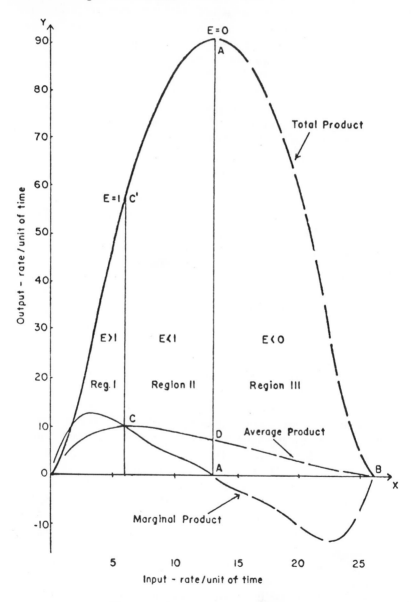

Figure 4. Factor-product relationships

The MPP curve in Region III would achieve a maximum negative value and reverse its direction to join *B* only if the TPP curve in Region III, under some special circumstances, were exactly symmetrical

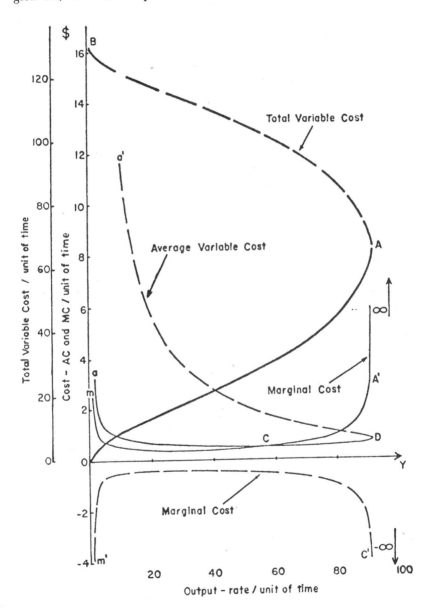

Figure 5. Cost-product relationships

(used here in the mathematical sense) to the TPP curve in *both* Regions I and II, i.e., if the TPP were symmetrical about the input value corresponding to the maximum TPP value. This is illustrated in Figure 4 where the TPP is symmetrical about input (X) value of 13. The MPP in Region III, therefore, is an exact mirror image of the MPP in Regions I and II. The corresponding cost functions are shown in Figure 5. Here the MC function in Region III, corresponding to the MPP behavior, is also an exact mirror image of the MC function in the first two regions. But this situation, as remarked earlier, is rather unusual. Theoretically, there is more reason to believe that the TPP curve would be nonsymmetrical than symmetrical. As Cassels stated [2, p. 109, n. 10], "since the *proportions* of the factors are less affected by each additional unit of the variable factor as we move to the right along the X-axis it is clear that *in general* the third phase must be more prolonged than the first."

REFERENCES

1. C. E. BISHOP AND W. D. TOUSSAINT, *Agricultural Economic Analysis.* New York 1958.

2. J. M. CASSELS, "On the Law of Variable Proportions," Am. Econ. Assoc., *Readings in the Theory of Income Distribution,* Vol. 3. Philadelphia 1946.

3. E. O. HEADY, *Economics of Agricultural Production and Resource Use.* New York 1952.

4. R. H. LEFTWICH, *The Price System and Resource Allocation.* New York 1958.

5. P. A. SAMUELSON, *Economics, An Introductory Analysis.* New York 1964.

6. M. M. SNODGRASS AND L. T. WALLACE, *Agriculture, Economics and Growth.* New York 1964.

7. G. J. STIGLER, *The Theory of Price,* Rev. ed. New York 1947.

8. W. S. VICKREY, *Microstatics.* New York 1964.

17

RETURNS TO SCALE AND THE SPACING OF ISOQUANTS *

Albert M. Levenson and Babette S. Solon †
teach at Queens College of the City University
of New York.

In the usual statement of production theory, average returns to scale
are specified in terms of scale elasticity: $E = (dQ/Q)/(dk/k)$, where
$Q = q(k\overline{X}, k\overline{Y})$, $k>0$, and $\overline{X}$ and $\overline{Y}$ are initial values of X and Y which
fix factor proportions when k, the scale coefficient, equals 1.[1] Further,
in the usual statement of production theory, the scale elasticity is related to the spacing of isoquants as follows: When $E>1$, the successively numbered isoquants are getting ever closer (which means that
the production surface, viewed from the origin, is getting steeper and
steeper; i.e., $q_k'' > 0$). When $E < 1$, the isoquants are getting ever farther
apart $(q_k'' < 0)$; and when $E = 1$, it is asserted that the isoquant spacing
does not change $(q_k'' = 0)$. It is the purpose of this note to show (1)
that isoquant spacing depends on marginal, not average, returns to
scale; and (2) that the above usually-stated relationships between average returns to scale and spacing of isoquants are accurate only for
homogeneous production functions.

Scale elasticity is the ratio of marginal returns to scale to average
returns to scale: $E = q_k'/(Q/k)$. In the case of a linear homogeneous
production function, q_k' and Q/k are both constant and equal and
$E = 1$. And since q_k' is a constant, the isoquants are equally spaced. For
homogeneous functions, where there are constantly increasing average
returns to scale, marginal returns to scale must always be greater than

---

* From the *American Economic Review*, Vol. LVI, No. 3 (June, 1966), pp. 501–505.
Reprinted by permission.

† The authors are indebted to Mr. Joel Stone, a student at Queens College, who
noted ambiguities in the usual discussions of the spacing of isoquants.

[1] The only exception that we have been able to find in a check of the literature
appears in Schneider [1, p. 149]. Professor Schneider defines constant, increasing,
and decreasing returns to scale as follows:

$dx/d\lambda$ is constant
$dx/d\lambda$ increases as λ increases
$dx/d\lambda$ diminishes as λ increases

where x represents output and λ represents the scale coefficient (our k).

254

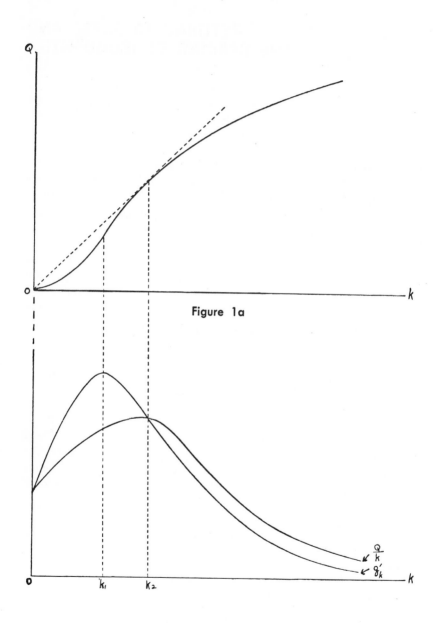

Figure 1a

Figure 1b

average returns to scale and also constantly increasing, E is a constant greater than 1, and the isoquants are spaced closer and closer together. For homogeneous functions where average returns to scale are constantly decreasing, $E<1$ and the isoquants are spaced farther and farther apart.

Figures la and lb show that these relationships do not necessarily hold for nonhomogeneous functions. These figures show increasing average returns to scale for values of k up to k_2 and decreasing average returns beyond k_2. (This is the usual assumption of economic theory.) Marginal returns are increasing up to the inflection point, k_1, and decreasing thereafter. Thus, while average returns to scale are increasing up to k_2, marginal returns to scale first increase, reach a maximum, and then decrease, but they are always greater than average returns. In terms of isoquants, this would mean that up to k_1 the isoquants are getting ever closer and beyond k_1 ever farther apart. But since the marginal returns are greater than the average returns, $E > 1$ up to k_2. These diagrams have thus shown that the usually posited relationships between average returns to scale (and E) and spacing of isoquants are violated in the case of a nonhomogeneous production function.

We now show the *general* relationship between scale elasticity and the spacing of isoquants along a ray from the origin. We begin with the definition of scale elasticity:

(1)
$$E = \frac{q'_k}{\dfrac{Q}{k}}.$$

Differentiating with respect to k:

$$\frac{dE}{dk} = \frac{d}{dk}\left[q'_k\frac{k}{Q}\right] = q''_k\frac{k}{Q} + \frac{1}{Q}q'_k - \frac{k}{Q^2}[q'_k]^2.$$

Substituting (1) in the above, we have:

(2)
$$\frac{dE}{dk} = q''_k\frac{k}{Q} + \frac{1}{Q}q'_k(1-E).$$

For homogeneous functions, E is a constant, and therefore, $dE/dk = 0$.[2] In addition we assume $k > 0$[3] and $q'_k > 0$. It follows from (2) that:

$$q''_k\frac{k}{Q} = -\frac{1}{Q}q'_k(1-E)$$

[2] $q(k\overline{X}, k\overline{Y}) = k^iq(\overline{X}, \overline{Y})$; $q'_k = ik^{i-1}q(\overline{X}, \overline{Y})$; $\dfrac{Q}{k} = \dfrac{k^iq(\overline{X}, \overline{Y})}{k} = k^{i-1}q(\overline{X}, \overline{Y})$

$\text{E} = \dfrac{q'_k}{\dfrac{Q}{k}} = \dfrac{ik^{i-1}q(\overline{X}, \overline{Y})}{k^{i-1}q(\overline{X}, \overline{Y})} = i \text{ (a constant)}$; $\dfrac{dE}{dk} = \dfrac{d}{dk}(i) = 0.$

[3] In Figures la and lb we show $k = 0$ at the origin. This is the case where no output is being produced. For algebraic exposition, it is convenient to neglect the trivial case where no output is being produced; i.e. $k = 0$.

and

(3)
$$\frac{q_k''}{q_k'} = \frac{E-1}{k}.$$

Thus, when $E > 1$, $q_k'' > 0$ (isoquants are ever closer)
    when $E = 1$, $q_k'' = 0$ (isoquants are equally spaced)
    when $E < 1$, $q_k'' < 0$ (isoquants are ever farther apart).

The spacing of isoquants is not discussed at length in the literature; where it is discussed, it is implicitly or explicitly in terms of homogeneous production functions. For nonhomogeneous functions, we investigate first the case where scale elasticity is positive and increasing, i.e., $dE/dk > 0$. Again we assume $k > 0$ and $q_k' > 0$. From (2):

$$\frac{dE}{dk} = q_k'' \frac{k}{Q} + \frac{1}{Q} q_k' (1-E) > 0$$

and

(4)
$$\frac{q_k''}{q_k'} > \frac{E-1}{k}.$$

If $E > 1$, $q_k'' > 0$
    $E = 1$, $q_k'' > 0$
    $E < 1$, $q_k'' \gtrless 0$.

Of more importance for economic analysis is $dE/dk < 0$, i.e., a stage of increasing returns to scale followed by constant and/or decreasing returns to scale. Our assumptions are now $dE/dk < 0$, $k > 0$, and $q_k' > 0$. Then (2) gives:

$$\frac{dE}{dk} = q_k'' \frac{k}{Q} + \frac{1}{Q} q_k' (1-E) < 0$$

(5)
$$\frac{q_k''}{q_k'} < \frac{E-1}{k}.$$

If $E > 1$, $q_k'' \gtrless 0$
    $E = 1$, $q_k'' < 0$
    $E < 1$, $q_k'' < 0$.

Referring to Figure 1b, we see that, with the usual assumption of an initial stage of increasing returns to scale followed by a stage of constant average returns to scale and then a stage of decreasing average returns to scale, $E > 1$ in the first range, $E = 1$ in the second range, and $E < 1$ in the third range. We have shown, however, that marginal returns to scale may be increasing, constant, and decreasing when average returns are increasing; but marginal returns must be decreasing at the point of diminishing average returns to scale and thereafter. Thus, the most general production function diagram would show isoquants along a ray from the origin initially ever closer, then equally spaced, and finally ever farther apart within the range of increasing average returns (up to k_2 in Figure 1b) and continuingly ever farther apart in the stage of decreasing average returns.

REFERENCE

1. E. SCHNEIDER, *Pricing and Equilibrium*. New York 1962.

18

MARGINAL COST CONSTANCY
AND ITS IMPLICATIONS *

HANS APEL is Professor Emeritus at the University of Bridgeport; he was formerly at Middlebury College.

To judge from some recent indications, it almost seems that the proposition of marginal cost linearity resembles the hydra of mythical fame: it continues to thrive in spite of much well-founded criticism against it. One can observe a dangerous tendency to misinterpret the evidence of the case and to build on insufficiently tested ground.[1] Perhaps it is the very extent of the discussion concerning this problem that has made the evidence behind it appear much stronger than it actually is. Two recent contributions which have attempted to draw implications from this assumed cost linearity demonstrate the issue well: they are Professor Hansen's article on "Cost Functions and Full Employment," [2] and Professor Eitemen's communication dealing with the "Factors Determining the Location of the Least Cost Point." [3] Since they refer not only to interesting aspects of theory but also bear directly on matters of great practical importance, it becomes imperative to appraise the validity of these arguments after drawing attention once more to the status of the cost-curve controversy with which they are so intimately connected.

I

In order to gain from the start a somewhat clarified picture of the empirical evidence that has accumulated so far, the pertinent studies so frequently quoted in this discussion are roughly characterized in the table on page 259.

* From the *American Economic Review*, XXXVIII (December, 1948), pp. 870–885. Reprinted by permission.
[1] This seems to account for the strange presentation found in the latest edition of Professor Froman's textbook *Principles of Economics* (R. D. Irwin, Chicago, 1946), when the various pertinent strands are tied together. While apparently accepting the evidence for cost linearity at its face value, he nevertheless assumes a "very sharply" rising marginal cost curve (pp. 342, 343, 379n, 390n, 391).
[2] *Am. Econ. Rev.*, Vol. XXXVII, No. 4 (Sept., 1947), pp. 552–65.
[3] *Am. Econ. Rev.*, Vol. XXXVII, No. 5 (Dec., 1947), pp. 910–18.

The three studies in group I are of a more general nature and cannot by their very nature contribute much to the complex problem of the cost function. The latter, it must be kept in mind, is a *ceteris paribus* proposition that demands an intricate processing of the normally available accounting data, if these are to yield the hidden relationship which the cost function represents.

The Topkis and Hall-Hitch studies, both primarily concerned with other aspects of their investigation, get their results mainly from unprocessed accounting data, the former obviously including "labor overhead costs," the latter, general overhead as well as selling costs. This, of course, introduces the very elements of complexity which under the *ceteris paribus* qualification should be eliminated before the true cost function can be established. Apart from this procedural shortcoming, the evidence presented for marginal cost linearity is not impressive. Only one of the firms interviewed by Hall-Hitch reported decreasing

Cost Studies

Year of publication	Author	Industry studied	Number of firms studied
I. General Cost Studies			
1936	Topkis[a]	Cement	12
1939	Hall-Hitch[b]	Miscellaneous	38
1941	Oliver[c]	All industry	—
II. Cost Function Studies			
A. Based on data within "normal" range of output			
1933	Ehrke[d]	Cement	1
1935	Topkis-Rogers[e]	Steel	15
1940	Yntema[f]	U. S. Steel Corporation	1
1941	Ezekiel-Wylie[g]		
1941	Dean[h]	Leather belts	1
1941	Dean[i]	Hosiery mill	1
1946	Lester[j]	Miscellaneous	58
B. Based on data for entire output range			
1940	Whitman[k]	Department store	1

a B. H. Topkis, "Labor Requirements in Cement Production," *Mo. Lab. Rev.*, Vol. XLII (Mar. 1936), p. 575.
b R. L. Hall and C. J. Hitch, "Price Theory and Business Behaviour," *Oxford Economic Papers*, No. 2 (May, 1939).
c H. M. Oliver, Jr., "The Relationship between Total Output and Man-Hour Output in Manufacturing Industry," *Quart. Jour. Econ.*, Vol. LV (Feb., 1941), pp. 239–54.
d Kurt Ehrke, *Die Uebererzeugung in der Zementindustrie von 1858–1913*, (Jena, 1933), pp. 251–310. [Footnotes continued on p. 260]

marginal cost "up to full capacity"; of the twelve others with decreasing marginal costs, five were clearly operating at low depression outputs, and there is no clear indication that the same was not true of the remaining seven firms.[4]

The cement industry, which Topkis studied, has a rather uncommon technology. Each plant usually has several kilns. A kiln must be operated at full capacity if at all; so output variations are effected by operating fewer or more kilns. Kilns of the same type and size, working at uniform full capacity, cannot possibly have different cost functions. This means that the decreasing costs which the study reveals must necessarily be traced to the influence of overhead costs.

Oliver's investigation undertakes a comparison between aggregate production and employment data for the period 1933–1938, these data being taken from Federal Reserve Board and Bureau of Labor statistics. Since average industrial output during this period was certainly close to the least cost point on a conventionally shaped cost curve, constant or slightly decreasing costs such as he establishes are to be expected.[5]

If we turn now to an appraisal of the more specific cost function studies as listed in group II, the following basic strictures apply:

1. Of the studies under (A), five were admittedly based upon plant operations considerably short of the peak capacity technically possible. The two others, while claiming validity for the entire output range,

---

e United States Steel Corporation, T.N.E.C. Papers (U. S. Steel Corp., New York, 1940), pamph. 6.

f B. H. Topkis and H. O. Rogers, "Man-Hours of Labor per Unit of Output in Steel," *Mo. Lab. Rev.*, Vol. XL (May, 1935), p. 1161.

g M. Ezekiel and K. H. Wylie, "Cost Functions for the Steel Industry," *Am. Stat. Assoc. Jour.*, Vol. XXXVI (Mar., 1941), pp. 91–99.

h Joel Dean, *The Relation of Cost to Output for a Leather Belt Shop* (Nat. Bur. Econ. Research, New York, 1941).

i Joel Dean, *Statistical Cost Functions of a Hosiery Mill* (Univ. of Chicago Press, Chicago, 1941).

j R. A. Lester, "Shortcomings of Marginal Analysis for Wage-Employment Problems," *Am. Econ. Rev.*, Vol. XXXVI, No. 1 (Mar., 1946), pp. 67–75.

k See "Round Table on Cost Functions and their Relation to Imperfect Competition," *Am. Econ. Rev.*, Vol. XXX (May, 1940), pp. 400–02.

4 To judge from Hall-Hitch's "Appendix E," only 12 out of the 38 firms questioned gave pertinent answers, the above mentioned 10 firms indicating decreasing, the other 3 increasing costs. Footnote 1 on page 20 of their article, however, refers to 13 firms with decreasing, 4 with constant, and 2 with increasing costs.

5 The author recognizes this when he says: "During that period recovery never progressed to the point where there was no longer . . . a considerable amount of unused capacity" (*op. cit.*, p. 253).

do not substantiate this claim satisfactorily.[6] The linearity conclusions drawn from these studies consequently do not apply to the extreme right of the output range which is the very region of crucial importance in regard to the behavior of the marginal cost curve. The only study, listed under (B), which definitely refers to the entire range, establishes constant cost under normal conditions but steeply rising marginal costs at the seasonal Christmas peak. Conventional assumptions of severely diminishing returns at extreme levels of output are thus clearly upheld.

2. The adequacy of the methods and techniques used in these studies which deal with an inherently very difficult problem, must seriously be doubted, as shown in the critical appraisals listed below.[7] These pertinent strictures can be summarized as follows:

a. Empirical studies of the cost function run up against a host of difficult problems; these consist in eliminating effects from (a) technological change, (b) change in the size of equipment, (c) changes in factor prices, (d) changes in the rate, direction, permanence, and spread of output; and in (e) measuring a diversified output, and (f) separating costs, unless they are in the most immediate sense direct ones, into those which depend on lapse of time and those which depend on utilization.[8] Only if all this is

---

[6] This refers to the cases of Ehrke and Lester. With regard to Ehrke, Staehle (see footnote 7) states on page 328 that he is the "only one to have secured observations . . . on (the) extreme reaches of the total cost curve. . . ." This, however may be doubted because he refers to only one such case in which the highest rate of output is not more than 7 per cent beyond the one obtainable at least unit cost. Professor Lester's claim of covering output ranges up to full capacity falls to the ground as soon as one doubts that he has succeeded in establishing a clear concept of "capacity."

[7] G. J. Stigler, "Production and Distribution in the Short Run," *Jour. Pol. Econ.*, Vol. 47 (June, 1939), pp. 312-22.

R. Ruggles, "The Concept of Total Linear Cost Output Regressions," *Am. Econ. Rev.* Vol. XXXI, No. 2 June, 1941), pp. 332-35.

C. R. Noyes, "Certain Problems in the Empirical Study of Costs," *Am. Econ. Rev.*, Vol. XXXI, No. 3 (Sept., 1941), pp. 473-92.

Hans Staehle, "Statistical Cost Functions: Appraisal of Recent Contributions," *Am. Econ. Rev.*, Vol. XXXII, No. 2, Pt. 2 (June, 1942), pp. 321-32.

Caleb Smith, "Cost-Output Relation for U. S. Steel," *Rev. Econ. Stat.*, Vol. XXIV (Nov., 1942), pp. 166-76.

Cost Behavior and Price Policy (Nat. Bur. Econ. Research, New York, 1943).

Everet Straus, "Cost Accounting and Statistical Cost Functions," *Am. Econ. Rev.*, Vol. XXXV, No. 3 (June, 1945), pp. 430-31.

[8] *Cf.* Staehle, *op. cit.*, p. 324; Smith, *op. cit.*, p. 166; Noyes, *op. cit.*, p. 491; *Cost Behavior*, pp. 52-77; Straus, *op. cit.*, pp. 431-32; and Stigler's comment in "Round Table on Cost Functions," *Am. Econ. Rev.*, March, 1940, p. 401.

successfully done, is the *ceteris paribus* condition which the theoretical cost function implies fulfilled.

b. Even very slight deviations from cost linearity are sufficient to
cause considerable curvature in the marginal cost curve. But such
deviations, though existing in reality, are likely to disappear due
to biases in the procedure which specifically flow from (a) the generally used method of straight line depreciation, (b) the use of a
fairly long output unit leading to average output rates, and (c)
from the fact that statisticians frequently prefer the adoption of
a linear equation regression.[9]

c. While all these objections question the reliability of the results
shown by the various empirical studies, the possibility of cost
linearity if viewed as an exceptional and special case only, is in
no way excluded by conventional marginal theory. Cost functions,
either almost or fully linear, should be expected wherever given
conditions of production are inherently unfavorable to diminishing returns, as may be the case where the capital/labor ratio is
small, or where a high degree of flexibility is built into a plant, or
where a plant is designed for uniform peak performance.[10]

It is pertinent to point out that these criticisms have not been refuted, but have been reaffirmed in the exhaustive "Cost Behavior"
study.[11]

3. The sample is small and unrepresentative. The two studies which
provide the bulk of the evidence, in so far as numbers of firms are
concerned, are the least convincing. The Topkis-Rogers investigation
of 15 steel producers represents the situation of these mills at a time
when they were operating at 55–60 per cent of their capacity. This
means that the stricture referred to under (1) applies. The Lester study,
which relates to 58 firms, suffers from particularly severe procedural

[9] *Cf.* Smith, p. 166; Ruggles, p. 334; Staehle, p. 329; *Cost Behavior*, pp. 88 and 96.
[10] *Cf.* Stigler, "Production and Distribution in the Short Run," *Jour. Pol. Econ.*,
June, 1939, pp. 312–22; *Cost Behavior*, pp. 111–13.
[11] *Cf. Cost Behavior*, pp. 110–11, where the following conclusion is offered: "The
examination of empirical studies in Sections 2 and 3 concluded that in the cases
explored a linear cost function was the most probable relation *within the observed range* of fluctuations of output, although *basic difficulties in the methods
and techniques made it impossible to place sufficient confidence in the solution to
preclude marginal cost curves with considerable curvature.* This conclusion *certainly does not justify the statement that all cost functions are linear,* but it does
suggest that the conditions underlying discussions of 'diminishing returns' not
only need to be re-examined, but *may* not be as typical as presumed. *Indeed,
even so cautious a conclusion as this must be qualified.* The results of the several
types of empirical studies designed to measure cost-output relationship must be
substantially influenced by the accounting conventions for allocating costs over
different periods" (italics supplied).

defects: such as the exclusive use of so unreliable a method as the questionnaire technique and of an undefined and highly ambiguous concept of "capacity." [12] There is also good reason, supported by Professor Lester's own argument, to doubt the representative character of the firms he has investigated.[13]

4. It is this writer's contention that the Ehrke study has been misinterpreted with regard to the cost-linearity conclusion. Ehrke himself, it is true, makes this claim, which Staehle has also accepted.[14] But a close inspection of Ehrke's chart opposite page 305 shows, particularly with regard to the lines representing the periods of 1888–89 and 1897, that the linearity is only apparent and not real. Marginal costs derived from his figures in Table 9, p. 304, are in six cases out of the eight that can be traced, sharply increasing, even while unit costs continue to decline. It is wholly implausible to assume that the sharply rising trend in the marginal cost curve before it cuts the average curve should not continue beyond the latter. And this is exactly what happens in the only recorded case where production is carried beyond the least cost point.[15] The linearity conclusion is not borne out at all by these

---

[12] Professor Machlup, in his article on "Marginal Analysis and Empirical Research," *Am. Econ. Rev.*, Vol. XXXVI, No. 4, Pt. 1 (Sept., 1946), pp. 550–52, has already criticized this procedure. This writer feels even more strongly in this regard, and considers the use of an undefined "capacity" concept, the ambiguity of which is stressed even in elementary economics, an outrightly "objectionable" course. Professor Lester has countered such criticism with the assertions that "definition was not necessary" and "would only have been confusing and fruitless." See his "Marginalism, Minimum Wages, and Labor Markets," *Am. Econ. Rev.*, Vol. XXXVII, No. 1 [March, 1947], p. 138.) May this not indicate that Professor Lester, recognizing the difficulties of his project, preferred to evade them rather than to overcome them? After all, he himself admits at least the partial justification of the criticisms when he says that "*most* of the businessmen I have talked with *seem* to think of plant capacity" in the way assumed by him (*ibid.*, italics supplied); and such different answers as "Theoretical 100% is likely to produce too many strains" and "By reducing from more than 100% of capacity to 100%, costs are likely to fall" testify clearly to the underlying confusion. *Cf.* "Shortcomings of Marginal Analysis," *Am. Econ. Rev.*, March, 1946, pp. 68, 70.

[13] He remarks that "the flexibility of many plants is, however, extremely limited, especially those designed for earlier stages of manufacturing such as the smelting, refining, compounding, and rolling of materials" (*ibid.*, p. 73). Not one of the 58 firms investigated by Professor Lester belongs in this important group in which conditions of diminishing returns are likely to be more accentuated.

[14] *Op. cit.*, p. 326.

[15] The figures show this strikingly: average unit costs are 5.73, 4.89, 4.88, and 5.12 accompanying outputs of roughly 6.000, 9.700, 10.500, and 11.000 units; marginal costs for the last three output figures are 3.56, 4.74, and 10.00. If one takes into consideration that net price was around 11.00, output only 7% beyond the optimal cost point, it almost seems that conscious marginal considerations may have dictated output determination.

facts. The fact that this firm, with one exception, always operated within the decreasing cost range admits of two alternative explanations: either capacity was always kept ahead of demand, or this was a case of a plant designed for high capacity production. The latter fact would naturally express itself in a cost curve on which the least cost point would lie relatively far to the right.

The following propositions, it would seem, are fair conclusions summing up the evidence as related to the present status of the cost curve controversy:

1. The evidence suggests that the normal range of output, apart from the extremes of a cost curve, may frequently have constant unit costs rather than the slightly decreasing and increasing cost behavior shown in the conventional diagrams.

2. The main assumption, flowing from the concept of diminishing returns, that the marginal cost curve must show steep extremes has not been disproved. On the contrary, it was upheld in the few cases where a reliable test was possible.

3. A conclusion as to what actually is the "typical" shape of the cost curves cannot be drawn from the evidence. Since, on *a priori* grounds it seems doubtful whether a "typical" cost curve can result from the diversity of cost conditions, the conventional type of presentation still retains its merits.

4. Considering, as Stigler does, flexibility as the potential clue to cost linearity, and viewing the achievement of greater flexibility as one aspect of the general process of technological improvement, one may venture the idea that a trend towards cost linearity over the normal range of output is indicated. If, through more refined methods, which would have to remove the linear bias in our empirical approach, such linearity would be supported, a double-kinked shape in which the two kinks would separate the steep extremes from an almost or entirely flat middle range, might then emerge as most representative of general cost behavior.[16] But if such functional dependence on the state of technological development should prevail, this might imply the existence of a great many cost curve shapes "typically" related to specific industries. It might be a fruitful suggestion for researchers to work in this direction.

II

Professor Hansen, in his previously mentioned article, investigates the specific effects that cost linearity would exercise upon the achievement of a full-employment economy. Since, within the context of his thesis, only the linearity at the extreme right of the cost curve matters and since this has been shown to be a not sufficiently supported proposition, his entire argument becomes exceedingly hypothetical.

Although there are several references to the "tentative" character of the empirical results upon which the argument is based, Professor Hansen's procedure is not sufficiently careful to avoid misinterpretation, or even misrepresentation, of the results. In all the three instances in which Professor Hansen points to the support which the cost linearity thesis has found, his presentation is incomplete and misleading: Keynes, contrary to Professor Hansen's interpretation, had definitely refused to accept this thesis.[17] The "Cost-Behavior" study is cited as support without any reference to the severe strictures against the validity of much of the research methods involved.[18] And, finally, the criticism of Lester's grave procedural defects which Professor Machlup had supplied in great detail, is by-passed with the remark, relegated to a footnote, that it contained no successful attack against the empirical findings.

Apart from its weak foundation, the argument contains a number of inconsistencies, and the crucial part of the underlying theoretical reasoning lacks validity.

[17] Relevant passages of Keynes' article are cited as indicative of a change of heart: "Is it the assumption of increasing marginal cost in the short period which we ought to suspect? Mr. Tarshis finds part of the explanation here, and Dr. Kalecki is inclined to infer approximately constant marginal cost. . . . We should all agree that if we start from a level of output very greatly below capacity, so that even the most efficient plant and labour are only partially employed, marginal real cost may be expected to decline with increasing output, or, at the worst, remain constant. *But a point must surely come, long before plant and labour are fully employed,* when less efficient plant and labour have to be brought into commission or the efficient organization employed beyond the optimum degree of intensiveness. Even if one concedes that the course of the short-period marginal cost curve is downwards in its early reaches, Mr. Kahn's assumption *that it eventually turns upwards is, on general common-sense grounds, surely beyond* reasonable question; and that this happens, moreover, on a part of the curve which is highly relevant for practical purposes. *Certainly it would require more convincing evidence than yet exists to persuade me to give up this presumption.* . . . Nevertheless it is of great practical importance that the statisticians should endeavour to determine at what level of employment and output the short-period marginal cost curve for the composite product as a whole begins to turn upward and how sharply it rises after the turning-point has been reached" (italics supplied). (In "Relative Movements of Real Wages and Output," *Econ. Jour.*, March, 1939, pp. 44–45.)

[18] *Cf.* Hansen's statement, "The Committee concludes that empirical studies indicate with few exceptions a linear cost-output relationship" (*op. cit.*, p. 560), with the cautious wording cited in footnote 11.

First, the linearity thesis itself is used in a highly inconsistent manner throughout the argument. The latter rests basically on the assumption that the marginal cost curve, in accordance with results established by recent empirical research, can be assumed to be linear *up to full capacity*. A number of passages are fully in line with this view.[19] But others are not.[20] They indicate merely the assumption that linearity prevails *over large ranges of output*, but not over the extreme right of the cost curve. Since these two propositions represent the crucial difference in the entire cost-curve controversy in which Professor Hansen takes so decided a stand, he cannot logically have both opinions at the same time. For the sake of his argument, however, both views prove to be convenient: the first is used to overcome the difficulties of a transition period to full employment in which the economy is not "perched high up on *steeply* rising marginal cost curves," [21] while only the second one is able to support the overcapacity-argument which Professor Hansen so greatly emphasizes for the period of established full employment.

Secondly, it seems inconsistent to combine the thesis of induced overcapacity during full employment and the belief in prevailingly linear marginal cost curves. If this belief is justified in regard to present conditions, it should be no less appropriate for conditions of full employment.[22] If, on the other hand, marginal costs remain constant, or even decrease up to capacity, the overcapacity assumption becomes absurd.

Thirdly, there is certainly a lack of coherence when the role of marginal costs in the price-determining process is highly stressed on one side, and, on the other side, Professor Lester's empirical findings, which attempt to undermine this role, are upheld.[23] Finally, Professor

---

[19] ". . . as boom conditions are approached" (*ibid.*, p. 559): ". . . as boom conditions of demand develop (*ibid.*, p. 557); ". . . assumptions usually made with respect to sharply rising marginal cost curves" and ". . . without the economy being perched high up on steeply rising marginal cost curves" (*ibid.*, p. 561).

[20] ". . . Keynes . . . concluded that possibly the cost curves were flatter than he had formerly supposed" (*ibid.*, p. 559); ". . . The suggestion that marginal costs approach the 'horizontal over large ranges of output' is of the utmost significance . . ." (*ibid.*, p. 560); "If these assumptions are correct, it means that we shall be compelled to operate for a period under conditions of high marginal cost . . ." and ". . . until we become sufficiently saturated with plant and equipment so that cost functions would again become linear" (*ibid.*, p. 563).

[21] Italics supplied by this writer.

[22] As argued on p. 281, cost linearity appears to be much more feasible under established full employment than it is now.

[23] See Topkis, "Labor Requirements in Cement Production," *Mo. Lab. Rev.*, March, 1936, p. 560, footnote 4.

Hansen's two statements mentioned below [24] present a hardly recon-
cilable contradiction, unless "vigorous" booms are assumed not to be
"short-lived," which is certainly not a generally valid proposition.

The main criticism, however, rests primarily on objections against
the two fundamental tenets of the argument: one, the implication that
"the structure of *costs*, prices and profits" (italics supplied)[25] holds
the clue to the problem of full employment; the other, that linear cost
functions "are a highly favorable fact for full-employment policy." [26]
Compared with these objections, some others related to the role which
overcapacity would have to play under attained full employment, and
to the oversimplified solution of the problem of possible labor short-
ages, play a relatively minor role.

Professor Hansen does not state clearly what specific relationships
he has in mind when he refers to this "structure of costs, prices and
profits." From the entire context, however, one must conclude that
it refers specifically to the influence that marginal costs are bound to
exercise upon prices and profits. Without going into the complex
processes which govern price determination, Professor Hansen seems
to assume that steeply rising marginal costs alone are responsible for
the "abnormally high profits" that cause general instability and fateful
distortion of income distribution.[27] It is not easy to see how this assumption can be backed up. Under perfect competition there can be no
direct price-determining influence from marginal costs; these bear only
on output determination which, in turn, influences aggregate supply
which, finally, affects price. Under conditions of monopolistic competition, output and price-determination are mutually related and depend upon the assumed shape of the demand curve. Where prices are
administered, marginal costs can hardly be assumed to have any effect,
because this would introduce the very price instability which this technique attempts to prevent.

While the preceding brief remarks show in which direction the cost
effects must be traced, one must keep in mind that the marginal principle does not operate automatically and frictionless. In practice, it will
tend to be impaired. The rational conduct which it presupposes is
often absent in businessmen, and it is particularly admitted that its

[24] During the short-lived boom "there is neither time nor incentive to bring capacity
up to . . . low unit cost" (*op. cit.*, p. 558); during sufficiently vigorous booms,
"capacity tends to be adjusted to the 'peak load' so that total unit costs, even at
high output, are fairly flat" (*ibid.*, p. 564).
[25] *Ibid.*, p. 553. A determining relationship between marginal costs on one side,
prices and profits on the other is also assumed on pages 562, 564.
[26] *Ibid.*, p. 560.
[27] Various references can be found on pages 553, 558, 561, 564.

force is weakest under the extreme conditions of either depressions or booms where other considerations often take precedence.[28] Under this aspect, it is likely that the case for the effects of marginal costs on prices is overstated when one assumes unimpaired rational behavior on the part of those concerned.

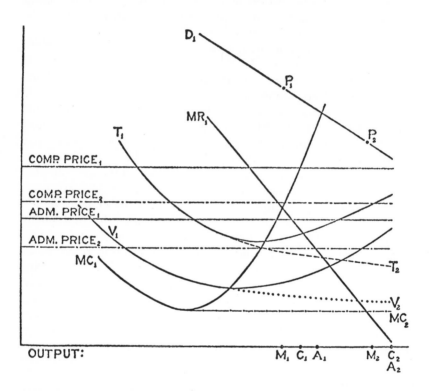

It is possible to show in a simple way that the effects of the two relevant shapes of marginal cost curves on profits are not at all so clear as Professor Hansen suggests. The diagram above attempts to present the case. The lines, curves, and positions denoted with the subscript (1) are identical with those relating to boom conditions in Professor Hansen's three diagrams; those denoted by the subscript (2) describe the changed conditions under constant marginal costs.

Inspection of the diagram in connection with the guiding remarks previously laid down reveals that:

a. Under perfect competition the boom demand curve and the con-

[28] *Cf.* Keynes, *op. cit.,* sec. V, pp. 46–47; also Machlup, *op. cit.,* pp. 520–21.

stant marginal cost curve can never meet. This does not prove the marginal principle wrong, but implies only that whenever price is above marginal costs—as certainly is to be expected in the boom—output tends theoretically to infinity, and practically to peak capacity. This new output C_2 is 30 per cent higher than C_1 was. If one assumes the *aggregate* demand curve to have an elasticity of 2 over the relevant range, which cannot vary much from Professor Hansen's underlying assumptions, a 30 per cent increase in supply would lead to a 20 per cent reduction in price which is represented on the diagram by a new line marked (Comp. Price$_2$).

b. The intersection of the newly introduced constant marginal cost curve (MC$_2$) with the marginal revenue curve (MR$_1$) leads to the new price and output positions (P$_2$) and (M$_2$) for the firms operating under conditions of monopolistic competition.

c. The situation representative of administered price conditions permits two alternatives, depending on whether the businessmen concerned will or will not anticipate maintenance of full employment. In the latter case, they will cling to the previous price because they want to be sure to cover at least their variable costs even at low depression outputs; in the former, however, one should assume that they are willing to reduce price to a level which would yield unit profits characteristic of a "normal sales" output, as indicated by Professor Hansen's last diagram; this is represented by the new line marked (Adm. Price$_2$). Once this price is considered a datum for the whole range of output, profit maximization would of course be reached at full capacity.

The relationships thus established can be easily summarized in precise figures; listed in the following table, they indicate the percentage change that cost linearity would produce in comparison with cost curvilinearity.

	Perfect competition (per cent)	Monopolistic competition (per cent)	Administered price [29] (per cent)	
			I	II
Unit profit	− 5	− 20	+ 550	+ 150
Total profit	+ 29	+ 6	+ 700	+ 215
Output	+ 35	+ 32	+ 30	+ 30
Sales	+ 10	+ 6	+ 30	± 0
Prices	− 20	− 20	± 0	− 20

[29] In the light of Professor Hansen's remark on page 559, the very high percentage increases shown below reflect the utterly low profits of the base period rather then implausibly high profits under the new conditions.

Certainly, these results, which claim only approximate validity, do not bear out Professor Hansen's contention but show a tendency towards even higher total profits on the whole, and towards that greater instability to which they are inherently linked.

It is this latter aspect to which Professor Hansen's second fundamental tenet refers. His assumption of the favorable effects of linear cost functions which is identical with a belief in their stabilizing effects, flows logically from the wrong and unsubstantiated idea that they would mitigate high profits to a considerable extent. Apart from the preceding evidence to the contrary which undermines the very foundation of this tenet, it is, however, hard to see how Professor Hansen could ignore a most definite warning which he could hardly have overlooked. For, his pertinent statement is made almost as the continuance of a quotation from the "Cost Behavior" study which ushers in exactly the opposite conclusion of greater instability.[30] Such instability might imply favorable effects in a period of general under-employment, but not under boom conditions. In the former case, cost linearity would be conducive to a low price policy which, in turn, due to greater *instability*, would favor increased output levels. In the latter case, the cost effect on prices will be overshadowed by the pressure from supply and demand conditions, and output levels forced up to peak capacity are no unmixed blessing. Under boom conditions, U-shaped marginal costs, if they have an influence on profits at all, take on the character of a brake and do not render the situation more precarious. This is only a reiteration of the maladjustment concept that underlies so much of accepted business cycle theory. The dilemma which confronts us in the boom, which Professor Hansen seems to have overlooked in this connection, is that both low as well as high costs can produce the same high profits, because these are a function of costs *and* prices reflecting only their relative and not their absolute magnitudes.

A further criticism must be directed against Professor Hansen's thesis that full employment, "if maintained for a considerable period and on a basis such that people expect it to persist," would tend to produce large overcapacity favorable for low-cost production and for

[30] The two versions compare as follows: "If marginal costs approach the horizontal over large ranges of output, small changes in demand make for larger changes in output. An economic system with linear cost functions is more unstable than one with markedly U-shaped marginal cost functions" (*Cost Behavior*, pp. 109–10). "The suggestions that marginal costs approach the 'horizontal over large ranges of output' is of the utmost significance since, if this is so, small changes in demand will tend to permit large changes in output without significant price increases. If the economic system has linear cost functions, this is a highly favorable fact for full-employment policy" (Hansen, *op. cit.*, p. 560).

a tendency towards an equilibrium profit rate.[31] With the qualification which this conditional clause contains, the cart is obviously put before the horse. If cost-price-profit relationships should actually be as unfavorable for the establishment of full employment as Professor Hansen attempts to show they may not be, both its maintenance for a considerable period and the belief of people in such maintenance cannot very well materialize.

But even if one assumes these preconditions as given, Professor Hansen's conclusions would seem to be justified only under highly competitive general conditions. That full employment should automatically create a thoroughly competitive atmosphere is neither a reasonable proposition nor has Professor Hansen suggested it. Barriers to easy entrance into the most important fields of industry would therefore remain at best as formidable as they are today; and without strong and rather universal pressure from new entrants it seems doubtful that businessmen should easily turn to the overcapacity thesis. After all, they are not going to live in a stationary economy after establishment of full employment. Full and even intensified continuation of dynamic forces with their attendant aspects of change and uncertainty, the tendencies toward the "bunching" of innovations along the lines of Schumpeterian thought, and the fact that increase of plant capacity normally cannot be secured in small continuous increments but necessitates certain jumps, do not make it likely that businessmen will readily agree to march always far ahead of prevailing demand schedules.

Ironically enough, Professor Hansen has overlooked a much simpler solution of the cost problem under securely established full-employment conditions. Assurance of a sustained demand should certainly influence the type of plants that businessmen will build. Therefore, they are likely to build for constant peak performance in the way suggested by Professor Stigler's previously quoted exposition and represented by marginal cost curves decreasing up to full capacity. This would obviously be a solution much preferable to that of maintaining vast over-capacity.

With regard to Professor Hansen's labor shortage argument, it is hard to imagine that the three circumstances which he seems to appraise as a sufficient remedy, could produce more than a very slight alleviating effect. The margin of flexibility represented by "turnover" unemployment appears to be more apparent than real. Bottlenecks resulting from a real shortage of labor relative to the vastly increased capacity of plant could certainly not be remedied in this way. How,

31 *Ibid.*, pp. 558, 564. See also the remarks on p. 266 with regard to the inconsistency implied in the overcapacity assumption.

secondly, growth factors in the labor supply which definitely represent a long-term phenomenon, should sufficiently influence short-run bottlenecks, is also not easy to comprehend. The final reference to possible improvements in the technique of job classifications and wage structures carries only the claim that they would "tend to ease" bottleneck pressures. This limited claim one may grant.

III

The origin of Professor Eiteman's article, no doubt, lies also in the impact of the misinterpreted thesis of cost linearity "up to full capacity" that resulted from Professor Lester's apparently convincing investigation. Accepting these results without reservation, he has attempted to add a further explanation for this phenomenon. If, in conformity with the analysis of the first section of this paper, one doubts severely that its prevalence has been established at all, one may well feel that his effort cannot yield significant results. Yet, it certainly calls for consideration and appraisal.

Again, there is reason to start with an objection against procedure. In his attempt to pit the new doctrine against tradition, Professor Eiteman unnecessarily overstates the cleavage. His Figure 1, supposed to be "typical" in the sense that it portrays "practically all average cost curves used for illustrative purposes in textbook discussions," [32] represents an extreme of which this writer has been unable to detect even a single example.[33]

[32] Eiteman, *op. cit.*, p. 910, first paragraph.

[33] In Figure 1 he draws a "Typical Cost Curve" with the least-cost-point at 35% of total capacity, and in Figure 2 an output curve with the point of highest returns to the input factor at 25% only. In fourteen of the most widely used textbooks, selected at random, this writer found cost curves with the least-cost-point in one case at 40%, in two at 80; the average was 64, the median and the mean 60. True, the *output curve* of Figure 2 is taken from one of these textbooks which, however, displays a *cost curve* with the least-cost-point at about 65%. It almost looks as if Professor Eiteman subconsciously introduced the output approach because he had not at hand a case of a cost curve portrayal with a sufficiently strict curvature, and then submitted to a process of rationalization. It is, of course, not strange to find output diagrams more easily than cost diagrams which show the unabated influence of "diminishing returns," because the former go often directly back to empirical findings related to agriculture, while the latter are meant to depict industrial conditions where the influence of diminishing returns is definitely more subdued. If one wants to establish the "typical" cost curve, thus ignoring all the mental reservations which every alert instructor probably makes when he draws such a curve on the blackboard, the least-cost-point would have to be shown at about two-thirds of the total range.

The central suggestion offered by Professor Eiteman is to the effect that prevailingly linear cost functions at the extreme right of a cost curve result when an "engineer designed the plant so as to cause the variable factor to be used most efficiently when the plant is operated close to capacity." [34] Thus stated, the proposition is certainly true, but, so it seems, not new at all. Whenever a plant is built for performance at one and the same capacity level only, this excludes the necessity—and very likely the possibility also—for its adaptability to changing inputs. This case of "zero adaptability" has been presented by Stigler, and clarified by a diagram which shows in principle the same shape of a cost curve decreasing up to the point of highest capacity which would correspond to Eiteman's Figure 3.[35] Actually, what distinguishes Eiteman's suggestion from Stigler's is only a different evaluation of its practical significance. While Eiteman thinks that it relates to a prevailing phenomenon, Stigler states that it "is indeed unlikely that this case would ever arise in practice. . . ." [36]

It is, however, the specific conclusion which Professor Eiteman reaches and presents for acceptance that invites criticism. From the unquestionably correct assumption that a plant built for uniform peak performance must have been designed by an engineer, he develops, though clearly as a logical *nonsequitur,* the corollary that the most relevant dichotomy is between plants in which the "fixed factor was designed *by engineers"* . . . or "whether it was supplied *by nature." * [37] This, however, is a highly misleading proposition, because one might easily conclude that it is only a matter of hiring engineering talent to build those ideal plants with cost linearity up to peak capacity; while actually the real difficulty involved is the question posed to a businessman as to whether he would be better off with a plant built for uniform peak capacity or with a plant well adaptable to varying capacities. This will, on the part of the businessman, invite the same type of cal-

<hr/>

[34] *Ibid.,* p. 913.

[35] "Production and Distribution in the Short Run," *Jour. Pol. Econ.,* June, 1939, pp. 310, 313, 314, Fig. 2(A). The only difference in Stigler's diagram is that his plant shows the uniform and unadaptable position at a relatively low output level. It almost seems that this representation is somewhat inconsistent with the assumed condition, because the fact that marginal costs at this capacity become vertical makes it the point of peak capacity. It may be also noted that Eiteman, on p. 914, objects to this representation of the marginal cost situation. He says: "The truth of the matter is that the MC curve does not rise vertically at the point of capacity output: it ENDS there." This, for all practical purposes, is correct, but shows also that Eiteman interprets Stigler's diagram as implying the same case he makes.

[36] *Ibid.,* p. 310, (d).

[37] *Op. cit.,* p. 915 (italics in the text).

culation related to profit maximization to which Stigler has referred in connection with the similar problem of deciding upon a wanted degree of flexibility.[38]

The proper dichotomy, therefore, may be suggested as follows: On one side there are plants largely influenced by natural conditions of "diminishing returns," and those built for fluctuating conditions of output. The latter, most suitable for our present cycle-affected economy, are, as a rule, certainly built by engineers. On the other side, there may exist special conditions favoring plants in which their "normal" capacity coincides with peak capacity—and these, of course, are *also* built by engineers!

It may well be that Professor Eiteman—in 1947—had more reason to point to the importance of the type of plant he has in mind, than Stigler had in 1939. War conditions with their call for constant peak performance and with no uncertainty about maintenance of demand, are, in contrast to the output fluctuations characteristic of peace conditions, exactly those in which the type of plant envisaged by Professor Eiteman had a proper place. But all that this proves is that under appropriate conditions such plants can be built, and not that engineering talent will be the solution to U-shaped marginal cost curves such as are likely to prevail in an economy subject to high fluctuations of output levels.

[38] *Op. cit.,* p. 316.

19

WHAT DO ENTREPRENEURS SEEK? *

GEORGE J. STIGLER teaches at the University of Chicago; he was formerly at Columbia University.

In order to predict how firms will behave, we must know what their owners seek. The entrepreneur could have, and historically has had, very diverse goals: to be his own boss, to maintain a customary standard of living, to obtain money and economic power, to obtain political power, etc. In modern economics it is customary to attribute to him one overriding goal: the maximization of profits.

No economist would deny that all entrepreneurs are subject also to other desires that may conflict with profit maximization, nor even that some of these other forces may be widespread and important. Rather, the position is that profit maximization is the strongest, the most universal, and the most persistent of the forces governing entrepreneurial behavior. This is a judgment based upon wide observation of entrepreneurs under innumerable sets of conditions: of the need for profit incentives to obtain maximum output even in war; of the enormous risks and the monotonous toil that are incurred because of the prospect of profits; and especially, from the success of predictions based on this assumption.

Of course this overstates the degree of confidence placed in the assumption by most economists. Some wish to give an important role to "the desire for security," although they have not yet indicated what an entrepreneur wishes to be secure against that requires non-profit-maximizing behavior. Others wish to introduce a goal of "fair profits" which reflect a social consciousness and obligation to the community (especially under monopolistic conditions), so far without exploring the rubbery concept of fairness. Still others wish to make the entrepreneur the passive bearer of his cultural tradition and seek to explain economic structure in terms of a broader institutional structure.

The reason for not adopting such alternative goals is that unless they are developed in content and their scope of operation and strength are approximately determined, they impoverish rather than enrich eco-

* From *Theory of Price*, (New York: The Macmillan Company, 1952), pp. 148–150. Reprinted by permission.

nomic analysis. If, for example, an undefined and unmeasured "sense of fairness" is put into the theory of the firm, we can no longer predict anything the firm will do. With a rise in wage rates, for example, the firm may restrict output at the ruling price to maximize profits, or it may leave output unchanged to avoid discharging workers, or it may increase output because buyers suffer even more from the wage increase. There is no objection in principle to these alternative goals, but in their present undeveloped state they are seldom useful in general analysis. And I would support the controversial position that persistent patterns of entrepreneurial behavior can usually be explained on profit maximizing grounds.[1]

The profit-maximizing assumption confers great definiteness on economics. The variables in a firm's policy that affect profits are usually more or less quantifiable, and the rule of maximum profits is simple: equate marginal cost to price. So long as price exceeds marginal cost of output, expansion of output will increase profits. If the marginal cost exceeds price, a contraction of output will increase profits. This simple rule (which, however, is not always simple to apply) gives specific content to predictions of the behavior of the firm.

We should note, however, that the rule, marginal cost equals price, is only a shorthand rule and that it is subordinate to a more basic rule: maximize profits. Thus, if marginal cost equals price at several outputs, or at none, one must go back to profit maximizing. More important, profit maximizing itself is ambiguous unless the profit rate is constant through time. Consider the two following annual profit streams:

Profit stream	Years in future		
	0	1	2
I	$100	$200	$ 50
II	100	50	220

One cannot assert that one of these streams is bigger than the other.

When the profit rate fluctuates we must shift to the most basic formulation of the entrepreneur's goal: maximizing the present value of the firm. The present value of the firm is the discounted value of its future income, so if we know the proper interest rate, we can always tell which income stream is most preferable. A few values of the above profit streams are tabulated below for selected interest rates:

---

[1] Yet one should beware of the temptation to define profit so broadly that it includes every possible motive.

Interest rate (per cent)	Profit	Stream
	I	II
5	$335.83	$347.17
10	323.14	327.27
15	311.72	309.83
20	301.39	294.44
25	292.00	280.80

Thus the first profit stream is more valuable at high interest rates, and the second stream at low interest rates; they are equally valuable at an interest rate of 13.3 per cent.

20

THE BREAKUP OF THE
MAXIMIZATION PRINCIPLE *

GERALD L. NORDQUIST teaches at the University
of Iowa.

This paper arises from the recurrent proposal that the theory of
price is in an unsatisfactory state largely because of shortcomings in the
theory of the firm. This proposition is summarily rejected by many, if
not most, academic economists, but it has exhibited remarkable persistence and resiliency despite determined efforts to put it down. The
issue has been openly and, at times, hotly debated among economists
for more than 20 years and is far from being resolved at present. Like
an ill-fated ship, the theory of the firm came under fire almost immediately after being launched and subsequently became the subject of one
round of criticism after another, virtually without rest. Among the
critics there are wide differences as to what is wrong with the theory
and little agreement on what should be done—whether it should be
refitted, retired, or simply scuttled to make way for a completely new
model, revised from stem to stern.

Although structural defects allegedly have been spotted in every
compartment, the chief trouble with the traditional theory of the firm
seems to be in its propulsion—in the principle that business firms are
motivated by the desire to maximize profit. Criticism of this conventional assumption ranges from assertions that firms typically maximize
something other than profit (viewed as the excess of total revenue over
total outlays) to claims that they do not maximize, cannot maximize,
and do not even care to maximize.

On the other hand, the traditional theory of the firm has staunch
defenders. Many prominent academic economists maintain that there
is nothing essentially wrong with the theory or its structural components, including the principle of profit maximization. Rather, if shortcomings exist, they belong to the critics who often understand neither
the nature nor the proper use of theory in economics. As a conse-

* From *Quarterly Review of Economics and Business,* Vol. V, (Fall, 1965), pp. 33–46.
Copyright © by the Board of Trustees, University of Illinois. Reprinted by permission of the Bureau of Economic and Business Research.

quence, they claim, the debate is a patent waste of time and energy which should be devoted to more rewarding tasks.

At the risk of being charged with perpetuating an overly long series of misguided efforts, I shall address myself to a general assessment of what I believe is still an open issue in economics. Specifically, my objectives are (1) to review the unfolding of the controversy over the neoclassical theory of the firm, drawing special attention to the maximization principle and including a brief statement on where things stand today; and (2) with respect to the theory of price, cost, and output, to consider the consequences of dropping the traditional maximization assumption and replacing it with some other principle which does not attribute to business managers knowledge and clairvoyance which they do not possess.

Discussion in this paper is confined to the main stream of the controversy, to the internal debate among economists. Since my chief concern is with the kind of behavioral explanations and predictions economists are prome to make, perhaps the bias can be excused and any shortcoming in the scope of the essay will be compensated for by a gain in manageability. This is not necessarily the best possible choice, but merely one of several acceptable alternatives I now see. I can only proceed with the hope that the outcome will exceed or at least match the expectation.

THE ASCENDENCY OF THE FIRM

In the 1920's, the neoclassical theory of value was still reigning supreme, after several decades of preeminence. This was a relatively settled period in the history of economic thought; price and distribution theory was firmly established and well grounded in the works of Marshall, Edgeworth, Clark, and Wicksteed, to mention a few of the architects of this outstanding tradition. There were, of course, vigorous and articulate critics of the neoclassical school (such as Veblen, Schumpeter, Tawney, the Webbs, and H. L. Moore) with all its formalism, apparent neglect of history, and preoccupation with perfect competition; but the occasional dissenters did little to shake the prevailing view.

In this period the theory of the firm was an integral, yet only vaguely recognizable, part of the branch of value theory dealing with production, costs, and supply. Cournot[1] had long before provided most of the ideas and tools for it, including the mathematical approach,

---

[1] Augustin Cournot, *Researches into the Mathematical Principles of the Theory of Wealth*, translated by N. T. Bacon (London: Macmillan, 1897).

a clear expression of the producer's demand and cost functions, a rough morphology of markets, and the principle of profit maximization. As is well known, however, Cournot was overlooked or ignored for several decades after he wrote. In the meantime the marginal economists, reacting to the heavy emphasis on costs in the theory of political economy, set about building up their theory of value on the side of demand, giving scant attention to the determinants of supply. This bias was soon to be corrected in the skillful hands of Marshall; without neglecting demand, he focused attention once again on the producer by reintroducing the laws of returns and elements of cost into economic theory.[2]

Curiously enough, despite the swingback of interest to considerations of production and cost following the immensely successful publication of Marshall's *Principles,* there was no great rush to examine the market behavior of the individual firm. This lack of interest in the firm as a distinct and complex market agent prevailed for nearly 40 years.[3] Marshall, no doubt, was in good measure responsible. Because of his preoccupation with equilibrium in commodity markets and resolute presumption of competition, the firm was completely overshadowed by the industry. The anomalous case of monopoly aside, in the early neoclassical view the firm had significance only because it was a very small element in the makeup of the competitive industry. Consequently, it was afforded no perceptible economic power, no function other than to organize production efficiently and adjust passively to impersonally determined market forces. Cournot's more balanced view of market prototypes made no discernible impression on Marshall, although in the Preface to the first edition of his *Principles,* he acknowledged his debt to Cournot for other things. But on the primacy of competition, which was the great legacy of his classical predecessors, he would not be swayed.

There remained, however, a stubborn paradox in the neoclassical structure which finally proved to be its undoing, namely, that unlimited competition is incompatible with the technical condition of increasing returns. The inimitable Cournot with characteristic precision had put his finger on the problem,[4] and perhaps this was one of the reasons he felt obliged to treat perfect competition as a limiting case. Marshall, on the other hand, made such a good argument for the ex-

---

[2] Alfred Marshall, *Principles of Economics* (1st ed.; London: Macmillan, 1890).

[3] Cf. P. J. D. Wiles, *Price, Cost and Output* (Oxford: Basil Blackwell, 1956), pp. 1–4.

[4] Cournot observed: "It is, moreover, plain under the hypothesis of unlimited competition, and where, at the same time, the function $\phi_k{}^1(D_k)$ should be a decreasing one, that nothing would limit the production of the article." *Op. cit.,* p. 76.

istence of increasing returns in manufacturing industries that he was
really never able to extricate himself from the difficulty, although
through his "representative firm" and "external economies" he made
an overture toward reconciliation.[5]

It was not until the late 1920's, as a consequence of the discussion
arising from the appearance of Sraffa's article on the laws of returns,[6]
that the most convinced Marshallians finally had to face up to this
distressing dilemma. The conclusion had to be that if "competition is
perfect, and if no frictions prevent firms from growing to their equilibrium size, then falling costs for the individual firm cannot occur." [7]
Still, the condition of falling cost would not give way.

The emergence of the theory of imperfect competition as a result of
the controversy over returns is by now well documented. The actual
modifications in the new theory were slight—the producer was given
some measure of influence on demand, and some geometry was added
—but the consequences seemed to be little short of revolutionary. An
entirely new market morphology was created. After more than a century of supremacy, unlimited competition was relegated to the status
of extreme case; oligopoly, with some trouble, was brought into the
family of market structures; and in general there was a rush to examine the multifarious consequences of introducing monopoly into competition.

There was also a marked shift in focus from the industry to the
firm,[8] and fresh doubts began to emerge over the meaning of supply.
The new theory was hailed as more realistic, but it also was much less
tidy. Most of Marshall's analysis of costs had to be reworked, and the
distressing condition of indeterminateness of equilibrium was more
frequently encountered. Consumer sovereignty was dealt a sharp blow,
and, worst of all, there was nothing at hand to replace the regulatory
function of unlimited competition except government control.

Economic theorists thereafter were to pay closer attention to their

---

[5] Marshall, *op. cit.*, p. 666 n.

[6] Piero Sraffa, "The Laws of Returns Under Competitive Conditions," *Economic
Journal*, Vol. 36, No. 144 (December, 1926), pp. 535–50. For references to a num-
ber of other articles in this general discussion see the editor's note, *Economic
Journal*, Vol. 40, 157 (March, 1930), p. 79.

[7] Joan Robinson, "Imperfect Competition and Falling Supply Price," *Economic
Journal*, Vol. 42, No. 168 (December, 1932), p. 544.

[8] Much later Wiles observed: "It is not sufficiently realized that the descriptive
economics of the entrepreneur began with imperfect competition; before then
we studied industries, not firms. Thus Birck and Taussig, writing immediately
before 'imperfect competition' treat the marginal cost of an industry as the average cost of the marginal firm." *Op cit.*, p. 3.

assumptions. It became necessary to be more explicit about such things as the nature of the product, the conditions of entry, the size of the firm relative to the market, and the state of the entrepreneur's knowledge, including the nagging question of uncertainty. Theorists were also more explicit on the motivational assumption, but on this point, at least for a while, there was little to quarrel about; the maximization principle was retained intact from the Marshallian theory. Indeed, because of the emphasis now placed on the firm, this principle became an indispensable element in the determination of the firm's equilibrium.

THE GATHERING STORM

After a long time in preparation the theory of the firm was fully launched, but it ran into trouble almost immediately. As the assumptions of the theory were subjected to closer scrutiny, not only with respect to their logical consistency, but in view of their proximate correspondence to observed business behavior and conditions, the voices of dissent began to multiply. In particular, there soon developed a growing uneasiness, if not outright skepticism over the appropriateness of the maximization principle.

One source of reservation was a consequence of recognizing the importance of monopoly elements in the market economy. Since the monopolist ordinarily earns above normal returns, why should he maximize? In imperfectly competitive industries where barriers to entry are effective, the firm ordinarily does not have to walk the tightrope of zero economic profits. Instead, the existence of monopoly power provides a certain latitude for error and inertia; the range of viable alternatives is much wider than under conditions of perfect competition. Why, then, should the firm always seek the profit-maximizing alternatives?

J. R. Hicks was one of the first to express this reservation:

> It seems not at all unlikely that people in monopolistic positions will very often be people with sharply subjective costs; if this is so, they are likely to exploit their advantage much more by not bothering to get very near the position of maximum profit, than by straining themselves to get very close to it. The best of all monopoly profits is a quiet life.[9]

In the cases of large-group competition it could be argued that profit

[9] J. R. Hicks, "Annual Survey of Economic Theory: The Theory of Monopoly," *Econometrica*, Vol. 3, No. 1 (February, 1935), p. 8.

maximization exists *ex definitione,* as a necessary condition for ultimate equilibrium, but it became clear that this reasoning would not hold in analyses of industries characterized by the conditions of fewness and restricted entry.

An attempt was soon made to patch up this source of indeterminacy in models of imperfect competition by introducing an entrepreneurial preference function which would allow treatment of objectives other than profit maximization. The idea was first proposed by Higgins [10] who suggested that the entrepreneur orders his preferences with respect to income and other rewards, such as leisure and prestige, in a way that is consistent with the axioms of rational choice. Thus under conditions of imperfect competition, price and output may be fully determinate, but it is highly unlikely that the equilibrium will coincide with the profit-maximizing solution.

Other expressions of doubt arose in this period as to the appropriateness of the maximization principle. The studies of Berle and Means, Burnham, and Gordon [11] in various degrees showed that many large corporations are not controlled by their owners largely because ownership is so widely diffused. Rather, control often rests in salaried professional managers who frequently have little or no equity in the corporations they operate. The question then is, Why should management of this kind be compelled to maximize profits, particularly when other objectives and motives exist? In the colorful language of Wiles, "If *homo economicus* is suspect, then *corporatio economicus* is rubbish."

The Hall and Hitch study [12] published in 1939 represented the first reasonably systematic attempt to examine how prices and outputs are determined in the firm. The results appeared not to support the marginal analysis and the postulate of profit maximization. One of the more important conclusions was that the businessmen in the sample tended to follow a "full cost" policy in setting prices, knowing little or nothing of the cost and revenue functions of marginal analysis. In following this policy, price is established by calculating the full average cost per unit of output including a conventional markup for profit. The quantity sold is then determined simply by what the market will

[10] B. Higgins, "Elements of Indeterminacy in the Theory of Imperfect Competition," *American Economic Review,* Vol, 29, No. 3 (September, 1939), pp. 468-79.

[11] A. Berle and G. Means, *Modern Corporation and Private Property* (New York: Commerce Clearing House, Inc., 1932); J. Burnham, *The Managerial Revolution* (New York: John Day, 1941); R. A. Gordon, *Business Leadership in the Large Corporation* (Washington: Brookings Institution, 1945).

[12] R. L. Hall and C. J. Hitch, "Price Theory and Business Behavior," *Oxford Economic Papers,* No. 2 (May, 1939), pp. 12-45.

take. It appeared highly fortuitous that profits would be maximized under these conditions.

It was this period also that economists began formally to wrestle with the problem of uncertainty in the decision-making process. Gerhard Tintner showed precisely how the objective function of the producer would have to be modified to incorporate this element.[13] Under conditions of uncertainty, according to Tintner, the producer attempts to maximize a subjective preference functional, that is, an expectation of return based on a probability distribution whose parameters can only be subjectively estimated. There were at least two implications in this work for the theory of the firm. First, in showing how the firm might maximize under conditions of uncertainty, Tintner and others incidentally displayed the true complexity of the decision-making process; secondly, they demonstrated that the equilibrium under uncertainty is likely to be very different from that established under conditions of perfect foresight.

Although the decade following the appearance of the Robinson-Chamberlin theories was a period of rapid developments in the theory of the firm, it was also a time of foreboding and increasing perplexity. The theory of the firm was now expected to conform more closely to the observed facts of business organization and behavior, but somehow it appeared to be as remote from reality as ever. The Sraffa concession to realism merely opened a Pandora's box of deficiencies, not the least of which were the emerging doubts as to the validity of the maximization principle.

In surveying the developments of this period, Boulding concluded that the main trouble with the Cambridge theory was that it ignored the element of time in business activity. As he perceived it, the concept of the firm in this theory was nothing more "than a rough—though useful—first approximation." But he also saw in the preceding decade a building up of a more accurate picture of the enterprise, one which explicitly took into account the elements of time and uncertainty. Under these conditions, he noted, it cannot be assumed that the firm seeks to maximize net revenue because the entrepreneur may prefer to forgo profit in the present for larger returns in the future. "The problem,

---

[13] Gerhard Tintner, "The Theory of Choice Under Subjective Risk and Uncertainty," *Econometrica*, Vol. 9, No. 384 (July–October, 1941), pp. 298–304; *idem*, "The Price Theory of Production Under Technological Risk and Uncertainty," *op cit.*, pp. 305–12; *idem*, "The Theory of Production Under Non-Static Conditions," *Journal of Political Economy*, Vol. 50, No. 5 (October, 1942), pp. 646–67; and *idem*, "A Contribution to the Non-Static Theory of Production," in Lange, McIntyre, and Yntema, eds. *Studies in Mathematical Economics and Econometrica* (Chicago: University of Chicago Press, 1942), pp. 92–109.

'What does the entrepreneur maximize?' therefore, becomes an acute one." [14]

THE MARGINALIST CONTROVERSY

By 1946 the stage was set for a direct encounter between the disciples of the neoclassical theory of the firm and a growing group of dissenters. It is difficult to tell exactly where the line was drawn, but roughly speaking the more theoretical economists tended to be on one side and the more applied, on the other. The clash of opposing points of view was sharp and heated; few who cared failed to choose a side and do battle. Neither side achieved a decisive victory, and there ensued a cold war between the major combatants which remains unsettled even today.

The controversy began when Machlup mounted a counterattack on the critics of the marginal theory, concentrating in particular on an article by Richard A. Lester which appeared in the March, 1946, *American Economic Review*. Lester had reported on the results of a survey of some 50 business firms which was intended to determine, among other things, how employers respond to changes in wage rates. He claimed that business firms do not alter output and employment according to the principles of marginal productivity theory and, therefore, the theory must be wrong. He concluded that most employers do not think in terms of marginal variables and pointed to several "insuperable" problems of applying the marginal analysis to the modern multiprocess firm.

The reply by Machlup was brilliantly executed and on many points seemed to be totally devastating. He took on not only Lester but all critics of conventional economic theory who "from time to time voice surprise at the general acceptance of marginalism and the confidence of the textbook writers in the validity of the marginal analysis." His objective was to show that "the alleged inapplicability of marginal analysis is often due to a failure to understand it, to faulty research techniques, or to mistaken interpretations of 'findings.'" The chief aim of the marginal theory, he declared, is not to provide a complete explanation of business conduct but rather to show the probable effects of certain changes in market forces. Machlup also argued that Lester's results could be fully harmonized with marginal analysis. And he left little room for doubting that he had to his own complete satisfaction dispatched Lester and, for that matter, all others of the same bent:

[14] Kenneth Boulding, "The Theory of the Firm in the Last Ten Years," *American Economic Review*, Vol. 32, No. 4 (December, 1942), p. 793.

I conclude that the marginal theory of business conduct of the firm has not been shaken, discredited or disproved by the empirical tests discussed in this paper. I conclude, furthermore, that empirical research on business policies cannot assure useful results if it employs the method of mailed questionnaires, if it is confined to direct questions, without carefully devised checks, and if it aims at testing too broad and formal principles rather than more narrowly defined hypotheses.[15]

Thus opened a debate which must rank as one of the most lively slugging matches in the annals of economic thought. Dozens of articles and notes on the topic poured out of the journals in the next five or six years. Of particular interest were the discussions by Lester, Machlup, H. M. Oliver, Jr., F. H. Blum, and R. A. Gordon in the *American Economic Review*. The controversy was fanned by the "findings" of several studies of production costs in the firm, some of them dating back to the late 1930's.[16] In essence, these cost studies challenged the validity of the concept of diminishing returns to variable factors, or the principle of rising variable cost per unit of output. Several of the studies found constant unit costs, and more than one claimed that unit costs tend to decline right up to the point of short-period capacity. Although the results of these studies were at first sight unsettling, it was quickly pointed out that, at least in imperfectly competitive markets, the condition of falling cost is perfectly consistent with equilibrium.

After having raged among American economists for several years, the controversy jumped the Atlantic and flared up in Great Britain between the neo-Marshallians of Cambridge and a group of empirically oriented economists at Oxford. An attempt by Andrews [17] to reconstruct the theory of the firm along the lines of full-cost pricing was the immediate cause of the debate. The Cambridge economists reproached the applied economists for not fully understanding the theories of imperfect competition and for proposing an alternative theory (amounting to little more than an account of pricing ritual) without first confronting existing theories with a set of opposing and unreconcilable facts. And so on somewhat different ground the dispute continued.

Looking back on the marginalist controversy, there is evidence that

[15] Fritz Machlup, "Marginal Analysis and Empirical Research," *American Economic Review*, Vol. 36, No. 4 (September, 1946), pp. 519-54.

[16] For a bibliography and critique of these studies, see Hans Apel, "Marginal Cost Constancy and Its Implications," *American Economic Review*, Vol. 38, No. 5 (December, 1948), pp. 870-85.

[17] P. W. S. Andrews, *Manufacturing Business* (London: Macmillan, 1949).

both sides argued from positions of strength but were also extremely vulnerable in certain places. The empiricists' orientation to the facts had an enormous appeal; yet their attacks on the existing theory were often blunted by haphazard statistical work and ill-considered findings. The guardians of the theory, on the other hand, had fortification in long-standing tradition, and displayed matchless skill in polemics; yet they countered with scant empirical evidence of their own.

After the heat of the battle subsided and some of the smoke cleared it became apparent that the principal issues were not settled. Neither were there any major compromises struck nor concessions granted. But it was also obvious that things were not, and could never again be, as they were before. The pronouncements of the defenders were as staunch as ever, but the unavoidable conclusion was that the traditional theory of the firm had been badly shaken.

THE AFTERMATH: REAFFIRMATION AND RECONSTRUCTION

The early 1950's marked the beginning of a period of agonizing reappraisal in an atmosphere of much confusion. Some, like Papandreou,[18] were in a diagnostic mood, gravely trying to identify the various shortcomings of the existing theory. Boulding,[19] in taking stock of the situation exactly 10 years after his first review, was asking whether the marginal analysis ought to be banned from the textbooks in favor of something along the lines of his own reconstructions. Mrs. Robinson [20] referred to her "scholastic book . . . directed to analyzing the slogans of textbooks twenty years ago . . . ," and appeared to repudiate many of the principles she had so solemnly advanced in the earlier days. Chamberlin [21] was busy explaining why his theory was superior to that of the Cambridge group and arguing that the full-cost principle did not conflict with monopolistic competition theory. This was a very perplexing time, but it marked the beginning of a more constructive phase in the turbulent course of the theory of the firm.

Developments in the last 10 years or so have tended to follow the

18 A. G. Papandreou, "Some Basic Problems in the Theory of the Firm," and comments, in B. F. Haley, ed., *A Survey of Contemporary Economics*, Vol. II (Homewood: Irwin, 1952), pp. 183–222.

19 K. E. Boulding, "Implications for General Economics of More Realistic Theories of the Firm," *American Economic Review*, Vol. 42, No. 2 (May, 1952), pp. 35–44.

20 J. Robinson, "Imperfect Competition Revisited," *Economic Journal*, Vol. 63, No. 251 (September, 1953), pp. 579–93.

21 E. H. Chamberlin, " 'Full Cost' and Monopolistic Competition," *Economic Journal*, Vol. 62, No. 246 (June, 1952), pp. 318–25.

schism arising out of the marginalist controversy. The marginalists have sought to reaffirm the classical tradition by perfecting a methodological defense and by countering with supporting empirical evidence. The opposing side has continued to assail the tradition with the "facts" of business behavior and has attempted to revise or reconstruct the theory of the firm along new lines. I shall merely mention a few of the suggested revisions in order to provide an outline of the situation as it presently exists.

REAFFIRMATION OF THE TRADITION

In the wake of the series of sharp attacks upon the neoclassical theory of the firm, the guardians of the tradition reacted by erecting a methodological defense which has indeed proved to be formidable. They began to argue that the widespread concern over the reality of assumptions is a waste of time because one never tests the validity of a theory by whether or not the assumptions are descriptively realistic, as they almost never are. The crucial question is whether they are sufficiently good approximations for the purpose at hand, and this question can only be answered by testing the hypotheses derived from the assumptions. In granting that the profit-maximization assumption is unrealistic, the theory is not in the least impugned; the important thing is that the maximization principle, when combined with other, perhaps equally unrealistic assumptions, leads to hypotheses that accurately predict certain facets of business behavior.[22]

Efforts have also been made in recent years to present empirical evidence supporting the marginal analysis. One such attempt was made by J. S. Earley who conducted a survey of 110 "excellently managed" manufacturing companies and concluded that the assumptions of the traditional theory of the firm are both reasonable and realistic.[23] He based his conclusions on certain indirect evidence, namely on the discovery that the firms in his sample used accounting methods which provide a "marginalist" type of information. However, the marginalist behavior he found was somewhat different from that pictured in the

[22] This methodological debate continues to the present. See the papers and discussions on problems of methodology in the *American Economic Review*, Vol. 53, No. 2 (May, 1963), pp. 204–36.

[23] J. S. Earley, "Marginal Policies of 'Excellently Managed' Companies," *American Economic Review*, Vol. 46, No. 1 (March, 1956), pp. 44–70. See also his "Recent Developments in Cost Accounting and the 'Marginal Analysis,'" *Journal of Political Economy*, Vol. 63, No. 3 (June, 1955), pp. 227–42. A recent book on the subject is, J. R. Nelson, ed., *Marginal Cost Pricing in Practice* (Englewood Cliffs: Prentice-Hall, 1964).

textbook of price theory: "What seems to be typical of these companies is not 'marginalism-sitting,' short or long run, but 'marginalism-on-the-wing.' " [24]

Mention should also be made of a defensive argument which arises from a particular twist on the "viability" hypothesis.[25] Under conditions of intense competition—including the rivalry of capital in many overlapping markets—the firms surviving in the long run will be those which have made the "right," or profit-maximizing, decisions, regardless of whether or not the managers of these firms have consciously sought this objective. Consequently, economists are justified in constructing a theory of the firm based on the maximization principle because all viable firms will act "as if" profit maximization were the primary objective.[26]

ALTERNATIVE THEORIES OF THE FIRM

Although it is not easy to classify the many suggestions which have been made to revise or reconstruct the theory of the firm, it is convenient to group them roughly according to how the motivational assumption is to be modified. In one category may be included a few writers who have suggested that the principle of maximization be retained but that some other concrete, or directly observable, variable be substituted for realized profit. Perhaps the frequently heard assertion that the typical firm attempts to maximize long-run rather than short-run profit should be cited here, despite the obvious difficulties of advancing a concrete and objectively satisfying definition of long-run profit. There have been other, more specific suggestions. Baumol [27] has recently proposed a modification which has attracted widespread interest; based on his experience as a management consultant he has suggested that the firm strives to maximize sales revenue, subject to the realization of some minimum level of profit. And another writer has argued that profit maximization takes different forms depending on who controls the firm—for example, the stockholder-controlled firm

[24] Earley, "Marginal Policies of 'Excellently Managed' Companies," *op. cit.*, p. 66.
[25] A. A. Alchian, "Uncertainty, Evolution, and Economic Theory," *Journal of Political Economy*, Vol. 58, No. 3 (June, 1950), pp. 211–21.
[26] S. Enke, "On Maximizing Profits: A Distinction Between Chamberlin and Robinson," *American Economic Review*, Vol. 41, No. 4 (September, 1951), pp. 566–78.
[27] W. Baumol, *Business Behavior, Value and Growth* (New York: Macmillan, 1959), esp. Chs. 6 and 7. For criticisms, see M. H. Peston, "On the Sales Maximization Hypothesis," *Economica*, Vol. 26, No. 102 (May, 1959), pp. 128–36, and R. L. Sandmeyer, "Baumol's Sales-Maximization Model: Comment," *American Economic Review*, Vol. 54, No. 6 (December, 1964), pp. 1073–81.

tries to maximize dividend payments, whereas the management-controlled firm tries to maximize undistributed profit.[28]

A number of writers have advocated scrapping the maximization principle altogether. Boulding's attempt to revise the theory of the firm by advancing the interesting idea of "balance-sheet homeostasis" might fall in this category.[29] Borrowed from physiology, the concept of homeostasis applied to the firm supposes that there is some desired set of accounting ratios that management attempts to maintain—an equilibrium of the balance sheet—and that whenever this equilibrium is disturbed, a control mechanism goes into operation to restore the equilibrium. Stability is of prime importance and therefore the quest for profit assumes a subsidiary role. The firm maximizes only in the sense that it seeks to establish some ideal, or optimal, set of balance sheet ratios.

Another approach stems from attempts to reconstruct the theory around the full-cost principle of price determination, a hypothesis arising from empirical studies of the price and output behavior of business firms. In this approach the maximization principle is rejected as being incompatible with the actual circumstances of business decision-making, especially in view of the problem of uncertainty and in recognition of the multifarious nature of business objectives. The firm is merely assumed to seek a satisfactory level of profit.

A movement to develop a theory of the firm along "behavioral" lines has received considerable attention in recent years, particularly as a result of the work of Cyert and March and their associates.[30] The rationale for this work stems from the proposition that a full understanding of economic forces requires knowledge of the internal operation of the firm as well as the external environment. It amounts to a full-scale assault on the question of how the addition of organizational variables might modify and enrich the theory of oligopoly. This approach relies heavily on empirical studies and the use of computer techniques which are combined in a kind of "laboratory method" to test hypotheses on business motivation, organization, and behavior.

The earliest attempts to revise the theory of the firm, and the most frequently encountered modification in contemporary literature on the subject, stem from an observation that the objective function of the firm be defined in terms of an ordinal index of utility rather than

[28] J. R. Wilson, "Maximization and Business Behavior," *Economic Record*, Vol. 28, No. 54 (May, 1952), pp. 29ff.

[29] K. E. Boulding, *A Reconstruction of Economics* (New York: Wiley, 1950).

[30] R. M. Cyert and J. G. March, "Organizational Structure and Pricing Behavior," *American Economic Review*, Vol. 45, No. 1 (March, 1955), pp. 129–39, and *idem*, *A Behavioral Theory of the Firm* (Englewood Cliffs: Prentice-Hall, 1963).

profit.[31] In the contemporary version, management (the peak authority) behaves rationally with respect to a well-defined ordering of preferences—that is, it acts as if it were trying to maximize a multivariate preference function subject only to any limitations or constraints, which inhibit the effort.[32] Thus, for example, the desire for leisure, the need for liquidity and control, and the quest for profit are all incorporated in management's generalized problem of constrained maximization.

The utility-index hypothesis has the advantage of putting the theory of the firm on an equal footing with the theory of consumer choice. Furthermore it tends to remove some of the objections to the assumption in the traditional theory that the entrepreneur has enough objective information to maximize profit. In the revised theory the business decision-maker, like the consumer, merely makes a choice from among the set of all feasible alternatives which will put him on the highest indifference locus.

If utility maximization seems to be an improvement on profit maximization, the gain may be largely illusory. The utility revision seems to have greater generality and flexibility, but it may turn out to be so general and so elastic that it becomes incapable of producing meaningful and refutable hypotheses. Most of the suggestions considered thus far for revising the theory can be subsumed under the general hypothesis of utility maximization, including those that propose maximizing some directly observable variable, such as sales revenue, as well as those that advocate scrapping the maximization principle altogether. Moreover there is the nagging conceptual problem of whether or not it makes sense to speak of a well-ordered set of preferences for the firm in view of the size and complexity of most business operations. In short, the utility hypothesis may merely provide us with a more imposing and intriguing box which upon inspection turns out to be even more empty than the others.

WHITHER THE THEORY OF THE FIRM?

Developments in the theory of the firm cover a span of 125 years. What we now refer to as the traditional theory of the firm was nearly three-quarters of that time in the making, its form being only partly visible

[31] Hicks, op. cit. See also Higgins, op. cit.; T. Scitovsky, "A Note on Profit Maximization and Its Implications," Review of Economic Studies, Vol. 11, No. 1 (Winter, 1943), pp. 57–60; and M. Reder, "A Reconsideration of Marginal Productivity Theory," Journal of Political Economy, Vol. 55, No. 5 (October, 1947), pp. 450–58.

[32] Cf. J. Encarnacion, Jr., "Constraints and the Firm's Utility Function." Review of Economic Studies, Vol. 31, No. 86 (April, 1964), pp. 113–19.

in the classical analyses of cost, output, and price. When at last it was completed, it ran into trouble, largely because of increasing doubt over the validity of the maximization principle.

As a consequence of nearly three decades of criticism there has been a break-up in the maximization principle and with it the theory of the firm. This conclusion is virtually inescapable as we survey the contemporary literature, noting the variety of suggestions on how the theory might be rescued and observing the defensive efforts of its more staunch adherents.

In the present state of confusion one can only speculate on the future course of the theory of the firm. Two identifiable streams of activity seem to be emerging. The first, at least in precedence, involves an elaboration of the traditional theory into a general framework of optimal choice wherein the assumption of profit maximization is replaced by constrained preference maximization. The second approach seeks to develop process-oriented models of the firm, based upon close observation of actual decision behavior in real business settings.

Neither of these approaches, however, has as yet produced an alternative which has attained enough recognition to replace the traditional theory of the firm. Despite the scores of assaults on it over a period of more than 20 years, the battered and bruised neoclassical theory somehow manages to stand as the principal model of the firm's output, cost, and price behavior. How is this remarkable viability to be explained? Surely it cannot be attributed entirely to the stubborn influence of tradition.

Of course one answer is that the neoclassical theory continues to stand because of its ability to produce meaningful and empirically verified hypotheses. There is much merit in this argument, especially if one is not much concerned about the crudeness of the hypotheses produced or the stringency of the empirical tests being applied. That is, so long as we are satisfied with qualitative propositions such as "an increase in demands leads to a rise in both output and product prices" or "a rise in wage rates causes a fall in employment" and then rely on *ceteris paribus* to rescue us when the facts appear to arrange themselves in contradiction, the traditional theory probably passes the test. (Perhaps this statement should be amended to say that the perfectly competitive model passes these tests because in markets where the number of buyers or sellers is small it usually happens that we cannot even derive these crude, qualitative propositions. No one really knows whether "supply function" is a meaningful concept under conditions of fewness, much less what its slope or elasticity might be.)

It may also be true that the traditional theory predicts as well as or better than any of the alternative theories proposed thus far. But given the quality of these predictions and the difficulties of testing them, I doubt that we can take much comfort in this. Against the mathematical standards of prediction employed in most of the physical sciences, the achievements of microeconomic theory would hardly be registered. It is hard to believe that the viability of the neoclassical theory of the firm can be explained in these terms.

I should like to suggest that the true explanation lies in a combination of things including not so much our successes in prediction as our failures. To state the general proposition positively, the dominant place of the neoclassical theory is assured so long as the following circumstances prevail: (1) economic propositions continue to spring from the postulate of rationality, (2) the dynamic aspects of choice continue to defy generalization, and (3) we continue to prefer in theory construction antecedent conditions whose terms are directly observable.

The assumption of rationality, of course, in general form merely asserts that the decision-maker perceives a set of contemporaneous alternatives which he is able to rank in a consistent preference ordering and then proceeds to choose from among a subset of *available* alternatives the one most preferred. Hence, rational behavior implies the existence of a maximizing procedure; the rational decision-maker always maximizes over some relevant set of alternatives.[33] We must hasten to add, however, that what is always maximized is an index of preference and not necessariliy the pecuniary rewards associated with the alternatives perceived.

Unfortunately, when the decision problem is analyzed in a framework of dynamics, the task of explaining the meaning of rational behavior is enormously, perhaps hopelessly, complicated. Rationality still implies some kind of maximizing activity, but the alternatives perceived and the choices involved are not of the simple, once-over variety. Instead, they are alternative courses of action, each composed of an irreversible series of choices spread out through time. In his attempt to maximize over this complex set of alternatives, the decision-maker is plagued by uncertainty. The selection of any particular course of action and the specific choices which must be made to initiate it will have an unknown, conditioning effect on the shape of future alternatives; the return from each plan has to be viewed as an unknown sum of an

[33] Rational behavior does not require that all possible alternatives are known any more than it requires that the outcomes are known with certainty. It is simply false to assert, as many casual observers are prone to do, that people typically behave irrationally because they make choices without considering all the alternatives.

uncertain stream of returns projected indefinitely into the future; and the composition of future alternatives and projected returns depends not only on the decision-maker's own sequence of choices but on the indeterminable choices of countless others. If maximization is to be employed, it cannot be "maximization-sitting" as it is in the framework of statics, but instead it has to be a kind of "maximizing-on-the-wing." [34] But we have not as yet worked out an unambiguous set of rules which describes this behavior. [35]

By putting the presumption of rationality in economic theorizing together with the failure to solve the puzzle of rationality in the context of dynamics and uncertainty, some idea of why the neoclassical theory of the firm continues to survive despite all the attacks on it begins to take shape. We need only add the further observation that there continues to be a marked preference among economists for a theory of the firm which has antecedent propositions containing terms that are directly observable. This preference probably exists because of difficulties and disappointments resulting from testing derived predictions. Thus it is still preferable to develop the foundations of theory primarily in terms of the kinds of costs and returns which can be estimated against the measuring stick of money. Now this would hardly be necessary if there were more confidence in the hypotheses produced by the theory. In any case, the presumption of rational behavior in a world where the preferences of business authorities are supposed to vary directly with money returns, and where the elements of time and uncertainty have to be sidestepped, leads inevitably to the marginal analysis of the firm.

This perspective also sheds light on why most of the alternative theories of the firm, such as the model of full-cost pricing and Boulding's homeostasis theory, have not attracted much attention or additional elaboration. They often begin more "realistically" by defining equilibrium in a way consistent with the kind of information business managers usually possess and shunning the notion of maximization, but the solutions usually turn out to be hopelessly indeterminate. In

[34] My debt to Earley, "Marginal Policies of 'Excellently Managed' Companies," *op cit.*, is obvious.

[35] There is, however, considerable interest and activity in this sphere even though unification and integration of the results thus far have not been achieved. Much of this activity is being stimulated by developments in decision theory, optimal inventory policy, and dynamic programming. Definitive works include R. D. Luce and H. Raiffa, *Games and Decisions* (New York: Wiley, 1957); K. J. Arrow, S. Karlin, and H. Scarf, *Studies in the Mathematical Theory of Inventory and Production* (Stanford: Stanford University Press, 1958); and R. E. Bellman, *Dynamic Programming* (Princeton: Princeton University Press, 1957).

order to get these models to work it becomes tempting to assume the existence of more information which in turn leads to some form of the rationality postulate, whether it is called "achieving," "striving," "trying to do better," or whatever. Yet in following this course it soon becomes apparent that the differences between the alternative and the traditional model are so slight that they can be neglected. In lieu of proposing specific behavioral hypotheses which take into account the elements of time and uncertainty, one can always sidestep them altogether and possibly come up with a determinate solution. All this means is that when the problem is narrowed down to a contest between equilibrium and realism, the latter is almost sure to lose.

Is it justifiable to conclude that there really has been a breakup in the maximization principle and with it the theory of the firm? I think the answer is definitely in the affirmative although it has to be qualified by the observation that as yet a suitable replacement has not been found. Until a workable dynamic framework for analyzing business decisions is developed, the conventional theory of the firm with all of its shortcomings is not likely to be discarded.

> Humpty Dumpty had a great fall,
> But patched up and righted
> Is back on the wall.

No doubt we should be grateful for that.

SECTION IV

MARKET ORGANIZATION

21

MONOPOLY AND COMPETITION: A CLASSIFICATION OF MARKET POSITIONS *

FRITZ MACHLUP teaches at Princeton University; he was formerly at the University of Buffalo.

More discussion of the terminological and conceptual disorder is needed before the theory of the blendings of monopoly and competition can progress further after its great advance in the last decade. Attempts at clarification, at clearer definitions, and at a more uniform use of words have been undertaken recently.[1] A classification of the various forms of competition or the various positions on the selling market will be attempted here. As in any classification, the lines drawn between the different types are artificial, but such dividing lines are necessary for clear reasoning.

As criteria of classification we may choose the types of considerations and reflections in the mind of the seller when he pictures the quantities he could sell at various prices. The main division is that between sellers whose calculations or deliberations include expected reactions of rival sellers and, on the other side, sellers who do not engage in such complicated reflections. The latters' thought is concerned with the buyers' reactions only. No account is taken of what rival sellers may do in consequence of his action. For want of a shorter expression we call this type of seller the *seller heedless* of rivals' reactions, and contrast it with the *seller conscious* of rivals' reactions. The latter anticipates not only the buyers' reactions on his higher or lower selling prices, but also, and sometimes primarily, his rivals' reactions. When he raises the selling price, when he lowers it, will the rivals (or the rival) follow suit or not; if so, fully or partly, immediately or with some delay? The customers' reactions and thus the effects of a price change, cannot be estimated or imagined by the seller if he fails to take into account the most probable of the rivals' reactions.

If the seller expects the reactions of his rivals to take place without

* From the *American Economic Review*, Vol. XXVII (September 1937), pp. 445–451, copyright © by the American Economic Assoc. Reprinted by permission.

[1] Horace G. White, "A Review of Monopolistic and Imperfect Competition Theories," *Am. Econ. Rev.* vol. xxvi, 1936, pp. 636–649; Paul M. Sweezy, "On the Definition of Monopoly," *Quart. Jour. of Econ.*, vol. 51, 1936, pp. 362–363.

any delay, then the estimate of these reactions often precedes the estimate of buyers' reactions. If he expects some delay in his rivals' reactions, then he may first make an estimate of buyers' reactions for the
period between his price change and his rivals' reactions (*i.e.*, a short-
period demand curve); second, an estimate of rivals' reactions, and
finally, one of buyers' reactions subsequent to his rivals' adjustments
(*i.e.*, the long-period demand curve). How many customers will he be
able to take from his rivals; how many will he lose to them? This question becomes of foremost importance to the rival-conscious seller. And,
the demand curve, *i.e.*, the schedule of quantities which the seller believes [2] to be salable at various prices, acquires a still greater degree of
vagueness, because each point may refer to a different set of anticipated
reactions of rivals.

It will be clear from what we have said about the rival-conscious
seller that duopoly and oligopoly are the cases in point. It may be
worth while to distinguish between oligopolists with standardized
products and oligopolists with differentiated products. The differentiation of the product in this case where sellers are few does not, however, change essentially the type of sellers' reflections; it will merely
diminish the ease with which in their belief customers can be detached
from their rivals or lost to their rivals. In other words, the differentiation of the product will make for a smaller elasticity of demand in the
minds of the individual sellers; but these elasticities are in any case
smaller than infinity because of the fewness of sellers.

With few sellers in the market the sellers must be rival-conscious,
that is to say, they have to make guesses about their rivals' reactions
together with guesses about the buyers' reactions. This is not so in the
case where there is only one seller, or in the case where there are very
many sellers. Both the monopolist and the competitor in a market of
very many sellers are unconcerned with rivals' reactions; the one because he has not any, the other because he has too many.

The monopolist's product has of course (distant) substitutes and is,
therefore, in rivalry with many other products. The monopolist "competes" with all sellers of all different products for the consumer's dollar. This, however, is too wide a concept of competition for the
purposes of our classification. The competition of commodities outside
the industry—beyond the "gap in the chain of substitutes—" [3] is so

---

[2] Consistent methodological individualism calls for an interpretation of demand
curves as pictures of typical sellers' estimates. What the "actual facts" do is to
influence and reshape the estimates of the sellers who learn by experience.

[3] Joan Robinson, "What is Perfect Competition?" *Quart. Jour. of Econ.* vol. 49,
1935, pp. 104–120.

anonymous and so nebulous that expectations as to the policy of their sellers are excluded. The perfect monopolist has no rival whose reactions to his own price policy concern him.

One seller in a market of very many sellers has, of course, many direct competitors, but he has so many that he does not expect they would care about what he does. He is conscious of his small share in the market and he knows or thinks that none of his competitors would feel any tangible effect of his actions. Thus he will not be expectant of possible reactions of rivals.

The distinction between the competition of homogeneous or standardized products offered by many sellers, and the competition of differentiated products of many sellers is important. In the first case, that of pure competition, every single seller knows or thinks that he could not sell a single unit of his product should he ask a price higher than the market price, and that he could sell any quantity he cares to sell without charging less than the market price. In other words, the demand conceived by any such single seller is infinitely elastic. In the second case, that of monopolistic competition, each seller knows or thinks that he could keep some of his customers even if he raised his price, and that he could sell some more, but still very limited quantities of his product, if he lowered his price. In other words, the demand conceived by the monopolistic competitor is less than infinitely elastic because of the attachment of customers to the slightly differentiated product or service they get from the individual sellers.

I put the seller under monopolistic competition (*i.e.*, the seller in a market of many sellers offering differentiated products) and the seller under oligopoly with differentiated products (*i.e.*, the seller in a market of few sellers offering differentiated products) in different groups, and venture to hold that the case of the latter is much more adequately treated as an oligopoly case and that little is gained by treating it as a case of monopolistic competition. What the "small" or "great" number of sellers in the market mainly does is to affect the policy of the individual seller. "Sellers are few" means that the single seller is afraid his actions will be felt by, and cause reactions of, his rivals. "Sellers are many" means that the single seller is not conscious of any reactions of rivals. And it will be agreed that the difference in the sellers' reflections in the two cases is essential.

These are the types which we have distinguished so far:

A. *Sellers conscious of their rivals' reactions*
   (1) Duopoly
   (2) Oligopoly with differentiated products
   (3) Oligopoly with standardized products

B. *Sellers heedless of rivals' reactions*
  (1) Monopoly
  (2) Competition with differentiated products (monopolistic competition)
  (3) Competition with standardized products (pure competition)

The seller under monopolistic competition has sometimes been regarded as a monopolist in his particular product; since neither the monopolist nor the monopolistic competitor care for rivals' reactions, it may seem hard to see any distinguishing characteristic between the two. One might be satisfied with a difference in the degree of substitutability of products and hence of elasticity of demand. Monopolistic competition would then comprise the cases of closer substitutes and more elastic demand curves, while monopoly would comprise those of remote substitutes and steeper demand curves. Or one might make a mere physical comparison of products and call the monopolistic sellers of physically very similar products monopolistic competitors.

Another aspect of these market positions, however, yields distinguishing characteristics of much greater significance. It is the chance of supernormal profits and the ease of entry into the industry which have to be examined. And such examination will also suggest the proper place in our classification for the concepts of imperfect competition and imperfect monopoly.

The distinction between pure competition and perfect competition, suggested by Professor Chamberlin [4] was felicitous. It can be carried through further than he himself may have done. The two pairs of antonyms can be shown in four different combinations; competition may be pure and perfect, pure and imperfect, monopolistic and perfect, monopolistic and imperfect.

Pure competition, *i.e.,* the competition of very many sellers of a homogeneous product, implies infinitely elastic demand curves for each individual seller. Perfect competition means uniform prices for homogeneous goods and uniform earnings for equal services, hence the absence of supernormal or subnormal earnings. In geometrical language pure competition means a demand curve parallel to the x-axis, that is, a demand curve coinciding with the corresponding marginal revenue curve. (Average revenue equal to marginal revenue.) While pure competition refers, thus, to the *shape* of the demand curve, perfect competition refers to its *position* in relation to the cost curves. If under

---

[4] *Theory of Monopolistic Competition,* pp. 6–7 and 25–26. The suggested "distinction of terms does not seem to have impressed recent writers on the subject," as Mr. White (*op. cit.* p. 641) states with regret. Is it hoping against hope that writers of the Cambridge school may occasionally adopt foreign-coined terms?

perfect competition abnormal returns are excluded, selling price and average cost must be equal for the output chosen (*i.e.*, for the output for which marginal revenue and marginal cost are equal) and this implies that the demand curve must be tangent to the average cost curve. It can be easily seen that the demand curve may be parallel to the *x*-axis without being tangent to the average cost curve, or that it may be tangent to the average cost curve without being parallel to the axis, or that it may be both at the same time, or that it may be neither.

If competition is pure but imperfect,[5] the demand curve to the individual seller will, due to the great number of sellers and to the homogeneity of the product, be infinitely elastic, but not tangent to the respective average cost curve, thus leaving profits under or above normal. This will be due to frictions, which stand in the way of quick transference of productive factors (including entrepreneurial capacity) between different industries, and to the costs of transference, which prevent such adjustment until price differentials or profit margins are large enough to pay for the switching of factors between localities and occupations.[6]

If competition is perfect but monopolistic, the demand curve conceived by the individual seller will be less than infinitely elastic because of the differentiated service which he offers, but it will be tangent to the average cost curve. If the demand for products of this and similar kinds rises, and the demand curves conceived by the individual sellers have a tendency to be higher than tangent to the respective average cost curves, the prospect of supernormal returns in this industry would instantly bring about an influx of new firms [7] and thus push the demand curves of the single firms back to tangency to the respective average cost curves. In other words, the free and easy entry of new

[5] Our use of the concept "imperfect" competition must not be confused with Mrs. Robinson's. See *op. cit.* and *Economics of Imperfect Competition*.

[6] Space does not permit discussion here of the notion of "normal profits." Mrs. Robinson (*op. cit.*, p. 106–107) objects to linking "normal profits" with the concept of competition, chiefly because "entrepreneurship" is not homogeneous. If an industry is licensed by the state, are entrepreneurs with license and those without license heterogeneous factors? Should physical, psychical and legal inabilities, natural and institutional obstacles to perfect substitution, all be treated alike? It is the economist's view as to control and flexibility of institutions that is back of his thought that certain inabilities give rise to a "normal" difference, others to an "abnormal" difference in earnings. Yet, there is a meaning in the application of these terms and I cannot share Mrs. Robinson's verdict that they cease to be of use.

[7] Perfection of competition does not depend on perfect fluidity of all units of all factors. The fluidity of a certain portion of the total amount of each factor would suffice to produce the assumed result, *i.e.*, equal earnings of equal factors.

firms into the industry (which turns out products not homogeneous but similar) does not allow abnormal returns to be reaped. With any prospect of such returns new firms offering a close substitute would be attracted and the demand for the products of the existing firms thus pressed down. This pressure stops only when returns are reduced to normal so that no more firms are attracted. Geometrically expressed, the demand curve is tangent to the average cost curve.[8]

If competition is monopolistic and imperfect, so that the influx of new firms into the industry (or the withdrawal of old firms) is delayed, abnormal returns can appear.[9] Whether or not the profits of these sellers under monopolistic imperfect competition should be considered monopoly profits is not an urgent question. That they appear at all is due to the imperfection of competition, but they are possibly higher than if competition were pure, because of the sloping demand curve and the output restriction of each monopolistic competitor who keeps the selling price above marginal cost.

The absence of supernormal returns is a distinctive feature of monopolistic perfect competition [10] as against perfect monopoly. This distinguishing characteristic, however, fails if monopolistic competition is imperfect. The delayed emergence of new firms allows the existing monopolistic competitors in this industry to reap supernormal ("monopoly") profits. The only criterion that then distinguishes monopolistic imperfect competition from monopoly is the time element. Competition is imperfect if it works slowly, being hampered and delayed because of frictions and costs of moving. But if enough time is allowed, the results approach those of perfect competition. Monopoly, on the other hand, is not based on mere frictions, time-lags, and costs of moving. It is based on more reliable and more enduring conditions. From a short-run point of view, monopoly and monopolistic imperfect

---

[8] The nature of the average cost curve can be conceived in either of two ways. If "differential rents" are included in long-run average cost, then the above statement is adequate. If, on the other hand, "differential rents" are excluded from cost, the statement is true only of the "marginal firm."

[9] When the product differentiation is considerable, monopolistic competition will most likely be imperfect as well. This is because the uncertainty involved in the establishment of new firms will be much greater than if products are less differentiated or even homogeneous. Firms with established good-will or well known trade-marks are often given as illustrations of monopolistic and imperfect competition. Most of these cases, however, should more appropriately be treated as oligopolies with differentiated products.

[10] "Perfect monopolistic competition" would sound better but it might be read as "perfectly monopolistic" while "perfect" ought to refer to competition.

competition are the same. It is from a long-run point of view that they are different. In the long run the "imperfections of adaptation" will be overcome, while the conditions constituting a monopoly position may survive.

Monopoly may be perfect or imperfect. It is imperfect if the factors making for the monopoly position are such that the seller can depend upon their endurance only within limits.[11] There may be serious limits for his price policy, limits set by the seller's fear of government interference, and limits set by the seller's fear of "potential competition." This last possibility interests us most in our classification because it bears on the distinction between the rival-conscious seller and the non-rival-conscious seller. The perfect monopolist has no rivals who are of concern to him, but the imperfect monopolist may have "potential rivals." The latter may be afraid that above certain prices his monopoly position could be terminated through the appearance of rivals offering the same product or close substitutes. Yet this type of rival-consciousness is different from the one observed with the duopolist or oligopolist. The imperfect monopolist has a range of prices where he feels himself entirely free from possible reactions of rivals. He shies merely from going above a limit where, even though only in the long run, rivals may come into existence.

The potential competition of the imperfect monopolist finds its geometrical expression in the shape of the long-run demand curve conceived by the seller: above a certain price range the demand curve would rapidly flatten out toward the left. That is to say, at certain high prices the monopolist would expect rivals to appear on the market so that from then on a slight price increase would cause a relatively great loss of sales. It should be noted how differently the "potential competition of the imperfect monopolist" and "monopolistic imperfect competition" are to be represented in geometry and as types of conduct. In the former case there is the sudden turn to high elasticity in the upper part of the long-period demand curve; in the latter case there is a sloping demand curve which as a whole will be reshaped and shifted more and more to the left and downward as times goes on and the imperfections of the market are gradually overcome. In the former case the shape of the long-period curve is conceived by the seller who avoids the high price ranges because of the potential competition. In the latter case the movement of the demand curve in the long run is a succession of revised demand anticipations of the seller; it need not be subject to any specific measures in his price policy; it is simply the

11 One may question whether cases of perfect monopoly exist in reality.

realization of pressure on the market due to the gradual emergence of suppliers of close substitutes.[12] This pressure, realized only gradually, may not be foreseen by the seller, but if it is foreseen, then it may lead him to a policy contrary to that of the monopolist. He may, for instance, pursue a consciously short-run policy because he knows that after some time the market will be spoiled by the unfailing appearance of more sellers.

The price policy of the seller under monopolistic imperfect competition who is aware how short-lived is his favorable market position borders again rather closely on the policy of sellers conscious of their rivals' reactions. There is indeed no great difference between the type of policy which an oligopolistic seller of differentiated products may pursue when he believes that his rivals will take only delayed reactions on his actions, and the case of monopolistic imperfect competition which we have just described. But the classification here offered does not attempt to create water-tight compartments in which to force the specimens of all cases observed in reality.

We have seen that a subdivision of the groups and sub-groups of our classification seems appropriate, distinguishing perfect from imperfect monopoly, perfect from imperfect monopolistic competition, perfect from imperfect pure competition. But we have still to bear in mind that the kinds of imperfections are so manifold and different that it is hardly permissible to label the various market positions satisfactorily with the few tags now currently in use.

<hr/>

[12] Paul M. Sweezy, *op. cit.*, p. 362, includes in his monopoly definition the condition that the demand curve for the product is independent of the profit made. This formulation allows of at least two interpretations. It may mean, first, that the monopolist is not afraid that the profits he makes will attract others to supply substitutes, and thus the long-run demand curve conceived by the monopolist will not show in its shape any expected loss of sales to other suppliers. Second, it may mean that the profits of the monopolist will "actually" not attract others to supply substitutes so that the "actual" demand curve for his product will not be shifted to the left and downward. This difference between events expected by the seller, and events "actually" in store for the seller is, I hope, clearly brought out in the text.

22

MONOPOLISTIC COMPETITION
IN RETROSPECT *

GEORGE J. STIGLER teaches at the University of
Chicago; he was formerly at Columbia University.

Before the Great Depression, that chasm between darkness and light,
economists had generally looked upon the economy as a mixture of
industries that approximated conditions of perfect competition and
industries that were "monopolies." The competitive industries, it was
believed, were satisfactorily analyzed by the theory of competition, and
although the "monopolies" were diverse in structure and power, they
could be informatively analyzed by a discriminating use of the theory
of monopoly. Individual economists varied considerably in the relative
importance they attached to these two groups of industries, of course,
but they varied surprisingly little in the type of analytical system they
deemed appropriate to the analysis of economic events. This is not to
say that the details of the analytical system were, or were thought to be,
definitive: indeed certain portions of the system, such as duopoly,
admittedly were (and are) in wretched shape.

Then came the works of Mrs. Robinson and Professor Chamberlin,
who criticized this viewpoint and demanded a new orientation of our
thought. Because of the high quality of their volumes, and because it
was the " 'thirties," they were enthusiastically received. Then too, their
messages seemed to reinforce one another, but this was a confusion that
was quickly detected by, and almost only by, Professor Chamberlin.

Of Mrs. Robinson's work I need say little. It is amply clear, on a rereading at this distant date, that her message was in no sense revolutionary, although at times her language was rebellious. Her two basic
theses were: (1) that price theory is capable of great improvements in
elegance and significant improvements in logic; and (2) that the theory
of monopoly is the appropriate instrument of analysis of all real situations in which the assumptions of perfect competition are not completely and exactly fulfilled. If she gave no evidence for her second

* From *Five Lectures on Economic Problems*, (New York: The Macmillan Company,
1949). pp. 12–24. Reprinted by permission of George J. Stigler.

thesis, to which I shall return later, she contributed much to the fulfillment of the first. Her volume marks no break with the tradition of neo-classical economics; indeed it contains, I think, too uncritical an acceptance of the substantive content of orthodoxy.

Professor Chamberlin was a true revolutionary. Instead of assimilating observed market structures into exclusive classes such as competition and monopoly, he told us, we must throw off our theoretical heritage and look at the world with clear and candid eyes. Then we shall find that no simple dichotomy does justice to the rich variety of industrial organization. True, there are (a very few) industries that closely resemble those studied by the economist of perfect competition. True, there are (perhaps more) firms that partake of the nature of monopoly as this concept was used in neo-classical economics. But vastly more often the firm displays a mixture of insulation from other rivals, by means of real or fancied product differences, and of indirect rivalry by way of (1) the willingness of some consumers to shift among products and (2) the ability of firms to change their products. As a result, there are important—in fact, typical—phenomena which cannot be explained, or can be explained only with serious error, if economic reality is forced into the neo-classical categories.

Let us spell out Professor Chamberlin's *Weltanschauung* in a bit more detail. Suppose our primary interest is (or perhaps I should say, begins with) the housing of the people who work in New York City. Even casual observation indicates the prominence of two characteristics in this housing market: (1) a great variety of products; and (2) a certain "unsystematism" or irregularity or randomness in the interrelationships among these products. (1) The housing facilities range from incredible estates to unbelievable slums. Every unit is unique in a rigorous technological sense and, more relevant, there are thousands of classes of dwellings whose rents need not move in strict proportion on threat of wholesale vacancy or queuing up. Our housing facilities, moreover, roam far afield. They extend to several states directly, and—through summer and winter places and other channels—ultimately to the whole world. They very probably extend also to automobiles, fur coats, and trips abroad, for the competition may well be stronger between these products and various classes of housing than the competition between some classes of housing. (2) Nor is there any systematic arrangement of this assemblage of products. The barriers between products are not of uniform height or thickness, nor is there any discernible order in their occurrence. It is not impossible that apartments A and B do not compete directly and yet are both in close rivalry with automobiles. The existence of many similar and closely situated apartments is compatible with pervasive duopoly.

This picture of economic life was not fundamentally new, but Professor Chamberlin's reaction was. Customarily the picture had led to some sort of "institutional" economics, that strange mixture of magnificent methodological pronouncements and skinny, *ad hoc* analyses. Chamberlin, however, persevered to construct an analytical system of recognizable type to deal with the picture: the co-ordinates of his diagrams would be price and quantity, not Church and State.

Chamberlin's vision was clearly a legitimate way of looking at economic life. One may even argue that it was more congruent with untutored observation, and in this sense more "realistic." But these are points, not of unimportance, but of complete irrelevance, despite the part they played in securing popularity for his theory. There is a question of minor interest: did Chamberlin develop from this viewpoint a logically consistent theory of economic events? And there is a question of paramount importance: does a theory incorporating this viewpoint contain more accurate or more comprehensive implications than the neo-classical theory? I wish to emphasize this second question because it is not true that a theory which is realistic in its assumptions—if any meaning can be attached to this—is necessarily realistic in its implications, a theme to which I shall return.

But let us return to Chamberlin's picture. How does he reduce this stupendous diversity and complexity to a manageable system without assuming away its essential characteristics?

1. THE FIRST ATTEMPT: CHAMBERLIN

One cannot long talk sensibly and simultaneously about a Connecticut estate, a Brooklyn walk-up, and a New Jersey hotel—to say very little of the fur coats and trips to Europe. And so Professor Chamberlin introduced the "group":

> The group contemplated is one which would *ordinarily* be regarded as composing one imperfectly competitive market: a number of automobile manufacturers, of producers of pots and pans, of magazine publishers, or of retail shoe dealers.[1]

[1] *Theory of Monopolistic Competition,* 5th edition, p. 81. Our interest at this point is in the early editions, but with two exceptions the quotations are identical in content and pagination in the first and fifth editions. The first exception is in the above quotation: "ordinarily" is not italicized in the early editions.

The ambiguity of the concept of a group is not removed by this enumeration or the references to competing monopolists; we are left with the strong impression that the Marshallian industry has reappeared and we do not understand its new role, for our new picture is one of diversity. But then our picture is not an analytical system; it is therefore necessary to turn to Chamberlin's use of the concept in order to discover its rôle in his analytical system.

The subsequent analysis indicates that the group is a collection of (producers of?) fairly close substitutes; and at least once Chamberlin refers to "groups of products that are close substitutes for each other" (p. 140). More formally, the group may be defined as the collection of firms whose cross-elasticities of demand exceed some pre-assigned value. We must suspend judgment on the usefulness of the concept until we see the results to which it permits Chamberlin to arrive, but several direct implications of the definition should be noticed at once:

1. It is perfectly possible, on Chamberlin's picture of economic life, that the group contain only one firm, or, on the contrary, that it include all of the firms in the economy. This latter possibility can readily follow from the asymmetry of substitution relationships among firms: taking any one product as our point of departure, each substitute has in turn its substitutes, so that the adjacent cross-elasticities may not diminish, and even increase, as we move farther away from the "base" firm in some technological or geographical sense.
2. The picture of diversity and unsystematism also makes it very likely, if the group contains several firms, that the products be heterogeneous from the technological viewpoint.
3. The picture also dictates that often, and perhaps usually, a large or dominant role is played by firms outside the group in determining prices and profits within the group.

The importance of the group concept for the theory of monopolistic competition must be emphasized. Chamberlin asks the reader: can not the conventional theory of monopoly cope with the problems of monopolistic competition? And he answers: No. "Monopolistic competition, then, concerns itself not only with the problem of an *individual* equilibrium (the ordinary theory of monopoly), but also with that of a *group* equilibrium (the adjustment of economic forces within a group of competing monopolists, ordinarily regarded merely as a group of competitors)" (p. 69). The group is no mere expedient to get the analysis started, it is the vehicle of Chamberlin's theory of interdependence of products.

What, then, can we say of the (perhaps) 100 products—dwellings and limousines—in the group? Further simplification is obviously necessary, and Chamberlin introduces what he calls the "uniformity" assumption:

> We therefore proceed under the heroic assumption that both demand and cost curves for all the "products" are uniform throughout the group (p. 82).

Again we must pause: the uniformity assumption is only temporary, we are promised, but even a temporary assumption should be meaningful. How can different products have uniform costs and demands? The quantity axes of the various product diagrams are simply not the same: one measures three-room apartments, another four-room houses, and perhaps still another, restaurant meals (an excellent substitute for a kitchen). We cannot translate one into another by the ratio of their prices, for we are constructing the apparatus to explain prices. We do not wish to say that two physically similar apartments are "really" the same. They are not the same if their prices differ, and perhaps even if they do not differ [2]—this is the fundamental picture. And we do wish to say that restaurant meals plus a bedroom may form a better substitute for a Manhattan apartment than does a Brooklyn apartment—this is also part of the picture.

And yet, by the uniformity assumption Chamberlin has implicitly defined the group as a collection of physically homogeneous products. The identity of costs and demands is otherwise meaningless, and so also is the demand curve he proceeds to draw for a firm on the assumption that "competitors' prices are always identical" (p. 90). We simply cannot attach meaning to the statement that physically diverse things have the same price. This physical homogeneity possibly destroys, at least temporarily, Chamberlin's monopolistic competition (except for spatially distributed firms), for he has also assumed that buyers have perfect knowledge (p. 73), in order further to simplify the analysis. With perfect knowledge and homogeneous products, must not the demand curve confronting each firm be infinitely elastic? But the uniformity assumption is only temporary, we recall.

---

[2] ". . . general uniformity of price proves nothing as to the freedom of competition from monopoly elements" (p 88).

So we have 100 products of various sorts (blinking the inconsistency) or of one sort, but with negatively sloping demand curves (dropping the assumption of perfect knowledge), what then? Our vision tells us that we are unlikely to find symmetry, continuity, or any sort of smoothness in the relationships among these products. To meet this problem, Chamberlin introduces what I shall term the "symmetry" assumption:

> Specifically, we assume for the present that any adjustment of price or of "product" by a single producer spreads its influence over so many of his competitors that the impact felt by any one is negligible and does not lead him to any readjustment of his own situation (p. 83).

It is now an anti-climax to notice that Chamberlin further assumes, throughout his entire volume, that (1) the only relationship between products is that of substitution—complementarity "is beyond the scope of our problem" (p. 39 n.), and (2) the Marshallian cost apparatus is acceptable *in toto*: the vision of diversity and unsystematism does not extend to the resources market.[3]

But now we have utterly abandoned the picture with which our analytical technique was designed to deal: there is no variety and there is only one possible type of interrelationship between products. We probably have a Marshallian industry. We appear also to have negatively sloping demand curves for individual products, because our picture and our group are inconsistent with our uniformity assumption. The tangency of average cost and demand curves which we now deduce is of little importance to us: this familiar result of competitive theory, I will argue later, is not enriched. Possibly of more importance is the finding that even under these extreme conditions our new variable, "product," cannot be "measured along an axis" (p. 79)—that is, cannot be measured. Each time "product" appears in the discussion, we are told to choose it to maximize profits, and nothing more.[4] As a result, for practical purposes the theory of monopolistic competition concerns

---

[3] Although, in strict logic, it must: there are no consumer goods that are purchased exclusively by consumers.

[4] "The difficulties of representing graphically the variation of 'product' render hazardous any attempt to define with precision the exact point of equilibrium. It would seem that the most that can be said is that it will be characterized by (1) the equation of cost and price, and (2) the impossibility of a 'product' adjustment by anyone which would increase his profits" (p. 97). This, of course, is a statement of the problem, not of its solution.

only consumers moving among products, and ignores products moving among consumers.

We hasten on to the sections in which the uniformity and symmetry assumptions are separately (but, oddly, never jointly) lifted. Oligopoly may, and perhaps usually will, enter if the symmetry assumption fails, and then we are reduced to the familiar uncertainty over assumptions and results (pp. 100–4), from which we salvage only the conclusion that prices may be higher than under competition (p. 104). The effect of diversity of demand and cost conditions is even more devastating: there may be monopoly profits throughout the group at equilibrium—and then again, there may not. Indeed, although Professor Chamberlin does not state the possibility, it is not even clear that equilibrium is attainable: under these vague conditions prices may continue to change, and new firms may continue to enter and old firms continue to leave the "group." This indeterminacy is especially likely if we recognize variety through time—the consumers' liking for novelty, which Professor Chamberlin should surely add to his picture. He sums up the effects of diversity:

> To sum up this phase of the matter, our statement of the group problem must be modified by recognizing that the demand curves are not adjusted uniformly to a position tangent to the cost curves. In so far as profits are higher than the general competitive level in the field as a whole or in any portion of it, new competitors will, *if possible*, invade the field and reduce them. If this were always possible, as hitherto assumed, the curves would always be tangent and monopoly profits would be eliminated. In fact it is only partially possible. As a result some (or all) of the curves may lie at various distances to the right of the point of tangency, leaving monopoly profits scattered throughout the group— and throughout the price system (p. 113).

It will be observed that the theory of monopolistic competition now contains no conditions of equilibrium, only a definition of equilibrium.

As a result, in the general case we cannot make a single statement about economic events in the world we sought to analyze. It is true that many such statements are made by Chamberlin, but none follows rigorously from the ambiguous apparatus. All of the definite comparisons with competition, for example, are made when there is uniformity and symmetry.[5] Indeed even these comparisons rest upon the further and technically inadmissible assumption that the cost curves of a firm will be the same under competition and monopolistic competition, although there is no presumption that the size of the "group" will be the same in the two situations if they really differ.[6]

And so the first attempt has failed.[7] Professor Chamberlin did not reduce his picture of reality to a manageable analytical system.

2. THE SECOND ATTEMPT: CHAMBERLIN-TRIFFIN

In the course of time and controversy, Professor Chamberlin indicated the probable desirability of abandoning the concept of the group, which in his system was, after all, an anachronistic vestige of neo-classical economics. When discussing the closely related concept of entry of new firms (into a group), he said:

> The upshot of the matter seems to be that the concept is not very useful and is even seriously misleading in connection with monopolistic competition. It is, in reality, a concept usually related to a market for a definite commodity, and the fundamental difficulty is that there is no such commodity under monopolistic competition beyond that produced by an individual firm (p. 201).

[5] This is recognized in a footnote (p. 78 n.), where it is said that if there is not tangency, the monopolistically competitive output of the firm may exceed the competitive output. This is held to be an unimportant exception because of "considerations introduced below in connection with the group problem." In the group discussion, under symmetry and uniformity, the footnote is recalled (p. 88) but not elaborated. The exception is forgotten when diversity of costs and demands is reached, although tangency of cost and demand curves has now vanished, and with it the improbability of the exception.

[6] The neglect of cost differences is justified on two grounds. (1) Many industries are constant cost industries—a result borrowed from Marshallian analysis, for which there is no presumption in the Chamberlin group. (2) The belief that even with increasing or decreasing cost industries, "the divergences from the norms of purely competitive theory are always of the same sort" (p. 87). This belief is without foundation.

[7] I pass over the theory of selling costs because my subject is monopolistic competition, not the economics of Professor Chamberlin. Selling costs played only one role in the discussion that we need notice: their existence was adduced as a criticism of the theory of perfect competition, for none would be needed with perfect knowledge. Professor Chamberlin was right in concluding that perfect competition is a poor instrument in analyzing selling costs. His results might have been more informative, however, if he had chosen to drop the assumption that the economy was stationary, rather than the assumption that the economy was competitive.

But he does not follow this line of thought to its conclusion:

> It is not meant by this argument to discard completely the concept of an "industry." In many connections, it is obviously useful to delimit a portion of the economic system and study it in some degree of isolation from the rest. And if this can be done, although entry is never "free," it is not wholly without meaning to speak of the *relative* ease with which this particular field may be entered, in the sense of the relative ease with which substitutes for the particular products which compose the "industry" may be produced. One emerges from any attempt to classify industries, however, with a feeling that it is all exceedingly arbitrary. The "common sense" definitions of industries in terms of which practical problems are likely to be studied seem to be based much more upon technological criteria than upon the possibility of market substitution (p. 202 n.).

Except for the last sentence, which is an indirect admission of the entire Marshallian system,[8] the tenor of the argument is that the group must go.

This is a most baffling state in which to leave the theory of monopolistic competition, for we recall that the theory differs from that of monopoly only in containing a group equilibrium. "As for monopoly, *as ordinarily conceived and defined,* monopolistic competition embraces it and takes it as a starting point" (p. 68, not in first edition). But if the group is suspect, if at best it is a notion "not wholly without meaning," the theory of monopoly seems to be also the final destination.

It was left for an able disciple, Dr. Robert Triffin, to carry the purification of the technique a step farther, in his *Monopolistic Competition and General Equilibrium Theory* (1940). He succeeds in making the analytical apparatus portray faithfully the original picture of variety and unsystematism. Costs, demand, and hence profits of each firm are functions of all prices in the economy, i.e. profits of firm $= \phi$ $(p_1, p_2, \ldots, p_n)$, where n is very large. The firm will maximize profits, subject to the usual uncertainties of oligopolistic situations—that is, it will equate marginal revenue and marginal cost.

---

[8] This last sentence is even more remarkable in the original article of which the above quotations are revisions: "It seems much easier and more defensible to set up classifications based upon technological criteria than upon the possibility of market substitution." (*"Monopolistic or Imperfect Competition?"* Q.J.E., LI (1937), 568 n).

And what of the group? It must go, for it is inconsistent with the fundamental vision. "In the general pure theory of value, the group and the industry are useless concepts" (p. 89). "Product differentiation robs the concept of industry of both its definiteness and its service-ability" (p. 188). How, then, are we to analyze the interrelationships among firms? Apparently we cannot; Dr. Triffin's chapter (III) on the theory of external interdependence consists only of an elegant classification of types of interdependence.

Dr. Triffin does not fail to draw the conclusion that monopolistic competition has nothing to say of the interdependence of firms; this silence is indeed hailed as an advance over the Marshallian theory (p. 189). The basis for this claim deserves our attention. Dr. Triffin visualizes the discipline as composed of two very different types of studies: the "general pure theory of value"; and the investigation of concrete economic problems—for example, the New York housing problem:

> Is anything gained by limiting the investigation to a group of close competitors, which we would call a group or industry? In an empirical, statistical study, yes: we can, in this way, reduce to a manageable size the research work involved, without any serious loss in precision or exhaus-tiveness. In the general statement of value theory, no: when competition is discussed in general abstract terms, we may just as well make the group (or industry) coextensive with the whole economic collectivity. The problems are the same, and the complexity is no greater.
>
> In other words, the value of these groupings is only a concrete, empirical one: it is never useful to speak of "in-dustries" or "groups" in a general, abstract way, but it may be very helpful to speak of the oil industry, the coal indus-try, the steel industry, etc. (p. 88).

And in his conclusion, Dr. Triffin goes on:

> Instead of drawing its substance from arbitrary assump-tions, chosen for their simplicity and unduly extended to the whole field of economic activity, our theory may turn to more pedestrian, but more fruitful methods. It will recog-nize the richness and variety of all concrete cases, and tackle each problem with due respect for its individual aspects. More advantage will be taken of all relevant factual infor-

mation, and less reliance will be placed on a mere resort to the pass-key of general theoretical assumptions (p. 189).

I would emphasize the separateness of these two types of economic analysis in Triffin's view of economics: there is neither substitution nor complementarity between the general theory and the specific economic investigation. The theory has nothing to learn from the study of specific problems because these problems are so diverse that no single inductive generalization is possible.[9] Conversely the study of specific problems has nothing to gain from the general theory, for the theory can provide no apparatus to raise relevant questions, to indicate relevant types of facts, or to guide the economist in handling the facts to reach useful conclusions.

This is a fundamentally mistaken rôle to assign to general theory. The study of economic theory is not defensible on æsthetic grounds— it hardly rivals in elegance the mathematics or physics our sophomores learn. The theory is studied only as an aid in solving real problems, and it is good only in the measure that it performs this function. Dr. Triffin's advice is fundamentally to give up theory, "to tackle each problem with due respect for its individual aspects." Chamberlin's picture of reality has finally led, when consistently followed, to the familiar reaction: *ad hoc* empiricism.

3. THE REASONS FOR FAILURE

Professor Chamberlin's failure to construct an analytical system capable of dealing informatively with his picture of reality is not hard to explain. The fundamental fact is that, although Chamberlin could throw off the shackles of Marshall's view of economic life, he could not throw off the shackles of Marshall's view of economic analysis. Marshall's technique was appropriate to the problem set to it: it deals informatively and with tolerable logic with the world of competitive industries and monopolies. But it is lost in the sea of diversity and unsystematism, and Chamberlin is lost with it.

Dr. Triffin's failure, on the other hand, seems to me attributable to his attempt to make the general theory an accurate description of all reality. It is as if an artist is commissioned to paint the picture of a typical skyscraper: and since skyscrapers are thick and thin, of vari-

---

9 Thus, after Dr. Triffin examines freedom of entry, he concludes, "Which type of entry prevails in any particular case is to be ascertained and 'explained' by an investigation of the facts. Analytical reasoning is powerless to deduce the answer from general, universally valid assumptions" (p. 123).

able height, of differing colours, with various architectural designs, his painting must be blank because it would violate reality if it contained a single identifiable detail. Dr. Triffin should have been warned by the Walrasian theory of general equilibrium he sought to generalize. This theory proved to be relatively uninformative, even when it had as many equations as unknowns; it was not likely to gain in usefulness when the unknowns were multiplied and the equations reduced.

4. CONCLUDING OBSERVATIONS

I wish to close by offering an estimate of the net contribution of the attempt to construct a theory of monopolistic competition. Before undertaking this appraisal, however, it is necessary to set forth certain methodological principles.[10]

The purpose of the study of economics is to permit us to make predictions about the behaviour of economic phenomena under specified conditions. The sole test of the usefulness of an economic theory is the concordance between its predictions and the observable course of events. Often a theory is criticized or rejected because its assumptions are "unrealistic." Granting for a moment that this charge has meaning, it burdens theory with an additional function, that of description. This is a most unreasonable burden to place upon a theory: the rôle of description is to particularize, while the rôle of theory is to generalize—to disregard an infinite number of differences and capture the important common element in different phenomena.

But this line of argument grants the ungrantable; it is often impossible to determine whether assumption A is more or less realistic than assumption B, except by comparing the agreement between their implications and the observable course of events. One can but show that a theory is unrealistic in essentials by demonstrating that its predictions are wrong.

Should monopoly or competition be used to analyze the New York housing market? The answer is: both. If we are interested in the effects of rent ceilings and inflation, the theory of competition provides informative predictions. If we are interested in why one location rents for more than another, the theory of monopoly may be an informative guide. Different theories, each with its particular assumptions, can be applied to the same phenomena to answer different questions.

These remarks are especially relevant to the theory of monopolistic

[10] The present interpretation of these principles is due to Professor Milton Friedman; see Talcott Parsons, *The Structure of Social Action*.

competition. A good deal of the support for this theory stems from the mistaken demand for correspondence between "reality" and premises. The theory is further supported by the erroneous view, for which Professor Chamberlin bears some responsibility, that if the premises of competitive theory depart (in a descriptive sense) from the facts, the implications of that theory must be wrong.[11]

This leads me to the specific contribution of the theory of monopolistic competition: the analysis of the many-firm industry producing a single (technological) product under uniformity and symmetry conditions, but with a falling demand curve for each firm. Chamberlin's analysis of this particular situation is essentially correct, and many economists appear to wish to incorporate it into neo-classical theory. It should be incorporated, not if it is a more "realistic" description of industries, but if it contains different or more accurate predictions (as tested by observation) than the theory of competition. I personally think that the predictions of this standard model of monopolistic competition differ only in unimportant respects from those of the theory of competition because the underlying conditions will usually be accompanied by very high demand elasticities for the individual firms. But this is a question of fact, and it must be resolved by empirical tests of the implications of the two theories (a task the supporters of the theory of monopolistic competition have not yet undertaken).

The general contribution of the theory of monopolistic competition, on the other hand, seems to me indisputable: it has led to reorientation and refinement of our thinking on monopoly. We are now more careful to pay attention to the logical niceties of definitions of industries and commodities. We are now more careful to apply monopoly theory where it is appropriate. The importance of the trade mark and of advertising, and the need for study of product structure and evolution, have become more generally recognized. These and other improvements may seem disappointing to the hopeful proposers of a proud new theory, but they should not be. This is the way sciences grow. One of the prominent lessons of the history of human thought is that new ideas do not lead to the abandonment of the previous heritage; the new ideas are swallowed up by the existing corpus, which is thereafter a little different. And sometimes a little better.

---

11 "In all of the fields where individual products have even the slightest element of uniqueness, competition bears but faint resemblance to the pure competition of a highly organized market for a homogeneous product" (p. 9).

23

THE THEORY OF MONOPOLISTIC COMPETITION AFTER THIRTY YEARS: THE IMPACT ON GENERAL THEORY *

Robert L. Bishop teaches at Massachusetts Institute of Technology.

The character and importance of the impact that the theories of monopolistic and imperfect competition have had on general theory obviously depend on whose general theory it is. As I judge the consensus of economists, Chamberlin's *Theory of Monopolistic Competition* and Mrs. Robinson's *Economics of Imperfect Competition* are acknowledged to have touched off, in 1933, a theoretical revolution whose relative importance in the microeconomic area was comparable to that of Keynesian analysis in macroeconomics. But there are also some significant minorities in the profession who would minimize or reject completely the positive value of the Chamberlinian and Robinsonian doctrines; so, for anyone like myself that happens to hold these theories in high esteem, it is important to test that judgment against the counterarguments of the opposition. Accordingly, I shall divide my remarks beween, first, a brief characterization of the merits and positive significance of Chamberlin's and Robinson's contributions and, second, a consideration of the nature and worth of some of the dissenting views.

Let me begin on a personal note. I was privileged to begin my own study of economics, as a freshman at Harvard, just before the Chamberlin-Robinson revolution—in the very year that their pioneering works were published. I confess that I was a better student of the received doctrines that were set before me than I was an observer of reality; and, among other things, I absorbed quickly the notion that "supply and demand" were the key to an understanding of how any market operates, including the occasional monopolistic one that was subject to a control and restriction of supply. Then, sometime during that first year, I heard someone talking about a distinction between buyers' markets and sellers' markets, according as buyers found it

* From the *American Economic Review*, Vol. LIV, No. 3 (May, 1964), pp. 33–43. Reprinted by permission.

320

easy to buy or sellers to sell. My own instant reaction was to classify the speaker as an emonomic illiterate; for it seemed perfectly apparent that, in any "competitive" market, the equilibrium price had to be at the level where demand and supply were equal, so that every buyer could readily buy, and every seller could no less readily sell, whatever respective quantities they pleased. When I subsequently learned that the speaker was indeed talking about relevant economic phenomena, not only did I make a belated mental apology to him for my similarly unspoken slur on his intelligence, but I also felt that I had acquired a justifiable grievance against the analytical tradition that had trapped me into placing my faith in the universality of the law of supply and demand. By this time, of course, I had become a student of monopolistic competition, having found readily convincing the judgment that the demands relevant for most sellers' price decisions were significantly less than perfectly elastic. This was a conclusion that seemed to me then, and still seems to me now, essentially inescapable as soon as the equilibrium of the individual firm was subjected to a more explicit and cogent analysis than, say, in Marshall's fuzzy device of a "representative firm."

Now I do not mean to suggest for a minute that my betters among pre-1933 economists were all equally and uniformly guilty of the same overliteralness in their understanding and analytical use of the law of supply and demand than I was as a freshman. I do believe, however, that they were frequently victims of the state of affairs in which their only explicit theory of competition involved what is now called pure or perfect competition. Furthermore, having only that theory, they were also subject to the persistent analytical bias of a wishful thinking that the world did indeed conform well enough, for the most part, to the conditions necessary for a relevant application of the only theory at their command. Nor has this bias altogether disappeared; it is still very much alive, for example, in such citadels as the University of Chicago. As always, it takes a theory to lick a theory. Accordingly, whether we call the phenomenon "monopolistic competition" as in this Cambridge or "imperfect competition" as in the other one, the intensive theoretical treatments of Chamberlin and Mrs. Robinson were essential in order to force upon the attention of the economics profession due regard for the fact that most product markets differ significantly from the traditional models of either simple monopoly or pure competition.

I can afford to sketch only briefly, and with a few selected examples, some of the ways in which these doctrines have made a difference in economic theory and in the views that most of us entertain as to the economic world around us. Example: as late as 1932, even as excellent an economist as J. R. Hicks was able to write a *Theory of Wages* in which he was still telling us that wages are typically equal to the value of labor's marginal product. In the commentary that he has recently published on that early work, he has himself acknowledged to some extent the seriousness of the defects attributable to his having so consistently and uncritically assumed perfect competition in both product and factor markets.[1]

A few examples concerning Marshall's economic theory are especially appropriate; for he was probably without peer in the delicate art of not letting his inadequate theory get too much in the way of his sensible view of reality. As to retail trade, for example, he was usually careful to mention that the competitive theory he was talking about did not apply.[2] Now, of course, we have a theoretical framework into which an analysis of many different kinds of retail trade can be fitted. Or consider the famous category of the decreasing-cost industry, whose existence Marshall had to explain by means of a very confusing set of comments about the internal and external economies reaped by the representative firm when demand for the industry's product went up, despite the fact (which he uneasily recognized) that unexhausted internal economies of scale are incompatible with purely competitive equilibrium. With product differentiation or oligopoly (or both), the possibility that increased demand may lead to lower prices becomes eminently comprehensible and plausible, without recourse to any mystique about an especially dubious type of external economy. Finally, consider the anomalousness of Marshall's view that price typically equals marginal cost except when demand is too low for the firm to cover its full costs, whereupon misgivings about "spoiling the market" are dragged in to explain why the firm does not suffer the even greater loss that would be implied if it were to continue to equate price to marginal cost (at least down to minimum average variable cost). This conception is revealed in all its naked implausibility by Frisch's graphical interpretation of Marshall's verbal exposition.[3]

As soon as we recognize that there are comparatively few markets in which "demand and supply" operate in the essentially symmetrical way that is the essence of that famous law, many things become analytically clear for the first time. Thus, in product markets where buyers are passive and prices are unilaterally administered by sellers,

[1] J. R. Hicks, *The Theory of Wages* (2nd ed., 1963), p. 310.
[2] A. Marshall, *Principles of Economics* (8th ed., 1920), p. 328.
[3] R. Frisch, "Alfred Marshall's Theory of Value," *Q.J.E.*, 1950, pp. 495–524.

the normal condition of price in excess of marginal cost explains why it is the sellers rather than the buyers who are eager for more transactions. Not only does this open the door to such phenomena as advertising and other forms of non-price competition, but it also helps explain why we are a race of eager sellers and coy buyers, with purchasing agents getting the Christmas presents from the salesmen rather than the other way around, and with "salesmanship" a familiar concept while "purchasemanship" does not even appear in the dictionary. We find here also, I am convinced, part of the explanation—even though not the whole—of the persistent producer-orientation of so many of the world's mercantilist policies, both ancient and modern, international and domestic.

Not the least of the contributions of these doctrines, in my opinion, is the improved sense that they make out of the major propositions that have emerged from Keynesian macroeconomic analysis. Keynes himself, of course, was still sufficiently Marshallian when he wrote the *General Theory* so that he based his theory on an assumption of universal pure competition, but with the anomalous extra feature of a perfectly elastic labor supply up to the full employment quantity, as based on a peculiarly strong and implausible "money illusion" on the part of the labor suppliers. This was Keynes's way of explaining how an underemployment equilibrium was possible without a persistent price deflation. In contrast to that rationalization, how much more natural and plausible it is to explain the necessary price and wage rigidities or "stickiness" with reference to the fact that the world is not predominantly purely competitive.

Similarly, it is only with reference to these doctrines that we can make analytical sense out of the more modern dilemma that really full employment is very hard to achieve without at least a creeping inflation. The difficulty is not at all that some prices and wage rates rise for the good competitive reason that otherwise there would be an excess of demand over supply, but rather that other prices not only fail to fall but are even capable of being increased when the opposite condition prevails. This asymmetry, whereby many prices and wage rates go up much more readily than they go down (save only in the deepest depression), is again traceable to the basic facts that (1) our price-determining machinery is preponderantly seller-dominated, and (2) the normal condition of such markets is that supply exceeds demand—in the relevant sense that sellers (whether of goods or labor) are willing and eager to sell more than they can actually sell at their current prices. To investigate the conflicting claims of demand-pull and cost-push theories of inflation without due regard for these considerations, as some scholars still do, is to omit a most important ingredient of the analysis.[4]

Widely accepted though the theories of monopolistic or imperfect competition have been, there are still some determined pockets of resistance. I turn, accordingly, to an examination of some of the views entertained in those quarters. The various misgivings can be disentangled to some extent, I think, under such headings as (1) ideological, (2) methodological, and (3) factual.

Even though ideological precommitment is a poor influence in shaping anyone's evaluation of a new theory, such ideological contamination has played a not inconsiderable role in just such areas as the present one. As always, ideology cuts at least two ways. Thus, in the atmosphere of the depressed 1930's, so conducive to the deepest disillusionment with the current performance of capitalist free enterprise, it was not surprising that many young Turks—and some old ones as well—were strongly predisposed to find in the theories of monopolistic or imperfect competition, not only a legitimate analytical framework, but also a device for dramatizing in an exaggerated way at least some of the sins of capitalism. Mrs. Robinson herself, I am told, has testified that the central motivation for her own book was to demonstrate the pervasiveness of the exploitation of labor; and her bias is further apparent in her failure to give a corresponding attention to monopoly power in labor markets. It is sometimes inadequately appreciated that, no matter how much labor a great corporation may hire, it exerts no monopsony power at all unless it is unable to get as much labor as desired at the current wage rate; conversely, if there is an excess of job seekers at that wage, the predominating influence in the situation is monopolistic, not monopsonistic.

On the other side, the central ideological resistance to a due acknowledgement of the widespread relevance of monopolistic competition comes from those theorists who have a strong emotional stake in an absolute and uncompromising defense of the optimality of unregulated markets. This is illustrated, for example, in the writings of Mises and Hayek. To Mises, imperfect or monopolistic competition is "mythology" (*Human Action,* 1949, p. 378). His argument is a curious one, however, for he concedes the existence of all of the basic phenomena with which the theory of monopolistic competition is concerned, including product differentiation and oligopoly (e.g., pp. 354–61). Indeed, he even concedes that "almost all consumers' goods are

[4] For example, R. T. Selden, "Cost-Push versus Demand-Pull Inflation, 1955–57," *J.P.E.*, Feb., 1959, pp. 1–20.

included in the class of monopolized goods" (p. 357). But, even more curiously, he also argues that it does not follow by any means that monopolists necessarily, or even presumptively, charge monopoly prices (e.g., p. 356). Now it should not be thought that Mises is talking about the *curiosum* of a "monopolist" who faces a perfectly elastic demand; for he is ludicrously confused about this. Thus, a bit farther on (pp. 381–82), in speaking of the various ways in which the individual consumer may react to monopoly prices, he says of one of the possibilities: "The consumer restricts his purchase of the monopolized commodity to such an extent that he spends less for it than he would have spent under the competitive price; he buys with the money thus saved goods which he would not have bought otherwise. (If all people were to react in this way, the seller would harm his interests by substituting a higher price for the competitive price; no monopoly price could emerge. . . .)" The cream of this little jest, of course, is that a monopolist with positive marginal cost maximizes his profit only where marginal revenue is also positive, or where demand exhibits the relative elasticity that Mises' case implies.

But if Mises' own discussion founders in this type of futility, he also invokes the aid of a much more careful and competent analyst when he cites (p. 278, n.) as "a refutation of the fashionable doctrines of imperfect and of monopolistic competition" two essays by Hayek in his *Individualism and Economic Order* (1948; pp. 92–118). Actually, however, Hayek's unhappiness with the concept of an "imperfect" market really rests primarily on his misgivings as to the unreal character of a "perfect" one and on what he describes as "the so-called theory of 'perfect competition'" (p. 92). Thus, his quarrel would seem to me to be less with Chamberlin and Mrs. Robinson than with such theorists as Friedman and Stigler, who defend the application of the perfectly competitive model in many situations where others of us regard it as very dubiously applicable.

Specifically, Hayek argues "that what the theory of perfect competition discusses has little claim to be called 'competition' at all and that its conclusions are of little use as guides to policy" p. 92). This reflects a methodological complaint that "the modern theory of competition deals almost exlusively with a state of what is called 'competitive equilibrium' in which it is assumed that the data for the different individuals are fully adjusted to each other, while the problem which requires explanation is the nature of the process by which the data are thus adjusted" (p. 94). In reply, it seems to me that no competent theorist regards static-equilibrium theory as the last word of economic analysis. Moreover, part of our interest in static equilibria concerns their stability conditions, from which the more general comparative-statics theorems are generated; and, beyond that, everyone stands ready to move on to explicitly dynamic analysis whenever necessary. But to argue, as Hayek seems to, that dynamic analysis can be wholly divorced from concepts of equilibrium seems to me anything but fruitful. In other words, even the dynamics of a market remain quite incomprehensible except as we can analyze them as movements toward or away from some equilibrium position, even when the data are changing so rapidly that at least the longer-run types of equilibria are never actually attained. In short, Hayek's discussion is less a "refutation" of what others call imperfections of competition—like Mises, he also willingly acknowledges the phenomena and balks only at what they are called—than it is an obscurantist effort to undermine all of the standard techniques of economic analysis.

On the other hand, Hayek is too sensible a man to hold consistently to his rejection of equilibrium analysis. Thus, his methodology does not prevent him from comparing "an 'imperfect' market . . . with a relatively 'perfect' market as that of, say, grain" (p. 102), despite his previous argument that competition has to be not only dynamic but personal pp. (96–97). On the latter point, he cites as "remarkable" Stigler's eminently perceptive statement that "economic relationships are never perfectly competitive if they involve any personal relationships between economic units" (in the sense, of course, that when demand equals supply in a perfectly competitive market, it makes no difference to any buyer or seller as to the identity of the other party or parties with whom he deals, and also in the sense that no buyer or seller is thereby frustrating any other person in his desire to make a similar purchase or sale at the competitive equilibrium price). My final comment is that, if Hayek finds such impersonal equilibria unrealistic, he is more than welcome to join the ranks of the converts to the theory of monopolistic competition. Nor, if he were to accept this invitation, should he fear that he would thereby be forced to give up what he cites as the "practical lesson of all this, . . . that we should worry much less about whether competition in a given case is perfect and worry much more whether there is competition at all" (p. 105). Surely, many of his presumed opponents agree wholeheartedly with that sentiment, and also with his further remark that "much more serious than the fact that prices may not correspond to marginal cost is the fact that, with an intrenched monopoly, costs are likely to be higher than necessary." To this I would only add that so may they be when oligopolists invite excess capacity with high-price policies and deliberately create excess capacity to discourage further entry, or when monopolistic competitors of any kind inflate their costs with certain types of sales-effort expenditures as an alternative to cutting prices. But even if Hayek rejects this invitation, the rest of us must at least be pardoned if we conclude that his discussion constitutes a pale and unconvincing "refutation" of the doctrines in question.

A quite different motive for either ignoring or minimizing market imperfections is rooted in the theorist's methodological bias in favor of the assumption of pure competition, because of its analytically tractable features. Sometimes this assumption is made in a properly apologetic way, as by Hicks in *Value and Capital*. Still, this does not keep him from consoling himself with the comforting thought: "I do not myself believe that the more important results of this work are much damaged by this omission [of imperfectly competitive influences]" (p. 7). And later, when he acknowledges that certain considerations do indeed have "to be met by sacrificing the assumption of perfect competition," he adds unhappily, "yet it has to be recognized that a general abandonment of the assumption of perfect competition, a universal adoption of the assumption of monopoly, must have very destructive consequences for economic theory" (p. 83). In other words, he feels that it is better to have a neat, inapplicable theory than to face up to the difficulties of formulating some relevant ones.

Where Hicks is at least frankly apologetic and defensive, however, others such as Friedman assume an aggressive initiative, even to the extent of finding positive merit in the failures of the purely competitive model to conform better than it does to the facts of a great variety of siuations. If I understand him aright, Friedman imposes on himself the heroic act of self-denial of choosing to work with only two abstract models (*Essays in Positive Economics,* pp. 35ff.). These involve: (1) a "competitive" firm, where "the demand curve for its output is infinitely elastic with respect to its own price for some price and all outputs, given the prices charged by all other firms"; and (2) a "monopolistic" firm, where "the demand curve for its output is not infinitely elastic at some price for all outputs." In a footnote, however, he breaks the latter category down into two types: (1) "the monopolistic firm proper, if the demand curve is nowhere infinitely elastic (except possibly at zero output)," and (2) "the oligopolistic firm, if the demand curve for its output is infinitely elastic at some price for some but not all outputs."

As to this weird oligopoly concept, it may first be noticed that oligopolistic suppliers of merely close (but not perfect) substitute products are not oligopolists at all to Friedman, but just monopolists. Thus, there is apparently no competition worth anaylzing at all between Ford and General Motors. Second, there is not even a clear distinction between competition and oligopoly in Friedman's scheme; for, whether the suppliers of perfect substitutes are two or two thousand, the demand confronting any one of them (with other prices constant, as Friedman specifies) is perfectly elastic only up to the total quantity demanded in the market as a whole at the common price. On the other hand, Friedman never puts his oligopolistic model to any analytical use anyway; so it does not really constitute a third model as an addition to the two basic ones.

Having only two such models at his disposal, then, he naturally needs a good deal of leeway in the discretion that he allows himself as to their use. Thus, as he makes perfectly clear in an example relating to the cigarette industry (pp. 37–38), either model is relevantly applicable depending on the problem at hand. First, however, no guidance whatever is offered as to the principles that might determine which of the two models is relevant, in advance of applying one or the other. Second, there is obviously a lot of room here for self-deception as to whether either model really applies at all satisfactorily. Thus Friedman says: "Suppose the problem is to determine the effect on retail prices of cigarettes of an increase, expected to be permanent, in the federal cigarette tax. I venture to predict that broadly correct results will be obtained by treating cigarette firms as if they were producing an identical product and were in perfect competition." There are some problems, however, as to how this conjecture might be tested. Thus, depending perhaps on the period allowed for the industry's adjustment, the gross price paid by consumers will presumably rise; but any such reaction can be tautologically rationalized after the fact with reference to either competitive or monopolistic theory, whether the price rises by an amount greater than, equal to, or less than the tax. Clearly, if competitive theory is to be relevantly applicable, Friedman must first find not only a supply curve for the cigarette industry, but the whole collection of successively relevant short-run and long-run supply curves; and he must then find that the cigarette industry does indeed behave "as if" it were constantly equating demand and supply. Now, actually, there is a test that can at least disprove what Friedman ventures to predict. In an industry that really is purely competitive, with the basic demand and cost data constant, a tax may cause the price to rise little, if at all, in a very short run; then it causes the price to rise more in each successively longer short run; and finally it rises most in the long run. But monopolists and oligopolists, in their wisdom as dynamic profit maximizers, often respond to a tax with an immediate, once-and-for-all price increase—quite unlike pure competitors. My own ventured prediction is that cigarette manufacturers do indeed respond in this oligopolistic manner, perhaps even rescinding part of the price increase in the longer run if a reduction of factor prices is induced by the curtailment of factor demand.

The same sort of determination to divide both reality and its economic analysis into the two neat boxes of competition and simple monopoly is also illustrated in Stigler's work. Thus, in one of his *Five Lectures on Economic Problems* (1950), he concludes that the theory of monopolistic competition is a "failure" (p. 22) because it embraces too many diverse conditions for any single, neat theory to cope with in a fruitful way. Then, in the last lecture, he gallantly undertakes to classify as best he can the industries of the United States into the two categories of "competition" and "monopoly" (with a monopolistic subcategory of "compulsory cartels"). "A competitive situation," he says (p. 48), "is characterized by price or product competition of the individual firm, leading to approximate equality of price and marginal cost in the long run." This is a constructive start, but it has two weaknesses: (1) the standard of "approximate equality" is not clear (should it be no more than a 2 percent disparity, for example, or would 10 percent be acceptable too?), and (2) what is the meaning and the justification of limiting the prescription to the long run? As to the first point, it is also important to appreciate that, with production divided into various vertical stages, the magnitude of price minus marginal cost is more relevantly compared with value added than with price. As to the reference to the long run, if this means only that price may temporarily exceed marginal cost by an appreciable percentage, for example in the early stages of major innovative change, then well and good; but if it means, as I fear it does, that price may acceptably be only slightly higher than long-run marginal cost at the same time that it is persistently or predominantly higher than short-run marginal cost by a much larger percentage, then I must respectfully protest. The point involved is an important one and the subject of quite widespread confusion, so I should like to spell out its implications.

First, in an industry that is really purely competitive, there is no need to indulge in any apologetics about short-run equilibrium. In any purely competitive equilibrium, whether short-run or long-run, price is always equal to the respectively relevant marginal cost. Furthermore, in long-run equilibrium, price is equal to both long-run and short-run marginal cost (provided only that they are both determinate.) This follows, of course, from the tangency or envelope relationship between long-run and short-run total cost. Then, according as output in the short run is either above or below the long-run equilibrium level, short-run marginal cost is also either above or below long-run marginal cost, respectively. Thus it does not follow that short-run marginal cost is either necessarily or presumptively below long-run marginal cost, despite a widespread belief to the contrary even among theorists who should know better. Accordingly, in any evaluation as to how "nearly" purely competitive a given industry may be, the relevant test is how nearly price corresponds to short-run marginal cost on the average through time. Therefore, an industry or firm which keeps price not too far above some version of long-run marginal cost on the average, but which consistently exhibits an appreciably higher excess of price over short-run marginal cost, should not get very good marks as to the closeness of its approximation to pure competition. Under these conditions, in other words, there is an unfailing indication that capacity is persistently in excess of what it should be for either purely competitive or efficient equilibrium. On the other hand, as already suggested above in connection with Hayek's observation about cost inflation, this is by no means an unusual case under conditions that are other than purely competitive.

Stigler's estimate as to the number of industries that adequately approximate pure competition or, as he puts it, "in which monopoly power is inappreciable" (p. 47), is further biased by his willingness to certify an industry as "competitive" if either of two conditions are met. The first concerns an industry's structure and the second concerns its performance (p. 47): "(1) It must possess a large number of independent firms, none dominant in size, and additional firms can enter the industry. (2) It may possess few firms, or a few firms of relatively large size, but the departures from a competitive situation are not large." I have already indicated my misgivings as to the excessive leniency of the second condition, since it rests on "approximate equality of price and marginal cost in the long run." Furthermore, the first condition is also too lenient, in that it allows an industry to qualify as "competitive" even if the gap between price and marginal cost is substantial. This may well be the case (1) because product differentiation alone is capable of raising price appreciably above marginal cost, even when the rival firms are numerous and entry is easy, and (2) because local oligopolistic relationships may also exist, even when firms are numerous throughout a broadly and loosely defined "industry."

Let me conclude with the almost obligatory reference to what remains for future research. Despite the methodological differences just indicated, it still seems to me that the basic conflicts between Cambridge and Chicago in this area are primarily factual, at least to the extent that we seem to agree that the relationships of price and marginal cost are of central importance. What we ideally need, accordingly, is a kind of profile of price, marginal-cost, and value-added relationships throughout the economy. Even if the whole job would be a staggering one, it would still be worth while to have it done if only on a piecemeal sampling basis. Only then would we really be in a position to evaluate definitively, for example, Stigler's conclusion that the U.S. economy is about 70 percent "competitive" or Harberger's ingenious but extraordinarily naïve estimate that resource misallocation in American manufacturing entails a cost of only about $2.00 per capita.[5] My own hostage to fortune is that the relevant data would reveal the disparities between price and marginal cost throughout the U.S. economy to be far greater than they are thought to be in Chicago.

[5] A. C. Harberger, "Monopoly and Resource Allocation," *A.E.R.*, May, 1954, pp. 77–87, esp. p. 84.

24

THE STATISTICS OF MONOPOLY
AND MERGER *

GEORGE J. STIGLER teaches at the University of
Chicago; he was formerly at Columbia University.

Three quantitative studies of the monopoly problem in the United
States have been made in recent years by Harberger, Kaplan, and Weston. In different ways the studies of Harberger and Kaplan tend to
show that the monopoly problem is not overly serious in our economy,
and Weston's study argues along a converging line that large firms are
chiefly the product of internal growth, not of mergers.

In the broad sweep of economic literature, studies which question
the importance of monopoly are but a tiny dissent from dominant
opinion: for every page of argument that competition is rampant,
there are surely a thousand which suggest its imminent extinction. But
these studies by serious and objective scholars do not seek to reach the
golden mean by counterexaggeration; rather they seem to imply that
even "reasonable" views have been rather one-sided. I wish to examine
these statistical invitations to change our view of the economic world.

I. HARBERGER

Professor Harberger seeks to measure the magnitude of the misallocation of resources and the consequent loss of welfare due to monopoly.[1]
As one who has strolled along the edge of this primrose path, it be-
hooves me to avoid criticisms of detail, and I raise questions chiefly on
the general theory underlying the measures.

Harberger assumes that all industries and firms have constant costs,
that all demand curves have unitary elasticity, that all industries were
in long-run equilibrium in 1924–28, and that Epstein's figures on rates

* From *The Journal of Political Economy*, Vol. XLIV (February, 1956), pp. 33–40,
copyright © by the University of Chicago Press. Reprinted by permission.
[1] A. C. Harberger, "Monopoly and Resource Allocation," *Proceedings of the American Economic Association* (May, 1954). I must thank Harberger for eliminating
an error from an earlier draft of this paper; of course, this does not imply his
agreement with the present version.

of return on investment for this period are tolerably precise. The central argument is now stated briefly:

> We can pick out the places where resources are misallocated by looking at the rates of return on capital. Those industries which are returning higher than average rates have too few resources; and those yielding lower than average returns have too many resources. To get an idea of how big a shift it would take to equalize profit rates in all industries, we have to know something about the elasticities of demand for the goods in question. In Figure 1, I illustrate a hypothetical case. The industry in question is earning 20 per cent on a capital of 10 million dollars, while the average return to capital is only 10 per cent. We therefore build a 10 per cent return into the cost curve, which leaves the industry with 1 million in excess profits. If the elasticity of demand for the industry's product is unity, it will take a shift of 1 million in resources in order to expand supply enough to wipe out the excess profits.[2]

If I may restate this argument in primitive symbols, it proceeds as follows. Costs of production per unit are a of labor and ic of capital (where i is the competitive interest rate), and a and c are constants if the industry has constant costs. The demand function has unitary elasticity, so $pq = S$ (where S is sales). The monopolist obtains a rate of return of mi on his investment. Then, if the price is to fall to the competitive level, output will rise in the ratio

$$\frac{S \,/\, (a + i\,c) - S \,/\, (a + mi\,c)}{S \,/\, (a + mi\,c)}$$

This expression simplifies to $(m - 1) \,/\, R_c$, where R_c is the ratio of all competitive costs to competitive capital costs (that is, $R_c = [(a + ic) \,/\, ic]$).

Armed with these assumptions and Epstein's data, Harberger measures the welfare loss due to monopoly in manufacturing. We may illustrate his measurements by the toilet preparations industry. In Epstein's sample this industry earned an average of 30.4 per cent on capital in 1924–28, while the "competitive" rate (that is, the average rate in all manufacturing) was 10.4 per cent. Hence monopoly profits were 20.0 per cent of capital, and, since capital was $16 million in 1928, monopoly profits were 0.20 × $16 million = $3.2 million. The competitive costs of the industry's output were therefore its $20 mil-

[2] *Ibid.*, p. 78.

lion sales minus $3.2 million, or $16.8 million, and we may choose such a unit of output that the industry was producing 16,800,000 units at a cost of $1.00 each. The monopoly price of these units was $20,000,000/16,800,000 = $1.19. With competition, the output would be 20,000,000 units and the price $1.00. Since the loss of welfare due to monopoly is taken as

$$\frac{\text{Increase in output} \times \text{reduction in price}}{2},$$

we may substitute our numbers,

$$\frac{3,200,000 \times \$0.19}{2} = \$304,000.$$

If we make this calculation for all manufacturing industries and convert the results roughly to 1953 prices, we find that the total welfare loss resulting from monopoly "comes out to be 225 million dollars, or less than $1.50 for every man, woman, and child in the United States." [3]

If this estimate is correct, economists might serve a more useful purpose if they fought fires or termites instead of monopoly. But there are several reasons for believing that it is too low.

1. The assumption of a demand elasticity of unity is objectionable. A monopolist does not operate where his marginal revenue is zero. A loosely co-ordinated set of oligopolists might operate where *industry* marginal revenue is zero, but only because their monopoly power was very weak—and it seems undesirable in such a study to *assume* that oligopolies are competitive. In any event, the assumption seems empirically objectionable: most industries have long-run demand curves which are elastic. And in Harberger's model, welfare losses go up when elasticity of demand increases.

2. If monopoly profits are capitalized, the capital of a monopolist grows in such a way that only competitive rates of return are being earned. Harberger finds that the elimination of intangibles has little effect,[4] but monopoly profits can be capitalized under many asset titles. He refers to Weston's finding that mergers accounted for only one-quarter of the total growth of assets of seventy-odd corporations,[5] but, even accepting Weston's techniques, the proportion should be recalculated for 1928, and then it would at least double. In that sample of

[3] *Ibid.*, p. 82.
[4] *Ibid.*, p. 83.
[5] *Ibid.*, p. 85.

companies, therefore, it would have been easy for monopoly profits to be capitalized as a by-product of revaluations for consolidations.

Pending a study of business valuation practices before 1929, it is not possible to form any good estimate of the probable force of this criticism of Harberger's method. Conceivably, he caught only the monopoly profits attributable to the procrastination of accountants; certainly, the estimate of welfare losses is biased downward on this score. One cannot believe that petroleum, meat-packing, railway equipment, and pianos were excessively competitive industries and that boots and shoes, planing mills, canned goods, and job printing were monopolistic.

3. If there are any monopoly gains in the payments to factors of production other than capital, they are not detected by the procedure.[6] The magnitude of monopoly elements in wages, executive compensation, royalties, and rents is possibly quite large. Garbarino found a high correlation between concentration ratios and increases in wage rates.[7]

4. The competitive rate of return on investment should be calculated for the entire economy, not just for the manufacturing sector. Welfare loss in manufacturing would be larger if the competitive rate of return were lower. On the other hand, monopoly is presumably somewhat more important in manufacturing than in the remainder of the economy taken together, and to this extent the loss due to monopoly is exaggerated.

No one knows the amount of welfare loss that would be found if all the appropriate modifications could be carried through. Perhaps it would come to only $2,000,000 a year for every economist. Whatever it may be, we may still properly devote much attention to monopoly. The loss would be much larger if we were less diligent in combating monopoly, and the cumulative effects of widespread cartelization would eventually move the losses into a new order of magnitude.

II. KAPLAN

Dr. A. D. H. Kaplan's recent study of *Big Enterprise in a Competitive System*[8] contains a new statitical investigation of the largest industrial corporations in the United States. Only this portion of his study will be examined here.

[6] I am indebted to Milton Friedman for this point.
[7] "A Theory of Interindustry Wage Structure Variation," *Quarterly Journal of Economics*, LXIV (1950), 300 ff.
[8] Washington: Brookings Institution, 1954.

336

READINGS IN MICROECONOMICS

Table 1.   Largest Industrial Corporations by Year of Entry into List

Companies still in List in	Companies in list of 100 largest appearing first in					To-tal
	1909	1919	1929	1935	1948	
1909	100	..	..	..	..	100
1919	53	47	..	..	..	100
1929	39	33	28	..	..	100
1935	41	28	20	11	..	100
1948	36	26	14	5	19	100

The hundred largest industrial corporations are listed for each of the years 1909, 1919, 1929, 1935, and 1948, using total assets as the measure of size in each year. There is considerable turnover in the list —205 names appear at one time or another. The general pattern of Kaplan's data may be summarized as in Table 1.[9] On the basis of these figures, Dr. Kaplan comments:

> These evidences of mobility of position among the 100 largest industrials do not accord with any general assumption that large-scale corporations enjoy secure entrenchment by virtue of their size. The record does hold an implication, however, that merits our later consideration—namely, that much of the strongest direct competition faced by a big business in its major lines is apt to be from other big firms or those growing into big business. One of the bases for acceptance of the competitive system—that it provides incentives to growth and change with commensurate rewards to those who contribute most effectively to an advancing economy—is suggested in this general picture of rise and decline among the giants of American industry.[10]

Before we consider this interpretation of Table 1, it is well to enter certain caveats concerning the underlying tables.

1. The lists in the early years reflect the effrontery of promoters as well as the sizes of companies. For example, a forlorn Utah venture, Greenwater Copper Mines and Smelting (No. 74 in 1909) suspended operations in November, 1909. Development Co. of America (No. 72 in 1909) failed a few years later.

[9] I have carried out the correction reported in a note to the tables (Kaplan, *op. cit.,* p. 155).
[10] *Ibid.,* pp. 142–43.

2. The lists are much influenced by variations in accounting practice. Some companies consolidated majority-owned subsidiaries, others consolidated only wholly owned subsidiaries, and still others excluded foreign subsidiaries. International Mercantile Marine, for example, had assets of $164.1 million in 1928 but only $78.0 in 1929, when foreign subsidiaries were excluded, so it fell off the list. Koppers was on the list in 1935, with assets of $331 million; in 1936 its assets fell to $130, when its accounting practices changed, and it disappeared from the list.

3. There are numerous errors in the tables. Among the companies erroneously omitted were Borden (1919); Pure Oil (1919); Mexican Petroleum (1919); Tide Water Associated Oil (1929); American Shipbuilding (1919); and Lehigh Valley Coal (1929)—to cite only cases of companies which were on the list in some other year. Western Electric was omitted from 1919 through 1935, although not in 1948. General Theatres Equipment is listed at $360.0 million in 1929 by Kaplan, at $110.4 million by Moody. Wilson and Company is a change of name for Schwarzchild and Sulzberger; this is not recognized in the tables. The express companies were lost after 1909, perhaps because Moody shifted them to public utility manuals.

In addition to these deficiencies, which, on balance, lead to considerable overstatement of the extent of turnover among the one hundred largest enterprises, there are three economic reasons for turnover that have little to do with rivalry among the enterprises.

1. When new companies in the list are created by antitrust actions, one should look to social policy rather than the forces of rivalry for an explanation. In Kaplan's list one finds, in 1919 and later years: Atlantic Refining, Standard Oil of New Jersey, Standard Oil of New York, Standard Oil of Indiana, Consolidated Oil, Ohio Oil, Glen Alden Coal, Vacuum Oil, Magnolia Petroleum, Reynolds Tobacco, Liggett and Myers, Lorillard, Prarie Oil, Prairie Pipe Line. These fourteen companies are perhaps one-sixth of the true number of displacements on the list.

2. Mergers of two or more firms on the list create vacancies for new firms, but no one should be inclined to hail the new names as evidence of rivalry. Indeed, in this context one should refer to the turnunder, not to the turnover, of firms. Kaplan lists in a note [11] but does not discuss some ten mergers. His list is incomplete; at a minimum, one should add: Guggenheim Exploration, Cambria Steel, Mexican Petroleum, Pierce Oil, Fox Theatre (in various guises), Vacuum Oil, Utah Copper, Wells-Fargo, Midvale Steel, Chile Copper, Greene

[11] *Ibid.*, p. 155.

Cananea Copper, Pan American Petroleum, Tidewater Pipe Line. These twenty-three disappearances amount to another third of the displacements on the true list.

3. A large part of the remaining turnover of names is due to the rise and decline of industries. Professor Adelman has estimated that forty-six of the names in the 1909 list that had disappeared by 1948 owed their disappearance to shifts in the relative importance of industries and that only sixteen companies disappeared because of intra-industry shifts.[12] Even if one shares Kaplan's view of the great force of interindustry competition (and I do not), this sort of turnover is on a different footing from intra-industry changes.

Even without these vast qualifications, Kaplan's data do not show that rivalry is strong among or in the neighborhood of these companies. The figures, in fact, show a steady decline in turnover: one may calculate the net rate of disappearance of companies, once they are on the list: 4.7 companies disappeared per year, 1909–19; 2.8 in 1919–29; 1.8 in 1929–35; and 1.5 in 1935–48. It appears that it is becoming harder and harder to enter the list of the one hundred largest companies and that soon one may expect only about one company to disappear each year, that is, once on the list, a company will, on the average, stay there for a century.

The statistical universe of the hundred or two hundred largest corporations is inappropriate to studies of monopoly and competition, and we may hope that this will be the last study to fall prey to its dramatic irrelevance. For Kaplan's central idea—that the extent of instability in the relative fortunes of leading firms is an informative symptom of competition—is important and deserves to be applied on a correct, industry basis.

III. WESTON

Professor J. Fred Weston's investigation of the role of mergers in the growth of large companies ranges over a series of problems of great interest to students of industrial organization.[13] But the most basic question his study raises—and the only one I discuss—is implicit in his title: How does one measure the role of mergers in the growth of a firm?

[12] "A Note on Corporate Concentration and Turnover," *American Economic Review*, June, 1954, pp. 392–96; see also J. W. Markham's review of Kaplan, *American Economic Review*, June, 1955.

[13] *The Role of Mergers in the Growth of Large Firms* (Berkeley: University of California Press, 1953).

The basic data for one company, now known as Socony-Mobil Oil, are given in Table 2.[14] One can measure the role of mergers in absolute growth, and this is the greater of Weston's efforts. Then one can divide the total growth of Socony from 1913 to 1948 (which is $1,443.0 − $103.4 = $1,339.6 million) into two parts: $618.3 million of assets acquired by merger and a residual of $721.3 million of assets, which is internal growth. Thus 46.2 per cent of the company's growth is due to merger.

This procedure (which is Weston's method B) purchases simplicity at a high price. I shall mention only two serious limitations. There is, first, a question of price levels. The assets of Vacuum Oil, in our example, were $240.5 million in 1930; if they were adequately maintained, they would be valued much more highly in 1948. One can use Daniel Creamer's price index for assets in petroleum refining to calculate "real" assets (Table 3).[15] We now find that 76.0 per cent of the total growth of real assets was due to merger. The share of growth due to mergers is considerably understated because Weston neglects this factor, for the price level of assets was much lower in the period of most active merging than it was in 1948.

Second, Weston's total (22.6 per cent of all growth due to merger) is a creature of his selection of companies. He chose a group of industries most of which had fairly high concentration ratios, and within these industries he apparently included those firms for which data were at hand. The particular totals and averages are calculated with no attention to industry weights or coverage ratios, so it is quite impossible to accept them as representative of any relevant section of the industrial community.

But the real interest of most students of the merger movement has been in the role of mergers in producing high concentration in some of our major industries, and for this problem the absolute growth of firms is irrelevant. The absolute growth ignores the size of industry and pays less attention to the absolutely small mergers by which Aluminum Company of America became a literal monopoly than to those by which a textile company acquires 1 per cent of its industry's capacity.

14 There are several differences between my figures and Weston's: (1) I reject the inconsistent figures for 1911 and 1912; and (2) I combine Magnolia Petroleum and Standard Oil when the latter got control of the former, not (as Weston may have done) when the formal merger occurred. Still he reports only $487.2 million of assets acquired by merger, which presumably means that General Petroleum was overlooked.

15 This index is implicit in his figures in *Capital and Output Trends in Manufacturing Industries, 1880–1948* (New York: National Bureau of Economic Research, 1954).

Absolute growth gives equal weight to vertical mergers that do not affect industry concentration and to horizontal mergers that may affect it radically. Absolute size may fall because a firm becomes a monop-

Table 2.   Asset History of Socony-Mobil Company, 1913–48*
(In Millions)

Year	Standard Oil of New York	Magnolia Petroleum	General Petroleum	White Eagle Oil and Refinery	Vacuum Oil
1913	$103.4	. . . . .	. . . . .	. . . . .	$ 34.5
1914	102.0	. . . . .	. . . . .	. . . . .	36.1
1915	117.3	$ 26.3	. . . . .	. . . . .	44.9
1916	168.7	50.2	. . . . .	. . . . .	57.5
1917	204.3	122.8	$ 32.2	. . . . .	76.2
1918	234.1	157.2	37.3	. . . . .	75.4
1919	299.6	182.0	42.2	. . . . .	79.6
1920	347.9	193.6	47.4	. . . . .	99.1
1921	333.2	190.9	64.1	. . . . .	109.7
1922	418.7	206.6	76.7	. . . . .	122.8
1923	418.6	213.4	106.6	. . . . .	127.7
1924	$619.0		114.4	. . . . .	133.2
1925	533.0		127.5	. . . . .	144.5
1926		$691.2		. . . . .	141.5
1927		678.1		$31.5	158.8
1928		695.4		33.4	186.9
1929		708.4		n.a.	205.7
1930		720.3		36.9	240.5
1931			$1,038.6		
1948			1,443.0		

* Sources: Annual reports and Poor's and Moody's manuals.

Table 3

	Million dollars
Total growth of Socony-Mobil, 1929 prices	892.6
Assets acquired by merger, 1929 prices:	
1923 Magnolia Petroleum	240.9
1925 General Petroleum	140.9
1930 White Eagle	39.4
Vacuum Oil	256.9
Total	678.1

oly.[16] To study the effects of merger on concentration, one must deal with the proportions of individual markets supplied by individual firms.

In the study of monopoly power, then, we must use the firm's share in the industry as the basic unit of measurement. Weston essays such a measure, but in a most peculiar fashion:

> First, the market occupancy percentage of the leading firms in an industry for the earliest year for which data are available was calculated. Second, data on external growth were deducted from absolute amounts of output or total assets of individual firms, but not for the industry as a whole. Third, the adjusted data of output or total assets for the firms were used to calculate market occupancy percentages of individual firms which would have obtained if the growth of the firms had occurred entirely by internal expansion. Fourth, the adjusted concentration ratios were compared with the concentration ratios of the earliest period to measure the extent of present concentration due to internal growth.[17]

We may illustrate Weston's procedure with a hypothetical example. Consider the history in Table 4. Company A had 40 per cent of the industry's assets in 1920 (Weston's step 1). It merges with Company B in 1930 and acquires $200 of assets. Subtract this $200 from A's total growth of $900 to get $700 (step 2). Hence, without merger, A's assets are held to have been $900 in 1950, and its share of the industry 45 per cent (step 3). The growth of A's share by internal growth was 45 − 40 = 5 per cent, and its growth by merger 10 per cent (step 4).

This arithmetic rests upon the unstated and undefended assumption that B would have ceased to grow in the absence of the merger. (In our earlier example, it is assumed that Magnolia Petroleum, General Petroleum, and Vacuum Oil would have stopped growing on the day of merger, although before the merger each was growing more rapidly than Standard Oil of New York.) Surely, a more reasonable procedure would be as follows: In 1930, by merger, the share of A rose from 40 to

[16] If the acquiring firm pays more in cash than the book value of the acquired company, a decline is registered; for example see Federal Trade Commission, *The Merger Movement* (Washington, 1948), pp. 79, 105, 112, 121, 131.

[17] *Op. cit.*, p. 44. We may ignore here a fifth step: "Fifth, these results were expressed in relative terms by dividing by the adjusted percentages of market occupancy."

Table 4

	Year	Assets		
		Company A	Company B	Industry
1920	. . . .	$200	$100	$ 500
1930	. . . .	400	200	1,000
1950	. . . .	$1,100		2,000

60 per cent. By 1950 A's share had fallen to 55 per cent. We may say that, over the entire period, A's share rose thus:

$$+20 \text{ per cent by merger}$$
$$- 5 \text{ per cent by internal growth}$$

$$+15 \text{ per cent net change}$$

In this procedure the implicit hypothesis is that in the absence of merger the acquired firms would have grown at the same rate as the industry. One might argue for alternative assumptions, such as that the merged firms would have grown at the same rate as the merger,[18] but I fail to see how a case could be made for Weston's procedure.[19]

The method of calculating the effect of mergers has large effects in real, as well as hypothetical, cases. Using refining capacity as the measure, Standard Oil of New York increased its share of the industry from 2.12 per cent in 1914 to 8.72 per cent in 1948. On Weston's procedure, 5.88 percentage points of the increase of 6.60 percentage points were achieved by internal growth; on the alternative procedure, 5.46 percentage points of 6.60 were acquired by merger.[20]

[18] On this assumption, the summary of growth would be:

$$+ 18.3 \text{ per cent by merger}$$
$$- 3.3 \text{ per cent by internal growth}$$

$$+ 15.0 \text{ per cent net change}$$

The most plausible base for measurement would be given by the assumption that the merged firms would have grown at the same rate as other firms of the same size that did not merge.

[19] Weston's procedure required knowledge of the industry's total assets, which is seldom known (if "industry" is defined properly), and his measure is dominated by large movements of price levels.

[20] The data for these calculations in thousands of barrels per day are as follows: the second figure of each set is the capacity of the industry: 1914, 20 (ca. 944); Magnolia, 69 (2,828); General Petroleum, 43 (2,853); White Eagle, 12 (3,766); Vacuum, 47.1 (3,943); and 1948, 526 (6,034).

Even with his biased measure, Weston finds that only three out of twenty-five firms could add as much as 10–15 per cent of the industry's output or assets to their shares, and eleven had negative increments, from internal growth. He lends support to the opinion that merger has been the basic method by which individual firms have acquired high shares in major industries in the United States.

25

MARKET STRUCTURE, BUSINESS
CONDUCT, AND INNOVATION *

Jesse W. Markham † teaches at Princeton University.

I

We rely heavily on the a priori relationships between market structure and business conduct and performance for providing meaningful interpretations of the activities of the approximately eleven million business enterprises that make up the private sector of the American economy. If firms are numerous and no one of them controls a significant share of the appropriately defined market, we predict reasonably competitive pricing; if firms are very few (concentrated oligopoly), we predict the contrary. Indeed, it is the assumed validity of these relationships that makes price theory something more than random speculations and public policy toward monopoly something more than the caprice of politicians and bureaucrats. There seems to be a general presumption, *ceteris paribus* and all that, in favor of low concentration as a structural goal on the grounds that this is more likely to assure the attainment of certain performance goals such as price-cost relationships compatible with efficient resource allocation.

It is generally agreed on a priori grounds also that market structure affects the level of innovational effort, but there is far less agreement on the magnitude and direction of the effect. Many economists adhere to the traditional view that competition begets technical progress [9, p. 317]. But the Schumpeterian hypothesis [13, Chap. 7], probably the oldest and most respectable on this subject, asserts that the possession of accumulated monopoly rewards, the prospects of additional such rewards in the future, and the security attending market power are prerequisites to undertaking the risks and uncertainties of innovational

* From the *American Economic Review*, Vol. LV, No. 2 (May, 1965), pp. 323–332. Reprinted by permission.

† I am greatly indebted to my colleague Professor Frederic M. Scherer for his valuable comments on this paper and to the Ford Foundation's Inter-University Research Program on the Micro-Economics of Technological Change and Economic Growth for financial assistance.

activities. Contemporary students of the problem have recently interpreted the hypothesis to state that the greater the profits and the degree of market power (the potential capability to earn monopoly rewards) or firm size, the greater should be the effort to innovate. The original and restated versions, while akin to each other in terms of their policy implications, are obviously not the same. The original Schumpeterian hypothesis simply stated that in the absence of uncommitted accumulated surpluses the undertaking of risky and uncertain innovational activities would not occur; and unless the prospective rewards to such innovational activities were high (relative to competitive returns), the incentive to undertake them did not exist. But for several important reasons this does not imply that the measurable innovational effort of a firm as expressed, say, in terms of its research and development expenditures should be a continuous and increasing function of market power, business size, or, for that matter, retained monopoly earnings.

First, it has not yet been demonstrated that industry concentration ratios are good surrogates for monopoly power or past or future monopoly profits. The lines of demarcation between census classifications of industries are drawn often faintly, often heavily, and sometimes arbitrarily. And the concentration ratio—the measure of market power most frequently used in empirical tests of the restated Schumpeterian hypothesis—is after all only one of the many possible points on the cumulative concentration curve and not a summary index of the entire curve. Accordingly, even if industries identically monopolistic by a true measure of monopoly always earned identical monopoly profits, one would surely still expect to find what we in fact find: considerable variation in reported profits among industries having concentration ratios of roughly the same magnitude.

Second, and this is much more important, there is no presumption in the Schumpeterian hypothesis as originally stated that innovational activity as measured in terms of research and development expenditures is the only use to which accumulated uncommitted profits will be put, or that any of such profits, simply because they exist, will be put to this use in the absence of appropriate opportunities. Schumpeter defined innovations broadly enough to include, among others, mergers, new organization, the new advertising campaign, the new product, and the new process. Only the last two are logical consequences of technical research and development activities conducted inside the business firm. What Schumpeter really said was that uncommitted balances were a prerequisite to engaging in highly uncertain commercial activities. Hence, to run regression analyses of research and development expenditures as reported, say, to the National Science Foundation (the most comprehensive source of research and development expenditures) and firm size, concentration ratios, or any other index of market structure, at best only determines the statistical relationship between a fraction of the Schumpeterian variable and some rather imprecise measures of monopoly.

Third, there is the fundamental question of whether, even if our indexes of monopoly power or business size were statistically unbiased and our quantitative measures of innovative effort conceptually complete and unambiguous, one would on logical grounds expect them to vary systematically and continuously with each other; and there are very persuasive practical and theoretical reasons why we would not expect them to vary proportional to each other. If we can predict cricket chirps from the temperature, then we can also predict the temperature from cricket chirps; so let us take a look at the policy implications of the presumed collinearity between monopoly and research and development outlays by interchanging the dependent and independent variables. Between 1930 and 1963 the private outlays of firms on research and development increased from $116 million to $5 billion—an increase of 4,310 percent. No one to my knowledge, even the most lugubrious observer of our antitrust policy, has estimated anything like a 43-fold increase in monopoly over this period. It could—and should—hastily be pointed out that these data must be deflated by some general economic indicator such as the gross national product as expressed in current dollars. In 1930 the outlays of private firms on research and development amounted to 0.1 percent of GNP, and in 1963 to 1.0 percent of GNP, a relative increase of 1,000 percent. To suggest the possibility that monopoly may have increased even tenfold over this period would surely horrify every Assistant Attorney General from Thurman Arnold to William Orrick. I believe we can rescue ourselves from this situation and restore the philosophical calm of our antitrust crusaders as well by interpreting Schumpeter's theory as a "threshold theory"; some departure from a state of perfect competition (or the presence of some monopoly) is a necessary concomitant of innovation, but it does not follow that twice this volume of departures, somehow measured, should lead to twice the volume of innovations.

Moreover, the number of scientists must surely be an important determinant of the volume of inventions and, in turn, volume of innovative activity. As Derek J. Price has pointed out [16, p. 517], for three hundred years now the number of scientists has doubled every ten years or so; which means that at any point in time in this three-hundred-year period it could be said that approximately 80 percent of all the scientists that ever existed, currently exist. Again it is difficult to equate, or even systematically relate, this apparent law of growth of the scientific population with monopoly power in the private sector of the economy.

There is also a good theoretical reason why we should expect at best a rather weak relationship between either the measurable input or output of a given innovative effort and firm size in any given industry, or between innovative effort and levels of concentration among industries. As will be demonstrated later in simple quantitative terms, innovative effort is heavily concentrated in oligopolistic industries where at least several strategies are available to each firm and the patterns of reaction among rivals are characterized by high orders of uncertainty. It is very likely that, as it is frequently contended, a significant portion of private research and development is imitative and competitive and not innovative in the Schumpeterian sense. This portion may possibly be distributed among firms selling in the same market in rough proportion to their size. But oligopolists have other Schumpeterian innovative strategies open to them, and at any given time one firm may easily reason that the best counter-strategy to another's increase in research and development outlays is not greater research and development outlays of his own, but the development of a new product line through acquisition or an increase in advertising outlays on product lines he currently produces. The Cournot reaction paths among oligopolists with respect to research and development outlays could therefore conceivably be multidimensional and could tend toward some rough equilibrium bearing no systematic relationship to firm size.

The important question, however, is not so much whether the recent voluminous and, on the whole, excellent empirical work constitutes effective tests of the Schumpeterian hypothesis. Schumpeter, more than any other economist of his generation, assigned great importance to the innovational activities of the business firm and suggested certain of their implications for economic welfare and public policy. The hypothesis itself was the product of empirical observation and, by the crude and limited test employed, was of course delivered to us already pretested by Schumpeter himself. As he put it, speaking of the sources of economic progress in a capitalistic society: "As soon as we go into the details and inquire into the individual items in which progress was most conspicuous, the trail leads not to the doors of those firms that work under conditions of comparatively free competition but precisely to the doors of the large concerns" [13, p. 82]. In the context of Schumpeter's basic thesis he left no doubt that he viewed the "large firm" as synonymous with "large firm with market power."

By the same crude tests, the hypothesis is as consistent with observable facts now as it was then. We need only consult any recent *Survey* of the National Science Foundation [6, p. 20] to remove any serious doubt that company-financed research and development effort is highly concentrated in large firms making up, for the most part, the economy's more highly concentrated industries. In 1961 an estimated 11,800 manufacturing and other companies performed research and development; a smaller number financed research and development out of their own funds. Three hundred and ninety-one firms having 5,000 or more employees amounted to only 3 percent of the total number of firms performing research and development, and for an insignificant one-hundredth of 1 percent of all industrial firms, but they accounted for slightly over 80 percent of the total company-financed research and development. In 1958, the 478 firms making up the 5,000 and over employee group accounted for 29 percent of total industrial employment and 26 percent of total sales. Firms having less than 1,000 employees accounted for 90 percent of the total number of firms and for 60 percent of total industrial employment, but for only 5 percent of total company-financed research.

Five industry groups containing most of the more narrowly defined industries making up the "oligopolistic core" of American industry accounted for nearly 75 percent of all company-financed R and D: chemical and allied products (19 percent), electrical equipment and communications (19 percent), motor vehicles and other transportation equipment (14 percent), machinery (13 percent), and aircraft and missiles (8 percent). At the opposite end of the spectrum are such industry groups as textiles, lumber, wood products and furniture, and other manufacturing and nonmanufacturing industries, which together account for about 5 percent of total company-financed research and development expenditures but for a considerable number of both the low concentration industries and the firms with 1,000 or less employees. To be sure, there are several spectacular examples of highly concentrated industries such as tobacco products and steel that rank low in research and development. Similarly, some of the firms included on *Fortune's* list of the largest 500 corporations spend a relatively small percentage of their sales on innovative activities. However, the data, now far more complete than those Schumpeter had before him, clearly support his hypothesis: the trail of innovative effort leads to the doors of the large concerns operating in markets distinctly not characterized by all the conditions of free competition. But it need not be inferred from this that all big firms and all oligopolists innovate. Schumpeter recognized the existence of both somnolent giants and oligopolists more disposed to preserving the calm than to participating in the "perennial gale."

The quantitative work of the past decade, while acknowledging Schumpeter as its inspiration and intellectual parent, has in fact been testing a different hypothesis and one having different policy implications. The restated hypothesis, since it has envisaged tests cast in terms of regression analysis, must also be stated in these terms. If one can sum up Schumpeter in the statement, give me factual evidence of innovational activity in the market economy and I can safely predict the presence of large firms having temporary monopoly power, the restated hypothesis is, give me x innovational activity and I will give you b_1, b_2, . . . b_n values showing how much of x can be "explained" in terms of firm size, the level of concentration, and similar a priori relevant variables. The policy implications of the original and restated versions are also different. Schumpeter simply argued that any indiscriminate assault on bigness and market power, taken out of their evolutionary context, would deprive the capitalistic process of its source of progress. The newer version proposes to tell us in quantitative terms, to the extent available data permit, how much, where, and up to what point innovative effort (and results) are attributable to such factors as firm size and market structure. Accordingly, it holds out the possibility of providing guidelines that can significantly enhance the efficiency of public policy toward the private sector. The historic dilemma of remedial action under our antitrust policy has been the problem of weighing the social benefit of more competition in the classical sense against the possible loss of scale economies and innovative effort that attend firm size and market power. Obviously, if something approaching probability values can be defined linking certain structural and behavioral attributes of markets with the intensity of innovative effort, we can reduce the risk, to use a favorite expression of Schumpeter's, of throwing the baby out with the bathwater. Instead, to extend the metaphor, we can at least distinguish the baby from the water and may even be able to salvage the clean before disposing of the dirty water.

II

A summary analysis of the neo-Schumpeterian literature cannot do full justice to its statistical subtleties and refinements. I shall deal here with the more essential findings, including their significant qualifications, and their public policy implications. The statistical results obtained by D. Hamberg [1], Frederic Scherer [10] [11], Edwin Mansfield [4] [5], Jacob Schmookler [12], James Worley [15] and others support the generalization that, at least beyond a certain size level, the ratio of research and development expenditures to some index of firm size does not increase significantly with size, and may not increase at all. But this, like most generalizations, must be qualified. Scherer [10] found that within the 500 largest corporations on *Fortune's* list, the largest 100 accounted for slightly smaller percentages of total R and D expenditures and patents than of total sales. This suggests that size, at least after a firm has made the list of 500, has no favorable effect on innovative or inventive effort. Mansfield found that the largest firms measured in terms of sales in petroleum, drugs, and glass spent a smaller percentage of their sales on research and development than did "somewhat smaller firms" [5, p. 334], that in chemicals the largest firms spent relatively more, and that in steel they spent relatively less but the computed difference was not statistically significant [5, p. 334]. My own unpublished data on the ethical drug industry (as distinguished from the drug industry) are consistent with Mansfield's findings on the drug industry generally, but they suggest that the ratio of research and development expenditures to sales increased markedly up to the firm size of $100 million annual sales and beyond this point declined slightly. However, between 1946 and 1958 the differences in the ratios among size classes declined substantially as firms in the smaller size groups rapidly stepped up their research activities. In the "research revolution" in drugs, the larger firms were the innovators and the smaller firms the imitators. Worley found that in six out of eight two-digit industries, research and development personnel per 1,000 employees increased with total company employment. But in only two industries were the results statistically significant enough to warrant rejection of his null hypothesis that research and development effort increased no more than proportionately with size. In a more recent study of seventeen two-digit and three-digit industries, Hamberg reached results consistent with Worley's in all of the seven industries common to both studies. In twelve industries R and D intensity increased with firm size.

Before the consistency of these general findings be given too much emphasis, it should be pointed out that Worley's and Hamberg's results, because of differences in data and method, conflict with Mansfield's in the case of every individual industry common to the three studies: glass, petroleum, and chemicals. These conflicting results, however, can be easily reconciled, and this reconciliation points up the central finding of the recent statistical studies of market structure and innovational effort: up to a certain size, innovational effort increases more than proportional to size; at that size, which varies from industry to industry, the fitted curve has an inflection point and among the largest few firms innovational effort generally does not increase and may decline with size. For the three industry groups cited, Worley and Hamberg fitted curves to all the available observations and found

R and D intensity to be an increasing function of size. Mansfield, on the other hand, confined his analysis to the "very" largest firms: ten large chemical firms, nine large petroleum firms, and only four large glass firms. It is almost certain that Mansfield's petroleum and glass firms fell to the right of the inflection points of curves fitted to a wider range of firm sizes.

In a study soon to appear, Scherer [11] has demonstrated that in the regression equations used by Worley and Hamberg of the form:

$$\log Y_i = \log a + b \log X_i + E_i,$$

where Y_i is R and D employment, R and D outlays or patents of the ith firm and X_i is some size variable of the ith firm, such as total employment, sales, or assets, the regression coefficients b are greatly affected by (1) whether zero observations are included or excluded and (2) the size variable used. In his own regressions of patents (more appropriately regarded as an index of R and D output rather than inventive and innovative input) on the three different size variables—assets, sales and employment—for all usable observations for the 500 largest American corporations (ranging from 365 to 448), he obtained values of b ranging from .795 to 1.158, depending upon whether the zeros were deleted and upon which size variable was used. In all cases with zeros deleted, intensity of inventive activity as measured by patents tended to decline with firm size, and in all cases tended to increase with firm size when he adopted the convention of counting each zero patent as 0.5 patent to permit its inclusion in the logarithmic analysis. Also, in all cases, the values of b were higher (showing greater increases in patenting intensity with size) when firm size was measured in terms of employment. By using alternative regression equations Scherer found, as did Mansfield, that R and D employment inputs increased with firm size in chemicals, and that in five other two-digit industries R and D effort increased with size up to about $500 million sales size group and then tended to decline, except in primary metals, which U.S. Steel pulled back into a stage of increasing returns.

Clearly, any answer to how inventive and innovative efforts are affected by firm size hangs on an extraordinary slender reed that may alternatively bend upward or droop downward, depending on the species of statistical zephyrs blowing at the time.

Similarly, we are equally unsure about the precise relationship between market power and inventive and innovative effort. Mansfield has found that in petroleum and coal over the periods 1919–38 and 1939–58 the ratio of important innovations to market share for the four largest firms was high: 1.42 and 1.26 for petroleum and 2.46 and

2.31 for coal [4, p. 561]; on the other hand, the corresponding ratio for steel was very low: 0.48 and 0.69. It would seem from the poor showing of steel and the previously indicated relationship in primary metals between size and research and development effort that the principal conclusion on the steel industry is that U.S. Steel tries hard but does not meet with spectacular success. Hamberg [1, pp. 74–75] found 1958 R and D expenditures and R and D to sales ratios in seventeen two-digit and three-digit industry groups positively correlated with their weighted concentration ratios, but concluded that only 30 percent of the variance in research and development intensity could be explained by industrial concentration. Horowitz, running similar correlations [2, pp. 300–01], reached a similar conclusion: a positive but weak correlation exists between R and D intensity and the level of industrial concentration.

The difficulty with such regression analyses as these is not so much their statistical as their conceptual inconclusiveness. It is clear that oligopoly theory in its present state is highly inadequate for purposes of generalizing on such traditional variables as price and output. In a Cournot model, price and output move monotonically from pure monopoly to pure competition equilibrium positions as the number of firms increases. In a Chamberlinian model, at some threshold point on the spectrum of firm numbers between one and many, the monopoly solution collapses and is replaced by a competitive one. And in game theory models almost anything can happen. Moreover, the facts on oligopoly lead us to look with considerable pessimism for neat and continuous relationships between variables characterized by far less uncertainty than inventive and innovative effort. For example, the synthetic fibers and cigarette industries both have concentration ratios of approximately .80, but over the period 1953–60 synthetic fibers had a price flexibility index of 0.87, cigarettes an index of only 0.02; and primary aluminum with a concentration ratio of 1.00 had more flexible prices than paperboard boxes with a concentration ratio of only 0.16. Until these diverse patterns of the commonplace variables of oligopoly have themselves been explained more satisfactorily, it is difficult to say much more about the statistical analysis of R and D than that it reveals far more stable and systematic relationships than those found for variables about which we are supposed to know much more. I, for example, would consider a computed correlation coefficient that explained one-third of the rate of return variance in American industry a computation of some significance.

The recent statistical analysis of inventive activity obviously is not without policy implications. It is true that it provides no basis for either condemning or beating the drums for bigness or for concentration on the grounds that they either stifle or promote technical progress. But this may be a much more significant contribution than it first appears. Only a short decade ago one of the nation's most respected public officials, not having the essential facts available, could state without fear of committing serious error that "Big Business" was the nation's greatest spur to technical progress [3]. A prominent spokesman from industry, equally unaware of the facts, could state with equal assurance in the same year that the essential feature of our large corporations was their failure to engender progress, except in the single case of the household garbage grinder [8]. Such statements could diminish in the light of the recently developed stubborn facts. The large corporation and some degree of market power appear to be concomitants of organized innovative effort, but corporate size and market power in excess of Schumpeterian threshold levels appears to be with us, and for this and other reasons are still legitimate concerns of public policy.

REFERENCES

1. D. Hamberg, "Size of Firm, Oligopoly, and Research: The Evidence," *Canadian J. of Econ. and Polit. Sci.*, Feb., 1964, pp. 62–75.
2. Ira Horowitz, "Firm Size and Research Activity," *S. Econ. J.*, Jan., 1962, pp. 298–301.
3. David E. Lilienthal, *Big Business, A New Era* (Harper & Bros., 1953).
4. Edwin Mansfield, "Size of Firm, Market Structure, and Innovation," *J.P.E.*, Dec., 1963, pp. 556–76.
5. ———, "Industrial Research and Development Expenditures: Determinants, Prospects, and Relation of Size of Firm and Inventive Output," *J.P.E.*, Aug., 1964, pp. 319–40.
6. National Science Foundation, *Research and Development in Industry, 1961* (NSF 64–9).
7. W. Nutter, "Monopoly, Bigness, and Progress," *J.P.E.*, Dec., 1956, pp. 520–27.
8. T. K. Quinn, *Giant Business: Threat to Democracy* (New York: Exposition Press, 1953).
9. *Report of the Attorney General's Committee to Study the Antitrust Laws* (Washington, 1955).
10. Frederic M. Scherer, "Firm Size, Market Structure, Opportunity, and the Output of Patented Inventions" (unpublished).
11. ———, "Size of Firm, Oligopoly, and Research: Comment," soon to appear in the *Canadian J. of Econ. and Polit. Sci.*

354 READINGS IN MICROECONOMICS

12. Jacob Schmookler, "Bigness, Fewness, and Research," *J.P.E.*, Dec., 1959, pp. 628–35.
13. Joseph A. Schumpeter, *Capitalism, Socialism and Democracy* (Harper & Bros., 1942), Chap. 7.
14. Henry Villard, "Competition, Oligopoly, and Research," *J.P.E.*, Dec., 1958., pp. 483–97.
15. J. S. Worley, "Industrial Research and the New Competition," *J.P.E.*, 1961, pp. 183–86.
16. Bernard Barber and Walter Hirsch, eds., *The Sociology of Science* (Free Glencoe Press, 1962), pp. 516–38.

26

NEW DEVELOPMENTS ON
THE OLIGOPOLY FRONT *

FRANCO MODIGLIANI teaches at Carnegie Institute
of Technology.

I

In my opinion the two books reviewed in this article [1] represent a
welcome major breakthrough on the oligopoly front. These two contributions, which appeared almost simultaneously, though clearly quite
independently, have much in common in their basic models and
method of approach to the problem. But, fortunately, they do not
significantly repeat each other; for, having started from the same point
of departure, the authors have followed divergent paths, exploring
different implications of the same basic model.

Sylos deals almost exclusively with *homogeneous* oligopoly defined
as a situation in which all producers, actual and potential, are able to
supply the identical commodity (more generally, commodities that are
perfect substitutes for each other) and have access to the very same
long-run cost function. He thus focuses on barriers to entry resulting
from economies of scale. Bain, on the other hand, also analyzes the
effect of competitors being altogether unable to produce perfect substitutes—that is, product-differentiation barriers—or being able to do
so only at higher costs—absolute cost-advantage barriers. Furthermore,
Bain's book is greatly enriched by fascinating empirical data, pains-
takingly collected through a variety of means, and by a courageous
attempt at an empirical verification of the implications of his model.
However, Bain is concerned primarily with the analysis of long-run
market equilibrium, while Sylos devotes more than half of his book to
examining the implications of his model for many other issues, such as

* From *Journal of Political Economy*, Vol. LXVI (June, 1958), pp. 215–232, copyright © by the University of Chicago Press. Reprinted by permission.

[1] A review article of Paolo Sylos Labini, *Oligopolio e progresso tecnico* ("Oligopoly
and Technical Progress"). Milan: Giuffrè, 1957. Pp. 207. L. 1,000. Joe S. Bain,
Barriers to New Competition. Cambridge, Mass.: Harvard University Press, 1956.
Pp. xi + 329. $5.50. A preliminary edition of Sylos' book was published in 1956
for limited circulation. References in this article are to the final edition.

(1) the effect of short-run or cyclical variations in demand and costs, (2) the validity of the so-called full-cost pricing model, (3) the effect of technological progress, and (4) the impact of oligopolistic structures on the formation and reabsorption of unemployment. His analysis is primarily theoretical and does not purport to provide new empirical evidence, with one rather significant exception. In an appendix to the introductory chapter Sylos presents indexes of concentration for various sectors of the American economy, based on the Gini coefficient.[2] Sylos finds that, according to this measure, concentration has tended to increase appreciably over the period considered—generally from the first decade of the century to the end of the 1940's—for all but one of the distributions analyzed. These include the distribution of plants by value added and by value of sales for manufacturing as a whole and by size of labor force for all manufacturing and for selected industries [3] and the distribution of corporations by size of assets. These findings are rather striking, since they run counter to widely accepted views based on well-known studies of the share of the market of the four or eight largest firms. They will undoubtedly deserve close scrutiny by the experts on the subject.

It would be impossible within the scope of a review article to summarize adequately the content of both books and take a good look at the promising new horizons they open. Under these conditions it appears wise to devote primary attention to Sylos' work. The reader can do full justice to Bain's contribution by reading the original, while in the case of Sylos this possibility is open only to the "happy few." With respect to Bain's book, therefore, my only goal will be to whet the reader's appetite.

II

Until quite recently little systematic attention has been paid in the analysis of monopoly and oligopoly to the role of entry, that is, to the behavior of potential competitors. This neglect is justified for monopoly, which is generally defined as the case of a single actual as well as potential producer whose demand curve is not significantly in-

---

[2] The Gini coefficient is a measure of the area lying between the actual Lorenz curve and the equidistribution Lorenz curve.

[3] The individual industries, chosen on the ground that their definition has remained reasonably stable over time, are: (1) steel works and rolling mills; (2) electrical machinery; (3) petroleum refining; (4) lumber and timber products; and (5) shipbuilding and iron and steel. For these industries indexes are given for 1914 and 1947. The distribution for lumber is the single instance in which concentration has decreased.

fluenced, either in the short or in the long run, by his price policy. Oligopoly could also be defined to exclude entry, fewness being then the result of the impossibility, for firms not now in the group, of producing the commodity—whether for physical or legal reasons. And, undoubtedly, the impossibility of entry is frequently at least implicitly assumed in the analysis of oligopoly, following the venerable example of Cournot, with his owners of mineral wells. But such a narrow definition leaves out the far more interesting case where fewness is the result of purely economic forces, entry being prevented by—and within the limits of—certain price-output policies of existing producers. This is precisely the essence of homogeneous oligopoly analyzed by both Sylos and Bain.

One might suppose that, as long as potential entrants have access to a long-run cost function identical in all respects to that of existing firms, entry must tend to occur whenever the market price is higher than the minimum long-run average cost. (Cost is used hereafter in the sense of opportunity cost, including therefore an appropriate allowance for "normal" profits.) But then long-run market equilibrium would have to involve a price equal to minimum average cost and a corresponding output [4] and would be undistinguishable from perfectly competitive equilibrium. This supposition is, however, invalid whenever the output of an optimum size firm represents a "non-insignificant" fraction of pre-entry output. The price that is relevant to the potential entrant is the price *after* entry. Even if the pre-entry price is above the lowest achievable cost, the additional output he proposes to sell may drive the price below cost, making the entry unprofitable.

Unfortunately for the theorist, the exact anticipated effect of the entry on price is not independent of the (anticipated) reaction of existing producers. The more they are willing to contract their output in response to the entry, the smaller will be the fall in price; in the limiting case the price may even be completely unaffected. Both authors have wisely refused to be stopped by this difficulty. They have instead proceeded to explore systematically the implications of the following well-defined assumption: that potential entrants behave as though they expected existing firms to adopt the policy most unfavorable to them, namely, the policy of maintaining output while reducing the price (or

---

[4] This is in fact, the conclusion reached by H. R. Edwards, "Price Formation in Manufacturing Industry and Excess Capacity," *Oxford Economic Papers*, VII, No. 1 (February, 1955), 194–218, sec. 4.2, which is, in turn, an elaboration of the model developed by P. W. S. Andrews in *Manufacturing Business* (London: Macmillan & Co., 1949). In other respects Edwards' stimulating analysis anticipates many of the conclusions of Sylos and Bain.

accepting reductions) to the extent required to enforce such an output policy. I shall refer to this assumption as "Sylos' postulate" because it underlies, more or less explicitly, most of his analysis, whereas Bain has also paid some attention to the possibility of potential entrants, assuming a less belligerent behavior on the part of existing firms.

The significance of Sylos' postulate lies in the fact that it enables us to find a definite solution to the problem of long-run equilibrium price and output under homogeneous oligopoly, or at least a definite upper limit to the price, to be denoted by P_0 and a corresponding lower limit to aggregate output, say, X_0. Both authors have essentially reached this conclusion, though through somewhat different routes.

I shall not attempt to reproduce faithfully their respective arguments, but shall instead concentrate on developing the logical essence of their approach. To this end, let $X = D(P)$ denote the market demand curve for the product and let P' denote the pre-entry price, $X' = D(P')$ being then the corresponding aggregate output. Under Sylos' postulate the prospective entrant is confronted not by an infinitely elastic demand at the price P' but by a sloping demand curve which is simply *the segment of the demand curve to the right of* $\mathbf{P}'$. I shall refer to this segment as the marginal demand curve. Note that it is uniquely determined by the original demand curve and the pre-entry price P'. Suppose P' to be such that the corresponding marginal demand curve is *everywhere* below *the* long-run average cost function. Clearly, under these conditions, entry will not be profitable; that is, such a P' is an *entry-preventing price*. The critical price P_0 is then simply the *highest* entry-preventing price, and the critical output X_0 is the corresponding aggregate demand, $D(P_0)$. Under perfect competition, where the output of an optimum size firm is negligible relative to market demand, the marginal demand curve is itself infinitely elastic *in the relevant range;* hence the familiar conclusion that the long-run equilibrium price cannot exceed minimum average cost. But, where the output of an optimum plant is not negligible, P_0 will exceed minimum cost to an extent which depends on the nature of the demand and the long-run cost function.

In order to explore the factors controlling P_0, let us denote by $\bar{x}$ the optimum scale of output, that is, the scale corresponding to the lowest point of the long-run average cost curve. (If this scale is not unique, $\bar{x}$ will mean the smallest scale consistent with minimum cost.) If k denotes the corresponding minimum average cost, then the perfectly competitive equilibrium price is $P_c = k$, and the corresponding equilibrium output is $X_c = D(P_c) = D(k)$. Finally, let us define the size of the market, S, as the ratio of the competitive output to the optimum scale; $S = X_c/\bar{x}$. (This definition is not the same as that of either Sylos or Bain; it appears, however, to be the most convenient for theoretical purposes, even though it may have drawbacks for empirical investigations.)

Now, following Bain, consider first the simplest case in which the technology of the industry is such that, at a scale less than $\bar{x}$, costs are prohibitively high, so that an entrant can come in only at a scale $\bar{x}$ or larger. In this case the entry-preventing output X_0 is readily found to be

$$X_0 = X_c - \bar{x} = X_c\left(1 - \frac{\bar{x}}{X_c}\right) = X_c\left(1 - \frac{1}{S}\right), \qquad (1)$$

or $(100/S)$ per cent below the competitive output. Suppose in fact that aggregate output were smaller; it would then be profitable for a firm of scale $\bar{x}$ to enter. Indeed, the post-entry output would then still be smaller than X_c, and hence the post-entry price would be larger than P_c, which is in turn equal to the entrant's average cost. By the same reasoning an output X_0 (or larger) would make entry unattractive. The critical price P_0 corresponding to X_0 can be read from the demand curve or found by solving for P the equation $X_0 = D(P)$. The relation between P_0 and the competitive equilibrium price P_c can be stated (approximately) in terms of the elasticity of demand in the neighborhood of P_c; if we denote this elasticity by η we have

$$P_0 \simeq P_c\left(1 + \frac{1}{\eta S}\right),$$

or $100/\eta S$ per cent above P_c.[5]

We can now replace the very special cost function assumed so far with the more conventional one, falling, more or less gradually, at least up to $\bar{x}$. In this general case the critical output may be somewhat larger, and the critical price may be lower, than indicated in the previous paragraph. Indeed, while at the output X_0 given by (1) it is not profitable to enter at the scale $\bar{x}$, it *may* still be profitable to come in at a *smaller* scale.

This possibility and its implications can be conveniently analyzed by means of the graphical apparatus presented in Figure 1. (This graphical device is not to be found in either of the books under re-

[5] This approximation will not be very satisfactory for small values of S. In particular, if the demand curve has constant elasticity, then, for small values of S, the extent of price rise will be significantly underestimated.

view, but I believe that it is quite helpful in bringing out the essence of the authors' arguments.) [6] In panels *IA* and *IIA,* the light lines falling from left to right are the (relevant portions of the) market demand curve. For the sake of generality it is convenient to take $\bar{x}$ (the optimum scale) as the unit of measurement for output X and to take k (the corresponding minimum cost) as the unit of measurement for price, P. It follows that the competitive equilibrium price is by definition, unity, while the corresponding output is precisely the size of the market S. Thus panel *IA* of Figure 1 relates to an industry of

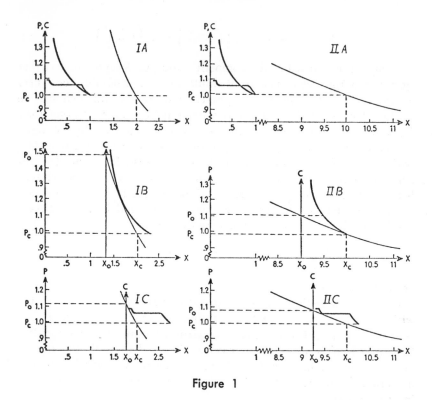

Figure 1

size 2 and panel *IIA* to an industry of size 10. The two demand curves have constant unit elasticity in the range shown, but, as will become apparent, the effect of different assumptions about the elasticity of demand can readily be handled.

The two heavy lines in each of the two panels represent alternative

[6] In the case of Sylos, I am less sure of my ground, since his argument rests almost entirely on a detailed analysis of two numerical examples.

cost curves, graphed on the same scale as the demand curve, for outputs up to $\bar{x}$ (that is, for values of X up to 1). Because of the choice of units, each curve shows the behavior of costs, in percentage of minimum cost, as a function of plant scale, expressed in percentage of optimum scale. The steeper of the two curves is the kind of traditional, well-behaved cost function that underlies Bain's analysis and involves marked economies of scale. It is, in fact, based on the information reported by him for the cement industry, which appears to have more marked economies of scale than any other of the twenty industries analyzed in his book. It is obtained by joining with a smooth curve the data provided there for discrete scale sizes. The other cost curve, involving less pronounced economies of scale, depicts the kind of cost function that underlies Sylos' numerical examples. Sylos explicitly assumes, on grounds of presumed realism, the existence of very pronounced discontinuities in the available technologies. Plants can thus have only sizes that are very specific and far apart—only three sizes in his examples and in my graph. The rounded portions of the curve result from the fact that, beyond certain critical outputs, it pays to shift to a plant of a larger size, even though such a plant could not be utilized to capacity.[7]

The critical price and output, P_0 and X_0, for a given cost curve can now be readily located by means of the following simple device. Slide the cost curve to the right parallel to itself, together with its co-ordinate axis, until no point of this curve lies inside the demand curve. This step is illustrated in panels *IB* and *IIB* for the steeper cost curve and in panels *IC* and *IIC* for the flatter one. The point at which the *Y*-axis so displaced cuts the demand curve represents P_0; the point at which it cuts the *X*-axis is X_0. For, clearly, the portion of the demand curve to the right of the displaced axis is precisely the marginal demand curve when the aggregate output of the existing firms is X_0. If the cost curve is nowhere below this marginal demand curve, there is no possibility of profits for a new entrant.

As can be seen from Figure 1, the cost curve in its terminal position may be either tangent to the demand curve, as in *IB,* or may touch it at a "corner," as in *IC* and *IIC,* or, finally, may touch it at its lower extreme, as in *IIB.*[8] The X co-ordinate of the point where the two curves touch, referred to the axis of the cost curve, indicates the size of

---

[7] If Sylos' assumption is taken literally, the portions of the curves shown as straight lines parallel to the X-axis should really have a scalloped shape. This refinement can, however, be ignored, since it does not affect the results.

[8] It may, of course, also have several discrete points of contact with the demand curve or overlap a portion of it.

firm which represents the most immediate threat of entry. Where this immediate threat comes from an optimum size plant, as in *IIB*, X_0 is precisely that given by formula (1) above; it is now seen that this possibility represents a limiting case—and that, in general, the formula provides only a lower bound to X_0.

With the help of Figure 1 we can also establish several interesting propositions in comparative statics. First, by comparing panel *IB* with *IC* and *IIB* with *IIC*, we see that, for given market size, P_0 will tend to be higher the steeper the cost curve, that is, the greater the economies of scale. The common sense of this result is apparent: when economies of scale are important, the effective threat will tend to come from large-scale plants, which must widen the gap between X_0 and X_c. Similarly, by comparing *IB* with *IIB* and *IC* with *IIC*, it appears that, for a given cost curve and elasticity of demand, P_0 will tend to fall with the size of the market; it will, in fact, approach unity (the competitive price) as the size of the market approaches infinity. Furthermore, since, for given size S, a higher elasticity of demand implies a rotation of the cost curve in a counterclockwise direction around the competitive point, it is apparent that a higher elasticity will act in the same direction as a larger size with given elasticity; that is, it will tend to lower P_0.

In summary, under Sylos' postulate there is a well-defined, maximum premium that the oligopolists can command over the competitive price, and this premium tends to increase with the importance of economies of scale and to decrease with the size of market and the elasticity of demand.[9]

III

I have now laid down the basic long-run equilibrium model common to both Bain and Sylos. Hereafter, their roads part, and I shall first follow Sylos in his explorations of some of the fascinating implications of the model.

The first of these implications refers to the size distribution of firms (or, more precisely, of plants) within the group—its *internal structure,* as I shall call it. If we look, for example, at panel *IC*, we see that the price P_0 is considerably above the average cost of the medium-size firms and even slightly above that of the smallest. If then any such firm *happened* to be a member of the group—Sylos here, in good Walrasian

---

[9] As Bain points out, it is conceivable, though not likely, that P_0 will be higher than the price that "maximizes the profit" of the existing firms, in which case it will have no bearing on long-run equilibrium. See below, Sec. VIII.

tradition, speaks of the initial structure as "criée par hasard"—it could survive and even prosper.

But would it not be profitable for the larger firms to expand, eliminating the smaller ones and securing for themselves the small firms' share of the market? In Sylos' model this possibility can be largely dismissed, thanks to his assumption of sharp technological discontinuities. Suppose, for instance, that there are only two possible scales: *(a)* large plants, producing 10,000 units, and *(b)* small plants, producing 500 units. Suppose further that X_0 is 15,000 and that this output is initially produced by one large firm and ten small ones. There is, then, no real incentive for the large firm to drive the small ones out of the market, for, in order to produce the extra 5,000 units, it would, in fact, have to operate ten small plants (at least as long as the average cost of a small plant is less than the average incremental cost of producing an extra 5,000 units by operating two large plants at 75 per cent of capacity). But the cost of a small firm must be such as to yield very little, if any, abnormal profit at the price P_0. In fact, this price must be such as not to give an inducement to enter the market with a small plant. Hence there will generally be no incentive for the large firm to undertake the price war necessary to eliminate the smaller firms.

If there existed a technology of intermediate size, say, size 5,000, the situation might look somewhat different, since at price P_0 such a plant would make some profits. However, even in this case the elimination of small firms would involve a costly price war. The price would have to be kept below prime cost of the small firms for a time long enough to induce them to fold up or below their average cost until their fixed plant wears out. Sylos suggests that usually the war will not be worth the prize and that it will be preferable for the larger firms not to disturb the delicate balance that always prevails in a homogeneous oligopoly structure.

Are we then to conclude that any structure, "criée par hasard," will tend to perpetuate itself as long as it is consistent with a price not higher than P_0? Sylos does not investigate this issue systematically, confining himself to illustrating various possibilities on the basis of his specific numerical examples. I suggest, however, that with the help of Sylos' model it is possible to throw some interesting light on this question. To this end I shall first introduce a definition. Consider any two structures A and B consistent with no inducement to entry: let us say that A is more rational than B if the total profits accruing to the members of the group are larger under structure A than under B.[10] It fol-

---

[10] It is apparent that this notion bears a close affinity to that of *dominance* in the theory of games.

lows from this definition and our previous analysis that there exists a *most rational* structure, namely, that structure (not necessarily unique) which produces at the smallest total cost the output X_0 that can be sold at price P_0.[11] This most rational structure has two features worth mentioning: (1) From a welfare point of view, it has certain optimal properties in that X_0 is being produced at the smallest (social) cost; but it still involves a departure from the usual conditions of Pareto optimality in that the output X_0 is, generally, too small and P_0 too high. (2) From a technological point of view, it has the property that the total capacity of the plants of a given size must necessarily be no larger than the capacity of one plant of the next larger size.

It seems reasonable to suppose that, if a structure B is less rational than a structure A, it will be less likely to be observed. For there is some incentive to a shift from B to A, since such a shift is accompanied by a net gain; that is, losses, if any, are more than compensated by gains. But there will be no corresponding incentive to move back from A to B. It does not follow, however, that structures other than the most rational have no chance at all of ever existing or surviving. As Sylos rightly points out, moving from one structure to another generally involves costs—at best, the cost of reaching an agreement; at worst, that of war—and the potential gain may not be worth the cost, especially when the gain, and even more the cost, may be problematic and uncertain.

The conclusions to which we are led are therefore, as it were, of a probabilistic nature. Less rational structures are less likely to be observed than more rational ones, and very irrational structures are unlikely to maintain themselves for any length of time. But certainly structures other than the most rational can exist and survive, especially in a world that is moving and in which the most rational structure is itself continuously changing. Similar considerations apply to the price; while we should not expect prices higher that P_0 to be long maintainable, lower prices may have a certain degree of permanence. But, again, a gap between P and P_0 will provide a stimulus to reorganization of the structure, and this stimulus will be more powerful, and hence more likely to produce a response, the greater the gap.

By drawing together the analysis of market equilibrium and that of

[11] This statement is valid only to a first approximation. It is possible that the output X_0 cannot be produced with an integral number of plants of various sizes working at capacity, in which case profit maximization may involve an output somewhat above X_0. However, the departure from X_0 will tend to be negligible, at least as long as the output of the smallest size consistent with P_0 represents a minor fraction of X_0.

internal structure, we may venture some tentative conclusions about the factors which, according to Sylos' model, tend to control the degree of scatter in the size distributions of firms. We already know that only those sizes can survive whose average cost is no larger than P_0. From an analysis of the figure it can therefore be inferred that the possible range of the scatter of sizes will tend to be greater the smaller *(a)* the economies of scale, *(b)* the size of the markets, and *(c)* the elasticity of demand.

These implications, as well as those relating to P_0, are in principle testable. Indeed, it is to both Bain's and Sylos' credit that, by moving us away from conjectural variations and similar subjective notions and focusing instead on objective market and technological data, they have provided us with theories rich in empirical content and capable of being disproved by the evidence. To be sure, such tests may not be easy to carry out, especially with the information presently available, as is amply attested by Bain's gallant efforts in this direction. But, with a clear theoretical framework available as a guide in the collection of data, one may hope that more reliable and abundant evidence will sooner or later accumulate.

Even at this stage, ingenuity can do much to remedy inadequacies of the data. For instance, in order to compute the actual value of P for a given industry, one would need to know not only the market price but also the minimum average cost of an optimal plant. Bain ingeniously suggests that, even in the absence of precise information on this point, some notion of the relative height of P for various industries may be gotten by ranking them in terms of the rate of profits of the largest firms in each industry, since the average cost of such firms will presumably tend to be reasonably close to the minimum.[12] It should be

---

[12] In his book and in earlier contributions Bain measures the rate of profit as the rate of return, net of taxes, on the book value of equity. It would seem preferable to use the rate of return before taxes and interest on the book value of assets, since such a measure is not affected by financial structure. Perhaps a still more relevant measure, for the purpose of testing the model, could be derived from the rate of profit on sales. In fact, letting p denote the market price, we have

$$P = \frac{p}{k} = \frac{px}{kx} = \frac{\text{Sales}}{\text{Sales} - \text{Profit}} = \frac{1}{1 - (\text{Profit}/\text{Sales})}$$

By profit I mean here earnings over and above a "normal" rate of return on the book value of assets, which may not be easy to estimate in practice. One may also have some reservations about the assumption that minimum long-run average cost can be approximated from the actual average cost of the dominant firms in the industry. Franklyn Fisher has suggested that a better approximation may be obtained by utilizing, at least as supplementary evidence, the rate of profit on sales of the most profitable firms.

noted, however, that, contrary to what Bain seems to imply in some of his empirical tests, there is no reason to expect any simple association between P_0 (or its proxy, the rate of profit) and the degree of scatter in plant sizes, at least within Sylos' model. While it is true that a large scatter is not to be expected when P_0 is very close to unity—for then only firms of near-optimum size can survive—it does not follow that there is a positive association between P_0 and scatter. The only safe statement we can make is that, for given P_0, the scatter should tend to be smaller the steeper the cost curve and that, for given cost curve, the association between P_0 and scatter should be positive, both variables tending to decline as the size of the market and the elasticity of demand increase. A cursory examination of Bain's data for those industries in which product-differentiation and absolute-cost advantages are not supposed to be dominant does not seem to contradict this inference conspicuously. Unfortunately, the data in question provide no information on the elasticity of demand and, what is more serious, leave too much room for personal judgment in ranking industries in terms of any variable.

IV

It is tempting to explore the extent to which the implications we have derived from Sylos' model would be affected if we relaxed some of his very rigid assumptions. This question is especially pressing with respect to his assumption of technological discontinuities. Indeed, Bain has emerged from his empirical investigation with a strong conviction that, although there exists a fairly definite scale $\bar{x}$ at which average cost reaches its minimum, costs do not generally tend to rise for scales larger than $\bar{x}$. This possibility in no way affects our analysis of long-run equilibrium price and output but has considerable bearing on the conclusions concerning the size structure. Clearly, under a Bain-type cost function, the "most rational structure" must be such that all the output X_0 is produced by plants of size $\bar{x}$ or larger. It would follow that structures involving smaller plant sizes would tend to be unstable, especially where the cost function is steep in the range of (relative) costs from 1 to P_0.

The reader can decide for himself just how serious this conclusion is for Sylos' construction.[13] I shall limit myself to suggesting that Sylos'

---

[13] Rosenstein-Rodan has pointed out to me that Bain's long-run cost function may not be too relevant where plant is very long lived. For, even though it may be possible to design a plant having cost k at sizes larger than $\bar{x}$, nonetheless an existing firm wishing to undertake a moderate expansion may have to utilize a smaller-scale technique with higher costs.

case may be considerably strengthened when we recognize the existence of product differentiation of a type not altogether inconsistent with the notion of homogeneous oligopoly, such as spatial differentiation or modifications in product design to meet customers' specifications. Under these conditions the area of the market supplied by smaller firms may be such that the dominant firms would have little to gain by capturing it, either because they have no cost advantage or because this would require an unprofitable price policy on other lines of product.

Consider, for example, the case of spatial differentiation. Suppose the large firm has a cost of 10 and the cost of transportation to a given distant market is 1. Suppose further that the highest f.o.b. price preventing entry that the large firm can charge is 12. The delivered price in the given market is then 13, and it may well be that, at this price, the market can be profitably supplied by a small local firm at, say, a cost of 12.5. In order to capture that relatively small market, the large firm would have to keep the price well below 11.5 for some considerable length of time and then keep it no higher than 11.5 indefinitely— a policy which may well be unprofitable.[14] There is thus room for smaller firms in the industry, but this room is generated by market "exploitation" on the part of the large firm, and all customers are paying a higher price (by 2 per unit) than under competitive equilibrium.

Consider next the case of product modifications. It may well be that a class of customers is willing to pay an extra premium of 1 for a specific variation of the standard product. If the large firm charges 12 for the standard line, even though it has a cost of 10, these customers are therefore willing to pay 13. Now, suppose that, given the size of the market for the specialty, the average cost of the product is again, say, 12.5, whether it is produced by the larger firm or by a smaller one specializing in that line. If such a smaller firm exists, it is not worthwhile for the large firm to try to capture the market. But note once more that the existence of the smaller firm is made possible by the larger firm's oligopoly power. Under competitive conditions the small firm could not exist, since, if customers could get the standard product for 10, they would not be willing to pay enough for the specialty to cover its production cost of 12.5.

---

[14] It is assumed that the alternative, and more profitable, course of quoting a delivered price of 12.5 is not available. It is interesting to note in this connection that the prohibition of freight absorption as an antitrust measure will have a desirable effect if it induces the producer to choose a lower price in order not to lose distant markets to smaller local firms but that it will have an undesirable outcome if the producer finds it more advantageous to abandon those markets, in which case the demand will be supplied at a higher social cost.

In short, in many situations the presence of a variety of sizes may be rendered reasonably stable by the fact that the larger firms find it advantageous to skim the fattest segment of the market, leaving it for smaller firms to supply less profitable pockets. Nor should one forget altogether, even within the realm of pure theory, the public relations advantages that tend to accrue to the large firms from the coexistence of smaller and weaker partners. The argument that prices cannot be lowered without playing havoc with large numbers of honest and industrious small enterprises is always one of great public appeal. And, where antitrust laws are a potential threat, the advantages of having smaller competitors is even more evident.[15]

V

Before closing the subject of long-run static analysis, I must report one more observation on which Sylos lays a great deal of stress and which has to do with the effects of technological progress. While improvements in technology that are applicable to all scales must necessarily tend to depress price and expand output, he argues that improvements applicable only at, or near, the largest scale will not affect the critical price and hence will tend to result in higher profits for the larger firms. Furthermore, Sylos seems to feel that technological changes are very commonly of this type, and he is inclined to account in this fashion for a presumed tendency of the profit margin of large firms to grow over time. Here, however, I cannot avoid feeling that Sylos is going too far. For, in the first place, even a change that affects only the largest scale may well lower P_0 when the immediate threat is, in fact, from firms of size x; and, in the second place, any innovation that affects only plants of suboptimal size (and such innovations are by no means inconceivable) will also result in a fall in the critical price and thus will reduce the profit of the largest firms whose costs have

---

15 The considerations of this section clearly point to the importance of factors other than those discussed in Sec. III above in controlling the scatter of the size distribution of firms and plants. In particular, under a Bain-type cost function, the model has nothing to say about the size distribution of firms above the optimum size $\bar{x}$. Here one may have to fall back on stochastic models of the type advanced, for example, by H. Simon in *Models of Man* (New York: John Wiley & Sons, 1957), chap. ix. In any event the analysis presented casts most serious doubts on the argument advanced by some authors and well exemplified by the following quotation: "Actually, we find that in most industries firms of very different sizes survive, and we may infer that commonly there is no large advantage or disadvantage to size over a very considerable range of ouputs" (George Stigler, *The Theory of Price* [New York: Macmillan Co., 1952], p. 144).

remained unchanged. There is therefore serious doubt whether Sylos' argument can account for a long-run relative rise in large firms' profits, not to mention the equally serious doubt whether such a relative rise has in fact occurred. The model does suggest, however, that changes in technology may cause radical changes in the most rational structure and thus eventually may lead to pervasive changes in the actual structure, including the possible elimination of whole layers of small-scale plants.

VI

I now proceed to consider with Sylos some implications of the model for the effect of short-run changes in demand and cost conditions. Note, first, that in the analysis of market equilibrium I have made no mention of the standard categories of monopolistic competition theories, namely, marginal cost and marginal revenue. To be sure, with sufficient ingenuity, the analysis could be forced into that cast,[16] but such an undertaking would be merely an exercise in semantics and formal logic and would in no way increase our understanding of what it involved. On the other hand, our result can readily be recast in the framework of the so-called full-cost pricing principle. According to this principle, prices are determined by adding to prime cost a markup to cover overhead per unit and by adding further an "appropriate" profit margin. So far, however, it has never been convincingly explained just at what level of output the overhead charge is computed or what determines the "appropriate" profit margin. Sylos' and Bain's models do provide answers to both questions. The large firms, which typically set the pace in the market, must base their price on long-run average cost (so that the overhead must normally be computed at capacity operation, with due allowance for normal seasonal and cyclical variations in the rate of utilization) and apply to this cost the largest profit markup that "the traffic will bear," namely, the markup P_0—for P_0, it will be recalled, is precisely the ratio of the highest possible price to average cost.

The usefulness of translating the result of the static analysis into the language of full-cost pricing becomes fully apparent when we proceed to examine the effects of a variation, say, an increase, in some element of prime cost. Such a change will generally affect all firms and hence will raise the long-run cost curve more or less uniformly. This development in turn will raise the level of the critical price and make it

16 For such an attempt see, for example, J. R. Hicks, "The Process of Imperfect Competition." *Oxford Economic Papers*, VI (February, 1954), 41–54.

profitable to raise the actual price to this new level. Now it can be verified that, at least for moderate variations in costs and well-behaved demand functions, a good approximation of the new critical price can be obtained precisely by adding to the new average cost the very same profit margin that prevailed before the change; and nearly as good an approximation can be obtained by applying to the new prime cost the original total percentage markup. Thus full-cost pricing may well represent a very useful rule of thumb in reacting to cost changes affecting the entire industry, at least as long as such changes are not too drastic.

Now that we have a solid rationale for the full-cost principle, we need not have qualms about acknowledging two other sets of factors that tend to give it further sanction. (1) In an oligopolistic situation, with its precarious internal equilibrium, there is much to be gained from simple and widely understood rules of thumb, which minimize the danger of behavior intended to be peaceful and cooperative being misunderstood as predatory or retaliatory.[17] (2) The experience of those who, like myself, have conducted extensive personal interviews with executives suggests that these respondents have a strong propensity to explain their behavior in terms of simple mechanical principles, especially when they feel that these principles are blessed by general respectability.

So much about the effect of variations in costs. Let us now turn to the effect of cyclical variations in demand. For the sake of concreteness, let us start out from the prosperity phase, in which plants are being operated at, or near, capacity rates. If the demand curve now shifts to the left as a result of a fall in aggregate income, our model suggests that the optimum markup may have a slight tendency to increase. There are two main reasons for this contention: (1) the critical price P_0 tends to rise when the size of the market falls and (2), with substantial idle capacity and sharply reduced profits, or even losses, prevailing in the industry, even a price somewhat higher than P_0 is not likely to encourage entry, especially where the effective threat is from plants large enough to require a substantial investment. This tendency for the critical markup to rise may partly be offset or even more than offset if, as the demand shifts, its elasticity increases; it will be reinforced if the elasticity falls—a case which Sylos regards as more typical, though, in our view, not very convincingly.

17 See, for example, A. Henderson, "The Theory of Duopoly," *Quarterly Journal of Economics*, LXVIII (November, 1954), 576–79, Sec. VII, and T. C. Schelling "Bargaining, Communication, and Limited War," *Conflict Resolution*, I (March, 1957), 19–36.

On the whole, then, the critical price P_0 may have some mild tendency to rise; but this does not mean that the actual markup will necessarily rise, for, with much idle capacity, the temptation for individual members of the oligopolistic group to secure a large share of the shrunken business is very strong. Thus the self-discipline of the group may well tend to break down, with a resultant fall in the effective price if not in the officially quoted one.

In the course of the recovery the markup will of course tend to retrace the path followed in the contraction. But here some new interesting possibilities arise which Sylos himself has not considered. In an expanding economy the recovery will tend to push demand to levels higher than previous peaks. As a result of a rise in demand that is rapid and larger than expected, or as a result of circumstances beyond its control, such as war, the industry may be caught with capacity inadequate to satisfy the demand at the critical price P_0. In terms of traditional patterns of thinking, one would expect firms in the industry to be eager to exploit the situation by charging higher prices. But such a price policy may not be so appealing to the larger firms whose long-run interest is to secure for themselves as much as possible of the additional demand at the profitable price P_0. A higher price may tend to encourage entry, which would not only reduce their share but possibly also threaten the maintenance of self-discipline in periods of depressed demand. Thus the dominant firms may have an incentive to "hold the price line" by such devices as lengthening delivery schedules and informal rationing (even at the risk of gray markets), while at the same time expanding capacity—but only to an extent that seems warranted by the anticipated long-run demand at the price P_0. These considerations may help to explain the otherwise rather puzzling behavior of certain important sectors of the economy in the early postwar period.[18]

On the whole it would appear that no very definite general conclusion can be reached about the cyclical behavior of the markup, although the model may have a good deal to say for well-defined classes

[18] A similar explanation is advanced in Edwards, op. cit., and in Kuh and Meyer, The Investment Decision (Cambridge, Mass.: Harvard University Press, 1957), esp. chap. xii. It has also been suggested that the price policies in question may be explained by the concern that higher prices and consequent higher profits would have led to irresistible pressure for wage concessions, difficult to reverse. By contrast, the abnormally high profits of dealers or gray-market operators could be counted on to disappear automatically as the supply gradually caught up with demand. I am indebted to Albert G. Hart and Richard Cyert for stimulating discussions on the relevance of Sylos' model to the explanation of the postwar experience.

of situations. One might, however, go along with Sylos on the following two tentative generalizations: (1) on the average, the markup is not likely to change much in the course of the cycle, but one should expect some scatter around this central tendency, and (2) prices should tend on the average to fluctuate more in relation to prime cost where there is more chance for the discipline of the group to break down, and this chance presumably should tend to increase with the size of the group and decrease with degree of concentration (in Sylos' sense). These generalizations appear to be consistent with the evidence assembled by Stigler in his well-known criticism of the kinky demand curve,[19] though they may be less easy to reconcile with certain empirical studies of price flexibility.[20]

Sylos attempts to dispose of the latter evidence by an ingenious argument which is not entirely convincing in this context but which is of interest on its own merit. Specifically, he suggests that, where the full-cost principle is widely adhered to, it may be in the interest of the larger firms to sustain the prices of factors entering into prime cost; in fact, provided that the shifted demand curve has a sufficiently low elasticity, such a policy will increase the over-all profit of the industry. Where the large firms are themselves important producers of some critical raw materials, they may best achieve this purpose by sustaining these particular prices; where this is not possible, they may acquiesce to an increase in real wages.[21] However, the advantage of an increase in prime costs is realized only where full-cost pricing is adhered to in spite of widespread excess capacity. Hence this policy can be sensible only where discipline is maintained, which, as suggested earlier, may be related to small number and heavy concentration. Sylos suggests that these considerations may help to explain certain empirical results indicating a positive association between cyclical wage rigidity and degree of concentration.[22]

[19] George Stigler, "The Kinky Oligopoly Demand Curve and Rigid Prices," *Journal of Political Economy*, LV (October, 1947), 432-49.

[20] Richard Ruggles, "The Nature of Price Flexibility and Determinants of Relative Price Changes in the Economy," in *Business Concentration and Price Policy* (A Conference of the Universities–National Bureau Committee for Economic Research [Princeton, N.J.: Princeton University Press, 1955]), pp. 441-505.

[21] Note that this argument is applicable even to long-run equilibrium analysis. That is, when the market demand is sufficiently inelastic, an increase in wage rates may increase the total excess of receipts over (opportunity) costs accruing to the group. It may then be profitable for existing firms to tolerate high wages, as long as these are enforced by a trade union strong enough to impose the same wage scale on any potential entrant.

[22] The major piece of evidence quoted in this connection is J. W. Garbarino, "A Theory of Inter-industry Wage Structure Variation," *Quarterly Journal of Economics*, LXIV (May, 1950), 282-305.

VII

The last two parts of Sylos' book expound the thesis that monopolistic and oligopolistic market structures are an important factor contributing to the development of unemployment, especially technological unemployment. In spite of the importance of the subject, this part will be reviewed in very sketchy form, both for lack of space and because Sylos' argument is not so convincing as his partial equilibrium analysis.

The main thread of his argument in Part II seems to run as follows. Starting from a stationary situation with full employment, a labor-saving innovation initially displaces labor. The reabsorption of this unemployment requires some net saving to be invested in the equipment necessary to outfit the displaced workers. (The alternative possibility of a fall in real wages leading to an appropriate change in capital coefficients is excluded by assumption.) Under perfectly competitive market structures, the fall in cost would lead to higher real income for all those who have not lost their employment, and this rise in real income, especially profits, supposedly produces the saving and investment necessary for the reabsorption. On the other hand, under oligopolistic structures, the fall in cost will frequently not be accompanied by a proportionate fall in prices and will thus result in an increase in the value added of the sector where costs have fallen. (I have already expressed some doubt about the validity of this conclusion in Sec. V above.) To the extent that the increase in value added is absorbed by higher wages, the necessary saving will not be forthcoming, since, by an assumption which is particularly unpalatable to me, workers have a marginal propensity to consume equal to 1. To the extent that the increase in value added results in higher profits—and even if these profits give rise to savings—there may still be difficulties. Sylos suggests in fact that the entrepreneurs to whom the profits accrue will be disinclined to invest outside their own industry, whereas the investment required should be spread throughout the economy.

The conclusion Sylos draws is that, with widespread oligopolistic market structures, the forces making for reabsorption, though not entirely absent, will be lagging and weak. In a world of continuous technological change this weakness is sufficient, in his view, to account for a substantial permanent pool of unemployment, whose continuing existence is therefore an essentially dynamic phenomenon. He further argues that the kind of innovations the larger firms in the oligopolistic group will be inclined to adopt are likely to aggravate the technological displacement of labor. He maintains in fact that, though these firms will tend to be quite progressive in searching for, and adopting, innovations that cut costs at current level of output, they will nonetheless shun improvements that would cut costs only at a large scale of operation. But this argument is not quite consistent with his own model, since the new, larger-scale, and cheaper technique may itself become the immediate threat to entry. Nor is it clearly relevant—for it does not per se establish a bias in favor of labor-saving innovations.

Part III purports to explore the implications of the previous analysis for the standard Keynesian theory of effective demand. This part again contains many interesting observations but also has its shortcomings. In particular, the author does not seem to be sufficiently aware that the implications of the analysis of Part III are profoundly different for an economy poor in capital and savings like the Italian economy and for one in which the main threat to unemployment springs from a lack of effective demand. In the former case, labor-saving innovations may indeed tend to aggravate the problem of unemployment, especially when coupled with powerful units and downward wage rigidity. But, in the latter case, such innovations are, as it were, a blessing, since they increase the required stock of capital and thus make possible the absorption of full-employment saving.

This sketch of Parts III and IV may well fail to do justice to Sylos' argument. But such a failure would serve to confirm the earlier statement that these final chapters do not quite match the high level of performance that characterizes the rest of this remarkable book.

VIII

Let us now look briefly at that part of Bain's analysis that does not overlap Sylos'.

Still with respect to barriers from economies of scale, Bain makes a halfhearted attempt to explore the consequences of dropping Sylos' postulate (see Sec. II). Unfortunately, as long as we are dealing with homogeneous oligopoly, it is hard to find a well-defined sensible alternative. Certainly, the diametrically opposite assumption that existing firms will adopt a policy of maintaining price, by contracting their output, would generally be a rather foolish one for the entrant to make. It implies that established firms will graciously allow the entrant to carve out for himself whatever slice of the market he pleases, while suffering losses on two accounts: (1) by losing sales and (2) by incurring a higher average cost, at least in the short run and possibly even in the long run, if their original plant was of no more than optimal size. Furthermore, such a policy, if consistently followed, would unavoidably result in the original members' being gradually squeezed out of the market.

The only alternative systematically explored by Bain is for the entrant to assume that price will be maintained but only provided he is contented with a share of the market no larger than that of the existing firms—which are conveniently assumed, for this purpose, to be all of equal size. There is, then, in general, a well-defined critical price (and corresponding output) such that entry is unprofitable even if a prospective entrant proceeds on the stated "optimistic" assumption.[23]

As Bain is well aware, his alternative assumption is but one of a large class of assumptions that could be constructed and explored. But he has wisely refrained from following this line, which is rather unpromising at this stage. For the moment, at least, we must be satisfied with the conclusion that there exists a well-defined upper limit to the price that can be maintained under oligopoly in the long run, and this upper limit is P_0, obtained under Sylos' postulate. It is the upper limit because, at a price higher than this, entry will be profitable even if the existing firms are bent on doing the entrant as much damage as they possibly can.[24] But a price lower than P_0 cannot be excluded a priori, even in the long run, especially where P_0 would cover the cost at a scale of output which represents a small fraction of X_0 and where a plant of such scale would require a relatively small investment. But, broadly speaking, these are precisely the conditions under which P_0 is close to 1, and the classical competitive model may provide a reasonable approximation. Conversely, Sylos' postulate may well provide a reasonable approximation precisely where it makes a real difference—where it implies a value of P_0 appreciably above unity.

Dropping the assumption that all producers, actual and potential, have access to identical cost functions enables us to analyze another set

[23] It is easy to verify that the stated critical price, say, p_0, and corresponding output are given by the simultaneous solution of the following two equations:

$$X = D(p) \tag{1}$$

$$p = c \frac{X}{(n+1)}, \tag{2}$$

where $c(q)$ denotes the minimum long-run average cost of producing the quantity q, and n is the number of plants. In general, p_0 is an increasing function of n and is larger than the competitive price, at least as long as n is larger than S. Furthermore, for sufficiently large n, each firm is of less than optimal size, and the equilibrium bears a close resemblance to that described by Chamberlin in *Monopolistic Competition*, Chap. v, Sec. 5.

[24] A somewhat higher price could conceivably be maintained if the industry produced an output smaller than X_0, but had enough capacity to produce X_0 or more and a record of readiness to exploit the extra capacity to *expand* output in the face of entry. Such behavior would presumably require more or less open collusion, of a nature likely only with a very small and well-disciplined group.

of forces which can account for a long-run excess of price over cost, and which Bain labels "absolute cost advantages." Such differential costs, arising from factors like control of scarce resources, patents and trade secrets, and generally superior technical and managerial know-how, have already been extensively analyzed and understood in the received body of theory. They underlie the traditional theory of monopoly, oligopoly without entry, and rents. Of course, with cost differential in the picture, there is no longer a specific entry-forestalling price, even under Sylos' postulate. Rather the critical price depends on the cost of the most efficient potential entrant and, hence, on just which firms are already in the group. It may then not be in the interest of existing firms to try to prevent the entry of very efficient producers, since this might require an unprofitably low price. When the price-output policy of existing firms is not intended to discourage potential entrants, Bain speaks of "ineffectively impeded" entry, in contrast to "effectively impeded" entry, in which price and output policy is designed to make entry unprofitable, and to "blockaded entry," in which the price and output policy that is most advantageous to the group, without regard to entry, happens to make entry unattractive.

But Bain's most significant finding about absolute cost barriers is probably at the empirical level. He finds in fact that, at least for his sample of twenty industries, such barriers are generally not important. Natural scarcity appears to be a significant factor in at most two industries—copper and possibly steel. In only three other cases do patents and/or technical know-how possibly play some role and apparently not a major one.

Bain also provides a valuable tabulation of available information on the size of the investment required by a new entrant (with an optimum scale plant). These capital requirements represent a somewhat special type of barrier to entry whose possible significance has been repeatedly mentioned earlier.

The remaining barrier to entry—resulting from the inability of potential competitors to produce a commodity that is a perfect substitute for the product of existing firms—is again one that has received considerable attention in the past. Bain's new contribution in this area consists of a penetrating empirical investigation of the specific barriers that impede the production of perfect or near-perfect substitutes for each industry and their consequences. The main factors may be classified roughly as follows: (1) Allegiance to brands, supported by large advertising outlays, and possibly also, by a long record of reliability; this factor is found to provide the main barrier, and a significant one, almost only in the case of inexpensive durable or non-durable consumers' goods such as cigarettes, liquor, and soap. (2) Control by the manufacturer of an extensive and exclusive dealers' organization attending to the sale and the servicing of the product; as one might expect, this phenomenon is of major importance for expensive durable goods, such as automobiles, typewriters, and tractors and other farm machinery, but it is apparently also of some significance for other commodities, such as petroleum and rubber tires. (3) Patents protecting some feature of the product or related auxiliary services. (4) Special services provided to customers. These last two factors are rarely mentioned and generally do not seem to offer very effective protection.

It is worth noting that factors (2) and (3), and in part also factor (1), could be largely treated as economies of scale in marketing. Both Bain and Sylos are aware of this possibility; in fact, the latter—though he pays only passing attention to product differentiation fostered by advertising—hints that the effect of this type of barrier could be analyzed along lines similar to those utilized in the homogeneous oligopoly model. That is, a new entrant could hope to match the profit performance of the successful large firms only by securing a market of the same absolute size. But, given the over-all size of the market, even if the entrant succeeded in capturing a share comparable to that of existing firms, each member would be left with too small a market, so that the final result of the entry would be to make the business unattractive for all.

After evaluating for his twenty industries the over-all barriers to entry resulting from the joint effect of economies of scale, absolute cost advantages, and product differentiation and after summarizing the effects that these over-all barriers should have on various aspects of market performance on the basis of his theoretical analysis, Bain proceeds to check his deductions against available evidence on actual performance. To be sure, the present evidence on barriers to entry as well as on market performance is frequently far from adequate, and one may have reservations about the details of some of the test procedures. Nonetheless, Bain's courageous attempt at systematic testing and his candid admission of occasional failures of his predictions is a highly welcome novelty and one whose importance can hardly be overestimated.

Finally, the implications of the analysis for public policy designed to foster workable competition are set forth in a very cautious and restrained spirit in the concluding chapter viii. On the whole, the outlook for effective public policy is not too optimistic, although it is by no means as gloomy as that of Sylos. But, then, Sylos' gloom is understandable. His inspiration comes from the Italian economy, where markets are naturally small and are made still smaller by tariffs and other artificial restrictions. According to his own model, the tendency to oligopolistic structures, and their power of market exploitation, will tend to be greater the smaller the size of the market.

I hope I have succeeded in justifying the glowing statement with which this review begins and in showing how well the two books complement each other. To be sure, much work still remains to be done in the area of oligopolistic market structures. In particular, the analysis of both authors is still largely limited to a static framework, and there is reason to believe that certain aspects of oligopolistic behavior can be adequately accounted for only by explicitly introducing dynamic elements into the analysis.[25] In my view, the real significance of Bain's and Sylos' contributions lies not merely in the results that they have already reached but at least as much in their having provided us with a framework capable of promising further developments and leading to operationally testable propositions. In addition, Bain deserves high credit for having led the way on the path of empirical testing.

[25] Some promising beginnings in this direction are already to be found in Sylos and, even more, in Bain. The latter's notion of ineffectively impeded entry, for example, is an essentially dynamic one. Similarly, Sylos hints that, where demand is growing, existing firms, to discourage entry, may have to keep their capacity somewhat larger than X_0 and their markup somewhat below P_0. Needless to say, the mere emphasis on the problem of entry is, per se, a significant movement in the direction of a dynamic analysis.

THEORY OF DISTRIBUTION

27

ALTERNATIVE THEORIES
OF DISTRIBUTION *

NICHOLAS KALDOR teaches at King's College, Cambridge; he was formerly at Cambridge University.

According to the Preface of Ricardo's *Principles,* the discovery of the laws which regulate distributive shares is the "principal problem in Political Economy". The purpose of this paper is to present a bird's-eye view of the various theoretical attempts, since Ricardo, at solving this "principal problem". Though all attempts at classification in such a vast field are necessarily to some extent arbitrary, and subjective to the writer, in terms of broad classification, one should, I think, distinguish between four main strands of thought, some of which contain important sub-groups. The first of these is the Ricardian, or Classical Theory, the second the Marxian, the third the Neo-Classical or Marginalist Theory and the fourth the Keynesian. The inclusion of a separate "Keynesian" theory in this context may cause surprise. An attempt will be made to show, however, that the specifically Keynesian apparatus of thought could be applied to the problem of distribution, rather than to the problem of the general level of production; that there is evidence that in its early stages, Keynes' own thinking tended to develop in this direction—only to be diverted from it with the discovery (made some time between the publication of the *Treatise on Money* and the *General Theory*) that inflationary and deflationary tendencies could best be analysed in terms of the resulting changes in output and employment, rather than in their effects on prices.

The compression of a whole army of distinguished writers, and schools of thought, between Ricardo and Keynes (Marx aside) under the term of Neo-Classical or Marginalist Theory is harder to justify. For apart from the marginalists proper, the group would have to include such "non-marginalists" or quasi-marginalists (from the point of

---

* From *Essays in Value and Distribution* (London: Gerald Duckworth, 1960). Originally published in *The Review of Economic Studies,* Vol. XXIII, No. 2 (1955–56), pp. 83–100. Reprinted by permission of the author and *The Review of Economic Studies.*

view of distribution theory) as the Walrasians and the neo-Walrasians,[1] as well as the imperfect competitionists, who though marginalist, do not necessarily hold with the principle of Marginal Productivity. But as I shall hope to show, there are important aspects which all these theories have in common,[2] and which justifies bringing them under one broad umbrella.

Ricardo prefaced his statement by a reference to the historical fact that "in different stages of society the proportions of the whole produce of the earth which will be allotted to each of these (three) classes under the names of rent, profit and wages will be essentially *different*".[3] To-day a writer on the problem of distribution would almost be inclined to say the opposite—that "in different stages of (capitalist) society the proportions of the national income allotted to wages, profits, etc., are *essentially similar*". The famous "historical constancy" of the share of wages in the national income—and the similarity of these shares in different capitalist economies, such as the U.S. and the U.K.— was of course an unsuspected feature of capitalism in Ricardo's day. But to the extent that recent empirical research tends to contradict Ricardo's assumption about the variability of relative shares, it makes the question of what determines these shares, more, rather than less, intriguing. In fact no hypothesis as regards the forces determining distributive shares could be intellectually satisfying unless it succeeded in accounting for the relative stability of these shares in the advanced capitalist economies over the last 100 years or so, despite the phenomenal changes in the techniques of production, in the accumulation of capital relative to labour and in real income per head.

Ricardo's concern in the problem of distribution was not due, or not only due, to the interest in the question of distributive shares *per se*, but to the belief that the theory of distribution held the key to an understanding of the whole mechanism of the economic system—of the forces governing the rate of progress, of the ultimate incidence of taxation, of the effects of protection, and so on. It was through "the laws

---

[1] By the term "neo-Walrasians" I mean the American "linear programming" and "activity analysis" schools, as well as the general equilibrium model of von Neumann (*Review of Economic Studies*, 1945–6, Vol. XIII (1)) whose technique shows certain affinities with Walras even though their basic assumptions (in particular that of the "circularity" of the production process) are quite different. From the point of view of distribution theory, however, the approach only yields a solution (in the shape of an equalibrium interest rate) on the assumption of constant real wages (due to an infinitely elastic supply curve of labour); it shows therefore more affinity with the classical models than with the neo-classical theories.

[2] With the possible exception of the "neo-Walrasian" group referred to above.

[3] Preface (my italics).

'which regulate distributive shares" that he was hoping to build what in present-day parlance we would call "a simple macro-economic model".[4] In this respect, if no other, the Ricardian and the "Keynesian" theories are analogous.[5] With the neo-Classical or Marginalist theories, on the other hand, the problem of distribution is merely one aspect of the general pricing process; it has no particular theoretical significance apart from the importance of the question *per se.* Nor do these theories yield a "macro-economic model" of the kind that exhibits the reaction-mechanism of the system through the choice of a strictly limited number of dependent and independent variables.

I. THE RICARDIAN THEORY

Ricardo's theory was based on two separate principles which we may term the "marginal principle" and the "surplus principle" respectively. The "marginal principle" serves to explain the share of rent, and the "surplus principle" the division of the residue between wages and profits. To explain the Ricardian model, we must first divide the economy into two broad branches, agriculture and industry and then show how, on Ricardo's assumptions, the forces operating in agriculture serve to determine distribution in industry.

The agricultural side of the picture can be exhibited in terms of a simple diagram (Fig. 1), where Oy measures quantities of "corn" (standing for all agricultural produce) and Ox the amount of labour employed in agriculture. At a given state of knowledge and in a given natural environment the curve $p\text{-}Ap$ represents the product per unit of labour and the curve $p\text{-}Mp$ the marginal product of labour. The existence of these two *separate* curves is a consequence of a declining tendency in the average product curve—i.e. of the assumption of diminishing returns. Corn-output is thus uniquely determined when the quantity of labour is given:[6] for any given working force, OM, total

4 "Political Economy", he told Malthus, "you think is an enquiry into the nature and causes of wealth—I think it should rather be called an enquiry into the laws which determine the division of the produce of industry amongst the classes who concur in its formation. No law can be laid down respecting quantity, but a tolerably correct one can be laid down respecting proportions. Every day I am more satisfied that the former enquiry is vain and delusive, and the latter only the true object of the science." (Letter dated 9 October, 1820, *Works* (Sraffa edition), Vol. VIII, pp. 278-9).
5 And so of course is the Marxian: but then the Marxian theory is really only a simplified version of Ricardo, clothed in a different garb.
6 This abstracts from variations in output per head due to the use of more or less fixed capital relative to labour—otherwise the curves could not be uniquely drawn, relative to a given state of technical knowledge. As between fixed capital and labour therefore the model assumes fixed coefficients; as between labour and land, variable coefficients.

output is represented by the rectangle $OCDM$. Rent is the difference between the product of labour on "marginal" land and the product on average land, or (allowing for the intensive, as well as the extensive, margin) the difference between average and marginal labour productivity which depends on the elasticity of the p–Ap curve, i.e. the extent to which diminishing returns operate.

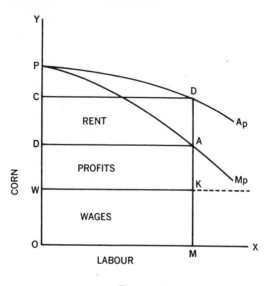

Figure 1

The marginal product of labour (or, in classical parlance, the "produce-minus-rent") is not however equal to the wage, but to the sum of wages and profits. The rate of wages is determined quite independently of marginal productivity by the supply price of labour which Ricardo assumed to be constant in terms of corn. In modern parlance, the Ricardian hypothesis implies an infinitely elastic supply curve of labour at the given supply price, OW.[7] The demand for labour is not

---

[7] The basis of this assumption is the Malthusian theory of population, according to which numbers will increase (indefinitely) when wages are above, and decrease (indefinitely) when they are below, the "subsistence level". In Ricardo's hands this doctrine had lost its sharp focus on a biologically determined quantum of subsistence to which the supply price of labour must be tied; he emphasised that habits of restraint engendered in a civilised environment can permanently secure for labour higher standards of living than the bare minimum for survival. Yet he retained the important operative principle that in any given social and cultural environment there is a *"natural* rate of wages" at which alone population could remain stationary and from which wages can only deviate temporarily. The hy-

determined however by the p–Mp curve, but by the accumulation of capital which determines how many labourers can find employment at the wage rate OW. Hence the equilibrium position is not indicated by the point of intersection between the p–Mp curve and the supply curve of labour, but by the aggregate demand for labour in terms of corn—the "wages fund".[8] As capital accumulates, the labour force will grow, so that any addition to the total wage fund, through capital accumulation—the *agricultural* wages fund is indicated by the area $OWKM$—will tend to be a horizontal addition (pushing the vertical line KM to the right) and not a vertical one (pushing the horizontal line WK upwards).[9]

For any given M, profits are thus a residue, arising from the difference between the marginal product of labour and the rate of wages. The resulting ratio, $\dfrac{\text{Profits}}{\text{Wages}}$ determines the rate of profit % on the capital employed; it is moreover *equal* to that ratio, on the assumption that

---

pothesis of an infinitely elastic supply curve of labour thus did not necessarily imply that this supply price must be equal to the bare minimum of subsistence. Yet this assumption was inconsistent with another (implied) feature of his model discussed below, that wages are not only *fixed* in terms of "corn" but are entirely (or almost entirely) *spent* on corn.

8 Total wages depend on—and are "paid out of"—capital simply because production takes time, and the labourers (unlike the landlords) not being in the position to afford to wait, have their wages "advanced" to them by the capitalists. This is true of fixed as well as circulating capital but since, with the former, the turnover period is relatively long, only a small part of annual wages is paid out of fixed capital; the amount of circulating capital was therefore treated as the proper "wages fund". Despite his analysis of the effect of changes in wages on the amount of fixed capital used relative to labour, i.e. on the proportions of fixed and circulating capital employed in production (Professor Hayek's celebrated "Ricardo effect"), for the purpose of his distribution theory this ratio should be taken as given, irrespective of the rate of profit.

9 The feature which the modern mind may find most difficult to swallow is not that capital accumulation should lead to a rise in population but that the reaction should be taken as something so swift as to ignore the intervening stage, where the increase in the wages fund should raise the rate of wages rather than the numbers employed. The adjustment of population to changes in the demand for labour would normally be treated as a slow long-run effect whereas changes in the demand for labour (caused by capital accumulation) may be swift or sudden. Ricardo, however, conceived the economy as one which proceeds at a more or less steady rate of growth in time, with the accumulation of capital going on at a (more or less constant) rate; while he conceded that *changes* in the rate of capital accumulation will temporarily raise or lower wages, he assumed that the rate of population growth itself is adapted to a certain rate of capital accumulation which had been going on for some time.

the capital is turned over once a year, so that the capital employed is equal to the annual wages-bill. (This latter proposition, however, is merely a simplification, and not an essential part of the story.)

In a state of equilibrium, the money-rate of profit % earned on capital must be the same in industry and in agriculture, otherwise capital would move from one form of employment to the other. But it is the peculiarity of agriculture that the money-rate of profit in that industry cannot diverge from the rate of profit measured in terms of that industry's own product, i.e. the corn-rate of profit. This is because in agriculture both the input (the wage outlay) and the output consist of the same commodity, "corn". In manufacturing industry on the other hand, input and output consist of heterogeneous commodities— the cost per man is fixed in corn, while the product per man, in a given state of technical knowledge, is fixed in terms of manufactured goods. Hence the only way equality in the rate of profit in money terms can be attained as between the two branches is through the prices of in- dustrial goods becoming dearer or cheaper in terms of agricultural products. The money-rate of profit in manufacturing industry there- fore depends on the corn-rate of profit in agriculture; [10] the latter, on the other hand, is entirely a matter of the margin of cultivation, which in turn is a reflection (in a closed economy and in a given state of technical knowledge) of the extent of capital accumulation. Thus "diminishing fertility of the soil", as James Mill put it, "is the great and ultimately only necessary cause of a fall in profit".

To make the whole structure logically consistent it is necessary to suppose, not only that wages are fixed in terms of "corn" but that they are entirely spent on "corn", for otherwise any change in the relation between industrial and agricultural prices will alter real wages (in terms of commodities in general) so that the size of the "surplus", and the rate of profit on capital generally is no longer derivable from the "corn-rate of profit"—the relationship between the product of labour and the cost of labour working on marginal land. Assuming that agri- cultural products ("corn") are wage-goods and manufactured products are non-wage-goods (i.e. ignoring that *some* agricultural products are consumed by capitalists, and *some* non-agricultural products by wage- earners), the whole corn-output (the area $OCDM$ in the diagram) can be taken as the annual wages fund, of which $OWKM$ is employed in agriculture and $WCDK$ in the rest of the economy. Any increase in

[10] The analytical basis for this conclusion, given above, was never, as Sraffa remarks, stated by Ricardo in any of his extant letters and papers though there is evidence from Malthus's remarks that he must have formulated it either in a lost paper on the Profits of Capital or in conversation (cf. *Works*, Vol. I, Introduction, p. xxxi).

OWKM (caused, e.g., by protection to agriculture) must necessarily lower the rate of profit (which is the source of all accumulation) and thus slow down the rate of growth.[11] Similarly all taxes, other than those levied on land, must ultimately fall on, and be paid out of, profits, and thus slow down the rate of accumulation. Taxation and agricultural protection thus tend to accelerate the tendency (which is in any case inevitable—unless *continued* technical progress manages to shift the *p–Ap* and *p–Mp* curves to the right sufficiently to suspend altogether the operation of the Law of Diminishing Returns) to that ultimate state of gloom, the Stationary State, where accumulation ceases simply because "profits are so low as not to afford [the capitalists more than] an adequate compensation for their trouble and the risk which they must necessarily encounter in employing their capital productively".[12]

II. THE MARXIAN THEORY

The Marxian theory is essentially an adaptation of Ricardo's "surplus theory". The main analytical differences are: (1) that Marx paid no attention to (and did not believe in) the Law of Diminishing Returns, and hence made no analytical distinction between rent and profits; (2) that Marx regarded the supply price of labour (the "cost of reproduction" of labour) as being fixed, not in terms of "corn", but of commodities in general. Hence he regarded the share of profits (including rent) in output as determined simply by the surplus of the product per unit of labour over the supply price (or cost) of labour—or the surplus of production to the consumption necessary for production.[13]

There are important differences also as between Marx and Ricardo in two other respects. The first of these concerns the reasons for wages being tied to the subsistence level. In Marx's theory this is ensured through the fact that at any one time the supply of labour—the number of workers seeking wage-employment—tends to exceed the demand

11 The evil of agricultural protection is thus not only that income is reduced through the transfer of labour to less productive employments, but that owing to the reduction in the rate of profit, industrial prices fall in terms of agricultural prices; income is thus transferred from the classes which use their wealth productively to classes which use it unproductively.

12 Ricardo, *Principles,* p. 122 (Sraffa Edition).

13 Ricardo himself abandoned in the *Principles* the idea that wages *consist* of corn (to the exclusion of manufactures), but whether he also abandoned the idea that the agricultural surplus is critical to the whole distribution process through the fixity of wages in terms of *corn only* is not clear. (Cf. Sraffa, *op. cit.,* pp. xxxii–xxxiii.)

for labour. The existence of an unemployed fringe—the "reserve army" of labour—prevents wages from rising above the minimum that must be paid to enable the labourers to perform the work. Marx assumed that as capitalist enterprise progresses at the expense of pre-capitalistic enterprise more labourers are released through the disappearance of the non-capitalist or handicraft units than are absorbed in the capitalist sector, owing to the difference in productivity per head between the two sectors. As long as the growth of capitalist enterprise is at the cost of a shrinkage of pre-capitalist enterprise the increase in the supply of wage labour will thus tend to run ahead of the increase in the demand for wage labour.

Sooner or later, however, the demand for labour resulting from accumulation by capitalist enterprise will run ahead of the increase in supply; at that stage labour becomes scarce, wages rise, profits are wiped out and capitalism is faced with a "crisis". (The crisis in itself slows down the rate of accumulation and reduces the demand for labour at any given state of accumulation by increasing the "organic composition of capital", so that the "reserve army" will sooner or later be re-created.)

The second important difference relates to the motives behind capital accumulation. For Ricardo this was simply to be explained by the lure of a high rate of profit. Capitalists accumulate voluntarily so long as the rate of profit exceeds the minimum "necessary compensation" for the risks and trouble encountered in the productive employment of capital. For Marx, however, accumulation by capitalist enterprise is not a matter of choice but a necessity, due to competition among the capitalists themselves. This in turn was explained by the existence of economies of large-scale production (together with the implicit assumption that the amount of capital employed by any particular capitalist is governed by his own accumulation). Given the fact that the larger the scale of operations the more efficient the business, each capitalist is forced to increase the size of his business through the re-investment of his profits if he is not to fall behind in the competitive struggle.

It is only at a later stage, when the increasing concentration of production in the hands of the more successful enterprises removes the competitive necessity for accumulation—the stage of "monopoly capitalism"—that in the Marxian scheme there is room for economic crises, not on account of an excessive increase in the demand for labour following on accumulation, but on account of an insufficiency of effective demand—the failure of markets resulting from the inability of the capitalists either to spend or to invest the full amounts of profits (which Marx called the problem of "realising surplus value").

Marx has also taken over from Ricardo, and the classical economists generally the idea of a falling rate of profit with the progressive accumulation of capital. But whereas with the classicists this was firmly grounded on the Law of Diminishing Returns, Marx, having discarded that law, had no firm base for it. His own explanation is based on the assumed increase in the ratio of fixed to circulating capital (in Marxian terminology, "constant" to "variable" capital) with the progress of capitalism; but as several authors have pointed out,[14] the law of the falling rate of profit cannot really be derived from the law of the "increasing organic composition" of capital. Since Marx assumes that the supply price of labour remains unchanged in terms of commodities when the organic composition of capital, and hence output per head, rises, there is no more reason to assume that an increase in "organic composition" will yield a lower rate of profit than a higher rate. For even if output per man were assumed to increase more slowly than ("constant" plus "variable") capital per man, the "surplus value" per man (the excess of output per man over the costs of reproduction of labour) will necessarily increase faster than output per man, and may thus secure a rising rate of profit even if there is diminishing productivity to successive additions to fixed capital per unit of labour.

While some of Marx's predictions—such as the increasing concentration of production in the hands of large enterprises—proved accurate, his most important thesis, the steady worsening of the living conditions of the working classes—"the immiseration of the proletariat" [15]—has been contradicted by experience, in both the "competitive" and "monopoly" stages of capitalism. On the Marxian model the share of wages in output must necessarily fall with every increase in output per head. The theory can only allow for a rise of wages in terms of commodities as a result of the collective organisation of the working classes which forces the capitalists to reduce the degree of exploitation and to surrender to the workers some of the "surplus value." [16] This hypothesis, however, will only yield a constant share of wages on the

---

[14] Cf., in particular, Joan Robinson, *An Essay in Marxian Economics*, pp. 75–82.

[15] It is not clear, in terms of Marx's own theoretical model, why such a progressive immiseration should take place—since the costs of reproduction of labour appear to set an *absolute* limit to the extent to which labour can be exploited. Some parts of *Das Kapital* could, however, be construed as suggesting that wages can be driven below the (long run) reproduction cost of labour, at the cost of a (long run) shrinkage in the labour force: and with the increasing organic composition of capital, and the rise of monopolies, the demand for labour may show an equally declining tendency.

[16] Marx himself would have conceived a reduction in the "degree of exploitation" in terms of a reduction in the length of the working day rather than a rise in real wages per day. In fact both have occurred side by side.

extremely far-fetched assumption that the rate of increase in the bargaining strength of labour, due to the growth of collective organisation, precisely keeps pace with the rate of increase in output per head.

III. THE NEO-CLASSICAL THEORIES

(A) MARGINAL PRODUCTIVITY

While Marx's theory thus derives from Ricardo's surplus principle, neo-classical value and distribution theory derives from another part of the Ricardian model: the "marginal principle" introduced for the explanation of rent (which explains why both Marx and Marshall are able to claim Ricardo as their precursor). The difference between Ricardo and the neo-classics is (1) that whereas Ricardo employed the "principle of substitution" (or rather, the principle of "limited substitutability"—which is the basic assumption underlying all marginal analysis) only as regards the use of labour relative to land, in neo-classical theory this doctrine was formalised and generalised, and assumed to hold true of any factor, in relation to any other; [17] (2) whereas Ricardo employed the principle for showing that a "fixed" factor will earn a surplus, determined by the gap between the average and marginal product of the variable factor, neo-classical theory concentrated on the reverse aspect—i.e. that any factor variable in supply will obtain a remuneration which, under competitive conditions, must correspond to its marginal product. Thus if the total supply of *all* factors (and not only land) is being taken as given, independently of price, and all are assumed to be limited substitutes to one another, the share-out of the whole produce can be regarded as being determined by the marginal rates of substitution between them. Thus in terms of

[17] As well as of any particular commodity in the sphere of consumption. The utility theory of value is really Ricardian rent-theory applied to consumption demand. In fact, as Walras has shown, limited substitutability in consumption might in itself be sufficient to determine distributive shares, provided that the proportions in which the different factors are used are different in different industries. His solution of the problem of distribution, based on "fixed coefficients" of production (intended only as a first approximation) is subject, however, to various snags since the solution of his equations may yield negative prices for the factors as well as positive ones and it cannot be determined beforehand whether this will be the case or not. If the solution of the equations yields negative prices the factors in question have to be excluded as "free goods"; and the operation (if necessary) successively repeated until only factors with positive prices are left. Also, it is necessary to suppose that the number of different "factors" is no greater than the number of different "products"; otherwise the solution is indeterminate.

our diagram, if we assumed that along Ox we measure the quantity of any particular factor of production, x, the quantities of all the others being taken as fixed, p–Mp will exhibit the marginal productivity function of the variable factor. If the actual employment of that factor is taken to be M, AM will represent its demand price per unit, and the rectangle $OBAM$ its share in the total produce. Since this principle could be applied to any factor, it must be true of all (including, as Walras and Wicksell have shown, the factors owned by the entrepreneur himself) hence the rectangle $BCDA$ must be sufficient, and only just sufficient, for remunerating all other factors but x on the basis of their respective marginal productivities. This, as Wicksteed has shown,[18] requires the assumption that the production function is homogeneous of the first degree for all variables taken together—an assumption which he himself regarded as little more than a tautology, if "factors of production" are appropriately defined.[19] From the point of view of the theory, however, the *appropriate* definition of factors involves the elimination of intermediate products and their conversion into "ultimate" or "original" factors, since only on this definition can one assume the properties of divisibility and variability of coefficients. When factors are thus defined, the assumption of constant returns to scale is by no means a tautology; it is a restrictive assumption, which may be regarded, however, as being co-extensive with other restrictive assumptions implied by the theory—i.e. the universal rule of perfect competition, and the absence of external economies and diseconomies.

The basic difficulty with the whole approach does not lie, however, in this so-called "adding-up problem" but in the very meaning of "capital" as a factor of production.[20] Whilst land can be measured in acres-per-year and labour in man-hours, capital (as distinct from

---

18 *The Co-ordination of the Laws of Distribution* (1894).

19 *The Co-ordination of the Laws of Distribution* (1894), p. 53. "We must regard every kind and quality of labour that can be distinguished from other kinds and qualities as a separate factor; and in the same way, every kind of land will be taken as a separate factor. Still more important is it to insist that instead of speaking of so many £'s worth of capital we shall speak of so many ploughs, so many tons of manure, and so many horses or footpounds of power. Each of these may be scheduled in its own unit." Under these conditions it is true to say that "doubling all factors will double the product", but since these "factors" are indivisible in varying degrees, it does not mean that the production function is a linear and homogeneous one in relation to incremental variations of output. Also a change in output may be associated with the introduction of *new* factors of production.

20 For a general equilibrium system, capital goods cannot be regarded as factors of production *per se* (in the manner suggested by Wicksteed), otherwise the same things are simultaneously treated as the parameters and the unknowns of the system.

"capital goods") cannot be measured in terms of physical units.[21] To evaluate the marginal product of labour it is necessary to isolate two situations containing identical "capital" but two different quantities of labour, or identical amounts of labour, and two differing quantities of "capital", in precise numerical relationship.[22]

Marshall, without going into the matter in any detail, had shown in several passages that he was dimly aware of this; and in carefully re-defining marginal productivity so as to mean "marginal *net* productivity" (*net* after deduction of all associated expenses on other "factors") he shied away from the task of putting forward a general theory of distribution altogether.[23]

In fact, in so far as we can speak of a "Marshallian" theory of distribution at all, it is in the sense of a "short period" theory, which regards profits as the "quasi-rents" earned on the use of capital goods of various kinds, the supply of which can be treated as given for the time being, as a heritage of the past. The doctrine of the "quasi-rent" as-similates capital as a factor of production to Ricardian land: the separate *kinds* of capital goods being treated as so many different kinds of "land". Here the problem of the measurement of capital as a factor of production does not arise: since, strictly speaking, no kind of change or reorganisation in the stock of intermediate products is permitted in connection with a change in the level or composition of production. It was this aspect of Marshall which, consciously or sub-consciously, pro-vided the "model" for most of the post-Marshallian Cambridge theo-rising. Prices are equal to, or determined by, marginal prime costs; profits are determined by the difference between marginal and average prime costs; prime costs, for the system as a whole, are labour costs (since raw-material costs, for a closed economy at any rate, disappear if

---

21 Measurement in terms of value (as so many £'s of "capital") already assumes a certain rate of interest, on the basis of which services accruing in different periods in the future, or costs incurred at different dates in the past, are brought to a measure of equivalence.

22 The product of the "marginal shepherd" is the difference in terms of numbers of sheep, between 10 shepherds using 10 crooks and 11 shepherds using 11 slightly inferior crooks, the term "slightly inferior" being taken to mean that the 11 crooks in the one case represent precisely the same amount of "capital" as the 10 crooks in the other case. (Cf. also Robertson, "Wage Grumbles", in *Economic Fragments*, 1931).

23 "The doctrine that the earnings of a worker tend to be equal to the net product of his work, has by itself no real meaning; since in order to estimate the net product, we have to take for granted all the expenses of production of the com-modity on which he works, other than his own wages." Similarly, the doctrine that the marginal efficiency of capital will tend to equal the rate of interest "can-not be made into a theory of interest, any more than a theory of wages, without reasoning in a circle". (Cf. *Principles*, 8th edition, Book VI, Chapter I, paras. 7-8.)

all branches of industry are taken together); ultimately therefore the division of output between profits and wages is a matter depending on the existence of diminishing returns to labour, as more labour is used in conjunction with a *given* capital equipment; and is determined by the elasticity of labour's average productivity curve which fixes the share of quasi-rents.

Marshall himself would have disagreed with the use of the quasi-rent doctrine as a distribution theory, holding that distributive shares in the short period are determined by long-period forces.[24] Clearly even if one were to hold strictly to the assumption that "profit margins" are the outcome of short-period profit-maximisation, this "short-period" approach does not really get us anywhere: for the extent to which diminishing returns operate for labour in conjunction with the capital equipment available to-day is itself a function of the price-relationships which have ruled in the past because these have determined the quantities of each of the kinds of equipment available. The theory does not therefore really amount to more than saying that the prices of to-day are derived from the prices of yesterday—a proposition which is the more true and the more trivial the shorter the "day" is conceived to be, in terms of chronological time.

For the true neo-classical attempt to solve the general problem of distribution we must go to Wicksell who though that by integrating the Austrian approach to capital with Walrasian equilbrium theory he could provide a general solution, treating capital as a two-dimensional quantity, the product of time and labour. The "time" in this case is the investment period or waiting period separating the application of "original" factors from the emergence of the final product, and the marginal productivity of capital the added product resulting from an extension of "time". This attempt, again, came to grief (as Wicksell himself came near to acknowledging late in life): [25] (i) owing to the impossibility of measuring that period in terms of an "average" of some kind; [26] (ii) owing to the impossibility of combining the investment periods of different "original" factors in a single measure.[27]

24 Cf., in particular, *Principles*, 8th edition, Book V, Chapters V and VI, and Book VI, Chapter VIII, para. 4.
25 Cf. the concluding passage of his posthumous contribution to the Wieser Festschrift. *Die Wirtschaftstheorie der Gegenwart* (1928), Vol. III, pp. 208–9; also his "Analysis of Akerman's Problem", reprinted in *Lectures*, Vol. I, p. 270.
26 Since owing to compound interest, the weights to be used in the calculation of the average will themselves be dependent on the rate of interest.
27 For a more extended treatment cf. my articles on capital theory in *Econometrica*, April, 1937, and May, 1938; also Joan Robinson, "The Production Function in the Theory of Capital", *Review of Economic Studies*, Vol. XXI (1953–4), p. 81, and "Comment" by D. G. Champernowne, *ibid.*, p. 112.

In fact the whole approach which regards the share of wages and of profits in output as being determined by the marginal rate of subtsitution between Capital and Labour—with its corollary, that the constancy of relative shares is evidence of a unit-Elasticity of Substitution between Capital and Labour [28]—is hardly acceptable to present-day economists. Its inadequacy becomes evident as soon as it is realised that "the marginal rate of substitution" between Capital and Labour—as distinct from the marginal rate of substitution between labour and land—can only be determined once the rate of profit and the rate of wages are already known. The same technical alternatives might yield very different "marginal rates of substitution" according as the ratio of profits to wages is one thing or another. The theory asserts, in effect, that the rate of interest in the capital market (and the associated wage rate in the labour market) is determined by the condition that at any lower interest rate (and higher wage rate) capital would be invested in such "labour-saving" forms as would provide insufficient employment to the available labour; whilst at any higher rate, capital would be invested in forms that offered more places of employment than could be filled with the available labour.

Quite apart from all conceptual difficulties, the theory focuses attention on a relatively unimportant feature of a growing economy. For accumulation does not take the form of "deepening" the structure of capital (at a given state of knowledge) but rather in keeping pace with technical progress and the growth in the labour force. It is difficult to swallow a theory which says, in effect, that wages and profits are what they are for otherwise there would be too much deepening or too little deepening (the capital/output ratios would be either too large or too small) to be consistent with simultaneous equilibrium in the savings-investment market and in the labour market.

(B) The "Degree of Monopoly" Theories of Distribution

Monopoly profit was always regarded as a distinct form of revenue in neo-classical theory, though not one of any great quantitative importance since the mass of commodities was thought of as being produced under competitive conditions. But the modern theories of imperfect competition emphasise that monopoly profit is not an isolated feature. Profits in general contain an *element* of monopoly revenue—an element that is best defined as the excess of the actual profit margin in output over what the profit margin would have been under perfectly competitive conditions. Under Marshallian "short-period" assumptions

---

[28] Cf. Hicks, *The Theory of Wages* (1932), Chapter VI, passim.

the perfectly-competitive profit margin is given by the excess of marginal cost over average prime costs. The additional monopoly element is indicated by the excess of price over marginal cost. The former, as we have seen, is a derivative of the elasticity of labour's productivity curve where capital equipment of all kinds is treated as given. The latter is a derivative of the elasticity of demand facing the individual firm. The novel feature of imperfect competition theories is to have shown that the increase of profit margins due to this element of monopoly need not imply a corresponding excess in the rates of profit on capital over the competitive rate; through the generation of excess capacity (i.e. the tendency of demand curves to become "tangential" to the cost curves) the latter may approach a "competitive" or "normal" rate (as a result of the consequential rise in the capital/output ratio) even if the former is above the competitive level.

Kalecki [29] built on this a simplified theory of distribution, where the share of profits in output is shown to be determined by the elasticity of demand alone. This was based on the hypothesis that in the short period, labour and capital equipment are largely "limitational" and not "substitutional" factors, with the result that the short-period prime cost-curve is a reverse L-shaped one (prime costs being constant up to full capacity output). In that case marginal costs are equal to average prime costs; the ratio of price to prime costs (and hence, in a closed economy, the ratio of gross profits to wages) is thus entirely accounted for by the elasticity of the firm's demand curve.

On closer inspection, however, the elasticity of the demand curve facing the individual firm turned out to be no less of a broken reed than its counterpart, the elasticity of substitution between factors. There is no evidence that firms in imperfect markets set their prices by reference to the elasticity of their sales-function, or that short-period pricing is the outcome of any deliberate attempt to maximise profits by reference to an independent revenue and a cost function. Indeed the very notion of a demand curve for the products of a single firm is illegitimate if the prices charged by different firms cannot be assumed to be independent of each other.[30]

[29] The original version appeared in *Econometrica*, April, 1938. Subsequent versions appeared in *Essays in the Theory of Economic Fluctuations* (1938), Chapter I, *Studies in Economic Dynamics* (1943), Chapter I, and *Theory of Dynamic Economics* (1954) Part I.

[30] The theory of the "kinked" demand curve is in fact no more than a recognition of the fact that the demand curve of the firm (in the sense required for the purpose of deriving price from the postulate of profit maximisation) is nonexistent. Since the position of the "kink" *depends* on the price, it cannot *determine* the price; it thus leaves the profit margin completely undetermined.

In the later versions of his theory Kalecki abandoned the link between the "degree of monopoly" and the elasticity of demand, and was content with a purely tautological approach according to which the ratio of price to prime costs was *defined* simply as the "degree of monopoly". Propositions based on implicit definitions of this kind make of course no assertion about reality and possess no explanatory value. Unless the "degree of monopoly" can be defined in terms of market relationships of some kind (as, for example, in terms of the cross-elasticities of demand for the products of the different firms) [31] and an attempt is made to demonstrate how these market relationships determine the relation between prices and costs, the theory does not provide a hypothesis which could be affirmed or refuted.

There is no need, of course, to follow Kalecki in the attempt to lend spurious precision to the doctrine through implicit theorising—a vice which afflicts all theories which we grouped together as "neo-classical" in varying degrees. Fundamentally, the proposition that the distribution of income between wages and profits depends on market structures, on the strength or weakness of the forces of competition, is not a tautological one; it asserts *something* about reality (which may in principle be proved false) even if that "something" cannot be given a logically precise formulation. Just as the positive content of the marginal productivity theory can be summed up by the statement that the rate of profit on capital (and the margin of profit in output) is governed by the need to prevent the capital/output ratio from being either too large or too small, the positive content of the "degree of monopoly" theory can be summed up in the sentence that "profit margins are what they are because the forces of competition prevent them from being higher than they are and are not powerful enough to make them lower than they are". Unfortunately neither of these statements get us very far.

Dissatisfaction with the tautological character and the formalism of the "marginal revenue-equals-marginal cost" type of price theory led to the formulation of the "full cost" theories of pricing,[32] according to which producers in imperfect markets set their prices independently of the character of demand, and solely on the basis of their long-run costs of production (including the "normal" rate of profit on their own capital). If these theories asserted no more than that prices in manu-

---

[31] The "cross-elasticities" of demand indicate the degree of interdependence of the markets of different firms and are thus inversely related to monopoly power in the usual sense of the word.

[32] Cf. Hall and Hitch, *Oxford Economic Papers*, 1939; P. W. S. Andrews, *Manufacturing Business* (1949).

facturing industry are *not* determined by the criterion of short-run profit-maximisation, and that profit margins can be fairly insensitive to short-period variations in demand [33] (the impact effect of changes in demand being on the rate of production, rather than on prices), they would provide a healthy antidote to a great deal of facile theorising. When, however, they go beyond this and assert that prices are determined quite independently of demand, they in effect destroy existing price theory without putting anything else in its place. Quite apart from the fact that a "full cost" theory is quite unable to explain why some firms should be more successful in earning profits than others, the level of the "normal profit" on which the full cost calculations are supposed to be based is left quite undetermined. The very fact that these full cost theories should have received such widespread and serious consideration as an alternative explanation of the pricing process is an indication of the sad state of vagueness and confusion into which the neo-classical value theory had fallen.

IV. THE KEYNESIAN THEORY

Keynes, as far as I know, was never interested in the problem of distribution as such. One may nevertheless christen a particular theory of distribution as "Keynesian" if it can be shown to be an application of

[33] This, I believe, was the intention of the original Hall-Hitch article. Cf. Marshall, *Principles*, Book VI, Chapter VIII, paragraph 4: "We see then that there is no general tendency of profits on the turnover to equality; but there may be, and as a matter of fact there is, in each trade and in every branch of each trade, a more or less definite rate of profits on the turnover which is regarded as a 'fair' or normal rate. Of course these rates are always changing in consequence of changes in the methods of trade; which are generally begun by individuals who desire to do a larger trade at a lower rate of profit on the turnover than has been customary, but at a larger rate of profit per annum on their capital. If however there happens to be no great change of this kind going on, the traditions of the trade that a certain rate of profit on the turnover should be charged for a particular class of work are of great practical service to those in the trade. Such traditions are the outcome of much experience tending to show that, if that rate is charged, a proper allowance will be made for all the costs (supplementary as well as prime) incurred for that particular purpose, and in addition the normal rate of profits per annum in that class of business will be afforded. If they charge a price which gives much less than this rate of profit on the turnover they can hardly prosper; and if they charge much more they are in danger of losing their custom, since others can afford to undersell them. This is the 'fair' rate of profit on the turnover, which an honest man is expected to charge for making goods to order, when no price has been agreed on beforehand; and it is the rate which a court of law will allow in case a dispute should arise between buyer and seller." Cf. also Kahn, *Economic Journal*, 1952, p. 119.

the specifically Keynesian apparatus of thought and if evidence can
be adduced that at some stage in the development of his ideas, Keynes
came near to formulating such a theory.[34] The principle of the Multiplier (which in some ways was anticipated in the *Treatise* but without
a clear view of its implications) could be alternatively applied to a
determination of the relation between prices and wages, if the level of
output and employment is taken as given, or the determination of the
level of employment, if distribution (i.e. the relation between prices
and wages) is taken as given. The reason why the multiplier-analysis
has not been developed as a distribution theory is precisely because it
was invented for the purpose of an employment theory—to explain
why an economic system can remain in equilibrium in a state of underemployment (or of a general under-utilisation of resources), where the
classical properties of scarcity-economics are inapplicable. And its use
for the one appears to exclude its use for the other.[35] If we assume that
the balance of savings and investment is brought about through variations in the relationship of prices and costs, we are not only bereft of a

[34] I am referring to the well-known passage on profits being likened to a "widow's
cruse" in the *Treatise on Money*, Vol. I, p. 139. "If entrepreneurs choose to
spend a portion of their profits on consumption (and there is, of course, nothing
to prevent them from doing this) the effect is to *increase* the profits on the sale
of liquid consumption goods by an amount exactly equal to the amount of
profits which have been thus expended. . . . Thus, however much of their profits
entrepreneurs spend on consumption, the increment of wealth belonging to entrepreneurs remains the same as before. Thus profits, as a source of capital increment for entrepreneurs, are a widow's cruse which remains undepleted however much of them may be devoted to riotous living. When on the other hand,
entrepreneurs are making losses, and seek to recoup these losses by curtailing
their normal expenditure on consumption, i.e. by saving more, the cruse becomes
a Danaid jar which can never be filled up; for the effect of this reduced expenditure is to inflict on the producers of consumption-goods a loss of an equal
amount. Thus the diminution of their wealth as a class is as great, in spite of
their savings, as it was before." This passage, I think, contains the true seed of
the ideas developed in the *General Theory*—as well as showing the length of the
road that had to be traversed before arriving at the conceptual framework presented in the latter work. The fact that "profits", "savings" etc. were all defined
here in a special sense that was later discarded, and that the argument specifically
refers to expenditure on consumption goods, rather than entrepreneurial expenditure in general, should not blind us to the fact that here Keynes regards entrepreneurial incomes as being the resultant of their expenditure decisions, rather
than the other way round—which is perhaps the most important difference between "Keynesian" and "pre-Keynesian" habits of thought.

[35] Although this application of Keynesian theory has been implicit in several discussions of the problem of inflation. (Cf. e.g. A. J. Brown, *The Great Inflation*,
Macmillan, 1955.)

principle for explaining variations in output and employment, but the whole idea of separate "aggregate" demand and supply functions—the principle of "effective demand"—falls to the ground; we are back to Say's Law, where output as a whole is limited by available resources, and a fall in effective demand for one kind of commodity (in real terms) generates compensating increases in effective demand (again in real terms) for others. Yet these two uses of the Multiplier principle are not as incompatible as would appear at first sight: the Keynesian technique, as I hope to show, can be used for both purposes, provided the one is conceived as a short-run theory and the other as a long-run theory—or rather, the one is used in the framework of a static model, and the other in the framework of a dynamic growth model.[36]

We shall assume, to begin with, a state of full employment (we shall show later the conditions under which a state of full employment will *result* from our model) so that total output or income (Y) is given. Income may be divided into two broad categories, Wages and Profits (W and P), where the wage-category comprises not only manual labour but salaries as well, and Profits the income of property owners generally, and not only of entrepreneurs; the important difference between them being in the marginal propensities to consume (or save), wage-earners' marginal savings being small in relation to those of capitalists.[37]

Writing S_w and S_p, for aggregate savings out of Wages and Profits, we have the following income identities:

---

[36] I first thought of using the Multiplier technique for purposes of a distribution theory when I attempted to analyse the ultimate incidence of profits taxation under full employment conditions in a paper prepared for the Royal Commission on Taxation in 1951. The further development of these ideas, and particularly their relationship to a dynamic theory of growth, owes a great deal to discussions with Mrs. Robinson, whose forthcoming book, *The Accumulation of Capital*, contains a systematic exploration of this field. I should also like to mention here that I owe a great deal of stimulus to a paper by Kalecki, "A Theory of Profits" (*Economic Journal*, June–September, 1942) whose approach is in some ways reminiscent of the "widows' cruse" of Keynes' *Treatise* even though Kalecki uses the technique, not for an explanation of the share of profits in output, but for showing why the *level* of output and its fluctuations is peculiarly dependent on entrepreneurial behaviour. (In doing so, he uses the restrictive assumption that savings are entirely supplied out of profits.) I have also been helped by Mr. Harry Johnson and Mr. Robin Marris, both in the working out of the formulae and in general discussion.

[37] This may be assumed independently of any skewness in the distribution of property, simply as a consequence of the fact that the bulk of profits accrues in the form of company profits and a high proportion of companies' marginal profits is put to reserve.

$$Y \equiv W + P$$
$$I \equiv S$$
$$S \equiv S_w + S_p$$

Taking investment as given and assuming simple proportional savings functions $S_w W = s_w$ and $S_p = s_p P$, we obtain:

$$I = s_p P + s_w W = s_p P + s_w (Y - P) = (s_p - s_w) P + s_w Y$$

Whence

$$\frac{I}{Y} = (s_p - s_w)\frac{P}{Y} + s_w \qquad \ldots (1)$$

and

$$\frac{P}{Y} = \frac{1}{s_p - s_w}\frac{I}{Y} - \frac{s_w}{s_p - s_w} \qquad \ldots (2)$$

Thus, given the wage-earners' and the capitalists' propensities to save, the share of profits in income depends simply on the ratio of investment to output.

The interpretative value of the model (as distinct from the formal validity of the equations, or identities) depends on the "Keynesian" hypothesis that investment, or rather, the ratio of investment to output, can be treated as an independent variable, invariant with respect to changes in the two savings propensities s_p and s_w. (We shall see later that this assumption can only be true within certain limits, and outside those limits the theory ceases to hold.) This, together with the assumption of "full employment", also implies that the level of prices in relation to the level of money wages is determined by demand: a rise in investment, and thus in total demand, will raise prices and profit margins, and thus reduce real consumption, whilst a fall in investment, and thus in total demand, causes a fall in prices (relatively to the wage level) and thereby generates a compensating rise in real consumption. Assuming flexible prices (or rather flexible profit margins) the system is thus stable at full employment.

The model operates only if the two savings propensities differ and the marginal propensity to save from profits exceeds that from wages, i.e. if:

$$s_p \neq s_w$$

and

$$s_p > s_w$$

The latter is the stability condition. For if $s_p < s_w$, a fall in prices would cause a fall in demand and thus generate a further fall in prices, and equally, a rise in prices would be cumulative. The degree of stability of the system depends on the *difference* of the marginal propensities, i.e. on $1/(s_p - s_w)$ which may be defined as the "coefficient of sensitivity of income distribution", since it indicates the change in the share of profits in income which follows upon a change in the share of investment in output.

If the difference between the marginal propensities is small, the co-efficient will be large, and small changes in I/Y (the investment/output relationship) will cause relatively large changes in income distribution P/Y; and vice versa.

In the limiting case where $s_w = 0$, the amount of profits is equal to the sum of investment and capitalist consumption, i.e.:

$$P = \frac{1}{s_p} I.$$

This is the assumption implicit in Keynes's parable about the widow's cruse—where a rise in entrepreneurial consumption raises their total profit by an *identical* amount—and of Mr. Kalecki's theory of profits which can be paraphrased by saying that "capitalists earn what they spend, and workers spend what they earn".

This model (i.e. the "special case" where $s_w = 0$) in a sense is the pre-cise opposite of the Ricardian (or Marxian) one—here wages (not profits) are a residue, profits being governed by the propensity to in-vest and the capitalists' propensity to consume, which represent a kind of "prior charge" on the national output. Whereas in the Ricardian model the ultimate incidence of all taxes (other than taxes on rent) falls on profits, here the incidence of all taxes, taxes on income and profits as well as on commodities, falls on wages.[38] Assuming however that I/Y and s_p remain constant over time, the share of wages will also re-main constant—i.e. real wages will increase automatically, year by year, with the increase in output per man.

If s_w is positive the picture is more complicated. Total profits will be reduced by the amount of workers' savings, S_w; on the other hand, the sensitivity of profits to changes in the level of investment will be

---

[38] The ultimate incidence of taxes can only fall on profits (in this model) in so far as they increase s_p, the propensity to save out of *net* income after tax. Income and profits taxes, through the "double taxation" of savings, have of course the oppo-site effect: they reduce s_p, and thereby make the share of *net* profits in income larger than it would be in the absence of taxation. On the other hand, discrim-inatory taxes on dividend distribution, or dividend limitation, by keeping down both dividends and capital gains, have the effect of raising s_p. (All this applies, of course, on the assumption that the Government *spends* the proceeds of the tax—i.e. that it aims at a balanced budget. Taxes which go to augment the budget surplus will lower the share of profits in much the same way as an increase in workers' savings.)

greater, total profits rising (or falling) by a greater amount than the change in investment, owing to the consequential reduction (or increase) in workers' savings.[39]

The critical assumption is that the investment/output ratio is an independent variable. Following Harrod, we can describe the determinants of the investment/output ratio in terms of the rate of growth of output capacity (G) and the capital/output ratio, v:

$$\frac{I}{Y} = Gv \qquad \qquad \ldots \ (3)$$

In a state of continuous full employment G must be equal to the rate of growth of the "full employment ceiling", i.e. the sum of the rate of technical progress and the growth in working population (Harrod's "natural rate of growth"). For Harrods' second equation:

$$\frac{I}{Y} = s$$

we can now substitute equation (1) above:

$$\frac{I}{Y} = (s_p - s_w)\frac{P}{Y} + s_w.$$

Hence the "warranted" and the "natural" rates of growth are not independent of one another; if profit margins are flexible, the former will adjust itself to the latter through a consequential change in P/Y.

This does not mean that there will be an *inherent* tendency to a smooth rate of growth in a capitalist economy, only that the causes of cyclical movements lie elsewhere—not in the lack of an adjustment mechanism between s and Gv. As I have attempted to demonstrate elsewhere [40] the causes of cyclical movements should be sought in a disharmony between the entrepreneurs' *desired* growth rate (as influenced by the degree of optimism and the volatility of expectations) which governs the rate of increase of output capacity (G), and the natural growth rate (dependent on technical progress and the growth of the working population) which governs the rate of growth in output

---

[39] Thus if $s_p = 50\%$, $s_w = 10\%$, $I/Y = 20\%$, P/Y will be 25%; but a rise in I/Y to 21% would raise P/Y to 27.5%. If on the other hand $s_w = 0$, with $s_p = 50\%$, P/Y would become 40%, but an increase in I/Y to 21% would only increase P/Y to 42%. The above formulae assume that average and marginal propensities are identical. Introducing constant terms in the consumption functions alters the relationship between P/Y and I/Y, and would reduce the *elasticity* of P/Y **with** respect to changes in I/Y.

[40] *Economic Journal*, March, 1954, pp. 53–71. [See my *Essays on Economic Stability and Growth*, pp. 213–32.]

over longer periods (let us call this G'). It is the excess of G over G'—not the excess of s over $G'v$—which causes periodic breakdowns in the investment process through the growth in output capacity outrunning the growth in production.[41]

Problems of the trade cycle however lie outside the scope of this paper; and having described a model which shows the distribution of income to be determined by the Keynesian investment-savings mechanism, we must now examine its limitations. The model, as I emphasised earlier, shows the share of profits P/Y, the rate of profit on capital P/vY, and the real wage rate W/L,[42] as functions of I/Y which in turn is determined independently of P/Y or W/L. There are four different reasons why this may not be true, or be true only within a certain range.

(1) The first is that the real wage cannot fall below a certain subsistence minimum. Hence P/Y can only attain its indicated value, if the resulting real wage exceeds this minimum rate, w'. Hence the model is subject to the restriction $W/L \geq w'$, which we may write in the form:

$$\frac{P}{Y} \leq \frac{Y - w'L}{Y} \qquad \ldots \quad (4)$$

(2) The second is that the indicated share of profits cannot be below the level which yields the minimum rate of profit necessary to induce capitalists to invest their capital, and which we may call the risk "premium rate", r. Hence the restriction:

$$\frac{P}{vY} \geq r \qquad \ldots \quad (5)$$

(3) The third is that apart from a minimum rate of profit on capital there may be a certain minimum rate of profit on turnover—due to imperfections of competition, collusive agreements between traders, etc., and which we may call m, the "degree of monopoly" rate. Hence the restriction:

$$\frac{P}{Y} \geq m \qquad \ldots \quad (6)$$

---

[41] I/Y will therefore tend to equal Gv, not $G'v$. It may be assumed that, taking very long periods, G is largely governed by G' but over shorter periods the two are quite distinct, moreover; G' itself is not independent of G, since technical progress and population growth are both stimulated by the degree of pressure on the "full employment ceiling", which depends on G. The elasticity of response of G' to G is not infinite however: hence the greater G, the greater will be G' (the *actual* trend-rate of growth of the economy over successive cycles) but the greater also the ratio G/G' which measures the strength of cyclical forces.

[42] Where $L =$ labour force.

It is clear that equations (5) and (6) describe *alternative* restrictions, of which the higher will apply.

(4) The fourth is that the capital/output ratio, v, should not in itself be influenced by the rate of profit, for if it is, the investment/output ratio Gv will itself be dependent on the rate of profit. A certain degree of dependence follows inevitably from the consideration, mentioned earlier, that the value of particular capital goods in terms of final consumption goods will vary with the rate of profit,[43] so that, even with a *given technique, v* will not be independent of P/Y. (We shall ignore this point.) There is the further complication that the relation P/Y may affect v through making more or less "labour-saving" techniques profitable. In other words, at any given wage-price relationship, the producers will adopt the technique which maximizes the rate of profit on capital, P/vY; this will affect (at a given G) I/Y, and hence P/Y. Hence any rise in P/Y will reduce v, and thus I/Y, and conversely, any rise in I/Y will raise P/Y. If the sensitiveness of v to P/Y is great, P/Y can no longer be regarded as being determined by the equations of the model; the *technical* relation between v and P/Y will then govern P/Y whereas the savings equation (equation (2) above) will determine I/Y and thus (given G) the value of v.[44] To exclude this we have to assume that v is invariant to P/Y,[45] i.e.:

$$v = \bar{v} \qquad \qquad \dots (7)$$

If equation (4) is unsatisfied, we are back at the Ricardian (or Marxian) model. I/Y will suffer a shrinkage, and will no longer correspond to Gv, but to, say, γv where $\gamma < G$. Hence the system will not produce full employment; output will be limited by the available capital, and not by labour; at the same time the classical, and not the Keynesian, reaction-mechanism will be in operation: the size of the "surplus" available for investment determining investment, not investment savings. It is possible however that owing to technical inventions,

[43] Cf. p. 391 above. In fact the whole of the Keynesian and post-Keynesian analysis dodges the problem of the measurement of capital.

[44] This is where the "marginal productivity" principle would come in but it should be emphasised that under the conditions of our model where savings are treated, not as a constant, but as a function of income distribution, the sensitiveness of v to changes in P/Y would have to be very large to overshadow the influence of G, of sp and of s_w on P/Y. Assuming that it is large, it is further necessary to suppose that the value of P/Y as dictated by this technical relationship falls within the maximum and minimum values indicated by equations (4)–(6).

[45] This assumption does not necessarily mean that there are "fixed coefficients" as between capital equipment and labour—only that technical innovations (which are also assumed to be "neutral" in their effects) are far more influential on the chosen v than price relationships.

etc., and starting from a position of excess labour and underemployment (i.e. an elastic total supply of labour) the size of the surplus will grow; hence I/Y and γ will grow; and hence γ might rise above G' (the rate of growth of the "full employment ceiling", given the technical progress and the growth of population) so that in time the excess labour becomes absorbed and full employment is reached. When this happens (which we may call the stage of *developed* capitalism) wages will rise above the subsistence level, and the properties of the system will then follow our model.

If equations (5) and (6) are unsatisfied, the full employment assumption breaks down, and so will the process of growth; the economy will relapse into a state of stagnation. The interesting conclusion which emerges from these equations is that this may be the result of several distinct causes. "Investment opportunities" may be low because G is low relatively to G', i.e. the entrepreneurs' expectations are involatile, and/or they are pessimistic; hence they expect a lower level of demand for the future than corresponds to potential demand, governed by G'. On the other hand, "liquidity preference" may be too high, or the risks associated with investment too great, leading to an excessive r. (This is perhaps the factor on which Keynes himself set greatest store as a cause of unemployment and stagnation.) Finally, lack of competition may cause "over-saving" through excessive profit margins; this again will cause stagnation, unless there is sufficient compensating increase in v (through the generation of "excess capacity" under conditions of rigid profit margins but relatively free entry) to push up Gv, and hence I/Y.

If, however, equations (2)–(6) are all satisfied there will be an inherent tendency to growth and an inherent tendency to full employment. Indeed the two are closely linked to each other. Apart from the case of a developing economy in the immature stage of capitalism (where equation (4) does not hold, but where $\gamma < G$), a tendency to continued economic growth will only exist when the system is only stable at full employment equilibrium—i.e. when $G \geq G'$.

This is a possible interpretation of the long-term situation in the "successful" capitalist economies of Western Europe and North America. If G exceeds G', the investment/output ratio I/Y will not be steady in time, even if the *trend* level of this ratio is constant. There will be periodic breakdowns in the investment process, due to the growth in output capacity outrunning the possible growth in output; when that happens, not only investment, but total output will fall, and ouput will be (temporarily) limited by effective demand, and not by the scarcity of resources. This is contrary to the mechanics of our model, but several reasons can be adduced to show why the system will not be flexible enough to ensure full employment in the short period.

(1) First, even if profit margins are assumed to be fully flexible in a downward, as well as an upward, direction the very fact that investment goods and consumer goods are produced by different industries, with limited mobility between them, will mean that profit margins in the consumption goods industries will not fall below the level that ensures full utilisation of resources in the consumption goods industries. A *compensating* increase in consumption goods production (following upon a fall in the production of investment goods) can only occur as a result of a transfer of resources from the other industries, lured by the profit opportunities there.

(2) Second, and more important, profit-margins are likely to be inflexible in a downward direction in the short period (Marshall's "fear of spoiling the market") even if they are flexible in the long period, or even if they possess short period flexibility in an upward direction.[46]

This applies of course not only to profit margins but to real wages as well, which in the short period may be equally inflexible in a downward direction at the *attained* level,[47] thus compressing I/Y, or rather preventing an *increase* in I/Y following upon a rise in the entrepreneurs' desired rate of expansion. Hence in the short period the shares of profits and wages tend to be inflexible for two different reasons—the downward inflexibility of P/Y and the downward inflexibility of W/L—which thus tend to reinforce the long-period stability of these shares, due to constancy of I/Y, resulting from the long-period constancy of Gv and $G'v$.

We have seen how the various "models" of distribution, the Ricardian-Marxian, the Keynesian and the Kaleckian are related to each other. I am not sure where "marginal productivity" comes in, in all this—except that in so far as it has any importance it does through an extreme sensitivity of v to changes in P/Y.

---

[46] Cf. the quotation from Marshall, note 33, page 397 above.

[47] This operates through the wage-price spiral that would follow on a reduction in real wages; the prevention of such a wage-price spiral by means of investment rationing of some kind, or a "credit squeeze", is thus a manifestation of downward inflexibility of W/Y.

28

AN EXPOSITION OF THE EQUILIBRIUM OF THE FIRM: SYMMETRY BETWEEN PRODUCT AND FACTOR ANALYSES *

JACK HIRSHLEIFER teaches at The University of California at Los Angeles; he was formerly with the Rand Corporation in California.[1]

The standard textbook presentation of the equilibrium of the firm is marred by an imperfect symmetry—at least in the usual diagrammatic representations—between the analysis conducted in terms of product units and concepts and the analysis conducted in terms of factor units and concepts. In this brief note I attempt to repair the defect.[2] Apart from mere improvement of elegance, the symmetrisation will bring out a rather significant ambiguity in the usual concept of marginal cost that has not received its due from authors of textbooks.

In what follows I shall for starkest simplicity assume that the firm produces only one product while employing only one factor. The first

* From *Economica*, Vol. XXIX (August, 1962), pp. 263–268. Reprinted with the compliments of the author and the Economica Publishing House, London School of Economics and Political Science.

[1] Any views expressed in this paper are those of the author. They should not be interpreted as reflecting the views of the RAND Corporation or the official opinion or policy of any of its governmental or private research sponsors.

[2] I would not wish to claim that the relationships between the factor and product analyses developed here are entirely novel. A correct verbal statement for the perfectly competitive case will be found in A. P. Lerner, *The Economics of Control*, New York, 1914, chs. 6 and 9. Even in Lerner's book, however, the symmetry of the analyses is more latent than explicit, and has not been carried over to the cases of imperfect competition in factor and product markets. J. R. Hicks also provides the beginnings of a symmetrical factor-product treatment, for the competitive case only, in *Value and Capital*, second ed., Oxford, 1946, ch. 6. Hicks's formulation also suggests the inverted nature of the symmetry. I have been unable to find any other works which go further than Hicks and Lerner in providing a correct symmetrical treatment for the equilibrium of the firm in both product and factor units. It is certain that standard textbooks fail to make this symmetry clear to students; so far as I know, it has never been displayed diagrammatically before. Nevertheless, this note is offered as an exposition and integration of basically known relationships rather than as a new contribution to analysis.

assumption is a common one; the second is not. The generalisation to
a multi-product, multi-factor situation will follow directly from my
algebraic formulation—but I do not spend time on it as the essential
points I want to emphasise stand out most clearly in the simplest
possible case.

I shall use upper-case letters (Q, P, etc.) to denote *product* quantity,
price, or other concepts referring or relating to product units, and
lower-case letters (q, p, etc.) for the corresponding *factor*-unit concepts.
The following abbreviations are used in the text and in the diagrams:

P = product price.

Q = product quantity.

MC = marginal cost.

AC = average cost.

AR = average revenue.

MR = marginal revenue.

CMF = cost of the marginal
    quantity of factor (required to
    produce one unit of product).

p = factor price.

q = factor quantity.

mfc = marginal factor cost.

afc = average factor cost.

vmp = value of the marginal
    product.

mrp = marginal revenue product.

mp = marginal physical product.

In Figure 1 we see the usual diagrammatic formulations of the
product-unit equilibrium where MR equals MC (at Q_o, with the corresponding P_o being the price along the product demand curve $AR =$
P), and the factor-unit equilibrium where mrp equals mfc (at q_o, with
the corresponding p_o being the price along the factor supply curve
$afc = p$). The asymmetry is obvious to the eye, although its source in
terms of economic concepts may not be immediately evident. After all,
one might think, does not vmp in the factor diagram correspond to AR
in the product diagram—since $vmp = mp \cdot AR$? Similarly, does not
mrp correspond to MR, since $mrp = mp \cdot MR$; afc correspond to AC;
and mfc correspond to MC? This analogy is plausible, but does not
lead to a symmetrical formulation. The reason is that as output rises
MC, in particular, incorporates *both* the effect on cost due to rising
factor prices (represented in the factor diagram by mfc) and the effect
of diminishing marginal productivity [3] (represented in the factor diagram only in the shape of vmp and mrp). The true symmetry is not, in
fact, the direct one sketched above but rather an inverse one—just as
the factor-cost relation between mfc and afc is an inverse analogue of
the product-revenue relation between MR and AR, so the product-cost

[3] That rising marginal cost may reflect both diminishing marginal productivity
and rising factor supply price is, of course, a very familiar proposition. See, for
example, T. Scitovsky, *Welfare and Competition*, Chicago, 1951, p. 312.

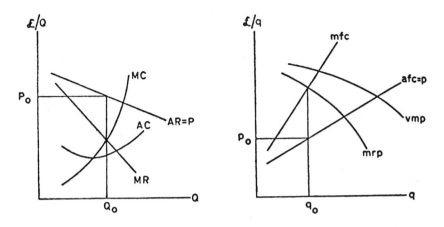

Figure 1. Product and factor diagrams—usual formulation

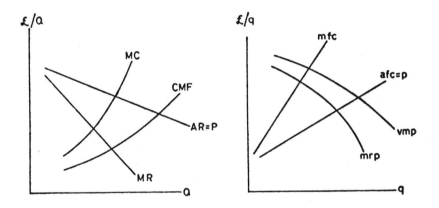

Figure 2. Product and factor diagrams, general solution—
symmetric formulation

concepts must be made inversely analogous to the factor-revenue concepts of *vmp* and *mrp*.

The proper symmetry is displayed in Figure 2. The average cost curve, *AC*, has been deleted from the product diagram. It is no more needed than is its inverse concept, value of the *average* product (average physical product × average revenue) in the factor diagram. However, we have added a curve which stands in relation to *MC* as *vmp* does to *mrp*. The curve labelled *CMF* (cost of the marginal quantity of factor) shows the cost of the marginal unit of output in terms of the quantity of factor input required valued at the factor price, p. It may be defined as afc/mp; it has the dimensions of price (pounds/Q). CMF is the inverse analogue of vmp, which is of course $AR \cdot mp$. We can now see explicitly that MC, the conventional marginal-cost concept, shows not only the cost of the quantity of factor purchased to produce the marginal unit of output, but also take into account the effect on cost through the higher prices that must be paid to the infra-marginal factor units. Definitionally, it is mfc/mp; it is the inverse analogue of mrp, or $MR \cdot mp$.

Figure 2 incorporates a special assumption about the shapes of the curves which is designed to convey to the eye the inverse nature of the symmetry. It is assumed that the demand curve for the product (on the left-hand side of Figure 2) and the supply curve for the factor (on the right) are both straight lines, so that the corresponding marginal curves, MR and mfc, are also straight lines. In general, changes for market reasons alone in factor or product value measures are indicated by straight lines. On the other hand, when value measures change with increasing output because of internal cost reflections of the law of diminishing returns, a curve of increasing (absolute) slope is utilized. When such internal cost changes are combined with market changes, a curve of increasing slope is required *a fortiori*. In Figure 2, then, vmp is a curve of increasing slope because it reflects both declining mp (law of diminishing returns) and declining P.[4] Similarly, CMF is a curve of increasing slope (in the inverted direction, of course) because it represents increasing quantities of factor per unit of product (the inverse of declining mp) together with rising factor supply price, p.

The solutions, of course, are the product and factor prices and quantities determined by the (equivalent) conditions $MR = MC$ and $mrp = mfc$. The auxiliary lines by which the solutions would ordinarily be indicated (see Figure 1) have been omitted in the other Figures in order to enhance the visual effect of the symmetry.

Figures 3 and 4 carry the analogy further by displaying equilibrium

---

[4] It may not be amiss here to warn against a common student error in the interpretation of vmp, which applies correspondingly to its inverse analogue CMF. The student is sometimes tempted, by the textbook definition of vmp as $mp \cdot P$, to think that mrp ($mp \cdot MR$) falls faster than vmp because the latter assumes a constant product price, P, while the former is based on calculations with the falling marginal revenue, MR. Of course, MR cannot be falling unless P is also falling. If P really is constant, therefore, $vmp = mrp$. The distinction between vmp and mrp, when the two differ, is that the former multiplies marginal physical product, mp, by a falling P while the latter multiplies it by a more rapidly falling MR. An exactly corresponding argument can be formulated for the relationship between CMF and MC.

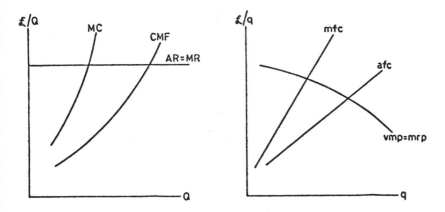

Figure 3. Product and factor diagrams, perfect competition in product market

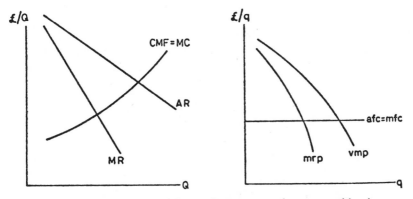

Figure 4. Product and factor diagrams, perfect competition in factor market

solutions in the two most interesting special cases: perfect competition in the product market only (Figure 3), and perfect competition in the factor market only (Figure 4), the other market in each case remaining subject to monopsonistic or monopolistic influence by the firm. The reader will note that the left-hand diagram of Figure 3 is an inverted analogue of the right-hand diagram of Figure 4, and along the other diagonal a similar relationship holds.

Finally, for completeness, Figure 5 shows the familiar solutions for the firm facing perfectly competitive markets for both factor and product. Here, of course the inverted nature of the symmetry is unmistakeable.

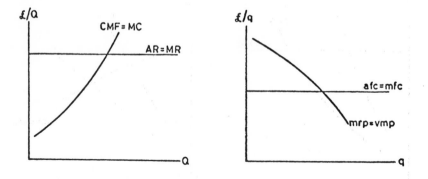

Figure 5. Product and factor diagrams, perfect competition in both
product market and factor market

In the table below, the definitions of the basic concepts are sum-
marised in such a way as to bring out the inverse symmetries. I have
also incorporated the equilibrium conditions to illustrate their algebraic correspondences. The correspondences follow immediately from
the definitions in the one-product, one-factor case. Thus, to show that
$MC = MR$ is equivalent to $mrp = mfc$:

$$1 = \frac{MR}{MC} = \frac{MR}{mfc/mp} = \frac{MR.mp}{mfc} = \frac{mrp}{mfc} = 1$$

Table of Inverse Symmetries

Definitions	Product concept	Factor concept
	$AR = R/Q$	$afc = C/q$
	$MR = \Delta R/\Delta Q$	$mfc = \Delta C/\Delta q$
	$CMF = afc/mp$	$vmp = AR.mp$
	$MC = mfc/mp$	$mrp = MR.mp$
Equilibrium conditions:		
General	$MC = MR$	$mrp = mfc$
Perfect competition in product market	$MC = MR = AR$	$mrp = vmp = mfc$
Perfect competition in factor market	$MC = CMF = MR$	$mrp = mfc = afc$

Let me close by citing one application of this analysis. It is now a
familiar argument that while a profit-seeking monopolist will set
$MC = MR$, a monopoly operated in the interests of social efficiency
should set output so as to equate MC with price, or AR. While the pros

and cons of this recommendation have been widely discussed, it is not
so widely recognised that the efficiency argument leading to the recommendation $MC = AR$ fails if what is meant is the ordinary private
marginal cost—what I have called MC in contrast with CMF. Setting
MC equal to AR is equivalent to setting mfc equal to vmp [5]—that is, to
exploiting monopsony power in the factor market while refraining
from exploiting monopoly power in the product market. The correct
efficiency rule, in factor units, is to set afc equal to vmp—that is, to set
factor price, measuring the opportunity cost of production foregone
elsewhere, equal to the value of the marginal product of the factor in
the employment under consideration. In product units, this is equivalent to setting $CMF = AR$—the cost of the marginal quantity of factor
valued at factor price (not the private marginal cost) equal to product
price.[6] This corrected rule of marginal-cost pricing forbids the firm to
use either its monopolistic power in the product market or its monopsonistic power in the factor market [7]—output will be greater, and price
lower, than under the ordinary interpretation of the marginal-cost
pricing rule, which implies using the latter market power with attendant restriction of output.

[5] Since $\dfrac{vmp}{mfc} = \dfrac{AR.mp}{mfc} = \dfrac{AR}{mfc/mp} = \dfrac{AR}{MC}$

[6] Since $\dfrac{vmp}{afc} = \dfrac{AR.mp}{afc} = \dfrac{AR}{afc/mp} = \dfrac{AR}{CMF}$

[7] While I am sure that theoretical economists would agree that what I have called
the *corrected* marginal-cost pricing rule is the valid one, I have not seen it explicitly espoused anywhere except by Lerner, who is perfectly clear on this point
(*op. cit.*, p. 99).

29

ALTERNATIVE THEORIES
OF LABOR'S SHARE *

MELVIN W. REDER teaches at Stanford University.

The present state of distribution theory is most unsatisfactory. This statement would probably always command a large measure of assent, irrespective of time or place; but today, in view of some recent contributions, it has perhaps more than ordinary pertinency. This is not because of the poor quality of the recent work, but because of its excessive compartmentalization. The authors who adopt an aggregative approach often write as though relative factor quantities had nothing to do with relative shares. On the other hand, the writers on the Cobb-Douglas function and related matters hardly consider the possibility that wage rigidities, unemployment, and the like might furnish alternative hypotheses to explain their findings. The students who stress profit margins, labor union pressure, and various institutional forces constitute a third stream of thought. And, finally, we have the data gatherers; these hewers and drawers pay little attention to what the theorists are cooking, except for an occasional—and usually correct—remark to the effect that the proposed bill of fare cannot be prepared from the ingredients at hand.

The purpose of this paper [1] is twofold: (1) to compare the more important theories of labor's share with one another and (2) to study the capacity of two of them to explain empirically the behavior of labor's share in the United States.

* From *The Allocation of Economic Resources: Essays in Honor of Bernard Francis Haley,* ed., Moses Abramovitz and others (Stanford University Press, 1959), pp. 180–206, © by the Board of Trustees of the Leland Stanford Junior University. Reprinted by permission.

[1] This paper benefited greatly from discussions of its author with K. J. Arrow, R. M. Solow, and Lorie Tarshis. Dr. J. C. Harsanyi made a number of valuable comments on an earlier draft, and Tibor Scitovsky's editing substantially improved both style and contents. The ground rules of this volume prevented me from showing the manuscript to Bernard Haley; however, his continuing interest in this subject and his many sagacious remarks upon it have sustained my own interest and greatly influenced my ideas. Mrs. Mary Girschick performed the computations for Table A and the extensive experimentation that preceded them.

I

Let us first examine the various theories. These may be placed in three classes: marginal productivity, or, more accurately, supply and demand theories; "mark-up" theories; and "widow's cruse" theories.

MARGINAL PRODUCTIVITY THEORIES

With reference to an individual firm, this theory needs no further exposition; it is a staple item in general works on economic theory. In these works, the demand of a firm for a specific factor service is determined (under pure competition) by the firm's production function, the prices of the outputs it produces and of the various factor services it uses or might use. (The monopoly and/or monopsony cases present inessential complications but no serious difficulties so long as the relevant demand and/or supply functions are known.) To get the aggregate demand curve for any one factor service, given the prices of other factors and products, is simply a matter of summing the demands of the various firms at the relevant prices of the factor in question. By an analogous though usually neglected operation, the aggregate supply function of labor and of certain other factor services) is derived from the preference functions of the economy's households. The equilibrium of the system determines the quantities and prices of the various factors used and products turned out, given the production functions of the firms and preference functions of the households.

The relative share of any factor in net output is the ratio of its total reward (price per service unit times the number of service units used) to the net product of the system. On this theory, changes in the relative share of a factor can be explained only by shifts in production functions and/or by changes in the preference functions of the households that furnish factor services and buy products. Therefore, in order to use this theory to explain the actual behavior of a factor's share, it is necessary to relate the behavior of that share to shifts in the above functions. In a more old-fashioned terminology, this theory seeks to explain the variations in factor shares (and related phenomena) as the result of changes in tastes, techniques, and resources—and nothing else. That is, factor quantities and factor prices are supposed, in this theory, to vary in an interrelated fashion with changes in tastes, techniques, and resources.

Obviously this theory requires an hypothesis as to how these parameters (i.e., tastes, techniques, and resources) of the economic system change, and how their changes affect factor shares. Thus far, only one such hypothesis has been seriously offered: this is the hypothesis related to the construction of "aggregate production functions," particularly the Cobb-Douglas function. The details of this hypothesis will be discussed below (pp. 423–435) when we consider its empirical validity. For the present, it will suffice to mention one of its features: it implies that such market imperfections as would be reflected in a difference between the value of the marginal product of a factor and its rate of remuneration are either (1) nonexistent or (2) uncorrelated with the quantities of any output or input.

The second of these possibilities should be noted carefully; use of the marginal productivity theory via an aggregate production function does not imply an acceptance of the idea that departures from competitive conditions are negligible. It implies only that these departures are uncorrelated with the variables in terms of which the theory operates (i.e., quantities of factors and products). I do not find this possibility absurd *a priori*; it is merely one of those approximations, such as "constancy" of tastes, which is certainly untrue in detail but which *may* be justified heuristically. Whether it *is* justified can be determined only after considering the empirical results that it helps us to obtain. However, this implication of the marginal productivity theory is inconsistent with the idea that market imperfections, monopoly power, policies governing profit-margins, etc., play a role in distribution theory.[2] Some, perhaps most, economists find this unacceptable and have, therefore, looked hopefully toward some sort of "mark-up" theory.

"MARK-UP" THEORIES

I define as "mark-up" theories those which make the distribution of the receipts of a firm, industry, group of industries, or an entire economy depend solely upon the relative prices of factor services and products, but regard these prices as being independent of relative quantities. That is, the ratio of price to average cost is "explained" as the outcome of oligopolistic agreements (explicit or implicit), conventional profit margins, and the like, and not by the presence and amount of excess capacity (of capital goods). Similarly, the wage rate is supposed to

[2] It is easy, in principle, to develop a distribution theory (of the supply and demand type) which makes the demand and supply functions of the factors to individual firms depend upon the relevant degrees of monopoly and monopsony power. At the purely formal level this has been done, in good part, by Mrs. Robinson (1, 2). However, this analysis is of virtually no assistance in empirical work because of the fact that we have no way of measuring, or even indicating the direction of movement of the weighted average elasticities of the various product demand and factor supply curves in any given time period.

reflect union and employer bargaining power rather than the amount and sign of the excess demand for labor.

Now the mark-up theorists do not assert that excess demand in a market has no influence upon price in that market; they would probably concede that a great deal of unemployment would tend *(cet. par.)* to reduce wage rates and that "excess capacity" would *(cet. par.)* tend to reduce profit margins. However, they would insist that other forces are also important in determining such variables as wage rates and profit margins, and that these forces should not be treated as mere "disturbances." This is not, *prima facie,* an unreasonable position; my only objection is that no theory has ever been offered that relates, *in a testable way,* either factor prices or profit margins to such forces as bargaining power, oligopoly agreements, etc. Indeed, these forces have not been defined in such a way that we could ever know when they had increased or decreased, except by looking at their alleged effects. Needless to say, this makes it impossible to refute or confirm any statements about the effect of these forces on the variables (e.g., wage rates or profit margins) whose behavior they are supposed to explain.[3]

These remarks can be made more concrete if we consider the outstanding example of an explicit mark-up theory: Kalecki's theory of income distribution.[4] In essence, this theory divides the "value added" by each firm into two parts, prime costs and the remainder; and it is focused on the expression, *product price minus average prime cost.* For any one firm, average prime cost consists exclusively of wages and raw material costs, but, for a closed economy, raw material costs will "wash-out" and we may, after aggregating, identify prime costs with wage payments.[5] Therefore, summing the above expression over all firms, we obtain the nonwage share of national income and, by subtracting this from the total, the wage share.

Of itself, this asserts nothing about the behavior of the relative shares. But Kalecki adds the assumption that the marginal cost curves of firms are, "on the average," [6] horizontal up to capacity output. If this is granted, we may, for our purposes, substitute marginal for av-

[3] See below (pp. 418-19) our comment on the alleged effect of union power on wage rates.

[4] Cf. M. Kalecki (3), especially pp. 201-8; also (4), Chap. I.

[5] Kalecki, whose principal point of reference is Great Britain, usually treats the ratio of average wage cost to average raw material cost as a parameter, whose level may affect relative shares. However, our simplification changes nothing of importance.

[6] The construction of this average is a much more difficult matter than Kalecki's discussion [in (3), pp. 201-4] would suggest; it involves several implicit assumptions about noncorrelation of relevant variables.

erage prime cost in the above ratio. This makes the nonwage share (in each firm) depend exclusively upon Lerner's measure of the "degree of monopoly power"; i.e., *price minus marginal cost.* As can readily be seen, the truth of this statement is guaranteed as soon as average prime cost is assumed equal to marginal cost. Hence, the only empirically refutable statement that Kalecki makes is that marginal cost curves (in some aggregative sense) are horizontal up to capacity output.

Now, it is very unlikely that this statement is consistent with the facts.[7] However, as the issue is not relevant to our main argument, let us accept it. What follows? One and only one thing: given the stock of plant and equipment, the relative shares of labor and other factors depend upon neither the scale of output nor the relative quantities of the factors used. That is, this theory denies that the marginal productivity theory helps to explain labor's share, but does not tell us what does explain it. Advertising, oligopoly agreements, union pressure, anything and everything that could conceivably affect the "degree of monopoly power" might—for all that Kalecki's theory implies—do so.[8]

Indeed, it is apparent on careful examination that if there should be a *long-run* change [9] in the labor-capital ratio, this might also affect the relative shares. That is, if capital charges per unit of output should rise relative to average prime costs, Kalecki's theory does not deny that this might lower the wage share—or do the reverse. All that it says is that any influence must alter the "average degree of monopoly power"; whether it *will* do so is not discussed.

The mark-up theory of distribution has a strong appeal to those who wish to emphasize the role of unions in determining labor's share, since it makes it possible to portray the distribution of income as a struggle between unions and employers. Such a portrayal may be a useful and harmless expository device so long as it is not taken for a theory of distribution. The temptation to do this, however, seems difficult to resist.

---

[7] I have argued this point elsewhere: M. W. Reder (5).

[8] We are discussing Kalecki's theory as though it sought to explain the remuneration of all labor. Actually, it refers only to manual labor, so that shifts between manual and other kinds of labor also affect the relative shares.

[9] In a rather neglected article, "A Theory of Long-Run Distribution of the Product of Industry" (6), Kalecki has offered a "long-run" theory of distribution which is quite different from the more famous (short-run) theory we are discussing in the text. It makes the wage share depend crucially upon the degree of utilization of equipment, as well as upon mark-up policy and the ratio of average wage cost to average material cost. In this article, as in his latest statement [(4), pp. 28–31], Kalecki retreats from his earlier denial that factor proportions and level of output can affect relative shares, and thereby ceases to offer a theory of distribution.

Consider the argument of Phelps-Brown and Hart who makes unions an important factor in the determination of the level of wage rates and leave the distribution of income to be determined by the interaction of the levels of wage rates and product prices.[10] Whether the level of product prices reflects mark-up policy, the forces of supply and demand, both, or some other factors, is not specified. These writers do not claim that unions have an appreciable influence on long-term movements in labor's share, but feel that in certain types of situations, union pressure has exerted a detectable upward pressure on the wage share. Specifically, they argue that where unions are aggressive and product markets "hard" (i.e., product prices do not rise appreciably), labor's share tends to rise. As a description of what has happened this is acceptable; but it explains nothing.

For, as Phelps-Brown himself points out, in some (though not all) cases, hard markets lead to downward pressure on wage rates despite determined union resistance. How are we to know whether unions were more "aggressive" when wage rates rose despite hard product markets, than when (under similar circumstances) wages fell? It is possible that unions were actually "more aggressive" in the cases where wages fell, but employer resistance was still more obstinate. Unless we have some independent measures of union aggressiveness and employer resistance,[10a]—and these have not yet been furnished—using "union aggressiveness" as an explanatory factor of wage behavior is simply to affirm the consequent.

Someone may yet discover that a genuine influence is exerted by unionism upon labor's share; but so far the available evidence is entirely compatible with the view that unionism has had but a negligible effect upon labor's share.[11] In section III, we shall suggest a hypothesis

[10] E. H. Phelps-Brown and P. E. Hart (7). The main argument of this justly famous article is not affected by this particular criticism.

Phelps-Brown and Hart are not alone in arguing in this fashion. It is a common type of argument which stems from a (commendable) desire to treat relative bargaining power as an explanatory variable though there is no way to determine its direction of movement. Because of this, bargaining power is identified with a residual; i.e., what cannot be explained otherwise is attributed to bargaining power. This is not, per se, objectionable—though it is always risky. To minimize the risk, it is necessary to analyze the impact of as many as possible of the other pertinent variables.

[10a] In correspondence, Professor Phelps-Brown has indicated that he has further evidence of a qualitative nature that indicates, independently of the results, that unions became more aggressive in certain of the periods to which he refers.

[11] The available evidence is well summarized by Kerr (8), especially p. 279 ff. The reader interested in the relevant literature will find ample guidance in Kerr's footnotes.

that is consistent with such a lack of influence; but, in any event, we shall henceforth ignore unionism as a determinant of labor's share.

THE "WIDOW'S CRUSE" THEORY

We now turn to a quite different, though related, kind of theory. Based on the analogy of the widow's cruse, it has been expounded in various forms by a number of writers, notably K. E. Boulding [12] and (more recently) Nicholas Kaldor.[13] As Kaldor's version is directly concerned with labor's share, we shall base our exposition on his paper, although many of our comments are applicable to the literature as a whole.

The widow's cruse theory starts with the proposition that, for the system to be in equilibrium, *ex ante* saving and *ex ante* investment must be equal. From this it follows that if the economy is divided into sectors, each with a different marginal (and average) propensity to save, the equilibrium of the system requires that the distribution of income among these sectors be such as to generate the amount of *ex ante* saving that will equal the *ex ante* amount of investment undertaken. In the aggregate, however, the level of income, as well as its distribution, is determined by the condition that *(ex ante)* saving equals investment. This leaves us, in effect, with one equation to determine two unknowns: the level of income and its distribution into classes.[14]

Kaldor gets out of this difficulty by considering separately the two cases of full employment and underemployment. In the former case, the level of real income is determined exogenously by the (given) stock of capital and state of productive technique—accepting for the moment the debatable assumption that the full employment of the labor force coincides with the full-capacity utilization of the stock of capital. In this case, with the level of income exogenously determined, the savings-investment equation determines relative shares.

In the underemployment case, it is assumed that the marginal physical product of labor is constant at less than capacity outputs,[15] so that

---

[12] Boulding (9), Chap. XIV, and (10), Chap. VI. Also see Bronfenbrenner (11). The present article was completed before the appearance of Weintraub's *An Approach to the Theory of Income Distribution* (12).

[13] N. Kaldor (13), especially pp. 94–95.

[14] In general, the number of unknowns is equal to n, where n is the number of income classes. This is because one variable, the level of income, plus the income received by dwellers in $n-1$ income classes determines income received by dwellers in the nth class. Where, as in our case, $n = 2$, we are "short" one equation.

[15] "Capacity output" refers only to the technical capacity of the capital stock. It is assumed that the labor supply is sufficient to utilize the capital stock to its "capacity." There may be more than enough labor to accomplish this (i.e., there

marginal cost depends on the wage rate but not on the level of output.[16] The price level is also independent of output, being some multiple of marginal cost; and this multiple is assumed to be an unique function of the mark-up ratio. Thus, the relative shares are independent of national income, being determined uniquely by the ratio of product price to wage cost per unit of output. Given this ratio, exogenously-determined fluctuations in investment will affect the level of (real) national income but not its distribution so long as there is unutilized capital equipment.

In short, for this case of underemployment Kaldor, in effect, adopts Kalecki's "theory" of income distribution but (properly) does not seriously consider it a theory. Instead, he focusses his attention on the full-employment case,[17] where both factors are fully used and the elasticity of supply of output is zero. In this case, the level of real income is fixed, and any increase of investment implies an increase in the ratio of investment to national income and, therefore, also an increase in the ratio of saving to income. Assuming fixed propensities to save of both wage earners and others, such an increase leads (if the system is stable) to a shift of income from the sector with the lower to that with the higher propensity to save.

To see what this means, assume (with Kaldor) the wage rate to be constant and wage earners to have a lower propensity to save than do others. Then, an increase in investment must (assuming stability) lead to a rise in product prices which implies a reduction in the wage share (because the quantities of both labor and capital are fixed) sufficient to increase the saving ratio by the same amount as the increase in the in-

---

may be unemployment), but this is irrelevant, as unemployment is not permitted to affect the wage rate.

[16] I.e., the marginal cost curve has a reverse "L" shape.

[17] Kaldor further restricts the applicability of his model to cases where two minimum profit conditions and one minimum real wage condition are satisfied. The last condition states that the profit share must not be so large that the full employment wage level lies below a subsistence minimum. One minimum profit condition states that the rate of return on invested capital must not be less than the minimum necessary to induce capitalists to risk it, and the other states that there is a minimum rate of return on sales, reflecting market imperfections. (These restrictions are alternative to one another, only the higher of the two being applicable.) The theory that Kaldor advances is restricted in its application to the range of relative factor shares where these restrictions simultaneously apply. Kaldor further restricts the applicability of the theory to situations where the capital-output ratio is independent of the relative distributive shares of labor and capital. This restriction precludes application of the marginal productivity theory, except in the special case where the aggregate production function is of the Cobb-Douglas variety (pp. 435–440).

422 READINGS IN MICROECONOMICS

vestment ratio. If the wage rate rises, for whatever reason, the price level must rise even more in order to achieve the same result.[18]

To put the theory into algebra, consider the following identities (borrowed from Kaldor):

$$Y \equiv W + P \equiv C + I \tag{1}$$

where Y is national income; W wage income; and P other income, identified (for simplicity) with profit; C is consumption expenditure and I investment. From the usual savings-investment identity, we obtain

$$I \equiv S = s_w W + s_p P \tag{2}$$

where S is aggregate saving, s_w is the marginal (and average) propensity to save from wage income and s_p the analogous fraction for profits. Dividing (2) by Y and using (1), we obtain:

$$I/Y \equiv (s_p - s_w) P/Y + s_w \tag{3}$$

where $s_w < s_p$ and $s_w(W/Y) + s_p(P/Y) < I$.[19] As can be seen from (3), an increase in I/Y, the investment ratio, must be offset by an increase in P/Y, the profit share, if $s_p > s_w$.

The only characteristic of these identities worthy of comment is the special form of the consumption functions implied by (2). To treat the savings ratios, s_w and s_p, as constants independent of the level of income is to accept, by implication, a particular and controversial view of the relation of saving to income. This point is elaborated in the next section.

Since Kaldor's theory can be stated in a series of identities, the reader might well ask what state of affairs could conceivably refute it; or, less politely, isn't this "theory" a disguised tautology? *The answer is that the empirical content of the theory lies in the implicit assumption* [20]

18 Alternatively, we could assume the price level to be constant and discuss the behavior of the wage rate. What is at issue is whether the ratio of the wage level to the price level is determinate (given I/Y, the ratio of investment to income) and stable with respect to displacements in I/Y. Kaldor's discussion in the aforementioned article (13) is very incomplete. In a later article [(14), especially pp. 604–14], he offers a somewhat better discussion of stability conditions.

19 Stability requires $s_w < s_p$, provided that $d(P/Y)/d(I/Y) > 0$. This assumption is plausible; but it is not based on empirical investigation.

20 From Kaldor's discussion in "A Model of Economic Growth" (14), it seems clear that he regards s_w and s_p as roughly constant for long periods of time. It is, of course, possible that Kaldor's theory might be empirically meaningful even though s_p and s_w change frequently. In this case, the test of the theory would lie in the observed pattern of covariation of s_p/s_w and I/Y. However, we do not have observations on s_p and s_w at different moments of time, and therefore if the theory is to be tested on time series, s_w and s_p must be assumed to be constant. Of course, it is also possible that the theory might be useful in explaining international or interregional variations in relative shares, irrespective of temporal fluctuations in s_p and s_w, when suitable data become available.

that the saving coefficients, s_p, and s_w, are parameters which do not vary over time. If s_p and s_w are constant over time, then it immediately follows from (3) that changes in the investment ratio must be matched by corresponding changes in the nonwage share.

Obviously, we might construct on these lines a "theory of income distribution" between any *two* [21] sectors of the economy; e.g., rich and poor, peanut-sellers and nonpeanut sellers, etc. Whether any one of these theories is of empirical interest depends entirely upon whether the difference between their respective marginal propensities to save is sufficiently large, relative to variations in investment and the sizes of the various disturbances affecting the parameters of the relevant consumption functions, to account for the observed movements in the division of the national product between the two sectors. Whether the division between wage and nonwage incomes can be usefully explained by Kaldor's model is, therefore, a matter for statistical investigation. To this subject we turn in the next section.

II

To understand the empirical significance of any theory, it is necessary to specify precisely how it is tested. For the purpose of testing we express Kaldor's theory in equations (4) and (4a). Equation (4) defines d, the difference between the actual and estimated values of I/Y. [The sole purpose of writing (4) and (4a) is to contrast them, presently, with (5).]

$$d = I/Y - \text{est. } I/Y \qquad (4)$$

$$\text{est. } I/Y = s_g + .14\,P/Y + .04\,W/Y \qquad (4a)$$

The expression (4a) is the empirical counterpart of (3), with numerical values assigned to s_w and s_p and the new term s_g added: s_g is the ratio of "Government Surplus on Income and Product Transactions to National Income"; we must insert this term in (4a) in order that, on Department of Commerce definitions, savings equal investment. As soon as we insert numerical values for s_g, P/Y, and W/Y, (4a) provides us, in each year, with an estimate of I/Y on the hypothesis that $s_w = .04$ and $s_p = .14$.

Looked at in this way, the test of Kaldor's theory is its performance as a predictor of movements in the investment ratio, I/Y.[22] What ob-

---

[21] Of course, it is also possible to have three (or more) sectors. But then we need an additional equation for each additional sector (see footnote 14).

[22] Since Kaldor's theory is concerned with labor's share, W/Y, and not with I/Y, the reader may wonder why we have not tested the theory by its ability to predict W/Y. It would, of course, have been possible to do so; however, such a test would have been logically equivalent to the one used and would have involved extra calculations.

servations are relevant to the test? Clearly, not all observations, for the theory is supposed to apply only to situations of full employment. Hence, the depression years 1930–39 are irrelevant and, for the moment, we shall ignore them. Nothing that Kaldor says would exclude the war years (1915–19 and 1942–45) from the purview of his theory; however, it is generally believed that the savings ratios during these periods were considerably above their normal peacetime levels (i.e., during these periods s_w and s_p temporarily increased), and so we shall also abstract, temporarily, from these years.[23]

What of the remaining years? Are they "full-employment" years in the sense required by Kaldor's theory? Probably not, in a literal sense, for it is unlikely that an "aggregate" marginal cost curve would have the required reverse L shape. Nonetheless, 1909–14, 1923–29, and 1946–56 were periods of reasonably full employment during which variations in I/Y might have been expected to affect S/Y primarily by redistributing income—or by altering savings ratios—and only to a limited degree by shifting the level of current output and employment. Let us assume, therefore, that the aforementioned periods were sufficiently good approximations to full employment (in the United States) to use for testing Kaldor's theory.

The test to be made is how well the annual levels of I/Y can be predicted, with the aid of equation (4a), from the annual levels of W/Y and P/Y. The success of the theory in meeting this test is indicated by the resulting size of d in equation (4). Kaldor's theory implies that d will be as small in each full-employment period as in the base period 1948–50, whose data were used for calculating the values of s_p and s_w on the assumption that d is approximately zero. (Actually, d is not zero but $+ .002$ for the base period with the values of s_p and s_w used.) The annual values of d, and of the variables from which it is computed, are presented in Appendix Table A; a summary of which is presented in Table I below.

As column 4a of Table I shows, the average size of d was $+ .002$ in the base years of 1948–50. For the logic of the argument, the values assigned to s_w and s_p should be considered to be arbitrary; however, they were chosen from among the possible pairs that would make d roughly zero in the base period, with an eye to realism.[24] For the period

[23] The selection of the particular years included in the "war periods" was made, frankly, *ex post facto*. That is, we looked at the data to see which years had unusually high saving ratios and defined the "war periods" accordingly. The depression decade was defined arbitrarily as 1930–39.

[24] The coefficients chosen are roughly consistent with the available estimates of s_w and various parts of s_p made from budgetary data for the period 1948–50. The published estimates to which we refer are in Table 5 of Friedman (15), p. 71. Also see Brady (16), Table H-9, p. 157.

1946–56, the average value of d was $-.004$; for 1923–29 it was $+.005$; for 1921–29 it was $-.001$; and for 1909–14 it was $+.020$. I interpret the values of d for either 1921–29 or 1923–29 and for 1946–56 as "small"; i.e., as being not inconsistent with the acceptance of Kaldor's theory. One reason for this interpretation is that the average values of d in each of these periods lies within one standard deviation of the annual values of d when these values are measured from zero. Another reason is that in 1949–56, the average value of d was only about $1/200$ of I/Y and in 1923–29, about $1/20$ of I/Y.

Table I. Average Values of d Computed from Equations; (4a) and (5) for Selected Period °

	(4a)	(5)
Base period 1948–50	$+.002$	$-.003$
Full employment periods		
1946–56	$-.004$	$-.007$
1923–29	$+.005$	$+.004$
1921–29	$-.001$	$+.003$
1909–14	$+.020$	$+.021$
Other periods		
1915–19	$+.097$	$+.100$
1930–39	$-.084$	$-.085$
1942–45	$+.122$	$+.118$

* Data from Appendix Table A.

The data for 1909–14 are not so easily reconciled with Kaldor's theory. They suggest that s_w or s_p (or both) might have been higher before World War I than thereafter.[25] However, the quality of the pre-1919 data is such as to inhibit inference. It may be that the greater size of d in 1909–14, as compared with the other "full-employment" periods, is merely a statistical artifact.

But to assert that a set of data are or are not reasonably consistent with a particular hypothesis requires that we also test their consistency with some alternative hypothesis. One obvious alternative to (4a) is that $s_w = s_p$; i.e., the saving ratio is the same for both groups of income receivers. This hypothesis is expressed by (5) which is an analogue of (4a), the only difference being that in (5) we assume that $s_w = s_p = .08$.

$$\text{est. } I/Y = s_g + .08 \qquad (5)$$

[25] The standard deviation of the annual observations in 1909–14 was .021. Hence the difference between the entries in Table I for 1909–14 and 1946–56 is about two standard deviations of the latter period and one of the former. This would be insufficient to reject the hypothesis that the coefficients for the two periods were the same if one chose to believe it.

The results of applying (5) to the data of Appendix Table A are summarized in column (5) of Table I. Comparing columns (4a) and (5) of Table I shows that the hypothesis that $s_w = s_p$ does just about as well as Kaldor's theory; i.e., the differences between the entries for the base period (1948–50) and the given periods are about the same (and small) in both columns.[26] This judgment is confirmed by the fact that the difference between the entries in any row of Table I is substantially less than the standard deviation of annual values of d on either hypothesis.

In other words, it is difficult to choose between Kaldor's theory and our "dummy" alternative expressed by (5).[27] However, while this does not preclude the possibility that variations in the relative shares of national income "explain" variations in the savings ratio, it does mean that variations in the distribution of wage income among workers; of nonwage income among its recipients (especially the ratio of corporate to noncorporate profits); and of exogenous shifts in the savings functions of households, governments, and firms have so combined as to have had just about the same effect upon the savings ratio as shifts in relative shares. If we could state that the coefficients in (4a) were more realistic than those in (5)—and I think they are—this would be a point in favor of Kaldor's hypothesis. However, the method of selecting these coefficients precludes any such argument.

So far, we have considered the relative performance of equations (4a) and (5) in years of peacetime full employment. Now let us consider briefly the other periods. During the years of World Wars I and II, and their aftermaths, d (on both Kaldor's theory and our alternative) is large and positive. This is readily explained on the hypothesis that a

---

[26] Since both entries for the base period are very close to zero, the reader may, for convenience, treat the absolute size of the various entries as indicating the extent of their disagreement with the hypothesis under consideration.

[27] The reader might also wonder whether the coefficients we have chosen for equations (4a) and (5) might not be improved upon. While it might be possible to choose "better" sets of coefficients for these equations, it is not likely that they would greatly improve the performance of either of the hypotheses considered. Examination of Table I shows that the performance of both (4a) and (5), especially the former, was extremely good for the periods 1946–56 and 1921–29 (or 1923–29). Any attempt to improve performance during 1909–14, would almost certainly worsen performance in the other periods—if s_w and s_p are assumed constant. Put in a slightly different way, the "trouble" with Kaldor's theory is not that (4a) does so badly, but that the alternative, (5), does so well.

One reason (4a) and (5) show such similar results is the limited, though genuine, variation in the relative shares in years of peacetime full employment. This means that though Kaldor's theory might be (empirically) valid, it is not in itself a very important factor in explaining the observed behavior of relative shares.

household's expenditure tends to lag its income; therefore, in periods (such as major wars) when income is rising rapidly, aggregate saving ratios tend to be higher than usual. This would cause estimates of savings based on customary saving ratios to be lower than actual savings (and investment). Conversely, during the 1930's actual saving ratios were below customary ones, and our estimates of S/Y were correspondingly in excess of the observed levels of I/Y.[28] As d exhibits the same general pattern during the World Wars and the 1930's, irrespective of which hypothesis we accept, and because Kaldor's theory does not refer to such periods, I shall not attempt to discriminate between the hypothesis on the basis of evidence from these periods.

III

Let us now consider the empirical evidence bearing upon the marginal productivity theory. To test this theory it is necessary that we specify a functional relation among factor prices and quantities so that we can deduce a theoretical pattern of price-quantity covariations with which to compare the actual covariations. In practice, we do this by assuming (1) that the production function either remains unchanged or varies in some particular way, so that the demands for factor services can be deduced once the parameters are estimated and factor and product prices are given. It is further assumed (2) that the supply functions of the factors shift over time, and that the observed price-quantity points (assumed to represent, save for random disturbances, equilibrium positions) are traced out by the intersections of the shifting factor supply curves with the factor demand curves deduced from the fitted production function.

The price-quantity points thus generated are supposed to be positions of "general equilibrium." That is, they are positions where (apart from random disturbances) every firm and every market is in equilibrium, and where each factor is so allocated that the value of its marginal physical product is equal in all uses. There is no point

[28] This view is similar to that expounded as part of the "permanent income hypothesis" by Milton Friedman in "A Theory of the Consumption Function" (15). However, the lag hypothesis mentioned in the text may be rationalized on several different hypotheses.

It might also be mentioned that the savings functions given in equation (2) are of a specific kind which imply that savings are a constant fraction of income (i.e., are independent of the level of income). This form of savings function was specified, without discussion, by Kaldor. However, it is an essential part of Friedman's permanent income hypothesis that savings functions should be of this form.

in arguing whether these assumptions are "sufficiently realistic." The only way to find out is to accept them and see what follows.

To discuss the relative size of two factor shares, those of "labor" and "capital," involves considerable violence to the facts. There are many different kinds of labor and capital, and there is good reason to believe that the quantities of the various grades of labor, at least, have not varied proportionately over time.[29] Consequently, to treat sums of (equally-weighted) hours of labor at different moments of time as though they were homogeneous magnitudes is a tour de force, whose only justification (if any) is pragmatic. The problem of valuing the services of capital goods produced at different dates and possessing varying "technical" capacities creates similar difficulties. However, if the argument is not to be grounded at the start, we must brush these difficulties aside and proceed as if they did not exist.

To derive the demand curves for the two factors, labor and capital, the usual procedure is to fit an "aggregate"[30] production function to annual data of quantities of labor and capital used and output produced. In principle, a variety of functional forms could be fitted to the available data. However, for several reasons that will become apparent, we prefer to concentrate upon the Cobb-Douglas function given by:

$$P = aL^kK^j, \tag{6}$$

where P is product, L is labor, and a, K, and j are estimated parameters.

Estimating the parameters of aggregate production functions (in particular the Cobb-Douglas) from their fits to time series is subject to well-known statistical difficulties.[31] However, these difficulties are largely overcome in a recent paper by R. M. Solow.[32] Solow advances the hypothesis (1) that technical progress is neutral and stochastically independent both of relative factor quantities and the level of output, and (2) that there is constant returns to scale. That is, it is hypothesized that the relative marginal physical productivities of two factors are determined uniquely by the ratio of their quantities. Put in a slightly different way, this states that the aggregate production function is, at any moment of time, identical with what it was at any previous moment, save for a vertical displacement.

[29] That is, the number of unskilled workers has declined relative to the total. This implies that there has been a secular improvement in the quality of the aggregate labor input unit; the consequences of this for the estimated parameters of the Cobb-Douglas function are discussed by Zvi Griliches (17), especially pp. 14–16.

[30] I.e., a function involving the operations of more than one firm.

[31] These have been pointed out by a long list of authors; and most recently by Professor E. H. Phelps-Brown (18).

[32] R. M. Solow, "Technical Change and the Aggregate Production Function" (19).

Solow shows that where a production function of two factors is homogeneous of degree one, the percentage change in output, at any moment of time, will equal the "rate of technical progress" [33] plus the share of capital times the percentage change in the ratio of capital to labor. If technical progress is neutral, then the aggregate production function takes the multiplicative form,

$$P = A(t)aL^kK^{1-k} \qquad (6a)$$

where $A(t)$ is a variable which reflects technical progress and all economic forces correlated therewith.

The legitimacy of (6a) depends crucially upon the hypothesis of neutrality in technical progress. The evidence in favor of this hypothesis is as follows: if technical progress were neutral and independent of the level of output, then the (percentage) changes in output would be uncorrelated with the percentage changes in the ratio of capital to labor. Solow constructed a scatter diagram of these two variables and, finding no relation whatever between them, concluded that the evidence supported the hypothesis of neutrality. Though at least one other possibility remains,[34] the hypothesis of neutrality has thus far been substantiated and (6a) may therefore be accepted, tentatively, as an aggregate (private nonfarm) production function, for the United States in the period 1909–53.

The principal advantages of (6a) over (6) are as follows; (6a) is fitted to the time series

$$(P/L)/A(t) \text{ and } (K/L)^{1-k} \text{ (see footnote 35)}$$

neither of which contains a trend; i.e., we are correlating variables largely free of auto-correlation.[36] Consequently, the statistical insta-

[33] Defined as the percentage increase in product, per time period, with given factor inputs.

[34] I.e., that the production function is not homogeneous of degree one and is "biased" in such a way as to offset the underlying pattern of association of technical progress with changes in factor ratios.

There is some independent evidence for the hypothesis that the production function is homogeneous of the first degree. Professor Solow has told me that he has, since publication, fitted a Cobb-Douglas function where the exponents of L and K were determined independently; i.e., $j + k$ was not forced to equal one. It turned out that the fitted function was $P/A = aL^{.6181}K^{.3381}$. (The agreement of the implied capital share, .3381, with the actual capital share is obvious.) The sum of the exponents, .9562, is within one standard error of unity, as the standard error of the sum of the exponents is .048.

[35] That is, Solow divides (6a) through by L and then by $A(t)$, so that after taking logs we have log $[P/L/A(t)] = \log a + 1-k [\log (K/L)]$.

[36] The series used by Solow are P/L, $A(t)$, and K/L. $A(t)$ is the factor reflecting technical progress. The K/L series does exhibit an upward trend from 1909 to 1923, but none thereafter.

bility which has plagued previous attempts to fit Cobb-Douglas functions is largely avoided.[37]

A further though related advantage is that while the ordinary Cobb-Douglas function makes no allowance whatever for technical progress, (6a) does. Ignoring technical progress is contrary to common sense and may have been responsible for some of the difficulties in obtaining sensible estimates of the coefficients of the fitted functions.[38] A further "practical" improvement of Solow's work over most previous efforts is that he uses labor employed, rather than the size of the labor force, as a measure of L and also corrects K (conceptually) for idle capacity.

There is one important difference between Solow's own discussion of his results and ours. We have focussed our attention on the Cobb-Douglas function, while Solow fitted five different functions. Among these five, the Cobb-Douglas gave as good a fit as any, but there is no purely statistical reason for preferring it to three of the others.[39] However, the Cobb-Douglas function (when it is homogeneous of the first degree) is the only function which has the property of implying that the factors receive the same relative shares *whatever* their (non-negative) quantities.[40] Put differently, the Cobb-Douglas is the only func-

[37] Unfortunately, the standard errors of the coefficients of (6a) are not available. However, Professor Solow has told me in conversation that he recalls the coefficients as being many times greater than their standard errors, indicating a high degree of statistical stability. In the calculation mentioned in footnote 34, Solow found that the standard error of the labor exponent is .0662, and of the capital exponent, .0405; i.e., the labor exponent is more than nine times its standard error and the capital coefficient more than eight times its standard error.

[38] For example, negative exponents for capital have been obtained for American manufacturing for the 1920's.

[39] I.e., the correlation coefficient between observed and estimated values of $P/A(t)$ was for all functions better than .99 for all functions.

[40] This can be shown as follows: let the total income of capital be equal to rK and the wage-bill be wL where r is the rate of return per unit of capital service and w is the wage rate. The value of output, P, is identically equal to $rK + wL$; $P \equiv rK + wL$. Now the marginal productivity theory implies, assuming (6) to be the production function, $w = \partial P/\partial L = k(P/L)$ and $r = \partial P/\partial K = j(P/K)$; alternatively $L(\partial P/\partial L) = kP = wL$ and $K(\partial P/\partial K) = jP = rK$. Substituting,

$$P \equiv (j + k)P;$$

therefore $k + j = 1$. The share of labor is kP/P, and of capital jP/P; hence the ratio of the shares is k/j or $k/(1-k)$ where j and k are constants and independent of relative factor quantities and output.

To obtain this result it is necessary that $L(\partial P/\partial L) = kP$ and $K(\partial P/\partial K) = jP$, j and k being constants whose sum equals unity. Otherwise $L(\partial P/\partial L)$ and $K(\partial P/\partial K)$ could not be constant fractions of product, independent of the levels of P, L and K. But kP/L and jP/L are the derivatives of the Cobb-Douglas function which has a unit elasticity of substitution at all points (assuming first-degree homogeneity).

This means that if labor's share is constant over time, and if factor markets are cleared by the forces of supply and demand, we must either accept the Cobb-Douglas function as the proper relation among the aggregates of output, labor, and capital or argue that the constant shares result from secularly constant ratios of factor quantities and factor prices. This second possibility is not to be dismissed lightly; however, from Solow's data it appears that for the period 1909–53 employed capital per man-hour varied from a low of \$2.06 to a maximum of \$3.33 (a variation of 47 per cent about the mid-point of the range). It is pointless to argue abstractly as to whether this is little or much variation; it was sufficient variation to fit a statistical regression of $P/A(t)$ on K/L with "satisfactory" results, but it was not sufficient variation to prevent several different functions (all homogeneous of the first degree) from giving very good fits to the data. In short, in the United States during 1909–53, the fit of the Cobb-Douglas function is to a range of observations not sufficiently "wide" to enable us to choose (on statistical grounds) from among several functions, all homogeneous of the first degree. Our choice of the Cobb-Douglas function must rest upon its analytical properties; e.g., the fact that it implies constant shares.

We must next consider two separate, but related questions: is labor's share (and therefore that of its complement) constant over time; and if so, is the size of the share equal to that implied by the coefficients of the fitted Cobb-Douglas function (or nearly so)?

(1) Before discussing the constancy of labor's share, it is necessary to specify what we include in that share. In Section II we defined labor's share as the share of Employee Compensation in National Income. For our present purpose, this definition is unacceptable; what we need is a concept that includes the value of the services of the self-employed as well as of the wage earners. Also, it is desirable to avoid the complications stemming from the growing economic role of government; clearly the employee share of government product is fictitiously high (judged by the standard of private accounting rules) because of the absence of profits and of charges for the services of government-owned capital. Hence, we restrict our discussion to the private sector of the economy. Finally, because Solow's data exclude Agriculture (they refer to the private nonfarm sector) we are also

---

tion; therefore, only the Cobb-Douglas function is consistent with (1) constant relative shares, (2) variations in L/K, and (3) the production function being homogeneous of the first degree.

compelled—if we wish to make use of his results—to confine our argument to the (private) nonfarm sector.[41]

The difference between the definition used in this section of the paper and that used in Section II is very important. The share of Employee Compensation (the concept used in Section II) is *not* secularly constant; on the contrary it has risen appreciably since 1910.[42] However, the share of wage earners plus the imputed earnings of the self-employed (what is sometimes called labor's functional share) in Private non-Farm Product behaves quite differently. It is quite possible that, despite the upward trend in the share of Employee Compensation, labor's functional share has stayed constant in the United States since 1910 or thereabouts. First let us consider the period 1929–52; the salient facts for which are presented in Table II. It is clear that, for the economy as a whole, the share of Employee Compensation rose during this period. However, if we look at the various sub-sectors of the "ordinary business sector," there is no evidence of an upward trend in the employee share in any one of them. This suggests, and Table III confirms, that the economy-wide increase in the share of employees results principally from an increase in their relative numbers in industries with more than average employee shares.

One very important example of such a shift is the relative decline of Agriculture as a labor user with its very low employee share.[43] (The reason for the low employee share in Agriculture is the large fraction of labor furnished by farm operators and their families, most of which is not reported as wages.) Another instance of such a shift is the rise in importance of government which has an unusually high employee share. The relative growth of government employment is primarily responsible for the marked rise in the employee share in "all other sectors" (shown in Table II).

Because of these and similar facts, Denison concludes that, during prosperous peacetime years,[44] there is "substantial stability" in the

41 Another reason is that there is considerable evidence that the marginal productivity of labor is lower in agriculture than in industry, so that shifts out of the former and into the latter would be inconsistent with the hypothesis on which an aggregate production function is based. On the difference between the marginal productivity of labor in agriculture and industry, see M. W. Reder [(20), especially pp. 78–79].

42 See D. Gale Johnson (21); also E. F. Denison (22, 23). Johnson's article contains references to the earlier literature.

43 There is evidence of a positive trend in labor's functional share within agriculture, but this is not so marked as to upset the argument of the text.

44 I.e., these statements do not apply to the depression years of the 1930's or to the war years, 1942–45.

Table II. Compensation of Employees as a Percentage of National Income by Sectors, Selected Years

Sector	1929	1941	1948	1949	1950	1951	1952	Average 1948–1952
Entire economy	58.1	61.9	62.7	64.7	63.8	64.3	66.3	64.3
Ordinary business:								
Nonfarm corporations	74.1	72.6	74.2	75.3	73.3	72.9	75.2	74.2
Nonfarm proprietorships and partnerships	48.4	47.1	49.0	49.4	49.5	50.3	51.9	50.0
Farms	16.5	13.9	14.4	17.8	16.4	15.4	16.1	16.0
All other sectors	45.2	65.9	68.9	69.7	68.5	71.0	71.4	69.9

Source: E. F. Denison, "Income Types and the Size Distribution," *Papers and Proceedings of the 66th Annual Meeting of the American Economic Association*, May 1954, p. 257.

employee share of income in the ordinary business sector, when account is taken of structural changes in that sector.[45] Excluding government confines our analysis (approximately) to the ordinary business sector, and excluding agriculture eliminates most of the structural change in the ordinary business sector from which Denison abstracts. The remaining major source of structural change is the shift from wage earning to self-employment; but as this does not affect labor's *functional* share, we may interpret Denison's conclusion as tantamount to saying that labor's functional share of private nonfarm output was constant during the prosperous peacetime years of 1929–52.

Table III. Analysis of Changes in Employee Share in National Income,
1941–52

Year	Actual change from 1929	Change due to shifts in industry weights	Change due to share shifts within industries
1941	− 0.8	0.8	− 1.6
1948	− 0.4	0.4	− 0.8
1949	1.7	1.2	0.5
1950	0.8	1.6	− 0.8
1951	0.8	1.8	− 1.0
1952	3.1	2.3	0.8
Average 1948–52	1.2	1.5	− 0.3

Source: E. F. Denison, "Income Types and the Size Distribution," *Papers and Proceedings of the 66th Annual Meeting of the American Economic Association,* May 1954, p. 258.

For the longer period, 1900–1909 to 1947–52, Johnson estimates that the (functional) share of labor in the private sector of the economy rose from 68.0 to 71.5 per cent. Part of this small increase was fictitious (because of differences in living costs in rural and urban areas), and Johnson seems to attribute the remainder to the shift of workers away from agriculture. In view of the limitations of the data, it is not stretching matters too far to say that there is general agreement between Johnson's and Denison's estimates. In any case, if we confine our attention to the private nonfarm sector, both Johnson's and Denison's data would be consistent with the hypothesis of a secularly-constant distribution of income between labor and capital during "prosperous peacetime years."

(2) Now let us turn briefly to the second question. Does labor's share, as computed from the modified Cobb-Douglas function, (6a),

[45] E. F. Denison (23), especially pp. 258–59.

agree with the actual share? The available estimate of labor's functional share, Johnson's [46] places it from 68 to 71.5 per cent in the
period 1900–1909 to 1947–52. Now Solow's published estimate of the
exponent of L in (6a) is

$$1 - .353 = .647.$$

Unfortunately, the standard error of this coefficient is unavailable, but
in a subsequent calculation Solow obtained an exponent for L of .6181
with a standard error of .0662.[47] This estimate of L, plus two standard
errors, is .7405; .6181 and .7405 comfortably span Johnson's estimate.
In short, the marginal productivity theory, in this form, is not refuted
by the facts.[48]

One further "advantage" of the marginal productivity theory, with
the Cobb-Douglas accepted as the appropriate form of the aggregate
production function, is that it explains why unionism has had little
effect on labor's share. That is, the theory thus limited implies that
the mechanisms of product and factor substitution have been such
that whatever pressure unions have been able to bring to bear upon
wage rates has been offset, insofar as any effect on relative shares is
concerned.

IV

Thus, there is some merit in the marginal productivity explanation
of relative shares.[49] However, let us not go overboard; the data refer
only to one historical period in one country. And, even in this case,
the data are not such as to guarantee that the results bear the interpretation placed upon them. An even more fundamental objection
to our argument is that, unless we can relate an aggregate production
function to the production functions of individual firms, our aggre-

[46] D. Gale Johnson (21).

[47] The difference between this estimate and that published is due to the fact that
this estimate was made "directly"; i.e., was not computed as a residual from one
minus the exponent of capital. (See footnote 34 above.)

[48] It should be noted that Johnson's data refer to the private sector as a whole, and
not to the nonfarm sector exclusively. However, the difference between labor's
functional share in agriculture and elsewhere is not very great. Johnson (24) has
estimated that labor's functional share in Agriculture is of the order of 65 per
cent.

[49] A further advantage of the Cobb-Douglas function, as compared with Kaldor's
theory, is that (after adjustment for unemployment of labor and underutiliza-
tion of capital) it applies to all years and not merely to those of peacetime full
employment.

gate function is "floating in air." And we know very little about the production functions of individual firms, or even of industries.[50] In fact, within individual industries there is also very substantial stability (over time) of the wage share.[51] Thus, we may need an aggregate Cobb-Douglas function for individual industries, of which an economy-wide Cobb-Douglas function must be a "super-aggregate." Whether this program of constructing aggregate production functions can be carried out consistently remains to be seen.[52]

But what of Kaldor's theory; how does it fit together with marginal productivity, if at all. The answer is that, contrary to Kaldor's opinion,[53] the theories need not be inconsistent. Kaldor's theory "explains" the secular rise in the share of Employee Compensation, while the marginal productivity theory (as we have developed it) "explains" the secular constancy of labor's functional share. To see what it means for both theories to hold simultaneously, suppose that factor markets are cleared but the share of Employee Compensation is too big to generate enough savings to prevent inflation. Then, assuming stability, the employee share would tend to fall as wage earners became self-employed, thereby acquiring higher propensities to save.[54] Whether a dynamic

[50] A promising beginning has been made by H. S. Houthakker (see 25).

[51] In a forthcoming paper, R. M. Solow points out that, within the manufacturing sector, the evidence for temporal stability of the share of wages within individual industries is at least as persuasive as that for stability in the aggregate.

[52] Many years ago, I criticized severely the then current interpretation of Cobb-Douglas functions in "cross-sectional" studies. [M. W. Reder (26).] Nothing said here is in any way inconsistent with this criticism. Indeed, I think the "cross-section" studies are subject to a more serious criticism than the one made in the earlier article.

The cross-section functions imply, as does any Cobb-Douglas function, that the rewards per service unit of either factor must vary with the ratio of the factors used; i.e., partially differentiating $P = aL^kK^j$ with respect to L, we have
$$\partial P/\partial L = k(P/L).$$
As P/L obviously varies in the same direction as K (and in the opposite direction from L), the marginal productivity of labor, $\partial P/\partial L$, and hence the wage rate, must be different for differing quantities of either capital or labor. But this is inconsistent with the assumption that all units of labor (or capital) are homogeneous; hence the properties of the fitted cross-section functions mirror either the effect of qualitative differences in factor inputs or of exogenous factors that are correlated with industry size, but not the marginal productivity of (homogeneous) factors.

[53] Cf. Kaldor, pp. 592–93 in (14). Kaldor also argues that it is arbitrary to separate movements along a production function from shifts in it [see (14), pp. 595–98]; by implication, this impugns the validity of (6a). Certainly, the distinction in question is arbitrary, but its justification derives entirely from the results that it helps us obtain and charges of arbitrariness are irrelevant.

[54] This assumes that self-employed persons have a higher propensity to save than wage earners with the same income.

mechanism such as this exists is far from obvious; but it is by no means absurd to suppose that it might.[55]

This mechanism can be visualized by means of Figure 1, on whose vertical axis we measure I/Y and S/Y (as defined in Section II), and on whose horizontal axis we measure fractions of national income. (All points in Figure 1 refer to positions of full employment of both labor and capital.) The line $(I/Y)_0$ gives the actual value of I/Y, which is determined exogenously; the SS' curve relates the aggregate saving ratio to wage share. (The wage share and labor's functional share are measured from the vertical axis; their complements are measured from the unity line.) Equilibrium is reached where SS' cuts the $(I/Y)_0$ line; i.e., where the wage share is OW.[56] Labor's functional share is given by the vertical line, L, so that if the wage share were OW, the share of the self-employed would be WL. Disequilibrium would lead to changes in the ratio WL/OW; that is, in the ratio of Employee Compensation to the income of the self-employed. L is a vertical line because we assume arbitrarily that labor's functional share is deduced from a Cobb-Douglas function and independent of I/Y.[57] However, if the production function were of some other form, labor's functional share might be related to I/Y by some relation such as ZZ_1. (Unity minus OL is the nonlabor share, which is also derived from a Cobb-Douglas function.) Thus it is possible that Kaldor's theory and the marginal productivity theory both hold.

Figure 1 suggests that a satisfactory explanation either of labor's share or the share of Employee Compensation is simpler than it really is. Actually, the distribution of income is determined by the entire set of prices and quantities that the economy generates. Hence, any very large aggregates will be interrelated via the different relative weights attached to their various common components. To investigators of cautious temperament, this undeniable fact will always be adequate reason for eschewing models of the kind we have been considering. Perhaps such caution is justified, and it is foolish to take aggregative distribution theories seriously.

However, I venture the following self-serving opinion: even though

---

[55] Note that an important type of shift from self-employment to wage earning is movement from agriculture to "industry."

[56] Assume the position is stable; i.e., that if $S/Y > (I/Y)$, the wage share increases and vice versa.

[57] It will not generally be true that the coefficients of a Cobb-Douglas function will be independent of the income share of the self-employed. I.e., a shift in the aggregate propensity to save will very likely shift the pattern of final demand and hence the coefficients, or possibly the functional form, of the aggregate production function. However, for simplicity, we confine ourselves to the special case where such independence obtains.

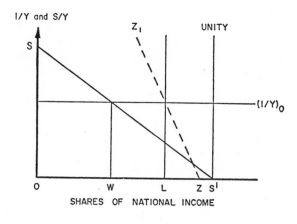

Figure 1

we never succeed in creating a generally accepted aggregative distribution theory—and there is a good chance that we will not—the attempt to do so is likely to uncover a number of interrelations between different aggregates of which some will prove helpful in formulating and testing theories about other aspects of the economy. Put in another way, any theory about the whole economy will have corollaries about income distribution; Kaldor's theory and marginal productivity are two illustrations of this. To deduce and test these corollaries cannot help but improve our understanding of the operation of the economy.

Table A. Estimated Components of Savings and (Actual) Investment, 1909–56

	(1) S_w	(2) S_p	(3) S_g	(4) Sum (1)—(3)	(5) I/Y	(6) * (5)—(4)
1909	.023	.060	.009	.092	.115	.023
1910	.023	.058	.008	.089	.138	.049
1911	.024	.057	.009	.090	.087	−.003
1912	.023	.058	.013	.094	.135	.041
1913	.024	.057	.016	.097	.100	.003
1914	.024	.056	.007	.087	.095	.008
1915	.023	.060	.009	.092	.173	.081
1916	.022	.063	.018	.103	.212	.109
1917	.021	.067	−.044	.043	.165	.122
1918	.024	.056	−.159	−.079	.022	.101
1919	.022	.061	−.071	.012	.082	.070

Table A—(*Continued*)

1920	.026	.049	.026	.101	.153	.052
1921	.028	.042	.016	.086	.055	−.031
1922	.025	.052	.014	.091	.074	−.017
1923	.025	.051	.022	.098	.120	.022
1924	.026	.051	.024	.101	.081	−.020
1925	.025	.053	.021	.099	.122	.023
1926	.025	.051	.026	.102	.113	.011
1927	.026	.049	.029	.105	.102	−.003
1928	.025	.051	.023	.099	.090	−.009
1929	.023	.051	.026	.100	.115	+.015
1930	.025	.053	−.003	.075	.041	−.034
1931	.026	.046	−.042	.030	−.048	−.078
1932	.030	.038	−.034	.034	−.143	−.177
1933	.030	.036	−.028	.038	−.135	−.173
1934	.028	.042	−.041	.029	−.078	−.107
1935	.026	.049	−.030	.045	−.013	−.058
1936	.026	.047	−.039	.038	−.004	−.042
1937	.026	.049	+.007	.082	.052	−.030
1938	.026	.046	−.020	.052	−.006	−.058
1939	.026	.048	−.026	.048	.014	−.034
1940	.026	.051	−.008	.069	.062	−.007
1941	.025	.053	−.032	.046	.084	.038
1942	.025	.053	−.211	−.133	.002	.131
1943	.026	.050	−.244	−.168	−.032	.136
1944	.026	.048	−.260	−.186	−.049	.137
1945	.027	.046	−.198	−.125	−.040	+.085
1946	.026	.049	+.021	.096	.097	−.001
1947	.026	.050	+.061	.137	.106	−.031
1948	.026	.053	+.033	.112	.119	+.007
1949	.026	.049	−.013	.062	.061	−.001
1950	.026	.051	+.031	.108	.107	−.001
1951	.026	.050	+.020	.096	.106	+.010
1952	.027	.047	−.010	.064	.074	+.010
1953	.027	.046	−.020	.053	.057	+.004
1954	.028	.043	−.019	.052	.052	0
1955	.027	.043	+.007	.077	.074	−.003
1956	.028	.041	+.013	.082	.083	+.001

Sources: 1909–28: *Economic Almanac, 1953–1954* (Crowell, New York, 1953), pp. 504–5 (data derived from unpublished estimates of the Department of Commerce), and Raymond Goldsmith, *Study of Saving in the United States* (Princeton University Press, Princeton, 1956). 1929–56: *Survey of Current Business*, February 1957 and July 1957.

* Components may not precisely equal total because of rounding.

1909–1929

Column 1 .04 × $\dfrac{\text{Employee Compensation}}{\text{National Income}}$ from *Economic Almanac* pp. 504–505.

| Column 2 | $.14 \times$ | $\dfrac{\text{1 minus Employee Compensation}}{\text{National Income}}$ | $\dfrac{\textit{Economic Almanac}}{\textit{op. cit.}}$ |

Column 3 $\qquad \dfrac{\text{Sum columns 7 and 8, Table T-1, Goldsmith}}{\text{Column 2, Table N-1, Goldsmith}}$

Column 5 $\qquad \dfrac{\text{Column 1, Table T-1, Goldsmith minus (Sum of Column 5, Table T-8 and Column 5, Table A-3, Goldsmith)}}{\text{Column 2, Table T-1, Goldsmith}}$

1929–1956 (*Survey of Current Business,* February and July, 1957)

Column 1 $.04 \times \dfrac{\text{Compensation of Employees}}{\text{National Income}}$

Column 2 $.14 \times \dfrac{\text{1 minus Employee Compensation}}{\text{National Income}}$

Column 3 $\qquad \dfrac{\text{Government surplus on income and product transactions}}{\text{National Income}}$

Column 5 $\qquad \dfrac{\text{Gross Investment minus (Business Depreciation Charges plus Accidental Damage to Fixed Business Capital)}}{\text{Net National Product}}$

APPENDIX

Table A contains the figures on which text Table I is based. Column 1 (S_w), in each year, is the share of Employee Compensation in National Income multiplied by the assumed marginal (and average) propensity to save, .04. The entries in column 2 (S_p) are found by multiplying one minus the share of Employee Compensation in National Income by the assumed marginal (and average) propensity to save, .14. This last figure is an amalgam of the appropriate propensities of households to save nonwage income and of corporations to retain (pre-tax) [1] earnings. Column 3 (S_g) is the ratio of the government surplus or deficit to National Income; [2] as S_g plays no role in Kaldor's theory it is measured directly for each year. But, though S_g plays no role in the theory, it is necessary to include it in order to satisfy the savings-investment identity. [3]

Column 5 (I/Y) is the ratio of Net Investment to National Income. Conceptually, we have aimed at getting our estimates of Y and $I \equiv S$ as close as possible to Net National Product (National Income at market prices) and net investment; i.e., Gross Investment minus (Business

---

[1] We are concerned with pre-tax profits because the saving propensities of the other components of S_p are defined with reference to Personal Income rather than Disposable Income.

[2] "Government" includes all government plus Government surplus on income and product transactions plus Statistical Discrepancy equals Gross Investment.

[3] I.e., Gross Private Saving plus Government surplus on income and product transactions plus Statistical Discrepancy equals Gross Investment.

depreciation plus Accidental damage to fixed business capital). These definitions of saving and investment exclude purchases of durable consumer goods; this choice of concepts was made for reasons of statistical convenience only.

REFERENCES

1. Joan Robinson, *The Economics of Imperfect Competition*. Macmillan, New York, 1933. Books VII–IX.

2. Joan Robinson, "Euler's Theorem and the Problem of Distribution," *Economic Journal*, 1934, pp. 398–414.

3. M. Kalecki, "The Distribution of the National Income," in William Fellner and B. F. Haley (eds.), *Readings in the Theory of Income Distribution*. Blakiston, Philadelphia, 1946, pp. 197–217.

4. M. Kalecki, *Theory of Economic Dynamics*. Rinehart, New York, 1954, Chap. I.

5. M. W. Reder, "Rehabilitation of Partial Equilibrium Theory," *American Economic Review*, May 1952, pp. 182–97.

6. M. Kalecki, "A Theory of Long-Run Distribution of the Product of Industry," *Oxford Economic Papers*, June 1941, pp. 31–41.

7. E. H. Phelps-Brown and P. E. Hart, "The Share of Wages in National Income," *Economic Journal*, June 1952, pp. 253–77.

8. Clark Kerr, "Labor's Income Share and the Labor Movement," in G. W. Taylor and F. C. Pierson (eds.), *New Concepts in Wage Determination*. McGraw-Hill, New York, 1957, pp. 260–98.

9. K. E. Boulding. *A Reconstruction of Economics*. Wiley, New York, 1950, Chap. 14.

10. K. E. Boulding, in D. M. Wright (ed.), *The Impact of the Union*. Harcourt, Brace, New York, 1951, Chap. VI.

11. M. Bronfenbrenner, "A Contribution to the Aggregative Theory of Wages," *Journal of Political Economy*, December 1956.

12. S. Weintraub, *An Approach to the Theory of Income Distribution*. Chilton, Philadelphia, 1958.

13. N. Kaldor, "Alternative Theories of Distribution," *Review of Economic Studies*, XXIII (2), No. 61 (1955–56), 83–100.

14. N. Kaldor, "A Model of Economic Growth," *Economic Journal*, December 1957, pp. 591–614.

15. Milton Friedman, *A Theory of the Consumption Function*. National Bureau of Economic Research. Princeton University Press, Princeton, 1957.

16. D. S. Brady, "Family Saving, 1888 to 1950," in Goldsmith, Brady, and Menderhausen, *A Study of Saving in the United States*. Princeton University Press, Princeton 1957, Vol. III, Table H-9, 1957.

17. Zvi Griliches, "Specification Bias in Estimates of Production Functions," *Journal of Farm Economics*, February 1957, pp. 8–20.

18. E. H. Phelps-Brown, "The Meaning of the Fitted Cobb-Douglas Function," *Quarterly Journal of Economics*, November 1957, pp. 546–60.

19. R. M. Solow, "Technical Change and the Aggregate Production Function," *Review of Economics and Statistics*, August 1957, pp. 312–20.

20. M. W. Reder, "Wage Determination in Theory and Practice," in N. W. Chamberlain *et al.* (eds.), *A Decade of Industrial Relations Research*. Harper, New York, 1958, pp. 64–97.

21. D. Gale Johnson, "The Functional Distribution of Income in the United States, 1850–1952," *Review of Economics and Statistics*, May 1954, pp. 175–82.

22. E. F. Denison, "Distribution of National Income," *Survey of Current Business*, June 1952, pp. 16–23.

23. E. F. Denison, "Income Types and the Size Distribution," *American Economic Review*, May 1952, pp. 254–69.

24. D. Gale Johnson, "Allocation of Agriculture Income," *Journal of Farm Economics*, November 1948, pp. 724–49.

25. H. S. Houthakker, "The Pareto Distribution and the Cobb-Douglas Production Function Activity Analysis," *Review of Economics and Statistics*, XXIII (1), No. 60 (1955–56), 27–31.

26. M. W. Reder, "An Alternative Interpretation of the Cobb-Douglas Function," *Econometrica*, July 1943, pp. 259–64.

30

A "NEW" CONCEPT IN WAGE DETERMINATION: DISGUISED PRODUCTIVITY ANALYSIS *

E. E. LIEBHAFSKY† teaches at The University of Missouri; he was formerly at Texas A. and M.

Two new concepts in wage determination, offered in John T. Dunlop's essay, "The Task of Contemporary Wage Theory," [1] are alleged to define the points at which wage-making forces are concentrated, for they "help to focus attention upon the operation of demand and supply" and "suggest that product-market competition and conditions decisively influence the structure of wage rates." [2] The suggested reformulation of wage theory is accompanied by a rejection of marginal productivity analysis, which "has proved unsatisfactory as a tool of analysis." [3] If we are to accept the proposed reformulation, Dunlop must demonstrate that the new concepts (1) depart significantly from familiar concepts in productivity analysis and (2) are more effective than the received doctrine in focusing attention upon demand and supply and in accounting for the influence of product-market competition and conditions. The proposed reformulation can be accepted only with reservations, however, if the new concepts are disguised applications of an existing analytical tool.

I

Dunlop's indictment of marginal productivity analysis appears to rest upon a failure to distinguish, consistently, between the marginal

* From *Southern Economic Journal*, Vol. XXVI (October, 1959), pp. 141–146. Reprinted by permission.

† I am indebted to A. F. Chalk, W. G. Modrow, and L. H. Stern for their suggestions (some of which I accepted) on this paper.

[1] John T. Dunlop, "The Task of Contemporary Wage Theory," in George W. Taylor and Frank C. Pierson (eds.), *New Concepts in Wage Determination* (New York: McGraw-Hill, 1957), pp. 117–139. An earlier version of the essay appears in John T. Dunlop (ed.), *The Theory of Wage Determination*, Papers of a Conference Held by the International Economic Association (London: Macmillan, 1957), pp. 3–27. Subsequent references in this paper are to the version appearing in the volume edited by Taylor and Pierson.

[2] *Ibid.*, p. 139.

[3] *Ibid.*, p. 124.

productivity *theory* of J. B. Clark and the marginal productivity *doctrine* of Alfred Marshall.[4] Clark's theory, after all, predicts that wages tend toward the competitive level in the long-run stationary state, while Marshall's doctrine purports merely to explain the demand for labor.[5]

Dunlop indicts the Clarkian theory and the Marshallian doctrine indiscriminately in arriving at the conclusion that marginal productivity, like the wage-fund doctrine before it, has substantially collapsed on the supply side. He argues that "marginal productivity *theory*, with some notable exceptions, has not been widely applied to the complexities of wage structures," and that "the marginal productivity *analysis*," i.e., the doctrine that wages measure marginal productivity, "is not a theory of wage-rate determination" and "explains neither particular wages nor the general level." [6] Dunlop contends that "unions can no longer be treated as an aberration of the usual market determination," that "collective bargaining must be taken as the normal case," that "governmental action has impinged on wage-setting forces very generally," that the task of contemporary wage theory is "the formulation of a body of wage analysis more suitable to labor-market developments and to wage-setting institutions of the day, drawing upon the central body of economic analysis," and that "the questions that are posed for contemporary wage theory are quite different from those that challenged the wage-fund and marginal-productivity *doctrines*." [7]

These comments lead to the conclusion that Dunlop's attack is formulated in terms of the Clarkian theory and directed against the Marshallian doctrine. Dunlop recognizes that "strictly speaking, marginal productivity is not a theory of wages, but only a statement of the demand side," [8] yet his criticism appears to be directed against the Clarkian conclusion that wages will tend toward the competitive level. The author of this paper does not consider himself to be an "unabashed defender" of marginal productivity theory and finds him-

[4] An excellent analysis of the development of marginal productivity theory and of the distinctions between Clarkian and Marshallian contributions is contained in Allan M. Cartter, *Theory of Wages and Employment* (Homewood: Richard D. Irwin, 1959), pp. 11–44, especially pp. 18–20 and 22–25.

[5] *Ibid.*, pp. 21–23. Cartter offers the following quotation as illustrative of Marshall's view: "This doctrine has sometimes been put forward as a theory of wages. But there is no valid ground for any such pretension." Alfred Marshall, *Principles of Economics* (London: Macmillan, 1920), p. 518.

[6] Dunlop, *op. cit.*, p. 123. Italics mine.

[7] *Ibid.*, pp. 123, 125, 126, 138. Italics mine.

[8] *Ibid.*, p. 122.

self uncomfortable with "received" theory, if that term, as Dunlop uses it,[9] refers to marginal productivity theory based upon competitive assumptions in product and factor markets. Productivity analysis, i.e., analysis of a firm's demand for units of labor service, can be employed separately and distinctly from a commitment to acceptance of a long-run competitive equilibrium.

Dunlop's sketch of marginal productivity theory attributes to the theory the conclusion that the marginal value productivity of labor will equal the wage in both competitive and imperfectly competitive labor markets. That conclusion, however, is validly attributed to marginal productivity analysis only when it is assumed that the labor market is perfectly competitive, so that the supply of labor to the firm is infinitely elastic, and marginal labor cost equals average labor cost.

Following Samuelson,[10] Dunlop states: "Maximization of profits by the firm requires, simply as a logical deduction, that as an equilibrium condition the price of each factor of production be proportional to marginal physical productivity *and that the marginal value productivity of each factor be equal to its price.*" [11]

But, he adds: "This is true of any factor of production, including labor services, and holds regardless of the character of competition." [12]

Using Samuelson's definition of marginal value productivity as marginal revenue times marginal physical productivity, let us substitute the term *revenue productivity* (marginal revenue product) [13] for marginal value productivity in order to make more clear the distinction between the sales value of the marginal product and the addition to revenue resulting from the sale of the output produced by one additional unit of labor service. The profit-maximizing firm, then, will seek to hire that number of units of labor service at which revenue productivity equals marginal labor cost. Marginal labor cost equals average labor cost (the wage or the price of labor) only if the supply of labor to the firm is infinitely elastic, i.e., if the labor market is perfectly competitive. In an imperfectly competitive labor market, the supply curve of labor to the firm is less than infinitely elastic and slopes upward and to the right, so that marginal labor cost is above

9 *Ibid.*, p. 126.

10 Paul A. Samuelson, *Foundations of Economic Analysis* (Cambridge: Harvard University Press, 1947), pp. 87–89.

11 Dunlop, *op. cit.*, p. 122. Italics mine.

12 *Ibid.*

13 Samuelson, of course, uses the term "marginal revenue product" in his principles text, *Economics—An Introductory Analysis*, 3rd ed. (New York: McGraw-Hill, 1955), pp. 483–484, and in the Fourth Edition (1958), pp. 507–509.

average labor cost: the familiar case of monopsony or "employer wage determination." Under these conditions, as the firm equates revenue productivity and marginal labor cost, the wage it pays is below the corresponding marginal labor cost, and, consequently, below revenue productivity. A monopsonistic employer, then, exploits labor.[14] The marginal value productivity of labor is not equal to its price, precisely because the labor market is imperfectly competitive. The conclusion stated by Dunlop holds only if the character of competition in the factor market is perfect.

II

The tenor of Dunlop's essay is such that one would expect its reformulation of wage theory to be somewhat more consistent with rejection of the received doctrine. Dunlop's thesis is that the task to which contemporary wage theory must set itself is analysis of "the problem of setting and variation in the whole structure or complex of rates," [15] rather than the problem of single wage rate determination, and to indicate the interrelations between internal and external wage structures.[16] The analysis utilizes two new concepts: (1) *a job cluster* ("a stable group of job classifications or work assignments within a wage-determining unit" [17]) and (2) *a wage contour* ("a stable group of wage-determining units . . . which are so linked together . . . that they have common wage-making characteristics" [18]).

The 1954 Round Table Conference of the International Economic Association, at which the earlier version of the Dunlop essay was presented, apparently was organized upon the basis of the assumption that labor economists can be clearly distinguished from general theorists.[19] Although not to be specifically directed toward Dunlop's endeavors

[14] Joan Robinson, *The Economics of Imperfect Competition* (London: Macmillan, 1948), pp. 281–283.

[15] Dunlop, *op. cit.*, p. 128, i.e., a wage structure.

[16] *Ibid.*, pp. 128–129. The internal wage structure exists within "a bargaining unit, plant, firm, association or other grouping in which wage differentials are set by the same authorities," while the external wage structure is "the complex of interfirm or group structures each set by different agencies."

[17] *Ibid.*, p. 129.

[18] *Ibid.*, p. 131.

[19] Dunlop's introduction to the proceedings of the conference, *The Theory of Wage Determination*, p. xi, states: "Labour specialists have a contribution to make on such matters as the behaviour of labour organizations and managements, the degree of flexibility of the wage structure in response to relative changes in employment and other factors, and the impact of labour organizations on the operation of otherwise unorganized labour markets. General theorists, in turn, emphasize the common elements in the experience among countries: the role of

in "The Task of Contemporary Wage Theory," it would seem that Boulding's evaluation of the apparent conflict between economists and industrial relations specialists [20] is applicable to the popularity of the "whipping boy" approach in appraisals of marginal productivity analysis. It is disconcerting to find that rejection of the competitive model of marginal productivity theory is frequently accompanied by rejection of the marginal productivity doctrine, as well, and by the contention that contemporary analysis must forge new tools—when the tools, in reality, are familiar concepts parading under new labels.

III

A plant's wage structure, according to Dunlop, is comprised of a limited number of job clusters determined in the short run by concomitant institutional forces: technology, administrative organization, and/or social custom. A group of closely interrelated ·jobs requiring similar skills and training of the incumbents, with common promotion, transfer, and layoff patterns, becomes a job cluster.[21]

---

wages in inflation, the relations between wage policy and monetary and fiscal policy, the relations between wages and transfer payments, and the factors determining the structure of wage differentials."

[20] Kenneth E. Boulding, "Collective Bargaining and Fiscal Policy," *American Economic Review*, Proc., May, 1950, 40, p. 306. "The study of industrial relations has now spread so far beyond the limits of economics that the economist in these days has considerable difficulty in persuading students of labor that his discipline has anything to contribute to their studies. It is not enough for him to confess—as in all honesty he should—that economics comprises no more than about 20 per cent of the subject, and that the rest is sociology, social psychology, individual psychology, psychiatry, anthropology, law, engineering, political science, etc., with perhaps an occasional dash of philosophy, ethics, and even physics to improve the flavor. There is a strong (and to my mind a deplorable) tendency among the bright young labor specialists not merely to let economics go by default out of ignorance, as was customary among the older generation of writers on this subject, but to cast it out of the window bodily, with shrill cries of jubilation. One can hardly pick up a book on labor nowadays without finding the author jumping gleefully on what he thinks is the corpse of Demand-and-Supply, or proclaiming with trumpets, "The Labor Market is Dead, Long Live Human Relations.' "

[21] Dunlop, *op. cit.*, p. 129. E. Robert Livernash's essay in the same volume, "The Internal Wage Structure," elaborates upon the concept of a job cluster as a job group "within which internal comparison is most significant," (p. 148) and states that rates applicable to jobs within the groups are determined through comparison with the key job or jobs within the cluster. Livernash appears to contend (p. 149) that, while internal comparison serves as the basis of wage determination, a subjective element of "general judgment," rather than job-content, determines the appropriate wage relationship between clusters.

Dunlop cites the following examples of job clusters which are determined, in the short-run, by institutional forces: machinists operating various specialized machines (training and skill), the crew of a train or plane (technology), employees in a department (administrative organization), and sales girls in a department store or the stenographers in an office (social custom).[22] It would appear reasonable to assume that each unit of labor service within each of these examples of job clusters is employed in conjunction with approximately the same average quantity of fixed factors. Interchangeability of labor inputs within each of the groups exists as a possibility. The clustering of jobs (and of wage rates in most of these examples) is determined by the additions to revenue resulting from the outputs of additional inputs of labor service—as well as by the institutional forces cited by Dunlop.[23] The fact that wage rates applicable to units of labor service within a cluster may diverge from the revenue productivity of the marginal unit reflects, simply, the fact that labor is not infinitely divisible.[24]

Job clustering occurs, then, because an employer finds machinists, crew members, clerical employees, or department stores sales personnel to constitute relatively homogeneous groups in terms of skill, training, technology, or social custom—and productivity. The establishment of wage differentials between the key job or jobs and other jobs within the group is based upon differentials in productivities. The fact that "certain job clusters may be more closely related to some than to other clusters" [25] is further indication of the role of the revenue productivity associated with each unit of labor service within each of the clusters. The employer's demand for a particular kind of units of labor service reflects not only the relationship between jobs within a cluster but the

[22] *Ibid.*, pp. 129–130.

[23] Decisions by employers to hire a specific number of units of labor service, or to change the number of units employed, are based upon comparisons (whether they be conscious and calculated or of the trial-and-error variety) of revenue productivities and additions to labor cost. The job cluster, being determined by institutional forces, may describe some of the forces which affect the employer's demand for labor services. However, the employer's decision, although affected by institutional forces, seems still to be dependent upon the revenue productivity function. The basic question, it would seem, is whether the job cluster is a device which aids in the prediction of changes in wages and/or employment or is merely a rationalization of existing wage structures. When it is used for purposes of prediction, the job cluster must consider productivity and becomes "revenue productivity affected by institutional forces."

[24] The "range of indeterminateness," after all, is limited by the internal and external marginal products and reflects the elasticity of demand for labor. See J. R. Hicks, *The Theory of Wages* (New York: Peter Smith, 1948), pp. 24–26.

[25] Dunlop, *op. cit.*, p. 130.

interrelationship between clusters as well. Historical wage differentials and union wage scales would appear to serve as further reflections of productivity differentials. A job cluster might appropriately be redefined as consisting of a group of job classifications or work assignments which is stable because of the equivalence of the contributions of the clustered jobs to the firm's total revenue.

The stable group of wage-determining units—a wage contour—exhibits common wage-making characteristics reflecting "(1) similarity of product markets, (2) resort to similar sources for a labor force, or (3) common labor market organization. . . ." [26] The case for Dunlop's new concepts seems to rest upon their application to the union scale for motor-truck drivers in Boston for July, 1953. In fact, Dunlop considers this case to constitute "a kind of critical experiment," for a diversity of wage rates exists among "essentially similar and substitutable" teamsters "performing almost identical work, organized by the same union." [27] Dunlop expresses his belief that negative answers can be provided for the following questions relating to this case: "Are the disparities temporary? Do they arise from 'friction' or 'immobilities' in the labor market? Are they primarily the consequence of a monopolistic seller of labor discriminating among types of employers?" [28]

Certainly, Dunlop is entitled to his belief that the wage diversities do not arise from immobilities of labor between the various industries. But his essay does not demonstrate, either deductively or through the presentation of empirical evidence, that immobilities are to be dismissed as the possible explanations of the diversities.

Each hourly rate, according to Dunlop, "reflects a wage contour," and "is a reflection of the product market." [29] Differentials among contours reflect differences in product markets back into the labor market, and short-run differentials reflect the fact that "newer and expanding industries or contours, such as oil, have had to pay higher wages to attract labor in the evolution of wage scales." [30] Dunlop contends that historical precedent causes the relative rates among contours to be regarded as "proper." In addition, he states:

A minor part of the explanation lies in the fact that these wage rates are influenced by the wages of the groups of workers these employees tend to be associated with in work

[26] Ibid., p. 131.
[27] Ibid., pp. 134–135.
[28] Ibid., p. 135.
[29] Ibid.
[30] Ibid., p. 136.

operations. Teamsters hauling oil and building materials
come in contact with high-paid employees in their work
operations, while laundry and scrap drivers have more direct contact with lower-paid employees. *A larger emphasis
is to be placed on the fact that competitive conditions permit higher pay at the top end of the list.* Demand is less
elastic and wages tend to be a lower proportion of sales
revenue.[31]

The level of a wage contour is dependent upon the ability of an
employer to pay wage rates above, below, or equal to those associated
with existing contours. For instance, teamsters hauling oil come into
direct contact with more highly-paid employees than do laundry
drivers; and, of course, this would be expected. The higher value of
the product and the higher capital-labor ratio in the petroleum industry result in a higher productivity per unit of labor service. It
would seem, however, that the persistence of a wage diversity in the
case of teamsters in the two industries would stem, in the final analysis, from immobilities of truck drivers from laundries into the petroleum industry.

I would suggest that a wage contour might be redefined as a stable
group of wage-determining units which reflects (1) the amount of fixed
factors available for use by each unit of labor service, (2) the percentage of each firm's total cost accounted for by labor costs, and (3)
the ease with which each firm can pass on wage increases to purchasers
of its product.

The mirroring of the product market into the labor market tending
to determine the wage structure [32] and resulting in wage differentials
for virtually identical units of labor service is recognized by Dunlop
to "reflect different product-market competitive conditions." [33] Dunlop
also recognizes that the introduction of new plants into the com-
munities of a growing economy reflects higher productivities. He
states:

> The new industries may require higher standards of skill.
> The new plants may need several thousand employees as a
> minimum work force. A higher rate is needed to attract that
> number than if the plant were to grow gradually from a
> small figure. Labor costs are frequently a small fraction of

[31] *Ibid.* Italics mine.
[32] *Ibid.*
[33] *Ibid.*, p. 137.

total costs, and the product markets are often oligopolistic. These factors permit or encourage an enterprise to set a higher rate for the key jobs than would be paid for a comparable level of skill in other jobs in the community. The oil, chemical, atomic and television industries provide current examples. All this suggests that there is a tendency for new industries to push the wage level upward.[34]

In other words, the revenue productivity of a unit of labor service will be greater in a large firm than in a small firm; it will tend to be greater in an imperfectly competitive firm than in one which approaches the model of perfect competition.

IV

The introductory section of Dunlop's essay leaves the reader with the impression that the suggested reformulation will, at the very least, constitute a step toward a correction of the major deficiency of marginal productivity analysis: its collapse on the supply side. Labor economists appear to be in agreement with Dunlop's quotation from Robertson to the effect that "wages tend to measure the marginal productivity of labor" [35] and with Dunlop's statement that "this is not a theory of wage-rate determination." [36] A recognition of the failure of the marginal productivity theory to explain the supply of labor does not, however, appear to warrant the conclusion that the theory "has proved unsatisfactory as a tool of analysis," for the merit of modern marginal productivity analysis lies in its ability to provide a tool for analyzing the demand for labor, considering a variety of product market conditions. If the wage contour differs significantly from existing tools, it is a new concept; if it is conceptually similar to existing tools, it is a restatement of a useful portion of orthodox theory and is not, in reality, "new." If, on the other hand, the wage contour explains the supply of labor, it corrects the major deficiency of marginal productivity analysis.

The wage contour does not attempt to analyze the supply of labor. It does not, therefore, cope with the theory's major deficiency, and we are left with a system of analysis which does not explain wage-rate determination. The wage contour is, however, an analysis of the demand for labor, and its merits must rest upon its ability to provide an

[34] *Ibid.*
[35] *Ibid.*, p. 123.
[36] *Ibid.*

explanation of labor demand more adequate that that which is already available.

Since a wage contour is defined as "a stable group of wage-determining units . . . having common wage-making characteristics," [37] we must examine the forces which contribute to those common characteristics. Dunlop finds that wage contours reflect the elasticity of product demand and the firm's labor cost–total cost ratio by "mirroring" product market conditions.[38] In other words, each contour reflects the fact that the firms within the group of wage-determining units experience approximately the same labor-capital ratios and face similar marginal revenue functions in their product markets. The wage contour, then, is an industry-wide view of the addition to each firm's total revenue resulting from the output of one additional unit of labor service, but it seems to be no more effective than the received doctrine in focusing attention upon demand and supply and in accounting for the influence of product-market competition and conditions.

The wage contour of a particular firm of industry for a specific kind of labor service is a reflection of the forces which, according to marginal productivity analysis, affect (1) the slope of the marginal revenue product function, (2) shifts in the marginal revenue product function, and (3) the divergence of the marginal revenue product function from, or its identity with, the value of the marginal product function. The wage contour is the marginal revenue product function in an industry-wide disguise.

V

It was the purpose of this paper to question the basis upon which Dunlop's suggested reformulation of wage theory constitutes a departure from existing marginal productivity analysis. Perhaps Dunlop's analysis is "brilliant as far as it goes," [39] since it does provide two new terms to be utilized in analysis of wage determination. But does it, in the final analysis, warrant the assertion that the marginal productivity theory has "proved unsatisfactory as a tool of analysis" or that the new concepts suggest more effectively than does the marginal revenue product concept "that product market competition and conditions decisively influence the structure of wage rates"?

---

[37] See footnote 26.

[38] Dunlop, *op. cit.*, pp. 135–136.

[39] Sar A. Levitan, "Review of New Concepts in Wage Determination," *American Economic Review*, March, 1958, 48, pp. 222–224.

31

THE PROFIT CONCEPT AND THEORY: A RESTATEMENT *

J. FRED WESTON teaches at the University of
California at Los Angeles.

Profit theory has long been regarded as a vexed, confused, and unsatisfactory subject.[1] The recent writings in this area continue to
present divergent ideas.[2] It appears useful, therefore, to review the areas
of dispute, to indicate the reasons for the continuing disagreements,
and to attempt a restatement which may secure more general acceptance.[3]

* From *The Journal of Political Economy*, Vol. LXII (April, 1954), pp. 152–170,
copyright © by the University of Chicago Press. Reprinted by permission.

[1] For convenience in summarizing and referring to the different views held by the
writers in this area, code letters will designate the leading rival theories of profit.
This results in extreme over-simplification but serves to indicate the nature of
the positions held.

[2] Chronologically: J. F. Weston, "Profit as the Payment for the Function of Uncer-
tainty-bearing," *Journal of Business*, XXII (April, 1949), 106–18; "Enterprise and
Profit," *ibid.*, July, 1949, pp. 141–59; "A Generalized Uncertainty Theory of
Profit," *American Economic Review*, XL (March, 1950), 40–60 (U); Armen A.
Alchian, "Uncertainty, Evolution, and Economic Theory," *Journal of Political
Economy*, LVIII (June, 1950), 211–21 (U, A); Jean Marchal, "The Construction of
a New Theory of Profit," *American Economic Review*, XLI (September, 1951),
549–65 (MC, A); Stephen Enke, "On Maximizing Profits," *American Economic
Review*, XLI (September, 1951), 566–78 (U, A); R. G. Hawtrey, "The Nature of
Profit," *Economic Journal*, LXI (September, 1951). 489–504 (A); G. L. S. Shackle,
"The Nature and Role of Profit," *Metroeconomica*, III (December, 1951), 101–7
(U); Richard M. Davis, "The Current State of Profit Theory," *American Eco-
nomic Review*, XLII (June, 1952), 245–64 (U, Q); Boris Ischboldin, "Die Theorie
der Quasirente und des Profits," *Schmollers Jahrbuch*, LXXII (1952), 35–51 (U);
R. F. Harrod, "Theory of Profit," *Economic Essays* (London: Macmillan & Co.,
Ltd., 1952), pp. 188–207 (E, U, R); Peter L. Bernstein, "Profit Theory—Where
Do We Go from Here?" *Quarterly Journal of Economics* LXVII (August, 1953),
407–22 (A).

[3] I have greatly benefited from extended discussions with Armen A. Alchian, Martin Bronfenbrenner (by correspondence) Karl Brunner, Harry Markowitz, Frank
E. Norton, and R. Clay Sprowls. I am grateful for research assistance to the Bureau of Business and Economic Research, University of California, Los Angeles.

I. INTRODUCTION

The development of profit theory offers a fascinating study in the history of economic ideas. Since Knight covers the period up to the publication of his own landmark,[4] it is necessary to sketch here only the nature of the subsequent materials, with one notable exception. Although *Risk, Uncertainty, and Profit* includes references to the stationary state of Schumpeter's *The Theory of Economic Development,* it does not discuss his profit theory.[5]

Although only six books on "profit" have been published since 1921,[6] many others included substantial sections on this topic.[7] Especially good are Triffin's discussion of uncertainty, innovation, restrictions on entry, and recontracting and his emphasis on the individual rather than the firm.[8] Statistical studies of accounting net income purport to test some aspects of "profit" theory.[9] Textbook discussions have been influential, but this segment of the literature is too diverse for brief treatment.[10]

Surprisingly few journal articles on profit appeared during the thirty-year period, 1921-50.[11] Three contributions have been out-

[4] Frank H. Knight, *Risk, Uncertainty, and Profit* (Boston: Houghton Mifflin Co., 1921), pp. 22-50 (U).

[5] Joseph A. Schumpeter, *The Theory of Economic Development,* trans, R. Opie (Cambridge: Harvard University Press, 1934) (E).

[6] William Trufant Foster and Waddill Catchings, *Profits* (1925) (R, E); George O'Brien, *Notes on the Theory of Profit* (1929) (R); Clarence J. Foreman, *Efficiency and Scarcity Profits* (1930) (R, E, MC); H. P. Fairchild, *Profits or Prosperity* (1932) (W); James P. Beddy, *Profits* (1940) (MC); Hastings Lyon, *Risk, Profit, and Loss* (1943) (R).

[7] M. Dobb, *Capitalist Enterprise and Social Progress* (1925) (U, E); J. M. Keynes, *A Treatise on Money* (1930) (U); A. C. Pigou, *Economics of Welfare* (London: Macmillan & Co., Ltd., 1932) (R).

[8] Robert Triffin, *Monopolistic Competition and General Equilibrium Theory* (Cambridge: Harvard University Press, 1941), pp. 158-87 (U, E).

[9] S. H. Nerlove, *A Decade of Corporate Incomes* (Chicago: University of Chicago Press, 1932); R. C. Epstein, *Industrial Profits in the United States* (New York: National Bureau of Economic Research, 1934); R. T. Bowman, *A Statistical Study of Profits* (Philadelphia: University of Pennsylvania Press, 1934); W. L. Crum, *Corporate Size and Earning Power* (Cambridge: Harvard University Press, 1939); M. Taitel, *Profits, Productive Activities, and New Investment* ("T.N.E.C. Monograph," No. 12 [Washington, 1941]).

[10] I have not attained complete coverage of the foreign-language literature since 1920. Nor have I attempted to track down all unpublished doctoral dissertations on profit.

[11] L. Kotany, "A Theory of Profit and Interest," *Quarterly Journal of Economics,* 1921-22 (A); R. A. Lehfeldt, "Analysis of Profit," *Journal of Political Economy,*

standing: Hicks for his discussion of the nature and role of uncertainty; Gordon for delineating dominant patterns of ideas about profit and for a persuasive formulation of his own; Machlup for a remarkably clear exposition of the relationships between accounting and economic concepts and for his discussion of the many facets of restrictions on entry.

Important issues are raised by both the older and the more recent literature on profit: (1) the use of the profit concept in economic analysis; (2) the nature of risk and uncertainty; (3) the origin or source of profit (4) empirical testing of profit concepts and theories; (5) innovation, entrepreneurship, and profit; (6) profit and monopoly power; (7) profit, imputation, and quasi-rent; (8) profit and the income of social classes; (9) profit maximization; (10) profit and macroeconomics. These topics are discussed in the order listed.

II. IS A PROFIT CONCEPT USEFUL FOR ECONOMIC ANALYSIS?

Do we need a concept "profit"? A succinct statement of the distribution process provides an answer. Fundamentally, there are two types of payments for productive services—wages and rent. Since personal services cannot be capitalized and sold as a reservoir of services, payments for a stream of current services may be called "wages." The payment for the use of a capital asset is rent. Alternatively, a person may borrow loanable funds to buy a capital good and pay interest on his borrowings. Rent and interest may therefore be regarded as alternative methods of arranging for the possession and use of capital

1925 (R); G. E. Barnett, "The Entrepreneur and the Supply of Capital," *Economic Essays in Honor of John Bates Clark* (1927) (E); C. A. Tuttle, "A Functional Theory of Economic Profit" *Economic Essays in Honor of John Bates Clark* (1927) (E); J. R. Hicks, "The Theory of Uncertainty and Profit," *Economica*, 1931 (U); W. S. Hopkins, "Profit in American Economic Theory," *Review of Economic Studies*, Vol. I (October, 1933) (U, MN, MC); A. C. Littleton, "Contrasting Theories of Profit," *Accounting Review*, 1936, (E, A); R. A. Gordon, "Enterprise, Profits, and the Modern Corporation," *Explorations in Economics* (1936) (U, E, MN, MC); M. A. Hasan, "Enterprise and Profit," *Indian Journal of Economics*, 1937 (E); R. S. Tucker, "Is There a Tendency for Profits To Equalize?" *American Economic Review*, 1937 (A); N. S. Buchanan, "Toward a Theory of Fluctuations in Business Profits," *American Economic Review*, 1941 (A); L. R. Chenault, "Buchanan's Theory of Fluctuations in Business Profits," *American Economic Review*, 1942 (A); M. Kalecki, "A Theory of Profits," *Economic Journal*, 1942 (A); F. Machlup, "Competition, Pliopoly, and Profits," *Economica*, 1942 (R, MN, MC); J. H. Stauss, "The Entrepreneur: The Firm," *Journal of Political Economy*, 1944 (E).

goods. Under perfect competition and complete knowledge, each factor is paid the value of its marginal product. In accordance with Euler's theorem, total product will be exhausted in wage, rent, and interest payments.[12]

Planned total product and planned total costs, however, are likely to differ from those actually realized. If expectations are not realized, residuals will arise. These residuals represent an income-flow element contained in payments to owners of productive services. The residuals are not income flows parallel or correlative with the traditional categories—wages, rent, and interest—but components of these incomes. Thus any income has two elements, a functional segment and a nonfunctional segment, profit. Thus the profit concept is useful for identifying a distinctive income element. This concept of profit is explained further after a discussion of the key factor, uncertainty.

III. THE NATURE OF RISK AND UNCERTAINTY

A. DEGREES OF INFORMATION

Marschak has set forth a framework which is useful for making clear the nature of uncertainty.[13] He distinguishes four degrees of information (for convenience of reference, his numbering and symbols are followed):

3.1 The firm does not know (p).[14]
3.2 The firm does not know (p), but it knows data permitting it to estimate (p).
3.3 The firm knows (p).
3.4 The firm knows (p), and every element of (p) is either 0 or 1.

The relationships can be most clearly seen by a tabular summary of his explanatory comments.

Incomplete information, 3.1, nonstochastic case (ignorance)
Incomplete information, 3.2, stochastic case
Complete information, 3.3, stochastic case
Complete information, 3.4, nonstochastic case (certainty)

[12] Technically, total product is exhausted under two sets of conditions. Under constant returns to scale, this is true at any output. Exhaustion of product in distribution also obtains whenever the production function is tangent to any homogeneous function of the first degree, as is the case at long-run equilibrium.
[13] Jacob Marschak, "Role of Liquidity under Complete and Incomplete Information," *American Economic Review*, Suppl. XXXIX (May, 1949), pp. 183–84. Professor Marschak also helped me by commenting on an earlier draft of this section.
[14] (p) is the probability distribution of alternative outcomes.

The stochastic cases are amenable to rational solution through statistical decisions. The extreme cases are relatively unimportant for practical problems. Although Marschak acknowledges "obvious mixed cases" of other degrees of information, one of these mixed cases is of such importance that it deserves recognition as a distinct category. It is intermediate between his first and second situations and will be referred to here as "situation 3.11."

Under situation 3.11, the firm does not know p; it has some knowledge, but the information is such that p cannot be estimated on the basis of statistical relationships (because, for example, the observations are not drawn from a single or homogeneous universe; the observations are not from a stable universe; there are too few observations; etc.). Situations represented by 3.11 are of the greatest practical importance, since the great majority of important business and economic decisions fall into this category. A danger of Marschak's classification is its implication that business and economic decisions can ordinarily be handled as stochastic problems. One of the goals of statistical analysis and econometrics, of course, is to develop record-keeping and techniques which will transform 3.11 problems into 3.2 problems.[15] But the area of decision-making in which this has not yet been attained remains vast and doubtless will always remain so.

The use of distinct categories (as both Knight and Marschak have observed) is an idealization, since reality is a continuum of cases running from certainty to increasing degrees of uncertainty. Nevertheless, the concepts of uncertainty and risk are amenable to definition.

B. Definition and Nature of Uncertainty

The necessary condition for uncertainty is either incomplete information or a "short-run" stochastic situation. Differences in degree of uncertainty may be distinguished for stochastic cases by measures of the dispersion of the probability distribution. In the important 3.11 cases of incomplete probability distributions, it may not be meaningful to attempt to compare the degree of uncertainty associated with alternative courses of action. These circumstances pose difficult questions for formalizing the decision-making process, which Shackle seeks to surmount by the concept of the degree of potential surprise.[16] But if the decision-maker cannot assign probability values to alternative outcomes, it is difficult to understand how he can arrive at degrees of

15 The recent development of linear programming is an example of such effort.
16 G. L. S. Shackle, *Expectation in Economics* (Cambridge: At the University Press, 1949); also "On the Meaning and Measure of Uncertainty." I, *Metroeconomica*, IV (December, 1952), 99–103.

458 READINGS IN MICROECONOMICS

potential surprise. Shackle's analysis appears to represent a method of formulating subjective probability judgments.

The causes of uncertainty are (1) innovations, (2) exogenous changes, and (3) interactions between the two. Examples of exogenous changes are wars, alterations in the legislative-legal environment, differences in ability between businessmen (also reflected in innovations), spontaneous changes in tastes (including changes in spending habits of people, changes in preferences between income and leisure, etc.). The interaction of these forces produces changes in the total national product; these changes have unequal impact upon industries and firms, variations in income elasticities of demand being an important variable.

C. DEFINITION OF RISK

Two meanings of risk are in current usage. Many follow Knight, who identified risk with the insurable cases. Others use the word to indicate possible disappointment; in this use, risk is not a category parallel with those of certainty and uncertainty. Since insurable (more generally, transformable) situations no longer involve risk after the risk has been insured (transformed), what Knight calls "risk" may more informatively be referred to as "transformable uncertainty." [17] The word "risk" may then be reserved to refer to the possibility of an unfavorable outcome of an action taken under uncertainty. It is not necessarily the expected (actuarial) loss, since p may not be known. Risk may be measured in money or utility; or it may be expressed in terms of degrees of surprise, regret, disappointment, unattained pleasures, etc.

IV. THE UNCERTAINTY THEORY OF PROFIT

Under uncertainty, total product may not equal total costs (explicit and implicit) because plans are not fulfilled. How this occurs is briefly indicated. Two classes of owners of productive services are distinguished. First, those with rates of compensation fixed in advance of the determination of the results of operations are called "hired factors" and receive contractual returns. Second, those with rates of compensation dependent upon the results of operations are referred to as "unhired factors," who receive noncontractual or residual returns.[18]

[17] For elaboration of this position see my "A Generalized Uncertainty Theory of Profit," pp. 43–44.
[18] J. R. Hicks, *The Theory of Wages* (New York: Peter Smith, 1932), pp. 234–35. It will be noted that the above formulation avoids the use of that "mystery man" of economic history whose presence is always felt, who seems to be an important figure in the economic process, and yet whose identity is difficult to establish—the entrepreneur.

Whatever the basis upon which contractual relationships have been entered, actual results will not have been accurately foreseen, because of uncertainty. Hence, whatever the basis upon which contractual commitments have been made, events actually do not work out that way. This is the significance of economic profit. It is not possible to plan in advance exactly what total product or total costs will be.[19]

A. IDENTIFICATION OF PROFIT

It is uncertainty which gives rise to profit, yet makes difficult a clear exposition of its nature. Profit is the difference between *ex ante* and *ex post* returns.[20] If all compensation were actually a function of the results of operations, no profit would arise (except in the sense that if some other commitment of time or resources had been made, one's return would have been different, even though dependent upon the results of operations). But, in practice, compensation arrangements involve fixed commitments. Hence, after all protective strategies are taken into account, commitments are made on the basis of some subjective probability distributions. The difference between the expected outcomes defined by the basis upon which contracts are entered into and the results actually realized is a measure of profit.[21] This is what is meant when I state that profit is the difference between *ex ante* and *ex post* returns. It is not implied that the *ex ante* returns represent single-valued expectations or can be expressed as certainty equivalents.[22]

Another aspect of the uncertainty concept of profit is emphasized by means of an example using the concept "utility-equivalent income." [23] Let us postulate that a decision-maker is considering an action whose outcome is uncertain. We could offer him a series of certain incomes to determine the minimum certain income he would take for his uncertain alternative. We would thus determine the point at which he would be indifferent between an income with certainty and the uncertain situation. This income we will call the "utility-equivalent income." Profit may be defined as the difference between the income actually attained and the utility-equivalent income.

[19] Alchian, *op. cit.*, pp. 211–13.

[20] "A Generalized Uncertainty Theory of Profit," p. 51.

[21] But, of course, zero profits may occur with wide divergences which happen to cancel out.

[22] Another method of formulating the profit idea is to describe it as the difference between incomes which would have been received if no payments were contractual and incomes when some payments are contractual and others not.

[23] This formulation was suggested to me by Harry Markowitz of Rand Corporation.

However, there is lack of parallelism between the certainty equivalent and the uncertain incomes. If the decision-maker chooses the certain income, that ends the matter. But if he remains in the uncertainty situation, many other kinds of behavior are called for—flexibility, diversification, safety margins, etc. Thus the utility-equivalent-income idea is a useful analytical device, but it has severe limitations for indicating behavior strategy.

The uncertainty concept of profit may be further clarified by considering its emergence under different circumstances. With the aid of the classification presented under the discussion of the nature of uncertainty, the existence of profit under alternative situations may be diagramed (Table 1).

The only point requiring explanation, in connection with Table 1, is the distinction between profit in the short run and profit in the long run, in cases 3.2 and 3.3. As long as the problem is a statistical one, statistical errors may occur in the short run (the time dimension is not necessarily identical with the definition of the short-run production period). These errors will be associated with profit (unless perfect canceling occurs).

Table 1.   Profit under Alternative Situations

Degree of information	Category	Stochastic situation?	Uncertainty?	Profit?
Incomplete ..	3.1	No	Yes	Yes
Incomplete ..	3.11	No	Yes	Yes
Incomplete ..	3.2	Yes	Short run—yes; long run—no	Short run—yes; long run—no
Complete	3.3	Yes	Short run—yes; long run—no	Short run—yes; long run—no
Complete	3.4	No	No	No

B. PROFIT AS REWARD FOR UNCERTAINTY-BEARING

The uncertainty concept of profit is often misunderstood and frequently misrepresented. This is the case when profit is said to be the payment *for bearing* risk or uncertainty. That such a view still has many adherents results from its effective presentation by Pigou.[24] If each of a million people, having a vase worth £100 as a vase, but with equal probability of between 0 and £250 broken, break their

[24] Pigou, *op. cit.*, pp. 771–72.

vases, national wealth would be increased by £25 million.[25] From this example Pigou develops the idea of units of uncertainty-bearing and uncertainty as a fourth factor of production.

The commitment of funds or effort to economic activities is, indeed, analogous to "breaking the vase" in Pigou's example. But it is not bearing uncertainty as such which is the source of the gain. One can envisage many commitments under uncertainty which will involve loss. The source of the gain in Pigou's example is the fact that operations, on the average, yield outputs which exceed inputs. It is the productivity of economic activity which is the source of additional value. The bearing of risk or uncertainty as such is not productive.

Another reason why it is sometimes said that profit is the payment for bearing uncertainty or risk is the observation that higher-risk investments appear to provide higher yields than lower-risk investments. Thus Caa bonds appear to bear higher yields than Aaa bonds. Nominal yields of lower-grade bonds may be higher than nominal yields of higher-grade bonds, but whether they will be higher net of defaults is less certain. If a net differential obtained, it would not represent the payment for bearing risk but would represent different relative demand and supply conditions upon which many forces, in addition to the degree of uncertainty, operate.

V. SOME OBJECTIONS TO THIS UNCERTAINTY CONCEPT OF PROFIT

A. The Traditional Functions of Profit

One objection to this uncertainty concept of profit is its failure to perform the functions traditionally assigned to profit: (1) to constitute a distinctive distributive share and (2) to guide economic decisions.

Economic profit is not a distinctive share correlative with wages, interest, and rent. It is a component of each of these types of payments. Profit is the difference between the bases upon which the decisionmakers choose between alternative courses of action to enter into contractual commitments and the actual outcomes which are experienced.

[25] Calculation of the actuarial value of breaking the vases demonstrates this:

Probability (p)	Gain or Loss (X)	Probability Times Gain or Loss
0.5	0 less 100 = (100)	(50)
0.5	250 less 100 = 150	75
		$E(X) = $ 25

If decision-makers are overoptimistic, their incomes are smaller, and contractual incomes are larger, than they would have been if the decision-makers had possessed more knowledge. If decision-makers are overpessimistic (but not so much so that the total level of economic activity is reduced), the converse will obtain. It follows that profit is an element found in payments to the owners of all types of productive services. Profit should not, therefore, be regarded as a distinct distributive share.

A statement frequently expressed is that profit guides economic decisions, that it is the mechanism for allocating economic resources. It is strange how thinking is compartmentalized at times. A basic teaching of economics is that the price system allocates resources. A utility theory (theory of demand for products) plus a marginal-productivity theory (theory of demand for resources and a statement of the supply conditions of factors) are sufficient to explain simultaneously resource allocation and income distribution. Wage theory, interest theory, and rent theory (to the extent that we have them) in essence are applications of price theory, attempting to take account of differences in market forces in different institutional settings. Such theories are ingredients of the theory of a price system. Price theory involves maximization of incomes.[26] Since price theory and income maximization provide the basis for decisions resulting in resource allocation, it is not necessary to have a profit theory which does this uniquely. In fact, the attempt to do so runs into inconsistencies.

If the uncertainty concept of profit does not perform the traditional functions of profit theory, what function does it perform for economic analysis? First, it states explicitly a fact of economics—the divergence of plans and realizations. Second, it provides a basis for revising plans as in a sequential decision process. Decisions are based on (1) *ex post* data, (2) expectations with regard to the uncertain future, and (3) utility preferences of the decision-makers. A decision is made. Time elapses. If plans are not fulfilled (profit is the measure of the extent of nonfulfilment), plans will be revised.

Zero profit does not imply that plans may not be revised. The occurrence of zero profit is an additional amount of information. The subjective probability judgments of decision-makers will be influenced by the increased knowledge. Thus plans for the future will be influenced by (1) the amount of profit, and (2) the additional information upon which a course of action may be formulated.

---

[26] Qualification of income maximization under uncertainty and the distinction between profit maximization and income maximization are developed in the section "Is Profit Maximization Meaningful?"

The uncertainty concept of profit is not unique in this attribute. Many economic decisions involve uncertainty. When the opportunity of revising plans occurs, the decision will be influenced by experience subsequent to the previous decision. Indeed, most of life's activities involve sequential decision processes.

Hence the direct importance of the uncertainty concept of profit for economic theory is modest. What needs underscoring is the de-emphasis of the uncertainty theory on the role of profit, as such, in the economy. Ours is not a profit (and loss) system, as much as it is a (relative) price system. The role of profits (windfalls) is significant at times, but the price mechanism performs the functions ascribed to "profit" by various writers. Profit theory is important, not because of the significance of amounts of profit, but because of the need for a concept consistent with generally accepted economic principles.

What is loosely called "profit theory" is a concept or definition. The uncertainty definition or concept of profit follows from the definitions and theorems of economic doctrine. Theory flows from propositions derived from the profit concept.

B. Empirical Test of the Uncertainty Theory

Still, it is averred, the uncertainty theory of profit cannot be tested empirically.[27] Empirical testing of the uncertainty theory is a task of considerable dimensions, but the nature of the procedure can be briefly sketched. The previous discussion has made clear that payments for productive services of all kinds include profit elements. Hence data on wage, rent, and interest returns would be relevant. For illustrative purposes, we may utilize the studies of business net income data to test the theory.[28]

Stability in earnings would be inconsistent with the uncertainty theory. Great variability of earnings patterns would be consistent with the hypothesis and also would be consistent with some of the alternative profit theories. Epstein's data indicate some stability in the differ-

---

[27] Many citations, of course, can be marshaled to denounce any theory which cannot be so tested. "What is not measurable is not meaningful." A polite but firm reservation ought to be expressed. Some important ideas cannot be quantified and vice versa.

[28] The usual empirical studies of "profit" are actually studies of accounting net income. The main component of this conglomerate of economic returns is an interest return on invested capital. In addition, unimputed wage or rent returns are likely to be included. The "profit" category in national income statistics is aggregated corporate net incomes. Thus empirical studies of "profit" have not centered on the real issues of profit theory.

ences between levels of returns of firms in different industries.[29] But these are large firms in which, to a considerable extent, statistical averaging of results may take place. Bowman and Crum, using broader samples, observed great erratic tendencies.[30] In all these empirical studies the dispersion of earnings rates of firms is considerable. The observed diversity of experience and wide changes from year to year are predicted by the uncertainty theory of profit. Further investigations along these lines are indicated.

Another approach to empirical testing of the uncertainty theory utilizes internal accounting records of firms. To the extent that they are genuinely employed, budgets or *pro forma* statements represent expressions of the plans of firms.[31] Variable budgets express these plans not as single-valued certainty equivalents but as expected ranges of the variables. The uncertainty theory predicts that while budgets may provide rough guides to action, budgeted amounts will usually not be realized. The differences between the "plans" expressed in budgets and what actually happens provide a basis for some quantification of profit.

C. The Significance of the Uncertainty Theory of Profit for Behavior Strategies

The uncertainty concept of profit is significant, whether or not the magnitudes may be directly measured. Like other constructs of economic theory, the uncertainty profit concept is useful if meaningful statements (propositions) can be derived from it. The uncertainty profit idea meets this test better than possible alternatives, because it provides a model of economic behavior which suggests important types of activities that would not exist in the absence of uncertainty.

1. Because of uncertainty, which gives rise to profit, reasonable and prudent men hold different views of the future. The differences in expectations give rise to different forms of contractual relationships. It is differences of opinions (also differences in abilities and tastes) which make markets. This is the motivational significance of the uncertainty concept. Uncertainty leads some to take great chances, to innovate, to attempt to monopolize, etc. It leads some to avoid risky occupations and enterprises, to seek the quiet life.

[29] Epstein, *op. cit.*, pp. 79–86.

[30] Bowman, *op. cit.*, pp. 173–76; Crum, *op. cit.*, pp. 231–34.

[31] They may also represent strategic weapons in intra-firm struggles for allocation of resources. Such problems are highlighted by the discussion of budgeting under a different social setting in J. S. Berliner, "The Informal Organization of the Soviet Firm," *Quarterly Journal of Economics*, LXVI (August, 1952), 347–53.

2. Because of uncertainty, strategies and arrangements which provide some protection against the alternative contingencies are developed and utilized. Some of these devices are flexible machines and plants; diversification in many forms—multiproducts, multiplants, multisales outlets; reduced ratios of fixed to total costs; etc.

3. Since, because of uncertainty, it is not possible to reduce business decisions to virtual routine, the operations of a firm require continuous exercise of judgment. Judgment is decision-making on the basis of incomplete information. It is not possible to associate the exercise of judgment with a limited number of key personnel in a firm. Akin to the difference between the abilities of a baseball player in a major league versus one in a minor league, the difference in the extent of judgment exercised by functionaries at different levels in any authority hierarchy is a matter of degree, not of kind.

If these descriptions of the usefulness of the uncertainty concept of profit appear abstract, a practical application may be cited.[32] The uncertainty concept of profit is a basis for a wartime (or period of heightened preparedness) excess profits tax. An excess profits or excess income tax should remove those elements of income in excess of incomes likely to have been earned if the unusual exogenous factors (war, threat of war) had not occurred. For a wartime excess profits tax, this implies the use of historical earnings standards rather than an invested capital standard.[33] While practical problems of implementation abound, a defensible conceptual basis for a wartime excess profits tax is provided.

Other aspects of the uncertainty concept will be developed through a consideration of alternative theories of profit. One which has long commanded an important following is the innovation theory of Schumpeter.

[32] In this connection cf. Bernstein, *op. cit.*, pp. 407-22. I am sympathetic with Mr. Bernstein's emphasis on the practical aspects of profit theory. But his suggestion to have different profit theories for different circumstances violates any usable theory of knowledge. While behavior implied by a theory may find different forms of expression under differing circumstances, the theory need not be altered to fit different situations. Indeed, profit theory does not explain all kinds of facts and situations. Other theories may be applicable, *but not different profit theories.* The materials he discusses are important, but he needs other elements of economic theory to provide an understanding of some items he discusses. His paper reflects the tendency to attempt to label every explanation of dramatic business activity with the rubric "profit theory."

[33] Those who hold that a wartime excess profits tax should be levied on "high" profits as well as "war" profits will disagree on policy grounds. The applicability of the uncertainty profit concept holds, nevertheless.

VI. INNOVATION, ENTREPRENEURSHIP, AND PROFIT

A. SCHUMPETER'S SYSTEM

To explain the innovation theory of profit, it is necessary to summarize (briefly) Schumpeter's entire framework. Innovation is the act of changing production functions. This includes producing new products, improving processes, improving production methods. Schumpeter treats changes in tastes as changed production functions. (Influences from the demand side are thus thrown over into the supply side.) Without innovations, an economy would settle down into a stationary state —the circular flow (unless exogenous forces intervened).

The central figure in Schumpeter's scheme is the entrepreneur. The entrepreneur is defined as one who innovates. (Once Schumpeter has defined innovation, the rest of his system follows.) Profit arises from innovation; it is achieved through entrepreneurial activity; the entrepreneur is its recipient.

Schumpeter does not stop here, however. Because others imitate the innovator, his profits are finally wiped out. Hence the only way an innovator can continuously make profit is to innovate continuously. The tremendous social significance of Schumpeter's innovator is thus seen. He is an instrument of progress. Profit is the reward which induces him to innovate repeatedy, and by this device society is led to continuous progress.

Other central ideas in Schumpeter's theory are summarized in the following succinct statement:

> A word about the relation of profit to monopoly revenue. Since the entrepreneur has no competitors when the new products first appear, the determination of their price proceeds wholly, or within certain limits, according to the principles of monopoly price. Thus there is a monopoly element in profit in a capitalist economy. Let us now assume that the new combination consists in establishing a permanent monopoly, perhaps in forming a trust which need fear absolutely no competing outsiders. Then profit is obviously to be considered simply as permanent monopoly revenue and monopoly revenue simply as profit. And yet two quite different economic phenomena exist. The carrying out of the monopolistic organization is an entrepreneurial act and its "product" is expressed in profit. Once it is running smoothly the concern in this case goes on earning a surplus,

> which henceforth, however, must be imputed to those natu-
> ral or social forces upon which the monopoly position rests
> —it has become a monopoly revenue. Profit from founding
> a business and permanent return are distinguished in prac-
> tice; the former is the value of the monopoly, the latter is
> just the return from the monopoly condition.[34]

Here Schumpeter emphasizes the distinction between the act of innovating which results in profit and the continuing differential return which is capitalized or imputed to its sources. Any continuing differential in payments for services is not profit but a differential revenue return.

B. Comparison Between the Profit Theories of Schumpeter and Knight

The theories of Schumpeter and Knight are similar in many respects. Uncertainty and innovation are related. Innovation may be defined more generally than in Schumpeter's presentation (but consistent with it) as changing production *or* utility functions. An ultimate source of uncertainty is therefore innovation. But uncertainty and innovation are not identities, because innovation sets in force a series of influences with concomitant adjustments that, in addition, interact with exogenous factors—wars, new laws, etc.

The innovator positively engages uncertainty. To forsake the tried and familiar in creating change is clearly a situation in which the decision-maker has incomplete information. But decision-makers not attempting innovations also face uncertainty. Hence both Knight and Schumpeter devote considerable discussion to enterpreneurial activities. For Knight, the entrepreneur makes decisions dealing with uncertainty and then bears responsibility for those decisions. Schumpeter's entrepreneur innovates, an act involving uncertainty as well as a major source of uncertainty. Knight emphasizes that entrepreneurship is fundamentally judgment of men—innovation and other activities can be delegated. Schumpeter's later writing makes a similar emphasis: "Innovation itself is being reduced to routine. Technological progress is increasingly becoming the business of teams of trained specialists who turn out what is required and make it work in predictable ways."[35]

[34] *Op. cit.* p. 152.
[35] Joseph A. Schumpeter, *Capitalism, Socialism, and Democracy* (2d ed.; New York: Harper & Bros., 1947), p. 132.

This subsequent agreement suggests that Schumpeter's earlier position on the function of profit requires revision. The economic incentive to creation is seen to be income, whose nature is similar to payments for other types of productive services. This has been clearly stated by Harrod: "In value theory it has proved expedient to relate profit specifically to uncertainty-bearing, ability to direct a business being easily assimilable in theory to the category of highly skilled labour." [36] Machlup expressed the same view equally effectively: "The high 'profit' made by the entrepreneur who performs these services himself is really nothing but an implicit wage or an implicit rent." [37]

Thus, whether the payment is for creative services, whether compensation is on a contractual or residual basis, the return remains functional in nature. It is an income category appropriately labeled wages, rent, or interest; and it is likely to contain a nonfunctional component, profit.

VII. ENTERPRISE AND PROFIT

The discussion of Schumpeter's contribution leads to a treatment of other aspects of the relationship between entrepreneurship and profit. In specifying the unique function of the entrepreneur, writers have described him variously as (a) one who organizes and co-ordinates the other factors of production (peak co-ordinator); (b) one who exercises the joint and inseparable functions of responsibility (ultimate risk-bearing) and control (ultimate decision-making); (c) one who innovates (changing production or utility functions); and (d) one who is charged with the responsibility of dealing with uncertainty.[38]

A. THE NATURE OF ENTREPRENEURIAL RETURNS

Somehow it is felt that, since the acts of organizing, co-ordinating, directing, and changing the scope of enterprise are of special significance, some special terminology should be applied to the returns for these activities. But, regardless of the definition adopted, entrepreneurial activities are functional in nature. The returns to the entrepreneur in connection with his functional activities qua entrepreneur are not, therefore, profit. As the quotations above from Harrod and Machlup

[36] *Op. cit.*, p. 192.
[37] *Op. cit.*, p. 15.
[38] If there is little agreement on the nature of the entrepreneurial function or functions, there is even less on identification of the entrepreneur, i.e., the person performing the functions in different circumstances. Fortunately, it is not necessary to consider these problems here.

emphasize, the returns to entrepreneurs seem best looked upon as wage or rent returns.

This does not deny that executive leadership and creative activity in business are important or that adequate inducements for the performance of these functions should be provided through requisite incentives. If the value of such services could be forecast, compensation could be fixed accordingly. But since such forecasts cannot be made accurately, bonuses, profit-sharing, stock options, pensions, including arrangements to minimize taxes, are widely used in executive compensation arrangements. Executive incomes depend at least in part upon the results of operations; their incomes are partially residual in nature. This is another clear illustration of the proposition that wage returns may include a fluctuating component. The use of incentive payment schemes for piece-workers is still another. We may conclude, therefore, that functional returns to high ability in any form cannot be said to be profit but rather a type of rent or wage return.

B. THE FIRM AS ENTREPRENEUR

In this connection, Davis has proposed to "define the entrepreneur as the business enterprise itself and profit as the enterprise's net income." [39] While the firm is a useful unit of account and center for organizing economic activity, it is an institution whose function is best understood as a convenience of association for the purpose of achieving particular goals of individuals. As a consequence, the difficulties in adopting the suggested fiction are many.

It is logically fallacious, because the whole is made equal to one of its parts. What scope remains for the operation of the other types of productive services in the firm? The essential qualities of entrepreneurship are blurred. The nature of its origin and development are obscured. The conditions for the successful expression of the entrepreneurial functions cannot be discerned in such an orientation. The error of identifying the goals of the firm with the goals of all participating agents is aggravated. [40] While it may appear to be "remarkably convenient" for handling certain problems, it has not been shown that the adoption of this fiction is more useful than adherence to the

---

[39] Davis, *op. cit.*, pp. 251–52; see also Stauss, *op. cit.*, pp. 112–27.

[40] This criticism has been expressed most effectively by Triffin: "In fact, however, the firm is a mere abstraction: profit maximization is the concern, not of the legal entities called firms, but of human beings. Pure theory starts on the assumption that each man tries to maximize his income" (Triffin, *op. cit.*, p. 186; see also M. W. Reder, "A Reconsideration of the Marginal Productivity Theory," *Journal of Political Economy*, LV [October, 1947], 450–58).

realities of the situation. All the advantages for its adoption are also attained by regarding entrepreneurship as a function widely diffused among participants in the operation of a firm.

C. PROFIT AS THE INCOME OF A SOCIAL CLASS

It has also been proposed that profit can be identified as the income of a particular social class. Professor Davis states: "For many authors the purpose of distribution theory is to explain the sharing out of the total income among social groups."[41] He observes that this is a basis for the fundamental objection to the orientation of the uncertainty theory of profit.

If ownership of types of productive services coincided even roughly with the composition of social groups, it might be possible to apply distribution theory to the explanation of social incomes, as did the classical economists. But such a coincidence now obtains to an even smaller degree than formerly (for example, the time of the classical economists). To assume it now is not only inaccurate but also leads to a distortion of the basic nature and purpose of distribution theory—the pricing of productive services in their allocation among alternative uses.

Davis suggests that at one end of the spectrum of classification the terms "enterpreneur" and "businessman" may be treated as roughly equivalent.[42] But this is to define an ambiguous concept with an imprecise expression. What is a businessman? Are all executives businessmen? Do we include only top-level management? Do we include supervisory personnel? Are inactive bondholders businessmen? Are equally inactive common stockholders businessmen?

At the other end, Davis suggests that the firm be identified as the entrepreneur and profit be defined as the firm's net income. Aside from difficulties previously described, such a procedure fails to achieve Davis' objective of associating the receipt of profit with a particular social class. Thus whichever definition is followed, Davis' attempt to identify profit with the income of a social class fails.

With even greater emphasis, Marchal develops the doctrine that profit is the special type of income of a particular social class.[43] The methods by which entrepreneurs ("enterprise" and "entrepreneurship" are not defined) are said to seek to augment their gains are seen, upon reflection, to be those utilized by workers and capital owners alike. But the distinctive behavior of the entrepreneur, Marchal says, is to identify

[41] Davis, *op. cit.*, p. 248.
[42] *Ibid.*, p. 250.
[43] *Op. cit.*, pp. 549–65.

himself with the enterprise.[44] However, this is only asserted, not demonstrated. Even if true, identification of the entrepreneur with the enterprise is without economic significance, for the opportunity cost of the entrepreneur's services must be taken into account.

Furthermore, it should be observed that, although other types of factor owners are not identified with the enterprise, they enter the market and contract in fundamentally the same manner as enterprisers. Owners of other factor services may act on the market structure; they may attempt to change it; and they may attempt to engage in all types of predatory practices attributed to entrepreneurs by Marchal. Even more important, since elements of predatory behavior exist everywhere in varying proportions, the behavior is of unique relevance not to profit theory but to income distribution generally.

From this analysis of some recent theories of how profit may be related to the incomes of specific social classes, it appears clear that such attempts confuse, rather than clarify, the nature of profit and its significance.

D. PROFIT AS PROSPERITY RETURNS

Another critic has suggested a related approach. There are two types of returns—property returns and nonproperty returns or returns for labor services. Payments for labor services are called "wages." Returns to property involve fixed commitments. These returns are called "profits." This was essentially the practice of the classical economists. Profits formerly included all elements of returns for the contributions of the owners, whether land, capital, or personal services. One development in economic thought has been the peeling-off of the various segments of returns, leaving a pure economic profit element.

Gross residual returns (total receipts less contractual payments for labor services) are akin to accounting net income or profit.[45] However, accounting net income is not an adequate representation of economic profit, because the residual-income receivers contribute productive services. It would not be logical to label as profit the entire amount of the returns of residual-income receivers, when contractual payments for similar functional services performed by hired factors are labeled variously wages or interest. Not only would this be illogical from a classification standpoint, but it would also be unsound for practical reasons. It would not be possible for owners of a particular type of productive service to know whether the productive service could earn

44 *Ibid.*, p. 550.
45 Accountants themselves now avoid calling business net income "profit."

more on a contractual or on a residual basis, when the residual incomes of firms included payments for a combination of different types of productive services. Correct allocation and distribution decisions depend upon knowledge of the value imputed to services sold to the firm on a residual basis.

VIII. MONOPOLY AND PROFIT

Most opposing theories of profit existed prior to Knight's first exposition of the uncertainty theory. One of these was the view of profit as a monopoly return—a position which has repeatedly been expressed. Marchal's recent paper, "The Construction of a New Theory of Profit," is another presentation of it.[46]

Marchal's emphasis on improving a firm's situation by changing the economic structure is a useful one. His discussion implies, however, that most of the actual activity along this line has been in the direction of predatory activities by managements. This may be an unwarranted exaggeration for noncontinental economies. But, regardless of the degree of its empirical applicability, Marchal's contribution is not profit theory but rather a description and theory of predatory behavior.

The continued rejection of the uncertainty theory by those who view profit as a monopoly return is both understandable and surprising. It is understandable because the activity of increasing one's income by achieving a monopoly position and by engaging in restrictive activities and monopoly pricing is "obviously widespread." Here is another apparent ground for dissatisfaction with the uncertainty theory of profit—it does not seem to explain enough of the dramatic events of economic life which press upon our attention.

But the persistence of predatory theories of profit is surprising, since Schumpeter very early pointed out the basis for their invalidity.[47] The attainment of a monopoly situation is an act either of creation (innovation) or of chance (a windfall). But after the monopoly has been established, the prospective monopoly revenues or rents are imputed to the source of the monopoly advantage and/or capitalized. A clear illustration of this can be observed in the fact that when the common stocks of firms possessing such advantages are publicly traded, they sell on a low-yield basis (because of relative stability of prospective earnings and dividends). Although monopoly pricing and monopoly revenues may remain, the yields to current purchasers of the common stock are competitive.

The implications of the uncertainty theory of profit may be further

[46] Pp. 489–504.
[47] *Op. cit.*, p. 152; see also Harrod, *op. cit.*, pp. 198–206.

discerned by consideration of three remaining topics: (1) How can the profit element be identified in conventional diagrams of partial equilibrium analysis? (This question may also be expressed in another fashion: What are the nature and role of the imputation process and the implications for choices between alternative kinds of contractual relationships?) (2) Are profits really maximized? (3) What is the significance of profit theory for macroeconomics?

IX. PROFIT AS AN UNIMPUTABLE QUASI-RENT

The first question is most conveniently discussed in connection with the conventional diagram of a situation in which short-run "profits"

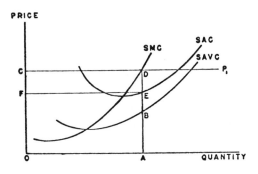

Figure 1. Short-period equilibrium

are obtained (Fig. 1). The area CDEF, is said to portray economic "profit." It is said to be the unimputed (and unimputable) surplus of the firm. The tale is told best in the following manner.[48] The future cannot be known with certainty. All resources are not freely and immediately transferable from one use to another. As a consequence of the twin influences of uncertainty and resource immobility, situations of the type portrayed in Figure 1 develop.[49] Factor prices are set by the entire framework of competitive conditions. A wholly unanticipated favorable change in demand conditions facing the industry takes place. This new situation facing the individual firm may be considered to be that portrayed by Figure 1. The firm has a surplus, DE, over costs, AE, which is called "profit." This "profit" calls forth a resource flow, which tends to eliminate such a surplus in the long run. This is quite a rea-

48 Cf. Davis, op. cit., pp. 247–48.
49 Both uncertainty and immobility are necessary conditions. Without uncertainty, the immobile resources would have been correctly located. Without immobilities, adjustments to change would involve no delays.

sonable, appealing, and convincing story; but it leaves a good many elements unsettled.

Does the diagram represent a planned or an *ex post* situation? Drawn in the Marshallian tradition, it is timeless with reference to clock time or represents an unstated arbitrary choice of one of many relevant clock-time periods. The situation is *ex ante,* in that the decision-makers have freedom of action with respect to the quantities of the variable factors which will be employed. With respect to the fixed factors, an unalterable monetary commitment has been made, so it is an *ex post* situation. Thus the conventional short-run situation is a mixture of *ex ante* and *ex post* elements.

The short period is conventionally defined as one in which it is useful to regard a particular set of costs as nonvariable. The division between the short run and the long run is based on the degree of fixity of costs. Although the Marshallian tradition does not distinguish between short and long run on the basis of demand considerations, it is not likely that demand conditions will remain fixed during the planning period implied by the selection of a particular set of costs for defining a short period.

Thus a contradiction is implied in the diagram. Given that the situation is the result of a wholly anticipated shift in economic conditions, is it realistic or meaningful to make the assumption that no further changes will take place for the duration of the planning period? If the industry is subject to windfall changes of this type, it is not meaningful to draw this type of diagram without showing the sales curve as a range of values.[50]

This leads to the question of imputation of a portion of quasi-rents. Quasi-rents of the firm are generally defined as "simply the excess of receipts over total variable costs."[51] Davis appears to have another definition.[52] He refers to *BD* (Stigler's quasi-rent per units of output)[53] as the net income of the firm per unit of output. He divides this into two segments. The segment *ED* is said to be unimputed and termed "profit." The segment *BE* is imputed to the assets which the firm owns, and this is termed "quasi-rent."

[50] Another interpretation is that insiders (firms already in the industry) have knowledge of these favorable conditions but that outsiders do not have this knowledge. However, this would be a permanent differential—a rent rather than a quasi-rent. If it is urged that the favorable conditions are only temporary, then it is not likely that their exact duration can be known, nor can the sales curve be known for the duration of "the" planning period.

[51] George J. Stigler, *The Theory of Price* (rev. ed.; New York: Macmillan Co., 1952), p. 193.

[52] Davis, *op. cit.,* p. 247.

[53] Refer to Fig. 1 again.

But the segment *ED,* which is often referred to as "profit," is a portion of the quasi-rents per unit of output. To the extent that it is meaningful to use the diagram, what is maximized is quasi-rent, not profit. This is not simply a matter of taste in choice of terminology. The components of total product are wage, rent, or interest returns. It is misleading to label a portion of the total revenues as profit, as distinct from wages, rent, and interest. A profit element may be, and probably is, contained in all three of these other returns. The differential is a temporary supernormal (or subnormal) return for some of the factors. Its allocation is determined by the nature of the contractual arrangements that have been agreed upon.

With regard to imputation, the role of uncertainty must be recognized and its institutional consequences considered. Given that situations of the type portrayed by Figure 1 develop because of uncertainty, it would be unrealistic not to acknowledge that owners of productive services are likely to take uncertainty into account in their decisions. Since the future cannot be wholly known, some resource payments cannot be fixed by contract before the results of operations are known. Some income receivers must therefore take a residual-income position.

Whether resource owners take a residual position or a contractual position depends in part upon differences in training, experience, opportunities, asset position, attitudes toward risk, noneconomic considerations, and, in part, differences in anticipations. The practical fact is, however, that the residual-income receivers are the recipients of the amounts remaining after the fixed-income receivers have been fully paid. Given the institutional consequences of uncertainty, the distribution of the element *EB* (as well as *ED*) is not a matter of imputation but a matter of contractual relationships. Theoretically, any type of arrangement could be envisaged. Wages of workers, salaries of executives, payments to "bond" holders, etc., could all be put on a contingent as well as a fixed basis. Given the presence of uncertainty, however, all returns could not be fixed (but all could be contingent).

The characteristics of contracts differ. The two most important elements of the difference are: (1) whether the return is fixed or residual [54] and (2) if fixed, the terminability of employment or the opportunity of either party for recontracting.

[54] However, the form of the contractual relationship is not a sufficient basis for distinguishing whether returns will fluctuate or be relatively stable. Uncertainty is associated with both contractual and noncontractual returns. Numerous examples could be cited to demonstrate this. Bondholders receive contractual returns, but very low-grade bonds fluctuate more, pricewise and incomewise, than high-grade common stocks do. Workers receive contractual returns, but what is the relevant time horizon? They receive contractual returns so long as they are employed, but employment may be interrupted.

But the noncontractual payments do not represent a different kind of economic return. A profit element, as here defined, may be contained in the returns of either form. The fixed return contains positive or negative profit if the return would have been lower or higher if all returns had been based on *ex post* data (strictly speaking, *mutatis mutandis* considerations make this statement somewhat inaccurate, but it conveys the basic idea). The noncontractual returns contain a positive or negative element of profit for exactly the same reason.

X. IS PROFIT MAXIMIZATION MEANINGFUL?

From time to time it has been suggested that a wider concept, e.g., preference-function maximization, be substituted for the traditional idea, profit maximization.[55] Alternative motives are cited: leisure or the quiet life, power and prestige, reluctance to experiment (aversion to uncertainty-bearing), and ideas of the "just price." [56] This approach emphasizes the role of noneconomic influences, whose relative importance has not yet been established by factual evidence.

On other grounds, Alchian and Enke discard profit maximization both as a *goal* and as a *criterion* for choosing between different actions.[57] Since unfavorable surprises may threaten the very survival of the firm, the use of expectation "begs the question of uncertainty by disregarding the variance." [58] The maximization of expected profits is therefore not a rational goal under uncertainty.

They set forth in detail the difficulties of profit maximization as a criterion for choosing between alternative actions. Behavior under incomplete knowledge involves the following: (1) the variability of the environment, (2) the multiplicity of factors that call for attention in choice, (3) the uncertainty attaching to all these factors and outcomes, (4) the nonavailability of a trial-and-error process converging to an optimum position, and (5) therefore the absence of an identifiable criterion for decision-making.[59]

The Alchian-Enke framework establishes that, under a complete uncertainty model, the economist can diagnose, predict, or explain resource allocation in the economy as a whole.[60] This is a somewhat sur-

---

[55] Cf. Andreas G. Papandreou, "Some Basic Problems in the Theory of the Firm," *Survey of Contemporary Economics,* Vol. II (Homewood, Ill.: Richard D. Irwin, Inc., 1952), p. 207.

[56] *Ibid.,* pp. 207–8.

[57] Alchian, *op. cit.,* pp. 211–12; Enke, *op. cit.,* pp. 569–70.

[58] Alchian, *op. cit.,* p. 213.

[59] *Ibid.,* p. 218.

[60] I am particularly indebted to Karl Brunner for suggestions leading to the materials in this and the following paragraph.

prising conclusion, and its demonstration is a valuable contribution. However, when the implications of such a model for individual decision-making are considered, we confront some difficulties. Under complete uncertainty, the optimum behavior strategy for the individual is a procedure which produces random actions. If some knowledge is admitted, but incomplete information remains, what is appropriate decision-making procedure? Alchian suggests imitation, adaptation, and innovation. The present writer would emphasize, in addition, the necessity for businessmen to exercise judgment.

But if profit maximization is denied, what is offered in its place? Some statements of positive position are offered. A maximizing solution is possible only under complete information. When information is complete, the probability distribution is known, so that it is rational to maximize the expected (long-run) value. Under complete information the individual maximizes his long-run income; the firm maximizes its long-run net receipts (the long-run income of the residual-income receivers).[61]

Under incomplete information, it is necessary to adopt some form of minimax [62] strategy. Even under the stochastic case in which the decision-maker knows data permitting him to estimate the probability distributions of alternative outcomes, he will make statistical errors (Type I or Type II).[63] Thus statistical decisions are all minimax procedures. Where only two hypotheses are admitted (h_o and h_1), we have a special case where h_1 represents the totality of unfavorable outcomes.[64] If knowledge is incomplete, the individual minimaxes his long-run income position; the firm minimaxes its long-run net receipts position.

While a situation of uncertainty implies that income maximization is not an appropriate goal or criterion, it does not imply that rational behavior will not be effective. Imitation, adaptation, and innovation are examples of rational strategies in the face of uncertainty. Subjective probability opinions may be formulated; but flexibility, diversification,

61 This formulation emphasizes that maximization of net receipts is the maximization of a conglomerate of economic returns, properly included under the broad title of "quasi-rents." Maximization of net receipts is indeed an important motivation. But I object to the undue emphasis on maximization of profits, as though decision-makers of firms were motivated by a particular kind of drive which was unique to them. Income maximization and rational behavior describe equally well the behavior of owners of all types of productive services.

62 The term is used in the general sense of minimizing maximum regret or maximizing the minimum gain.

63 A. M. Mood, *Introduction to the Theory of Statistics* (New York: McGraw-Hill Book Co., 1950), pp. 245–52.

64 *Ibid.*, p. 246.

and safety margins will be employed as well. These are all elements of a minimax strategy. They likewise involve the exercise of judgment and are influenced by the utility preference systems of the decision-makers. Sometimes greater uncertainty will be borne for the possibility of attaining higher income or net receipts, that is, the maximum potential loss possibility some are willing to chance may be greater or less than that of others.[65]

XI. PROFIT AND MACROECONOMICS

Davis' analysis of writings in this area is comprehensive, his criticisms searching, and his major conclusions well established.[66] He shows to be of doubtful validity Kalecki's generalization that gross margins reflect the degree of monopoly, which thus is said to determine the distribution of national income.[67] He points out that Boulding's macroeconomic profit theory rests upon an assumption that wage-earners have different consumption, investment, and liquidity preference functions than others.[68] Limited empirical studies raise considerable doubt that such fundamental differences exist. Davis suggests that more significant for macroeconomic theory than a division between total wages and property incomes (miscalled "profits" by many) is the distribution of income between people with large and small incomes, large and small holdings of total assets, and high and low ratios of liquid to other assets. His suggested emphasis on a division between households and firms may have some usefulness but, as he acknowledges, has little relation to the traditional profit theory he espouses.

The uncertainty theory of profit, however, can be shown to have significance for macroeconomics. Since some portions of income are unanticipated or relatively more uncertain than others, spending plans for such income are likely to be more flexible. They probably are influenced by the degrees of fluctuation of these incomes in previous periods as a guide to likely variations in the future. Thus the existence

---

[65] To a great degree business decisions are portfolio selection problems. Business behavior represents a combination of activities. If the correlation between outcomes of activities is not unity (positive), diversification exists, and uncertainty is reduced. Much of the analysis of portfolio selection will therefore apply (cf. Harry Markowitz, "Portfolio Selection," *Journal of Finance*, VII [March, 1952], 77–91).

[66] Davis, *op. cit.*, pp. 252–62.

[67] M. Kalecki, *Essays in the Theory of Economic Fluctuations* (New York: Farrar & Rinehart, 1939), chap. i, "The Distribution of the National Income."

[68] K. E. Boulding, *A Reconstruction of Economics* (New York: John Wiley & Sons, 1950), chap. xiv, "A Macroeconomic Theory of Distribution."

of profit implies an income-spending lag. The larger the absolute aggregate values of profits (and losses), the greater the uncertainty, and the greater are likely to be the portions of incomes which are subject to spending lags.[69]

The relationship of uncertainty (the source of profit) to production lags is mixed. On the one hand, uncertainty causes the disappointment of expectations, making the consequence of production lags more serious than otherwise. On the other hand, uncertainty causes decision-makers to introduce a wider amount of flexibility into operations; adjustments are made more quickly to altered market circumstances. Hence production lags are likely to be shorter.

Another aspect of macroeconomics in which the uncertainty theory of profit finds expression is in the divergence of the *ex post* from the *ex ante*. Whenever any of the planned magnitudes differ from the realized magnitudes, the influence of uncertainty is reflected, and profits emerge.

XII. CONCLUSIONS

The uncertainty theory of profit is not likely to secure general acceptance. The writings on profit theory since *Risk, Uncertainty, and Profit* (1921) afford abundant evidence of this. The entrepreneurial theories of profit secure adherents because they deal with dramatic and important economic behavior. The predatory theories offer opportunity for the expression of noble sentiments and moral indignation. Finally, it seems that there ought to be some special recompense for bearing risk and uncertainty.

While the uncertainty theory of profit presents challenges for investigating the many ramifications of the effects of uncertainty, it does not promise that these can be adequately catalogued. Nevertheless, it provides a framework for a better understanding of many types of economic practices and institutions, and it avoids the inconsistencies and dilemmas to which rival theories lead. It can be integrated into, and leads to, correct use of economic doctrine generally.

---

[69] It should not be implied that this is the only cause of the "Robertson" lag.

32

A RECONSIDERATION
OF THE THEORY OF RENT *

DEAN A. WORCESTER, JR. teaches at the University of Washington; he was formerly at the University of Georgia.

In most discussions of rent, it is customary to demonstrate how the remuneration due each segment of land may be determined by either residual or marginal productivity analysis, to note how this distributes land to its most important uses, and to conclude that, since social costs do not determine the supply of land, the receivers of rents can be taxed in special ways which would not otherwise be justified. It is usually argued, implicitly or explicitly, that the existence of rent does not increase prices and that social costs, therefore, are in harmony with the money prices paid by consumers.

To be sure, there is a growing group of economists who turn their backs on all such analysis and define rent in terms which apply equally well to any factor of production and which in any case include only part of the total payments to any productive agent. That both groups deal with matters of substance is hardly open to question. That the proponents of the two groups can understand each other is less certain. And it is inevitable that the neophyte will find his footing precarious. He must distinguish among at least three general groups of theorists: the classical, of whom Marshall and Taussig have probably presented the best arguments although neither is hardly a pure Ricardian; the neoclassical, which in this case is no more than a shorthand expression for those who, with Wicksteed, Jevons, Davenport and others, agree with the definitions and most of the conclusions of Marshall but who believe that the marginal productivity approach is superior to the residual approach; and the Paretian, which is followed in general by Joan Robinson, K. E. Boulding, H. D. Henderson and others and which involves fundamentally different conceptions. The purpose of this paper is, then, (1) to trace in rough outline the steps which have led us to the present ambiguities, and (2) to make some positive recom-

* From the *American Economic Review*, Vol. XXXVI (June, 1946), pp. 258–277, copyright © by the American Economic Assoc. Reprinted by permission.

mendations designed to unify the now divergent points of view so as to increase the content of rent theory.

The argument proceeds through the following stages: (a) an analysis of the necessity for and the steps involved in abandoning the classical position that rent does not affect the market price of commodities; (b) how this abandonment makes necessary two theories of rent, one based on opportunity costs and the other based on real costs; (c) the manner by which the conceptual relationship between the two theories can be preserved; (d) how the Paretian concept inserts much detail into the classical and neoclassical systems but seriously impairs the meaning of the word "rent"; (e) the advocacy of the use of the term "rent" to indicate the full opportunity cost (or remuneration) of a unit of land, as defined below, when this is computed on the level of the firm; (f) the need for a new term if the concepts of the various groups of theorists are to be brought together—"factor profits" is suggested and (g) subsidary reasons for preferring marginal productivity theory in the determination of rent.

In the following sections we shall consider, first, the manner in which the various viewpoints within classical and "neoclassical" theory came into being, and, second, the effect of the introduction of the Paretian concepts upon this structure. Such a recapitulation is most fruitful if based on Marshall's writings [1] since his entirely too clever defense seems to lie at the roots of most of our difficulties. In referring to Marshall we must raise again some of the old issues which were once discussed to the point of utter exhaustion and essential futility. But perhaps, at last, they may now reveal the basic points of view in such a way that, rather than end in deadlock, they can contribute to a more rounded theory.

SEMANTICS AND RENT THEORIES

We may begin by defining "land." We are not interested in the physical characteristics of the various agents of production with which we are confronted. Rather, their economic aspects draw our attention. Thus, for purposes of this discussion, land will be thought of as that group of productive agents whose fitness *for a particular use* is not likely to change as a result of a change or even the elimination of the remuneration of its owners. It is evident, then, that this paper is concerned with the analysis of a certain kind of supply condition, and not

---

[1] All references to Marshall will be to the eighth edition of his *Principles of Economics* (London, Macmillan, 1938).

with the classification of productive agents. No attempt will be made to discover an exact line between "land" and "capital." [2]

While "land" may be defined at the outset, this procedure is quite impossible for "rent." Some of the things to which it might refer are:

1. An entrepreneurial payment to certain agents of production.

2. Part of the entrepreneurial payments made to certain agents of production.

3. The income received by owners of certain productive resources.

4. Part of the incomes received by owners of certain productive resources.

There are some other ways in which various definitions might be expressed, which would multiply the possible number of precise meanings, but this list points up the main issue at stake. Numbers 1 and 3 can both be derived from a single operational definition.[3] So can numbers 2 and 4. But numbers 1 and 2, 3 and 4, clearly refer to different concepts, and can be only improperly labeled by the same term. Yet each group is accepted by large numbers of economists, who do employ the same terms in common. Those who prefer numbers 1 and 3, apparently believe that the essential characteristic of "rent" is that it is the full long-run remuneration of a certain group of productive agents called, collectively, "land," while the other group believes that the essential characteristic of rent is that it is a surplus return.

INADEQUACY OF THE CLASSICAL SYNTHESIS

At one time the concept of rent as a surplus return was not thought to be incompatible with the concept of the full long-run remuneration of the factor "land." Marshall apparently did not think so, although by his time there were a number of economists, including Mill,

[2] Some may contest the value of such a discussion on the ground that a better theory of distribution can be evolved using anonymous productive agents rather than four heterogeneous categories named "land," "labor," "capital" and "entrepreneurship." While the author has no objection to the generalized approach, the different supply conditions exhibited by different types of productive agents seem to justify quite different economic policies toward the owners of the various agents. The case of a "fixed" supply is valuable as a practical and as a limiting case even if it is not the most convenient concept when referring to the whole field of distribution, and, more particularly, to the problem of exhaustion of product. No one today would attempt to force all of economic reality into four types of supply conditions, but the intermediary cases will be more easily analyzed if the major limiting cases are understood.

[3] The author subscribes to the view developed in modern physics and generalized by the logical positivist philosophers who hold that a phenomenon is identical to the sum of the conditions which define it. Therefore, those conditions or operations necessary to isolate the occurrence are its best definition.

Jevons and Wicksteed, who were beginning to show some doubt. Marshall's case rests on the social point of view, and on that ground is correct, as will be pointed out later. But from the standpoint of the individual firm he was mistaken, and as a result of his ingenious efforts to reconcile the two irreconcilables he perpetuated and gave great impetus to the widening divergences between the various definitions of rent. It is to be emphasized, however, that the English economists of that day were agreed as to the definition of the factor which they were discussing. Wicksteed, for example, went to great length to prove the identity of the values computed by the marginal and by the residual methods.[4] Marshall admitted the validity of the marginal approach for theoretical purposes in his "Mathematical Appendix"[5] and used it in one place in his textual materials.[6]

[4] See Phillip H. Wicksteed, *Common Sense of Political Economy*, the 1935 reprint by George Routledge, pp. 563–68. The first edition appeared in 1910. See also S. J. Chapman "The Remuneration of Employers," *Econ. Jour.*, Vol. XVI (1906), pp. 523–28, quoted in G. J. Stigler, *Theory of Competitive Price* (New York, Macmillian, 1942).

[5] See Marshall, *op. cit.*, especially pp. 848 and 851.

[6] *Ibid.*, p. 535.

It may be helpful to sketch briefly Marshall's usual position. Typically, he thought of land as fixed in total supply, at least in old countries. When he turned to a consideration of an individual producer, he apparently decided that it was most realistic to assume that the land used by a single business man was also fixed, this time in the sense that it came in definite parcels of considerable size. He could then properly compute rent as a residual, with certain qualifications, after having determined the returns of such factors as might be variable by marginal productivity analysis. Each parcel of land would be allocated to its most important use in the long run as a result of the following process.

In the long run, or normal period, the entrepreneur would compare the productivity of each factor of production with the others with the sole exception of land. If it has been profitable to apply these factors intensively to land, a surplus return beyond the cost of the variable factors would result from the sale of the product, and this would give the firm the ability to pay rent. But other firms, and firms in other industries, might also be able to earn a surplus on any given piece of land. Competition would then take place for the whole unit of land resulting in its appropriation by the firm which could earn the greatest surplus with the particular parcel of land. Since the equilibrium rent is equal to the largest surplus, this would serve to allocate the various parcels of land to the same uses that a marginal approach would, assuming only that the land units were small enough so that all of each unit would be fully used by the successful bidder. This is a corollary of the demonstration that the computation of rent for any firm will yield the same result whether the residual or marginal productivity approach is used. Thus Marshall succeeds in allocating land without having it enter into the marginal elements of a firm's costs.

Jevons, Wicksteed, Davenport, and many others have argued against the Marshallian concept, holding that rent should not be measured as a surplus since

In more recent years another, the Paretian, concept of rent has gained prominence among English-speaking economists, including H. D. Henderson, Joan Robinson, Kenneth Boulding, Robert Triffin and Albert Meyers. Although they use the term "rent," the result of the operations which they prescribe to isolate it is completely different from the results of the operations outlined by the classical or the marginal productivity theorists. Rather than the normal return to a certain group of agents of production, rent is defined as being the return to any agent of production greater than that required to keep it in its present employment. It is a return over and above (or in the case of negative "rent," less than) the normal return to an agent, and is clearly a "surplus" return.

The manner in which the two major present-day definitions have grown apart can, perhaps, be best elucidated by reference to the ancient controversy within classical and neoclassical theory: Does or does not "rent enter into the costs of production" of commodities? The views expressed by Marshall postulated a harmony between market, or opportunity, costs and real costs. In taking this position Marshall seemed to maintain that rent did not "enter costs," and—by excluding it from the marginal costs of producers even in the long run—apparently based his conclusion on the Ricardian argument that the last units produced came from inputs of "labor" (and capital) on either the intensive or the extensive margins where the returns were just high enough to pay the "labor" (and capital) costs, leaving nothing for rent. He was, therefore, able to maintain the hypothesized harmony between social and private cost. While his basic argument is based directly on real costs rather than this argument, it, nevertheless, merits examination, since it has fathered the growth of contradictory definitions of rent.

---

it is unnecessary to do so, and it adds nothing to the explanation. Moreover, it makes the theory unnecessarily complex by putting rent on a basis different from other expenses and adds to the number of relatively unmanageable "surplus" returns. These theorists further believe that land is divisible and therefore may be properly regarded as a variable unit so far as each individual is concerned. Furthermore, they think that it *ought* so be regarded because of the smooth way in which it would then fit in the larger framework of economic theory. Marshall acknowledges the final point and condones it for this purpose, but not for general discussions. The dispute, then, was almost exclusively about the implications of the method and not the definition of the result. In either case, rent was defined as equal to the full normal return to land, a return which is equal to the maximum amount which it, with the cooperation of other agents, can add to the national income. The relative merit of these two approaches will be appraised in the final section of this paper. It is sufficient now to establish the identity of the definitions.

An examination of Marshall's arguments will reveal that his own logic fails to support the supposed harmony in some cases, and that in the other cases he preserves his position only by his often undetected switch to considerations based on real costs.

Because of this it is not entirely clear that Marshall meant to imply that rents may not affect the long-run *prices* of goods, as distinct from their costs. For example, he says: "A rise of ground values may be an indication of a scarcity of space that will tend to raise traders' prices";[7] and again: "A rise in rent does serve as a medium through which the growing scarcity of land available for hops and other produce obtrudes itself upon his notice." In this case, however, he concludes by saying that: "But it is worse than inexpedient to say that the rent of the land does enter into their [the hops'] price: that is false." [8]

To say that it does not enter price, as distinguished from (real) cost, however, is not consistent with his later statement that "land shares the influences of the laws of demand and of substitution . . . because the existing stock of it, like the existing stock of capital or of labor of any kind, tends to be shifted from one use to another till nothing could be gained for production by any other shifting. And . . . the income from a factory . . . is governed in the same way as is the income from land. In each case the income tends to equal the value of the marginal net product of the agent. . . ." [9] This is a clear statement of marginal theory in the short run and would make land rent as price-determining from the point of view of the individual producer as any other variable, for certainly land which is variable in the short run will be variable in the long run.

In whatever manner Marshall may have intended these statements, it is clear even on Ricardian premises that land rents do affect price in the case of those industries where the least efficient producers of a commodity must pay rent due to the competition of firms producing other products such as the "traders" referred to in footnote 7. In that case the pressure of others who desired to use the land eliminated all but the strongest traders who, to keep their places, had to pay the higher rent. This was possible because of the failure of the weaker traders, whose withdrawal affected a reduction of supply of certain commodities resulting in higher prices. It might be said that, as the price of land increased, the *industry* was forced to let some land go until the "marginal productivity" of the land was as high as its rent.

Another example in which all fixed elements are of positive value

[7] *Ibid.*, p. 452.
[8] *Ibid.*, pp. 436-37.
[9] *Ibid.*, p. 535.

may be found in Marshall's discussion of meteoric stones where he identifies the case where the stones "cannot be worn out or destroyed, and no more can be found" [10] with the rent of the land. He then says that they will be distributed by the price system to their most important uses and that the price paid for them will indicate the value of their services at the margins of application. The implication is clear that there are no marginal or no-rent stones and that the stones must be had if the product is to be produced. Thus the price paid is a price that the individual firm *must* pay if it is to continue to have the use of the stones, and is, therefore, a payment that must be made from the sale of the product produced with the aid of the stones if the "rent" is to be effective in allocating the stones to their most important uses. But Marshall does not draw this conclusion. Instead he turns to the point that it does not matter who receives the rents so far as the productivity of the stones now or ever is concerned. In other words, he turns at once from the individual to the social point of view and to matters of tax policy, both of which are related to real rather than opportunity costs. We shall come back to this shift in a moment, but first it may be well to inquire into the prevalence of the situation where the least efficient long-run producer must pay rent. At the moment we must note that, however correct his analysis of tax policy may be, it in no way disproves the possibility of commodity prices which are affected by the payment of rent.

Mill apparently decided that rent typically raised the price of manufactured, though not of agricultural, products.[11] The present author has difficulty in conceiving of any industry which does not find rent affecting the price charged by the "marginal," and hence all, firms. Certainly all retailing is carried on in areas where the worst usable locations are "superior" sites for hotels, apartments, or residences. Moreover, land to be put to any urban use must yield as much as the agricultural use that might be made of it, and this is almost certain to be positive near a city. Likewise "marginal" dairy land is likely to be superior for fattening animals, and land "marginal" for this purpose "superior" for growing certain grains or fibers, and this land is probably superior for stock-raising, and so on. Some sheep are raised on the public domain, and with them we may find a product which is raised in part on no-rent land and which, therefore, need cover only labor and capital costs to retain its marginal suppliers in the long run. But even in this case

10 *Ibid.*, p. 418.
11 J. S. Mill, *Principles of Political Economy*, Ashley ed. (London, Longmans. Green, 1909), p. 468.

we discover that the sheep are shorn and wintered in the lowlands where the land has alternative uses.[12]

In the case illustrated above, where—due to a scarcity of land suitable for certain uses—*all* competing producers must pay rent, an element heretofore passed over in this paper has been made explicit. So long as all producers had the practical alternative of using no-rent land, rent might properly be thought of as not belonging in the group of opportunity costs "entering into" the price of commodities. The full rent was then a "surplus" both from the viewpoint of price-determination and that of real costs of production, although its payment was unnecessary to secure the proper allocation of land. Now it seems clear that *part* of the return to land usually affects price; namely, that part equal to the average cost of land to the marginal producer of any product.

Marshall apparently never quite understood the problem in this manner and when he tried to answer Jevons on this point Marshall shifted his ground so as to make the parcel of land under discussion much more profitable in one use than in another so that there was no "simple numerical relation between the surplus, or rent, which the land would yield under oats and the marginal costs which the prices of hops must cover." [13] He then seems to assume that some of the units of the product yielding the highest rent on this particular parcel of land is grown on a no-rent margin.[14]

Thus Marshall seems to contend that the the price of a product will

12 Among others, Gustav Cassel has made a good deal of this point in his *The Theory of Social Economy*, translated by S. L. Barron (New York, Harcourt Brace, 1939), pp. 287–88.

13 Marshall, *op. cit.*, pp. 436–37.

14 See F. S. Oglivie, "Marshall on Rent," *Econ. Jour.*, Vol. 40 (1930), p. 1–24. This is not the interpretation given by Professor Oglivie to this passage. He seems to hold the opinion that since Marshall went on to say ". . . if for the purposes of a particular argument we take together the whole expenses of the production on that [rent-bearing] land, and divide these among the whole of the commodity produced; then the rent which we ought to count in is . . . that which it . . . [pays] when used for producing . . . [wheat]." P. 437n. Marshall admitted the crux of the arguments, against his position. But Marshall never denied the existence of rent, nor that firms on economically scarce land must pay rent. What he did say was that rent does not enter the calculations of the producer because the producer thinks of land as being fixed. This statement is in line with this view and yields nothing to the marginal productivity analysis. See also M. T. Holland, "Marshall on Rent—A Reply," *Econ. Jour.*, Vol. 40 (1930), p. 36, for a still different defense of Marshall's position. See also G. J. Stigler, *Production and Distribution Theories* (New York, Macmillan, 1940), p. 94. The interpretation given here, although based on quality of the product, yields a conclusion similar to ours.

rise if the producers cannot pay rents high enough to retain certain lands due to the application of their labor and capital to less productive soils. In this way, although prices rise, no rent is included in the cost of marginal units raised. Land, therefore, *need* not even be a supplementary cost since in the long run a firm may move to no-rent land. But this argument of Marshall's misses the mark. It is not enough to say that price is increased because the factors are forced to work poorer land. This may be true, but in the case under discussion it is also presumed that producers of many products will find that the least productive technically available land is scarce and commands a rental. In that case the producer does not have the alternative of moving to no-rent land, but only to this land which is worth a certain minimum rental. And this much, at least, must now be counted among the supplementary costs and must be covered in the long run. By a simple extension of this argument all payments necessary to keep certain parcels of land in a given industry will become supplementary costs and this will raise the normal price of most goods to a level higher than that which would prevail if land were free.[15]

It seems inevitable, then, that rents, or at least part of them, do "enter" opportunity costs and do usually result in higher equilibrium prices. This does not make rent a social cost, however, and it therefore destroys the harmony between social and private costs so earnestly sought by Marshall.

---

[15] Some may argue that this presentation ignores the basic consideration. It has been widely taught that the main issue is a matter of what is cause and what is effect, and that at least under conditions of increasing short-run average cost, prices must rise or fall *first* and rents then adjust themselves. This is logical enough when attention is paid to a single industry in which competing firms operate. But if as a result of a rise in the price of hops the rents on hop-lands rise, diverting land suitable for growing either hops or wheat to hop production, what will be the effect on wheat prices? Clearly, the acreage in wheat will be reduced, the supply of wheat will be shorter and prices higher in that order. The "final" cause of higher wheat prices, while not apparent, lies in the factors that raised the price of hops, but the immediate cause was a rise in the rent of wheat land which resulted in a reduction of supply, hence higher wheat prices. If the validity of this is admitted; then it becomes apparent that generalization as to "price-determining" *vs.* "price-determined" factor-payments are not possible. The problem is not one of cause and effect, as such arguments assume, but mutual determination.

It is, of course, apparent that under competitive conditions, the price of the product will still be equal to the cost of the last dose of labor-capital. What this argument does say is that, if land is still treated as a fixed factor, it must earn a "surplus" of a certain size if the firm is to stay in the industry. This is a queer kind of "surplus," and its magnitude may be found just as easily (if land be thought of as a variable) by finding the quantity of land the cost of whose marginal dose is also equal to the price of the product under competitive conditions.

We cannot pretend, as Smith, Ricardo and Marshall would have us, that all of "price-determining" cost must be accounted for by labor, past and present. It may be "wicked," as Edgeworth puts it, to come to this conclusion, but it is unavoidable.[16]

TWO THEORIES OF RENT ARE REQUIRED

It is proper to turn to real cost analysis, as Marshall does, in order to escape these conclusions if one is dealing with justice in taxation and similar problems. But in doing so one definitely leaves opportunity costs behind. The real cost concept is not a harmonious section of a single theory of rent which may be used to analyze social matters, but involves a separate theory based on real costs. Money costs, based on opportunity costs, yield a grossly distorted image of real costs.

To say this is in no way to detract from the value of the analysis of real, or social, costs. The "costs" which especially concerned Marshall are not the opportunity costs of the producers which we have been discussing, but are, rather, "the exertions of all the different kinds of labor that are directly or indirectly involved in making it; together with the abstinences or rather the waitings required for saving the capital used in making it: all these efforts and sacrifices together will be called the *real cost of production,* or, for shortness, its *expenses of production. . . ."*

Cost, then, is regarded by Marshall as being the sum of the efforts and sacrifices necessary for production.[17] Money cost is that payment necessary to secure the existence of adequate supplies of all qualities of the various factors of production. But land is defined as being the gift of nature and, in its basic characteristic, indestructible, although it may be severely "mined" in its subsidiary aspects.[18]

Since the author believes that the Marshallian analysis of real cost is

[16] Quoted in Oglivie, *op. cit.,* as appearing in Edgeworth's *Memorials,* p. 436.

[17] With such a definition of cost it is clear that Marshall's rigid insistence upon the distinction between rents and guasi-rents is quite proper. Quasi-rents involve real costs and rents do not. The supply conditions in the long run are crucial and similarity in demand factors or short-run divisibility will not alter the basic distinction. On the other hand, it is true that the supply of land can usually be reduced by literal or figurative "mining." The total return to land is typically a gross, not a net, return, and unless the proper deductions are made, the net rent may be overstated. If this occurs and more than the net return are taxed or withdrawn from the enterprise, a wasteful use of land will result which will involve lowering the quality of the land.

[18] The basic characteristic is conceded to be its extension. The fact that "land can be ruined" simply means that the user was not content with the *net* return, but took as income some of the "asset value" in addition. Such practices are discussed under the heading of royalties and are closely connected to the theory of interest.

essentially correct, and since he entertains a similar opinion about the validity of price theory based upon opportunity cost, it is desirable that some precise connection between the two be established.

THE RELATIONSHIP BETWEEN THE TWO THEORIES

A connection between Marshall's "money cost of production," *i.e.*, the money payments associated with real costs, and the total money cost of production may be preserved by a special use of the fixed factor analysis.[19] If we classify all real costs as variables but treat all non-real opportunity costs as fixed, the "expenses of production," as defined above, are equal to the average *variable* costs and the quantity indicated by the distance between this curve and the average cost curve at any point will measure the gap between real and money costs as expressed in dollars. A major point of this paper is that such a gap is to be expected in the case of marginal as well as other firms.[20]

This comment in no way invalidates the choice of the function which minimizes social cost as described by Ellis and Fellner, but it does suggest that price on the curve "excluding rent" does in fact only partially exclude it except in the special case presented by them. The non-real cost agents of production are scarce and productive. They, too, must be allocated to their most important uses and the basic consideration is that efficient use be made of all of the scarce productive factors taken together. Since in this case only real costs are placed with marginal costs, any excess of marginal revenue over marginal cost represents a net social gain. Under equilibrium conditions the output indicated by this analysis is the same as if all factors were variable, as indicated above.[21] And these, in turn, are identical to that indicated by Ellis and Fellner.

[19] This point was suggested by a consideration of the analysis made by H. S. Ellis and William J. Fellner in the article, "External Economies and Diseconomies," *Am. Econ. Rev.*, Vol. XXXIII, No. 3 (Sept., 1943), pp. 493–511. The author believes that the geometry used is based upon the implicit assumption that members of the industry have access to no-rent land because it shows a common origin for curves which show, on one hand, average cost including rent, β, and average cost excluding rent, δ, on the other (pp. 498–99). This is proper if land is regarded as variable or if land is regarded as fixed in quantity, but at least a small part of the total output is produced on no-rent land. The latter of these alternatives seems most proper here since the curves are relevant to a discussion of diminishing returns, apparently diminishing returns to land.

[20] This would have been clear from the diagrams of Ellis and Fellner, if, as the author believes proper, their β curve had at *all* points been greater, though by a diminishing amount, than the δ curve.

[21] See note 4 above.

Something more than the real costs are relevant in pricing, and social cost must recognize the loss which would result from an under-utilization of land. On the other hand, the *payments* made to the owners of fixed factors can be diverted to other uses without direct effect on production. Thus, the real cost is lower than the most desirable price from the social point of view. Social costs, as defined by Ellis and Fellner, cannot be identified with real costs except in the limiting case of industries which have access to technically useful no-rent land.

PARETIAN RENT AND CLASSICAL THEORY

We have seen how the attempted synthesis of business expenses and real costs led to certain difficulties in classical theory. We must now turn to another trouble spot in the analysis of rent.

Is rent the normal payment to land, including both surplus and cost elements, or is it just that part of the total payment comprising the surplus element? [22] Marshall's objection to the latter alternative seemed to be based on the contention that "there is no simple and numerical relation" between the surpluses raised by one product as compared to those raised by another. The Paretian conception provided an apparent answer.[23]

Pareto defines rent as equal to the *difference* between the two "surpluses." Thus there would be included in the total payment to land, as we have defined it, an opportunity cost (which affected prices and bore a "simple and numerical relationship" between the costs of two unlike products that could use the same land) plus a surplus, *i.e.*, a "rent" (which did not affect prices). This analysis has won over several influential English-speaking economists [24] who have sometimes termed the opportunity cost of land "transfer cost," to replace "rent" and quasi-rent as the principal return to fixed agents of production. "Rent," as defined by this group, is a true surplus but one that may disappear in the long run, and which will in no case affect the allocation of resources.

But the Paretian answer goes much further than this in its implica-

[22] The third alternative, that it be designated as the opportunity cost element alone, will be discussed and advocated presently. It cannot be given a separate place at this point, however, since it is not a standard conception.

[23] Vilfredo Pareto, *Cours d'Economie Politique, Librarie de l'Université* (Lausanne 1897), Vol. II, paragraphs 745–755 and related passages. Similar views are expressed in his later *Manual d'Economie Politique* in the section on rent. For a good treatment in English in a related vein, see Joan Robinson, *The Economics of Imperfect Competition* (London, Macmillan, 1934), chap. 8.

[24] See above, p. 261.

tions. If analysis is undertaken at the level of the individual firms, the importance of these implications is not so apparent, especially if the standard assumptions in regard to competition are made. The differences would seem to center about the assumptions regarding alternative uses and terminology. If all units of the particular agent employed by a firm have the same alternative employments and if the difference in productivity between the best and the next best uses is infinitesimal, the Paretian rents disappear, leaving nothing but "transfer costs" which, as Wicksteed pointed out, are equal to Marshallian rents. Since many very similar firms were thought to make up an "industry" in Marshallian economics, the various agents *would* have very good alternatives within the industry, and since the productive agents were thought of as being homogeneous, all would have the same opportunity costs. In this case, incidentally, if all firms were exactly alike all of rent would "enter into" price.

But even within the framework of Marshallian economics conceptual changes would be required. Paretian rents might be zero from the standpoint of all the firms, for horizontal supply curves for the factors offered to a firm seem logical. Not so for a whole industry. The supply curve of factors for an industry usually has positive slope, making the payments to factors with the poorer alternatives greater than that required, *i.e.*, than opportunity costs, thus introducing a finite "rent" element into a situation where an analysis of the firms had revealed only infinitely small "rents." Moreover, from the social point of view, rents are higher still, since few agents can insist on much more than subsistence, which, in the case of land, is zero.

All this may be fine in so far as it introduces greater flexibility into the theoretical economic system, but it leaves rent theory in a nebulous state, with the payment of rent related to different functions by different authorities and varying drastically in magnitude according to the level of analysis used if one of the groups of experts is followed. The fact is that very different concepts are defined by the prescription of the various authors. We will discover that ideas of the various authors can be profitably synthesized. To do so, however, we must adopt a terminology as flexible and exact as the prescriptions. Let us turn to this task.

RENT BEST DEFINED AS THE OPPORTUNITY COST OF LAND

In the following sections we will be primarily concerned with rent as analyzed at the level of the firm rather than that of the industry. Further analysis of real costs may be left to the standard treatments.

Space forbids expansion into the various levels intermediate to the firm and society as a whole at which "rent" might be determined, although such extension is not difficult. The author feels that the term "rent" should be applied to only one level, and suggests following Stigler's lead in the choice of terminology of the intermediary levels.[25] "Rent" may perhaps be most properly applied to the remuneration of a certain type of productive agent as the remuneration appears to the owner of the agent. This will usually depend on the opportunities available among firms, not industries.

Preference for the use of the term "rent" to refer to the opportunity cost of land may now be stated. This definition is in strict accord with the usage of neither of the groups of economists discussed above. But in no case would disruptive changes be involved. The "orthodox" economists who have thought of rent as the full payment to owners of land frequently make the assumption of homogeneity which eliminated that part of the payments which are of a non-opportunity cost character. Such economists would merely have to adopt Wicksteed's position. The other group could do their part in standardizing terminology by substituting the word "rent" where they now use "transfer cost" and adopting some new name for the group of "economic rents" which they have analyzed and which deserve a definite position in economic theory. Such a name is suggested in the following pages.

The choice of opportunity cost as a basis for the definition rests on several considerations. In the first place, it seems most in accord with common usage. To most people rent is still connected primarily with the use of durable agents rather than with surplus returns. It has come to be associated with surplus returns by professional economists largely as a result of several special arguments which can now be seen to be resting on special grounds. While there is little enough agreement of this matter of terminology within the ranks of economists, the proposed definition would probably minimize the total adjustment required to bring precision into our terminology, whether or not it were brought into accord with common usage.

Another reason for this choice is that no new name for the opportunity cost of land has been accepted. Some might say that "transfer cost" is such a name, but the author cannot recall seeing any listing of the functional shares of income that read "wages, interest, transfer cost, rent and profits."

A final reason is that the use to which the word "rent" is now being put by those who do not use it in connection with the normal returns to land seems misleading in important ways. As they use it, it is neither a real cost nor opportunity cost. Since many economists still think of

25 See below. footnote 34.

"rent" as a major branch of distribution theory, this sort of definition tends to confuse the issues. Moreover, the fact that such rents tend to disappear in the long run makes it particularly incomprehensible to students and laymen. Yet if the payment to the various agents' of production greater than that required to keep them in their present uses is not to be called "rent," what is it to be called?

TRUE SURPLUS RETURNS TO PRODUCTIVE AGENTS: FACTOR PROFITS

Paretian rents are not opportunity costs since they are defined as being the payment over and above opportunity costs. Neither are they real costs since they are payments which any agent may receive whether or not its supply, as suited to a particular use, would cease to exist if their owners were not paid. There is only one major share of functional income which is commonly thought of as having neither an opportunity cost nor a real cost character; that is pure profit. Let us then compare these surplus returns to profit.[26]

In the *Wealth of Nations,* profit was not clearly distinguished from interest. This practice, while modified by later English economists, was not changed sufficiently by them to exclude all non-cost returns until after Marshall's day, and some noted economists still regard entrepreneurial returns as being composed, in part at least, of opportunity and/or real cost elements.[27]

These economists, of whom Hawtrey and Taussig are representative, seem to find repugnant the idea that a single man can be at one and the same time a salaried manager, and a receiver of purely residual profits. It is, of course, true that some business men earn much more year after year than others, and it may be tempting to speak of the greater earning of some as a "rent of ability," as Hawtrey suggests. In doing so, however, he not only uses the word "rent" in the sense of payment greater than the opportunity cost of the entrepreneur, *i.e.,* in exactly the sense

26 Most of the characteristics of "profit" referred to below are suggested in the chapter on profits which appeared in the book by Robert Triffin, *Monopolistic Competition and General Equilibrium Theory* (Cambridge, Harvard Univ. Press, 1941), pp. 158 *ff.*

27 Marshall, *op. cit.,* p. 624n. It may be noted that if the manager is paid according to his ability and if insurable risks are also included in costs, the "excluded 4/5 of what are ordinarily classed as profits in England" becomes 5/5.

See also H. G. Hawtrey, "Competition from Newcomers," *Economica,* Vol. X, No. 39 (Aug., 1943), pp. 219 *ff.* It goes without saying that in this paper we have adopted ". . . what orthodox economists all over the world are teaching their students," rather than the view which he advocates in his article.

which is inappropriate and incompatible with the usage advocated here, but he also seems to be saying in another way that entrepreneurs are paid according to their productivity. Any implication that they are fixed factors and receive a residual return will not affect this observation.[28]

We take, therefore, as our definition of profits that share of income left over from sales after all costs have been paid including the opportunity costs of management, insurable risks, and payments to bondholders and stockholders sufficient to maintain the investment at its current level. It seems clear that profits are as likely to be negative as positive for any firm in a "normal" year, and that in the long run for the economy as a whole profits will be zero, although there will be very wide fluctuations about this level and some firms may show profits for very long periods of time.

There seem to be several points of similarity between the surplus return of pure profits and the surplus return to certain agents of production. In the first place, neither return need be paid by a firm in order to retain the services of the agents who receive the "surplus" payments. This is true for each individual firm as well as for society, a point which distinguishes this type of return from what we have defined as "rent." Rent (the opportunity cost of land) must be paid by the firms in order to secure the agent for the firm's use. Profits and the surplus returns to some units of specific agents are also alike in that neither the specific agents nor the profit-takers *need* be fixed in quantity or location in the ordinary sense of the word. They simply *will* not change their employment if their returns are reduced even if they could so long as they are not reduced below their opportunity costs. Thus taxes that fall on either profits or surpluses of this nature will affect neither output nor price directly whether or not the taxes are uniform, *i.e.*, reach the surpluses of all competing agents or firms on the same basis.[29]

This last statement must be qualified. If pure profits are taxed, unlike the surplus returns mentioned above, it is probable that people

[28] See page 483 above. Parenthetically, it may be added that the conception of opportunity cost seems unnecessarily restricted as it is used by Hawtrey. He apparently regards all opportunity past after the stripling youth has made his choice of profession, since his "opportunity" is what he might have expected to make in another profession. But the ordinary meaning of the term as used in America implies, on the contrary, a relatively short-run situation which would not exclude the entrepreneur, currently employing himself, from the alternative of becoming the manager of another *firm* in the same industry.

[29] The use to which the tax funds are put may, of course, affect the output and price.

will be less willing to become "profit-takers" since losses are likely to outweigh profits-minus-taxes. But this is a consideration that depends upon the nature of the supply of entrepreneurs [30] and, in any case, does not bear upon the problem of output and price where the entrepreneur can be called a fixed factor in the ordinary meaning of the term.[31]

Another point of similarity between "surplus rents" and entrepreneurial profits is suggested by Triffin who remarks that, "[A promoter's] purpose may be sheer exploitation of the bondholders and the stockholders . . . he may innovate by creating . . . profit-opportunities for himself, rather than for the corporation. . . ." [32] In this, too, the position of the profits-taker is similar to that of owners of other factors of

[30] Such nice calculations would probably not affect the supply of entrepreneurs if their supply depends, as some maintain, upon the "sweepstakes urge" where mindful of a better-than-even chance of loss, this chance is taken to make possible a very rich gain.

[31] To avoid confusion in matters of tax policy it may be well to contrast these surpluses with the opportunity cost of land. A uniform tax that takes the same percentage of the rent regardless of the purpose for which the land is used will affect neither the prices nor the outputs of the various goods produced with the aid of land. This conclusion follows only in the case that the tax does not change the relative position or at least the ordinal relationship of each agent; i.e., is in some sense of the word "uniform." But this is true of any factor of production, e.g., a uniform income tax (or a properly constructed progressive one) will leave all receivers of income in the same relative position where, at least, they can not shift so as to increase their money incomes after taxation.

It is to be noted, however, that unlike other factors, collateral effects on the physical supply of land or the extent of the use of land are avoided, since land has no real cost, with the exception of the case elaborated by K. E. Boulding ("Incidence of a Profits Tax," Am. Econ. Rev., Vol. XXXIV, No. 3 [Sept., 1944], pp. 567–72), where the owners do not try to squeeze all of the rent out of their holdings. (In general, I believe that his conclusions are stronger when applied to Paretian rents, rather than profits, since one can not count on the existence of positive profits, and it is generally conceded that business men will work pretty hard to avoid losses.)

As in the case of other factors, a tax on land which is devoted only to certain uses, if impinging on opportunity costs, will result in a changed use of some of the agents. The conclusions reached in regard to the surplus returns, and profits, in contrast, have application whether or not the tax is "uniform." Any tax smaller than the surplus will fail to result in the movement of an agent of production even if only scattered and random agents are taxed and all others escape entirely. This follows since the current employment remains the only one where returns greater than the opportunity returns are available.

We can hardly afford to use the word "rent" indiscriminately in matters of tax policy when the two commonly accepted payments defined as "rent" yield such different results when taxed.

[32] Triffin, op. cit., pp. 185–86.

production who receive returns greater than their opportunity costs. Bankers when lending their funds, workers when bargaining for their contracts, suppliers of materials and buyers of the finished product are all, in theory, working for their own, not primarily for their firm's welfare—a fact that may explain the predatory actions which all groups in business occasionally display.

If one whole group of productive agents is successful in gaining special returns, their special returns will affect output and price if the marginal cost curves are affected, and their returns, although "surplus" from the social point of view, reduce output and increase prices resulting in a monopoly profit which is appropriated by the privileged group. This eventuality is possible only if the industry or firm is monopolistic. In this case a tax on such a surplus will improve matters by transferring part of the fruits of the exploitative gain to the government, which is presumed to act in the general welfare. Again this type of analysis is identical to that typically used in discussing monopolistic "profits" rather than "surplus" elements in factor costs, but it appears to be appropriate.

This leads us directly to the consideration of a final point of similarity between pure profits and these surplus returns. From one point of view the surplus accruing to the individual agent *is* a profit. In a free economy each agent is responsible for finding its own employment and may be thought of as a little firm selling a productive service.[33] Any failure to follow market conditions may result in a loss (*i.e.*, receipts less than opportunity cost in the sense of next highest marginal value product) and any advantage taken of a fortuitous situation will result in profit (i.e., receipts greater than opportunity costs). If "profits" or "losses" become regular and lose their apparent "unusualness," the factor may impute the gain or loss to itself, thus raising or lowering its estimate of what it is worth in accordance with what it is paid, just as the entrepreneur of a firm will so revalue his fixed stocks. In using this term "fixed stocks," the true fixity of the "stock in trade" of the individual person is emphasized. This fixity, involving as it does a non-marginal, non-real cost situation, again underlines the parallel between the situation of the individual and the entrepreneur. Indeed, the latter is in the more favorable position today in that he can escape some of the risks involved in his actions through the application of various devices of business organization.

It is true that the difference between the scale of operations of the

---

[33] Wicksteed, *op. cit.*, pp. 360–70, must have had something of the same thing in mind when he said that undertakers might be dispensed with and in their stead have the owners of the various productive resources spontaneously combine them, each waiting for his remuneration until the product due his agent had been sold.

entrepreneur of a firm and the "entrepreneur" disposing of his personal
services is so great as to amount to a difference of kind. This difference
is perhaps great enough to justify a different term for these surpluses
which may accrue to any factor. Perhaps the term "non-cost outlay"
advanced by Stigler [34] will be found to be the most suitable. Another
possibility is "factor profits" as distinguished from "entrepreneural
profits." Either of these terms would give the proper impression—that
they are payments greater than opportunity costs to any factor of production—and their use would also avoid confusing surplus returns with
the return to land.

Of the two terms, "factor profits" may prove to be the more suitable
since Stigler's "non-cost outlay" is closely tied up to the industry concept. Throughout the last two sections of this paper, opportunity costs
have been defined in terms of alternative 'jobs" which a given agent is
able to secure. Thus a movie star whose next best *industry* is selling
does not show a "factor profit" embracing the difference between his
present salary and his possible earnings as, say, a brush peddler, but
only the difference between what he earns and what a rival studio is
prepared to offer. Thus "non-cost outlay," as Stigler defines it, belongs
most properly to the middle ground which we decided to eschew (see
page 492).

"Factor profits" refer to the everyday level where the great majority
of decisions are made which involve the allocation of resources. As
such, it is the most important level on which returns necessary to retain resources in their present use can be discussed. The industry
concept is not very useful here since job-opportunities cut across industry lines very freely.

LAND IS PREFERABLY TREATED AS A VARIABLE FACTOR

In the earlier discussions of this paper it seemed desirable to emphasize the identity of the results isolated using the concept of "fixed
factors" and those isolated using marginal productivity analysis. Now
that this need is past it is proper to point out the reasons why the
author prefers to use the marginal productivity approach.

Marshall defended the concept of "fixed factors" on the ground of
realism. Thus he wrote, ". . . in discussions written specially for mathematical readers it is no doubt right to be very bold in the search for
wide generalizations . . . but it is not in a treatise such as the present,
in which mathematics is used only to express in terse and more precise
language those methods of analysis and reasoning which ordinary peo-

[34] *Theory of Competitive Price,* pp. 105 *f.*

ple adopt, more or less consciously, in the affairs of everyday life." [35]
Marginal productivity theorists usually are interested in "wide generalizations." Wicksteed, for example, who attacked Marshall most vigorously in this respect, was the first to give a demonstration of exhaustion of product by marginal productivity analysis under competitive conditions. But it seems proper to question the rôle assigned to land—and here physical characteristics, not the fixity of supply, is basic —by Marshall as he looked through the eyes of a business man. Let us assume that the *total* amount of "land" in the world is fixed. Is it the most prominent fixed factor to the individual firm?

In the United States most of our farms are what is called "family-sized." While, before the war, seasonal labor was employed during the harvests, the size of the family is an important consideration influencing the amount of land that it will attempt to work. Even where the families own their farms there is continual bargaining for the use of part of one another's land. Thus the land is often more variable to the farmer than is his labor supply. On the other hand, it is likewise true that the United States merchant marine at least from the First World War until the Merchant Marine act of 1936, found its supply of ships, its capital, relatively fixed, whereas the land space required could be rented and was largely a variable factor. It may be objected that the second example is relevant primarily to the short run where Marshall agreed that capital might well be a fixed factor, but the point is not that capital is or is not fixed, but that, *from the point of view of the business man,* land may be regarded as being *more easily* varied than the supply of other factors in some important cases. If this is true, then the alleged necessity for putting rent on a different basis from wages or interest is not proved, and marginal productivity theory should be adopted, at least in certain cases, on grounds of realism as well as of theoretical beauty.

It may be that land is rigidly fixed in some employments, so that business men can not think in terms of adding or subtracting a small portion of their land even in the normal period. But this is certainly not true of farmers, and there are many business men of all kinds who rent their floor space and can easily acquire larger quarters if they so desire. From the viewpoint of a firm more of all factors can be obtained. The safest course on grounds of realism is probably to admit the validity of both types of analysis in so far as the economics of a firm is concerned, but to stress the marginal productivity approach.

Quite aside from the debatable element of realism, it should be noted that the presence of several surplus returns in the short run vastly

[35] Marshall, *op. cit.*, p. 851.

complicates the problem of income distribution in the short run.[36] Where only one surplus return is to be determined, it can be correctly found as a residual even if it could be determined by marginal productivity; but if there are several fixed factors, resort must be made to simultaneous equations on the theoretical level, a device that seems more out of touch with business practice than marginal productivity theory.

Marshall was aware of this difficulty, but seems to have preferred to leave this problem unresolved in the short run, and only partially resolved in the long run.[37] These difficulties are especially pressing when monopolistic competition is considered, a condition in which each firm must be able to evaluate each agent without reference to any industry. Since no two firms have the same product it would be impossible to apply simultaneous equations, making the division of income among two or more fixed agents quite arbitrary. In this case it would seem likely that costs would always be found equal to price simply because the "surplus" would be entirely imputed to land, at least in the long run, although a marginal analysis of rent might reduce it so as to indicate a high monopoly or other profit. In other words, a factor profit might displace the entrepreneurial profit simply because of a lack of precision of analysis. The use of marginal analysis seems to be the best way out of this impasse.

Finally, the marginal productivity theory avoids the welter of special issues which have impeded clear thinking for so long. All elements of cost, at least those which must be positive, are placed on the same basis. So far as the allocation of resources is concerned, what is true of one is true of another. And the true significance of real cost can be stated with vigor, albeit separately, without a fallacious and unconvincing argument which attempts to identify real costs and prices.

Two major difficulties involved in rent theory have been considered above. The first is the unfortunate result of a mistaken attempt to synthesize incompatible doctrines of cost, the second is a disagreement as to the essential characteristic of rent. Both of these difficulties should and can be overcome. One method for doing so has been proposed.

---

[36] For more detail on this problem as well as the distinction between rents and quasi-rents, see R. S. Meriam, "Quasi-rent," *Explorations in Economics* (New York, McGraw-Hill, 1936), Chap. X.

[37] Marshall, *op. cit.*, p. 626.

SECTION VI

WELFARE ECONOMICS

33

THE SIMPLE ANALYTICS
OF WELFARE MAXIMIZATION *

FRANCIS M. BATOR † is Deputy Special Assistant
to the President for National Security Affairs,
The White House, Washington, D.C. He was
formerly at Massachusetts Institute of Technology.

It appears, curiously enough, that there is nowhere in the literature
a complete and concise nonmathematical treatment of the problem of
welfare maximization in its "new welfare economics" aspects. It is the
purpose of this exposition to fill this gap for the simplest statical and
stationary situation.

Part I consists in a rigorous diagrammatic determination of the
"best" configuration of inputs, outputs, and commodity distribution
for a two-input, two-output, two-person situation, where furthermore
all functions are of smooth curvature and where neoclassical generalized diminishing returns obtain in all but one dimension—returns to
scale are assumed constant. Part II identifies the "price-wage-rent"
configuration embedded in the maximum problem which would ensure that decentralized profit- and preference-maximizing behavior by
atomistic competitors would sustain the maximum-welfare position.
Part III explores the requirements on initial factor ownership if market-imputed (or "as if" market-imputed) income distribution is to be
consistent with the commodity distribution required by the maximum-
welfare solution. Part IV consists in brief comments on some technical
ambiguities, *e.g.*, the presumption that all tangencies are internal; also
on a number of feasible (and not so feasible) extensions: more inputs,
outputs and households; elasticity in input supplies; joint and intermediate products; diminishing returns to scale; external interactions.
The discussion is still stationary and neoclassical in spirit. Then, in
Part V, the consequences of violating some of the neoclassical curvature
assumptions are examined. Attention is given to the meaning, in a
geometric context, of the "convexity" requirements of mathematical

* From the *American Economic Review*, Vol. XLVII (March, 1957), pp. 22–59. Reprinted by permission.
† The author is indebted to R. S. Eckaus and R. M. Solow for suggestive comment.

economics and to the significance of an important variety of nonconvexity—increasing returns to scale—for "real" market allocation, for Lange-Lerner type "as if" market allocation, and for the solubility of a maximum-of-welfare problem. Finally, Part VI contains some brief remarks on possible dynamical extensions. A note on the seminal literature concludes the paper.[1]

I. INPUTS, OUTPUTS AND COMMODITY DISTRIBUTION

Take, as given:

(1) Two inelastically supplied, homogeneous and perfectly divisible inputs, labor-services (L) and land (D). This "Austrian" assumption does violate the full generality of the neoclassical model; elasticity in input supplies would make simple diagrammatic treatment impossible.

(2) Two production functions, $A = F_A(L_A, D_A)$, $N = F_N(L_N, D_N)$, one for each of the two homogeneous goods: apples (A) and nuts (N). The functions are of smooth curvature, exhibit constant returns to scale and diminishing marginal rates of substitution along any isoquant (*i.e.*, the isoquants are "convex" to the origin).

(3) Two ordinal preference functions, $U_X = f_X(A_X, N_X)$ and $U_Y = f_Y(A_Y, N_Y)$—sets of smooth indifference curves convex to the origin— one for X and one for Y. These reflect unambiguous and consistent preference orderings for each of the two individuals (X and Y) of all conceivable combinations of own-consumption of apples and nuts. For convenience we adopt for each function an arbitrary numerical index, U_X and U_Y, to identify the indifference curves. But the functions have no interpersonal implications whatever and for any one individual they only permit of statements to the effect that one situation is worse, indifferent or better than another. We do require consistency: if X prefers situation α to situation β and β to γ, then he must prefer α to γ; indifference curves must not cross. Also, satiation-type phenomena and Veblenesque or other "external" effects are ruled out.

(4) A social welfare function, $W = W(U_X, U_Y)$, that permits a unique preference-ordering of all possible states based only on the positions of both individuals in their own preference fields. It is this function that incorporates an ethical valuation of the relative "deservingness" of X and Y.

The problem is to determine the maximum-welfare values of labor

---

[1] Anyone familiar with the modern literature will recognize my debt to the writings of Professor Samuelson. Reference is to be made, especially, to Chapter 8 of *Foundations of Economic Analysis* (Cambridge, 1947), to "Evaluation of Real National Income," *Oxford Econ. Papers*, Jan. 1950, II, 1–29; and to "Social Indifference Curves," *Quart. Jour. Econ.*, Feb. 1956, LXX, 1–22.

input into apples (L_A), labor input into nuts (L_N), land input into apples (D_A), land input into nuts (D_N), of total production of apples (A) and nuts (N), and, last, of the distribution of apples and nuts between X and Y (A_X, N_X, A_Y, N_Y).

A. FROM ENDOWMENTS AND PRODUCTION FUNCTIONS TO THE PRODUCTION-POSSIBILITY CURVE

Construct an Edgeworth-Bowley box diagram, as in Figure 1, with horizontal and vertical dimensions just equal to the given supplies, respectively, of D and L, and plot the isoquants for apples with the southwest corner as origin and those for nuts with origin at the northeast corner. Every point in the box represents six variables, L_A, L_N, D_A, D_N, A, N. The problem of production efficiency consists in finding the locus of points where any increase in the production of apples implies a necessary reduction in the output of nuts (and vice versa). The diagram shows that locus to consist in the points of tangency between the nut and apple isoquants (FF).

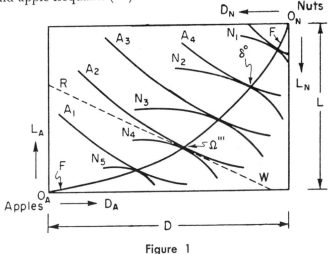

Figure 1

From this efficiency locus we can read off the maximal obtainable combinations of apples and nuts and plot these in the output (AN) space. Given our curvature assumptions we get the smooth concave-to-the-origin Pareto-efficient production-possibility curve $F'F'$ of Figure 2.[2] This curve, a consolidation of FF in Figure 1, represents input-

[2] This presumes, also, that the intrinsic factor intensities of A and N differ. If they did not, $F'F'$ would be a straight line—a harmless special case. (See V-3-c below.)

output configurations such that the marginal rate of substitution (MRS) of labor for land in the production of any given quantity of apples—the absolute value of the slope of the apple isoquant—just equals the marginal rate of substitution of labor for land in the production of nuts.[3]

The slope (again neglecting sign) at any point on the production-possibility curve of Figure 2, in turn, reflects the marginal rate of transformation (MRT) at that point of apples into nuts. It indicates precisely how many nuts can be produced by transferring land and labor from apple to nut production (at the margin), with optimal real-

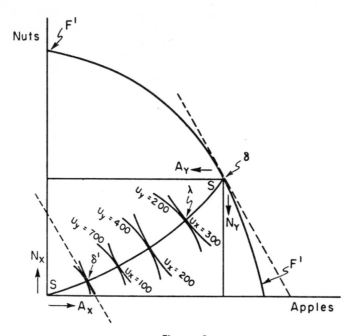

Figure 2

---

[3] In marginal productivity terms, MRS, at any point, of labor for land in, *e.g.* apple production—the absolute value (drop all minus signs) of the slope of the apple isoquant (Figure 1)—is equal to

$$\left[\frac{\text{marginal physical product of land}}{\text{marginal physical product of labor}} \right]$$

in apple production at that point. In the symbolism of the calculus

$$\left| \frac{\partial L_A}{\partial D_A} \right|_{\Delta A = 0} = \left(\frac{\partial A}{\partial D_A} \right) \div \left(\frac{\partial A}{\partial L_A} \right)$$

location of inputs in the production of both goods so as to maintain the
MRS-equality requirement of Figure 1. It is the marginal nut-cost of
an "extra" apple—or the reciprocal of the marginal apple-cost of nuts.

B. From the Production-Possibility Curve to the Utility-Possibility Frontier

Pick any point, δ, on the production-possibility curve of Figure 2: it
denotes a specific quantity of apples and nuts. Construct an Edgeworth-
Bowley (trading) box with these precise dimensions by dropping from
δ lines parallel to the axes as in Figure 2. Then draw in X's and Y's indifference maps, one with the southwest, the other with the northeast
corner for origin. Every point in the box again fixes six variables:
apples to X (A_X) and to Y (A_Y), nuts to X (N_X) and to Y (N_Y), and the
"levels" of satisfaction of X and Y as measured by the ordinal indices
U_X and U_Y which characterize the position of the point with respect to
the two preference fields. For example, at λ in Figure 2, $U_X = 300$,
$U_Y = 200$. Note again, however, that this 200 is incommensurate with
the 300: it does not imply that at λ X is in some sense better off than is
Y (or indifferent, or worse off).

The problem of "exchange-efficiency" consists in finding that locus
of feasible points within the trading box where any increase in X's
satisfaction (U_X) implies a necessary reduction in the satisfaction of Y,
(U_Y). Feasible in what sense? In the sense that we just exhaust the fixed
apple-nut totals as denoted by δ. Again, the locus turns out to consist
of the points of tangency, SS, and for precisely the same analytical
reasons. Only now it is the marginal subjective rate of substitution of
nuts for apples in providing a fixed level of satisfaction for X—the
absolute slope of X's indifference curve—that is to be equated to the
nut-apple MRS of Y, to the slope, that is, of *his* indifference curve.

From this exchange-efficiency locus,[4] SS, which is associated with
the single production point δ, we can now read off the maximal combinations of U_X and U_Y obtainable from δ and plot these in utility
$(U_X U_Y)$ space (S'S', Figure 3). Each such *point* δ in output space "maps"
into a *line* in utility space—the $U_X U_Y$ mix is sensitive to how the fixed
totals of apples and nuts are distributed between X and Y.[5]

---

[4] This is Edgeworth's contract curve, or what Boulding has aptly called the "conflict" curve—once on it, mutually advantageous trading is not possible and any
move reflecting a gain to X implies a loss to Y.

[5] Each *point* in utility space, in turn, maps into a line in output-space. Not just
one but many possible apple-nut combinations can satisfy a specified $U_X U_Y$ requirement. It is this reciprocal point-line phenomenon that lies at the heart of
Samuelson's proof of the nonexistence of community indifference curves such as

There is a possible short-cut, however. Given our curvature assumptions, we can trace out the grand utility-possibility frontier—the envelope—by using an efficiency relationship to pick just one point from each trading box contract curve SS associated with every output point δ. Go back to Figure 2. The slope of the production-possibility curve at δ has already been revealed as the marginal rate of transformation, via production, of apples into nuts. The (equalized) slopes of the two sets of indifference contours along the exchange-efficiency curve SS, in turn, represent the marginal rates of substitution of nuts for apples for psychic indifference (the same for X as for Y). The grand criterion for efficiency is that it be impossible by any shift in production *cum* exchange to increase U_X without reducing U_Y. Careful thought will suggest that this criterion is violated unless the marginal rate of trans-

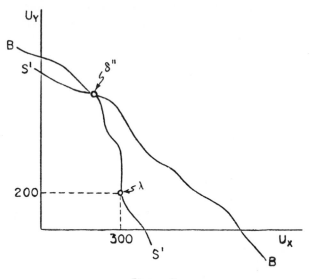

Figure 3

formation between apples and nuts as outputs—the slope at δ—just equals the common marginal rate of substitution of apples and nuts, as consumption "inputs," in providing psychic satisfaction.

If, for example, at δ one can get two apples by diverting resources

---

would permit the derivation of demand curves for apples and nuts. The subjective "community" MRS between A and N for given fixed A and N, e.g., at δ in Figure 2, would surely depend on how the A and N are distributed, i.e., on which $U_X U_Y$ point on SS is chosen. Hence the slope of a "joint" XY indifference curve at δ is not uniquely fixed by AN. (See citation [11] in bibliography.)

and reducing nut-output by one, a point on SS where the (equalized) marginal rate of substitution of apples for nuts along indifference curves is, *e.g.*, one to one, permits the following "arbitrage" operation. Shift land and labor so as to produce two more apples and one less nut. Then, leaving X undisturbed take away one nut from Y and replace it by one apple. By our assumption that MRS = 1 both X and Y are left indifferent: U_x and U_Y remain unaltered. But we have an extra apple left over; since this permits raising U_X and/or U_Y, the initial situation was not on the $U_X U_Y$ frontier.[6]

To be on the grand utility-possibility frontier (*BB* of Figure 3), then, MRT must equal the (equalized) MRS of the indifference contours along the SS associated with δ. This requirement fixes the single $U_X U_Y$ point on SS that lies on the "envelope" utility-possibility frontier, given the output point δ. Pick that point on SS, in fact, where the joint slope of the indifference curves is exactly parallel to the slope at δ of the production-possibility curve. In Figure 2 this point is at δ′, which gives the one "efficient" $U_X U_Y$ combination associated with the AN mix denoted by δ. This $U_X U_Y$ combination can then be plotted as δ″ in Figure 3.[7]

Repetition of this process for each point on the production-possibility curve—note that each such point requires a new trading box—will yield the grand utility-possibility frontier of Pareto-efficient input-output combinations, *BB*. Each point of this frontier gives the maximum of U_X for any given feasible level of U_Y and vice versa.

C. From the Utility-Possibility Frontier to the "Constrained Bliss Point"

But *BB*, the grand utility-possibility function, is a curve and not a point. Even after eliminating all combinations of inputs and outputs that are nonefficient in a Paretian sense, there remains a single-dimensional infinity of "efficient" combinations: one for every point on *BB*. To designate a single *best* configuration we must be given a Bergson-Samuelson social welfare function that denotes the ethic that is to

---

[6] The above argument can be made perfectly rigorous in terms of the infinitesimal movements of the differential calculus.

[7] Never mind, here, about multiple optima. These could occur even with our special curvature assumptions. If, for example, both sets of indifference curves show paths of equal MRS that coincide with straight lines from the origin and, further, if the two preference functions are so symmetrical as to give an $SS_δ$ that hugs the diagonal of the trading box, then either every point on $SS_δ$ will satisfy the MRS = MRT criterion, or none will. For discussion of these and related fine points see Parts IV and V.

"count" or whose implications we wish to study. Such a function—it could be yours, or mine, or Mossadegh's, though his is likely to be non-transitive—is intrinsically ascientific.[8] There are no considerations of *economic efficiency* that permit us to designate Crusoe's function, which calls for many apples and nuts for Crusoe and just a few for Friday, as economically superior to Friday's. Ultimate ethical valuations are involved.

Once given such a welfare function, in the form of a family of indifference contours in utility space, as in Figure 4, the problem becomes fully determinate.[9] "Welfare" is at a maximum where the utility-possibility envelope frontier BB touches the highest contour of the W-function.[10] In Figure 4, this occurs at Ω.

Note the unique quality of that point Ω. It is the only point, of all the points on the utility frontier BB, that has unambiguous normative

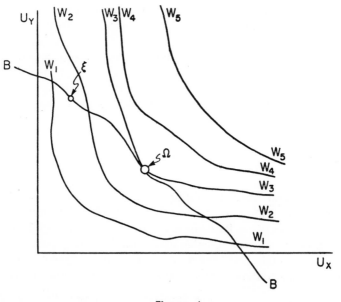

Figure 4

[8] Though it may provide the anthropologist or psychologist with interesting material for scientific study.

[9] In the absence of implicit income redistribution these curves cannot be transposed into output-space. They are not community indifference curves which would permit the derivation of demand schedules. See fn. 5 and 12, also IV–3.

[10] If there are several such points, never mind. If the "ethic" at hand is really indifferent, pick any one. If it doesn't matter, it doesn't matter.

or prescriptive significance. Pareto-efficient production and commodity-distribution—being on $F'F'$ and also on BB—is a necessary condition for a maximum of our kind of welfare function, but is not a sufficient condition.[11] The claim that any "efficient" point is better than "inefficient" configurations that lie inside BB is indefensible. It is true that given an "inefficient" point, there will exist *some* point or points on BB that represent an improvement; but there may well be many points on BB that would be worse rather than better. For example, in terms of the ethic denoted by the specific W-function of Figure 4, Ω on BB is better than any other feasible point. But the efficient point δ is distinctly inferior to any inefficient point on or northeast of W_2. If I am X, and if my W-function, which reflects the usual dose of self-interest, is the test, "efficient" BB points that give a high U_Y and a very low U_X are clearly less desirable than lots of inefficient points of higher U_X.[12]

D. From "Bliss Point" to "Best" Inputs, Outputs and Commodity-Distribution

We can now retrace our steps. To Ω on BB in Figure 4, there corresponds just one point, Ω', on the production-possibility curve $F'F'$ in Figure 5. (We derived BB, point by point, from $F'F'$ of Figure 2: and the $F'F'$ of Figure 5 is copied from that of Figure 2.). Ω' fixes the output mix: A and N. Then, by examining the trading-box contract curve S_aS_a associated with Ω' of $F'F'$, we can locate the one point where U_X and U_Y correspond to the coordinates of Ω in utility space. The equalized slope of the indifference curves will at that point, Ω'', just equal the slope of $F'F'$ at Ω'. Ω'' fixes the apple-nut distribution implied

---

11 Note, however, that Pareto-efficiency is not even a necessary condition for a maximum of just any conceivable W-function. The form of our type function reflects a number of ethically loaded restrictions, *e.g.*, that individuals' preference functions are to "count," and count positively.

12 Note, however, that no consistency requirements link my set of indifference curves with "my" W-function. The former reflects a personal preference ordering based only on own-consumption (and, in the more general case, own services supplied). The latter denotes also values which I hold as "citizen," and these need not be consistent with maximizing my satisfaction "*qua* consumer." X as citizen may prefer a state of less U_X and some U_Y to more U_X and zero U_Y. There is also an important analytical distinction. X's preference function is conceptually "observable": confronted by various relative price and income configurations his consumption responses will reveal its contours. His W-function, on the other hand, is not revealed by behavior, unless he be dictator, subjected by "nature" to binding constraints. In a sense only a society, considered as exhibiting a political consensus, has a W-function subject to empirical inference (*cf.* IV-3). The distinction —it has a Rousseauvian flavor—while useful, is of course arbitrary. Try it for a masochist; a Puritan. . . .

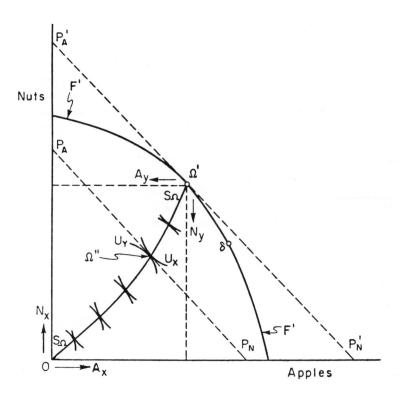

Figure 5

by the maximum of W: A_X, A_Y, N_X, and N_Y. Further, we can now locate the point Ω''' on the Pareto-efficient input locus, FF of Figure 1, that corresponds to Ω' of $F'F'$. It fixes the remaining variables, the factor allocations: L_A, D_A, L_N, and D_N. The maximum-welfare configuration is determinate. We have solved for the land and labor to be used in apple and nut production, for the total output of apples and nuts, and for their distribution between X and Y.

II. PRICES, WAGES AND RENTS

The above is antiseptically independent of institutional context, notably of competitive market institutions. It could constitute an intellectual exercise for the often invoked man from Mars, in how "best" to make do with given resources. Yet implicit in the logic of this purely "technocratic" formulation, embedded in the problem as it were, is a set of constants which the economist will catch himself thinking of as prices. And wisely so. Because it happens—and this "duality" theorem is the kernel of modern welfare economics—that decentralized decisions in response to these "prices" by, or "as if" by, atomistic profit and satis-faction maximizers will result in just that constellation of inputs, out-puts and commodity-distribution that our maximum of W requires.[13]

Can these constants—prices, wages, rents—be identified in our dia-grammatic representations?[14] Only partially so. Two-dimensionality is partly at fault, but, as we shall see, a final indeterminacy is implied by the usual curvature assumptions themselves.[15] The diagrams will, however, take us part way, and a little algebra will do for the rest.

The exercise consists in finding a set of four constants associated with the solution values of the maximum problem that have meaning as the price of apples (p_A), the price of nuts (p_N), the wage rate of labor (w), and the rental rate of land (r).[16]

First, what can be said about w and r? Profit maximization by the individual producer implies that whatever output he may choose as most lucrative must be produced at a minimum total cost.[17] The ele-mentary theory of the firm tells us that, for this condition to hold, the producer facing fixed input-prices—horizontal supply curves—must ad-just his input mix until the marginal rate of substitution (MRS) of labor for land just equals the rent-to-wage ratio. It is easy to see the "arbitrage" possibilities if this condition is violated. If one can substi-tute one unit of L for two units of D, and maintain output constant, with $w = \$10$ and $r = \$10$, it surely reduces total cost to do so and keep doing so until any further reduction in D by one unit has to be

[13] Note that this statement is neutral with respect to (1) genuine profit maximizers acting in "real" but perfectly competitive markets; (2) Lange-Lerner-type bureau-crats ("take prices as given and maximize or Siberia"); or (3) technicians using electronic machines and trying to devise efficient computing routines.

[14] To avoid institutional overtones, the theory literature usually attempts verbal dis-embodiment and refers to them as shadow-prices. The mathematically oriented, in turn, like to think of them as Lagrangean multipliers.

[15] These very assumptions render this last indeterminacy, that of the absolute price level, wholly inconsequential.

[16] Since we are still assuming that all the functions have neoclassical curvature properties, hence that, e.g., the production-possibility curve, as derived, has to be concave to the origin, we can impose the *strong* condition on the constants that they exhibit optimality characteristics for genuine, though perfect, markets. It will turn out, however, that two progressively weaker conditions are possible, which permit of some nonconvexities (e.g., increasing returns to scale), yet main-tain for the constants some essentially price-like qualities. More on this in Part V.

[17] In our flow model, unencumbered by capital, this is equivalent to producing the chosen output with minimum expenditure on inputs.

matched, if output is not to fall, by adding no less than one unit of L. In the usual diagrammatic terms, then, the producer will cling to points of tangency between the isoquants and (iso-expenditure) lines whose absolute slope equals r/w.

Reversing the train of thought, the input blend denoted by the point Ω''' in Figure 1 implies a shadow r/w ratio that just equals the MRS of labor for land in the production of both apples and nuts at that point Ω'''. MRS$_\Omega$ is given by the (equalized) slopes of the isoquants at Ω'''. The implicit r/w, therefore, must equal the slope of the line RW that is tangent to (both) the isoquants at Ω'''.[18]

The slope of RW identifies the rent: wage ratio implied by the maximal configuration. Essentially analogous reasoning will establish the equalized slope of the indifference curves through Ω'', in Figure 5, as denoting the p_A/p_N ratio implied by the solution. X, as also Y, to maximize his own satisfaction as measured by U_x, must achieve whatever level of satisfaction his income will permit at a minimum expenditure. This requires that he choose an apple-nut mix such that the psychic marginal-rate-of-substitution between nuts and apples for indifference just equal p_A/p_N. He, and Y, will pick Ω'' only if p_A/p_N is equal to the absolute slope of the tangent $(P_A P_N)$ at Ω''. This slope, therefore, fixes the Ω-value of p_A/p_N.[19]

Note that this makes p_A/p_N equal to the slope also of the production-possibility curve $F'F'$ at Ω'.[20] This is as it should be. If $p_A/p_N = 10$, i.e., if one apple is "worth" ten nuts on the market, it would be odd indeed, in our frictionlessly efficient world of perfect knowledge, if the mraginal rate of transformation of nuts into apples, via production, were different from ten-to-one. Producers would not in fact produce the apple-nut combination of Ω' if p_A/p_N differed from MRT at Ω'.

We have identified the r/w and p_A/p_N implied by the maximum of W. These two constancies provide two equations to solve for the four unknown prices. Unfortunately this is as far as the two-dimensional

---

[18] Again, absolute values of these slopes are implied throughout the argument. Recall from footnote 3 that the labor-for-land MRS, the absolute slope of the isoquants at Ω''' as given by RO_A/WO_A, is equal to the

$$\left[\frac{\text{Marginal physical product of land}}{\text{Marginal physical product of labor}}\right] \text{ratio.}$$

Our shadow r/w, then, turns out to be just equal to that ratio.

[19] The price-ratio relates reciprocally to the axes: $p_A/p_N = P_A O/P_N O$ in Figure 5. Along, e.g., X's indifference curve (U_X at Ω'') a rise in p_A/p_N, i.e., a steepening of $P_A P_N$, results in a substitution by X of nuts for apples; ditto for Y.

[20] Remember, in choosing the one point on $S_\Omega S_\Omega$ that would lie on the envelope in utility space, we chose the point where the indifference curve slopes just equaled the marginal rate of transformation (see p. 509 above).

diagrammatics will take us. None of the diagrams permits easy identification of the relationship between the input prices and the output
prices. Yet such a relationship is surely implied. By the theory of the
firm we know that the profit-maximizing producer facing a constant
price for his product—the horizontal demand curve of the perfectly
competive firm—will expand output up to where his extra revenue for
an additional unit of output, *i.e.*, the price, just equals the marginal
cost of producing that output.[21] And marginal cost, in turn, is sensitive to r and w.

It would be easy to show the implied price-wage or price-rent relationships by introducing marginal productivity notions. Profit maximization requires that the quantity of each input hired be increased
up to the point where its marginal physical product times the price of
the extra output, just equals the price of the added input. Since these
marginal physical productivities are determinate curvature properties
of the production functions, this rule provides a third relationship,
one between an output price and an input price.

Alternatively, given our assumption that production functions show
constant returns to scale, we can make use of Euler's "product exhaustion" theorem. Its economic content is that if constant returns to scale
prevails, the total as-if-market-imputed income of the factors of production just "exhausts" the total value of the product. This means, simply,
that $wL + rD = p_A A + p_N N$, and it provides a third relationship between w, r, p_A and p_N for the Ω-values of L, D, A and N.[22]

At any rate, the maximal solution implies a third price-equation,
hence we can express three of the prices in terms of the fourth. But
what of the fourth? This is indeterminate, given the characteristics of
the model. In a frictionless world of perfect certainty, where, for example, nobody would think of holding such a thing as money, only *relative*
prices matter. The three equations establish the proportions among
them implied by the maximum position, and the absolute values are of
no import. If the $p_A:p_N:w:r$ proportions implied by Ω are 20:15:50:75,
profit and satisfaction maximizers will make the input-output-consump-
tion decisions required for the maximum-of-W irrespective of whether

---

[21] Never mind here the "total" requirement—that this price exceed unit cost—if the
real-life profit-seeking producer is to produce at all. More on this in Part V.

[22] The condition also holds for each firm. In a competitive and constant-returns-to-
scale world the profit-maximum position is one of zero profit: total revenue will
just equal total cost. It should be said, however, that use of the Euler theorem
to gain a relationship between input price and output price involves a measure
of sleight of hand. It is only as a consequence of the relationships between price
and marginal productivity (*cf.* the preceding paragraph) that the theorem assures
equality of income with value of product.

the absolute levels of these prices happen to be just 20:15:50:75, or twice, or one-half, or 50 times this set of numbers. This is the implication of the fact that for the maximum problem only the various transformation and substitution *ratios* matter. In all that follows we shall simply posit that nuts are established as the unit of account, hence that $p_N = 1$. This then makes p_A, w and r fully determinate constants.[23]

Summarizing: we have identified diagrammatically two of the three shadow-price relationships implied by the solution to the welfare-maximum problem and have established, in a slightly more roundabout way, the existence of the third. The purpose was to demonstrate the existence, at least in our idealized neoclassical model, of a set of constants embedded in the "technocratic" maximum-of-welfare problem, that can be viewed as competitive market prices.[24] In what sense? In the sense that decentralized decisions in response to these constants, by, or "as if" by, atomistic profit and satisfaction maximizers will result in just that configuration of inputs, outputs and commodity-distribution that the maximum of our W requires.

III. FACTOR OWNERSHIP AND INCOME DISTRIBUTION

We have said nothing, so far, of how X and Y "pay" for their apples and nuts, or who "owns" and supplies the labor and the land. As was indicated above, the assumption of constant returns to scale assures that at the maximum welfare position total income will equal total value of output, and that total revenue from the sale of apples (nuts) will just equal total expenditures for inputs by the producers of apples (nuts). Also, the "solution" implies definite "purchase" of apples and of nuts both by X and by Y. But nothing ensures that the initial "ownership" of labor-hours and of land is such that w times the labor-hours supplied by X, wL_X, plus r times the land supplied by X, rD_X—X's income—will suffice to cover his purchases as required by Ω'', i.e., $p_A A_X + p_N N_X$; similarly for Y. There does exist some Pareto-efficient solution of inputs, outputs and distribution that satisfies the "income = outgo" condition for both individuals for any arbitrary pattern of ownership of the "means of production"—a solution, that is, that will place the system somewhere on the grand utility-possibility envelope frontier (BB in Figure 4). But only by the sheerest accident will that point on BB be better in terms of my W-function, or Thomas Jefferson's, or that of a "political consensus," than a multidimensional

---

[23] For the possibility of inessential indeterminacies, however, see Part IV–2.

[24] On the existence of such a set of shadow prices in the kinky and flat-surfaced world of linear programming, see Part V, below.

infinity of other points *on or off BB*. As emphasized above, only one point on *BB* can have ultimate normative, prescriptive significance: Ω; and only some special ownership patterns of land and of labor-services will place a market system with an "as imputed" distribution of income at that special point.[25]

The above is of especial interest in evaluating the optimality characteristics of market institutions in an environment of private property ownership. But the problem is not irrelevant even where all non-human means of production are vested in the community, hence where the proceeds of nonwage income are distributed independently of marginal productivity, marginal-rate-of-substitution considerations. If labor-services are not absolutely homogeneous—if some people are brawny and dumb and others skinny and clever, not to speak of "educated"—income distribution will be sensitive to the initial endowment of these qualities of mind and body and skill relative to the need for them. And again, only a very low probability accident would give a configuration consistent with any particular *W*-function's Ω.[26]

Even our homogeneous-labor world cannot entirely beg this issue. It is not enough to assume that producers are indifferent between an hour of X's as against an hour of Y's labor-services. It is also required that the total supply of labor-hours per accounting period be so divided between X and Y as to split total wage payments in a particular way, depending on land ownership and on the income distribution called for by Ω. This may require that X supply, *e.g.*, 75 per cent of total *L*; each man working $\frac{1}{2}L$ hours may well not do.[27]

But all this is diversion. For our noninstitutional purposes it is sufficient to determine the particular L_X, D_X, L_Y and D_Y that are consistent

---

25 It is of course possible to break the link between factor ownership and "final" income distribution by means of interpersonal transfers. Moreover, if such transfers are effected by means of costless lump-sum devices—never mind how feasible —then it is possible, in concept, to attain the Ω-implied distribution irrespective of market-imputations. But no decentralized price-market-type "game" can reveal the pattern of taxes and transfers that would maximize a particular *W*-function. "Central" calculation—implicit or explicit—is unavoidable.

26 If slavery were the rule and I could sell the capitalized value of my expected lifetime services, the distinction between ownership of labor and that of land would blur. Except in an "Austrian" world, however, it would not vanish. As long as men retain a measure of control over the quality and time-shape of their own services, there will always remain an incentive problem.

27 All this is based on the "Austrian" assumption that labor is supplied inelastically; further, that such inelasticity is due not to external compulsion, but rather to sharp "corners" in the preference-fields of X and Y in relation to work-leisure choices. More than this, the *W*-function must not be sensitive to variations in the $L_X L_Y$ mix except as these influence income distribution.

with Ω, given market-imputed, or "as if" market-imputed, distribution. Unfortunately the diagrams used in Part I again fail, but the algebra is simple. It is required that:

$$wL_X + rD_X = p_A A_X + p_N N_X,$$

and

$$wL_Y + rD_Y = p_A A_Y + p_N N_Y,$$

for the already-solved-for maximal Ω-values of A_X, N_X, A_Y, N_Y, p_A, p_N, w and r. Together with $L_X + L_Y = L$ and $D_X + D_Y = D$, we appear to have four equations to solve for the four unknowns: L_X, L_Y, D_X, and D_Y. It turns out, however, that one of these is not independent. The sum of the first two, that *total* incomes equal *total* value of products, is implied by Euler's theorem taken jointly with the marginal productivity conditions that give the solution for the eight variables, A_X, N_X, A_Y, . . . which are here taken as known. Hence, we have only three independent equations. This is as it should be. It means only that with our curvature assumptions we can, within limits, fix one of the four endowments more or less arbitrarily and still so allocate the rest as to satisfy the household budget equations.

So much for the income-distribution aspects of the problem. These have relevance primarily for market-imputed income distribution; but such relevance does not depend on "private" ownership of nonlabor means of production. Note, incidentally, that only with the arbitrary "Austrian" assumption of fixed supplies of total inputs can one first solve "simultaneously" for inputs, outputs and commodity-distribution, and only subsequently superimpose on this solution the ownership and money-income distribution problem. If L_X, D_X, L_Y, D_Y, hence L and D were assumed sensitive to w, r, the p's and household income levels, the dimensions of the production-box of Figure 1, hence the position of the production-possibility curve of Figures 2 and 5, etc., would interdepend with the final solution values of L_X, D_X, L_Y and D_Y. We would then have to solve the full problem as a set of simultaneous equations from the raw data: production functions, tastes (this time with an axis for leisure, or many axes for many differently irksome kinds of labor), and the W-function. Three (or more) dimensional diagrams would be needed for a geometrical solution.

IV. SOME EXTENSIONS

We have demonstrated the solution of the maximum problem of modern welfare economics in context of the simplest statical and stationary neoclassical model. Many generalizations and elaborations suggest themselves, even if one remains strictly neoclassical and restricts oneself to a steady-state situation where none of the data change and no questions about "how the system gets there" are permitted to intrude. To comment on just a few:

1. The problem could well be solved for many households, many goods, and many factors: it has received complete and rigorous treatment in the literature. Of course the diagrammatics would not do; elementary calculus becomes essential. But the qualitative characteristics of the solution of the m by n by q case are precisely those of the 2 by 2 by 2. The same marginal rate of transformation and substitution conditions characterize the solution, only now in many directions. Nothing new or surprising happens.[28]

2. The solution did skirt one set of difficulties that were not explicitly ruled out by assumption. We tacitly assumed that the two sets of isoquants would provide a smooth locus of "internal" tangencies, FF, in the production box of Figure 1; similarly, that we would get such an "internal" SS in the trading boxes of Figures 2 and 5. Nothing in our assumptions guarantees that this should be so. What if the locus of maximum A's for given feasible N's, should occur not at points of strict tangency *inside* the box, but at what the mathematician would call corner-tangencies along the edges of the box? Figure 6 illustrates this possibility. The maximum feasible output of A, for $N = 6000$, occurs at

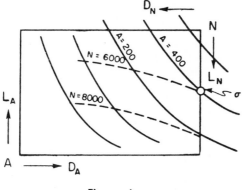

Figure 6

[28] Rigorous general treatment of the $m \times n \times q$ situation does highlight a number of analytical fine points that are of interest to the pure theorist, *e.g.*, the difficulties encountered if the number of factors exceeds the number of goods. But the qualitative economics is the same. For a full treatment from a nonnormative point of view, see P. A. Samuelson, "Prices of Factors and Goods in General Equilibrium," *Rev. Econ. Stud.*, 1953–1954, XXI(1), No. 54, 1–20.

σ, where $A = 400$; but at σ the two isoquants are not strictly tangent (they touch but have different slopes). The economic meaning of this is simple. With endowments as indicated by the dimensions of the production box in Figure 6, and with technology as denoted by the isoquants, it is not possible to reallocate inputs until the MRS of labor for land is the same in apple as in nut production. This is because apple technology (as depicted) is so land-using relative to nut production that the

$$\left[\frac{\text{marginal productivity of land}}{\text{marginal productivity of labor}}\right] \text{ratio}$$

in apple production exceeds that in nut production even when, as at σ, *all* land is devoted to apples.

Space precludes further analysis of such corner-tangency phenomena. They reflect the possibility that the maximum-welfare solution may require that not every input be used in producing every output (*e.g.*, no land in nut production or no brain surgeons in coal mining), and may even render one of the inputs a "free good," so that its total use will not add up to the total available supply. Let it suffice to assert that by formulating the maximum conditions, not in terms of *equalities* of various slopes, but rather in terms of *inequalities;* by explicit statement of the proper second-order "rate-of-change-of-slope" conditions; and by allowing inequalities in the factor-balance conditions; (*e.g.*, $L_A + L_N \leqq L$), such phenomena of bumping into the axes can be handled; further, that only inessential indeterminacies occur in the implied shadow-price configuration.[29]

[29] All this can perhaps be made clearer by two examples. The essential requirement for A_σ to be at a maximum for $N = 6000$ is that the intersection at the boundary be as in Figure 6 rather than as in Figure 7. In the latter, σ' gives a minimum of A for $N = 6000$; the true maximum is at σ''. The distinction between σ in 6 and σ' in 7 is between the relative rates of change of the two MRS's. The price indeterminacy implied by the maximum, *i.e.*, the fact that σ is consistent with an r/w that lies anywhere between the two isoquants, turns out to be inessential. A second example concerns the theory of the firm. It has been argued that if the marginal cost curve has vertical gaps and the price-line hits one of these gaps, then the $MC = p$ condition is indeterminate, hence that the theory is no good. As has been pointed out in the advanced literature (*e.g.*, by R. L. Bishop, in "Cost Discontinuities . . ." *Am. Econ. Rev.*, Sept. 1948, XXXVIII, 607–17) this is incorrect: What is important is that at smaller than equilibrum output MC be less than price and at higher outputs MC exceed price. It is true, but quite harmless to the theory, that such a situation does leave a range of indeterminacy in the price that will elicit *that* level of output. Such phenomena do change the mathematics of computation. Inequalities cannot in general be used to eliminate unknowns by simple substitution. On all this, see the literature of linear programming (*e.g.*, citations [10] and [13]).

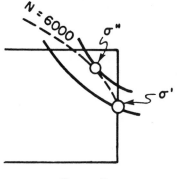

Figure 7

3. We stressed, above, the nonexistence of *community* indifference contours such as would provide a unique ranking, for the community as a whole, of various output combinations.[30] Individual marginal rates of substitution between, *e.g.*, apples and silk shirts, equalized along a trading-box contract curve to give a "community" MRS, are likely to be sensitive to the distribution of income [31] between gourmets and dandies; accordingly, community MRS at a given point in commodity space, *i.e.*, the slope of a curve of community indifference, will vary with movements along the associated utility-possibility curve. However, once the most desirable $U_X U_Y$ combination for a given package of A and N is fixed, MRS at that AN-point becomes determinate. It follows, as recently pointed out and proved by Samuelson,[32] that if the observed community continuously redistributes "incomes" in utopian lump-sum fashion so as to maximize, in utility space, over the W-function implied by a political consensus, then there does exist, in output space, a determinate *social* indifference function which provides a ranking for the community as a whole of all conceivable output combinations. This function, which yields conventionally convex social indifference contours, can be treated as though a single mind were engaged in maximizing it. Moreover, in concept and if granted the premise of continuous redistribution, its contours are subject to empirical inference from observed price-market data.

This existence theorem justifies the use of *social* indifference maps— maps "corrected" for distribution—in handling problems of production efficiency, international trade, etc.—a substantial analytical conven-

---

[30] See fn. 5.
[31] In terms of abstract purchasing power.
[32] See citation [11].

ience.[33] More important, it provides a conceptual foundation, however abstract, for prescription based not on just any arbitrary ethic, but rather on the particular ethic revealed by a society as reflecting its own political consensus.[34]

4. It is useful, and in a mathematical treatment not difficult, to drop the "Austrian" assumption of inelastically supplied inputs, and introduce leisure-work choices.[35] The analytical effect is to sensitize the production-possibility curve to the psychic sensibilities—the preference functions—of individuals. Note that the empirical sense of doing so is not confined to an institutional or ethical context of nonimposed choice. A dictator, too, has to take account of such choices, if only because of feasibility limitations on coercion.

5. We assumed away joint-product situations. This is convenient for manipulation but hardly essential; the results can be generalized to cover most kinds of jointness. It turns out, in fact, that in dynamical models with capital stocks, one means for taking account of the durability of such stocks is to allow for joint products. A process requiring a hydraulic press "produces" both stamped metal parts and a "one-year-older" hydraulic press.

6. In our system the distinction between inputs (L, D) and outputs (A, N) could be taken for granted. But the distinction is clear only in a world of completely vertically-integrated producers, all hiring "primary" nonproduced inputs and producing "final" consumable goods and services. In a Leontief-like system that allows for interproducer transactions and intermediate products, many outputs: electricity, steel, corn, beef, trucks, etc., are simultaneously inputs. It is of interest, and also feasible, to generalize the analysis to take account of, e.g., coal being used not only to heat houses, but to produce steel required in the production of mining machines designed for the production of coal. Moreover, none of the essential qualitative charac-

---

[33] Note, however, that none of this eliminates the need for a W-function: social indifference contours are a convex function of individual taste patterns of the usual ordinal variety taken jointly with an implicit or explicit W-function of "regular" content and curvature. Further, no ultimate superiority attaches to the W-function implied by a particular political consensus. One may disapprove of the power relationships on which such consensus rests, etc.

[34] Needless to say, feasibility is not here at issue. Even on this level of abstraction, however, matters become much more difficult once account is taken of the fact that the world is not stationary.

[35] If we assume only one commodity, say apples, and replace the second good by leisure (or by negative labor input); and if we let the second-good production function be a simple linear relation, our previous geometry will portray the simplest goods-leisure situation.

teristics of our maximum problem is violated by such generalization.[36]

7. What if instead of assuming that production functions show constant returns to scale, we permit diminishing returns to proportional expansion of inputs? This could be due either to inherent nonlinearities in the physics and topography of the universe, or to the existence of some unaccounted-for but significant input in limited, finite-elastic supply.[37]

Diminishing returns to scale, as distinct from increasing returns, does not give rise to serious trouble, either for the analytical solubility of the system, or for the market-significance of the intrinsic price-wage-rent constants. It does introduce some ambiguities, however. For one thing, the "value" of output will exceed the total of market-imputed income. This makes intuitive sense in terms of the "unaccounted-scarce-factor" explanation of decreasing returns; the residual unimputed value of output reflects the income "due" the "hidden" factor. If that factor were treated explicitly and given an axis in the production-function diagram, returns would no longer diminish—since, on this view, the relative inexpansibility of that input gave rise to decreasing returns to scale to begin with—and the difficulty would vanish.[38]

In a market context, this suggests the explicit introduction of firms as distinct from industries. In our constant-returns-to-scale world the number of apple- or nut-producing firms could be assumed indeterminate. Every firm could be assumed able to produce any output up to

36 Analytically, this is done by designating all produced goods as $X_1, X_2, X_3 \ldots$.
The gross production of, e.g., X_1 has two kinds of uses: It is partly used up as an input in the production of $X_2, X_3 \ldots$ and perhaps of X_1 (the automobile industry is a major user of automobiles). What remains is available for household consumption. The production functions have X's on the right- as well as the left-hand side.

37 If "output" varies as the surface area of some solid body and "input" as its cubic-volume, a doubling of input will less than double output—this is an example of the first kind. A typical example of the second is the instance where the production function for fishing does not include an axis for the "amount" of lake, hence where beyond a certain point doubling of man-hours, boats, etc. less than doubles the output. There is a slightly futile literature on whether the first kind could or could not exist without some element of the second. If *every* input is really doubled, so say the proponents of one view, output *must* double. The very vehemence of the assertion suggests the truth, to wit, that it is conceptually impossible to disprove it by reference to empirical evidence. Luckily, the distinction is not only arbitrary—it depends on what one puts on the axes of the production-function diagram and what is built into the curvature of the production surface; it is also quite unimportant. One can think of the phenomenon as one will—nothing will change.

38 The fact that the "hidden scarce factor" view is heuristically useful does not, however, strengthen its pretension to status as a hypothesis about reality.

A_Ω (or N_Ω) at constant unit cost. In fact, if we had a convenient way of handling incipient monopoly behavior, such as by positing frictionless entry of new firms, we could simply think of one giant firm as producing all the required apples (nuts). Such a firm would be compelled, nevertheless, to behave as though it were an "atomistic" competitor, *i.e.*, prevented from exploiting the tilt in the demand curve, by incipient competitors ready instantaneously to jump into the fray at the slightest sign of profit.

It is, however, natural, at least in a context of market institutions, to think of decreasing returns to scale, as associated with the qualitatively and quantitatively scarce entrepreneurial entity that defines the firm but is not explicitly treated as an input. Then, as apple production expands, relatively less efficient entrepreneurs are pulled into production—the total cost curve of the "last" producer and the associated shadow price of apples become progressively higher—and the intramarginal firms make "profits" due directly to the scarcity value of the entrepreneurial qualities of their "entrepreneurs." The number of firms, their inputs and outputs, are determinate. The last firm just breaks even at the solution-value of the shadow-price.[39]

At any rate, no serious damage is done to the statical system by decreasing returns to scale. When it is a matter of actually computing a maximum problem the loss of linearity is painful, but the trouble is in the mathematics.[40]

8. There is one kind of complication that does vitiate the results. We have assumed throughout that there exists no *direct* interaction among producers, among households, and between producers and households —that there are no (nonpecuniary) external economies or diseconomies of production and consumption. The assumption is reflected in four characteristics of the production functions and the preference functions:

a. The output of apples was assumed uniquely determined by the quantities of land and labor applied to apple production—A was assumed insensitive to the inputs and outputs of the nut industry; similarly for nuts. This voids the possibility that the apple production function might shift as a consequence of movements along the nut production function, *i.e.*, that for given D_A and L_A, A may vary with N, L_N and D_N. The stock example of such a "technological external economy" (or diseconomy) is the beekeeper whose honey output will

39 More precisely, the "next" firm in line could not break even. This takes care of discontinuity.
40 It should perhaps be repeated, however, that there remains considerable ambiguity about how the imbalance between income and outlay in decreasing-returns-to-scale situations is best treated in a general equilibrium setup.

increase, other things equal, if the neighboring apple producer expands *his* output (hence his apple blossom "supply").[41] The very pastoral quality of the example suggests that in a statical context such direct interaction among producers—interaction that is not reflected by prices—is probably rare. To the extent that it does exist, it reflects some "hidden" inputs or outputs (*e.g.*, apple blossoms), the benefits or costs of which are not (easily) appropriated by market institutions.

It should be emphasized that the assertion that such phenomena are empirically unimportant is defensible only if we rule out nonreversible dynamical phenomena. Once we introduce changes in knowledge, for example, or investment in changing the quality of the labor force via training, "external" effects become very important indeed.[42] But on our stratospheric level of abstraction such considerations are out of order.

b. The "happiness" of X, as measured by U_X, was assumed uniquely determined by his own consumption of apples and nuts. He was permitted no sensitivity to his neighbor's (Y's) consumption, and vice versa. This rules out not only Veblenesque "keeping up with . . ." effects, but such phenomena as Y tossing in sleepless fury due to X's "consumption" of midnight television shows; or X's temperance sensibilities being outraged by Y's quiet and solitary consumption of Scotch. Nobody with experience of a "neighborhood" will argue that such things are illusory, but it is not very fruitful to take account of them in a formal maximizing setup.[43]

c. X and Y were assumed insensitive, also, to the input-output configuration of producers, except as this affected consumption choices. Insensitivity to the allocation of their own working time is subsumed

---

[41] The other type of externality treated in the neoclassical literature, the type Jacob Viner labeled "pecuniary," does not in itself affect the results. It consists in sensitivity of input prices to industry output, though not to the output of single firms. External pecuniary economies (as distinct from diseconomies) do, however, signal the existence of either *technological* external economies of the sort discussed here, or of internal economies among supplier firms. These last reflect increasing returns to scale along production functions—a most troublesome state discussed at length in Part V.

[42] The full "benefits" of most changes in "knowledge," of most "ideas," are not easily captured by the originator, even with strong patent and copyright protection. If, then, the energy and resources devoted to "creating new knowledge" are sensitive to private cost-benefit calculation, some potential for social gain may well be lost because such calculation will not correctly account for cost and benefit to society at large. All this is complicated by the peculiarity of "knowledge" as a scarce resource: unlike most other scarcities, just because there is more for you there is not necessarily less for me. As for training of labor: the social benefit accrues over the lifetime services of the trainee; the private benefit to the producers accrues until the man quits to go to work for a competitor.

[43] For an important exception, however, see fn. 44 below.

in the "Austrian" assumption, but more is required. Y's wife must not be driven frantic by factory soot, nor X irritated by an "efficiently" located factory spoiling his view.

d. There is still a fourth kind of externality: X's satisfaction may be influenced not only by his own job, but by Y's as well. Many values associated with job-satisfaction—status, power, and the like—are sensitive to one's *relative* position, not only as consumer, but as supplier of one's services in production. The "Austrian" assumption whereby U_X and U_Y are functions only of consumption possibilities, voids this type of interaction also.

Could direct interaction phenomena be introduced into a formal maximizing system, and if so, at what cost? As regards the analytical solubility of some maximum-of-W problem, there is no necessary reason why not. The mathematics of proving the existence or nonexistence of a "solution," or of a unique and stable "solution," or the task of devising a computational routine that will track down such a solution should one exist, may become unmanageable. But the problem need not be rendered meaningless by such phenomena.

Unfortunately that is saying very little indeed, except on the level of metaphysics. Those qualities of the system that are of particular interest to the economist—(i) that the solution implies a series of "efficiency conditions," the Pareto marginal-rate-of-substitution conditions, which are necessary for the maximum of a wide variety of W-functions, and (ii) that there exists a correspondence between the optimal values of the variables and those generated by a system of (perfect) market institutions *cum* redistribution—those qualities are apt either to blur or vanish with "direct interaction." Most varieties of such interaction destroy the "duality" of the system: the constants embedded in the maximum problem, if any, lose significance as prices, wages, rents. They will not correctly account for all the "costs" and "benefits" to which the welfare function in hand is sensitive.[44]

In general, then, most formal models rule out such phenomena.

<hr />

[44] It should not be concluded, however, that the different types of direct interaction are all equally damaging. All will spoil market performance, almost by definition; but some, at least, permit of formal maximizing treatment such as will yield efficiency conditions analogous to those of Part I—conditions that properly account for full social costs and benefits. So-called "public goods," *e.g.*, national defense, which give rise to direct interaction since by definition their consumption is joint —more for X means not less but more for Y—are an important example. Maximizing yields MRS conditions that bear intriguing correspondence to those which characterize ordinary private-good situations. But these very MRS conditions serve to reveal the failure of duality. (Samuelson's is again the original and definitive treatment. See citation [12].)

There is no doubt that by so doing they abstract from some important aspects of reality. But theorizing consists in just such abstraction; no theory attempts to exhaust all of reality. The question of what kinds of very real complications to introduce into a formal maximizing setup has answers only in terms of the strategy of theorizing or in terms of the requirements of particular and concrete problems. For many purposes it is useful and interesting to explore the implications of maximizing in a "world" where no such direct interactions exist.

V. RELAXING THE CURVATURE ASSUMPTIONS: KINKS AND NONCONVEXITIES

None of the above qualifications and generalizations violate the fundamentally neoclassical character of the model. What happens if we relinquish some of the nice curvature properties of the functions?

1. We required that the production functions and the indifference curves have well-defined and continuous curvatures—no sharp corners or kinks such as cause indeterminacy in marginal rates of substitution. Such smooth curvatures permit the use of the calculus, hence are mathematically convenient for larger than 2 by 2 by 2 models. They are, however, not essential to the economic content of the results. The analysis has been translated—and in part independently re-invented— for a world of flat-faced, sharp-cornered, production functions: Linear programming, more formally known as activity analysis, is the resulting body of theory.[45] All the efficiency conditions have their counterparts in such a system, and the existence of implicit "prices" embedded in the maximum problem is, if anything, even more striking.[46]

2. Easing of the neoclassical requirement that functions be smooth is not only painless; in the development of analytical economics it has resulted in exciting new insights. Unfortunately, however, the next step is very painful indeed. In our original assumptions we required that returns to scale for proportional expansion of inputs be constant (or at least nonincreasing) and that isoquants and indifference curves be "convex to the origin." These requirements guarantee a condition that the mathematicians call *convexity*. The violation of this condition, as by allowing increasing returns to scale in production—due, if you wish, to the inherent physics and topography of the universe or to lumpiness and indivisibilities—makes for serious difficulties.

[45] Isoquants in such a setup consist of linearly additive combinations of processes, each process being defined as requiring absolutely fixed input and output proportions. This gives isoquants that look like that in Figure 8c.

[46] A little diagrammatic experimentation will show that the geometric techniques of Part I remain fully adequate.

The essence of convexity, a concept that plays a crucial role in mathematical economics, is rather simple. Take a single isoquant such as *MM* in Figure 8a. It denotes the minimum inputs of *L* and *D* for the production of 100 apples, hence it is just the boundary of all technologically feasible input combinations that can produce 100 apples. Only points on *MM* are both feasible and technologically *efficient,* but any point within the shaded region is *feasible:* nobody can prevent me from wasting *L* or *D.* On the other hand, no point on the origin side of *MM* is feasible for an output of 100 apples: given the laws of physics, etc., it is impossible to do better. *Mathematical convexity obtains if a straight line connecting any two feasible points does not anywhere pass outside the set of feasible points.* A little experimentation will show that such is the case in Figure 8a. In Figure 8b, however, where the isoquant is of "queer" curvature—MRS of *L* for *D* increases—the line connecting, *e.g.,* the feasible points γ and ϕ does pass outside the "feasible" shaded area. Note, incidentally, that an isoquant of the linear programming variety, as in Figure 8c, is "convex"—this is why the generalization of (1) above was painless.[47]

What kind of trouble does nonconvexity create? In the case of concave-to-the-origin isoquants, *i.e.,* nonconvex isoquants, the difficulty is

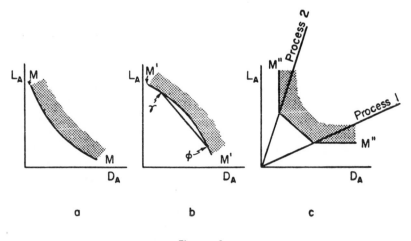

Figure 8

[47] It is important not to confuse mathematical convexity with curvature that appears "convex to the origin." Mathematical convexity is a property of *sets* of points, and the set of feasible output points bounded by a production-possibility curve, for instance, is convex if and only if the- production-possibility curve itself is "*concave* to the origin" (or a straight line). Test this by the rule which defines convexity.

easy to see. Look back at Figure 1 and imagine that the old nut-isoquants are really those of apple producers, hence oriented to the southwest, and vice versa for nuts. Examination of the diagram will show that the locus of tangencies, FF, is now a locus of minimum combinations of A and N. Hence the rule that MRS's be equalized will result in input combinations that give a minimum of N for specified A.[48]

3. This is not the occasion for extensive analysis of convexity problems. It might be useful, however, to examine one very important variety of nonconvexity: increasing returns to scale in production. Geometrically, increasing returns to scale is denoted by isoquants that are closer and closer together for outward movement along any ray from

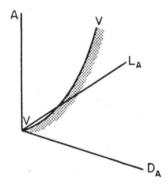

Figure 9

the origin: to double output, you less than double the inputs. Note that the isoquants still bound convex sets in the LD plane (they are still as in Figure 8a). But in the third or output dimension of a two-input, one-output production surface, slices by vertical planes through the origin perpendicular to LD will cut the production surface in such a way as to give a boundary such as VV in Figure 9. It is evident that VV bounds a nonconvex set of feasible points, so the full three-dimensional set of feasible input-output points is not convex.

The effect of such nonconvexity in input-output space can be classified with respect to its possible implications for (a) the slopes of producers' average cost (AC) curves; (b) for the slopes of marginal cost (MC) curves; (c) for the curvature of the production-possibility curve.

[48] A minimum, that is, subject to the requirement that no input be "wasted" from an engineering point of view, i.e., that each single producer be on the production function as given by the engineer.

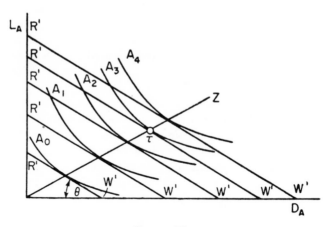

Figure 10

a. *Increasing returns to scale and* AC *curves.* It is a necessary consequence of increasing returns to scale that at the maximal configuration
of inputs outputs and input prices, producers' AC curves decline with
increasing output. By the definition of increasing returns to scale at a
given point τ of a production function, successive isoquants in the
neighborhood of τ lie closer and closer together for movement "northeast" along the ray from the origin through τ (Z in Figure 10). As
Figure 10 is drawn, the ray Z happens also to correspond to an expansion path for the particular r/w ratio denoted by the family of isocost
lines $R'W'$: each $R'W'$ is tangent to an isoquant along Z. Given
$r/w = |$ tangent $\theta |$, a profit-maximizing apple producer will calculate
his minimum total cost for various levels of output from input-output
points along Z. But along Z the equal cost $R'W'$ tangents in the
neighborhood of τ lie closer and closer together for increasing output,
as do the isoquants. This implies that the increase in total cost for equal
successive increments in output declines. *Ergo,* the AC curve at τ for
$r/w = |$ tangent $\theta |$ must be falling.

Suppose the expansion path for $r/w = |$ tangent $\theta |$ happened not to
correspond to the ray Z, but only to cross it at τ. The intersection of
A_4 with Z would not then mark the minimum-cost input-mix for an
output of A_4, hence the increase in minimized total cost between A_3
and A_4 would be even less than in Figure 10: the negative effect on
AC would be reinforced. The point is, simply, that if for movement
along a ray from the origin cost per unit of output declines, AC will
decline even more should production at minimized total cost call for
changes in the input-mix, *i.e.*, departure from the ray Z.

What, then, if the maximum-of-W input-output combination required of this particular producer is denoted by the point τ? It has just been shown that AC at τ is falling. A falling AC implies a marginal cost curve (MC) that lies *below* the average. But if τ is Ω'''-point, the shadow-p_A will just equal MC of τ. It follows that the maximum-of-W configuration requires $p_A < AC$, *i.e.*, perpetual losses. Losses, however, are incompatible with real life (perfect) markets; hence where increasing returns to scale prevails correspondence between market-directed and W-maximizing allocation fails. In an institutional context where producers go out of business if profits are negative, markets will not do.[49]

Increasing returns to scale has also a "macro" consequence that is associated with $p < AC$. For constant returns to scale, we cited Euler's theorem as assuring that total factor incomes will just equal total value of output. In increasing-returns-to-scale situations, total imputed factor incomes will exceed the total value of output: $rD+wL > p_A A + p_N N$.[50]

b. *Increasing returns to scale and* MC *curves.* Where nonconvexity of the increasing-returns-to-scale variety results in falling AC curves, real-life (perfect) markets will fail. What of a Lange-Lerner socialist bureaucracy, where each civil-servant plant-manager is instructed to maximize his algebraic profits in terms of centrally quoted "shadow" prices regardless of losses? Will such a system find itself at the maximum-of-W configuration?

It may or may not. If AC is to fall, MC must lie below AC, but at the requisite Ω-output, MC's may nevertheless be rising, as for example at ϵ in Figure 11. If so, a Lange-Lerner bureaucracy making input and output decisions as atomistic "profit-maximizing" competitors but ignoring losses will make the "right" decisions, *i.e.*, will "place" the system at the maximum-of-W. Each manager equating his marginal cost to the centrally quoted shadow price given out by the maximum-of-W solution, will produce precisely the output required by the Ω-configuration. By the assumption of falling AC's due to increasing returns to scale either one or both industries will show losses, but these are irrelevant to optimal allocation.[51]

---

49 Needless to say, comments on market effectiveness, throughout this paper, bear only on the analogue-computer aspects of price-market systems. This is a little like talking about sexless men, yet it is surely of interest to examine such systems viewed as mechanisms pure and simple.

50 The calculus-trained reader can test this for, say, a Cobb-Douglas type function: $A = L_A{}^\alpha D_A{}^\beta$, with $(\alpha+\beta) > 1$ to give increasing returns to scale.

51 There is an ambiguity of language in the above formulation. If at the maximum-of-W configuration losses prevail, the maximum profit position "in the large" will be not at $p = MC$ but at zero output. Strictly speaking, a Lange-Lerner bureaucracy must be instructed to equate marginal cost to price or profit-maximize "in

What if for a maximum-of-W producers are required to produce at points such as ϵ', where $p = MC$ but MC is declining?[52] The fact that ϵ' shows $AC > MC = p$, hence losses, has been dealt with above. But more is involved. By the assumption of a falling MC-curve, the horizon-

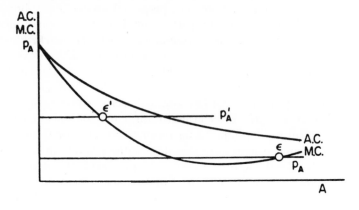

Figure 11

tal price line at ϵ' cuts the MC curve from below, hence profit ϵ' is not only negative: it is at a *minimum*. A "real-life" profit maximizer would certainly not remain there: he would be losing money by the minute. But neither would a Lange-Lerner bureaucrat under instruction to maximize algebraic profits. He would try to increase his output: "extra" revenue (p_A) would exceed his MC by more and more for every additional apple produced. In this case, then, not only would real life markets break down; so would simple-minded decentralized maximizing of profits by socialist civil servants.[53]

Paradoxically enough, the correct rule for all industries whose MC is falling at the Ω-point is: "minimize your algebraic profits." But no such rule can save the decentralized character of the Lange-Lerner

the small" without regard to the absolute value of profit. "Make any continuous sequence of small moves that increase algebraic profits, but do not jump to the origin." It is precisely the ruling-out of the zero-output position, unless called for by $MC > p$ everywhere, that distinguishes Lange-Lerner systems from "real-life" perfect markets, both viewed as "analogue computers."

[52] This would necessarily be the case, for instance, with Cobb-Douglas type increasing-returns-to-scale functions. Such functions imply ever-falling MC curves, for whatever r/w ratio.

[53] Note that a falling MC curve is simply a reflection of nonconvexity in the total cost curve.

scheme. In a "convex" world the simple injunction to maximize profits in response to centrally quoted prices, together with raising (lowering) of prices by the responsible "Ministries" according to whether supply falls short of (exceeds) demand, is all that is needed.[54] Nobody has to know *ex ante*, e.g., the prices associated with the Ω-point. In fact the scheme was devised in part as a counter to the view that efficient allocation in a collectivized economy is impossible due simply to the sheer administrative burden of calculation. With increasing returns to scale, however, the central authority must evidently know where MC's will be falling, where rising: it must know, before issuing any instructions, all about the solution.

c. *Increasing returns to scale and the production-possibility curve.* What is left of "duality"? Real-life markets and unsophisticated Lange-Lerner systems have both failed. Yet it is entirely possible, even in situations where the Ω-constellation implies $AC > MC$ with declining MC, that the maximizing procedure of Part I remains inviolate, and that the constants embedded in the maximum problem retain their price-like significance. To see this we must examine the effect of increasing returns to scale on the production-possibility curve. There are two possible cases:

i. It is possible for both the apple and the nut production functions to exhibit increasing returns to scale, yet for the implied production-possibility curve to be concave to the origin, *i.e.*, mathematically convex (as in Figure 2). While a proportional expansion of L_A and D_A by a factor of two would more than double apple output, an increase in A at the expense of N will, in general, not take place by means of such proportional expansion of inputs. Examination of FF in Figure 1 makes this clear for the constant-returns-to-scale case. As we move from any initial point on FF toward more A and less N, the L_A/D_A and L_N/D_N proportions change.[55]

The point is that if, as in Figure 1, land is important relative to labor in producing apples, and vice versa for nuts, expansion of apple production will result in apple producers having to use more and more of the relatively nut-prone input, labor, in proportion to land. Input proportions in apple production become less "favorable." The oppo-

---

54 Not quite all. Even in a statical context, the lump-sum income transfers called for by Ω require central calculation. And if adjustment paths are explicitly considered, complex questions about the stability of equilibrium arise. (*E.g.*, will excess demand always be corrected by raising price?)

55 Only if FF should coincide with the diagonal of the box will proportions not change. Then increasing returns to scale would necessarily imply an inward-bending production-possibility curve.

site is true of the input proportions used in nuts as nut production declines. This phenomenon explains why with constant returns to scale in both functions the production-possibility curve shows concave-to-the-origin curvature. Only if FF in Figure 1 coincides with the diagonal: *i.e.*, if the intrinsic "usefulness" of L and D is the same in apple production as in nut production, will $F'F'$ for constant returns to scale be a straight line.

The above argument by proportions remains valid if we now introduce a little increasing returns to scale in both functions by "telescoping" each isoquant successively farther towards the origin. In fact, as long as the FF curve has shape and curvature as in Figure 1, the production-possibility curve, $F'F'$ in Figures 2 and 5, will retain its convexity.

In this "mild" case of increasing returns to scale, with a still convex production-possibility curve, the previous maximizing rules give the correct result for a maximum-of-W. Further, the constants embedded in the maximum problem retain their meaning. This is true in two senses: (1) They still reflect marginal rates of substitution and transformation. Any package of L, D, A and N worth \$1 will, *at the margin* be just convertible by production and exchange into any other package worth \$1, no more, no less: a dollar is a dollar is a dollar. . . .[56] (2) The total value of maximum-welfare "national" output: $p_A A + p_N N$, valued at these shadow-price constants, will itself be at a maximum. A glance at Figure 5 makes this clear: at the price-ratio denoted by the line $P'_A P'_N$, Ω' is the point of highest output-value. As we shall see, this correspondence between the maximum welfare and "maximum national product" solutions is an accident of convexity.

ii. It is of course entirely possible that both production functions exhibit sufficiently increasing returns to scale to give, for specified totals of L and D, a production-possibility curve such as $F''F''$ in Figure 12.[57] This exhibits nonconvexity in output space. What now happens to the results?

If the curvature of $F''F''$ is not "too sharp," the constants given out by the maximum-of-W problem retain their "dollar is a dollar" meaning. They still reflect marginal rates of substitution in all directions. But maximum W is no longer associated with maximum shadow-value of output. A glance at Figure 12 confirms our geometric intuition that in situations of nonconvex production possibilities the bliss point coincides with a minimized value-of-output. At the prices implied, as de-

---

[56] For the infinitesimal movements of the calculus.
[57] Try two functions which are not too dissimilar in "factor intensity."

noted by $|\tan \psi|$, the assumed Ω-point ρ is a point of minimum $p_A A + p_N N$.[58]

But with nonconvexity in output space, matters could get much more complicated. If the production-possibility curve is *sharply* concave outward, relative to the indifference curves, it may be that the "minimize-profits" rule would badly mislead, even if both industries show declining MC's. Take a one-person situation such as in Figure 13. The production-possibility curve $F'''F'''$ is more inward-bending than the indifference curves (U), and the point of tangency Δ is a point of *minimum* satisfaction. Here, unlike above, you should rush away from Δ. The maximum welfare position is at Δ'—a "corner tangency" is involved. The point is that in nonconvex situations *relative* curvatures are crucial: tangency points may as well be minima as maxima.[59]

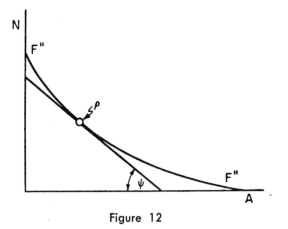

Figure 12

[58] For $p_A/p_N = |\text{tangent } \psi|$, $(p_A A + p_N N)$ is at its maximum at the intersection of $F''F''$ with the A-axis. Recall, incidentally, that in situations of falling MC producers were required to *minimize* profits.

[59] Recall that in our discussion of Part IV corner-tangencies were important in situations where no feasible internal tangencies existed. Here there exist perfectly good and feasible internal tangencies—but they are loci of minima rather than maxima. The second-order conditions, expressed as inequalities, constitute the crucial test of optimal allocation.

It is tempting, but a mistake, to think that there is a unique correspondence between the curvature of the production-possibility curve, and the relative slopes of the nut and apple MC curves. It is true that the $[MC_A/MC_N]$ ratio associated with a point such as Ω' in Figure 5 must be smaller than $[MC_A/MC_N]$ at any point of *more A* and *less N* on $F'F'$ (e.g., δ): the absolute slope of $F'F'$ has been shown to equal $pA/p_N = [MC_A/MC_N]$, and at Ω' the slope is less steep than at δ.

[Footnote 59 continued on page 536]

So much for nonconvexity. In its mildest form, if isoquants and indifference curves retain their normal curvature and only returns to scale "increase," nonconvexity need not violate the qualitative characteristics of the maximum-of-W problem. The marginal-rate-of-substitution conditions may well retain their validity, and the solution still could give out a set of shadow prices, decentralized responses to which result in the maximal configuration of inputs, outputs and commodity distribution. But certain nonmarginal *total* conditions for effective real-life market functioning, *e.g.*, that all producers have at least to break even, are necessarily violated. The shortcoming is in market institutions: the maximum-of-W solution requires such "losses." The important moral is that where increasing returns to scale obtains, an idealized price system is not an effective way to raise money to cover costs. It may, however, still be an effective device for the rationing of scarcities.[60]

VI. DYNAMICS

We have examined in some detail what conditions on the allocation and distribution of inputs and outputs can be derived from the maximization of a social welfare function which obeys certain restrictions.[61] We have done so, however, using a statical mode of analysis and have ignored all the "dynamical" aspects of the problem. To charge that

---

It is also true that along a nonconvex production-possibility curve, such as that of Figure 12, an increase in A and a decrease in N are associated with a decline in $[MC_A/MC_N]$. But it does not follow, *e.g.*, in the first case of Figure 5, that at Ω' MC_A must be rising for an increase in A sufficiently to offset a possibly falling MC_N. (Remember, in moving from Ω' to δ we move to the right along the A-axis but to the left along the N-axis.) For any departure from Ω' will, in general, involve a change in input shadow-prices, hence *shifts* in the MC curves, while the slopes of the curves at Ω' were derived from a total cost curve calculated on the basis of the given, constant, Ω-values of w and r. The point is that cost curves are partial-equilibrium creatures, evaluated at *fixed* prices, while movement along a production-possibility curve involves a general-equilibrium adjustment that will *change* input prices. Hence it is entirely possible that at say Ω', in Figure 5, both MC_N and MC_A are falling, though $F'F'$ is convex.

[60] No mention has been made of the case that is perhaps most interesting from an institutional point of view: production functions that show increasing returns to scale initially, then decreasing returns as output expands further. No profit-seeking firm will produce in the first stage, where AC is falling, and A_Ω and N_Ω may only require one or a few firms producing in the second stage. If so, the institutional conditions for perfect competition, very many firms, will not exist. One or a few firms of "efficient" scale will exhaust the market. This phenomenon lies at the heart of the monopoly-oligopoly problem.

[61] See fn. 11.

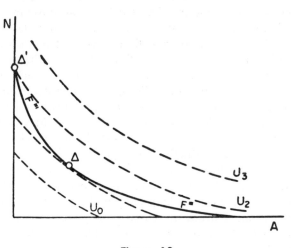

Figure 13

such statical treatment is "unrealistic" is to miss, I think, the essential meaning and uses of theorizing. It is true, however, that such treatment buries many interesting problems—problems, moreover, some of which yield illuminating insight when subjected to rigorous analysis. Full dynamical extension is not possible here, but some indication of the directions which such extension might take is perhaps warranted:

1. The perceptive reader will have noticed that very little was said about the dimensions of A, N, L_A, D_A, L_N, and D_N. The static theory of production treats outputs and inputs as instantaneous time rates, "flows"—apples per day, labor-hours per week, etc. This ignores the elementary fact that in most production processes outputs and the associated inputs, and the various inputs themselves, are not simultaneous. Coffee plants take five years to grow, ten-year-old brandy has to age ten years, inputs in automobile manufacture have to follow a certain sequence, it takes time to build a power station and a refinery (no matter how abundantly "labor and land" are applied). One dynamical refinement of the analysis, then, consists in "dating" the inputs and resultant outputs of the production functions, relative to each other. In some instances only the ordinal sequence is of interest; in others, absolute elapsed time, too, matters—plaster has to dry seven days before the first coat of paint is applied.

2. Another characteristic of production, on this planet at least, is that service flows are generated by stocks of physical things which yield

their services only through time. Turret-lathe operations can be generated only by turret-lathes and these have congealed in them service flows which cannot be exhausted instantaneously but only over time. In a descriptive sense, a turret-lathe's services of today are "joint" and indivisible from some turret-lathe's services of tomorrow. Strictly speaking, this is true of most service flows. But some things, like food, or coal for heating, or gasoline, exhaust their services much faster than, e.g., streamrollers, drill presses, buildings, etc. The stock dimension of the former can be ignored in many problems; this is not true of the latter set of things, which are usually labeled as fixed capital.[62] A second dynamical extension, then, consists in introducing stock-flow relationships into the production functions.

3. Lags and stock-flow relations are implied also by the goods-in-process phenomenon. Production takes place over space, and transport takes time, hence seed cannot be produced at the instant at which it is planted, nor cylinder heads the moment they are required on the assembly line. They have to be in existence for some finite time before they are used.

4. One of the crucial intertemporal interrelations in allocation and distribution in a world where stocks matter and where production takes time, is due to the unpleasant (or pleasant) fact that the inputs of any instant are not manna from heaven. Their supply depends on past output decisions. Next year's production possibilities will depend, in part, on the supply of machine tools; this, in turn, partly depends on the resources devoted this year to the construction of new machine tools. This is the problem of investment. From today's point of view investment concerns choice of *outputs*; but choice of what kinds and amounts of machines to build, plants to construct, etc., today, makes sense only in terms of the *input-uses* of these things tomorrow. Input endowments, L and D, become unknowns as well as data.

5. Tomorrow's input availabilities are also affected by how inputs are used today. The nature and intensity of use to which machines are subjected, the way in which soil is used, oil wells operated, the rate at which inventories are run down, etc., partly determine what will be left tomorrow. This is the problem of physical capital consumption, wear and tear, etc.—the problem of what to subtract from gross investment

---

[62] Much depends on arbitrary or special institutional assumptions about how much optimization we leave in the background for the "engineer." For example, machines of widely varying design could very likely yield a given kind of service. "A lathe is not a lathe is. . . ." Further, no law of nature precludes the rather speedy using-up of a lathe—by using it, e.g., as scrap metal. In some situations it could even be economic to do so.

to get "net" capital formation, hence the net change in input supplies.

How do these five dynamical phenomena fit into the maximum-of welfare problem? Recall that our W-function was assumed sensitive to, and only to, X's and Y's consumption. Nothing was said, however, about the timing of such consumption. Surely not only consumption of this instant matters. In a dynamic context, meaningful welfare and preference functions have to provide a ranking not only with respect to all possible current consumption mixes but also for future time. They must provide some means for weighing apples next week against nuts and apples today. Such functions will *date* each unit of A and N, and the choice to be made will be between alternative time-paths of consumption.[63]

Given such a context, the above five dynamical phenomena are amenable to a formal maximizing treatment entirely akin to that of Parts I, II and III. They are, with one qualification,[64] consistent with the convexity assumptions required for solubility and duality. The results, which are the fruit of some pathbreaking work by R. M. Solow and P. A. Samuelson, define intertemporal production efficiency in terms of time-paths along which no increase in the consumption of any good of any period is possible without a decrease in some other consumption. Such paths are characterized by the superimposition, on top of the statical, one-period or instantaneous efficiency conditions, of certain intertemporal marginal-rate-of-substitution requirements. But the statical efficiency requirements retain their validity: for full-fledged dynamical Pareto-efficiency it is necessary that at any moment in time the system be on its one-period efficiency frontier.[65]

Incidentally, the geometric techniques of Part I are fully adequate to the task of handling a Solow-Samuelson dynamical setup for a 2 by 2 by 2 world. Only now the dimensions of the production box and hence the position of the production-possibility curve will keep shifting, and the solution gives values not only for inputs, outputs and prices but also for their period-to-period changes.

---

[63] Note how little weight is likely to be given to current consumption relative to future consumption if we pick short unit-periods. This year certainly matters, but what of this afternoon versus all future, or this second? Yet what of the man who knows he'll die tomorrow? Note also the intrinsic philosophical dilemmas: *e.g.*, is John Jones today the "same" person he was yesterday?

[64] Capital is characterized not only by the fact of durability, but also by lumpiness or indivisibility "in scale." Such lumpiness results in nonconvexity, hence causes serious analytical troubles.

[65] For possible exception to this, due to sensitivity of the volume of saving, hence of investment, to "as imputed" income distribution, *cf.* my "On Capital Productivity, Input Allocation and Growth," *Quart. Jour. Econ.*, Feb. 1957, LXXI, 86–106.

There are many dynamical phenomena less prone to analysis by a formal maximizing system than the five listed above. The qualitative and quantitative supply of labor-input in the future is influenced by the current use made of the services of people.[66] There are, also, important intertemporal interdependences relating to the fact of space—space matters because it takes time and resources to span it. Moreover, we have not even mentioned the really "difficult" phenomena of "grand dynamics." Production functions, preference functions, and even my or your welfare function shift over time. Such shifts are compounded by what in a sense is the central problem of nonstationary dynamics: the intrinsic uncertainty that attaches to the notion of future.[67] Last, the very boundaries of economics, as of any discipline, are intrinsically arbitrary. Allocation and distribution interact in countless ways with the politics and sociology of a society . . . "everything depends on everything." But we are way beyond simple analytics.

A HISTORICAL NOTE ON THE LITERATURE [68]

The foundations of modern welfare theory are well embedded in the soil of classical economics, and the structure, too, bears the imprint of the line of thought represented by Smith, Ricardo, Mill, and Marshall. But in classical writing prescription and analysis are inseparably intertwined, the underlying philosophy is unabashedly utilitarian, and the central normative concern is with the efficacy of market institutions. In contrast, the development of modern welfare economics can best be understood as an attempt to sort out ethics from science, and allocative efficiency from particular modes of social organization.

The classical tradition reached its culmination in Professor Pigou's *Wealth and Welfare* [4]. Pigou, the last of the great premoderns was also, as witness the *Economics of Welfare* [5], among the first of the moderns. But he was not the first. Vilfredo Pareto, writing during the first years of the century, has a pre-eminent claim [6]. It is his work,

---

66 Although labor is in many respects analytically akin to other kinds of physical capital—resources can and need be invested to expand the stock of engineers, as to expand that of cows and machines. Machines, however, are not subject to certain costless "learning" effects.

67 While formal welfare theory becomes very silent when uncertainty intrudes, much of economic analysis—e.g., monetary theory, trade fluctuations—would have little meaning except for the fact of uncertainty.

68 For a short but substantive history of the development of thought in this field, the reader is referred to Samuelson's synthesis (nonmathematical), pp. 203–19 of *Foundations* [1]. See also Bergson, "Socialist Economics," *Survey of Contemporary Economics*, Vol. I [2] and Boulding, "Welfare Economics," *Survey*, Vol. II [3].

and Enrico Barone's after him [7]—with their focus on the analytical implications of maximization—that constitute the foundations of the modern structure. Many writers contributed to the construction, but A. P. Lerner, Abram Bergson, and Paul Samuelson come especially to mind [8]. Bergson, in particular, in a single article in 1938, was the first to make us see the structure whole. More recently, Kenneth Arrow has explored the logical underpinnings of the notion of a social welfare function in relation to social choice [9]; T. C. Koopmans, Gerard Debreu and others have tested more complicated systems for duality [10]; Samuelson has developed a meaningful species of social indifference function [11] and derived efficiency conditions for "public goods" [12]; and Robert Solow and Samuelson, in work soon to be published, have provided a dynamical extension [13, 14].

There is, also, an important modern literature devoted to the possible uses of the structure of analysis for policy prescription. Three separate sets of writings are more or less distinguishable. There was first, in the 'twenties and 'thirties, a prolonged controversy on markets versus government. L. von Mises [15] and later F. A. Hayek [16] were the principal proponents of unadulterated *laissez faire,* while H. D. Dickinson, Oscar Lange, Lerner and Maurice Dobb stand out on the other side [17]. The decentralized socialist pricing idea, originally suggested by Barone and later by F. M. Taylor, was elaborated by Lange to counter the Mises view that efficient allocation is impossible in a collectivized economy due simply to the sheer scale of the administrative burden of calculation and control.

Second, in the late 1930's, Nicholas Kaldor [18] and J. R. Hicks [19] took up Lionel Robbins' [20] challenge to economists not to mix ethics and science and suggested a series of tests for choosing some input-output configurations over others independently of value.[69] Tibor Scitovsky pointed out an important asymmetry in the Kaldor-Hicks test [21] and Samuelson in the end demonstrated that a "welfare-function" denoting an ethic was needed after all [22]. I. M. D. Little tried, but I think failed, to shake this conclusion [23].[70] The Pareto conditions are necessary, but never sufficient.

Third, there is a body of writing, some of it in a partial-equilibrium

[69] The Hicks-Kaldor line of thought has some ties to an earlier literature by Marshall, Pigou, Fisher, etc., on "what is income."

[70] While I find Little's alternative to a welfare function ("an economic change is desirable if it does not cause a bad redistribution of income, and if the potential losers could not profitably bribe the potential gainers to oppose it" [p. 105]) no alternative at all, his is a provocative evaluation of modern welfare theory. For an evaluation, in turn, of Little, see K. J. Arrow, "Little's Critique of Welfare Economics," *Am. Econ. Rev.,* Dec. 1951, XLI, 923-34.

mode, which is concerned with policy at a lower level of abstraction. Writings by Harold Hotelling, Ragnar Frisch, J. E. Meade, W. A. Lewis, are devoted to the question of optimal pricing, marginal-cost or otherwise, in public utility (M.C.<A.C.) situations [24]. Hotelling, H. P. Wald, M. F. W. Joseph, E. R. Rolph and G. F. Break, Little, and more recently Lionel McKenzie, have, in turn, analyzed alternative fiscal devices for covering public deficits [25]. Last, a number of the above, notably Lerner, Kaldor, Samuelson, Scitovsky, Little, McKenzie and, most exhaustively, Meade, as well as R. F. Kahn, Lloyd Metzler, J. de V. Graaf, H. G. Johnson and others have applied the apparatus to questions of gains from international trade, optimal tariffs, etc. [26].

BIBLIOGRAPHY

[1] P. A. Samuelson, *Foundations of Economic Analysis* (Cambridge, 1947).

[2] A. Bergson, "Socialist Economics," in H. S. Ellis, ed., *A Survey of Contemporary Economics,* Vol. I (Philadelphia, 1948).

[3] K. E. Boulding, "Welfare Economics," in B. F. Haley, ed., *A. Survey of Contemporary Economics,* Vol. II (Homewood, Ill., 1952).

[4] A. C. Pigou, *Wealth and Welfare* (London, 1912).

[5] ———, *The Economics of Welfare,* 4th ed. (London, 1932).

[6] V. Pareto, *Manuel d'économie politique* (Paris, 1909).

[7] E. Barone, "The Ministry of Production in the Collectivist State," transl. in F. A. Hayek, *Collectivist Economic Planning* (London, 1935).

[8] See A. P. Lerner, *The Economics of Control* (London, 1944); A. Bergson (Burk), "A Reformulation of Certain Aspects of Welfare Economics," *Quart. Jour. Econ.,* Feb. 1938, LII, 310–14, reprinted in R. V. Clemence, ed., *Readings in Economic Analysis,* Vol. I (Cambridge, 1952); P. A. Samuelson, *op. cit.,* Ch. 8.

For other works, see references in Samuelson, *op. cit.,* p. 219, and in Bergson's and Boulding's *Survey* articles [2, 3].

[9] See K. J. Arrow, *Social Choice and Individual Values* (New York, 1951).

[10] P. A. Samuelson, *Market Mechanisms and Maximization* (unpublished, RAND Corporation Research Memo., 1949).

T. C. Koopmans, *Activity Analysis of Production and Allocation* (New York, 1951); also R. Dorfman, "Mathematical or 'Linear' Programming," *Am. Econ. Rev.,* Dec. 1953, XLIII, 797–825.

[11] P. A. Samuelson, "Social Indifference Curves," *Quart. Jour. Econ.,* Feb. 1956, LXX, 1–22.

[12] ———, "The Pure Theory of Public Expenditure," *Rev. Econ. Stat.,* Nov. 1954, XXXVI, 387–89.

———, "Diagrammatic Exposition of a Theory of Public Expenditure," *Rev. Econ. Stat.,* Nov. 1955, XXXVII, 350–56.

[13] R. Dorfman, R. M. Solow and P. A. Samuelson, *Linear Programming and Economic Analysis* (RAND Corporation, forthcoming), esp. Ch. 11, 12. Ch. 14 contains a most elegant exposition by R. M. Solow of modern welfare theory in linear programming terms.

[14] Four other works should be mentioned: M. W. Reder, *Studies in the Theory of Welfare Economics* (New York, 1947), is a book-length exposition of modern welfare theory; Hla Mynt's *Theories of Welfare Economics* (London, 1948), treats classical and neoclassical writings; W. J. Baumol in *Welfare Economics and the Theory of the State* (London, 1952), attempts an extension to political theory; in a different vein, Gunnar Myrdal's *Political Elements in the Development of Economic Theory,* transl. by Paul Streeten (London, 1953), with Streeten's appendix on modern developments, is a broad-based critique of the premises of welfare economics.

[15] For the translation of the original 1920 article by Mises which triggered the controversy, see F. A. Hayek, ed., *Collectivist Economic Planning* (London, 1935).

[16] See esp. F. A. Hayek, "Socialist Calculation: The Competitive Solution," *Economica,* May 1940, VII, 125–49; for a broad-front attack on deviations from *laissez faire* see Hayek's polemic, *The Road to Serfdom* (Chicago, 1944).

[17] H. D. Dickinson, "Price Formation in a Socialist Economy," *Econ. Jour.,* Dec. 1933, XLIII, 237–50; O. Lange, "On the Economic Theory of Socialism" in Lange and Taylor, *The Economic Theory of Socialism,* B. E. Lippincott, ed. (Minneapolis, 1938); A. P. Lerner, *op. cit.*; M. Dobb, "Economic Theory and the Problem of the Socialist Economy," *Econ. Jour.* Dec. 1933, XLIII, 588–98.

[18] N. Kaldor, "Welfare Propositions in Economics and Interpersonal Comparisons of Utility," *Econ. Jour.,* Sept. 1939, LXIX, 549–52.

[19] J. R. Hicks, "The Foundations of Welfare Economics," *Econ. Jour.,* Dec. 1939, LXIX, 696–712 and "The Valuation of the Social Income," *Economica,* Feb. 1940, VII, 105–23.

[20] L. Robbins, *The Nature and Significance of Economic Science* (London, 1932).

[21] T. Scitovsky, "A Note on Welfare Propositions in Economics," *Rev. Econ. Stud.,* 1941–1942, IX, 77–78.

———, "A Reconsideration of the Theory of Tariffs," *Rev. Econ. Stud.,* 1941–1942, IX, 89–110.

[22] P. A. Samuelson, "Evaluation of Real National Income," *Oxford Econ. Papers,* Jan. 1950, II, 1–29.

[23] I. M. D. Little, *A Critique of Welfare Economics* (Oxford, 1950).

[24] H. Hotelling, "The General Welfare in Relation to Problems of Taxation and of Railway and Utility Rates," *Econometrica*, July 1938, VI, 242–69, is the first modern formulation of the problem that was posed, in 1844, by Jules Dupuit ("On the Measurement of Utility of Public Works," to be found in *International Economic Papers*, No. 2, ed. Alan T. Peacock *et al.*).

[25] See esp. Little, "Direct versus Indirect Taxes," *Econ. Jour.*, Sept. 1951, LXI, 577–84.

[26] For a comprehensive treatment of the issues, as well as for references, see J. E. Meade, *The Theory of International Economic Policy*, Vol. II: *Trade and Welfare* and *Mathematical Supplement* (New York, 1955).

LINEAR PROGRAMMING

34

MATHEMATICAL, OR "LINEAR," PROGRAMMING: A NONMATHEMATICAL EXPOSITION *

ROBERT DORFMAN, teaches at Harvard University; he was formerly at the University of California, Berkeley.

This paper is intended to set forth the leading ideas of mathematical programming [1] purged of the algebraic apparatus which has impeded their general acceptance and appreciation. This will be done by concentrating on the graphical representation of the method. While it is not possible, in general, to portray mathematical programming problems in two-dimensional graphs, the conclusions which we shall draw from the graphs will be of general validity and, of course, the graphic representation of multidimensional problems has a time-honored place in economics.

The central formal problem of economics is the problem of allocating scarce resources so as to maximize the attainment of some predetermined objective. The standard formulation of this problem—the so-called marginal analysis—has led to conclusions of great importance for the understanding of many questions of social and economic policy. But it is a fact of common knowledge that this mode of analysis has not recommended itself to men of affairs for the practical solution of their economic and business problems. Mathematical programming is based on a restatement of this same formal problem in a form which is designed to be useful in making practical decisions in business and economic affairs. That mathematical programming is nothing but a reformulation of the standard economic problem and its solution is the main thesis of this exposition.

* From the *American Economic Review*, Vol. XLIII (December, 1953), No. 5, Part I, pp. 797–825. Reprinted by permission.

[1] The terminology of the techniques which we are discussing is in an unsatisfactory state. Most frequently they are called "linear programming" although the relationships involved are not always linear. Sometimes they are called "activities analysis," but this is not a very suggestive name. The distinguishing feature of the techniques is that they are concerned with programming rather than with analysis, and, at any rate, "activities analysis" has not caught on. We now try out "mathematical programming"; perhaps it will suit.

The motivating idea of mathematical programming is the idea of a "process" or "activity." A process is a specific method for performing an economic task. For example, the manufacture of soap by a specified formula is a process. So also is the weaving of a specific quality of cotton gray goods on a specific type of loom. The conventional production function can be thought of as the formula relating the inputs and outputs of all the processes by which a given task can be accomplished.

For some tasks, *e.g.*, soap production, there are an infinite number of processes available. For others, *e.g.*, weaving, only a finite number of processes exist. In some cases, a plant or industry may have only a single process available.

In terms of processes, choices in the productive sphere are simply decisions as to which processes are to be used and the extent to which each is to be employed. Economists are accustomed to thinking in terms of decisions as to the quantities of various productive factors to be employed. But an industry or firm cannot substitute Factor A for Factor B unless it does some of its work in a different way, that is, unless it substitutes a process which uses A in relatively high proportions for one which uses B. Inputs, therefore, cannot be changed without a change in the way of doing things, and often a fundamental change. Mathematical programming focusses on this aspect of economic choice.

The objective of mathematical programming is to determine the optimal levels of productive processes in given circumstances. This requires a restatement of productive relationships in terms of processes and a reconsideration of the effect of factor scarcities on production choices. As a prelude to this theoretical discussion, however, it will be helpful to consider a simplified production problem from a common-sense point of view.

I. AN EXAMPLE OF MATHEMATICAL PROGRAMMING

Let us consider an hypothetical automobile company equipped for the production of both automobiles and trucks. This company, then, can perform two economic tasks, and we assume that it has a single process for accomplishing each. These two tasks, the manufacture of automobiles and that of trucks, compete for the use of the firm's facilities. Let us assume that the company's plant is organized into four departments: (1) sheet metal stamping, (2) engine assembly, (3) automobile final assembly, and (4) truck final assembly—raw materials, labor, and all other components being available in virtually unlimited amounts at constant prices in the open market.

The capacity of each department of the plant is, of course, limited.

We assume that the metal stamping department can turn out sufficient stampings for 25,000 automobiles or 35,000 trucks per month. We can then calculate the combinations of automobile and truck stampings which this department can produce. Since the department can accommodate 25,000 automobiles per month, each automobile requires 1/25,000 or 0.004 per cent of monthly capacity. Similarly each truck requires 0.00286 per cent of monthly capacity. If, for example, 15,000 automobiles were manufactured they would require 60 per cent of metal stamping capacity and the remaining 40 per cent would be sufficient to produce stampings for 14,000 trucks. Then 15,000 automobiles and 14,000 trucks could be produced by this department at full operation. This is, of course, not the only combination of automobiles and trucks which could be produced by the stamping department at full operation. In Figure 1, the line labeled "Metal Stamping" represents all such combinations.

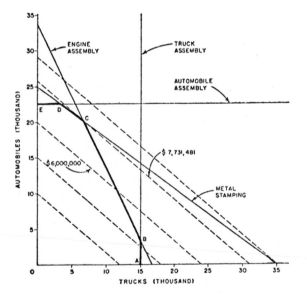

Figure 1. Choices open to an automobile firm

Similarly we assume that the engine assembly department has monthly capacity for 33,333 automobile engines or 16,667 truck engines or, again, some combination of fewer automobile and truck engines. The combinations which would absorb the full capacity of the engine assembly department are shown by the "Engine Assembly"

line in Figure 1. We assume also that the automobile assembly department can accommodate 22,500 automobiles per month and the truck
assembly department 15,000 trucks. These limitations are also represented in Figure 1.

We regard this set of assumptions as defining two processes: the
production of automobiles and the production of trucks. The process
of producing an automobile yields, as an output, one automobile and
absorbs, as inputs, 0.004 per cent of metal stamping capacity, 0.003
per cent of engine assembly capacity, and 0.00444 per cent of automobile assembly capacity. Similarly the process of producing a truck
yields, as an output, one truck and absorbs, as inputs, 0.00286 per cent
of metal stamping capacity, 0.006 per cent of engine assembly capacity,
and 0.00667 per cent of truck assembly capacity.

The economic choice facing this firm is the selection of the numbers
of automobiles and trucks to be produced each month, subject to the
restriction that no more than 100 per cent of the capacity of any department can be used. Or, in more technical phraseology, the choice
consists in deciding at what level to employ each of the two available
processes. Clearly, if automobiles alone are produced, at most 22,500
units per month can be made, automobile assembly being the effective
limitation. If only trucks are produced, a maximum of 15,000 units per
month can be made because of the limitation on truck assembly. Which
of these alternatives should be adopted, or whether some combination
of trucks and automobiles should be produced depends on the relative
profitability of manufacturing trucks and automobiles. Let us assume,
to be concrete, that the sales value of an automobile is $300 greater
than the total cost of purchased materials, labor, and other direct costs
attributable to its manufacture. And, similarly, that the sale value of a
truck is $250 more than the direct cost of manufacturing it. Then the
net revenue of the plant for any month is 300 times the number of automobiles produced plus 250 times the number of trucks. For example,
15,000 automobiles and 6,000 trucks would yield a net revenue of
$6,000,000. There are many combinations of automobiles and trucks
which would yield this same net revenue; 10,000 automobiles and
12,000 trucks is another one. In terms of Figure 1, all combinations
with a net revenue of $6,000,000 lie on a straight line, to be specific,
the line labelled $6,000,000 in the figure.

A line analogous to the one which we have just described corresponds to each possible net revenue. All these lines are parallel, since
their slope depends only on the relative profitability of the two activities. The greater the net revenue, of course, the higher the line. A few
of the net revenue lines are shown in the figure by the dashed parallel
lines.

Each conceivable number of automobiles and trucks produced corresponds to a point on the diagram, and through each point there passes one member of the family of net revenue lines. Net revenue is maximized when the point corresponding to the number of automobiles and trucks produced lies on the highest possible net revenue line. Now the effect of the capacity restrictions is to limit the range of choice to outputs which correspond to points lying inside the area bounded by the axes and by the broken line ABCDE. Since net revenue increases as points move out from the origin, only points which lie on the broken line need be considered. Beginning then with Point A and moving along the broken line we see that the boundary of the accessible region intersects higher and higher net revenue lines until point C is reached. From there on, the boundary slides down the scale of net revenue lines. Point C therefore corresponds to the highest attainable net revenue. At point C the output is 20,370 automobiles and 6,481 trucks, yielding a net revenue of $7,731,481 per month.

The reader has very likely noticed that this diagram is by no means novel. The broken line, ABCDE, tells the maximum number of automobiles which can be produced in conjunction with any given number of trucks. It is therefore, apart from its angularity, a production opportunity curve or transformation curve of the sort made familiar by Irving Fisher, and the slope of the curve at any point where it has a slope is the ratio of substitution in production between automobiles and trucks. The novel feature is that the production opportunity curve shown here has no defined slope at five points and that one of these five is the critical point. The dashed lines in the diagram are equivalent to conventional price lines.

The standard theory of production teaches that profits are maximized at a point where a price line is tangent to the production opportunity curve. But, as we have just noted, there are five points where our production opportunity curve has no tangent. The tangency criterion therefore fails. Instead we find that profits are maximized at a corner where the slope of the price line is neither less than the slope of the opportunity curve to the left of the corner nor greater than the slope of the opportunity curve to the right.

Diagrammatically, then, mathematical programming uses angles where standard economics uses curves. In economic terms, where does the novelty lie? In standard economic analysis we visualize production relationships in which, if there are two products, one may be substituted for the other with gradually increasing difficulty. In mathematical programming we visualize a regime of production in which, for any output, certain factors will be effectively limiting but other factors will be in ample supply. Thus, in Figure 1, the factors which effectively limit production at each point can be identified by noticing on which limitation lines the point lies. The rate of substitution between products is determined by the limiting factors alone and changes only when the designation of the limiting factors changes. In the diagram a change in the designation of the limiting factors is represented by turning a corner on the production opportunity curve.

We shall come back to this example later, for we have not exhausted its significance. But now we are in a position to develop with more generality some of the concepts used in mathematical programming.

II. THE MODEL OF PRODUCTION IN MATHEMATICAL PROGRAMMING

A classical problem in economics is the optimal utilization of two factors of production, conveniently called capital and labor. In the usual analysis, the problem is formulated by conceiving of the two factors as cooperating with each other in accordance with a production function which states the maximum quantity of a product which can be obtained by the use of stated quantities of the two factors. One convenient means of representing such a production function is an "isoquant diagram," as in Figure 2. In this familiar figure, quantities of labor are plotted along the horizontal axis and quantities of capital along the vertical. Each of the arcs in the body of the diagram correspond to a

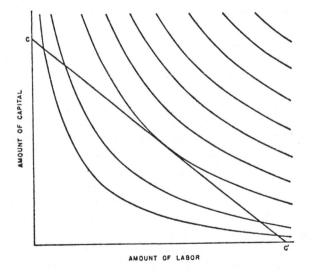

Figure 2. An isoquant diagram

definite quantity of output, higher arcs corresponding to greater quantities.

If the prices per unit of capital and labor are known, the combinations of labor and capital which can be purchased for a fixed total expenditure can be shown by a sloping straight line like CC' in the figure, the slope depending only on the relative prices. Two interpretations follow immediately. First, the minimum unit cost of producing the output represented by any isoquant can be achieved by using the combination of labor and capital which corresponds to the point where that isoquant is tangent to a price line. Second, the greatest output attainable with any given expenditure is represented by the isoquant which is tangent to the price line corresponding to that expenditure.

This diagram and its analysis rest upon the assumption that the two factors are continuously substitutable for each other in such wise that if the amount of labor employed be reduced by a small amount it will be possible to maintain the quantity of output by a *small* increase in the amount of capital employed. Moreover, this analysis assumes that each successive unit decrement in the amount of labor will require a slightly larger increment in the amount of capital if output is to remain constant. Otherwise the isoquants will not have the necessary shape.

All this is familiar. We call it to mind only because we are about to develop an analogous diagram which is fundamental to mathematical programming. First, however, let us see why a new diagram and a new approach are felt to be necessary.

The model of production which we have just briefly sketched very likely is valid for some kinds of production. But for most manufacturing industries, and indeed all production where elaborate machinery is used, it is open to serious objection. It is characteristic of most modern machinery that each kind of machine operates efficiently only over a narrow range of speeds and that the quantities of labor, power, materials and other factors which cooperate with the machine are dictated rather inflexibly by the machine's built-in characteristics. Furthermore, at any time there is available only a small number of different kinds of machinery for accomplishing a given task. A few examples may make these considerations more concrete. Earth may be moved by hand shovels, by steam or diesel shovels, or by bulldozers. Power shovels and bulldozers are built in only a small variety of models, each with inherent characteristics as to fuel consumption per hour, number of operators and assistants required, cubic feet of earth moved per hour, etc. Printing type may be set by using hand-fonts, linotype machines or monotype machines. Again, each machine is available in only a few models and each has its own pace of operation, power and space requirements, and other essentially unalterable characteristics. A moment's reflection will bring to mind dozens of other illustrations: printing presses, power looms, railroad and highway haulage, statistical and accounting calculation, metallic ore reduction, metal fabrication, etc. For many economic tasks the number of processes available is finite, and each process can be regarded as inflexible with regard to the ratios among factor inputs and process outputs. Factors cannot be substituted for each other except by changing the levels at which entire technical processes are used, because each process uses factors in fixed characteristic ratios. In mathematical programming, accordingly, process substitution plays a rôle analogous to that of factor substitution in conventional analysis.

We now develop an apparatus for the analysis of process substitution. For convenience we shall limit our discussion to processes which

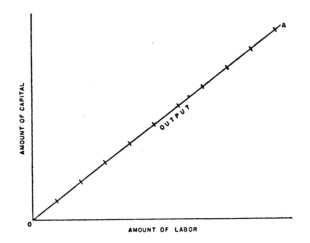

Figure 3. A process

consume two factors, to be called capital and labor, and produce a single output. Figure 3 represents such a process. As in Figure 2, the horizontal axis is scaled in units of labor and the vertical axis in units of capital. The process is represented by the ray, OA, which is scaled in units of output. To each output there corresponds a labor requirement found by locating the appropriate mark on the process ray and reading straight down. The capital requirement is found in the same manner by reading straight across from the mark on the process line. Similarly, to each amount of labor there corresponds a quantity of output, found by reading straight up, and a quantity of capital, found by reading straight across from the output mark.

It should be noted that the quantity of capital in this diagram is the quantity used in a process rather than the quantity owned by an economic unit; it is capital-service rather than capital itself. Thus, though more or less labor may be combined with a given machine—by using it more or fewer hours—the ratio of capital to labor inputs, that is, the ratio of machine-hours to labor hours—is regarded as technologically fixed.

Figure 3 incorporates two important assumptions. The fact that the line OA is straight implies that the ratio between the capital input and the labor input is the same for all levels of output and is given, indeed, by the slope of the line. The fact that the marks on the output line are evenly spaced indicates that there are neither economies nor diseconomies of scale in the use of the process, *i.e.*, that there will be strict proportionality between the quantity of output and the quality of either input. These assumptions are justified rather simply on the basis of the notion of a process. If a process can be used once, it can be used twice or as many times as the supplies of factors permit. Two linotype machines with equally skilled operators can turn out just twice as much type per hour as one. Two identical mills can turn out just twice as many yards of cotton per month as one. So long as factors are available, a process can be duplicated. Whether it will be economical to do so is, of course, another matter.

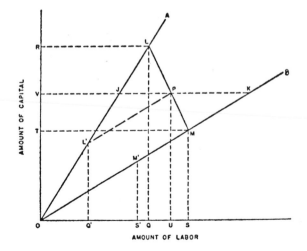

Figure 4. Two processes

If there is only one process available for a given task there is not much scope for economic choice. Frequently, however, there will be several processes. Figure 4 represents a situation in which two procedures are available, Process A indicated by the line OA and Process B indicated by OB. We have already seen how to interpret points on the lines OA and OB. The scales by which output is measured on the two rays are not necessarily the same. The scale on each ray reflects the productivity of the factors when used in the process represented by that ray and has no connection with the output scale on any other process ray. Now suppose that points L and M represent production of the same output by the two processes. Then LM, the straight line between them, will represent an isoquant and each point on this line will correspond to a combination of Processes A and B which produces the same output as OL units of Process A or OM units of Process B.

To see this, consider any point P on the line LM and draw a line through P parallel to OB. Let L' be the point where this line intersects OA. Finally mark the point M' on OB such that OM' = L'P. Now consider the production plan which consists of using Process A at level OL' and Process B at level OM'.[2] It is easy to show that this production plan uses OU units of labor, where U is the labor coordinate of point P, and OV units of capital, where V is the capital coordinate of point P.[3]

Since the coordinates of point P correspond to the quantities of factors consumed by OL' units of Process A and OM' units of Process B, we interpret P as representing the combined production plan made up of the specified levels of the two processes. This interpretation implies an important economic assumption, namely, that if the two processes are used simultaneously they will neither interfere with nor enhance each other so that the inputs and outputs resulting from simultaneous use of two processes at any levels can be found by adding the inputs and outputs of the individual processes.

In order to show that P lies on the isoquant through points L and M it remains only to show that the sum of the outputs corresponding to points L' and M' is the same as the output corresponding to point L or point M. This follows at once from the facts that the output cor-

[2] An alternative construction would be to draw a line through point P parallel to OA. It would intersect OB at M'. Then we could lay off OL' equal to M'P on OA. This would lead to exactly the same results as the construction used in the text. The situation is analogous to the "parallelogram of forces" in physics.

[3] Proof: Process A at level OL' uses OQ' units of labor, Process B at level OM' uses OS' units of labor, together they use OQ' + OS' units of labor. But, by construction, L'P is equal and parallel to OM'. So Q'U = OS'. Therefore, OQ' + OS' = OQ + Q'U = OU units of labor. The argument with respect to capital is similar.

responding to any point on a process ray is directly proportional to the length of the ray up to that point and that the triangles LL'P and LOM in Figure 4 are similar.[4] Thus if we have two process lines like OA and OB and find points L and M on them which represent producing the same output by means of the two processes then the line segment connecting the two equal-output points will be an isoquant.

We can now draw the mathematical programming analog of the familiar isoquant diagram. Figure 5 is such a diagram with four process lines shown. Point M represents a particular output by use of Process A and points L, K, J represent that same output by means of Processes B, C, D, respectively. The succession of line segments connecting these four points is the isoquant for that same output. It is easy to see that any other succession of line segments respectively parallel to those of

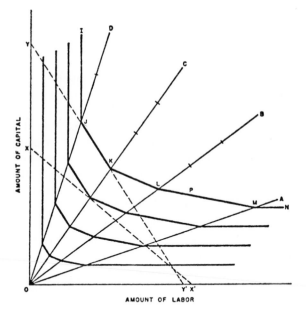

Figure 5. Four processes

[4] Proof: Let Output (X) denote the output corresponding to any point, X, on the diagram. Then Output (M')/Output (M) = OM'/OM and Output (L')/Output (L) = OL'/OL. By assumption: Output (L) = Output (M). So Output (M')/Output (L) = OM'/OM. Adding, we have:

$$\frac{\text{Output (M')} + \text{Output (L')}}{\text{Output (L)}} = \frac{OM'}{OM} + \frac{OL'}{OL} = \frac{L'P}{OM} + \frac{OL'}{OL} = \frac{L'L}{OL} + \frac{OL'}{OL} = 1.$$

MLKJ is also an isoquant. Three such are shown in the figure. It is instructive to compare Figure 5 with Figure 2 and note the strong resemblance in appearance as well as in interpretation.

We may draw price lines on Figure 5, just as on the conventional kind of isoquant diagram. The dashed lines XX' and YY' represent two possible price lines. Consider XX' first. As that line is drawn, the maximum output for a given expenditure can be obtained by use of Process C alone, and, conversely, the minimum cost for a given output is also obtained by using Process C alone. Thus, for the relative price regime represented by XX', Process C is optimal. The price line YY' is drawn parallel to the isoquant segment JK. In this case Process C is still optimal, but Process D is also optimal and so is any combination of the two.

It is evident from considering these two price lines, and as many others as the reader wishes to visualize, that an optimal production program can always be achieved by means of a single process, which process depending, of course, on the slope of the price line. It should be noted, however, that the conventional tangency criterion is no longer applicable.

We found in Figure 5 that an optimal economic plan need never use more than a single process for each of its outputs.[5] That conclusion is valid for the situation depicted, which assumed that the services of the two factors could be procured in any amounts desired at constant relative prices. This assumption is not applicable to many economic problems, nor is it used much in mathematical programming. We must now, therefore, take factor supply conditions into account.

III. FACTOR SUPPLIES AND COSTS

In mathematical programming it is usual to divide all factors of production into two classes: unlimited factors, which are available in any amount desired at constant unit cost, and limited or scarce factors, which are obtainable at constant unit cost up to a fixed maximum quantity and thereafter not at all. The automobile example illustrates this classification. There the four types of capacity were treated as fixed factors available at zero variable cost; all other factors were grouped under direct costs which were considered as constant per unit of output.

The automobile example showed that this classification of factors is adequate for expressing the maximization problem of a firm dealing in competitive markets. In the last section we saw that when all factors are unlimited, this formulation can be used to find a minimum average cost point.

---

[5] Recall, however, that we have not taken joint production into account nor have we considered the effects of considerations from the demand side.

Both of these applications invoked restrictive assumptions and, furthermore, assumptions which conflict with those conventionally made in studying resource allocation. In conventional analysis we conceive that as the level of production of a firm, industry or economy rises, average unit costs rise also after some point. The increase in average costs is attributable in part to the working of the law of variable proportions,[6] which operates when the inputs of some but not all factors of production are increased. As far as the consequences of increasing some but not all inputs are concerned, the contrast between mathematical programming and the marginal analysis is more verbal than substantive. A reference to Figure 4 will show how such changes are handled in mathematical programming. Point J in Figure 4 represents the production of a certain output by the use of Process A alone. If it is desired to increase output without increasing the use of capital, this can be done by moving to the right along the dotted line JK, since this line cuts successively higher isoquants. Such a movement would correspond to using increasingly more of Process B and increasingly less of Process A and thus, indirectly, to substituting labor for capital. If, further, we assume that unit cost of production is lower for Process A than for Process B this movement would also correspond to increasing average cost of production. Thus both marginal analysis and mathematical programming lead to the same conclusion when factor proportions are changed: if the change starts from a minimum cost point the substitution will lead to gradually increasing unit costs.

But changing input proportions is only one part of the story according to the conventional type of analysis. If output is to be increased, any of three things may happen. First, it may be possible to increase the consumption of all inputs without incurring a change in their unit prices. In this case both mathematical programming and marginal analysis agree that output will be expanded without changing the ratios among the input quantities and average cost of production will not increase.[7] Second, it may not be possible to increase the use of some of the inputs. This is the case we have just analyzed. According to both modes of analysis the input ratios will change in this case and average unit costs will increase. The only difference between the two approaches is that if average cost is to be plotted against output, the marginal analyst will show a picture with a smoothly rising curve while the mathematical programmer will show a broken line made up of increasingly steep line segments. Third, it may be possible to increase

6 Cf. J. M. Cassels, "On the Law of Variable Proportions," in W. Fellner and B. F. Haley, eds., Readings in the Theory of Income Distribution (Philadelphia, 1946), pp. 103–18.

7 Cf. F. H. Knight, Risk, Uncertainty and Profit (Boston, 1921), p. 98.

the quantities of all inputs but only at the penalty of increasing unit prices or some kind of diseconomies of scale. This third case occurs in the marginal analysis, indeed it is the case which gives long-run cost curves their familiar shape, but mathematical programming has no counterpart for it.

The essential substantive difference we have arrived at is that the marginal analysis conceives of pecuniary and technical diseconomies associated with changes in scale while mathematical programming does not.[8] There are many important economic problems in which factor prices and productivities do not change in response to changes in scale or in which such variations can be disregarded. Most investigations of industrial capacity, for example, are of this nature. In such studies we seek the maximum output of an industry, regarding its inventory of physical equipment as given and assuming that the auxiliary factors needed to cooperate with the equipment can be obtained in the quantities dictated by the characteristics of the equipment. Manpower requirement sudies are of the same nature. In such studies we take both output and equipment as given and calculate the manpower needed to operate the equipment at the level which will yield the desired output. Studies of full employment output fall into the same format. In such studies we determine in advance the quantity of each factor which is to be regarded as full employment of that factor. Then we calculate the optimum output obtainable by the use of the factors in those quantities.

These illustrations should suffice to show that the assumptions made in mathematical programming can comprehend a wide variety of important economic problems. The most useful applications of mathematical programming are probably to problems of the types just described, that is, to problems concerned with finding optimum production plans using specified quantities of some or all of the resources involved.

IV. ANALYSIS OF PRODUCTION WITH LIMITED FACTORS

The diagrams which we have developed are readily adaptable to the analysis of the consequences of limits on the factor supplies. Such

---

8 Even within the framework of the marginal analysis the concept of diseconomies of scale has been challenged on both theoretical and empirical grounds. For examples of empirical criticism see Committee on Price Determination, Conference on Price Research, *Cost Behavior and Price Policy* (New York, 1943). The most searching theoretical criticism is in Piero Sraffa, "The Laws of Returns under Competitive Conditions," *Econ. Jour.*, Dec. 1926, XXXVI, 535–50.

limits are, of course, the heart of Figure 1 where the four principal lines represent limitations on the process levels which result from limits on the four factor quantities considered. But Figure 1 cannot be used when more than two processes have to be considered. For such problems diagrams like Figures 3, 4, and 5 have to be used.

Figure 6 reproduces the situation portrayed in Figure 5 with some additional data to be explained below. Let OF represent the maximum amount of capital which can be used and thus show a factor limitation. The horizontal line through F divides the diagram into two sections: all points above the line correspond to programs which require more capital than is available; points on and below the line represent pro-

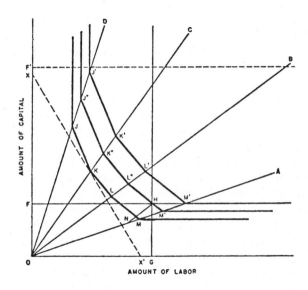

Figure 6. Four processes, with limitations

grams which do not have excessive capital requirements. This horizontal line will be called the capital limitation line. Points on or below it are called "feasible," points above it are called "infeasible."

The economic unit portrayed in Figure 6 has the choice of operating at any feasible point. If maximum output is its objective, it will choose a point which lies on the highest possible isoquant, i.e., the highest isoquant which touches the capital limitation line. This is the one labelled J'K'L'M', and the highest possible output is attained by using Process A.

Of course, maximum output may not be the objective. The objective may be, for example, to maximize the excess of the value of output over labor costs. We shall refer to such an excess as a "net value." The same kind of diagram can be used to solve for a net value provided that the value of each unit of output is independent of the number of units produced [9] and that the cost of each unit of labor is similarly constant. If these provisos are met, each point on a process ray will correspond to a certain physical output but also to a certain value of output, cost of labor, and net value of output. Further, along any process ray the net value of output will equal the physical output times the net value per unit and will therefore be proportional to the physical output. We may thus use a diagram similar to Figure 6 except that we think of net value instead of physical output as measured along the process rays and we show isovalue line instead of isoquants. This has been done on Figure 7, in which the maximum net value attainable is the one which corresponds to the isovalue contour through point P, and is attained by using process C.

It should be noted in both Figures 6 and 7 that the optimal program consisted of a single process, that shifts in the quantity of capital available would not affect the designation of the optimal process though they would change its level, and that the price lines, which were crucial in Figure 5, played no rôle.

The next complication, and the last one we shall be able to consider, is to assume that both factors are in limited supply. This situation is portrayed in Figure 6 by adding the vertical line through point G to represent a labor limitation. The available quantity of labor is shown, of course, by the length OG. Then the points inside the rectangle OFHG represents programs which can be implemented in the sense that they do not require more than the available supplies of either factor. This is the rectangle of feasible programs. The greatest achievable output is the one which corresponds to the highest isoquant which touches the rectangle of feasible programs. This is the isoquant J"K" L"M", and furthermore, since the maximum isoquant touches the rectangle at H, H represents the program by which the maximum output can be produced.

This solution differs from the previous ones in that the solution-point does not lie on any process ray but between the rays for Processes A and B. We have already seen that a point like H represents using Process A at level ON and Process B at level NH.

Two remarks are relevant to this solution. First: with the factor limitation lines as drawn, the maximum output requires two processes.

[9] This is a particularly uncomfortable assumption. We use it here to explain the method in its least complicated form.

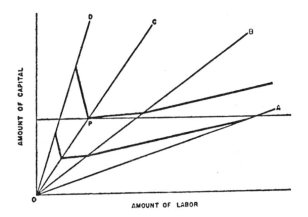

Figure 7. Four processes with isovalue lines

If the factor limitation lines had been drawn so that they intersected exactly on one of the process rays, only one process would have been required. If the factor limitation lines had crossed to the left of Process D or to the right of Process A, the maximizing production plan would require only one process. But, no matter how the limitation lines be drawn, at most two processes are required to maximize output. We are led to an important generalization: maximum output may always be obtained by using a number of processes which does not exceed the number of factors in limited supply, if this number is greater than zero. The conclusions we drew from Figures 6 and 7 both conform to this rule, and it is one of the basic theorems of mathematical programming.

Second: although at most two processes are required to obtain the maximum output, which two depends on the location of the factor limits. As shown, the processes used for maximum output were Processes A and B. If somewhat more capital, represented by the amount OF' were available, the maximizing processes would have been Processes C and D. If two factors are limited, it is the ratio between their supplies rather than the absolute supplies of either which determines the processes in the optimum program. This contrasts with the case in which only one factor is limited. Just as the considerations which determine the optimum set of processes are more complicated when two factors are limited than when only one is, so with three or more limited factors the optimum conditions become more complicated still and soon pass the reach of intuition. This, indeed, is the *raison d'être* of the formidable appartus of mathematical programming.

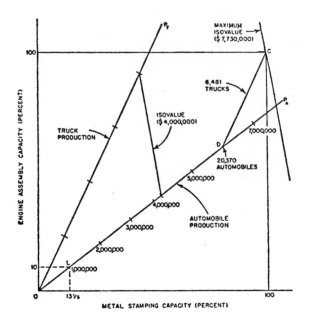

Figure 8. Automobile example, optimal plan

We can make these considerations more concrete by applying them to the automobile example. Referring to Figure 1, (p. 549), we note that the optimum production point, C, lay on the limitation lines for engine assembly and metal stamping, but well below the limits for automobile and truck assembly. The limitations on automobile and truck assembly capacity are, therefore, ineffective and can be disregarded. The situation in terms of the two effectively limiting types of capacity is shown in Figure 8.

In Figure 8 the ray P_A represents the process of producing automobiles and P_T the process of producing trucks. These two processes can be operated at any combination of levels which does not require the use of more than 100 per cent of either metal stamping or engine assembly capacity. Thus the rectangle in the diagram is the region of feasible production programs. The optimal production program is the one in the feasible region which corresponds to the highest possible net revenue.[10] Thus it will be helpful to construct isorevenue lines, as we

[10] Since the objective of the firm is, by assumption, to maximize revenue rather than physical output, we may consider automobile and truck production as two alternative processes for producing revenue instead of as two processes with disparate outputs.

did in Figure 7. To do this, consider automobile production first. Each point on P_A corresponds to the production of a certain number of automobiles per month. Suppose, for example, that the scale is such that point L represents the production of 3,333 automobiles per month. It will be recalled that each automobile yields a net revenue of $300. Therefore, 3,333 automobiles yield a revenue of $1,000,000. Point L, then, corresponds to a net revenue of $1,000,000 as well as to an output of 3,333 automobiles per month. Since (see page 549), 3,333 automobiles require $13\frac{1}{3}$ per cent of metal stamping capacity and 10 per cent of engine assembly capacity, the coordinates of the $1,000,000 net revenue point on P_A are established at once. By a similar argument, the point whose coordinates are $26\frac{2}{3}$ per cent of metal stamping capacity and 20 per cent of engine capacity is the $2,000,000 net revenue point on P_A. In the same manner, the whole ray can be drawn and scaled off in terms of net revenue, and so can P_T, the process ray for truck production. The diagram is completed by connecting the $4,000,000 points on the two process lines in order to show the direction of the isorevenue lines.

The optimum program is at point C, where the two capacity limits intersect, because C lies on the highest isorevenue line which touches the feasible region. Through point C we have drawn a line parallel to the truck production line and meeting the automobile production line at D. By our previous argument, the length OD represents the net revenue from automobile production in the optimal program and the length DC represents the net revenue from trucks. If these lengths be scaled off, the result, of course, will be the same as the solution found previously.

V. IMPUTATION OF FACTOR VALUES

We have just noted that the major field of application of mathematical programming is to problems where the supply of one or more factors of production is absolutely limited. Such scarcities are the genesis of value in ordinary analysis, and they generate values in mathematical programming too. In fact, in ordinary analysis the determination of outputs and the determination of prices are but two aspects of the same problem, the optimal allocation of scarce resources. The same is true in mathematical programming.

Heretofore we have encountered prices only as data for determining the direct costs of processes and the net value of output. But of course the limiting factors of production also have value although we have not assigned prices to them up to now. In this section we shall see that the

solution of a mathematical programming problem implicitly assigns
values to the limiting factors of production. Furthermore, the implicit
pricing problem can be solved directly and, when so solved, constitutes
a solution to the optimal allocation problem.

Consider the automobile example and ask: how much is a unit (1
per cent) of each of the types of capacity worth to the firm? The
approach to this question is similar in spirit to the familiar marginal
analysis. With respect to each type of capacity we calculate how much
the maximum revenue would increase if one more unit were added, or
how much revenue would decrease if one unit were taken away. Since
there is a surplus of automobile assembly capacity, neither the addition
nor the subtraction of one unit of this type would affect the optimum
program or the maximum net revenue. Hence the value of this type of
capacity is nil. The analysis and result for truck assembly are the
same.

We find, then, that these two types of capacity are free goods. This
does not imply that an automobile assembly line is not worth having,
any more than, to take a classic example, the fact that air is a free good
means that it can be dispensed with. It means that it would not be
worth while to increase this type of capacity at any positive price and
that some units of these types could be disposed of without loss.

The valuation of the other types of capacity is not so trivial. In
Figure 9 possible values per per cent of engine assembly capacity are
scaled along the horizontal axis and values per per cent of metal stamping capacity are scaled along the vertical axis. Now consider any possible pair of values, say engine assembly capacity worth $20,000 per
unit and metal stamping worth $40,000. This is represented by point A
on the figure. Applying these values to the data on pages 548–49, the
values of capacity required for producing an automobile is found to
be: $(0.004 \times \$40,000) + (0.003 \times \$20,000) = \$220$ which is well under
the value of producing an automobile, or $300.[11] In the same way, if
engine assembly capacity is worth $60,000 per per cent of capacity and
metal stamping capacity is valued at $30,000 per unit (point B), the
cost of scarce resources required to produce an automobile will be
exactly equal to the value of the product. This is clearly not the only
combination of resource values which will precisely absorb the value of
output when the resources are used to produce automobiles. The automobile production line in the figure, which passes through point B, is
the locus of all such value combinations. A similar line has been drawn
for truck production to represent those combinations of resource values
for which the total value of resources used in producing trucks is equal

[11] These unit values are also marginal values since costs of production are constant.

to the value of output. The intersection of these two lines is obviously the only pair of resource values for which the marginal resource cost of producing an additional automobile is equal to the net value of an automobile and the same is true with respect to trucks. The pair can be found by plotting or, with more precision, by algebra. It is found that 1 per cent of engine assembly capacity is worth $9,259 and 1 per cent of metal stamping capacity is worth $68,056.

To each pair of values for the two types of capacity, there corresponds a value for the entire plant. Thus to the pair of values represented by point A there corresponds the plant value of (100 × $20,000) + (100 × $40,000) = $6,000,000. This is not the only pair of resource values which give an aggregate plant value of $6,000,000. Indeed, any pair of resource values on the dotted line through A corresponds to the same aggregate plant value. (By this stage, Figure 9 should become strongly reminiscent of Figure 1, page 549). We have drawn a number of dotted lines parallel to the one just described, each corresponding to a specific aggregate plant value. The dotted line which passes through the intersection of the two production lines is of particular interest. By measurement or otherwise this line can be found to correspond to a plant value of $7,731,500 which, we recall, was found to be the maximum attainable net revenue.

Let us consider the implications of assigning values to the two limiting factors from a slightly different angle. We have seen that as soon as unit values have been assigned to the factors an aggregate value is assigned to the plant. We can make the aggregate plant value as low as we please, simply by assigning sufficiently low values to the various factors. But if the values assigned are too low, we have the unsatisfactory consequence that some of the processes will give rise to unimputed surpluses. We may, therefore, seek the lowest aggregate plant value which can be assigned and still have no process yield an unimputed surplus. In the automobile case, that value is $7,731,500. In the course of finding the lowest acceptable plant value we find specific unit values to be assigned to each of the resources.

In this example there are two processes and four limited resources. It turns out that only two of the resources were effectively limiting, the others being in relatively ample supply. In general, the characteristics of the solution to a programming problem depend on the relationship between the number of limited resources and the number of processes taken into consideration. If, as in the present instance, the number of limited resources exceed the number of processes it will usually turn out that some of the resources will have imputed values of zero and that the number of resources with positive imputed values will be equal to the number of processes.[12] If the number of limited resources equals the number of processes all resources will have positive imputed values. If, finally, the number of processes exceeds the number of limited resources, some of the processes will not be used in the optimal program. This situation, which is the usual one, was illustrated in Figure 6. In

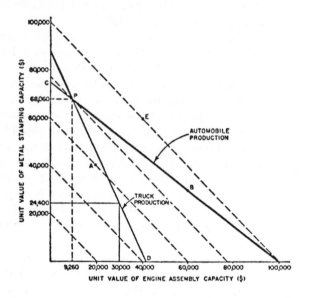

Figure 9. Automobile example, implicit values

this case the total imputed value of resources absorbed will equal net revenue for some processes and will exceed it for others. The number of processes for which the imputed value of resources absorbed equals the net revenue will be just equal to the number of limited resources and the processes for which the equality holds are the ones which will appear at positive levels in the optimal program. In brief, the determination of the minimum acceptable plant value amounts to the same thing as the determination of the optimal production program. The programming problem and the valuation problem are not only closely related, they are basically the same.

This can be seen graphically by comparing Figures 1 and 9. Each figure contains two axes and two diagonal boundary lines. But the boundary lines in Figure 9 refer to the same processes as the axes in Figure 1, and the axes in Figure 9 refer to the same resources as the

---

[12] We say "usually" in this sentence because in some special circumstances the number of resources with positive imputed values may exceed the number of processes.

diagonal boundary lines in Figure 1. Furthermore, in using Figure 1 we sought the net revenue corresponding to the highest dashed line touched by the boundary; in using Figure 9 we sought the aggregate value corresponding to the lowest dashed line which has any points on or outside the boundary; and the two results turned out to be the same. Formally stated, these two figures and the problems they represent are *duals* of each other.

The dualism feature is a very useful property in the solution of mathematical programming problems. The simplest way to see this is to note that when confronting a mathematical programming problem we have the choice of solving the problem or its dual, whichever is easier. Either way we can get the same results. We can use this feature now to generalize our discussion somewhat. Up to now when dealing with more than two processes we have had to use relatively complicated diagrams like Figure 6 because straightforward diagrams like Figure 1 did not contain enough axes to represent the levels of the processes. Now we can use diagrams modeled on Figure 9 to depict problems with any number of processes so long as they do not involve more than two scarce factors. Figure 10 illustrates a diagram for four processes and is, indeed, derived from Figure 6. In Figure 10 line A represents all pairs of factor values such that Process A would yield neither a profit nor a

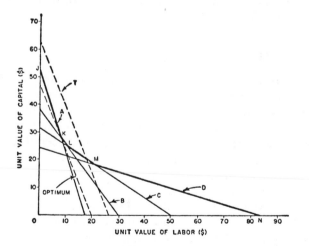

Figure 10. The valuation problem, four processes

loss. Lines B, C, and D are similarly interpreted. The dashed line T is a locus along which the aggregate value of the labor and capital available to the firm (or industry) is constant. Its position is not rele-

vant to the analysis; its slope, which is simply the ratio of the quantity
of available labor to that of capital, is all that is significant. The broken
line JKLMN divides the graph into two regions. All points on or above
it represent pairs of resource values such that no process gives rise to
an unimputed surplus. Let us call this the acceptable region. For each
point below that broken line there is at least one process which does
have an unimputed surplus. This is the unacceptable region. We then
seek for that point in the acceptable region which corresponds to
the lowest aggregate plant value. This point will, of course, give the
set of resource values which makes the accounting profit of the firm as
great as possible without giving rise to any unimputed income. The
point which meets these requirements is K, and a dotted line parallel
to T has been drawn through it to indicate the minimum acceptable
aggregate plant value.

At point K Processes A and B yield zero profits, and Processes C and
D yield losses. Hence Processes A and B are the ones which should be
used, exactly as we found in Figure 6. To be sure, this diagram does not
tell the levels at which A and B should be used, any more than Figure
6 tells the valuation to be placed on the two resources. But finding the
levels after the processes have been selected is a comparatively trivial
matter. All that is necessary is to find the levels which will fully utilize
the resources which are not free goods. This may be done algebraically
or by means of a diagram like Figure 8.

VI. APPLICATIONS

In the first section we asserted that the principal motivation of mathematical programming was the need for a method of analysis which
lent itself to the practical solution of the day-to-day problems of business and the economy in general. Immediately after making that claim
we introduced a highly artificial problem followed by a rather extended
discussion of abstract and formal relationships. The time has now
come to indicate the basis for saying that mathematical programming
is a practical method of analysis.

The essential simplification achieved in mathematical programming
is the replacement of the notion of the production function by the
notion of the process. The process is a highly observable unit of activity
and the empirical constants which characterize it can be estimated
without elaborate analysis. Furthermore in many industries the structure of production corresponds to operating a succession of processes,
as we have conceived them. Many industrial decisions, like shutting
down a bank of machines or operating an extra shift, correspond natu-

rally to our concept of choosing the level of operation of a process. In brief, mathematical programming is modelled after the actual structure of production in the hope that thereby it will involve only observable constants and directly controllable variables.

Has this hope been justified? The literature already contains a report of a successful application to petroleum refining.[13] I have made a similar application which, perhaps, will bear description. The application was to a moderate-sized refinery which produces premium and regular grades of automotive gasoline. The essential operation studied was blending. In blending, ten chemically distinct kinds of semirefined oil, called blending stocks, are mixed together. The result is a saleable gasoline whose characteristics are approximately the weighted average of the characteristics of the blending stocks. For example, if 500 gallons of a stock with octane rating of 80 are blended with 1,000 gallons of a stock with octane rating of 86 the result will be $500 + 1,000 = 1,500$ gallons of product with octane rating of $(1/3 \times 80) + (2/3 \times 86) = 84$.

The significant aspect of gasoline blending for our present purposes is that the major characteristics of the blend—its knock rating, its vapor pressure, its sulphur content, etc.—can be expressed as linear functions of the quantities of the various blending stocks used. So also can the cost of the blend if each of the blending stocks has a definite price per gallon. Thus the problem of finding the minimum cost blend which will meet given quality specifications is a problem in mathematical programming.

Furthermore, in this refinery the quantities of some of the blending stocks are definitely limited by contracts and by refining capacity. The problem then arises: what are the most profitable quantities of output of regular and premium gasoline, and how much of each blending stock should be used for each final product. This problem is analogous to the artificial automobile example, with the added complication of the quality specifications. The problem is too complicated for graphic analysis but was solved easily by arithmetical procedures. As far as is known, mathematical programming provides the only way for solving such problems. Charnes and Cooper have recently published the solution to a similar problem which arose in the operations of a metal-working firm.[14]

An entirely different kind of problem, also amenable to mathemat-

[13] A. Charnes, W. W. Cooper and B. Mellon, "Blending Aviation Gasolines," *Econometrica*, Apr. 1952, XX, 135–59.

[14] A. Charnes, W. W. Cooper, and Donald Farr and Staff, "Linear Programming and Profit Preference Scheduling for a Manufacturing Firm," *Jour. Operations Research Society of America*, May 1953, I, 114–29.

ical programming, arises in newsprint production. Freight is a major element in the cost of newsprint. One large newsprint company has six mills, widely scattered in Canada, and some two hundred customers, widely scattered in the United States. Its problem is to decide how much newsprint to ship from each mill to each customer so as, first, to meet the contract requirements of each customer, second, to stay within the capacity limits of each mill, and third, to keep the aggregate freight bill as small as possible. This problem involves 1,200 variables (6 mills × 200 customers), in contrast to the two or four variable problems we have been discussing. In the final solution most of these variables will turn out to be zero—the question is which ones. This problem is solved by mathematical programming and, though formidable, is not really as formidable as the count of variables might indicate.

These few illustrations should suffice to indicate that mathematical programming is a practical tool for business planning. They show, also, that it is a flexible tool because both examples deviated from the format of the example used in our exposition. The petroleum application had the added feature of quality specification. In the newsprint application there were limits on the quantity of output as well as on the quantities of the inputs. Nevertheless mathematical programming handled them both easily.

On the other hand, it should be noted that both of these were small-scale applications, dealing with a single phase of the operation of a single firm. I believe that this has been true of all successful applications to date. Mathematical programmers are still a long way from solving the broad planning problem of entire industries or an entire economy. But many such broad problems are only enlarged versions of problems which have been met and solved in the context of the single firm. It is no longer premature to say that mathematical programming has proved its worth as a practical tool for finding optimal economic programs.

VII. CONCLUSION

Our objective has been only to introduce the basic notions of mathematical programming and to invest them with plausibility and meaning. The reader who would learn to solve a programming problem—even the simplest—will have to look elsewhere,[15] though this paper may serve as a useful background.

15 The standard reference is T. C. Koopmans, ed., *Activity Analysis of Production and Allocation* (New York, 1951). Less advanced treatments may be found in A. Charnes, W. W. Cooper, and A. Henderson, *An Introduction to Linear Programming* (New York, 1953); and my own *Application of Linear Programming to the Theory of the Firm* (Berkeley, 1951).

Although methods of solution have been omitted from this exposition, we must emphasize that these methods are fundamental to the whole concept of mathematical programming. Some eighty years ago Walras conceived of production in very much the same manner as mathematical programmers, and more recently A. Wald and J. von Neumann used this view of production and methods closely allied to those of mathematical programming to analyze the conditions of general economic equilibrium.[16] These developments, however, must be regarded merely as precursors of mathematical programming. Programming had no independent existence as a mode of economic analysis until 1947 when G. B. Dantzig announced the "simplex method" of solution which made practical application feasible.[17] The existence of a method whereby economic optima could be explicitly calculated stimulated research into the economic interpretation of mathematical programming and led also to the development of alternative methods of solution. The fact that economic and business problems when formulated in terms of mathematical programming can be solved numerically is the basis of the importance of the method. The omission of methods of solution from this discussion should not, therefore, be taken to indicate that they are of secondary interest.

We have considered only a few of the concepts used in mathematical programming and have dealt with only a single type of programming problem. The few notions we have considered, however, are the basic ones; all the rest of mathematical programming is elaboration and extension of them. It seems advisable to mention two directions of elaboration, for they remove or weaken two of the most restrictive assumptions which have here been imposed.

The first of these extensions is the introduction of time into the analysis. The present treatment has dealt with a single production period in isolation. But in many cases, successive production periods are interrelated. This is so, for example, in the case of a vertically integrated firm where the operation of some processes in one period is limited by the levels of operation in the preceding period of the processes which supply their raw materials. Efficient methods for analyzing such

16 Walras' formulation is in *Éléments d'économie politique pure ou théorie de la richesse sociale*, 2d ed. (Lausanne, 1889), 20e Leçon. The contributions of A. Wald and J. von Neumann appeared originally in *Ergebnisse eines mathematischen Kolloquiums*, Nos. 6, 7, 8. Wald's least technical paper appeared in *Zeitschrift für Nationalökonomie*, VII (1936) and has been translated as "On some Systems of Equations of Mathematical Economics," *Econometrica*, Oct. 1951, XIX, 368–403. Von Neumann's basic paper appeared in translation as "A Model of General Economic Equilibrium," *Rev. Econ. Stud.*, 1945–46, XIII, 1–9.

17 G. B. Dantzig, "Maximization of a Linear Function of Variables Subject to Linear Inequalities," T. C. Koopmans, ed., *op. cit.*, pp. 339–47.

"dynamic" problems are being investigated, particularly by George Dantzig.[18] Although the present discussion has been static, the method of analysis can be applied to problems with a time dimension.

The second of these extensions is the allowance for changes in the prices of factors and final products. In our discussion we regarded all prices as unalterable and independent of the actions of the economic unit under consideration. Constant prices are, undeniably, a great convenience to the analyst, but the method can transcend this assumption when necessary. The general mathematical theory of dealing with variable prices has been investigated [19] and practical methods of solution have been developed for problems where the demand and supply curves are linear.[20] The assumption of constant prices, perhaps the most restrictive assumption we have made, is adopted for convenience rather than from necessity.

Mathematical programming has been developed as a tool for economic and business planning and not primarily for the descriptive, and therefore predictive, purposes which gave rise to the marginal analysis. Nevertheless it does have predictive implications. In so far as firms operate under the conditions assumed in mathematical programming it would be unreasonable to assume that they acted as if they operated under the conditions assumed by the marginal analysis. Consider, for example, the automobile firm portrayed in Figure 1. How would it respond if the price of automobiles were to fall, say by $50 a unit? In that case the net revenue per automobile would be $250, the same as the net revenue per truck. Diagrammatically, the result would be to rotate the lines of equal revenue until their slope was 45 degrees. After this rotation, point C would still be optimum and this change in prices would cause no change in optimum output. Mathematical programming gives rise, thus, to a kinked supply curve.

On the other hand, suppose that the price of automobiles were to rise by $50. Diagrammatically this price change would decrease the steepness of the equal revenue lines until they were just parallel to the metal stamping line. The firm would then be in a position like that illustrated by the YY' line in Figure 5. The production plans corresponding to points on the line segment DC in Figure 1 would all yield

[18] "A Note on a Dynamic Leontief Model with Substitution" (abstract), *Econometrica,* Jan. 1953, XXI, 179.

[19] See H. W. Kuhn and A. W. Tucker, "Non-Linear Programming," in J. Neyman, ed., *Proceedings of the Second Berkeley Symposium on Mathematical Statistics and Probability* (Berkeley, 1951), pp. 481–92.

[20] I reported one solution of this problem to a seminar at the Massachusetts Institute of Technology in September 1952. Other solutions may be known.

the same net revenue and all would be optimal. If the prices of automobiles were to rise by more than $50 or if a $50 increase in the price of automobiles were accompanied by any decrease in the price of trucks, the point of optimal production would jump abruptly from point C to point D.

Thus mathematical programming indicates that firms whose choices are limited to distinct processes will respond discontinuously to price variations: they will be insensitive to price changes over a certain range and will change their levels of output sharply as soon as that range is passed. This theoretical deduction surely has real counterparts.

The relationship between mathematical programming and welfare economics is especially close. Welfare economics studies the optimal organization of economic effort; so does mathematical programming. This relationship has been investigated especially by Koopmans and Samuelson.[21] The finding, generally stated, is that the equilibrium position of a perfectly competitive economy is the same as the optimal solution to the mathematical programming problem embodying the same data.

Mathematical programming is closely allied mathematically to the methods of input-output analysis or interindustry analysis developed largely by W. W. Leontief.[22] The two methods were developed independently, however, and it is important to distinguish them conceptually. Input-output analysis finds its application almost exclusively in the study of general economic equilibrium. It conceives of an economy as divided into a number of industrial sectors each of which is analogous to a process as the term is used in mathematical programming. It then takes either of two forms. In "open models" an input-output analysis starts with some specified final demand for the products of each of the sectors and calculates the level at which each of the sector-processes must operate in order to meet this schedule of final demands. In "closed models" final demand does not appear but attention is concentrated on the fact that the inputs required by each sector-process must be supplied as outputs by some other sector-processes. Input-output analysis then calculates a mutually compatible set of output levels for the various sectors. By contrast with mathematical programming the conditions imposed in input-output analysis are sufficient to determine the levels of the processes and there is no scope for finding an optimal

21 T. C. Koopmans, "Analysis of Production as an Efficient Combination of Activities," in T. C. Koopmans, ed., op. cit., pp. 33–97; P. A. Samuelson, "Market Mechanisms and Maximization" (a paper prepared for the Rand Corp., 1949).
22 W. W. Leontief, The Structure of American Economy 1919–1939, 2nd. ed. (New York, 1951).

solution or a set of "best" levels. To be sure, input-output analysis can be regarded as a special case of mathematical programming in which the number of products is equal to the number of processes. On the other hand, the limitations on the supplies of resources which play so important a rôle in mathematical programming are not dealt with explicitly in input-output analysis. On the whole it seems best to regard these two techniques as allied but distinct methods of analysis addressed to different problems.

Mathematical programming, then, is of significance for economic thinking and theory as well as for business and economic planning. We have been able only to allude to this significance. Indeed, apart from the exploration of welfare implications, very little thought has been given to the consequences for economics of mathematical programming because most effort has been devoted to solving the numerous practical problems to which it gives rise. The outlook is for fruitful researches into both the implications and applications of mathematical programming.

SECTION VIII

ECONOMETRICS

35

THE COSTS OF AUTOMOBILE MODEL
CHANGES SINCE 1949 *

Franklin M. Fisher, Zvi Griliches, and Carl
Kaysen † Professors Fisher and Griliches teach
at the Massachusetts Institute of Technology and
the University of Chicago, respectively. Professor
Kaysen is Director, Institute for Advanced Study,
Princeton University; he was formerly at Harvard
University.

I. INTRODUCTION: AIMS OF THE STUDY

This paper reports estimates of the costs to the consumer of the changes
in private automobile specifications that took place during the 1950's.
Throughout we concentrate on the costs that would not have been expended if cars with the 1949 [1] model lengths, weights, horsepowers,
transmissions, and other specifications had been produced in every
year. As there was technological change in the industry, we are thus
assessing not the expenditure that would have been saved had the 1949
models themselves been continued, but rather the expenditure that
would have been saved had such cars been continued but been built
with the developing technology.

We count as costs not only the costs to the automobile manufacturers
themselves of special retooling for new models, but also the direct costs
of producing larger, heavier, and more powerful cars, plus the costs of
automatic transmissions, power brakes, and the like. Finally, we include the secondary costs not paid out by the automobile companies
but paid nevertheless by the consuming public in the form of increased
expenditures for gasoline necessitated by the "horsepower race."

This procedure clearly counts as "changes" *all* changes in those speci-

---

* From *The Journal of Political Economy*, Vol. LXX (October, 1962), No. 5, pp.
433–451, copyright © by the University of Chicago Press. Reprinted by permission.
† The authors have written an abstract of this article which may be of benefit to
readers who do not have any background in statistics. The abstract appears at
the end of the full paper.
[1] 1949 is the earliest year for which all necessary data are available. It will be evident from the data that choice of 1950, 1951, or 1952 as the base year would not
substantially alter the results.

fications which directly relate to the appearance or performance of the automobile. We do not count alterations in design of the car that do not *directly* change the package the consumer thinks he is buying. Thus, we assume that horsepower is a dimension of the car that enters directly into the utility function of the car-buyer, but that engine displacement is not. This is not to say that changes in engine displacement are not relevant; it is to say that such changes are relevant only insofar as they influence one of the performance or appearance variables under consideration.

We have mentioned a consumer's utility function. The use of this concept carries with it the clear implication that the changes we consider may all have been desired by the car-buying public.[2] The question thus naturally arises: why not cost only those changes which were essentially "frills"? Why include in the estimates such things as automatic transmissions that were quite arguably improvements? The answer is that there is always a presumption of consumer sovereignty in the market economy and that it would be wholly arbitrary for us to say "this change was an improvement, and this was unnecessary" without detailed information on the utility functions of consumers. If tailfins were a frill, what about increased horsepowers? What about *extremely* increased horsepowers? Where there are costs, there are likely to be benefits as well, and, while the automobile market is not perfectly competitive, it seems likely to us that for most of the period in question the car manufacturers were giving the public what it wanted, save perhaps for overshooting in some respects.

We thus wish to avoid having this study taken as an indictment of the automobile companies. We are rather in the position of one who observes another man drinking various liquors. We do not blame the bartender for anything save that he occasionally gives the man more than he asks for of some expensive drink; nor do we question the man's right to drink; nor do we distinguish between "good" liquors and "bad." We do, however, present the bar bill. Since the argument is sometimes advanced that the resources spent on automobile model changes could be put to better use in the public sector,[3] it is clearly worth investigating the order of magnitude of the resources involved.

Section II considers the direct costs of model changes as well as the effect on advertising expenditures. Section III discusses retooling expenditures, and Section IV gasoline consumption. The results are combined and summarized in the final section, where we return to the question whether the estimated costs were worth incurring.

[2] We say "may," not "must," for the market in question is far from perfect.
[3] See, for example, J. K. Galbraith. *The Affluent Society* (Boston: Houghton Mifflin Co., 1958),p. 352 and elsewhere.

II. DIRECT COSTS AND ADVERTISING EXPENDITURES [4]

In this section we present estimates of the increases in consumer expenditures on automobiles associated with the changes in size and horsepower that have occurred since 1949. We discuss here how much more it cost to produce the, say, average 1958 car, given the 1958 levels of costs and technology, than it would have cost (at 1958 prices and with 1958 retooling expenditures) to produce a car of 1949 average specifications with the average 1949 level of "attachments." We shall treat the additional cost of the 1958 technology (above the 1949 level) —and the cost of retooling—in Section III. The "cost" estimates in this section consist of estimates of the increase in price due to increases in size and horsepower; the increase in expenditures due to the wider use of automatic transmissions, power steering, and power brakes; and the increase in price due to the increase in advertising expenditures above the 1949 levels.[5]

Only the effects of changes in size and horsepower present a difficult estimation problem, and hence only the solution to this particular problem will be discussed in some detail here. Ideally a group of engineers and cost accountants could produce the appropriate estimates of what it would cost to produce an average 1949-specifications car in each of the subsequent years. Unfortuately, we lack both the specialized knowledge and the resources required for such calculations. Instead, we make use of the apparent close relation between selected dimensions (specifications) of an automobile and its price at a point in time to estimate what the price would have been, at the same point of time, for a car with a different set of specifications.[6]

Table 1 presents the results of annual regressions of the logarithm of car prices (list) for different makes and models on the horsepower,

[4] We are indebted to G. S. Maddala for research assistance with this section. Some of the computations reported in this section, originally designed for other purposes, were supported by a grant from the National Science Foundation to the University of Chicago to allow Griliches to engage in econometric studies of technological change.

[5] The last item belongs more properly in the section dealing with the cost of a given "technology" but is discussed in this section for reasons of convenience.

[6] For a more detailed discussion of the problems associated with relating cross-sectional differences in the price of a commodity to difference in "quality," dimentions, or specifications see Z. Griliches, "Hedonic Price Indexes for Automobiles: An Econometric Analysis of Quality Change" (Bureau of the Budget-NBER Price Statistics Review Committee Staff Report No. 3, printed in United States Congress, Joint Economic Committee, *Government Price Statistics*, Hearings . . . January 24, 1961, [Washington, Government Printing Office, 1961], pp. 173–96), and the literature cited there.

weight, and length of these cars, and on a set of classificatory ("dummy") variables for other "qualities such as whether a car has a V-8 engine, whether an automatic transmission is included in the list price (is "standard" equipment), and so forth. As can be seen from these results, the use of three numerical variables (horsepower, weight, and length) and several dummy variables explains, on the average, 90 per cent or more of the cross-sectional variance in the logarithm of list prices at a point of time. While the coefficients of particular dimensions are not very stable, the direction of their change over time (for example, the fall in the relative "price" of horsepower [7] and length) is consistent with other evidence and what we know about the industry.[8]

The regressions presented in Table 1 are used to estimate what would have been the list price of a car with the specifications of the average 1949 car each year since 1949.[9] This series and that of the average list prices of the cars actually produced move closely together until about 1954 when they begin to diverge, the difference (shown in col. [1] of Table 2) reaching its maximum in 1959 and then declining slightly. During the 1956–61 period the difference between the average list price of the cars actually produced and the predicted price for the average 1949 car averaged approximately $450 per car, or about 17 per cent of the actual average list price.

The calculated price differences shown in column (1) of Table 2 are subject to several reservations. First of all they are based on list prices and may not represent the trend of actual prices adequately. In particular, if actual prices paid fell relative to list prices, the actual difference in price will be overestimated by our procedure. If, for example,

[7] In particular, the fall in the relative "price" of horsepower clearly stems from the technological change in horsepower-engine size relation studied explicitly in Sec. IV below.

[8] Similar regressions were also run in linear form (rather than the semi-log form reported here) and using "piston displacement in cubic inches" as an additional variable without any improvement over the reported results. The "insignificance" of the displacement variable is due to its extremely high correlation with horsepower. Since we are primarily interested in costing horsepower, we introduce it here directly rather than going through a circuitous procedure such as that necessary in Sec. IV.

Estimates were also made using several cross-sections at a time, imposing the condition that the various slope coefficients be the same for different years, but allowing the level of average prices ("technology") to shift "neutrally" over time, by assigning a separate constant term for each cross-section. The results were similar to those reported here and, since they do not lead to substantially different estimates or interpretations, are not reproduced here. Some of these estimates have been presented in Z. Griliches, "Hedonic Price Indexes . . . ," op. cit.

[9] In view of the form of our regressions, if profit margins and wholesale-retail markups are roughly constant in percentage terms, or at least uncorrelated with the various specification variables, this is also an estimate of "costs."

Table 1. Coefficients of Single-Year Cross-Sectional Regressions Relating
Logarithm of New United States Passenger-Car Prices to Various
Specifications, Annually 1950–61

Model year	No.	Constant	Coefficients* of				R^2
			H	W	L	V	
1950	72	1.2709	.158	.0484	.832	− .024	.892
			(.048)	(.0285)	(.115)	(.014)	
1951	55	1.4329	.117	.017	.818	.012	.909
			(.054)	(.031)	(.116)	(.013)	
1952	51	1.7174	.097	.105	.578	− .020	.927
			(.042)	(.030)	(.127)	(.015)	
1953	54	1.9328	.113	.103	.471	− .034	.891
			(.044)	(.038)	(.136)	(.020)	
1954	65	2.3766	.202	− .026	.398	− .024	.857
			(.037)	(.042)	(.106)	(.014)	
1955	55	2.4570	.118	.095	.202	− .050	.871
			(.059)	(.050)	(.128)	(.026)	
1956	87	2.3359	.065	.163	.192	− .052	.907
			(.027)	(.027)	(.079)	(.016)	
1957	95	2.7370	.051	.059	.171	− .011 plus significant	.967
			(.013)	(.017)	(.057)	(.010) coefficients for T, A, P, B	
1958	103	3.0389	.007	.142	− .073	.005 plus T, A, P, B	.906
			(.018)	(.026)	(.092)	(.021)	
1959	87	3.1077	.052	.103	− .068	− .031 plus T, A, P	.939
			(.013)	(.017)	(.065)	(.016)	
1960	78	2.9723	.052	.059	.065	− .017 plus T, A, P, C	.951
			(.009)	(.020)	(.073)	(.011)	
1961	99	2.2530	.026	.132	.309	.011 plus T, P, C	.940
			(.011)	(.017)	(.080)	(.012)	

* Dependent variable—logarithm of "list" (advertised delivered) price. Logarithms to the base 10. To convert the results to natural logarithms multiply all coefficients by 2.3. The resulting coefficient, if multiplied by 100, would measure the *percentage* impact on price of a *unit* change in a particular specification or "quality," holding the other specifications constant.

H, advertised brake horsepower, in 100's.

W, shipping weight in 1,000 pounds.

L, over-all length, in hundreds of inches.

V, 1 if the car has a V-8 engine; 0 if it has a 6-cylinder or less engine.

T, 1 if the car is a hardtop; 0 if not.

A, 1 if automatic transmission is "standard" equipment (included in price); 0 if not.

P, 1 if power steering is "standard"; 0 if not.

B, 1 if power brakes are "standard"; 0 if not.

C, 1 if the car is designated as a "compact"; 0 if not.

Source: *Specifications and prices, 1949, 1951–53:* Annual statistical issues (March 15) of *Automotive Industries* and annual issue of *Automotive News Almanac. 1954–60:* Various issues of National Automobile Dealers Association's *Used Car Guide*, Washington. *1955–58:* Data are from the February issue of the corresponding year. For 1954 models, figures are taken from July, 1959, issue, for 1959 models, from January, 1959, issue: and for 1960, from December, 1959, issue. *1950 and 1961: Red*

discounts from list price increased from zero in 1949 to an average of about 15 per cent in 1960, then the average figure given for 1956–61 should be about $380 per car rather than the estimated $450.[10] On the other hand, we have priced *all* cars at their four-door sedan prices, not taking into account the faster growth in the number of higher priced station wagons, convertibles, and other car models. Since our equations make percentage changes in price depend on changes in absolute specification levels, a higher "true" average price would lead also to a higher estimate of the difference.

Third, these and later calculations are based on "predictions" from statistically estimated equations that do not fit the data perfectly and hence are subject to error. The probable magnitude of this error can be calculated, however. The standard error of the regression line (the "standard" prediction error at the mean levels of the independent variables) is quite high for any one year. It averaged about $170 in the 1956–61 regressions. Thus, there is some doubt whether any *one* particular annual difference is statistically significantly different from zero. The consistency in the sign of these differences leaves little doubt, however, about their significance for the 1956–61 period as a whole. The quoted figures should thus provide a good estimate of the orders of magnitude that are involved here, since in no case were the average 1949 specifications outside the range of the observed variation in the specifications of later model-year cars. We are always interpolating rather than extrapolating to get at our "predictions."

The next set of "cost" estimates is very simple. Columns (2)–(4) of

Book: *Official Used Car Appraisals* (Chicago: National Market Reports, Inc.). November 14, 1956, and January 1–February 14, 1961. Some 1961 data are also based on *Car Fax* (Vol. VI, No. 1, 1961 ed., New York). Power brakes data for some years are taken from various issues of *Ward's Automotive Yearbook*. Prices of automatic transmissions, power steering, and power brakes are taken from various issues of *Automotive News Almanac* and from October 1–November 14, 1958, issue of the *Red Book*.

Production Data: 1956–60 by model years by makes is taken from *Automotive Industries*, March 15, 1961. 1961 model-year data are from *Automotive News*, August 7, 1961. For 1955 it was assumed that the model year began in November of the previous year; for 1954 that the model year was January–October, model-year production by makes was computed from monthly production figures by make given in the 1955 and 1956 March 15 issues of *Automotive Industries*. For 1949–53 it was assumed that the model year coincided approximately with the calendar year; calendar-year production data by makes were taken from *ibid*. Data on models within makes and on V-8 engine, automatic transmissions, and power steering and brakes installations were available only for calendar years based on registration data (*Ward's Automotive Yearbook*, various issues). These data were transformed into percentages of a particular make, and these calendar-year within-make percentages were used to break down the model year production figures by makes to arrive at model-year production figures by makes *and* models. For 1961 we used 1960 calendar-year data on models within makes to break down the 1961 model-year production data by makes.

[10] For data on discounts see A. F. Jung, "Price Policy and Discounts in the Medium- and High-priced Car Market," *Journal of Business*, October 1960, pp. 342–47.

Table 2. Total "Direct" Costs of Automobile Change since 1949

Model Year	Per car cost of increase in						Total passenger car production (000's)	Total "direct" cost of model change† ($ millions)
	Size and horsepower*	Use of optional equipment			Advertising Expense	Total		
		Automatic transmission	Power steering	Power brakes				
	(1)	(2)	(3)	(4)	(5)	(6)	(7)	(8)
1950	$-13	$12	...	...	$-3	$-4	6,659	-27
1951	17	33	$2	...	-2	50	5,331	267
1952	58	38	9	$1	0	106	4,337	460
1953	11	35	22	3	0	71	6,135	436
1954	160	55	21	7	3	246	4,359	1,072
1955	279	70	23	9	10	391	6,201	2,425
1956	377	72	14	6	14	483	6,295	3,040
1957	518	86	25	9	13	651	6,218	4,048
1958	410	86	31	10	16	553	4,256	2,354
1959	520	87	30	9	14	660	5,568	3,675
1960	447	75	31	9	13	575	6,011	3,456
1956–60 average	...	...	...	...	...	584	...	3,315

Source: See Table 1.
* The regressions presented in Table 1 were used to predict the price of a car with average 1949 specifications. The specifications of the average 1949 car used in these predictions were: horsepower—104.24, weight—3,289.5 pounds, length—200.84 inches, and fraction with V-8 engines—0.4067.
† Col. (6) × col. (7).

Table 2 present the estimated cost (per car) of the increased use of automatic transmissions, power steering, and power brakes. In each case we took a time series of list prices, a time series on the increase in the percentage use of these items (since 1949) as optional equipment (not already included in the price as "standard" equipment), and computed the "cost" per car as the product of these two series. Again, these "costs" reach their peak in 1958 or 1959.

Column (5) of Table 2 presents the estimated increases in advertising expenditures associated with the above-described model changes. We took a time series of advertising expenditures per car (for calendar years) from *Advertising Age*. These data are of doubtful quality but are used for lack of a better source. The main difficulty here is to devise a measure of the 1949 *quantity* of advertising per car in subsequent prices. We attempt to approximate such a measure by inflating the 1949 average advertising expenditures per car by the implicit GNP deflator. This deflator probably rises less than advertising *rates,* but the real cost of reaching and informing a particular consumer must have fallen somewhat during this period. Television rates, for example, have clearly not risen in proportion to the increase in the number of viewers. If anything, these calculations probably underestimate the "real" increase in the *quantity* of advertising per car. We estimated the "cost" of increased advertising as the difference between current advertising expenditures per car and the 1949 advertising expenditure level in current prices. Again these "costs" reach their peak in 1958.

The total direct cost of model changes (col. [8]) is estimated for each year by totaling the above described estimates (col. [6]) and multiplying them by the annual passenger-car production figures (col. [7]). For 1956–60 these costs averaged about $3.3 billion annually. This is probably an underestimate since we have left out of our calculations such other changes as the optional purchase of higher horsepower engines, power seats, power windows, various optional "trim" items, and so forth. On the other hand, allowing for the growth of discounting would reduce this figure to about $2.8 billion annually. In addition, the "prediction error" (two standard deviations) associated with these figures could lead them to be too high *or* too low by about $1.0 billion.

III. RETOOLING EXPENDITURES [11]

The most obvious cost of automobile model changes is the expenditure by the automobile manufacturers for the new tools, jigs, and dies

[11] We are grateful to Lloyd Dollett, of the Securities and Exchange Commission, for his courtesy and assistance. The computations in this section were performed by Felicity Skidmore. We are indebted to members of the Harvard Research Seminar in Quantitative Economics for suggestions.

needed to produce new models. Were models to remain unchanged, such expenditures would clearly be reduced to the level necessary to replace existing equipment as it wears out.

Of course, such expenditures on the physical equipment of production are not the only ones directly associated with model changes. There are, in addition, the costs of research and development and of design of the new models. Unlike the expenditures for retooling, however, the latter costs are not available, and we shall thus not be able to include them in our estimates. The exclusion of these costs, however, is not *wholly* undesirable. In the preceding section and in the following one we charge as "costs" expenditures that could have been avoided by producing cars with 1949 specifications *with the current technology*. It would clearly be inconsistent to charge also the costs of securing that technology. Since the development in which we are interested has been largely in engine design (see the next section), taking the form of reducing the "cost" of horsepower, it seems likely that the costs of securing that technology are a much larger part of research and development and design costs than of retooling expenditures. It follows that we are largely avoiding double counting here.[12]

It may appear, however, that we are double counting by including retooling expenditures as well as the direct costs discussed in the last section. Retooling expenditures are costs to the automobile companies and are presumably reflected in the prices of new cars which we already used in the regressions and computations of the previous section. It seems to follow that we have already included retooling expenditures (and research and development and design costs) implicitly in our estimates of direct costs. This is not the case, however. We used the regressions of the last section to estimate the direct costs of producing cars with 1949 specifications with current technology. But the costs of retooling (which are reflected in our regressions) are also reflected in such estimates. Hence our estimated direct costs for 1949 specification cars are *overestimates* of the costs that would have been incurred had no model changes taken place, since in the latter event the prices of all cars would have been lower because of the elimination of retooling costs. It is thus not double counting to add retooling expenditures at this point.[13]

[12] Since we are not estimating "secondary" costs other than gasoline consumption, we feel safe in saying that the inclusion of retooling expenditures leaves our estimates on the low side.

[13] One qualification is necessary. If the recoupment of retooling costs in car prices is correlated with specifications, we have already counted some of it. In view of the semi-logarithmic form of our regressions, however, this effect will cancel out if it is roughly proportional to car price. This seems likely, since retooling expenditures per car are probably greater for high-priced models. In any case, such a

As our estimates of retooling expenditures, we took the expenditures for special tools included in additions to plant and property reported by the automobile firms to the Securities and Exchange Commission [14] and charged by them to current costs. The relevant figures are available by calendar year; for the most part we have interpreted them as applicable to the model year following that calendar year.[15] The figures are available for the full period we consider, save that the Ford figures are only available beginning with the 1953 model year, and figures for Studebaker are not available before the merger with Packard. These problems were handled as follows.[16]

> *Ford.*—In 1953, Ford retooling expenditures were 10 per cent of the total. We have added 10 per cent to the totals for the preceding years.
> *Studebaker.*—In 1954, expenditures by Packard were 1.3 per cent of the total (adjusted to include Ford). In 1955, expenditures by Studebaker-Packard were 3.7 per cent. We therefore added 2.4 per cent to the total for each year before 1955.

Clearly, the first adjustment is the only one of any importance; it seems conservative in view of higher Ford expenditures in later years.

To allow for normal replacement of worn-out equipment, we ignored the fact that 1949 was a year of substantial model change and assumed that all expenditure for that model year was for replacement of worn-out equipment; this yielded an upper limit of $190 billion for normal replacement expenditures. Taking into account model changes

---

bias in our results cannot be large, for despite the huge increase in retooling expenditures over the period, our regressions show declining "prices" for specifications even after technological change in engine design practically ceased (as evidenced by our results of the next section). Moreover, the double counting engendered by this effect applies only to a part of the full retooling expenditure. We therefore feel fairly safe in neglecting it.

[14] Form 10K, Schedule V.

[15] The only exceptions are Willys-Overland and Nash and later American Motors, which report for the year ended September 30. (Neither of these is a large part of the total, and the first is clearly negligible.) We have still assumed that such expenditures took place at the *end* of the reporting year and were for the *following* model year. This seems clearly to have been the case since about 1955 but is less certain before that time. Readjustment to account for this (if needed) would be only one of timing and would make very little difference in the industry totals in any case.

[16] Figures for Hudson in 1953 and Kaiser in 1950 are also missing. We did not bother to adjust the totals for this, because the first figure was clearly only about 1 per cent of the total at the most, and the second was much less.

in 1949, $150 billion seems more than ample as an estimate of normal replacement expenditures (especially in view of the expenditure of only $175 million on retooling in 1950) and we used this figure adjusted for changes in the wholesale price index for metalworking machinery. The resulting costs and costs per car (including 8 per cent for taxes that would have been saved) are presented in Table 3.

IV. GASOLINE CONSUMPTION [17]

A. The Data

This section deals with the saving in gasoline consumption that would have been effected had the "horsepower race" not occurred—had 1949 specifications been continued. To estimate this saving requires detailed

Table 3.   Retooling Costs of Model Changes since 1949

| Model year | Millions of current dollars | | Cost per car* (current dollars) (3) |
	Total expenditures for special tools (1)	Retooling costs attributable to model changes (2)	
1950	175.3	19.6	2.9
1951	208.5	45.2	8.5
1952	262.8	81.7	18.8
1953	419.5	246.5	40.2
1954	439.1	263.5	60.5
1955	632.7	469.2	75.7
1956	523.3	336.2	53.4
1957	947.3	771.7	124.1
1958	827.8	625.7	147.0
1959	745.8	532.1	95.6
1960	756.5	536.6	89.3
1961	896.5	678.9	125.6
1956–60 average	760.1	560.5	98.9

* Production data 1950–60 from Table 2; 1961 estimated production from *Automotive News*, August 7, 1961.

[17] We should like to thank our research assistants, Stephen A. Resnick and David Shapiro, who secured most of the data here discussed; George Delehanty, who computed the weights for the relative importance of makers' models within automobile makes; and Felicity Skidmore and Cynthia M. Travis, who performed most of the computations directly relevant to gasoline consumption. The materials in this section of the study and based on work done for other purposes under a grant from Resources for the Future, Inc., to Massachusetts Institute of Technology to allow Fisher to study quantitative aspects of the economics of supply and demand in the petroleum industry.

data by model on miles per gallon performance of automobiles. The only such data available are the figures on miles per gallon during the period of ownership reported by Consumers Union and Consumer Research (principally the former) for 185 different models tested over the period 1948–July, 1961.[18]

B. Fuel Economy and Engine Size

There has been considerable technological progress in engine design over the last fifteen years. In particular, as the automobile manufacturers moved toward higher and higher horsepower cars in the middle and late fifties, they also redesigned engines to secure higher horsepower for a given engine size. This had the dual effect of reducing the extra gasoline consumption attendant on horsepower increases and (as noted in Sec. II) of reducing the direct cost of horsepower. Accordingly, we had to find some way of measuring such progress in engine design in order to estimate the gasoline consumption that would have occurred had cars with 1949 horsepowers been built in each successive year *with the developing technology.*

Since the available test statistics for any given year are too scanty to allow us to analyze each year's models wholly separately (as in Sec. II)— our solution was a compromise between the need for enough data to perform any analysis and the impossibility of pooling the test data in any simple way because automobiles with different types of transmission cannot be simply lumped together for such purposes. We proceeded to break the problem into two parts: the relation of engine size to gasoline consumption and the effect of horsepower on engine size. The former relation was studied by pooling all test data for cars with a given transmission; the latter effect was studied by analyzing engine data for each successive year separately. This procedure involved the assumption that technological change was largely restricted to changes in engine design or in the type of transmission employed (we were able to use a moderately fine breakdown by transmission types) rather than acting to alter the effects of existing transmissions without changing their type.[19]

Consumer Reports each year presents a statistic which they term "Fuel Economy Factor" and which we shall denote by F. This statistic is "the cubic feet of cylinder volume swept by the pistons on their suc-

---

[18] Other reported data are generally either for constant-speed tests, or highly aggregated.

[19] Visual inspection of the residuals from our regressions seems to bear this out, as there does not seem to be any tendency for the scatter in the relation of gasoline consumption to engine size, given transmission type, to change over time.

tion strokes while the car travels one mile in high gear." [20] If engine displacement (D) is measured in cubic inches and the number of engine revolutions per mile in top gear is denoted by R, then:

$$F = \frac{R}{2}\left(\frac{D}{1728}\right). \tag{1}$$

R, in turn, is dependent on wheel size and axle ratio, while D, as we shall see, is highly correlated with horsepower for a given engine type. Statements in *Consumer Reports* clearly imply that, if these data are segregated by type of transmission, they should be related to F.[21] This indeed turns out to be the case.

As already stated, F is defined for the performance of the car in its top gear. It would be possible to construct similar variables which measure performance in lower gears, but these would of course be almost perfectly correlated with F, for either manual or automatic transmissions, given the limited number of forward gears. However, even if we were to use such similar variables for lower gears, it would still be incorrect to regress gasoline consumption on them, pooling observations for cars with a different number of forward gears; the distribution of mileage over the different forward gears will not be the same for a car with four such gears as for a car with three or two. It follows that the coefficients in such regressions will be different for cars with a different number of forward gears. This being so, our data must be segregated by the number of forward gears before F can be used as the only "displacement-type" variable in the regression.[22] Accordingly, we segregated the data into 2-speed automatics, 3-speed automatics, 4-speed automatics, manuals without overdrive, and manuals with overdrive. Fortunately, the test data are sufficiently numerous to support the ensuing analysis.[23] We therefore regressed gallons per 10,000 miles of car travel (denoted by G) on F for each of the five transmission categories.

As already remarked, the true relationship we are seeking is one between G and variables similar to F reflecting performance in various gears as well as during idling periods. Given our segregation by transmission type, such variables are almost perfectly correlated with F, and we thus use F alone. However, the goodness of fit of the true relationship—and, therefore, of our estimated one as well—clearly depends on

[20] "U.S. Autos 1961," *Consumer Reports*, XXVI, No. 4 (April, 1961), 176.

[21] *Ibid.*

[22] F can be used also as the sole explanatory variable in the regressions, because such other variables as automobile weight enter principally into the determination of the characteristics and especially the size of the engine.

[23] For the period 1949–61, there are almost no tests of semi-automatic transmissions, but the number of cars with such transmissions is negligible.

the stability of the distribution of mileage over the various forward speeds or gears (and, less importantly, of the distribution of time between idling and motion) over the tests reported. Since this distribution is not very stable, we expect to find somewhat low (though statistically significant) correlations.[24] On the other hand, the relative stability of this distribution will depend on how much choice is left to the driver as to when to shift gears. We should, therefore, expect to find higher correlations for automatic-transmission cars than for manual-transmission cars, other things being equal. A similar argument leads us to expect higher correlation for 2-speed automatics than for 3-speed ones, for 3-speed automatics than for 4-speed ones, and for cars with manual transmissions than for those with overdrive.[25]

All these predictions as to the relative size of the R^2's are borne out by the results (Table 4). Their agreement with our predictions gives us some confidence in their relevance.

C. Engine Size and Horsepower [26]

The present section is concerned with the effects of horsepower on F, our measure of engine size. These effects are assumed to operate only on engine displacement, D, the principal determinant of F, an innocuous assumption as the number of engine revolutions per mile, R, the other variable in equation (1), does not vary greatly from model to model.

As our measure of horsepower, we take "maximum advertised horsepower" (as in Sec. II), despite the fact that this variable is based on stripped engine performance rather than on actual power delivered to the rear wheels.[27] We considered the effects of transmission characteristics in the previous section. Moreover, if advertised horsepower is what the car-buyer thinks he is buying, it is advertised horsepower whose cost we wish to ascertain.

For a given type of engine and given engine efficiency, engine displacement (D) and horsepower (H) are theoretically proportional. Ac-

---

24 Cf. comments on the test statistics in "Road-test Report on the Full-size 'Low-priced' V-8's," *Consumer Reports*, XXVI, No. 2 (February, 1961), 107.

25 Since the variability of the distribution of mileage over forward speeds can be expected to be relatively high (*ceteris paribus*) when the number of forward speeds is large and the amount of shifting among them consequently great.

26 We are indebted to A. R. Rogowski, of the Department of Mechanical Engineering at M.I.T., for preliminary discussion of some of the technical matters covered in this section. He is emphatically not to be held responsible for our opinions, conclusions, results, or especially errors, nor for the evidently rudimentary state of our information on automotive mechanics.

27 Cf. "U.S. Autos 1961," *op. cit.*, p. 176.

tual engines, however, were redesigned during the 1950's to permit the construction of high-horsepower engines at relatively lower displacements.[28] Accordingly, we did not pool observations from different years but estimated instead the relationship separately for each year.[29]

The fact that, for a given engine type, horsepower and displacement are roughly proportional implies that technological change takes the form of shifting a ray through the origin. Not all developments in engine design, however, can be applied to all horsepowers. Hence, while the points for a given engine type lie on a ray through the origin, not all points on that ray can represent actual engines. Successive techno-

Table 4. Regressions of Gasoline Consumption (G) on Consumer Reports' Fuel Economy Factor (F)

Transmission type	Regression equation	r^2	No.
2-speed automatic	$G = 214 + 2.38*F$ (0.287)	.748	27
3-speed automatic	$G = 248 + 2.18*F$ (0.179)	.693	68
4-speed automatic	$G = 380 + 1.54*F$ (0.359)	.368	35
Manual without overdrive	$G = 240 + 1.79*F$ (0.388)	.422	31
Manual with overdrive	$G = 308 + 1.68†F$ (0.648)	.233	24

* Significant at 0.1 per cent level.   † Significant at 2 per cent level.

logical changes which are aimed at higher horsepower engines become applicable at successively higher horsepower levels. Thus our regressions, save for the early years, are estimates not primarily of the relationship between displacement and horsepower for a given engine type but of the relationship between engine design and horsepower.[30] We are estimating the effect of higher horsepower on the availability of displacement-horsepower ratio reducing techniques. The fact that we obtain such a good fit leads us to accept a linear form for that relation-

[28] This redesign took the form largely of raising compression ratios and of shifting the torque-rpm curve. The rising octane content of gasoline also helped.

[29] The observations in these computations were on engines rather than on cars. We eliminated observations on other models produced by a given company that had the same engine.

[30] Since the correlation between horsepower and displacement is so high for each year, and this is the relationship of interest, there is no need to introduce the effect on compression ratios as an explicit step..

Table 5. Regressions of Displacement (D) on Maximum Advertised
          Horsepower (H)

Model year	Regression equation	r^2	No.
1948	$D =$ 0.738 + 2.30*H (17.0) (0.155)	.880	32
1949	$D =$ 6.24 + 2.17*H (12.0) (0.106)	.938	30
1950	$D =$ 6.29 + 2.14*H (13.8) (0.120)	.908	34
1951	$D =$ 11.4 + 2.04*H (11.1) (0.0963)	.930	36
1952	$D =$ 30.0† + 1.80*H (11.1) (0.0900)	.917	38
1953	$D =$ 70.3* + 1.42*H (12.2) (0.0946)	.851	41
1954	$D =$ 82.2* + 1.26*H (14.1) (0.0987)	.798	43
1955	$D =$ 112* + 0.938*H (10.8) (0.0595)	.883	35
1956	$D =$ 103* + 0.950*H (10.4) (0.0505)	.912	36
1957	$D =$ 108* + 0.860*H (11.1) (0.0472)	.910	35
1958	$D =$ 109* + 0.856*H (11.6) (0.0444)	.921	34
1959	$D =$ 101* + 0.914*H (10.4) (0.0390)	.945	34
1960	$D =$ 109* + 0.851*H (19.2) (0.0783)	.797	32
1961	$D =$ 73.4* + 1.07*H (12.2) (0.0564)	.914	36

* Significant at 0.1 per cent level.
† Significant at 1 per cent level.

ship, and our faith in it is further bolstered by the fact that in every
year the range of horsepowers covered in the data is extremely wide.
Further, the 1949 horsepowers are all inside that range, so that we shall
be interpolating between actual figures in applying our results to them.

It is important to realize that the relationship between D and H is
exactly what we want. To take a given engine type and extend the line
for high-horsepower cars backward toward the origin would give a
most misleading overestimate of the extent to which the developing
technology could have been used to effect gasoline economies at 1949
horsepowers. The engine redesigns for high-horsepower cars simply
could not have been applied to these lower levels. Our estimates, how-

ever, provide precisely the required information: the extent to which advances in engine design are applicable at *given* horsepowers.

The results of these regressions are presented in Table 5.[31] We report standard errors for the constant terms, as the question of whether the regression line passes through the origin is obviously of interest. These results show a clear pattern. Starting with the expected ray through the origin in 1948, there is a slight decline in the slope to 1950–51, without much change in intercept. From 1952 to 1955, the slope diminishes rapidly and the intercept rises substantially.[32] From 1955 through 1961 the coefficients remain roughly constant.[33]

This pattern is to be expected from the preceding discussion. Starting with the ray through the origin which represents the displacement-horsepower relation for a given engine type, minor improvements took at first the form of lowering the slope of that ray slightly (making horsepower cheaper in terms of displacement). With the start of the horsepower race, this effect was accompanied by the introduction of new rays, with lower slopes, attainable only at higher and higher horsepowers. The result in regression terms is depicted schematically in Figure 1, with R_1, R_2, and R_3 representing three engine types, representative of a whole spectrum of techniques (largely higher compression ratios and efficient use of high octane gasoline) available at higher horsepowers. The dashed portion of each ray represents that part of the ray which is unavailable, while the dotted circle shows the range of observations on the ray. *BC* is the resulting estimated regression line. As the horsepower race progressed, new rays became available to the right of R_3 at higher horsepowers, while existing techniques were used to produce higher horsepower engines at given displacements. The effect of all this was to shift *BC* upward and lower its slope. Finally, with the slackening of the horsepower race and the introduction of the compact cars, existing techniques were used to produce the required

[31] We present the results for the model years 1948–61 inclusive since the pattern seems of interest.

[32] Note that this change in the slope coefficients reflects itself (roughly) as a change in the direct cost of horsepower already reported in Sec. II.

[33] This pattern is not simply the result of sampling fluctuations. The hypothesis that all the regressions are from the same true relationship is emphatically rejected by covariance analysis, the relevant F statistic being 28.9, whereas the probability of observing an F even as high as about 2.1 if the hypothesis were true would be .001 (with 26 and 468 degrees of freedom). Moreover, such significant inhomogeneity is not merely due to the behavior of the intercepts. A further test of slope equality only yields an F statistic of 29.1, whereas the probability of observing an F even as high as about 2.7 if the slopes were all the same would be .001 (with 13 and 468 degrees of freedom). It is thus apparent that our results reflect real changes in structure for the period as a whole (similar tests would doubtless fail to reject the null hypothesis of no structural change for 1955–60).

lower horsepower engines, thus sliding the dotted circles back toward the origin, shifting the regression line *BC* downward and raising its slope slightly.

The magnitude of these effects is of some interest. Our results indicate that a car in the 80–90 horsepower range (slightly below the range encountered for most low-priced cars) would have had a roughly constant displacement up until 1961 when a very moderate decline in displacement would have occurred. At 100 horsepower, displacement fell from about 230 cubic inches in 1948 to 194 cubic inches in 1960 and 180 in 1961. At 200 horsepower, however, displacement fell from about 460 cubic inches in 1948 to about 280 in 1960 and 1961. At higher horsepowers, the fall was, of course, greater. In all cases, most of the reduction occurred in the 1951–55 period.

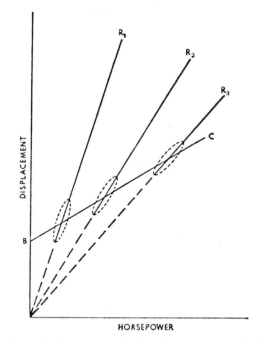

Figure 1. Illustration of technological change in the
horsepower-displacement relationship

D. GASOLINE COSTS OF MODEL CHANGES

The relations summarized in Tables 4 and 5 were used to estimate the saving in gasoline consumption that would have been expected had 1949 specifications been continued. First, we estimated the gasoline consumption per 10,000 miles of each actually produced automobile model. Where Consumer Union test data were unavailable, we estimated ("predicted") it from the appropriate equation in Table 4, using "fuel economy factors" computed from published engine displacement and rpm data. These "predictions," together with the actual test data, where available, were then aggregated to produce comparable figures for company brand names such as Chevrolet, Ford, and Dodge, using (as in Sec. II) weights constructed from model-year production data

Table 6. Miles Per Gallon Performance of New Actual and Constant 1949 Specification Cars

Model year	Miles per gallon, new actual cars	Miles per gallon, new 1949 specification cars	Extra cost of new actual cars per 10,000 miles* (current dollars)
1949	16.4	....	....
1950	16.4	16.7	3.1
1951	15.7	16.9	12.5
1952	16.0	17.1	11.4
1953	16.1	17.2	11.7
1954	15.6	17.3	18.4
1955	15.1	17.4	26.8
1956	14.8	17.7	34.6
1957	14.5	17.9	42.4
1958	14.4	17.9	43.2
1959	14.3	18.0	44.3
1960	15.3	18.0	30.6
1961	15.2†	18.5	37.2‡

* Valued at prices in Table 7 (below).
† 1960 weights used.
‡ At 1960 prices.

where available and from calendar-year registration data otherwise.[34] These figures were in turn averaged to secure average figures for the industry for each model year, 1949–60, using as weights actual production data by brand name, where available, or registrations as of July 1 of the year following the close of the model year.

To estimate the gasoline consumption that would have been incurred

[34] The basic assumption in the latter case was that the *internal* distribution of each brand name over the various maker's models it included was the same for the calendar year as for the model year. This involved a host of minor problems of comparability between successive year's models too numerous to discuss in detail. The registration data are collected by R. L. Polk & Co., and reported in several trade journals.

by cars with 1949 specifications, we took first each 1949 model's horse-power and used the results of Part C of this section to estimate what the model's displacement would have been in each successive year. From these estimates we selected as the displacement figure for each year the minimum of the displacements estimated for that model from 1950 to the year in question and the actual displacement for 1949. These displacements were then transformed into fuel economy factors using equation (1) from Part B and assuming that engine revolutions per mile in high gear would have been the same as in 1949. The result-ing values of F were then transformed into gasoline consumption per 10,000 miles by use of the results of Part B of this section.

These estimated gasoline consumption figures were aggregated into brand-name figures using the 1949 weights. The results were then ag-gregated in turn into industry figures using registrations of 1949 cars as of July 1, 1950.[35] The resulting estimates of miles per gallon per-formance for both the actual and the constant 1949 specification cars are given in Table 6 for model years 1949 through 1960.

Table 6 shows that, while gasoline mileage was declining from 16.4 miles per gallon in 1949 to 14.3 miles per gallon in 1959, it could have been rising to 18.0 miles per gallon had 1949 specifications been con-tinued. Even the rise to 15.3 miles per gallon that occurred with the introduction of the compacts in 1960 fell far short of the actual 1949 level, let alone the level that could have been achieved. In money terms, the average owner of a 1959 car (the most gasoline-consuming model year) was paying about $44 per 10,000 miles more for gasoline than would have been the case with 1949 specifications—about 20 per cent of his total gasoline expenditures. For high-price high-horsepower cars, the additional cost was even greater.

Unlike the costs discussed in the last two sections, the costs of extra gasoline consumption do not terminate with the building and sale of the car; they continue over the life of the automobile. We must there-fore estimate the total gasoline consumption of that part of the car *stock* consisting of cars built after 1949 that would have been avoided in each year with constant 1949 specification.[36]

35 We assume here and below that the distribution of 1949 cars by brand names would have been preserved had 1949 specification been continued. Since brand market shares have not changed very much, this is not an important assumption.

36 We must make here some assumption about the change in gasoline consumption over the life of a car. Since we are primarily interested in the *difference* between the gasoline consumption of the actual car stock and of one made up of 1949 specification cars, we have only to assume that the effect of age on gasoline con-sumption is linear and the same in both cases, so that with the same age distribu-tion of cars in the car stock, the difference in gasoline consumption will be unaffected.

To construct estimates of gasoline consumption by actual post-1949 cars for each year, we took the average gasoline consumption by brand name and model year derived above and multiplied them by the registration figure for that brand name and model year as of July 1 of the year in question. The basic assumption used in the construction of estimates of the gasoline consumption of the constant 1949 specification car stock was that the history of these cars would have duplicated the actual history of the 1949 models, so far as the distribution in any year t of such cars over brand names is concerned.[37]

The resulting estimates of gasoline consumption by post-1950 cars for both the actual and the 1949 specifications car stock assume that cars were driven 10,000 miles per year, on the average. However, the Bureau of Public Roads and the American Petroleum Institute estimate the actual average mileage of passenger cars at somewhat less than this, their estimates ranging between about 9,000 and 9,500 miles per year.[38] There is no need for great precision here, and we took 9,250 miles as the relevant figure for every year.

We valued gasoline consumption at the current retail prices for regular gasoline, including tax,[39] adding one cent per gallon as an adjustment for the higher price of premium grade gasoline.

The resulting estimates are given in Table 7. However, they do not tell the whole story. As mentioned earlier, gasoline consumption costs of model changes last throughout the life of the car. Thus, even if the 1962 and all later model years were to see a return to 1949 specifications, the additional gasoline expenditures due to the 1950–61 model changes would continue for the next decade at least. Assuming an average car life of ten years, and discounting the future at 10 per cent (surely an ample rate), the present value in 1961 of such expenditures (at 1960 prices) is about $7,109.5 million.

V. TOTAL COSTS AND CONCLUSIONS

The various components of costs estimated in previous sections are brought together in Table 8 and graphed in Figure 2.

---

[37] Other assumptions as to the composition of the car stock over brand names would have been more difficult to apply in practice and would make little difference to the totals. To assume that the total number of cars would have been less than actually was the case would have given a higher estimate of costs.

[38] American Petroleum Institute, *Petroleum Facts and Figures, 1959* (New York, 1960), pp. 252–53.

[39] We include taxes here as elsewhere as we are measuring expenditure by car owners. Taxes were about 7–10 cents per gallon during the period.

Table 7.   Gasoline Consumption Costs of Model Changes since 1949

Year	Extra gasoline consumption by post-1949 cars (million gals.)	Average per post-1949 car (gals.)	Per cent of actual gasoline consumption by such cars	Average retail price of gas including tax (current dollars per gal.)*	Gasoline costs of model changes	
					Per post-1949 car (current dollars)	Millions of total current dollars
1950	45.4	14.7	2.6	.2776	4.1	12.6
1951	126.1	15.1	2.7	.2815	4.3	35.5
1952	362.4	27.2	4.7	.2856	7.8	102.0
1953	542.7	29.8	5.2	.2969	8.8	161.1
1954	797.4	33.7	5.8	.3004	10.1	239.5
1955	1,237.7	42.1	7.2	.3007	12.7	372.2
1956	1,906.7	53.6	9.1	.3093	16.6	589.7
1957	2,523.6	62.7	10.5	.3196	20.0	806.5
1958	3,025.4	69.3	11.5	.3138	21.7	949.4
1959	3,642.0	77.0	12.7	.3149	24.2	1,146.9
1960	4,189.0	83.3	12.6	.3213	26.8	1,345.9
1956–60 av.	...	...	....	...	967.7

* One cent per gallon added (see text) to figures for 1950–58 in American Petroleum Institute, *Petroleum Facts and Figures, 1959*, p. 379; 1959–60 *Platt's Oilgram Price Service.*

Table 8.   Total Estimated Costs of Model Changes since 1949
(Millions of Current Dollars)

Year*	Total direct costs (1)	Retooling costs (2)	Gasoline costs (3)	Total costs† (4)
1950	−27	20	13	6
1951	267	45	36	348
1952	460	82	102	644
1953	436	246	161	844
1954	1,072	264	240	1,576
1955	2,425	469	372	3,266
1956	3,040	336	590	3,966
1957	4,048	772	806	5,626
1958	2,354	626	949	3,924
1959	3,675	532	1,147	5,354
1960	3,456	537	1,346	5,339
1956–60 average	....	...	....	4,843
Present value in 1961 of future gasoline costs already committed‡				7,110

* We have combined model-year and calendar-year figures. The actual timing of the various elements of the total is slightly different.

† Total may not equal sum of components due to rounding.

‡ Due to lack of data at time of writing, we do not present complete estimates for 1961. Preliminary estimates using 1961 figures presented in earlier sections indicate that costs in that year (including gasoline costs) continue well above $5 billion.

What can we say about these figures?

First, let us ask whether our estimates are likely to overstate or under-state the costs to the economy of model changes since 1949. The answer seems to be that our estimates understate the cost. Aside from items previously discussed, we have not attempted to estimate such possibly important secondary costs as the added traffic and parking problems due to greater car length, or the costs in human life and property damage that may have resulted from higher horsepowers.[40] Further, newer model cars (especially as automatic transmissions became more and more widespread) tended to have higher repair costs than would pre-sumably have been the case with 1949 specifications. None of these items has been included in our estimates.

Moreover, while we argued in Section III that the exclusion of de-sign and research and development costs was in part an avoidance of double counting, it is clear that large elements of such design and re-search and development costs hardly contributed to the technological change involved in our estimates. One need only mention the expendi-tures that Ford must have incurred in the introduction of the short-lived Edsel to realize that we have failed to include some sizable items in our analysis.

Next, we have assumed throughout that the number of cars would have been unchanged had 1949 specifications been continued. This may or may not be a good assumption, but it is difficult to argue that *more* cars would have been sold. It follows that, if anything, our results fail to cost the extra cars that were in fact produced.

Finally, in choosing the 1949 model year as a standard for specifica-tions, and in resting our analyses on the actual costs and gasoline consumption of domestically produced cars, we have not asked whether a more stringent standard could not be derived from the experience of various European car producers. Our cost estimates rest on the his-torical experience of the domestic industry. Had we chosen a European small-car standard, estimated costs clearly would have been higher.

For all these reasons, it seems to us that our estimates must err con-siderably on the low side, even after the greatest benefit of the doubt is given to the stochastic nature of our estimates. The order of mag-nitude of the cost of model changes is clearly greater than that indi-cated in our figures. On the other hand, we have not attempted to assess monetary benefits. For example, the increases in horsepower and in the use of power steering and automatic transmissions may have led to an

40 Potentially at least, these costs could be estimated. Some parking garages charge a higher fee for longer cars, and insurance claims paid presumably could be analyzed for variation with specifications, other things being equal. This would be a full-scale undertaking, however.

increase in the average speed of automobile travel of about 10 per cent.[41] Assuming that in the base period the average speed was about 30 miles per hour, that approximately 9,000 miles were traveled by a car per year, and that on the average there were about 1.5 passengers per car, we get an estimate of 45 man-hours saved per new car year. Valuing these hours at $1.00 per hour [42] leads us to a guess of $45 as the annual per car benefit from the time saving aspects of higher speeds. This is a large figure, of the same order of magnitude as our estimate of the costs of increased gasoline consumption per car, and would similarly persist throughout the life of the car. It is hard to think of many additional "benefits" of this sort. Their existence, however, is indicated by the apparent willingness of consumers to pay for at least some of these changes.

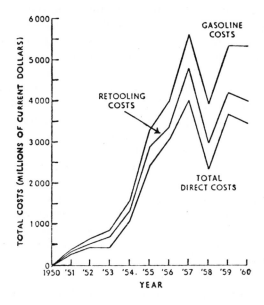

Figure 2. Total estimated cost of model changes since 1949

[41] This and the following figures are purely illustrative. We have been unable to find a consistent set of national data on this topic. The following calculation is only intended to indicate the possible magnitude of such benefits. These estimates are probably on the high side.

[42] This relatively low figure is used, since a substantial fraction of these passengers are women and children who are not in the labor force.

The costs of model changes since 1949 were thus a substantial part of expenditures on automobiles, especially in the last half of the 1950's, our estimates running about $5 billion a year.[43] Were such costs worthwhile? It is difficult to say. There is a presumption that consumer purchases are worth the money paid, yet one might argue that the fact that our figures for the late 1950's (about $700 in the purchase price per car, or more than 25 per cent, and $40 per year in gasoline expenses) will probably seem surprisingly high to consumers [44] is an indication that the costs in question were not fully understood by the consuming public.

On the other hand, one must not press such an argument too far. We have repeatedly stated that, in every model year considered, the *average* 1949 specifications lay inside the actual range of specifications encountered. The clear implication is that consumers could have bought such cars had they wished. Moreover, such items as automatic transmissions, power brakes, and power steering were separately available and had prices of their own. It is thus extremely hard to claim that at least some of the costs of model changes were not explicitly reflected in the prices set before consumers. Indeed, the only elements of such costs that were obviously not explicitly stated were the costs of retooling and advertising and (possibly) gasoline costs. Thus consumers knowingly purchased more costly cars than those with 1949 specifications, even in the presence of *some* explicit cost differential in favor of the latter.

All in all, save for the understatement of costs involved and the possibility that such costs were not fully understood by car-buyers, the model changes of the last decade seem to have been largely those desired by the consuming public, at least until the last years of the horsepower race. There are thus grounds for believing that car owners (at the time of purchase) thought model changes worth most of the cost. The general presumption of consumer sovereignty thus implies that these model changes *were* worth their cost.[45] How heavily that presumption is to be weighted in the presence of some cost understatement or in the presence of advertising directed at the formation or

---

[43] These figures include tax and are thus measures of expenditures by consumers. At factor costs they would still be over $4 billion a year.

[44] The Automobile Manufacturers Association clearly regards them as extremely high (see letter of Harry A. Williams [its managing director] in *The Nation*, February 17, 1962, p. 128).

[45] Indeed, one of the authors has used some of the same calculations to measure the improvement in the *quality* of automobiles since 1949 (see Griliches, "Hedonic Price Indexes . . . ," *op. cit.*).

changing of tastes [46] is not a question that can be readily decided. Nor, indeed, is it obvious in retrospect that a referendum among the same car owners on the desirability of model changes would now reveal (or would have revealed in 1949) the same preferences for model change that seem to have been revealed in the historical market place.

It is thus not easy to decide whether the costs reported in this paper were worth incurring. Unlike some other examples of product change, the issue seems difficult enough to be worth raising. No one would deny that the shift from the horse and buggy to the automobile and the change from the kerosene lamp to the electric light were worth their respective costs.[47] Such improvements were so large and obvious that the issue is easy to decide. Whether this is true of some or all of the changes from the 1949 automobile specifications seems to us to be at least an open question.[48]

---

[46] Or in the presence of external diseconomies of consumption in the case of some of the non-costed items mentioned earlier in this section.

[47] Cf. Williams, *op. cit.*, and *Barron's Weekly*, January 11, 1962, p. 7.

[48] "The 1949 car . . . was pretty advanced transportation for its day" (Williams, *op. cit.*).

ABSTRACT *

This paper reports estimates of the costs to the economy of the changes in private automobile specifications that took place during the fifties. In such costs are included not only the costs to the automobile manufacturers themselves of special retooling for new models but also the direct costs of producing larger, heavier, and more powerful cars, as well as the costs of automatic transmissions, power brakes, and the like. Finally, we include the secondary costs not paid out by the automobile companies but paid nevertheless by the consuming public in the form of increased expenditures for gasoline necessitated by the "horsepower race."

Throughout, we concentrate on the cost of the resources that would have been saved had cars with the 1949 model lengths, weights, horsepowers, transmissions, etc., been produced in every year. As there was technological change in the industry, we are thus assessing not the resource expenditure that would have been saved had the 1949 models themselves been continued but rather the resource expenditure that would have been saved had cars with 1949 specifications been continued but been built with the developing technology as estimated from actual car construction cost and performance data.[1]

In thus assessing the costs of automobile model change, we do not mean to deny that such changes also brought benefits. Indeed, it is quite clear that most or all of the changes involved were in fact desired by the consuming public (perhaps after advertising) and that the automobile companies were satisfying such desires. Nevertheless, the costs estimated seem so staggeringly high that it seems worth while presenting the bill and asking whether it was "worth" it, in retrospect.

The largest component of the cost of model changes since 1949 turns out to be the higher costs of automobile construction (as measured by automobile prices) attendant on higher horsepowers, greater lengths, greater weights, and so forth. As the cost of a given specification varies with technological change (in particular, that of horsepower clearly declines over time), such costs were estimated by a series of cross-section regressions of the list prices of a given year's models on the

---

* This abstract is from the *American Economic Review*, LII (May, 1962), pp. 259–261.
[1] The year 1949 was used as the earliest year for which all necessary data were available. The results would not be substantially altered if 1950 or 1951 were used.

specifications thereof.[2] From these regressions, estimates of the cost of construction of the average 1949 car in each successive year (given the retooling expenditures which actually took place) were constructed and compared with the average list price of actual models. Optional equipment was separately costed, as were advertising expenditures. The results showed an average cost per car (in current prices) over 1956–60 of $454 for size and horsepower plus about $116 for optional equipment and $14 for advertising. The total estimated costs of such items thus averaged about 3.3 billion dollars per year for the same period.

These estimates, however, make no allowance for the retooling expenditures which would have been saved had 1949 specifications actually been continued; they merely estimate the saving from producing cars with such specifications given the actual retooling expenditures. Accordingly, we next estimated the saving in retooling expenditure that would have occurred in the absence of model change, basing our estimates on the expenditures for special tools reported by the automobile companies to the Securities and Exchange Commission and charged by them to profit and loss. We concluded that, again in current prices, such savings would have averaged about $99 per car over the 1956–60 period, total savings coming to about 560 million dollars per year.

The total costs of model change as estimated so far came to about $700 per car (more than 25 per cent of purchase price) or about 3.9 billion dollars per year over the 1956–60 period. However, unlike the costs so far considered, there are other costs of model changes which are not exhausted with the construction of the car but are expended over its life. Chief among these (and the only one estimated by us) is the additional gasoline consumption due to changes in transmissions and especially to increases in horsepower.

This part of the study was broken into halves. First, we estimated the relation between over-all gasoline mileage as reported by *Consumer Reports* and the "fuel economy factor" reported by the same source.[3] This analysis was divided by type of transmission and number of forward speeds. We then proceeded (much as in our analysis of direct costs) to analyze the technologically changing relationship between advertised horsepower and displacement (the principal component of

[2] An extended discussion of these regressions (and some of the regressions themselves) may be found in Z. Griliches, "Hedonic Price Indexes for Automobiles: An Econometric Analysis of Quality Change," Bureau of the Budget—NBER Price Statistics Review Committee Staff Report, No. 3, printed in U. S. Congress, Joint Economic Committee, *Government Price Statistics*, Hearings. . . . Jan. 24, 1961, pp. 173–96.

[3] This is essentially a measure of displacement times engine revolutions per mile.

the fuel economy factor) by means of a series of cross-section regressions using the engines produced in successive model years. We interpreted the results in terms of engine redesign to secure higher horsepower at given displacement and used them to compute the displacement that could have been secured for the 1949 model horsepowers. We then used the relation between displacement and gasoline consumption via the fuel economy factor to estimate the gasoline consumption that would have been obtained with 1949 horsepowers. The result showed that whereas actual gasoline mileage fell from 16.4 miles per gallon in 1949 to 14.3 miles per gallon ten years later, then rising to about 15.3 in 1960 and 1961, the gasoline mileage of the average 1949 car would have *risen* to 18.0 miles per gallon in 1959 and 18.5 in 1961. This meant that the owner of the average 1956–60 car was paying about $40 more per 10,000 miles of driving (about 20 per cent of his total gasoline costs) than would have been the case had 1949 models been continued.

We then utilized these results to compute the cost of such additional gasoline consumption by the car stock, estimating this to average about 968 million dollars per year over the 1956–60 period in current prices. Moreover, since such additional expenditure continues over the life of the car, we estimated that even if 1962 and all later model years were to see a return to 1949 specifications, the 1961 present value (in 1960 prices) of additional gasoline consumption by cars already built through 1961 discounted at 10 per cent would be about 7.1 billion dollars.

We thus estimated costs of model changes since 1949 to run about 5 billion dollars per year over the 1956–60 period with a present value of future gasoline costs of 7.1 billion.[4] If anything, these figures are underestimates because of items not included. As stated at the outset, most of these costs were stated in the price of the car and it is difficult not to conclude that car owners thought the costs worth incurring at the time of purchase. Whether, in retrospect, this means that they were in fact worth incurring is a question we do not attempt to answer.

---

[4] We do not present complete figures for 1961 due to lack of data at time of writing. Preliminary estimates indicate that costs in that year (including gasoline consumption) continue well above 5 billion dollars.

DEC